KANT
Selections

Edited,
with Introduction, Notes, and
Bibliography by

LEWIS WHITE BECK

University of Rochester

A Scribner / Macmillan Book

Macmillan Publishing Company
NEW YORK

Collier Macmillan Publishers
LONDON

Macmillan Publishing Company
866 Third Avenue, New York, New York 10022

Collier Macmillan Canada, Inc.

Library of Congress Cataloging-in-Publication Data

Kant, Immanuel, 1724–1804.
  Kant selections.

  (The Great philosopher series)
  1. Philosophy. I. Beck, Lewis White. II. Title.
III. Series.
B2758 1988   193   87-18528
ISBN 0-02-307821-9

Printing: 1 2 3 4 5 6 7   Year: 8 9 0 1 2 3 4

ISBN 0-02-307821-9

KANT
Selections

THE GREAT PHILOSOPHERS

Paul Edwards, General Editor

Preface

Stories about how hard it is to read Kant, how one needs to diagram his sentences, how one must count on one's fingers the subordinate clauses encapsulated in other subordinate clauses, may be amusing, but they are false. Most common misunderstandings do not result from reading his own difficult writings, but from reading sympathetic efforts to simplify them or misguided efforts to set Kant up as an easily refuted straw man. The remedy for both is the same: read Kant himself. His "brilliantly dry" style (the characterization is Schopenhauer's) requires, and rewards, close reading.

This volume consists of my translations, or my revisions of others' translations, of most of Kant's principal works, together with my introductions. The translations by others have been thoroughly revised to conform to terminology which has become standard since their appearance, but I have made so many other changes too that some of the present versions might be considered almost new translations. I am indebted to a century of translators for preparing the way for these new versions. Editing this book has given me the opportunity to revise also my own previously published translations and to make them more accurate and readable.

The texts have been selected in the light of many years' teaching of Kant to both undergraduate and graduate students. Experience and experiment have convinced me that the best access to the *Critique of Pure Reason* is through the *Inaugural Dissertation* and the 1772 letter to Herz, with the *Critique* and *Prolegomena* then being read concurrently. I have found that the *Critique of Practical Reason* is best read by beginning students as a complement to the *Foundations of the Metaphysics of Morals*, and have chosen material from it which supplements but does not duplicate the *Foundations*. The greatest difficulty students have with the *Critique of the Faculty of Judgment* is in understanding its obscure organization. I therefore call special attention to my Introduction (pp. 331–340), in which I isolate, and then reintegrate, four questions to be answered; I believe this makes each part and the whole clearer than they otherwise would be. The remaining short works present parts of Kant's philosophy likely to be unduly neglected in courses that concentrate on the epistemology, ethics, aesthetics, and metaphysics of the *Critiques*.

I am grateful to Professor Ralf Meerbote for advice, and to Mrs. Lynne McCoy and Ms. Anna Harrison for cheerfully and skillfully helping me prepare the book for the press.

University of Rochester   LEWIS WHITE BECK

Contents

Introduction

KANT'S LIFE

Immanuel Kant was born April 22, 1724, in Königsberg, Prussia (now Kaliningrad, U.S.S.R.). His father was a harnessmaker, and the family were members of the Pietistic community — an evangelical sect comparable to the Methodists of the eighteenth century in England. Their religious life was based on the Lutheran belief in the priesthood of every believer, and consequently they had little room for catechistic orthodoxy and ecclesiastical liturgy. These lay Pietists emphasized, rather, the importance of purity of heart, good works, loving kindness, and moral conduct as a way of serving God.

When Kant entered the Pietist school in his hometown, however, he was suddenly caught in a web of religious practices which were alien to those of his family, and wholly repulsive to the eight-year-old boy. To the end of his life he would tell stories about the endless hours of prayer, meditation, confession, hymn-singing, catechizing, and self-examination which the boys had to endure in the school whose curriculum was designed to save them from their innate depravity. From his eight years in school Kant apparently acquired only the ability to write and speak in a good Latin style, a hatred of cant and hypocrisy, and a marked distaste for all formalities of religious observance.

At age sixteen, he enrolled in the University of Königsberg, and, by stratagems which have not come down to us, broke university regulations by not registering as a student in one of the higher faculties (like "choosing a major" in a modern university). Instead he heard lectures in all the faculties, especially in theology and medicine (where he even attended some surgical operations). When officially questioned about his unusual choice of courses, he replied that he took courses only out of intellectual curiosity and not to prepare himself for a profession (law, theology, or medicine). He must have been a plausible youngster, because he got himself exempted from requirements binding on less gifted students, and in consequence his education was broader than it would have been had he been confined to a single faculty.

The teacher who most influenced Kant was Martin Knutzen, a philosopher of the Leibniz-Wolffian school, which was then the dominant philosophy in most German universities. Knutzen opened to him not only the world of logic and metaphysics, but also mathematics, physics, and astronomy. Knutzen saw his talent, spent time talking with him, and apparently gave him access to his large library. It was in a copy borrowed from Knutzen that Kant first read

Newton, and Knutzen in all probability advised the young man on his first published book, *Thoughts on the True Measure of Living Forces* (1747).

Like many of his contemporaries, upon leaving the University without the doctor's degree Kant found employment as private tutor. He was *Hofmeister* to several families near Königsberg. Though he later confessed that he was probably the world's worst tutor, the boys apparently flourished under his care; several of them later studied under him at the University, and he maintained friendly relations with them and their families for many years. The period of his absence from Königsberg (1747 to 1754) contributed much to his own education. He had peace and quiet, devoted himself to study, and in all likelihood prepared the papers which he published when he first came back to the city. In addition, daily contact with ladies and gentlemen of the gentry and nobility gave Kant a proficiency in French conversation and a social ease which later raised him to a high place in the social life of Königsberg, where he was known as *der galante Magister,* and where his gallantry toward ladies, his courtesy, wit, apparently inexhaustible conversational resources, healthy enjoyment of good food and wine, and skill at billiards and card games made him an agreeable guest in the homes of the nobility and rich merchants.

Upon returning to town, he published a work which would have given him a place in the intellectual history of Europe even if he had not later become known as a major philosopher. It was the *Universal Natural History and Theory of the Heavens.* The title of the book is significant — it was to be a natural *history.* Newton had formulated the laws governing the state of the solar system after it had left, presumably, the hands of the Creator; Kant took a giant step forward and tried to show how, solely under Newton's laws, the solar system and the galaxy came to assume their present state, evolving from a chaos of matter to which they will return, only to be generated again under the same Newtonian laws. This theory, since known as the Kant-Laplace Hypothesis, was wrong in details, but right in direction — it moved astronomy toward modern cosmological speculation on the origin and evolution of the universe.

Other papers on geology and astronomy followed, and in 1755 Kant presented a dissertation in chemistry for the master's or doctor's degree (the titles were then interchangeable). Later in the same year he "habilitated," i.e., qualified for appointment as *Privatdozent* (licensed lecturer) in the University. The dissertation which earned him this appointment was his first philosophical work, a Latin treatise entitled *A New Exposition of the First Principles of Metaphysical Knowledge.*

As *Privatdozent,* he did not receive a salary, but only fees paid directly by students who attended his lectures. Fortunately Kant was a popular and versatile lecturer and, to earn a barely adequate income, he carried an incredible load of lectures (perhaps as many as twenty-eight hours per week) in a variety of subjects: mathematics, logic, ethics, metaphysics, geography, anthropology, mineralogy, and even fortification construction for military officers (sometimes Prussian, sometimes Russian, who occupied the city). During all this time he continued to publish papers in the sciences, mostly in geology.

In 1762 Jean-Jacques Rousseau published *Émile* and produced an intellectual sensation all over Europe. It is said that for two days Kant failed to take his afternoon walk (by which the *Hausfrauen* of Königsberg are said to have set their clocks) because he could not put Rousseau's book down. The influence of Rousseau upon him was perhaps even deeper than that of Newton ten years earlier. Kant explicitly compared Rousseau with Newton. Newton had discovered in external nature "order and regularity combined with simplicity"; Rousseau was the first to discover "under the manifold variety of shapes assumed by human beings the deeply buried nature of man, and the hidden law by obedience to which providence is justified." Rousseau not only gave him an idea which he developed later in his own ethical theory[1] but produced a sudden and profound change in Kant's whole orientation and philosophy of life. In a note written for his own eyes only, he said:

> By inclination I am an inquirer. I feel a consuming thirst for
> knowledge, the unrest which goes with the desire to progress in it,
> and satisfaction at every advance in it. There was a time when I
> believed this constituted the honor of humanity, and I despised the
> people, who know nothing. Rousseau corrected me in this. This
> blinding prejudice disappeared. I learned to honor man, and I would
> find myself more useless than the common laborer if I did not believe
> that this attitude of mine [as an inquirer] can give a worth to all
> others in establishing the rights of mankind.

Though Kant continued throughout his life to publish papers on the physical and biological sciences, it is perhaps to the influence of Rousseau that we should attribute the sudden broadening of his interests observable in the writings of the years 1762 to 1764.

One was a popular, gracefully written essay, *Observations on the Feeling of the Beautiful and the Sublime.* Another, of greater importance, was the Prize Essay written for the Berlin Academy (printed below as Selection I). After several disappointments at being passed over for promotion, Kant was finally appointed Professor of Logic and Metaphysics in 1770. His Inaugural Dissertation (Selection II in this volume) marks a decisive crisis in Kant's intellectual history: everything before it is called "precritical" and everything after it, "critical." The history of this change is given below in the Introduction to Selection III, Kant's Letter of 1772 to Marcus Herz.

His appointment as professor relieved Kant of financial dependence upon

---

[1] It is later said (see p. 15) that there was a "Rousseauistic Revolution" in Kant's ethical theory comparable to the "Copernican Revolution" in his theory of knowledge.

students' fees, so in the following years he reduced his teaching load significantly (but still, as full professor, he had about eighteen "contact hours" per week). In the 1770's, he was working on the *Critique of Pure Reason* but published nothing (a situation not unheard of in others after they have just previously achieved academic tenure). This so-called "silent decade" ended with the publication of the *Critique of Pure Reason* in 1781. He continued to enjoy the pleasures of society. Early in the 1780's he gave up his place at the *Stammtisch* of a local tavern where he had dined with anyone who wished to join him, and regularly had guests in his own home for dinners that lasted from one to four and even to six o'clock. Here his guests were the leading men of the city — ministers, government officials, merchants, writers, colleagues from the University, and distinguished strangers passing through Königsberg.

It was not in Kant to do vain boasting, but there was no humility in his estimate of the importance of the philosophical revolution he believed — and soon the world believed — he had made in his *magnum opus*. In 1781 he was fifty-seven years old, an old man by eighteenth-century standards. He had never been robust, and described himself as "never sick, though never well." He was, moreover, a hypochondriac, without much confidence that time would be given him to complete the revolution he had started. He was an old man in a hurry, writing against death. In the astonishing years from 1781 to 1790 he produced an *oeuvre* probably unmatched by any other philosopher in any one decade in the history of philosophy: *all* the works after 1781 from which selections have been taken in the remainder of this book with the exception of *Perpetual Peace*, one other book of size and importance *(Metaphysical Foundations of Natural Science)*, and thirteen other papers.

It was a period of growing fame for Kant: others began teaching his philosophy in other universities; students flocked to far-away Königsberg to hear him lecture; he was invited to other more prestigious universities at very high salaries; he was elected a member of the Royal Academy of Sciences in Berlin. Dining and balls in fashionable society almost ceased; it was a time of unremitting labor interrupted only by his long dinner hours. But there was trouble ahead.

In 1786 Frederick the Great, an enlightened despot, died and was succeeded by his nephew Frederick William II, who was more despotic and not at all enlightened. Kant was rector of the University at the time of the coronation, which took place in Königsberg, and the King favorably condescended to him and singled him out for compliments. But things changed rapidly for the worse. Von Zedlitz, the minister of justice and education in Berlin, to whom Kant had dedicated the *Critique of Pure Reason*, was dismissed. This outstanding man, who was a careful student of Kant's works and anxious to have knowledge of Kant's philosophy spread to other universities, was replaced by Johann Christoff Wöllner, whom Frederick the Great had called "a deceitful, intriguing parson, nothing more." In the name of a renewed religiosity of the most rigidly orthodox kind, Wöllner fed the King's feelings of guilt (the King was a bigamist), religious enthusiasm, and blatant superstition by exacting the most punctiliously orthodox lip-service from all clerics and professors in the Prussian Kingdom. Kant was singularly vulnerable to attack both because of his well-known unorthodox religious views and also because of his equally well-known sympathy for the revolutionary forces in France, on account of which he was often referred to as "the old Jacobin" and his books were burned. For six years there was harsh dispute between the forces of religious reaction and the more freethinking professors, publicists, and enlightened clerics. Kant was a leader in the campaign to warn of the consequences of both religious intolerance and the intervention of the state in matters of scholarship and private belief. Orders were issued from Berlin to freethinkers to keep their thoughts to themselves; spies were sent into churches and lecture halls (including Kant's) and censorship was imposed (although Kant, by complicated maneuvers, was able to evade it and publish his most unorthodox book, *Religion within the Boundaries of Reason Alone* in 1793).

Finally, on October 1, 1794, in a royal cabinet order addressed to Kant, he was ordered to refrain from writing or lecturing on any religious topic whatever, or else take "unpleasant consequences." Kant, expecting to be dismissed, had hoarded his savings against this eventuality and given thought to where he should seek refuge, now faced a problem of conscience. In a note of the kind he repeatedly wrote to clarify his own thoughts to himself, he said: "To withdraw or deny one's inner conviction is base, but to be silent in a case like this is a duty of a subject [to his sovereign]; and though everything that one says must be true, it is not one's duty also to say openly all the truth." And so, on October 12 "as Your Majesty's most faithful subject" Kant bowed to the will of the weak King whom he thought, good Lutheran that he was, he should obey.

But Kant had the last laugh in this miserable affair. Frederick William II died in 1797, and in 1798 Kant published *The Strife of the Faculties*, one part of which dealt with the relation between theology and philosophy interpreted as a question of academic organization of university faculties. Kant explained that in discussing a theological problem he was not infringing on his vow of obedience to the late King. He said that the words "as your Majesty's most faithful subject" meant "as *Frederick William*'s most faithful subject," and the King's death relieved Kant of obedience to that particular King. Some have seen this as a sophistry unworthy of the great moral philosopher; others take delight in the wisdom of the serpent instead of the innocence of the dove.

In spite of the disturbances of this troubled time, the period after the *Critique of Judgment* was one of fruitful work. Kant wrote three large books, *Religion Within the Boundaries of Reason Alone*, *The Strife of the Faculties*, and the two volumes of the *Metaphysics of Morals*. He prepared for the press the notes and texts which had been the foundation of his most popular lectures, *Anthropology from a Pragmatic Point of View*. In 1795 he published his most detailed political writing, *Perpetual Peace*, in which he argued for the establishment of a league of nations for the prevention of war, the members of which would have a republican constitution.[2]

Besides writing the papers published in the popular press concerning the religious controversies, several book reviews, and one last paper on geology and meteorology, Kant engaged in a public controversy with the Wolffian philosopher Eberhard, who professed to find the essentials of the *Critique of Pure Reason* in the Leibniz-Wolffian philosophy; Kant's side of the debate was presented in *On a New Discovery, Whereby Any New Critique of Pure Reason is Made Unnecessary by an Older One*. The Berlin Academy proposed a prize-essay contest on the topic: *What Real Progress Has Metaphysics Made in Germany Since the Time of Leibniz and Wolff?* Kant wrote an answer in defense of the originality of his own work, but he was unable to complete it and it was not published until after his death. In 1797, Kant gave up lecturing at the University but still continued to work on what has come to be known as the *Opus Posthumum* on the connection between metaphysics and physics, as well as many other topics with the earlier treatment of which he had become dissatisfied. The *Opus Posthumum* shows daring changes from Kant's published works, but also signs of increasing senility, and after a slow decline Kant died on February 12, 1804.

These are the outward facts of Kant's life. More could be added, but they would be simply more of the same kind, and would give us little or no additional insight into the nature and character of the man. Heinrich Heine said no one could write a life of Kant because Kant had no life. Of outward events there were few of significance; his life was one of inward development and intellectual expression. To a degree surpassed by almost no one, Kant's life *is* his thought. As the motto to the *Critique of Pure Reason* he quoted Bacon, but what Bacon had said of himself Kant was saying also of himself: It is the work that is important, *De nobis ipsis silemus* — "about ourselves we are silent."

Yet Kant was a creature of flesh and blood, not just of brain, and we should not let the common desiccated caricatures of Kant hide from us the traits which were obvious to his companions, many of whom did not understand his thought. They invariably speak of his cheerfulness, his childlikeness, his simplicity, his courtesy, his ability to put everyone at ease, his natural leadership to which everyone in his company deferred. In his old age, when he was famous, travelers through Königsberg would be anxious to pass on droll anecdotes about the great man, and they give us perhaps not less accurate,

[2] *Perpetual Peace* was the first book to bring Kant international renown beyond the confines of academic philosophy; it was translated into French (twice) and there were rumors — not wholly without foundation, but certainly exaggerated — that Kant was invited to come to Paris as consultant to the French government.

but certainly less sympathetic portraits: they show a man greedy in his eating, easily upset by trivial things, and sententious; a man who cannot understand those who disagree with him, a man in whom mechanical repetition sometimes replaces spontaneous good nature.

So we get a not unusual collection of diverse portraits. Those who knew him longest remembered the fresh traits of youth and maturity and overlooked the distressing signs of age. Those who knew him only in his senectitude saw his weaknesses and foibles, but not what had made him beloved by the others who were more tolerant of his failings.

I conclude with a word-picture by a man who had been his student back in the 1760s. Weight is to be given to his words, because their author had grown more and more distant from Kant as his own genius had flourished in new directions, leading him finally to a personal break in which he spoke angrily of his teacher. But Johann Gottlieb Herder later said:

> I have had the good fortune to know a philosopher. He was my teacher. In his prime he had the happy sprightliness of a youth; he continued to have it, I believe, even as a very old man. His broad forehead, built for thinking, was the seat of an imperturbable cheerfulness and joy. Speech, the richest in thought, flowed from his lips. Playfulness, wit, and humor were at his command. His lectures were the most entertaining talks. His mind, which examined Leibniz, Wolff, Baumgarten, Crusius, and Hume, and investigated the laws of nature of Newton, Kepler, and the physicists, comprehended equally the newest works of Rousseau . . . and the latest discoveries in science. He weighed them all, and always came back to the unbiased knowledge of nature and to the moral worth of man. The history of men and peoples, natural history and science, mathematics and observation, were the sources from which he enlivened his lectures and conversation. He was indifferent to nothing worth knowing. No cabal, no sect, no prejudice, no desire for fame could ever tempt him in the slightest away from broadening and illuminating the truth. He incited and gently forced others to think for themselves; despotism was foreign to his mind. This man, whom I name with the greatest gratitude and respect, was Immanuel Kant.

II
KANT'S THOUGHT

In his lectures on *Logic,* Kant said that philosophy comprises four questions:

1. What can I know?
2. What ought I to do?
3. What may I hope?
4. What is man?

Almost all the manifold topics and subjects Kant discussed are comprehended under these questions. They are not always sharply separated from
each other, but they provide helpful rubrics under which his writings over a
fifty-year period can be surveyed.

1. What Can I Know?

Kant deals with this question in the following Selections: I, II, III, IV, V,
and VIII. As Kant himself almost always did, we shall divide the discussion by
distinguishing two questions: (a) What can we know about nature, the world
we perceptually experience and explain by at least tacit reference to scientific observation, hypotheses, and laws? (b) What can we know about God,
the soul of man, the ultimate substances of the world, and other things
traditionally described as metaphysical? We shall see that Kant's answer to
the first question determines his answer to the second.

a. Natural Knowledge

From the time of Plato, when philosophers talk about knowledge they
mean not just awareness of what is the case, an awareness we presumably
share with other animals, but also some insight into why it is the case, and
even why, in the light of other things we know, it could not be otherwise.
Throughout the history of philosophy there have been competing accounts of
this feature of knowledge, but the lines of contest between them were never
more sharply drawn than in the seventeenth and eighteenth centuries.
Though individual philosophers may have taken something from both the
competing accounts, looking back upon their disputes we can see two ideal
paradigms, each claiming to tell the whole story. We call them rationalism
and empiricism.

Rationalists believed that the human mind had innate within it certain
ideas, a power to grasp directly (intuit) a small number of truths that could
not be doubted, and a power to test other knowledge-claims by establishing
their agreement or disagreement with these basic truths. In its most extreme
form in the philosophy of Christian Wolff, a leading German philosopher of
the eighteenth century, all knowledge was to be authenticated by the indis-
putable law of contradiction. A false proposition, fully analyzed, shows itself
to be self-contradictory. Wolff, of course, did not assert that all beliefs are in
fact tested in this way. He acknowledged that the finite human mind can see
nothing self-contradictory in most false judgments and most of the time we
do not try to establish the truth that the duck is in the water by showing the
self-contradictoriness of its contradictory — we simply look and see. But with
the development of scientific knowledge in which true judgments are woven
together into axiomatic systems and many observational truths are in fact
demonstrated, dependence upon sense perception seemed to be gradually
reduced by logical deduction from basic laws of mathematics and self-evident
principles, and it was thought that in the ideal system of omniscience there

would be no need for observation at all. Obviously in such a system metaphysical knowledge, which did not claim to have any observational base, could be even more certain than scientific facts which had to be, in spite of all, learned from some observation.

It was this system of philosophy which Kant was taught at the University, but never unquestioningly accepted. In the Prize Essay (Selection I) he argued that neither mathematics, the natural sciences, nor metaphysics followed the Wolffian model. Rather, science followed the Newtonian methodology of empiricism: observing, measuring, generalizing, deducing consequences, and observing again to see if the consequences are true. He proposed that it, or something closely analogous to it, should be practiced in metaphysics. (His assertion of the continuity between the methods of physics and those of metaphysics we shall call "the continuity thesis," p. 28.) In his scientific writings Kant followed this Newtonian model, but in 1766 he expressed doubt that metaphysics could be practiced in this way[3] and in the Inaugural Dissertation (Selection II) of 1770 he made a last effort to establish metaphysical truths along more orthodox Wolffian lines.

About 1772, however, he was awakened from his dogmatic slumber by a suggestion of David Hume's (below, p. 159). He had at last become aware of the significance of Hume's critical examination of the idea of necessary connection (causality) in his *Treatise of Human Nature*. Hume had shown, as Kant now understood him,[4] that the causal principle which relates one observed fact to other observed or unobserved facts was neither itself a logical truth (reducible to the law of contradiction) nor intuitively certain. It was, according to Hume, a mere subjective expectation that connections between future events would repeat those between past events; in Kant's somewhat gross words, Hume showed that the idea of causality is a bastard of the imagination impregnated by experience (p. 158) and not a necessary objective relation at all. Without use of the causal principle, however, our knowledge would be confined solely to what we directly perceive or remember, which is a very small portion of all that we think we know. Hence empiricism, consistently thought through, is skepticism.

Kant thus found himself without recourse to either the rationalistic or the empiricistic explanation of knowledge. At this time he perhaps remembered a statement of Leibniz's, which had only recently been published for the first time.[5] Leibniz, wishing to find a common ground with the empiricist Locke, had said, in agreement with him, that "There is nothing in the intellect which

---

[3] In *Dreams of a Spirit-Seer, Explained by the Dreams of Metaphysics* (1766) Kant describes, and is frankly puzzled by, Swedenborg's clairvoyant experiences, and skeptically compares explanations of extrasensory perception with the explanations given by metaphysicians for things not sensorily experienced, e.g., the soul.

[4] Kant, more likely under the influence of Crusius than of Hume, had already concluded (*Essay towards the Introduction of Negative Magnitudes in Philosophy*, 1763) that the causal relation is not a logical relation, but he did not then see the full significance of this.

[5] *New Essays Concerning the Human Understanding*, Bk. II, ch. i,ss § 2 (first published in 1765).

was not first in the senses," but added: "except the intellect itself." Thus the Cartesian theory of innate ideas, rejected by Locke and his empiricistic followers, was modified by Leibniz into the conception of innate faculties and rules of intellectual procedure. This was not a wholly new theory, and it left open the question that had plagued adherents of the theory of innate ideas: What is it that makes them *true?* Why should they conform to the truth any better than adventitious, empirically derived ideas? Kant mentioned this problem in his letter to Herz (Selection III), but had not then solved it. He might well have asked why the operations of the mind, which Leibniz said were inborn in the mind and not learned by experience, should give rise to truths about other realities.

Soon he had an answer to that question, and the critical philosophy, as his system is known, came into being. The content of knowledge, he said, comes from experience (a posteriori); *the formal structures and rules lie in the mind a priori, and the content conforms to the structures and rules, not the reverse.* This fundamental thought underlay what has come to be known as Kant's Copernican Revolution (pp. 88, 98). He himself called it transcendental idealism (pp. 125–126).

According to this theory we know a priori the formal spatio-temporal and conceptual structure of objects of experience, for they are only appearances to us, not things as they are in themselves. There is no reason for things in themselves to conform to our conceptual and sensible forms, but their appearances depend, in part, upon the cognitive faculties and operations of the beings to whom they appear, and these aspects of appearances which are dependent upon the mind can be known a priori.

The rest of the *Critique of Pure Reason* and the *Prolegomena* work out the consequences of this Copernican analogy. After appropriating the theory of space and time from the Inaugural Dissertation (where the first stage of the Copernican Revolution had already occurred), Kant established the categories and a priori synthetic principles that constitute the basic laws of nature, for instance: every change has a cause, every object of perception has a measurable magnitude, and the like. The specific laws of nature (e.g., the law of falling bodies) must be in conformity with these a priori principles, but cannot be derived from them. To know what specific laws hold in particular, therefore, one must observe and experiment but always within the framework of the a priori principles that are the laws the mind gives to nature, nature being nothing but phenomena (appearances) under law (p. 199).

Yet even in learning from experience, we are guided by some a priori principles. These are discussed in the *Critique of the Faculty of Judgment* (pp. 331–339). The first *Critique* shows that every change has a cause, but science is not just a collection of singular causal judgments; it is a systemic organization in which, for example, an apple's falling from a tree and the ebb and flow of the tides are known to instantiate the same law and to have the same cause.

We do not know a priori what the underlying law and cause are; we do not know even that there *is* a single underlying cause and single unifying law covering all of nature, but as a regulative heuristic principle we assume that one exists. This assumption is based on another analogy: that between human technique in the production of artifacts which serve human practical needs, and a "technique of nature" (p. 353) by which we explain how nature seems to meet our human cognitive need for simplicity and uniformity of explanation. To *know* that nature must conform to our regulative demands, however, would be to possess metaphysical knowledge about God and the design of the world. Can we have such knowledge?

b. Metaphysical Knowledge of What is Beyond Nature

Kant draws a distinction between a boundary and a limit (p. 219). A limit is simply the farthest point we have reached in our knowledge; next year the limit will be farther out in what is now our ignorance, and it may be said that our scientific knowledge is *limitless*, i.e., that there is no specifiable limit beyond which it cannot progress. A boundary, on the other hand, is a limit which cannot be breached. There is a boundary between all physics — wherever its temporary limit lies — and metaphysics, and this boundary is immovable and insurmountable. In saying this, Kant has given up the continuity thesis of the Prize Essay.

Metaphysics is the part of philosophy based upon pure reason working independently of experience. If pure reason is applied in experience, it is metaphysics "as a science," but if it is thought to apply to objects outside the possible experience of human beings (noumena, things in themselves) it is not science at all, though it is expressive of a deep, but insatiable, need of human reason for the *complete* explanation of experience. Traditional metaphysics claimed to give knowledge of noumena and things in themselves, to give knowledge which Kant called *transcendent* (not to be confused with *transcendental*) because it transcended the boundary of possible experience.

To save scientific knowledge from Humean skepticism, Kant had to forfeit the claims of transcendent metaphysics. Efforts to extend the categories and other cognitive functions to the realm of the supersensible lead invariably to a dialectic of illusory inferences and antinomies (contradictory propositions, each of which can be demonstrated). The categories give knowledge within experience, and nowhere else. Metaphysical ideas may serve at best as regulative principles, heuristic guides in the pursuit of more detailed empirical knowledge, and postulates of moral reasoning, but they give no knowledge of things as they are.

Suppose, however, that transcendent metaphysical knowledge could be shown to be possible. This would be a triumph of pure theoretical reason, i.e., of the human capacity to know. But it would be a disaster for human practical reason (reason operating in moral decision making) because metaphysics would then be a mere extension of physics (the continuity thesis of the Prize

Essay!) which has no room for God, freedom, immortality, values. "There-fore," Kant says, "I had to deny knowledge [of supersensible realities] to make room for faith [in the things which make morality intelligible]" (p. 103). The failure of metaphysics to achieve its traditional goal of certain knowledge of ultimate reality is the foundation on which Kant will establish the possibility of a moral system. That is why Kant said that "The inscrutable wisdom through which we exist is not less worthy of veneration in respect to what it denies us than in what it has granted" (p. 318).

2. What Ought I to Do?

In the Introduction to the *Critique of Practical Reason* Kant asked: "Who would want to introduce a new principle of morality and, as it were, be its inventor, as if the world had hitherto been ignorant of what duty is or had been thoroughly wrong about it?" Rather than formulate a new ethic, as Nietzsche attempted to do, Kant followed the path of Socrates, recovering what had been distorted by sophistry, or forgotten. Most of what had passed for ethical theory, Kant thought, was only a substitute for it, a theory about how to be happy and not a theory about how to be good. Because the conditions of happiness are different from those of goodness, and not only different but often in opposition, ethical theory as it had existed before his time was held by Kant to be incapable of explaining and justifying the ordinary moral judgments of the common man who, Kant thought, was more likely to be right than the philosopher acting on some theory (p. 256).

But the common man cannot speak for himself in these matters, and we have philosophical and psychological theories which explain away the most fundamental distinctions of lived morality. If believed, these theories corrupt the moral disposition of the common man by inducing him to think that his pursuit of happiness (which no one begrudges him) is the practice of virtue. The ordinary human being, Kant thinks, knows very well the difference between good and evil and between morality and prudence, but he needs someone — a philosopher — to speak for him against those who say that these differences are unimportant or do not exist, or at most are mere rationalizations of unconscious impulses.

Whether the common man would see Kant as his spokesman is another question not so easy to answer, for the common man never heard of Kant and does not understand him, thinking of him (if at all) as pedantic, Puritan, and Prussian. If he has heard of Kant, he probably has heard that his ethics is perhaps good in theory but will not work in practice because it demands too much of human nature, excludes too much of what the ordinary person esteems, disregards the consequences of actions, despises happiness, and takes an eighteenth-century code of an out-of-the-way provincial city as if it were a universal law for all rational beings.

A full estimation of these criticisms can be justly formed only when one has actually read Kant and does not depend upon second-hand accounts in elementary textbooks. The first two sections of the *Foundations of the Metaphysics of Morals* are the best place to find out if Kant is vulnerable to these criticisms. Kant's ethics does not stand alone, however, and is not just an appeal to common sense, which would not long stand up to the kinds of criticisms made of it by John Stuart Mill, for instance. Rather, it is an integral part of his entire project of seeing what pure reason can accomplish, and is not to be judged *simply* by reference to whether it is in agreement with the enlightened moral sense of mankind. It must be decided whether the subtle philosophical problems which have always attended moral ideas, and which have often raised questions about the genuineness of moral distinctions, are satisfactorily resolved by the Kantian philosophy as a whole. These connections between Kant's moral theory and the rest of his philosophy will principally concern us in this Introduction, whereas the details of the separate moral treatises printed in this book can be found in the Editor's Introductions to Selections VI and VII.

Kant's answer to the question: "What ought I to do?" in two words is: *act rationally*. But since reason and rationality are in the debatable center of Kant's entire philosophy, rational action must be related to Kant's theory of reason, which is different from the theories of most other philosophers.

All things in nature act according to laws, says Kant, but only rational beings act according to the *conception* of laws (p. 261). A body falls according to Galileo's law of falling bodies, and I would too if I stepped from a high place; but I do not step from high places because I act according to my *conception* of what follows from Galileo's law, a conception which tells me the consequences of my action. Only a rational being guides his behavior according to his conception of a law, whether it be a law telling what the speed of a falling body is, or a law fixing the maximum speed allowed an automobile. The human capacity to foresee consequences of actions, to place them in a perspective in which they can be weighed against alternatives, and to choose the appropriate means (causes) for accomplishing a purpose was called, by Aristotle, *practical reason*. We control our behavior in the light of these considerations so as to secure some specific goal. Especially when such control requires the frustration of incompatible desires and calls for sustained effort to accomplish the goal, it is called *will*. Thus will and practical reason are closely connected; Kant sometimes identified them.

Aristotle said that practical reason does not by itself move us to action, but only guides us in satisfying a want. Hume expressed the same idea by saying that reason is "the slave of the passions." For both, and for most philosophers between them, practical reason did its work only when something was desired. Through its rational conception of causal connections between means and ends, it prompted a person to do actions which, if effective, led to the desired object or state of affairs.

The constraint by reason, derived from knowledge of the conditions favoring the attainment of the object of desire, is experienced as an *ought,* or in what Kant called an *imperative.* For instance, if you want to build a dog house, reason and experience tell you that you ought to get a hammer; if you have a headache, you ought to take an aspirin, etc. In general, if you want *y* you ought to do the *x* which reason, *based upon past experience,* tells you is the causal condition of *y.* This rational formula applies to whatever you want, however "irrational" and foolish the desire may be. It also applies to the one desire which everyone properly and naturally has, the desire for happiness. You ought to do those things that will make you happy.

But, really, ought you do this? Are there not cases in which you ought to rein in your desire for happiness because there is something else, your duty, which you ought to do? Kant thinks so, and he thinks that the ordinary man in the street thinks so too. The account we have given of imperatives in the previous paragraph is correct and valid, but it is not a complete account of what we do, or at least think we ought to do. While it is not quite true that in making a moral decision we ought to disregard the happiness or unhappiness which will be effected by what we do (though Kant sometimes, but not always, writes as if this were so), it is true that in making moral decisions we must often overlook our *personal stake in the outcome,* and try to decide what we ought to do as if we were impartial spectators or disinterested judges, not potential beneficiaries of the action. The voice of duty does not say "Do *x* because it will make you happy" but "Do *x* because it is right" or "Do *x* because it is your duty." Each of these is an imperative of practical reason, but the second and third are categorical imperatives of *pure* practical reason, i.e., of practical reason which is not the slave of the passions.

Practical reason, moreover, cannot decide with assurance that doing *x* will make one happy. The concept of happiness is too vague and variable for us to know what will cause happiness, and the best laid plans of mice and men. . . . *Pure* practical reason, however, can decide *what x* ought to be done, and it can do so with certainty and necessity — in other words, a priori. It is what a person would do if he were a being of pure reason alone and not determined by desires and impulses arising from his sensuous nature. The categorical imperative, translated into the indicative mood, describes the actions of a being motivated solely by pure reason; it is in the imperative mood because we human beings do not, without constraint, do what pure reason requires. The various formulae of the categorical imperative derived from the concept of an imperative delivered by pure reason alone are to be found on pp. 278–279 and need not be repeated here.

A being following the law of pure practical reason not because of what it promises — for it promises nothing — must do so because he respects it as a law; this is equivalent to saying he does *x* because the moral law requires it and not because doing *x* will make him happy. Kant argues that a being capable of obeying a pure law of reason and not having to act from an impulse which would cause his action must possess a free will. A free agent, according to the *Critique of Pure Reason* (p. 133) is a noumenal being of which we can know nothing. But now we know something about this otherwise unknowable noumenon. Previously we had only the negative conception that, as a free being, it was independent of the causes working in nature; now we have a positive concept of its freedom, as self-determination, obedience to its own law. Using a political metaphor, Kant defines self-determination and positive freedom as *autonomy,* and says that the basic moral principle is that of the autonomy of the will (p. 281).

Here the influence of Rousseau on Kant is comparable to that of Copernicus. We may, indeed, speak of a Rousseauistic Revolution. Rousseau had defined political freedom as obedience to a law which the citizen had given himself, or in whose enactment the citizen had participated. Kant explains the respect for law which moves us to do our duty as respect for ourselves as noumenal legislators of a realm which ought to be brought into existence by our moral conduct. The slave obeys the law out of fear of consequences; the hedonist, out of hope for happiness; but the free moral individual, according to Kant, obeys it because, as a pure rational being, he participates in its legislation and thus has an interest in its faithful execution.

This is what we meant when we said Kant's answer to the question is: Act rationally. Another way of saying it is: *Act freely.* Still another way: *Act autonomously* as a member of a realm of ends, an ideal community of rational beings (p. 280).

Kant's ethics of the categorical imperative is not consequentialist, locating value in the achievement of some desired end, nor is it an ethic of specific actions according to which some actions (e.g., telling the truth) are intrinsically and universally right. It is, rather, an ethic of motive. The imperative does not exact a single specific action from all human beings; it requires, rather, that I act on a maxim that I would be content that all rational beings should act upon, e.g., the maxim of respecting human nature as an end in itself, the maxim of acting only on maxims that I will others also should follow. Kant's ethics does not stop there, of course. Sometimes he writes as if some acts were intrinsically right and others intrinsically wrong, and that the specific right action ought to be performed by all people. The truth lies somewhere between emphasis upon right motives and upon right actions; there are some actions which could not be done from a moral motive, and other actions which follow almost automatically from the possession of a moral motive. Most of the time, however, there are intermediate steps between motive and action, and these steps must be taken with a prudent regard for the facts of the individual case. No amount of so-called good will which is not followed by appropriate action and sincere effort to accomplish the intention can give moral stature to a person. But no action, however punctiliously one obeys the letter of the law or however effective it is in bettering the human condition, has genuine moral worth unless the motive is right and unless the act is undertaken because it is believed to be right. The end of Kant's ethics is like its beginning: The only thing in the universe good *without qualification* is a good will.

3. What May I Hope?

Kant's third question is somewhat surprising, for one would expect him to ask next: What may I believe? In the *Critique of Pure Reason* (p. 103) he said that he had denied knowledge in order to make room for faith (belief), and one would naturally expect that, having told us what it is we cannot know, he would next tell us what we may believe. Later in the *Critique* (A 805 = B 833) he phrased the question more precisely, relating it to the second question rather than the first. He stated it thus: "If I do what I ought to do, what may I then hope?"

Hope and belief are intimately connected. One may believe something but not hope for it, but one cannot hope for something unless one believes that it is at least possible (otherwise it is not hope, but empty wish). One can have beliefs about all manner of things, but Kant says hope is always directed to happiness or some component or condition of happiness. The beliefs Kant is interested in are *rational* beliefs, i.e., beliefs which reason creates for the sake of completing the rational systematic structure of its theoretical knowledge or practical commitment, but they are beliefs (not knowledge) because they lack a sufficient objective base to support them on the level of certainty which we require of knowledge. The hopes that one may entertain in consequence of doing what one ought to do are hopes for things in which we have rational belief. Knowing draws the conclusion that something is because something happens; hoping concludes that something is because something *ought* to happen. Hope infers that something is because human beings ought to do what the moral law requires. What hope infers is neither known nor merely believed: hope is belief that has a power of attraction and influence upon behavior.

We shall outline Kant's conception of hope under three headings: the hopes that can be fulfilled only in the supersensible world (eschatological hopes) and two hopes that may be fulfilled in the future history of mankind.

a. Eschatological Hopes

These hopes are discussed in the Dialectic of the *Critique of Practical Reason* (pp. 304–317).

There are two eschatological hopes, one for eternal life[6] and one for the *summum bonum*, the attainment of happiness proportionate to virtue. The latter is "the necessary highest end of a morally determined reason and a true object thereof (p. 307), and "to be in need of happiness and also worthy of it and yet not to partake of it would not be in accordance with the perfect volition of an omnipotent rational being" (p. 304). A basic premise for Kant's

[6]The argument for the justification of this belief and hope is found on p. 311.

entire argument is the assumption that the world is rationally organized, and that it would be irrational to suppose that the two ends of man, one natural and the other moral, could not be brought together.

Traditional argument, on the contrary, moves from the obvious discrepancies between happiness and virtue to the conclusion that God does *not* exist as moral governor of the universe. This is one of the standard solutions to the "problem of evil." Kant accepts the premise, but uses it to infer that it is necessary to believe in the existence of God as a necessary condition for the possibility of the *summum bonum,* which we are duty-bound to seek. Note that Kant does not claim to prove the existence of God in this way; he rejects as invalid all "proofs" of the existence of God (pp. 136–148), but here argues for the necessity of *believing* in God. Whether the belief is true is a matter beyond the boundary of human knowledge.

The argument goes as follows. The *summum bonum* does not arise in nature, because virtue is neither the cause nor the effect of happiness. Therefore in this life the *summum bonum* is not realized, but I am morally bound to seek it. We hope for it, therefore, in another (noumenal) world, and a necessary condition of this hope is the belief that it is possible. I can believe it possible only if I assume that there is a God who dispenses happiness in proportion to virtue. Therefore I must believe in the existence of God. This belief supports my hope for the *summum bonum.*

Whatever one may think of the soundness of this argument, there is a question as to whether it is consistent with the rest of Kant's moral philosophy. The danger is that the hope of happiness in the *summum bonum* will become the motive or incentive to virtue, and thus destroy virtue itself as autonomy. (Hoping for happiness in heaven is no better a moral incentive for virtue than hoping for it on earth.) Kant tries to show that the purity of the moral motive (acting out of respect for the law) need not be destroyed (though it often is) by the expectation and hope of celestial happiness (p. 315). Moral obligation stands even if there is no God, he says, and it ought to and can stand unmoved in the mind of anyone who believes, whether correctly or incorrectly, that there is a God. However, it stands also in the person who, however inconsistently, does his duty but believes that there is no God and no hope for the highest good; he instances Spinoza as a man of morals but without hope. Whether Kant was successful in maintaining both the autonomy of the virtuous will and the necessity of hope for the *summum bonum* has been a matter of debate among Kant scholars for generations.

Because the belief in God is founded on a moral argument, everything believed about God that has not to do with morality is, according to Kant, "the stupidity of superstition and the madness of fanaticism." Morality is wholly independent of religion, and religion is, or at least ought to be, nothing but taking the moral law as (as if) a divine command (p. 315). Kant rejects all the nonmoral arguments for the existence of God, and rejects all religious ceremonies and works of religion as having no moral significance (except a negative one — they may, and usually do, displace the true moral motive with the motives of fear and hope of divine favor). But the only way to worship God and to secure the peace of God is to respond to the moral calling, and hope.

Kant tells us nothing about the object of our eschatological hope except that it is an eternal life of continuous moral improvement. If such exist, it is in the transcendent world of which we know nothing. All religious talk about it is symbolical and metaphorical (p. 222). Kant, despising everything in religion except its moral import, was a biblical exegete skillful in uncovering moral meanings in scriptural texts, and with this interpretation of the Scriptures he claimed that there was an intimate connection between his moral philosophy and Christianity.

b. Hopes for Political Progress

These hopes are expressed and examined in *Idea for a Universal History, Perpetual Peace, What is Enlightenment?* (Selections IX, X, and XI in this book), and *The Strife of the Faculties* (1798).

Belief in the inevitable and endless progress of mankind was almost universal among eighteenth-century philosophers. Kant saw mankind as having in the past taken one momentous step from a state of nature (Hobbes' state of war of each against all) to a juridical state governed by laws, and projected this movement into the future. He foresaw two further steps which he believed mankind could and would take: one, from juridical societies with various constitutions (including those of despotism) to republican states in which human beings would govern themselves by laws in the enactment of which they had participated; and the second, from the state of nature now existing between nations, in which decisions are reached by war, to a league of nations under which states would regulate their external affairs by legal processes instead of violence. He believed that the first was a condition of the second, since citizens of a free state would not (at least if they are smart) wage aggressive war upon other peoples living in other self-governing states.

Kant was confident of the two goals of history because they are natural and not products of undependable moral enthusiasms of the people. It was natural for man to move from a state of nature to a juridical state, and it will be equally natural for him to move on to the two goals because the same natural propensity is responsible for all three. This is what Kant calls man's "unsocial sociability" (p. 417) — his antagonism to his fellows combined with his inescapable need for them. Just as a race of devils, provided they were intelligent, would leave Hobbesian nature for the benefits of civil society, so also could a race of devils establish a republican form of government and a league of nations, and do so out of prudence and without any moral aspiration (p. 443).

Nature has willed that human beings should develop their full potentialities, and this requires many generations and takes place in the whole of the race, not in single individuals here and now. But the hope for it in the indefinite future, inspired by the French and American Revolutions, gives a direction in which human beings will push history.

The life of mankind in a social union held together only by enlightened self-interest of the citizens (like a race of intelligent devils) is culture or civilization, a necessary but not sufficient condition for morality. We are civilized, Kant says, but far from having reached morality, and "Everything good that is not based upon a morally good disposition is nothing but pretense and glittering misery" (p. 422). A moral community requires something more than the intelligence of devils. Can we hope for something more?

c. The Hope for the Kingdom of God on Earth

This hope is examined in *Religion Within the Boundaries of Reason Alone.* (1793).

Morality cannot be enforced in a juridical commonwealth, for though the state may require certain actions, it cannot require that these actions be done out of a moral motive. Though the advent of the civil state lifts man from the state of nature, it does not raise him to an ethical state. If, however, human beings united in a civil society become motivated by the moral law while they obey the juridical laws of the society, they will see the laws of the society as morally right. Kant calls a community of human beings morally as well as juridically united an *ethical commonwealth.*

An ethical commonwealth cannot be established, like a state, by a human individual, for each individual has moral power only over his own character. Yet for the full moral development of human nature, human beings must be and must feel united with other moral agents who are worthy of being treated as ends in themselves and from whom respect and even practical love may be expected. For the establishment of an ethical commonwealth for which man hopes, he feels the need of divine assistance and thinks that, in the foundation of Christianity, he has had it. Consequently belief in God supports the hope of the triumph of good over moral indifferentism and evil in the course of history. The instrument of that triumph will be "the people of God" united in "the true church."

Fundamental to this (and to the dispute between Kant and the Berlin ministry—see p. 5) is the distinction between the *church visible* and the *church invisible.* The church visible is not based on pure rational faith but on ecclesiastical faith in historical documents and traditions. It enforces actions, and tries to enforce motives. It may be an arm of the state. It is not the ethical commonwealth Kant is speaking of. The *church invisible* comprises those who worship God by doing their duty from moral motives in the confident hope that the realm of ends will be established as the *summum bonum* in history and not in eternity only. The church visible derives morality from theology and history; the church invisible has no theological tenets except those implied by moral laws. It is the church invisible that represents the hope of rational religion for an ethical commonwealth:

. . . In the end religion will gradually be freed from all empirical
determining grounds and from all statutes which rest on history and
which, through the agency of ecclesiastical faith, provisionally unite
men for the requirements of the good. . . . We have good reason to
say . . . that *the kingdom of God is come unto us* once the principle of
the gradual transition of ecclesiastical faith to the universal religion of
reason, and so to a (divine) ethical state on earth, has become
general and has gained somewhere a public foot-hold, even though
the actual establishment of this state is still infinitely removed from us.[7]

4. What is Man?

Kant says this question sums up all the others. Long before formulating the
other questions, he had stated: "If there is any science which man really
needs, it is the one which I teach, [which instructs him] how properly to fill
the place assigned to man in creation, and from which he can learn what he
must be in order to be a man." Yet, paradoxical as it may seem, Kant nowhere
answers this question. Or, perhaps, on the contrary, his whole philosophy is
an answer to it. We cannot find a sentence or a paragraph containing the
answer; the answer if given at all must be found in the whole of his works.
With a task of such magnitude, it is little wonder that there is no unanimous
answer. The one I find most nearly satisfactory must include the following:

a. Man is a Citizen of Two Worlds
The Conclusion of the *Critique of Practical Reason* (p. 325 – 326) is only
one, albeit the most vivid, of the texts for this conception of man's dual
citizenship. The view of the starry heavens "annihilates, as it were, my
importance as an animal creature, which must give back to the planet (a mere
speck in the universe) the matter from which it came." As phenomenon, man
is almost nothing in the mechanism of nature. The contemplation of the
moral law, on the contrary, "infinitely raises my worth as that of an intelligence by my personality, in which the moral law reveals a life independent of
all animality and even of the whole world of sense." As noumenon, the
person is above price and has dignity; in the world of phenomena, man is
subject, almost a slave, to his fate determined by inexorable causal laws.

The conception of "two worlds" is a metaphor which should not be taken
literally. We generate problems for our understanding of Kant if we read him
as if there were two men instead of one — one living in the world of space and
time, one inhabiting an intelligible but unknowable world. Rather we must
take much more seriously and literally those regrettably few passages in
which Kant speaks of seeing *the same being* from two points of view: one from
that of scientists who want to explain human behavior under causal laws, and

---

[7] *Religion Within the Boundaries of Reason Alone* (transl. T. H. Greene and H. H. Hudson, New
York, 1960), pp. 112, 113.

one from a person's own point of view while making decisions (a point of view each person shares with those who hold him responsible for his actions). The worlds are perspectives from two points of view. Things do not look the same (either metaphorically or literally) from different points of view; the phenomenal man is understood in a conceptual context that does not apply to noumenal man, but there is only one man. Thus we can speak of man's dual citizenship, not of him as one being in one world and another in another world.

The distinction between the noumenal and the phenomenal man is not an ontological dualism. But we can ask which is the more fundamental, the more explanatory, of the two perspectives on the common being.

b. Man is a Creator

If the *Critique of Pure Reason* and the *Prolegomena* are correct, nature is the world of phenomena under laws which have been, as it were, enacted by the legislation of the human intellect. This is the Copernican Revolution in philosophy: as the astronomer impresses upon the astronomical phenomena the consequences of his own motion, so the human intellect impresses upon the phenomena the spatio-temporal and causal relations which not only make it possible for us to know something of nature a priori, but make nature itself (organized appearances of unknown and unknowable things in themselves) possible. Man is the creator of nature as phenomena under law.

In Kant's ethical writings, one comes upon what I have called his Rousseauistic Revolution. The question for Rousseau was: how can man obey laws and yet be free? His answer was: by participating in the law-making process, so that he is sovereign as much as subject. Kant raises this political theory to moral status, and calls the conception *autonomy*. Man is not only the executor but also the legislator of the moral law. He is sovereign in the realm of ends.

There are two other passages in our Selections which, though they do not occupy a very prominent programmatic place in Kant's philosophy as a whole, illustrate the creative role Kant ascribes to man. One is from the *Idea for a Universal History* (p. 417): "Nature has willed that man should, by himself, produce everything that goes beyond the mechanical ordering of his animal existence, and that he should partake of no other happiness or perfection than that which he himself, independently of instinct, has created by his own reason." Man is the creator of culture, without help from above.

Finally, man is a creator of art. "Genius is the talent or natural gift which gives the rule to art" (p. 381). Fine art is the art of genius; its essence is not that it imitates nature, but that through man the creative forces of nature are productive of beautiful things.

Thus man is a creator in nature, in morality, in history and culture, and in art. It would not be difficult to add to this list of creative functions Kant assigns to man. Creation is free and spontaneous and though it may produce rules, it does not follow rules dictated by some other metaphysical being.

c. Man is Finite

Kant, unlike his followers among the German idealists, never forgot that man's creativity is exercised in a world he never made. He is a creator within narrow limits, and a creator whose acts are incomprehensible to us.

The narrow limits of human creativity are set by things as they are in themselves. It is often said that the thing in itself is inconsistent with the rest of Kant's philosophy, and many Kantian philosophers have tried, with varying degrees of success, to purge Kantianism of this surd. It is, however, a constant reminder to Kant and to us that man does not create the world *ex nihilo,* but created the Euclidean, Newtonian world by applying laws of his mind to raw material which, so far as we know, might have been quite otherwise. Not all knowledge is a priori; the source of the brute a posteriori facts is something man did not create, and something he cannot understand. The "world" man creates is a perspective on a world he did not create. There is no metaphysical paranoia in Kant; while Kant's man exercises many functions previously assigned to God, man is not a god.

d. Man is a Being of Infinite Value

In a rational system all conditions are traced back to the unconditioned. Thus we look backward to the first cause of the world, and we look forward to the final end or purpose of the world. We look for the first cause, but since it is not within the boundaries of experience we cannot find it and know what it is. The final goal of all things, seen as some future event or state of affairs after which there will be nothing, the goal of creation having been attained, is likewise unknowable, not because our knowledge of the future is insufficient but because the end of the world[8] would be at a boundary of knowledge, the end of time. But we find that a teleological world in which every single thing may be regarded as having a purpose dependent upon supersensible reality does not constitute a single teleological system unless there is something that is the goal of all goals taken collectively. It is irrational that every thing should have a purpose, but everything should not. Kant finds the goal of creation in the human being, not in the human being as an animal organism but as a moral being, whose good will is the only thing in the universe of absolute and unqualified value — supremely good, but good for the sake of nothing else. Thus man as the vehicle of absolute and unqualified value, a being of dignity above price, is a being of infinite worth, whether he come at the end of time or in the present.

e. Man is a Mystery

To comprehend something is to show why it could not be otherwise. It is to state the conditions under which it must be what it is. The unconditioned cannot be comprehended, but we can comprehend its incomprehensibility (p. 298). If there is divine omniscience, it may know why we intuit objects in space and time, judge them as substances and causes and effects; it may know

---

[8] See Kant's essay, "The End of all Things," in *Kant on History.*

why our intuition is sensible instead of intellectual; it may comprehend the practical unconditional necessity of the moral law; but we do not. Perhaps Kant and we do not really know the answer to his last question: What is man?

NOTE ON THE TEXTS

The General Introduction has presented a survey of Kant's philosophy as a whole; the Editor's Introductions to each selection provide essential information about the historical context and philosophical content of the selected texts as well as expositions of their more difficult parts.

In the texts, Kant's footnotes are indicated by an asterisk * or a dagger †, the Editor's by arabic numbers. Words and phrases enclosed in square brackets have been inserted by the Editor.

The numbers in the margins of the selections from the *Critique of Pure Reason* refer to the pages of the second edition, 1787, but a few numbers preceded by the letter A are references to the first edition, 1781. References elsewhere to the *Critique of Pure Reason* are marked A for the first edition and B for the second. Since most modern editions show these numbers, and scholarly writing on Kant employs this system of reference, the use of commentaries and other secondary material is facilitated by this standard pagination.

Marginal numbers in the remaining texts refer to pages in the edition of the Royal Prussian Academy of Sciences, Berlin, 1902 to 1912. Again, since scholarly writing usually cites this edition, use of secondary writings is made easy by reference to these numbers.

Kant's typography was extravagant in its use of italics, boldface, and *Sperrdruck*. I have followed him only sparingly, making use of italics only where they definitely contribute to clarity, supply necessary emphasis, or conform to conventions of present-day printing.

Information on the source of translations used is given in the Editor's Introduction to each selection.

SUGGESTIONS FOR FURTHER READING

Beck, Lewis White. *Early German Philosophy. Kant and His Predecessors.* Harvard University Press, 1969. Chapter XVII.

Cassirer, Ernst. *Kant's Life and Thought.* Translated by James Haden. Yale University Press, 1981.

Copleston, Frederick. *A History of Philosophy,* vol. VI, Part ii: *Kant.* Garden City: Image Books, 1960.

DeVleeschauwer, Herman-J. *The Development of Kantian Thought.* Translated by A.R.C. Duncan. Edinburgh: Thomas Nelson & Son, 1962.

Körner, Stephan. *Kant.* Yale University Press, 1982.

Kroner, Richard. *Kant's Weltanschauung.* Translated by John E. Smith. University of Chicago Press, 1956.

I

An Enquiry into the Distinctness of the Fundamental Principles of Natural Theology and Morals

(The Prize Essay)

Editor's Introduction

The dominant philosophy in Germany when Kant was a young man was the Leibniz-Wolffian philosophy. It was heir to the rationalistic theory formulated by Descartes, according to which mathematics, the science which achieves the highest degree of certainty, was the proper model for all efforts at gaining knowledge. Descartes, Spinoza, Leibniz, Wolff, and countless lesser philosophers tried to imitate, or duplicate, the procedures of mathematics, as they understood them, in their metaphysical and general philosophical writings. Wolff was speaking almost a commonplace when he wrote in 1729: "The rules of philosophical method are the same as the rules of mathematical method" (*Preliminary Discourse on Philosophy in General,* Sec. 139).

In 1762 the Royal Academy of Sciences in Berlin, whose membership was divided almost equally between Wolffians and anti-Wolffians, announced a competition for the best essay answering the following questions: "Whether metaphysical truths generally, and in particular the fundamental principles of natural theology and morals, are capable of proofs as distinct[1] as those of geometry? And if not, what is the true nature of their certainty, to what degree can this certainty be developed, and is this degree sufficient for conviction?" Or, to put it more succinctly: Is the Wolffian mathematical ideal attainable in philosophy?

The prize was won by a leading Berlin philosopher of Wolffian persuasion, Moses Mendelssohn. He answered the first question affirmatively, though he acknowledged that metaphysical concepts and proofs are not as readily comprehensible as those of geometry. Although the Academy gave the prize to Mendelssohn, they voted to publish, along with Mendelssohn's, the essay by the then unknown Immanuel Kant. The two were published together in 1764.

Kant answered that mathematical certainty was not greater than metaphysical certainty but was of a quite different kind, and that the certainty proper to each was achieved by the use of wholly diverse methods. Mathematics, he said, proceeds synthetically. It moves from stipulative definitions through constructions of objects of these definitions in intuition to the derivation of new truths which render themselves

---

[1] Distinctness *(Deutlichkeit)* is one of the rationalistic criteria of truth, the other being clearness. Clarity has to do with the intuitive evidence of ideas; distinctness has to do with definitions, differences, classifications, and organization of ideas.

visible, as it were, to the mind's eye upon inspection of these constructions and whatever else they entail. Metaphysics, on the other hand, deals with concepts which cannot be intuited and constructed, and if they are defined at all it is at the end of philosophical examination, not at the beginning. The concepts are derived from experience, by an abstractive or analytic procedure, and then are synthesized and systematized. Rejecting the Leibniz-Wolffian mathematical paradigm, Kant wrote: "The genuine method of metaphysics is, in fundamentals, identical with that which was introduced into natural science by Newton. . . ." (p. 36). Kant held that metaphysics so conducted could establish the existence and attributes of God and is therefore an adequate foundation for natural theology. His answer to the question of the certainty achievable in morals is not as positive as his answer to the metaphysical part of the question; he leaves it an open question whether morals are based on reason or on feeling.

In the context of Kant's whole philosophy, two things stand out in this early essay. (1) Kant embarked on his long search for the foundations of mathematics and metaphysics.[2] The Prize Essay draws a sharp dividing line between mathematical and other rational knowledge, and this line was preserved with little or no change throughout the later writings. He defended this distinction by developing many of his later conceptions, such as those of pure intuition, the ideality of space, and the distinction between analytical and synthetical a priori judgments.

(2) In the metaphysical parts of the Prize Essay, Kant set out on a path he was later to abandon. Here he insisted upon a gradual transition between the knowledge we have from experience as worked up in natural science, and metaphysical knowledge which was simply a more abstract, universal, and synoptic extension of our scientific knowledge. We may call this "the continuity thesis." He later saw that if, following this thesis, we extend theoretical scientific knowledge without limit into the sphere of metaphysics, we threaten (or deny) the practical (moral) use of reason because the resulting metaphysics will be mechanistic and materialistic. Consequently, one of his tasks became the overthrow of the continuity thesis and the preservation of the purity (freedom from empirical content) of metaphysics. This radical shift in the relation of metaphysics to natural science becomes evident in the second selection, from the Inaugural Dissertation.

―――――――――――

The translation (complete) is by the Editor and was first published in Kant's Critique of Practical Reason and Other Writings on Moral Philosophy *(University of Chicago Press, 1949). A few minor emendations have been made in this reprinting.*

[2] Actually he had started this search in some Latin writings of the previous decade but had made little progress.

An Enquiry into the Distinctness of the Fundamental Principles of Natural Theology and Morals

(The Prize Essay)

Verum animo satis haec vestigia parva sagaci Sunt, per quae possis cognoscere caetera tute (For a keen-scented mind, these little footprints are enough to enable you to know all the rest. —LUCRETIUS

The question proposed is of such a kind that, if it can be properly answered, higher philosophy must in consequence achieve a definite form. Once we have established the method by which the highest possible certainty in philosophy can be achieved, and understood the nature of this assurance, an unchanging precept of instruction must bring thinkers together in the same kind of labor. It will replace the perpetual instability of opinions and school-factions, just as Newton's method in natural science changed the extravagance of physical hypotheses into an unequivocal procedure conforming to experience and geometry. But what kind of exposition should there be in this essay itself, in which metaphysics is to be shown both its true measure of certainty and the way in which this can be reached? If this exposition is itself metaphysics, its conclusion is just as uncertain as is the science which now hopes by this exposition to obtain some degree of consistency and stability; in this event all is lost. I shall, therefore, let certain empirical propositions and immediate inferences from them be the entire content of my essay. I shall trust neither the teachings of philosophers, the uncertainty of which is precisely the occasion of our present task, nor definitions, which often delude. The method I use will be both simple and cautious. Some ideas which may still be found uncertain will be of such a kind as serve only for elucidation but not for proof.

FIRST REFLECTION

GENERAL COMPARISON OF THE WAY OF ATTAINING CERTAINTY IN MATHEMATICAL KNOWLEDGE WITH THAT IN PHILOSOPHICAL KNOWLEDGE

I. Mathematics Achieves All Its Definitions Synthetically; Philosophy Achieves Its Analytically

We can reach any universal concept in two ways, viz., through arbitrary combination of concepts or through isolating those elements of knowledge

29

which have been made distinct by analysis. Mathematics formulates definitions only in the former way. We arbitrarily think, for example, of four lines inclosing a plane so that the opposite sides are not parallel, and we call this figure a trapezoid. The concept which I define is not given prior to the definition but only arises by means of it. Outside mathematics a cone may mean what it pleases; but in mathematics it arises from the arbitrary conception of a right triangle rotating on one of its legs. The definition obviously arises here and in all other cases through synthesis.

But the situation is entirely different with philosophical definitions. Here the concept of a thing is already given, though confusedly or insufficiently determined. I must analyze it, compare its isolated characteristics with the given concept in all kinds of cases, and make this abstract thought detailed and definite. Everyone has, for example, a concept of time; this is to be
277 defined. I must consider this idea in various kinds of relations in order to discover its characteristics by analysis; I must combine different abstract characteristics in order to see whether they give an adequate concept, whether they are consistent among themselves, and whether or not one of them partially contains the other. If I wished to try to arrive synthetically at a definition of time, what a fortunate accident would have to occur in order for this synthetic concept to be exactly that which fully expresses the idea given to us!

Still, we shall be told, philosophers sometimes define synthetically and mathematicians analytically. For instance, the philosopher arbitrarily thinks of a substance having the faculty of reason and calls it a mind. But I answer that such definitions of the meaning of a word are never philosophical definitions; if they are to be called definitions at all, they are only grammatical definitions. No philosophy at all is required to say what name I will attribute to an arbitrary concept. Leibniz thought of a simple substance which had only unclear ideas, and he called it a sleeping monad. In so doing, he did not define this monad; rather, he invented it, for the concept of it was not given to him but was created by him. On the other hand, mathematicians have sometimes defined analytically, I admit, but in every case it has been a mistake. Thus Wolff considered similarity in geometry with a philosophical eye in order to comprehend geometrical similarity under the general concept of similarity. But he could better have left that alone, for, when we think of figures in which the angles are equal and the sides proportional, this can in every case be regarded as the definition of the similarity of figures. It is the same with all other spatial similarities. The universal definition of similarity in general is of no concern to the geometer. When, as sometimes happens through a misunderstanding of his responsibility, the geometer concerns himself with such analytical definitions, it is fortunate for mathematics that he actually draws no conclusions from them, or that their immediate consequences constitute a basic mathematical definition. Otherwise this science would be exposed to the same unhappy dissension as is philosophy.

The mathematician deals with concepts — for example, with that of space

in general — which in many cases are subject to philosophical definition. But   278
he takes such a concept as given in accordance with the clear and ordinary
idea of it. Sometimes (chiefly in applied mathematics) he is given philosophical definitions from other sciences, for instance, the definition of fluidity.
That kind of definition does not arise in mathematics but is only used in it. It
is the business of philosophy to analyze concepts which are given as confused,
and to make them detailed and definite; but it is the business of mathematics
to combine and to compare given concepts of magnitude which are clear and
certain in order to see what can be inferred from them.

2. Mathematics in Its Analyses, Proofs, and Inferences Considers the Universal as Concretely within the Signs; Philosophy Considers the Universal Abstractly by Means of the Signs

Since we here deal with our theses only as immediate inferences from
experience, for the present one I appeal, first, to arithmetic, both to the
universal arithmetic of undefined magnitudes and to that which deals with
numbers, where the relation of magnitudes to unity is defined. In both,
instead of things themselves, their signs are posited together with special
indications of their increase or decrease, their ratios, etc. Thereafter we
proceed with these signs according to easy and certain rules of substitution,
addition, subtraction, and many other kinds of operations, so that the indicated things completely drop from sight until the meaning of the symbolic
consequence is finally deciphered. Second, for instance in geometry, in order
to know the properties of all circles, we draw a circle and then draw two
intersecting lines in it instead of all the possible ones. We show the relationship of these two, and in them we observe *in concreto* the universal rule of the
relationship of lines intersecting in any circle.

Compared to this, the procedure in philosophy is quite different. The signs
of philosophical observation are always verbal expressions. In their organization they cannot indicate the partial concepts which constitute the complete
idea expressed by the word, nor in their connections can they signify the
relationships between the philosophical thoughts. In this kind of knowledge,   279
therefore, we must always have the thing itself in view; we must think of the
universal *in abstracto* without being able to make use of the important simpli-
fication of dealing with single signs instead of general concepts of the things
themselves. If a geometer wishes to prove, for example, that space is infinitely divisible, he takes a straight line which stands perpendicular to two
parallels, and then from a point on one of these parallel lines he draws others
which intersect the perpendicular. In this symbol he recognizes with the
greatest certainty that the division must proceed without end. But if a philosopher wishes to prove that every body consists of simple substances, he must
first ascertain that a body in general is a whole of substances, that for these
substances combination is a contingent state without which they could still
exist, and thus that all combination in a body could be abolished in thought

and yet the substances of which a body is composed exist; and since that
which remains of a compounded body when all combination as such is abolished must be simple, he concludes that a body must consist of simple
substances. In this proof neither figures nor visible signs can express the
thoughts or their relations. No substitution of signs by rules can take the
place of abstract contemplation so that the philosopher could exchange the
conception of the things themselves for the clearer and easier conception of
signs; the universal must be considered *in abstracto.*

3. In Mathematics There Are Few Unanalyzable
Concepts and Indemonstrable Propositions,
but in Philosophy There Are Many

The concepts of magnitude as such — unity, quantity, space, etc. — are
unanalyzable at least within mathematics; that is, their analysis and definition do not belong to this science. I know very well that some geometers
mistake the boundaries between the sciences and sometimes wish to philosophize in mathematics in order to try to define this kind of concept, and this
280 in spite of the fact that in such cases the definition has absolutely no mathematical result. But it is certain that a concept is unanalyzable within a
particular discipline if it does not require a definition, at least in this science,
and this is true regardless of whether it may be defined elsewhere or not. And
I have said that there are few such concepts in mathematics; but I go even
further and state that actually none of them can be present in mathematics in
the sense that their definition by analysis of concepts belongs to mathematical knowledge, even granting that the definition is possible elsewhere. For
mathematics never defines by analyzing a given concept. Only by arbitrary
combination can it define an object, the thought of which is first made
possible by this combination.

Compare this with philosophy, and what a difference we see! In all its
disciplines, especially in metaphysics, we need every analysis that can be
made, for the distinctness of knowledge and the possibility of certain inferences depend upon it. But we can see in advance that by analysis we shall
inevitably arrive at unanalyzable concepts, whether these concepts are intrinsically unanalyzable or only unanalyzable for us. We also see that there
will be a good many of these, since it is impossible that universal cognitions of
such great complexity should be compounded from few fundamental concepts. Many concepts, for example, those of a representation,[3] of contiguity,
or of succession, can hardly be defined at all. Others can be defined only in

---

[3] *Vorstellung*, literally *presentation.* This is the word Kant most commonly used to refer to the
contents of consciousness, and is therefore largely equivalent to the Latin *repraesentatio* and to
Locke's word *idea.* Since Kant has another word *(Idee)* which must be translated as *idea* but
which has Platonic rather than a Lockean meaning, it is inadvisable to translate *Vorstellung* as
idea except in cases where the meaning is obviously unambiguous. *Vorstellung* will therefore be
translated generally as *representation*, except in informal contexts where it will be rendered in
nontechnical language as *conception, thought,* or (rarely) *idea.* On the use of *Idee*, see below,
p. 127 n.

part, as, for example, the concepts of space, time, and of many kinds of feelings of the human mind such as those of the sublime, of the beautiful, of the repulsive, etc. Without more exact knowledge and definition of these feelings, the urges of our nature cannot be adequately recognized; they cannot be fully defined even though a careful observer realizes that a [given] analysis is insufficient. I confess that definitions of pleasure and displeasure, of desire and aversion, and countless others of that kind have never been given by adequate analyses, and I do not wonder at their irresolvability. For distinguishable elementary concepts must be at the basis of concepts of such different kinds. The mistake made by some, who attempt to treat these kinds of cognition as though they could all be broken down into a few simple concepts, is an error like that into which ancient students of nature fell when they taught that all the matter of nature consisted of the so-called four elements—a view which has been superseded by better observation.

Furthermore, at the foundations of mathematics there are only few inde- 281 monstrable propositions. Even though they might be proved outside mathematics, within this science they are regarded as immediately certain. "The whole is equal to the sum of its parts." "Only one straight line can be drawn between two points." Mathematicians customarily state such axioms in the beginning to make one aware that only propositions as evident as these are presupposed as true and that all others will be rigorously proved.

If we compare philosophy, and especially metaphysics, with mathematics in this respect, I might well wish to see a table listing the indemonstrable propositions which lie at the foundation of this science in its entire scope. It would take up immeasurable space. The most important occupation of higher philosophy consists only in searching out these indemonstrable basic truths, and discovery of them will never cease so long as knowledge of this kind grows. For, whatever object we take, those characteristics of it which the understanding immediately perceives first are data for just that many indemonstrable propositions, and these then afford the basis on which definitions can be established. Before I even set out to define what space is, I distinctly see that, since this concept is given to me, I must first of all seek out by analysis those characteristics which are immediately thought in this concept. After that I notice that many parts in it are external to each other and that these are not substances (for I do not wish to know objects in space but space itself). Then I notice that space can have only three dimensions, etc. Propositions of this kind can very well be explained; one must see them *in concreto* in order to know them intuitively; but they can never be proved. For how could this be done when we realize that they constitute the first and simplest thoughts I can ever have of the object when I begin to think about it? In mathematics the definitions are the first thought I can have of the defined thing, because my concept of the object arises first from the definition; therefore it is absolutely absurd to consider definitions as demonstrable. In philosophy, where the concept of the thing to be defined is given to me, that which immediately and first of all is perceived in it must serve as an inde-

monstrable fundamental judgment. For, since I do not yet have the whole distinct concept of the thing but rather still seek it, that whole distinct concept is so far from demonstrated by these concepts that it rather serves to generate this distinct cognition and definition. Thus I must have the first
282 fundamental judgments prior to all philosophical definition of things, and I can fall into the error of considering what is merely a derivative characteristic to be a primordial one. In the following observation there will be remarks that will put this beyond doubt.

4. The Object of Mathematics Is Easy and Simple; That of Philosophy Is Difficult and Involved

Since magnitude is the object of mathematics, and since mathematical considerations have regard only to how many times something is posited, it is evident that this knowledge must rest on few and very clear basic theories of general mathematics, which is really universal arithmetic. The increase and decrease of quantities and their resolution into like factors in the theory of roots are easily seen to arise from few and simple basic concepts. A few fundamental concepts of space enable us to apply this general knowledge of quantity to geometry. To convince ourselves of this, we need only, for example, compare the ease in comprehending an arithmetic object which contains a tremendous multiplicity with the very great difficulty in comprehending a philosophical idea through which we try to know but little. The relation of a trillion to unity is very distinctly understood, while philosophers have not yet been able to make the concept of freedom intelligible from its unities, i.e., its simple and familiar concepts. That is, the qualities which make up the proper object of philosophy are infinitely many, and to distinguish between them is extraordinarily demanding; moreover, it is far more difficult to resolve complicated cognitions by analysis than to combine given simple cognitions by synthesis and to reach conclusions in this way. There are many, I know, who
283 find philosophy very easy in comparison with higher mathematics; but they call everything philosophy which is found in books bearing this title. The success shows the difference. Philosophical cognitions often have the fate of opinions and are like meteors whose brilliance holds no promise of duration; they disappear, while mathematics remains. Metaphysics is without doubt the most difficult of all human insights — but a metaphysics has never been written. The question which the Academy proposes shows that we have reason to reconnoiter the path by which we expect, first of all, to seek it.

SECOND REFLECTION

THE SOLE METHOD OF ACHIEVING THE GREATEST POSSIBLE CERTAINTY IN METAPHYSICS

Metaphysics is nothing else than a philosophy of the ultimate grounds of our knowledge; what has been shown in the preceding observation to be true

of mathematical knowledge in comparison with philosophy will hold also
with reference to metaphysics. We have seen noteworthy and essential differences between knowledge in the two sciences, and with reference to them
we can say, with Bishop Warburton, that nothing has been more harmful to
philosophy than mathematics; or better, there is nothing more harmful than
the idea of imitating mathematics as a method of thinking where it cannot
possibly be used; for, as concerns the application of mathematics in those
parts of philosophy where knowledge of quantities occurs, it is a different
matter, and there the usefulness of mathematics is immeasurable.

In mathematics I begin with the definition of my object, such as a triangle
or a circle. In metaphysics I can never so begin, and here the definition is so
far from being the first thing I know of an object that it is rather almost
invariably the last. In mathematics I have no concept whatever of my object
before the definition gives rise to it; in metaphysics I have a concept which is
already given, though confusedly, and I am to search out the distinct, detailed, and definite concept of the object. How can I then begin? Augustine
said, "I know what time is, but when someone asks me, I do not know it."
Many stages in the development of obscure ideas by means of comparison,
subsumption, and limitation must precede definition, and I dare say that, 284
although many acute and true things have been said about time, the real
definition of time has never been given. With regard to nominal definitions,
they help little or not at all, for even without them we understand the word
well enough not to misuse it. If we only had as many correct definitions as
appear under this name in books, with what certainty could we infer and what
conclusions could we derive from them! But experience teaches the contrary.

In philosophy and especially in metaphysics we can often distinctly and
with certainty know very much about an object and derive sure consequences
from it before we are in possession of its definition and even when we do not
undertake to give one. Various predicates of anything can be immediately
certain, although I do not yet know enough to state the definite itemized
concept of the thing, i.e., its definition. Though I might never define what
desire is, I would yet be able to say with certainty that every desire presupposes an idea of that which is desired, that this idea is an anticipation of
something in the future, that it is associated with the idea of pleasure, etc. All
this is constantly perceived by each person in the immediate consciousness of
desire. From comparing observations of this kind with each other, we could
perhaps eventually arrive at the definition of desire. But so long as we can
infer what we seek from some immediately certain characteristics of the
desire, even without a definition of it, it is unnecessary to venture on an
undertaking which is so precarious. In mathematics it is, as we know, entirely
different.

In mathematics the meaning of the signs is certain, because we can easily
know what meaning they were intended to have. In philosophy in general,
and in metaphysics in particular, verbal expressions have their meaning
through customary usage, except where their meaning has been more accu-

rately defined by logical limitation. But because the same expression is frequently used for very similar concepts which nevertheless contain a fair amount of hidden difference, in every application of the concept and even

285 when its designation appears from usage to be entirely fitting, we must carefully note whether it is really an identical concept which is associated with one and the same sign. We say that a man distinguishes gold from brass when he knows, for instance, that they have different densities. We say, moreover, that cattle distinguish one feed from another when they eat one and let the other alone. Here in two cases the word "distinguish" is used, although in the first case it means "to recognize difference," and this can never occur without making a judgment; but in the second it only indicates that, when there are different impressions, the actions are also different even when a judgment need not occur. Thus, in the case of cattle, we know only that they are driven to different actions by different sensations, and this is quite possible without their needing to judge about agreement or difference.

The rules of the only method by which the greatest possible metaphysical certainty can be achieved flow quite naturally from the preceding considerations. They are very different from those which have been previously followed, and, if applied, they promise an issue more favorable than anyone has been able to expect on any other path. The first and chief rule is that one should not begin from definitions, for then only verbal definitions would be sought—for example, "That is necessary, the opposite of which is impossible." But, even with these, there are only a few cases where one can confidently establish a distinctly defined concept at the very beginning. Rather one should carefully seek in one's object that of which one is immediately certain, even before one has a definition of it. One should draw inferences from it and seek to obtain only true and perfectly certain judgments on the object. Nor should one parade a hoped-for definition, or even risk it, until it offers itself manifestly in the most evident judgments and thus must finally be conceded.

The second rule is that one should particularly note immediate judgments of the object with respect to that which is first found with certainty in it; and, after one is certain that one such judgment is not included in the others, they should, like the axioms of geometry, be made the basis of all inferences. From this it follows that in metaphysical considerations one should particu-

286 larly indicate whatever is known with certainty, even though it be little. Though one can make experiments with uncertain cognitions in order to see if they might not lead to clues to certain knowledge, this should be done in such a way that it is not confused with the former. I do not cite the other rules which this method has in common with every other rational method but proceed to make them clear by examples.

The genuine method of metaphysics is, in fundamentals, identical with that which was introduced into natural science by Newton and which had such useful consequences there. It says that, by means of certain experiences and always with the aid of geometry, a search should be conducted for the rules according to which particular appearances of nature occur. Even though we do not understand the ultimate cause of appearances in bodies, it is nevertheless certain that they occur by this law [which Newton discovered], and we explain complicated natural events when we distinctly show how they are included under these well-proved rules. Similarly in metaphysics: through certain inner experience, i.e., self-evident consciousness, we should search for those characteristics which assuredly lie in the concept of any universal property; and, even though we may not know the entire essence of the thing, we can nevertheless make sure use of such characteristics in order to derive from them many properties of the thing.

Example of the Only Sure Method of Metaphysics in the Knowledge of the Nature of Bodies

For the sake of brevity, I refer to a proof, adduced briefly in the First Reflection at the end of § 2, and so use here as a basis the proposition that every body must consist of simple substances. Without establishing what a body is, I know certainly that it consists of parts which would exist even if they were not compounded together; and, if the concept of a substance is an abstract concept, it is without doubt abstracted from corporeal things in the world. But it is not at all necessary to call them substances; it suffices that from them we can infer with utmost certainty that a body consists of simple parts. The obvious analysis of this is easy but too lengthy for this place.[4] Now by means of infallible proofs of geometry I can show that space does not consist of simple parts; and the arguments for this are sufficiently well known not to need repeating. Accordingly, there are a definite number of parts of any body, each of which is simple, and an equal number of parts of the space occupied by the body, each of which parts is compound. From this it follows that each simple part (element) in a body occupies a space. Now if I ask, "What does occupying a space mean?" I become aware, without troubling myself about the essence of space, that if a space can be penetrated by any body without there being anything to resist it, one could certainly, if he wished, say that something was in this space but not that anything *occupied* it. From this I know that a space is occupied by something when there is something there which resists a moving body in its attempt to penetrate into it. This resistance is impenetrability. Consequently, bodies occupy space by impenetrability. Impenetrability, however, is a force, for it exerts resistance, i.e., an action opposing an external force. And the force which belongs to a body must belong to its simple parts. Therefore the elements of every body fill their space by the force of impenetrability. But I ask further: Are not the ultimate elements of a body extended, since each one fills a space? Here for

287

---

[4] It is given in Kant's Latin dissertation, *Physical Monadology*, Theorem II (*Kant's Latin Writings*, ed. L.W. Beck, New York, 1986, p. 118).

once I can offer an explanation which is immediately certain: that is extended which, taken absolutely and by itself, fills a space, just as each single body would fill a space even if I imagined that there were nothing except it. But if I consider an absolutely simple element taken alone and without connection with others, it is impossible that there should be in it a plurality of things outside each other or that it should by itself and absolutely occupy a space; therefore the simple element cannot be extended. But since the reason why the element occupies a space is that it directs against external things a force of impenetrability, I see that out of this flows a plurality in external action but not a plurality of internal parts. Consequently we cannot say, simply because an element occupies a space in the body in connection with others, that it is extended.

288   It will take only a few words to make it evident how superficial are the proofs of metaphysicians when they confidently infer from definitions once placed at the foundation, as is their custom. Their inferences are completely lost if the definitions are deceptive. It is well known that most Newtonians go further than Newton and assert that bodies directly attract each other at a distance (or, as they say, through empty space). I pass over the correctness of this proposition, which indeed has much to be said for it. I merely assert that metaphysics has not refuted it. First, bodies are separated when they are not in contact with each other. This is precisely the meaning of the word. Now if I ask, "What is understood by the word 'contact'?" I become aware, without bothering with the definition, that I judge in each case from the impenetrable resistance of another body that I touch it. For I find that this concept originally arises from feeling. By the judgment of sight I only surmise that one material body touches another, whereas through feeling the impenetrability of resistance I finally come to know it with certainty. Thus if I say, "A body affects a distant body directly," this means the same as, "It affects it directly but not by means of impenetrability." But it is not at all obvious why this should be impossible; to prove this, it would have to be shown that impenetrability is either the only force of a body or at least that one body could not be causally related to another except by virtue of their impenetrability. Since this has never been demonstrated and would presumably be hard to prove, metaphysics at least has no good reason to rebel against direct attraction at a distance.

However, let the arguments of the metaphysicians come forward. First there appears the definition: "Immediate reciprocal presence of two bodies is contact." From this it follows that, when two bodies have direct effects on each other, they are in contact. Things in contact are not separated. Consequently, two separated bodies never affect each other directly. And so forth. The definition is surreptitious. Not every immediate presence is contact, but only that which comes through impenetrability. The rest is built on air.

289   I proceed with my disquisition. It is clear from the examples given that we can say much with certainty about an object, in metaphysics as well as in other

sciences, without having defined it. For here neither body nor space has been defined, and yet on both we have trustworthy propositions. The main point I am aiming at is that in metaphysics we must proceed analytically throughout, for its business is in fact to resolve confused cognitions. If we compare with this the actual procedure of philosophers, as it is the fashion in all schools, how perverted shall we find it! The most highly abstract concepts, to which the understanding naturally proceeds only at the end, constitute their starting-point, because the itinerary of the mathematician is in their heads, and him they wish to imitate under all circumstances. But there is a peculiar difference between metaphysics and every other science. In geometry and other fields of mathematics we begin with the easier things and gradually ascend to more difficult exercises. In metaphysics the start is taken from what is most difficult, from possibility and existence in general, necessity and contingency, etc. These concepts demand much abstraction and attention, especially since in being applied their signs suffer many imperceptible modifications, and the differences between these must not be overlooked. Instead we are told the procedure must by all means be synthetic. Accordingly, one defines at the outset and confidently draws conclusions. Philosophers of this taste congratulate each other on having learned from the geometer the secret of thorough thinking; they do not notice that geometers obtain concepts by synthesis which philosophers can attain only by analysis and that this completely changes the method of thinking.

On the other hand, as soon as philosophers strike out on the natural path of sound reason, seeking first that which they assuredly know about the abstract concept of an object (e.g., space or time) without making any claim to definitions; when they infer only from these sure data; when they inquire at each changed application of a concept whether the concept itself has not changed even though its sign remains the same — then perhaps they will not have so many insights for sale, but those which they do offer will be of definite value. I will give one more illustration of the latter mistake. Most philosophers use as an example of obscure concepts those which we may have in deep sleep. Obscure notions are those of which we are not conscious. Now 290 some experiences show that in deep sleep we do have ideas *(Vorstellungen)*, and, since we are not conscious of them, they must have been obscure. Here *consciousness* has two meanings. Either one is not conscious of having an idea, or one is not conscious that one has had it. The former signifies the obscurity of the idea as it is in the mind; the latter shows no more than that he does not remember it. Now the given example shows only that there can be ideas which one does not remember when awake. But it does not follow that in sleep they could not have been clear to consciousness, as in Sauvage's example of a cataleptic person or in the ordinary actions of a somnambulist. By not giving, through attention to different cases, a definite meaning to the concept, and by jumping too quickly at a conclusion, a presumably great secret of nature is overlooked, namely, that in deepest sleep perhaps the greatest perfection of the mind might be exercised in rational thought. For we have no reason for asserting the opposite except that we do not remember the idea when awake. This reason, however, proves nothing.

It is far from the time for proceeding synthetically in metaphysics, only when analysis will have helped us to distinct concepts understood in their details will synthesis be able to subsume compounded cognitions under the simplest cognitions, as in mathematics.

THIRD REFLECTION

OF THE NATURE OF METAPHYSICAL CERTAINTY

1. Philosophical Certainty is of an Altogether Different Nature from Mathematical Certainty

One is certain in so far as he knows that a cognition cannot possibly be false. The degree of this certainty, when taken objectively, is a matter of the sufficiency of the marks of the necessity of a truth. But so far as it is considered subjectively, it is higher the more intuitive the cognition of this necessity is. In either case, objectively or subjectively, mathematical certainty is of a different kind from philosophical. I shall show this most clearly.

Human understanding, like any other force of nature, is bound by certain rules. We do not err because the understanding connects concepts without any rule, but because we deny to a thing some characteristic we do not perceive, and we judge that that of which we are not conscious in a thing does not exist. Now mathematics first arrives at its concepts synthetically, and it can say with certainty that what it did not intend to represent in its object by definition is not included in it. For the concept of the defined arises first from the definition, and it has no meaning at all other than that which the definition gives it. If we compare philosophy and especially metaphysics with mathematics in this respect, they are far more uncertain in their definitions when they do venture to give them, for the concept of that which is to be defined is already given. If we do not note one or another characteristic even if it belongs to the adequate discrimination of the object, and then judge that this characteristic is lacking in the full concept, the definition becomes false and deceptive. We could bring that kind of error to light by countless examples, but I refer to the example of contact, which I have already given.

Secondly, mathematics, in its inferences and proofs, considers its universal knowledge concretely, in its signs; while philosophy considers its knowledge abstractly, alongside its signs. This makes a noteworthy difference in the way each attains certainty, for, since the signs of mathematics are sensible instruments of knowledge, we can, with the same assurance we have in that which we see, also know that we have left no concept out of sight, that each individual comparison is made according to simple rules, etc. Attention to these matters is greatly facilitated by not having to consider the things in their universal sense but rather signs in the individual cognition we have of them. On the other hand, verbal expressions, as signs of philosophical knowledge, help in nothing but remembering the universal concepts they signify. We must always keep their meaning directly before us. Pure understanding must 292 be kept in a state of exertion, for how imperceptibly a characteristic of an abstract concept may slip away, since nothing given to the senses can reveal its omission! Then different things are held to be the same, and we bring forth erroneous cognitions.

It has now been shown that the grounds from which we can conclude the impossibility of having erred in a particular philosophical cognition are never equal to those we have in mathematics. Moreover, the intuition we have of the correctness of the cognition is greater in mathematics than in philosophy, since in the former the object is considered concretely in the sensible sign, while in the latter it is considered only in universal abstract concepts, the clear impression of which cannot be nearly as great as that of the former. In geometry, where the signs have, in addition, a similarity to the designated things, the evidence is even greater, though in calculations with letters the certainty is just as dependable.

2. Metaphysics Is Capable of a Certainty Which Is Sufficient for Conviction

Certainty in metaphysics is of the same kind as that in any other philosophical knowledge, as the latter can only be certain in so far as it conforms to the universal principles which metaphysics furnishes. We know from experience that on rational grounds even outside mathematics we can in many cases achieve certainty to the point of conviction. Metaphysics is only philosophy applied to more universal rational insights, and it cannot be otherwise with it.

Errors do not arise simply because we do not know some particular things but because we undertake to judge even though we do not know everything requisite. A large number of falsities — indeed, almost all of them — owe their origin to such rashness. You know some predicates of a thing with certainty? Very well, make these the basis of your inferences, and you will not err. But you wish to make a definition with them, although you are not certain 293 that you know everything requisite for a definition? If in spite of this you risk a definition, you fall into error. It is therefore possible to avoid errors if we seek certain and distinct cognitions without presuming to give definitions so readily. Further, you can infer a considerable part of a certain conclusion with assurance, but do not permit yourself to infer to the complete conclusion, however trivial the difference may seem to be. I concede that we have a good proof that the soul is not matter. But take care not to conclude that the soul is not of a material nature, for by this everyone understands not merely that the soul is not matter but also that it is not a simple substance such as an element of matter could be. This requires a special proof, namely, that this thinking being cannot be like a corporeal element in space and that, because of impenetrability, it could, with other corporeal elements, constitute an extended being or a mass. But actually no proof has yet been given of this; and the proof, were it discovered, would show the inconceivable manner in which a mind is present in space.

3. The Certainty of the Ultimate Fundamental Truths in Metaphysics Is of No Other Kind than That in Every Other Rational Knowledge, with the Exception of Mathematics

In our time the philosophy of Crusius* has undertaken to give metaphysics an altogether different form, because he does not concede to the law of contradiction the prerogative of being the universal and supreme principle of all knowledge; rather he has introduced many other immediately certain and indemonstrable principles and asserted that their correctness is grasped by the nature of our understanding according to the rule, "That which I cannot think except as true is true." He counts as such principles the following propositions, among others: what I cannot think of as existing has never existed, everything that exists must be somewhere at some time, and the like. In a few words I shall show the true property of the ultimate truths of metaphysics and also the true import of Crusius' method, which does not depart so far from the manner of philosophical thinking about these matters as one might think. From this one will be able to deduce the degree of certainty possible in metaphysics.

All true judgments must be either affirmative or negative. As the form of any affirmation consists in something being thought as a characteristic of a thing, i.e., as identical with the thing's characteristic, any affirmative judgment is true when the predicate is identical with the subject. And since the form of any negation consists in thinking something as conflicting with a thing, a negative judgment is true when the predicate contradicts the subject. The proposition expressing the essence of any affirmation and thus containing the supreme formula of all affirmative judgments, therefore, reads as follows: "For every subject there is a predicate which is identical with it." This is the law of identity. And the proposition which expresses the essence of all negation is: "No subject has a predicate which contradicts it." This is the law of contradiction, and hence this law is the basic formula of all negative

*I have found it necessary to mention the method of this new philosophy which has quickly become so famous and which has so much merit in respect to the better clarification of many views that it would be an essential lack, when metaphysics itself is discussed, to pass over it in silence. But what I am here dealing with is only the proper method of metaphysics; the difference in single propositions is not sufficient to indicate an essential difference between one philosophy and another.

[Christian August Crusius (1715–1775) was an influential anti-Wolffian philosopher generally held in high esteem by Kant. In several ways he anticipated Kant's own rejection of rationalistic metaphysics, which had insisted upon a mathematical model for metaphysics. — Ed.]

judgments. Both together constitute the supreme and universal principles, in a formal sense, of the entire human reason. And here most philosophers have erred in conceding to the law of contradiction a rank with respect to all truths which it actually has only in respect to negative truths. Every proposition is indemonstrable which is immediately thought under one of these supreme principles and which cannot be thought otherwise; that is, when either identity or contradiction lies directly in the concepts and neither can be nor needs to be seen by analysis through intermediate characteristics. All other propositions are demonstrable. That a body is divisible is a demonstrable proposition, since we can show the identity of the predicate with the subject by analysis, and hence indirectly. (A body is compound, and what is compound is divisible; therefore a body is divisible. The intermediate characteristic here is "compound.") Now in philosophy there are many indemonstrable propositions, as I have said. All of them stand under these formal ultimate principles, though indirectly; but, so far as they also contain grounds of other cognitions, they are the ultimate material principles of human reason. For instance, that a body is compound is an indemonstrable proposition, in so far as the predicate can only be thought as an immediate and primary characteristic in the concept of a body. Such material principles constitute, as Crusius correctly says, the foundation and stability of human reason, for, as we have said, they are the content to be defined and the data from which sure inferences can be drawn even when we have no definition.   295

Crusius is right in reproaching other schools of philosophers for having passed over these material principles and for having restricted themselves merely to formal principles. For from the latter alone nothing at all can be proved, because propositions are required which contain the mediating concept by which the logical relation of other concepts is to be recognized in a syllogism, and among these propositions there must be some which are fundamental. We can never attribute the status of material supreme principles to any propositions if they are not evident to every human understanding. But I hold that several of the principles Crusius adduces even permit of considerable doubt.

With respect to the supreme rule of all certainty which this celebrated man proposes to set before all knowledge and hence also before metaphysical knowledge — "What I cannot think except as true is true," etc. — it is easy to see that this proposition can never be a basis of the truth of any cognition. For if one admits that no other ground of truth can be given than that it would be impossible to regard it otherwise than as true, this is to admit that no further ground of truth can be given, and hence that the cognition is indemonstrable. Now there certainly are many indemonstrable cognitions, but the feeling of conviction with reference to them is an avowal that they are true and not a basis of proof of it.

Metaphysics, therefore, has no formal or material basis of certainty of any   296 other kind than geometry. In both the formal element of judgment occurs in accordance with the laws of identity and contradiction. In both there are indemonstrable propositions which are the foundations of inferences. But since the definitions in mathematics are the primary indemonstrable concepts of the defined things, in their stead various indemonstrable propositions in metaphysics must furnish the primary data. They can be just as certain, and they afford either the content for definition or the basis of sure implications. There is a certainty needed for conviction, and metaphysics is capable of it just as mathematics is, though mathematics is easier and partakes of a greater degree of intuition.

FOURTH REFLECTION

OF THE DISTINCTNESS AND CERTAINTY OF WHICH THE PRIMARY GROUNDS OF NATURAL THEOLOGY AND MORALS ARE CAPABLE

1. The Primary Grounds of Natural Theology Are Capable of the Greatest Philosophical Evidence

A thing can be most easily and distinctly differentiated from all others when it is the only possible thing of its kind. The object of natural religion is the only first cause; its attributes are so constituted that they cannot easily be mistaken for those of another. The greatest conviction is possible where it is absolutely necessary that precisely these and no other predicates apply to a thing; for with accidental attributes it is often difficult to discover the variable conditions of the predicates of a thing. The absolutely necessary being is therefore an object of such a kind that, as soon as one obtains a true clue to its concept, it seems to promise more certainty than most other philosophical cognitions. Concerning this part of the problem I cannot do more than direct attention to the possible philosophical knowledge of God in general, for it would take us too far afield to examine the actual theories of philosophers on this subject.

The chief concept which offers itself to the metaphysician in this field is
297   that of the absolutely necessary existence of a being.[5] In order to arrive at this concept, he could first ask whether it be possible that nothing at all existed. When he becomes aware that then neither existence nor anything that might be thought is given, and that no possibility takes place, he may investigate only the concept of the existence of that which must be the foundation of all possibility. This thought will broaden itself, and it will establish the definite concept of the absolutely necessary being. Without going particularly into this procedure, it is clear that as soon as the existence of the one and only

---

[5]This form of the ontological argument was first formulated by Kant in *A New Exposition of the Fundamental Principles of Metaphysical Knowledge* (a Latin dissertation of 1755), Proposition VII; and *The One Possible Basis for a Demonstration of the Existence of God* (1762), Observation IV.

most perfect and necessary being is known, the concepts of its other attributes will become much more precise, because they are without exception the greatest and most perfect, and they are much more certain since only those can be admitted which are necessary to the being. I wish, for example, to define the concept of divine omnipresence. I easily recognize that the being on which everything else depends, while itself independent, will determine by its presence the location of everything else in the world, but that it itself cannot have a location among them, for then it would belong, with them, to the world. Therefore, God is, properly speaking, in no place, but He is present to all things in all places where they are. Similarly I see that, since the successive things of the world are in His power, He does not take up a particular point in this series; thus I see that with respect to Him nothing is future or past. If I say that God foresees the future, that does not mean that He sees what is future with respect to Himself but what is future with respect to certain things in the world, that is, what follows on the condition in which they are. From this it is seen that knowledge of the future, past, and present with respect to the actions of the divine understanding is identical and that God sees them all as real things in the universe. Thus we can conceive of this prevision much more definitely and distinctly as belonging to God than as belonging to a thing which is a part of the world-whole.

In all cases where an analogy to contingency is not present, therefore, metaphysical knowledge of God can be very certain. But judgments of His free actions, of providence, of the ways of His justice and benevolence, even in the concepts which we have of these attributes in ourselves, are far less developed; in this science they can have either certainty only by approximation or certainty which is moral.

2. The Primary Grounds of Morals Are, in Their Present State, Not Yet Capable of All Requisite Evidence

298

In order to make this clear, I wish only to show how little even the primary concept of obligation is known, and how far removed we must therefore be in practical philosophy from proffering the distinctness and certainty of fundamental concepts and principles which are required for evidence. One ought to do this or that and leave something else undone; this is the formula under which every obligation is enunciated. Now that "ought" expresses a necessity of action and is capable of two meanings. That is, either I ought to do something (as a means) if I wish something else (as an end), or I ought directly to do something and make it real (as an end). The former we can call the necessity of means *(necessitatem problematicam)*, and the latter the necessity of ends *(necessitatem legalem)*. No obligation is present in necessity of the first kind; it only prescribes the solution of a problem, saying what are the means I must use if I wish to reach a particular end. When anyone prescribes to another the actions which he should do or refrain from doing if he wishes to promote his happiness, perhaps all the teachings of morals could be brought under precepts; but they are then no longer obligations but only like what might be called the obligation to make two arcs if I wish to bisect a line. That is, they are not obligations at all but only counsels to suitable actions if one wishes to attain a particular end. Since the use of means has no other necessity than that which pertains to the end, it follows that all actions which morals prescribe under the condition of particular ends are contingent and cannot be called obligations so long as they are not subordinated to an end necessary in itself. I ought, for example, to promote the greatest total perfection, or I ought to act according to the will of God; to whichever of these propositions all practical philosophy were subordinated, that proposition, if it is to be a rule and principle of obligation, must command the action as directly necessary, not commanding it merely under the condition of some

299 particular end. And here we find that such an immediate supreme rule of all obligation would have to be absolutely indemonstrable. For from no consideration of a thing or concept, whatever it be, is it possible to know and infer what we should do, unless what is presupposed is an end and the action a means. But this it must not be, because it would then be a formula not of obligation but only of skill in solving a problem.

Now I can briefly suggest, after long consideration of this subject, that I am convinced that the rule, *Do the most perfect thing that can be done by you* is the primary formal principle of all obligation of commission, and the proposition *Refrain from that whereby the greatest perfection possible through you is hindered* is the primary formal principle with respect to the duty of omission. And just as nothing follows from the primary formal principles of our judgments of truth except when primary material grounds are given, so also no particular definite obligation follows from these two rules except when indemonstrable material principles of practical knowledge are connected with them.

In these times we have first begun to realize that the faculty of conceiving the truth is cognition, while that of sensing the good is feeling, and that they must not be interchanged. Just as there are unanalyzable concepts of the true, that is, what is met with in the objects of knowledge considered by themselves, there is also an unanalyzable feeling for the good. (The good is never found in a thing by itself but always with relation to a feeling being.) It is a task of the understanding to resolve the compounded and confused concept of the good and to make it distinct by showing how it arises from simpler sensations of the good. But if the sensation of the good is simple, the judgment, "This is good," is completely indemonstrable and a direct effect of the consciousness of the feeling of pleasure associated with the conception of the object. And since there are many simple sensations of the good certainly in us, there are many simple unanalyzable conceptions of the good. Consequently, if an action is directly thought of as good without surreptitiously containing another particular good which can be found in it by analysis, and because of which it is called perfect, it follows that the necessity of

300 this action is an indemonstrable material principle of obligation. For in-

stance, "Love him who loves you" is a practical proposition which certainly and directly stands under the supreme formal and affirmative rule of obligation. For since it cannot be shown by further analysis why a particular perfection inheres in mutual love, this rule is not proved practically, i.e., by tracing it back to the necessity of another perfect action. Rather, it is directly subsumed under the universal rule of good actions. It may be that my example does not distinctly and convincingly prove my point; but the limits of an essay like the present one—which I have perhaps already exceeded—do not allow me the completeness which I would wish. There is an immediate deformity in an action which conflicts with the will of that Being from Whom our existence and everything good is derived. This deformity is clear even if no attention is given to the disadvantages which can accompany such conduct as its consequence. Therefore, the proposition that we should do that which conforms to the will of God becomes a material principle of morals standing formally, but directly, under the already mentioned supreme and universal formula. Just as in theoretical philosophy, so also in the practical we should not so readily consider something indemonstrable when it is not. Nevertheless, these principles cannot be dispensed with, for as postulates they contain the foundations of the rest of the practical propositions. In this respect, under the name of the "moral feeling," Hutcheson and others have provided a start toward some excellent observations.

From this it can be seen that, although it must be possible to achieve the highest degree of philosophical evidence in the primary bases of morality, the supreme principles of obligation must first be defined with more certainty. In this respect the task is greater in practical than in speculative philosophy, since it is still to be settled whether it is simply the cognitive faculty or whether it is feeling (the primary inner ground of the appetitive faculty) which decides the basic principles of practical philosophy.

POSTSCRIPT 301

These are the thoughts which I submit to the judgment of the Royal Academy of Sciences. I venture to hope that the principles I have expounded are of some significance for the desired clarification of the subject. I have preferred to be neglectful with respect to carefulness, proportion, and neatness of execution so that I should not, by attending to them, be hindered from transmitting these thoughts for examination within the allowed time, especially since this lack can easily be made up in the event that the essay is favorably received.

II

On the Form and Principles of
the Sensible and the Intelligible World

(The Inaugural Dissertation)

Editor's Introduction

In 1770 Kant was appointed Professor of Logic and Metaphysics in the University of Königsberg, and by the regulations of the University was required to prepare a Latin dissertation as the subject of debate (a "Disputation," it was called) by his students. Kant, already forty-six years old, had been impatient for this promotion, but it came at an unpropitious time for him, at a time when his philosophical views were unsettled and he was moving rapidly from some old to some new ways of thinking.

He had read Leibniz's *New Essays Concerning the Human Understanding* when it was first published several years before. This gave him a quite different picture of Leibniz's philosophy from the one that he had known before this time, and from it Kant got a new conception of "innate ideas." About 1768 Kant, apparently for the first time, read deeply in Plato, and the influence of Plato is clearly visible both in the subject matter and the terminology of the Inaugural Dissertation. In 1768 he discovered the "paradox of incongruent counterparts," which brought about a complete revolution in his theory of space (see p. 62). Apparently, in 1769 Kant came across the basic idea that led to the doctrine of the antinomies of pure reason. He said, "The year '69 brought great light," but before all these new ideas were illuminated by the great light he was forced by circumstances to write his Dissertation. It is no wonder, then, that old ideas appear side-by-side with new ones, and that they are not all completely consistent. Most of the Leibniz-Wolffian traditional metaphysics, which he was soon to give up, stands next to new ideas he was never again to surrender, such as the theory of space and time; mixed with them are new ideas he would seriously modify in his next book, *Critique of Pure Reason.* Truly, the Inaugural Dissertation deserves to be called a transitional book, it is a bridge from Kant's precritical and critical philosophy.

The basic new doctrine which underlies the Inaugural Dissertation is that there are two independent sources of, and kinds of, knowledge (§7). This replaces the Leibniz-Wolffian doctrine that there is one source of knowledge which appears in two forms, clear and obscure. Kant thinks the mind has two distinct faculties (abilities): the capacity to be affected by things (sense) and the faculty of spontaneous thought (reason). The objects of the first are sensible objects, phenomena, or appearances. Sensibility gives knowledge of things as they appear. Reason, on the other hand, has two functions. In its *logical* use (p. 55) it reflects on (abstracts, synthesizes, generalizes) the data of the senses and converts them into knowledge of the sensible world. In its *real* use reason goes wholly beyond the senses and gives us knowledge of noumena, of things as they are in themselves. Thus arises the so-called "two-world" theory, the Platonic theory that there is a sensible and an intelligible world, the former a mere appearance of the latter. With the acceptance of this theory, of course, the "continuity thesis" of the Prize Essay (p. 28) is given up.

Equally profound changes are made in the theory of sensible knowledge. According to the Leibniz-Wolffian philosophy with its one irreducible cognitive faculty, the structure of the world of sensibility is an implicit *logical* structure, since perception is only confused or obscure thought. Perhaps as a consequence of his treatment of the difference between mathematical and metaphysical thought in the Prize Essay, perhaps as a consequence of his discovery of the antinomy of space and time, and certainly as a consequence of the discovery of the paradox of incongruent counterparts, Kant argues now that sense perception has its own irreducible a priori forms different from the logical forms of thought or reason. They are space and time.

This makes a major contribution to a new theory of mathematical knowledge. Our a priori knowledge is not limited to logical necessities, but can be based on the forms of sensibility. Since space is a necessary form of our sense perception, we can know a priori that the truths of geometry apply to the phenomena perceived through the senses, because the phenomena perceived through the senses are the way things necessarily appear to creatures like us whose sensibility is spatio-temporal. This doctrine passes unchanged into the *Critique of Pure Reason* and the *Prolegomena.*

Kant is not yet ready to make an equally comprehensive revolution in his understanding of metaphysics. Metaphysics is the science[1] "which contains the first principles of the use of the pure intellect" (§8); it is knowledge by pure reason in its real use, unaided and unhindered by sensibility. So much for the continuity thesis! But Kant points out, in considerable detail, that most judgments claimed to be metaphysical in fact hide in themselves some tacit and surreptitious reference to space and time. The proper method of metaphysics is to ferret out and eliminate

---

[1] The English reader should be forewarned that *Wissenschaft,* translated *science,* is not restricted to what we in English call science, i.e., the natural and the social sciences. In German *Wissenschaft* means a well-ordered body of knowledge with an established methodology furthered by a community of more or less like-minded scholars or scientists. Thus it makes good sense in German to speak of a science of art history, a science of theology, and even, with Kant, a science of metaphysics. See below, Editor's Introduction to *Prolegomena,* p. 151.

this illegitimate influence of the senses, and to establish metaphysical truths wholly independent of experience and referring to things as they are. Kant ends by proposing (but not demonstrating) three such metaphysical propositions, which will appear again in the *Critique* under a different guise.

Students of Kant should make good use of the Inaugural Dissertation and the next Selection, the letter to Herz. It is not often that we can see a great philosopher slowly thinking out his problems in public, trying first one and then another solution. One of the best ways students have to understand the *Critique of Pure Reason* is to understand the Inaugural Dissertation (a relatively easy task) so well that they can see how plausible the development between 1770 and 1781 was.

The translation (complete except for the first Section, one paragraph in §14, and the Conclud-ing Note) is by John Handyside (Open Court Publishing Company, 1928), extensively revised by the present editor and published by Peter Lang Publishing, Inc., 1986, in a book entitled Kant's Latin Writings: Translations, Commentaries, and Notes. *Reprinted by permis-sion of Peter Lang Publishing, Inc.*

On the Form and Principles of the Sensible and the Intelligible World

(The Inaugural Dissertation)

SECTION II
ON THE DISTINCTION BETWEEN SENSIBLE THINGS AND INTELLIGIBLE THINGS IN GENERAL

II, 392 3. *Sensibility*[2] is the *receptivity* of the subject through which it is possible that its representative state should be affected in a certain manner by the presence of some object. *Intelligence* (rationality) is the *faculty* of the subject through which it is able to represent things which cannot by their own nature come before the senses of that subject. The object of sensibility is the sensible; that which contains nothing save what must be known through intelligence is the intelligible. The former was called, in the ancient schools, *phenomenon;* the latter, *noumenon.* Knowledge, so far as it is subject to the laws of sensibility, is *sensitive;* so far as it is subject to the laws of intelligence, it is *intellectual,* or rational.

4. Thus, on the one hand, all sensitive cognition depends upon the special nature of the subject, in so far as it is susceptible of being modified in diverse ways by the presence of objects. These modifications may differ in different subjects in accordance with variations in the nature of these subjects. But whatever is exempt from this subjective condition refers only to the objects. It is clear, therefore, that representations of things *as they appear* are sensitively thought, while intellectual concepts are representations of things *as they are.*

In representations of sense there is in the first place something that we may call *matter,* i.e., sensation; and something else that we may call *form,* i.e., that general configuration *(species)* of sensible things, which obtains when various things which affect the senses are co-ordinated by a certain natural law of the 393 things which affect the senses are co-ordinated by a certain natural law of the mind. Further, just as sensation, which constitutes the matter of sensible representation, involves indeed the presence of some sensible thing, but for

---

[2] *Sensualitas.* The adjective *sensualis* (= sensible) refers to the content and form of experience. The adjective *sensitiva* (= sensitive) refers to the cognition we have of sensible objects. Thus we have sensitive knowledge of the sensible world. The objects of intellectual knowledge (noumena) are called intelligible; accordingly we have intellectual knowledge of the intelligible world.

54

its quality depends upon the nature of the subject so far as it is in some way modifiable by the object, the form of the representation indicates a certain aspect or relation of the sensa and yet is not properly an outline or schema of the object, but only a certain law inborn in the mind co-ordinating with one another the sensa arising from the presence of the object. For objects do not strike the senses through their form or configuration. In order, therefore, that the various [representations of] objects which affect the senses may coalesce into some whole of representation, there is required an internal principle of the mind through which these various representations may take on a certain configuration *(speciem)* according to stable and innate laws.

5. To sensible cognition there thus belong, on the one hand, a matter which is sensation, and on account of which the cognitions are called *sensible* and on the other hand a form, on account of which representations are called *sensitive* even if it be found empty of all sensation.

As for *intellectual* cognitions, it is most important to notice that the use of the intellect, the superior faculty of the mind, is two-fold. By the first use, the very concepts of objects or relations are given, and this is the *real use*. By the second use, concepts, whencesoever given, are only subordinated to one another, the lower to the higher through common marks, and compared with one another according to the principle of contradiction; this is called the *logical use*. The logical use, but not the real use, is common to all the sciences. For a cognition, however given, is regarded as contained under a mark common to many or as different from them, and this either immediately and directly (as in judgments, which aim at distinct knowledge), or mediately (as in inferences [syllogisms] which aim at adequate [systematic] knowledge). Thus, sensitive cognitions being given, they are subordinated by the logical use of the intellect to other sensitive cognitions as to common concepts, and as phenomena to more general laws of phenomena.

But here it is of the greatest importance to note that these cognitions, no matter to what extent the logical use of the intellect has been exercised upon them, are still to be considered sensitive. For they are called sensitive on account of their origin, not on account of any comparison as to identity or difference. Hence the most general empirical laws are nonetheless sensible. Similarly those principles of sensitive form (i.e., of determinate relations in space) which are found in geometry, however much the intellect concerns 394 itself with them in arguing according to logical rules from what is sensitively given through pure intuition, do not pass out of the class of sensitive cognitions.

In things of sense and in phenomena, that which precedes the logical use of intellect is called *appearance,* and the reflective cognition which arises from the intellectual comparison of a number of appearances is called *experience.* Thus the only path from appearance to experience is by reflection according to the logical use of intellect. The common concepts of experience are called empirical, and its objects phenomena; the laws of experience and of all sensitive knowledge in general are called laws of phenomena. Thus empirical concepts do not become intellectual in the real sense and do not pass out of the species of sensitive cognition by being reduced to a greater universality. However high they ascend by way of abstraction, they always remain sensitive.

6. When we come to the objects of the intellect which are strictly such, in which the use of the intellect is real, the concepts involved, whether of objects or relations, are given through the very nature of the intellect, not abstracted from any use of the senses, and do not contain any form of sensitive cognition as such. But here it is necessary to take notice of a very great ambiguity in the word "abstract," which had best be disposed of at once lest it vitiate our treatment of intellectual concepts. Properly, we should say that we *abstract from something,* not that we *abstract something.* The first signifies that in a certain concept we do not attend to other things connected with it in some way. The second means that it is not given save in the concrete, and so has to be separated from what is conjoined with it. Hence an intellectual concept is not abstracted from the sensitive, but abstracts from all that is sensitive. Perhaps it would be more correctly called *abstracting* than *abstract.* It is therefore more appropriate to call intellectual ideas *pure,* and concepts given only empirically *abstract.*

7. From this it can be seen that it is wrong to regard the sensitive as that which is more confusedly known and the intellectual as being that of which our knowledge is distinct.[3] For these are merely logical distinctions and plainly do not concern those data which underlie all logical comparison. For that matter, the sensitive may be very distinct, and the intellectual extremely confused. This is shown, on the one hand, by geometry, the prototype of all sensitive knowledge, and on the other hand by metaphysics, the organon in all things [strictly] intellectual. Everyone knows how much labor metaphysics devotes to dispersing the clouds of confusion which darken the common intellect, though its work does not always have as happy an issue as that of geometry. Nonetheless, each kind of knowledge preserves the mark of its descent, so that the former kind, however distinct, is on account of its origin called sensitive, while the latter kind, however confused, remains intellectual. Moral concepts, for instance, though of this confused character, are known not by experience but by the pure intellect itself. But I fear that the illustrious Wolff by means of this (for him merely logical) distinction between the sensitive and the intellectual may to the great detriment of philosophy have quite destroyed the noblest enterprise of antiquity, the determin-

395

---

[3] In asserting that the difference between sensibility and intellect is not a matter of difference of clarity and distinctness, Kant separates himself from the rationalistic tradition from Leibniz to Wolff. It is absolutely basic to Kant's philosophy that there are two sources of knowledge, sense and thought (intuition and concepts) and that genuine knowledge (experience) is the elaboration of the former by the latter.

ing of the nature of phenomena and noumena, and turned men's minds from these investigations to what are frequently but logical minutiae.

8. That part of philosophy which contains the first principles of the use of pure intellect is *metaphysics*. Propaedeutic to it is the science which brings out the distinction between sensitive and intellectual knowledge, and of this science the present dissertation is a specimen. Since no empirical principles are to be found in metaphysics, the concepts there met with are not to be looked for in the senses, but in the very nature of the pure intellect, not as concepts connate to it but as concepts abstracted (by attention to its actions on the occasion of experience) from laws inborn in the mind, and to this extent as acquired concepts. Concepts of this sort are: possibility, existence, necessity, substance, cause, etc. with their opposites or correlates. These never enter into any sensual representations as parts of it, and could not, therefore, in any way be abstracted from it.

9. Intellectual concepts have two functions. In their first, *elenctic*, use they perform the negative service of keeping sensitive concepts from being applied to noumena. Though they do not advance knowledge a single step, they keep it from the contagion of errors. In their second, or *dogmatic*, use, the general principles of the pure intellect, such as are dealt with in ontology or rational psychology, issue in some exemplar conceivable only by the pure intellect, and is the common measure of all other things so far as real. This exemplar — *Perfectio Noumenon* — is perfection in either a theoretical* or in a 396 practical sense. In the former, it is the Supreme Being, God; in the latter, moral perfection. Thus moral philosophy, so far as it supplies first principles of moral judgment, is known only through the pure intellect and itself belongs to pure philosophy. Epicurus, who reduced the criteria of morals to the feeling of pleasure or displeasure, is therefore quite rightly condemned, along with certain moderns who, like Shaftesbury and his school, follow him in a much less thorough manner.

In every kind of things in which quantity is variable, the maximum is the common measure and principle whereby we have knowledge. The maximum of perfection, which is called by Plato an Idea (as in the Idea of the state) we now entitle an ideal. It is the principle of all that is contained under the general notion of any perfection, insofar as lesser degrees are supposed not to be determinable save by limiting the maximum. God, however, while as ideal of perfection is the principle of knowledge, is at the same time as really existing the principle of the coming into existence of all perfection whatsoever.

10. No intuition of things intellectual but only a symbolic [discursive] knowledge of them is given to man. Intellection is possible to us only through

---

*We regard a thing theoretically so far as we attend only to what pertains to existence, practically if we consider what, through freedom, ought to be in it.

universal concepts in the abstract, not through a singular concept in the concrete. For all our intuition is bound to a certain formal principle under which alone anything can be perceived by the mind immediately, that is, as singular and not as conceived merely discursively through general concepts.

But this formal principle of our intuition (space and time) is the condition under which anything can be an object of our senses, and being thus the condition of sensitive knowledge it is not a means to intellectual intuition. Further, all the matter of our knowledge is given by the senses alone, whereas a noumenon, as such, is not to be conceived through representations derived from sensations. Consequently, a concept of the intelligible as such is devoid of all that is given by human intuition. Thus for our minds, intuition is always passive and is possible only so far as something is able to affect our senses. But the divine intuition, which is the ground, not the consequence, of its objects, is, owing to its independence, archetypal and so is completely intellectual.

11. Although phenomena are, properly, semblances *(species),* not ideas, of things, and express no internal or absolute quality of the objects, knowledge of them is nonetheless perfectly genuine knowledge. For, in the first place, so far as they are sensible concepts or apprehensions, as being caused they bear witness to the presence of an object — which is opposed to idealism. On the other hand, consider judgments about things sensitively known: the truth of a judgment consists in the agreement of its predicate with the given subject. But the concept of the subject, so far as it is a phenomenon, can be given only by its relation to the sensitive faculty of knowledge, and it is also by the same faculty that the sensitively observable predicates are given. Hence it is clear that the representations of subject and predicate arise according to common laws, and so allow of a perfectly true knowledge.

12. All things which are presented as objects to our senses are phenomena; whatever does not affect the senses but contains merely the singular form of sensibility belongs to pure intuition (i.e., to intuition empty of sensations but not for that reason intellectual). The phenomena of outer sense are examined and expounded in physics, those of inner sense in empirical psychology. But a pure intuition (in man) is not a universal or logical concept *under* which, but a singular concept *in* which, any sensible things are thought. That is to say, it contains the concepts of space and time. Since these in no way determine the quality of sensible objects, they are not objects of science except in respect to their quantity. Pure mathematics considers space in geometry, time in pure mechanics. To these there is added a certain concept which, though itself indeed intellectual, yet demands for its actualization in the concrete the auxiliary notions of time and space (in the successive addition and simultaneous juxtaposition of a plurality), namely, the concept of number, treated of by arithmetic. Thus pure mathematics in dealing with the form of all our sensitive knowledge is the organon of all knowledge which is at once intuitive and distinct; and since its objects are not merely formal princi-

ples of all intuition but themselves original intuitions, it yields us quite genuine knowledge, and at the same time furnishes a model of the highest certainty for knowledge in other fields. *There is thus a science of sensible things,* though, since they are phenomena, the use of the intellect in reference to them is not real but only logical. From this it is clear in what sense those thinkers who derive their inspiration from the Eleatic School are to be understood as having denied scientific knowledge of phenomena.

SECTION III
ON THE PRINCIPLES OF THE FORM
OF THE SENSIBLE WORLD

13. A principle of the form of the universe is one which contains the ground of a universal connection, whereby all substances and their states belong to one and the same whole, which is called a world. A principle of the form of the sensible world is one which contains the ground of a universal connection of all things so far as they are phenomena. A form of the intelligible world recognizes an objective principle, that is, some cause in virtue of which there is a connection between things existing in themselves. But the world insofar as it is regarded as phenomenon, that is, in relation to the sensibility of the human mind, acknowledges no principle of its form except a subjective one, that is to say, a certain law of the mind on account of which all things which can, through their nature, be objects of the senses must *necessarily* be presented as belonging to the same whole. Thus whatever principle of the form of the sensible world may finally be acknowledged, it will include within its range only such existences as are deemed to fall within the range of the senses; and so extend neither to immaterial substances (which, as such, are by definition excluded altogether from the outer senses) nor to the cause of the world (which cannot be an object of the senses, since through it the mind itself exists and is endowed with the power of sense). I shall now show that there are two formal principles of the phenomenal universe which are absolutely primary and universal, and which are, as it were, the schemata and conditions of all human knowledge that is sensitive. I refer to time and space.[4]

14. *On Time.*

1. *The idea[5] of time does not originate in the senses, but is presupposed by them.* 399
The things that meet the senses can be represented either as simultaneous or as successive only through the idea of time; succession does not beget the

---

[4]What follows is the first presentation of Kant's mature theory of space and time, which appears most fully in the *Critique of Pure Reason* (below, pp. 105–107) and the *Prolegomena* (below, pp. 172–175).

[5]Kant's use of the word *idea* varies from time to time. On *idea* as representation, see above, p. 32 on *Idea* in contrast to concept of the understanding, see below, p. 127 n. Here *idea* means an intuitive representation, in contrast to concept *(notio)*.

concept of time, but presupposes it. Thus the notion of time regarded as acquired through experience is very badly defined in terms of the series of actual things existing after one another. For what the word *after* may signify, I know only by means of an antecedently formed concept of time. Things are one after another if they exist at different times, just as things are simultaneous if they exist at the same time.

2. *The idea of time is singular, not general.* For a time is not thought except as part of one and the same boundless time. If we think of two years we cannot represent them save by a determinate dating with regard to each other, and if one does not follow the other immediately we must think of them as joined to one another by some intermediate time. Which of different times is earlier, which later, can by no means be defined by any marks conceivable by the intellect, unless we are to fall into a vicious circle. The mind does not distinguish earlier and later except by a singular intuition. Further, we conceive all actual things as located *in* time, not as contained *under* its general notion as under a common mark.

3. *The idea of time is therefore an intuition.* And since the idea is conceived prior to all sensation as a condition of relations exhibited in sensible things, the intuition is not sensual but *pure.*

4. *Time is a continuous quantum.* It is the principle of the laws of continuity in the changes of the universe. For a quantum is continuous if it is not composed of simple [parts]. But since through time nothing is thought but relations, without any given things related to one another, it follows that in time as a quantum we have a composition of such a kind that when composition is thought of as completely removed, nothing remains. But any composite of which nothing remains when composition is wholly removed does not consist of simple parts; therefore, etc. Thus any part of time is a time, and the simples which exist in time, namely moments, are not parts of time, but limits between which there is a stretch of time. For, given two moments, a time is not given except in so far as in these moments existences succeed one another. Therefore, besides a given moment it is necessary that there be given a time in whose later part there is another moment.

The metaphysical law of continuity is this: all changes are continuous, or flow; i.e., opposite states do not succeed one another except through an intermediate series of different states. For since two opposed states are at different moments of time, and between two moments of time there is always some intervening time, and in the infinite series of its moments the substance 400 is not in either of the given states, nor yet in no state, it will be in different states, and so *in infinitum.* . . .

5. *Time is not something objective and real.* It is neither substance nor accident nor relation, but is a subjective condition, necessary because of the nature of the human mind, for the co-ordinating of all sensible things according to a fixed law, and it is a *pure intuition.* We co-ordinate both substances and accidents, as either simultaneous or successive, only through the concept

of time; and thus the notion of time, as a formal principle, is prior to the concepts of simultaneity and succession. Whether relations and aspects, so far as they are given to the senses, are simultaneous or successive involves nothing except their position which is to be determined in time, as either at the same or at different points of it.

Those who assert the objective reality of time conceive it in one or the other of two ways. Among English philosophers especially, it is regarded as a continuous real flux, and yet as apart from any existing thing—a most egregious fiction. Leibniz and his school declare it to be something real, abstracted from the succession of internal states. This latter view at once shows itself erroneous by involving a vicious circle in the definition of time, 401 and also by entirely neglecting simultaneity,* a most important mode of time. It upsets the whole use of sound reason, since, instead of requiring the laws of motion to be defined in terms of time, it would have time itself in its own nature defined by reference to the observation of moving things or some series of internal changes — a procedure by which, clearly, all the certainty of our rules is lost. But as for the fact that we cannot estimate quantity of time save in the concrete, either by motion or by the series of [our] thoughts, this is because the concept of time rests only on an internal law of the mind. For since the concept is not an intuition with which we are born, the action of the mind in co-ordinating its sensa is called forth only by the help of the senses. So far is it from being possible that anyone should ever deduce and explain the concept of time by help from the side of reason, that the very principle of contradiction presupposes it and requires it as a condition. For A and not-A are not incompatible unless they are thought of the same thing simultaneously (i.e., at the same time); but when they are thought of a thing successively (i.e., at different times) they may both belong to it. Hence the possibility of changes is thinkable only in time; time is not thinkable through changes, but *vice versa*.

6. But though time, posited in itself and absolutely, is an imaginary being, yet so far as it is related to an immutable law of sensible things as such it is a quite genuine concept and a condition of all intuitive representation extending *in infinitum* over all possible objects of the senses. For since simultaneous things as such cannot be presented to the senses except with the help of time, and changes are thinkable only through time, it is clear that the concept

---

*What is simultaneous is not made simultaneous simply by not being successive. For when succession is taken away there is removed a certain conjunction of things within the temporal series, but there does not on that account at once arise another genuine relation such as the conjunction of all at the same moment. For simultaneous things are joined in the same moment of time just as successive things at different moments. Thus though time possesses only one dimension, yet the ubiquity of time (to use Newton's manner of speaking), owing to which all things sensitively conceivable are at some time, adds to the quantum of actual things another dimension, so far as they hang, as it were, from the same point of time. For if you represent time by a straight line produced to infinity, and simultaneous things at any point of time by lines drawn perpendicular to it, the plane thus generated will represent the phenomenal world, both as to its substances and to its accidents.

contains the universal form of phenomena, and accordingly that all events observable in the world, all motions and all internal changes, necessarily 402 agree with any axioms which can be established in regard to time (such axioms as we have partly expounded), since only under these conditions can objects of the senses be, and be co-ordinated. It is therefore absurd to wish to incite reason against the first postulates of pure time (e.g., continuity, etc.) since these follow from laws than which nothing more primary or original can be found. Reason itself, in the use of the principle of contradiction, cannot dispense with the support of this concept of time, so primitive and original is it.

7. Thus *time is an absolutely primary formal principle of the sensible world.* For any things that are in any way sensible can be thought only as at the same or at successive times, and so as included and definitely related to each other within the course of one single time. Thus through this concept, primary to everything sensitive, there necessarily arises a formal whole which is not part of any other, i.e., the *phenomenal world.*

15. *On Space.*

A. *The concept of space is not abstracted from outer sensations.* For I cannot conceive anything as located outside me unless I represent it as in a space different from the space in which I myself am; nor can I conceive things as outside one another unless I place them in different parts of space. Therefore the possibility of outer perceptions as such presupposes, and does not create, the concept of space. Moreover, things which are in space affect the senses, but space itself cannot be derived from the senses.

B. *The concept of space is a singular representation,* including all spaces *in* itself, not an abstract common notion containing them *under* itself. For what we call different spaces are parts of the same boundless space, with a certain position relatively to one another; nor can we conceive a cubic foot except as bounded on all sides by surrounding space.

C. *The concept of space is thus a pure intuition,* since it is a singular concept not put together from sensations, but the fundamental form of all outer sensation. This pure intuition can be readily observed in the axioms of geometry and in every mental construction of postulates or problems. For that space has not more than three dimensions, that there is but one straight line between two points, that from a given point in a plane a circle can be described with a given straight line as radius, etc., are not inferred from any 403 universal notion of space, but can only be discerned in space in the concrete.

We cannot by any acuteness of intellect describe discursively, that is, with characteristic intellectual marks, the distinction in a given space between things which lie towards one quarter and things which are turned towards the opposite quarter. Likewise if we take solids completely equal and similar but incongruent, such as the right and left hands (so far as they are conceived only according to their extension), or spherical triangles from two opposite hemispheres, although in every respect which admits of being stated in terms intelligible to the mind through verbal description they can be substituted for one another, there is yet a diversity which makes it impossible for their boundaries to coincide. It is therefore clear that in these cases the diversity, that is, the incongruity, cannot be apprehended except by a certain pure intuition.

Hence geometry employs principles not only unquestioned and discursive, but also such as fall under the mind's direct vision. Evidence in demonstrations (meaning thereby the clearness of assured knowledge so far as this clearness can be likened to that of sense) is found in geometry not merely in the highest degree, but there alone among all the pure sciences. Geometrical evidence is thus the model for, and the means of attaining, all evidence in the other sciences. For since geometry contemplates the relations of space, the concept of which contains in itself the very form of all sensual intuition, there can be nothing clear and evident in things perceived by outer sense except through the mediation of the intuition which that science is occupied in contemplating. Furthermore, geometry does not demonstrate its universal propositions by thinking the object through a universal concept, as is done in the cognitions of reason, but by submitting it to the eyes in a singular intuition, as is done in sensitive cognitions.*

D. *Space is not something objective and real,* neither substance nor accident nor relation, but *subjective and ideal.* It is, as it were, a schema, issuing by a constant law from the nature of the mind, for the co-ordinating of all outer sensa whatsoever. Those who defend the reality of space either conceive it as an absolute and boundless receptacle of possible things (the view commends itself to most geometers, following the English), or hold that it is a relation of existent things, vanishing therefore if things be annihilated, and not think-   404 able except in actual things (as, following Leibniz, most of our countrymen maintain.) The former empty figment of reason, since it imagines an identity of true relations without any things so related, belongs in the world of fable. But those who adopt the second opinion fall into a much more serious error. For while the former only place a stumbling block in the way of certain concepts which are rational (i.e., which concern noumena) and which are in any case of a highly abstruse character (e.g., in questions concerning a spiritual world, omnipresence, etc.), the latter set themselves in opposition to the actual phenomena and to geometry, the most faithful interpreter of all phenomena. For — to pass over the obvious circle in which they are necessarily involved in their definition of space — they dash down geometry from the

---

*I here pass over the proposition that space must necessarily be conceived as a continuous quantum, since that is easily demonstrated. Owing to this continuity it follows that the simple in space is not a part, but a limit. A limit in general is that in a continuous quantum which contains the ground of its boundary. A space which is not the limit of a second space is complete, i.e., a solid. Thus there are three sorts of limits in space, just as there are three dimensions. Of these limits two, surface and line, are themselves spaces. The concept of limit has no application to quanta other than space and time.

supreme height of certainty and reduce it to the rank of those sciences whose principles are empirical. For if all the affections of space were learned through experience of external relations, geometrical axioms would not possess [genuine] universality but only that comparative universality which is acquired through induction and which holds only so far as it is observed; nor would they possess necessity, except such as depends on the stability of the laws of nature; nor would they have any precision save such as is a matter of arbitrary convention; and we might hope, as in empirical matters, some day to discover a space endowed with other primary affections, and perhaps even a rectilinear figure enclosed by two straight lines.

E. Although the *concept of space*, viewed as an objective and real being or affection, is imaginary, nevertheless *relatively to all sensible things (sensibilia)* it *is* not only *altogether true*, but the foundation of all truth in outer sensibility. For things cannot appear to the senses in any manner except by the mediating power of the mind, co-ordinating all sensations according to a constant law implanted in its nature. Nothing whatsoever, then, can be given to the senses save in conformity with the primary axioms of space and their consequences as taught in geometry. Though the principle of these axioms be only subjective, it will necessarily be in harmony with them because only so does it harmonize with itself. The laws of sensibility will be laws of nature, in so far as nature falls within the scope of the senses. Thus as regards all properties of space which are demonstrated from an hypothesis not invented but intuitively given as a subjective condition of all phenomena, nature is meticulously conformed to the rules of geometry, and only in accordance with them can nature be revealed to the senses. Certainly, unless the concept of space had been given originally through the nature of the mind (so that anyone who should labor to imagine any other relations than are anticipated in it would waste his pains, since he would have been forced to use this very concept in support of his fiction), the use of geometry in natural philosophy would be very unsafe, for it would be possible to doubt whether the notion of space obtained from experience would sufficiently harmonize with nature, since the determinations from which it would have been abstracted might perchance be denied — a suspicion which has indeed occurred to some thinkers. Space, therefore, is an absolutely first formal principle of the sensible world, not only for the reason that the objects composing the universe could not be phenomena save through the concept of space, but especially for this reason, that, by its essence, it must necessarily be single, embracing absolutely all outer sensible things, and so constitute a principle of totality, i.e., a whole which cannot be a part of another world.

Corollary. These, then, are the two principles of sensitive knowledge, not general concepts (as is the case in matters of the intellect), but singular intuitions which are yet pure. In these intuitions it is not true that the parts, and especially the simple parts, contain the ground of the possibility of the composite, as the laws of reason prescribe [in intellectual cognition]; instead, according to the pattern of sensitive intuition, the infinite contains the ground of every thinkable part and, finally, of the simple (or, rather, of the limit). For only if infinite space and infinite time be given can any definite space or time be marked out by limitation; neither a point nor a moment can be thought by itself, [for] they are conceived only as limits in an already given space or time. Thus all primary properties of these concepts are beyond the jurisdiction of reason and so cannot in any way be intellectually explained; but they are nonetheless presuppositions upon which the intellect rests when, with the greatest possible certainty and in accordance with logical laws, it draws consequences from the primary data of intuition.

Of these concepts, the one [i.e., space] properly concerns the intuition of an *object*, the other [i.e., time] of a *state*, namely that of representation. Thus space is applied as an image *(typus)* to the concept of time itself, representing it by a line, and its limits by points. But time approaches more nearly to a universal rational concept in that it embraces absolutely everything within its survey, even space itself, and in addition accidents which are not held together in space-relations, such as the soul's thoughts. Further, though time does not indeed prescribe laws to reason, it does establish the chief conditions by the help of which the mind can order its notions according to the laws 406 of reason. Thus I cannot decide that a thing is impossible except by predicating A and *not-A* of the same subject at the same time. It should be noticed above all that when the intellect is applied to experience, though the relation of cause and effect between outer objects requires space relations, nonetheless in all cases, both inner and outer, the mind can be informed what is earlier and what later (i.e., what is cause and what effect) only by means of the time relations. Indeed, even a spatial magnitude cannot be made intelligible unless we relate it to some measure as a unit and express it by a number. This can be done only if the manifold is an aggregate distinctly known by numeration, i.e., by the process of adding one to one successively in a given time.

Finally, the question naturally arises whether these concepts are connate or acquired. The latter alternative seems already refuted by our demonstrations, but the former is not to be rashly admitted, since in appealing to a first cause it opens the path to that lazy philosophy which declares all further research to be vain. Both concepts are without doubt acquired, being abstracted not from the sensing of objects (for sensation gives the matter, not the form, of human cognition) but from the action of the mind in coordinating its sensa according to unchanging laws — each being, as it were, an immutable type to be known intuitively. Though sensations excite this act of the mind, they do not become part of the intuition. Nothing is here connate save the law of the mind, according to which it combines in a fixed manner the sensa produced in it by the presence of the object.

SECTION IV
ON THE PRINCIPLE OF THE FORM
OF THE INTELLIGIBLE WORLD

16. Those who regard space and time as a real and absolutely necessary bond, as it were, of all possible substances and states think that nothing else is needed for conceiving how a certain original relation can belong to a plurality of existents as the primary condition of their possible influences [on each other] and as the principle of the essential form of the universe. For since, according to their view, all things that exist are necessarily somewhere, it seems to them superfluous to enquire why they are presented in a certain
407 specific manner, that being determined [according to their view] directly by the fact that space is a whole which includes all things. Apart, however, from the fact that the concept of space, as already proved, concerns rather the sensitive laws of the subject than conditions of the objects themselves, however much reality is assigned to the concept, it yet denotes only the intuitively given possibility of universal co-ordination. The question, which cannot be solved save by the intellect, thus still remains quite untouched: on what principle rests this relation of all substances, which when viewed intuitively is called space? Thus the question as to the principle of the form of the intelligible world hinges upon its being made clear how it is possible that a plurality of substances should stand in a relation of interaction and in this way belong to the same whole, called a world. We are here contemplating the world not as to its matter (whether the substances of which it consists are material or immaterial) but as to its form, that is, how in general the connection of many substances and the totality of all are brought about.

17. Given a plurality of substances, a principle of possible interaction between them is not given by their mere existence; something more is required from which their mutual relations may be understood. Through their mere subsistence they do not necessarily refer to anything else, except perhaps to their cause, but the relation of effect to cause is not one of interaction but of dependence. If, therefore, there be any interaction among them, there is required a special ground precisely determining it.

Herein consists the basic error of the doctrine of physical influence as commonly understood. It hastily assumes interaction of substances and transeunt forces as sufficiently comprehensible through the mere existence of the substances, and hence is not so much a system as the neglect of all philosophical systems as unnecessary in dealing with this question. But if we rid the concept of physical influence of this defect, we have the kind of interaction which alone deserves to be called real, and which also justifies us in speaking of a world as a whole which is real, not ideal or imaginary.

18. A whole of necessary substances is impossible. Since the existence of each is securely established apart from any dependence on anything else

(which clearly does not hold of necessary things), it is evident not only that the interaction of substances (i.e., the reciprocal dependence of their states) does not follow from their existence itself, but also that it cannot be attributed to them as necessary things at all.   408

19. Thus a whole of substances is a whole of contingent things, and a world, by its essence, consists of merely contingent things. Further, no necessary substance is connected with a world save as a cause is connected with its effect, and not as a part is connected with its complementary parts to form a whole. For the connection of joint parts is that of mutual dependence, which does not apply to a necessary being. Thus the cause of a world is an extramundane being; consequently, it is not the soul of the world, and its presence in the world is not local but virtual.

20. Mundane substances are beings [derived] from another, not, however, from different beings but all from one. For suppose them to be effects of a plurality of necessary beings; then, since the causes are without any mutual relation, the effects would not be in concord. Accordingly, unity in the conjunction of the substances in the universe is a consequence of the dependence of all of them upon one. The form of the universe bears witness to the cause of its matter, and only a single cause of all things can be the cause of its totality; there cannot be an architect of the world who is not also its creator.

21. If there were a plurality of necessary first causes with their effects, these would be worlds, not a world, because they would not be in any way connected to form the same whole. And vice versa, if there be a plurality of actual worlds outside one another, there is a plurality of first and necessary causes, with no interaction between one world and another, nor between the cause of one world and a world depending upon another cause.

It follows that a plurality of actual worlds outside one another is not impossible by its very concept (as Wolff wrongly concluded from the notion of a complex or aggregate, a notion which he deemed sufficient to a whole as such). It is impossible only under the condition that there exists one single necessary cause of all things. If more than one be admitted, a plurality of worlds (in the strictest metaphysical sense) external to one another will be possible.

22. We can conclude from a given world to a sole cause of all its parts. If we   409
could similarly argue, vice versa, from a given common cause of all things to their interconnection and so to the form of a world (though I confess that this inference does not seem to me equally clear), then owing to the substances' all being maintained by a common principle, the fundamental connection of the substances would be not contingent but necessary. The harmony arising from their very subsistence, resting upon this common cause, would proceed according to common rules. This kind of harmony I entitle *generally established harmony*. That which occurs only so far as each special state of a substance is adapted to the state of another substance I shall call *specially*

established harmony. According to the former, interaction is real and physical; according to the latter, ideal and sympathetic. Thus all interaction of the substances in the universe is externally established, through the cause common to all; and thus is either generally established through physical influence (in an amended sense) or is brought about for the states of each substance individually. In the latter case, it is either originally founded in the primary constitution of every substance *(preestablished harmony)* or imposed on the occasion of every change *(occasionalism)*. If owing to the maintenance of all substances by a unitary ground there be a necessary conjunction of all things whereby they constitute a unity, the universal interaction of substances will be by physical influence and the world will be real; if otherwise, the interaction will be sympathetic (i.e., harmony without real interaction) and the world only an ideal whole. In my view, though the former alternative has not been demonstrated, there are ample grounds for its acceptance.

Scholium. If it were legitimate to overstep a little the limits of apodictic certainty befitting metaphysics, it might be worth while to investigate certain questions concerning not merely the laws but also the causes of sensitive intuition which can be known through the intellect. The human mind, we might then say, is affected by outer things and the world lies open to its view *in infinitum* only so far as the mind, along with all other things, is sustained by
410 the infinite power of a single cause. For this reason it senses external things only through the presence of one sustaining common cause; and space, which is the sensitively known universal and necessary condition of the compresence of all things, can therefore be entitled *phenomenal omnipresence*. (For it is not because the cause of the universe is in the same place with each and every thing that it is present to them all; on the contrary, places, i.e., possible relations of substances, exist because the cause is inwardly present to all things.)

Again, the possibility of all changes and successions—the principle of which, so far as it is sensitively known, resides in the concept of time—presupposes the perdurability of a subject whose opposed states succeed one another. But that whose states change does not persist unless maintained by another; and thus the concept of time as single, infinite, and immutable* in which all things are and persist is the *phenomenal eternity* of the general cause.

The opinions just expounded are little different from Malebranche's, that we see all things in God. But it seems wiser to hug the shore of the knowledge granted us by the mediocrity of our intellect than, like him, to push out into the open seas of mystical inquiries.

---

*It is not the moments of time which seem to succeed one another, for in that case there would have to be presupposed another time for the succession of the moments; but in sensitive intuition actual things seem to descend, as it were, through a continuous series of moments.

SECTION V
ON THE METHOD OF DEALING WITH THE
SENSITIVE AND THE INTELLECTUAL IN METAPHYSICS

23. In all sciences whose principles are given intuitively, either by sensible intuition (experience) or by pure, though still sensitive, intuition (the concepts of space, time, and number) — that is to say, in mathematics and natural science — *practice gives rise to method.* After a science has reached some degree of comprehensiveness and order by trial and discovery, we are able to see by what method we must proceed in order to carry it to completion, clearing it of the stains of error and confused thought and so bringing it to its highest purity. It was in this way that grammar, after speech had been abundantly used, provided opportunity for rules and training; similarly with style, after high achievements in poetry and oratory. In the case of all sciences 411 whose primary concepts and axioms are given by sensitive intuition, the use of the intellect is only *logical,* i.e., only applied to subordinating cognitions in respect of their universality conformably to the principle of contradiction, as in subordinating phemonena to more general phenomena and the corollaries of pure intuition to the intuitive axioms.

In pure philosophy, however, such as metaphysics, the use of the intellect in dealing with principles is *real,* i.e., the primary concepts of things and relations, and the axioms themselves, are first given by the pure intellect itself. Since they are not intuitions, these concepts and axioms are not immune to error, and *method precedes all science.* Consequently all attempts at philosophizing made before a thorough investigation and firm establishment of its rules seem rashly conceived, and ought to be set aside as among the idle triflings of the mind. For since the right use of reason here constitutes the principles themselves, and since only by virtue of its own powers do the objects and the axioms which are to be thought about them first become known, the exposition of the laws of pure reason is the very beginning of the science, and the distinction of these laws from spurious ones is the criterion of truth.

At present the method of this science is not well known; though logic prescribes a method to all sciences in general, that which is suited to the special nature of metaphysics is completely ignored. That those devoted to this inquiry, with all the endless rolling of their Sisyphean stone, seem to have accomplished scarcely anything is not, therefore, surprising. I have neither the mind nor the space to speak here at length on so notable and far-reaching a question, but I shall briefly expound one point which constitutes an important part of this method, namely [preventing] *the contamination of intellectual knowledge by the sensitive.* This contamination not only misleads the unwary in the application of principles, but even introduces spurious principles in the guise of axioms.

24. The method of all metaphysics in dealing with the sensitive and the intellectual is reducible in the main to this all-important rule: *carefully prevent the principles proper to sensitive cognition from passing their boundaries and affecting the intellectual.*

In every intellectually enunciated judgment the predicate is a condition without which the subject is asserted to be unthinkable. The predicate is, in short, the principle in terms of which the subject is known. If it be a sensitive concept, it will be a condition only of possible sensitive cognition and will be in full accord only with the subject of a judgment whose concept is likewise sensitive. If it be applied to an intellectual concept, however, the judgment so constituted will be valid only according to subjective laws; it will not be predicable, nor capable of being objectively stated, of the intellectual notion itself. It can be asserted only as a condition without which there is no sensitive knowledge of the given concept.*

Since the tricks of the intellect in decking out sensitive concepts as intellectual marks may be called a fallacy of subreption (by analogy with the accepted meaning of the word "subreption"), the interchange of the intellectual and the sensitive will be the metaphysical fallacy of subreption (the fallacy of intellectualizing the phenomena, if a barbarism be permitted). An axiom thus hybrid (hybrid in that it proffers what is sensitive as being necessarily bound up with an intellectual concept) I call a subreptive axiom. Those principles of intellectual error which have most harmfully infested metaphysics have proceeded from these spurious axioms.

But we must go more deeply into this question, in order that we may have something ready to hand and clearly knowable to serve as a criterion and touchstone of these judgments, distinguishing them from those which are genuine. And since these judgments may seem to be firmly rooted in the intellect, we require also an art of assaying by the aid of which a just estimation may be made of how much may belong to the sensitive and how much to the intellectual. This, I think, requires a deeper investigation.

25. The principle of the reduction of any subreptive axiom is this: *if there be universally predicated of any intellectual concept anything belonging to the relations of space and time, it must not be enunciated as objective; it denotes only the condition*

---

*The use of this criterion is easy and fruitful in distinguishing principles which enunciate only laws of sensitive knowledge from those which propound something further about the objects themselves. For if the predicate be an intellectual concept, the reference of it to the subject of the judgment (however sensitively that subject may be thought), indicates always a mark belonging to the object itself. But if the predicate be a sensitive concept, then, since the laws of sensitive cognition are not conditions of the possibility of things themselves, it will not hold of the subject of the judgment as intellectually conceived, and so will not be capable of being objectively enunciated. Thus, since in the common axiom, "Whatever exists is somewhere," the predicate contains conditions of sensitive cognition, it will not be capable of being universally enunciated of the subject of the judgment, viz., every existent. So this formula, claiming something objective, is false. But if the proposition be converted so that the intellectual concept becomes the predicate, a completely true proposition will emerge, namely, "Whatever is somewhere exists."

without which the given concept is not sensitively knowable. That an axiom of the subreptive type is spurious and, if not false, at least rashly and hazardously asserted is clear from the fact that the subject of the judgment, being intellectually conceived, pertains to the object, whereas the predicate containing determinations of space and time pertains only to the conditions of human sensitive knowledge. Since this latter cognition does not necessarily qualify every [possible] cognition of the object, it cannot be universally enunciated of the given intellectual concept.

The reason why the intellect is so liable to this fallacy of subreption is that the deception takes place under cover of another rule which is genuine enough. We rightly suppose that what cannot be known through any intuition whatever is not thinkable, and thus is impossible. Since by no effort of mind can we attain even in imagination to another kind of intuition than that which takes place according to the form of space and time, it comes about that we regard as impossible all intuition which is exempt from the laws of the senses, such as the divine intuition which Plato calls an Idea; thus we would subject all possible things to the sensitive axioms of space and time.

26. All the pretenses of sensitive cognition masquerading as intellectual knowledge — from which arise the subreptive axioms — can be reduced to three kinds, of which the following are the general formulae:

1. The same sensitive condition under which alone the intuition of an object is possible is a condition of the possibility of the object itself.

2. The same sensitive condition under which alone data can be collected and compared for the formation of an intellectual concept of an object is a condition of the possibility of the object itself.

3. The same sensitive condition under which alone the subsumption of any object presented under a given intellectual concept is possible is also a condition of the possibility of the object itself.

27. A subreptive axiom of the first kind is: *Whatever is, is somewhere and*   414 *somewhen.** By this spurious principle, all beings, even if intellectually known, are bound in their existence by conditions of space and time. Thence are tossed to and fro those idle questions as to the position in the corporeal universe of immaterial substances. There is no sensitive intuition of immaterial substances nor any representation under such [spatial] form as to the seat of the soul or other vain questions of that kind. Thus improperly confounding the sensitive with the intellectual, like square with round things,

---

*Space and time are conceived as if comprehending in themselves all things which can in any way meet the senses. Thus, according to the laws of the human mind, no intuition of any being is given except as that being is contained in space and time. With this prejudice there can be compared another, not properly a subreptive axiom but a trick of the imagination, which might be expressed in the general formula: in whatever exists, there is space and time; that is, all substance is extended and in continual change. For though all those whose conceptions are somewhat gross are firmly tied down by this law of the imagination, they themselves readily see that this applies only to the efforts of the phantasy in its attempts to give an outline of the appearance of things, not to the condition of their existence.

one of the disputants commonly appears as it were to be milking a he-goat and the other to be holding a sieve under it. The presence of immaterial things in the corporeal world is virtual, not local, though it is often and improperly so called. Space contains the conditions of possible reciprocal actions only between material bodies. What constitutes the external relations of force [or influence] between one immaterial substance and another or between immaterial substances and bodies is a problem quite beyond the human intellect, as the truly perspicacious Euler, a great investigator and judge of phenomena, acutely noted in his letters to a German princess.

When philosophers come to the concept of a supreme and extra-mundane being, words cannot express the extent to which they are befooled by these shadows that flit before the intellect. They imagine the presence of God to be local, and involve God in the world as if He were comprised in infinite space all at once, although they themselves have to make up for this limitation by conceiving the locality as it were *per eminentiam*, namely, as infinite. But to be in a number of places at the same time is absolutely impossible because different places are outside one another, and consequently what is in more than one place is outside itself and externally present to itself, which is self-contradictory.

As regards time, philosophers involve themselves in an inextricable maze, for not only do they disconnect it from the laws of sensitive knowledge, but they carry it beyond the confines of the world to the extra-mundane being itself as a condition of the existence of such a being. Hence the absurd questions with which they torment their minds, e.g., why God did not fashion the universe many ages earlier. They persuade themselves that it can easily be conceived how God perceives things present, that is, things actual at the time in which He is; but how He foresees the future, that is, things which will be actual at a time in which He is not yet, they think difficult to understand. As if the existence of a necessary being must descend through all the moments of imaginary time, and as though, part of His duration already exhausted, He looked forward to the eternity He is yet to pass through and to the events of the world to take place in that time: All these difficulties vanish like smoke when the notion of time is rightly understood.

28. Preconceptions of the second kind are hidden still more deeply. Through the sensitive conditions by which the mind is bound they delude the intellect if it wishes in certain cases to arrive at an intellectual concept. One of these affects the knowledge of quantity, the other that of qualities generally. The former is: *every actual aggregate can be expressed by a number, and therefore every quantum is finite.* The latter is: *whatever is impossible is self-contradictory.* In neither case does the concept of time enter into the predicate notion itself, nor is it considered a mark of the subject, but it serves as the medium in which the concept of the predicate is formed, and so affects the intellectual concept of the subject as a condition, inasmuch as we attain the concept only by its aid.

As regards the former axiom, since every quantum and every series is distinctly known only by successive co-ordination, the intellectual concept of a quantum and multiplicity arises only by help of the concept of time and never attains completeness save when the synthesis can be completed in a finite time. Owing, therefore, to the limits of our intellect, an infinite series of co-ordinate things cannot be distinctly comprehended; accordingly, through a fallacy of subreption, it appears impossible. According to the laws of pure intellect every series of effects has its assignable ground of existence, and in a series of effects regress without limit is impossible; according to the laws of sensitive cognition every series of co-ordinate things has an assignable beginning. The latter proposition involves the measurement of the series, the former the dependence of the whole; but these propositions are wrongly held to be identical.[6]

In similar fashion, when the intellect proves that in a given substantial composite there are given also the elements of its composition, i.e., simples, there is combined with the [intellectual] argument a false principle borrowed from sensitive knowledge, namely, that in such a compound there cannot be an infinite regress in the composition of parts, i.e., that in every compound there is a definite number of parts. The meaning of this proposition is certainly not on all fours with that of the former, and it would therefore be rash to substitute it for the former. That the world, therefore, is limited in its quantity (and is not a maximum), that it manifests its cause, and that bodies consist of simples, can indeed be known on the trustworthy authority of reason. But that the universe with respect to its mass is mathematically finite, that its age is assignable in terms of a unit measure, and that there is a definite number of simples constituting any body, are propositions which openly declare their origin in the nature of sensitive knowledge; and whatever truth may belong to them, they nevertheless labor under the indubitable defects of their origin. 416

As regards the second subreptive axiom, it arises from rashly converting the principle of contradiction. To that primary principle the concept of time adheres, for given contradictorily opposed characters in the same thing at the same time, an impossibility is manifested, and is thus formulated: *whatever is and is not at the same time is impossible.* Since something is here predicated through the intellect in a case given according to the sensitive laws [of cognition], the judgment is perfectly true and evident. But if the maxim be converted, and it is asserted: *everything impossible both is and is not at the same time* (i.e., involves a contradiction), something is predicated universally of an object of reason through sensitive knowledge, and the intellectual concept of the possible or impossible is thereby subjected to conditions of sensitive knowledge, namely to the relations of time. It is altogether true that the laws [of sensitive knowledge] restrict and limit the human intellect, although

---

[6]Kant is here anticipating the theory of the Antinomy of Pure Reason (below, pp. 127–130).

they cannot be conceded objectively and universally. That is to say, our intellect recognizes impossibility only where it can remark the simultaneous enunciation of opposites about the same subject, i.e., only where a contradiction occurs. The human intellect can therefore make no judgment of impossibility in cases in which such a contradiction is not found. But it is a hasty conclusion, and involves regarding subjective conditions of judgment as objective, to say that no intellect whatsoever can do so, and that what does not involve a contradiction is for that reason possible. This is why, in the absence of the obstacle of contradiction, a host of fictitious forces fabricated at will are poured forth in multitudes by those of speculative mind or, if the description be preferred, by those whose minds are given to chimeras. For since force is nothing but the relation of a substance A to something else B (an accident) as ground to consequent, the possibility of any force does not rest upon the identity of cause and effect or of substance and accident, and consequently the impossibility of falsely imagined forces does not depend upon contradiction alone. It is therefore illegitimate to assume any primary force is possible, unless it be given by experience; by no acuteness of intellect can its possibil-

417 ity be conceived a priori.

29. The third species of subreptive axioms, while arising from conditions special to the subject and thence rashly carried over to objects, do not (as the second kind do) originate in our making the sensitively given [i.e., space and time] the only path to the intellectual concept, but in holding that only by their aid can the intellectual concept be applied to a case given by experience. That is to say, we maintain that only through them can it be known whether or not anything is contained under a certain intellectual concept. Of this type is the trite maxim of certain schools: *whatever exists contingently has at some time not existed.* This spurious principle arises from the poverty of the intellect, which for the most part discerns the nominal marks of contingency or necessity, seldom the real ones. Since, therefore, we can scarcely hope to determine, through marks derived a priori, whether the opposite of some substance is possible, we shall be able to do so only insofar as we have evidence that at one time the substance did not exist. It is truer that changes prove contingency than that contingency proves mutability, and accordingly, if nothing transient and perishable met us in the world, we could hardly have acquired any notion of contingency. Thus while the direct proposition is true: *whatever at some time was not is contingent,* its converse only points to conditions under which alone we can discern whether a thing exists necessarily or contingently. If, therefore, it be enunciated as a subjective law (as it really is), it should be expressed as follows: *if there be no evidence that there was a time when a certain thing did not exist, the common intelligence does not supply sufficient marks for [us to infer] its contingency.* This subjective law is later tacitly converted into an objective condition, as if without this condition there were no room at all for contingency. This being done, a spurious and erroneous axiom arises. Though this world exists contingently, it is everlasting, i.e., simulta-

neous with every moment of time, and therefore it would be wrong to assert that there ever was a time when it did not exist.

30. With these subreptive principles there are closely associated certain 418 others, which do not indeed communicate to the given intellectual concept any blemish of sensitive cognition, but which yet so play upon the intellect that it regards them as arguments drawn from the object. They are really commended to us only by the special nature of the intellect, owing to their service in its free and extended employment; so, like those already enumerated, they rest upon the conditions under which the intellect seems to itself to make easy and ready use of its perspicacity.[7]

Let me here, by way of conclusion, add some remarks upon these principles. So far as I know, they have never yet been properly expounded. I call principles serviceable [to the intellect] those rules of judgment to which we willingly submit and to which we cling as if they were axioms, solely for the reason that, *if we gave them up, scarcely any judgment about a given object would be possible for our intellect.* Into this class fall the following principles:

(1) *All things in the universe happen according to the order of nature.* Epicurus affirmed this principle without restriction, and all philosophers with one voice assert it as holding good, subject only to those very rare exceptions which may have to be admitted under stress of the most extreme necessity. We do not assume it because of our possessing so wide a knowledge of cosmic happenings according to the common laws of nature, or because we perceive the impossibility, or the small hypothetical possibility, of the supernatural. We do so because, if we departed from the order of nature, there would be no use at all for intellect, and because the hasty appeal to the supernatural is a couch upon which the intellect slothfully rests. For the same reason, we are careful to exclude comparative miracles from our exposition of phenomena; I mean the influence of spirits, since, as their nature is unknown to us, it would be greatly to the detriment of the intellect if it were diverted away from the light of experience — through which alone it has the means of judging between rival interpretations — to the shadows of forms and causes unknown to us.

(2) The second principle is due to that preference for unity so characteristic of the human mind. From it has issued the commonly accepted canon: *principles are not to be multiplied beyond what is absolutely necessary.* We accept this principle not because we have insight into the causal unity in the world, either by reason or by experience; we are driven to search for it by the impulsion of the intellect, which believes itself to have succeeded in the explanation of phenomena only insofar as it is enabled to descend from one and the same principle to the greatest number of consequences.

---

[7]These principles are the form in which the Analogies of Experience and the regulative Ideas of the *Critique of Pure Reason* make their first appearance in Kant's work. The first principle becomes the Second Analogy of Experience (below, pp. 117–120).

(3) The third principle of this kind is that *nothing material either comes into being or perishes*, and that all the changes of the world concern only its form. This postulate, on the recommendation of the common intellect, has pervaded all schools of philosophy, not because it has been regarded as ascertained fact or demonstrated by a priori arguments, but because if it were admitted that matter itself is transient and perishable, nothing stable and lasting would be left to serve in the further explanation of phenomena according to universal and constant laws, and so in the further use of the intellect.

So much, then, as regards method, especially in reference to the distinction of sensitive and intellectual knowledge. Should this method, by a more thorough investigation, ever be reduced to rule, it will occupy the place of a propaedeutic science, to the immense benefit of all who would explore the innermost recesses of metaphysics. . . .

III

Kant's Letter to Marcus Herz, February 21, 1772

Editor's Introduction

Marcus Herz was the student who publicly defended Kant's Inaugural Dissertation in 1770. He took copies of the Dissertation to the leading philosophers (including Mendelssohn) in Berlin when he went there to practice his profession as a physician. He and his wife, the famous and beautiful bluestocking hostess Henrietta Herz, became members of the various intellectual circles in Berlin, where he was seen as "Kant's envoy." He and Kant maintained a friendly correspondence for many years.

The letter of February 21, 1772 is of unusual biographical importance. In it Kant expresses some second thoughts he has had about the Dissertation, reports good progress in resolving the difficulties, and confidently asserts that he expects to have the *Critique of Pure Reason* ready for publication within a few months.

Herz's friends in Berlin had raised minor questions in their letters to Kant, but Kant was his own best critic. He put his finger on the weakest point in the Dissertation. How, he asked, can a concept of reason refer to a noumenon? A sensible concept can refer to a phenomenon because it is an effect of the object on our sensibility. This cannot, however, be the case with a rational concept, for then our knowledge of noumena would be as empirical and a posteriori as our knowledge of phenomena. Kant then runs through various answers which have been given to this or like problems, and accepts none of them.

But instead of giving, as one expects, his own answer, he abruptly turns to another problem: what precisely are the pure rational concepts (later to be called categories)? He reports to his friend that he has found a way of deriving them from "a few" cognitive operations[1] and, having done this, he apparently thinks that the heavy labor on the *Critique of Pure Reason* is done and that the book will be published shortly.

How little he knew! Shortly after writing this optimistic letter,[2] Kant was awakened from his "dogmatic slumber" by Hume, as he tells us in *Prolegomena* (below, p. 159). The consequence of his study of Hume was

---

[1] This is probably in anticipation of the Metaphysical Deduction of the Categories in *Critique of Pure Reason* (see below, pp. 110–112).

[2] Readers should be cautioned that there is lively debate among scholars about precisely *when* Kant was "awakened" by Hume. There is no unanimous agreement that it was 1772, though that appears to me to be the most probable date.

the denial that there can be any knowledge of noumena at all. Synthetic judgments cannot be made without sensible intuition; the Inaugural Dissertation, by excluding sensible intuition from metaphysical knowledge, made it impossible.

But let us not chide Kant for his simpleminded confidence in 1772. After all, we have the inestimable advantage over him and Herz of having read the *Critique of Pure Reason*.

The translation (omitting 52 lines) is by Arne Unhjem, revised by the present Editor. It was published in The Philosophical Forum, *volume 13, pp. 103–110 (1955) and is reprinted by permission of the Editor of* The Philosophical Forum.

Kant's Letter to Marcus Herz, February 21, 1772

Noble Sir, Esteemed Friend: X,129

If you become indignant at the complete absence of my replies, you certainly do me no injustice; but if you draw any disagreeable conclusions from it, I would like to appeal to your knowledge of my way of thinking. Instead of any excuse, I shall give you a brief account of the kind of things which have occupied my thoughts and which cause me to put off letter-writing even in my leisure moments.

After your departure from Königsberg I examined once more in the intervals between professional duties and my sorely needed relaxation, the plan of the views that we had debated, in order to adapt it to the whole of philosophy and other knowledge, and to understand its extent and limits.

I had already made considerable progress in the effort to distinguish the sensible from the intellectual in the field of morals and the maxims which spring from this distinction. I had also long ago outlined, to my tolerable satisfaction, the principles of feeling, taste, and the power of judgment, with their effects — the pleasant, the beautiful, and the good; and now I was making the plan of a work that might have some such title as *The Boundaries of Sensibility and Reason*. I planned it to consist of two parts, a theoretical and a practical. The first part in two sections. (1) General Phenomenology, and (2) Metaphysics, and that only in regard to its nature and method. The second likewise in two sections, (1) the universal principles of taste, feeling, and sensuous desire, and (2) the basic principles of morality. As I thought through the theoretical part in its whole scope and the reciprocal relations of its parts, I 130 noticed that I still lacked something essential, something which in my long metaphysical studies I, as well as others, had failed to pay attention to and which in fact constitutes the key to the whole secret of hitherto still obscure metaphysics. That is, I asked myself: On what ground rests the relation of that in us which is called representation to the object? If the representation contains only the manner in which the subject is affected by the object, then it is easy to see how it [the representation] is in conformity with the object as an effect in accord with its cause, and how this modification of our mind allows it to represent something, i.e., to have an object. The passive or sensible representations thus have an understandable relationship to objects, and the principles which are derived from the nature of our soul have an understandable validity for all things insofar as they are supposed to be objects of the senses.

In the same way, if that in us which is called representation were active with regard to the object, that is to say, if the object itself were created by the representation (as in the case when divine knowledge is conceived as the archetype of all things), the conformity of these representations to the object could be understood. Thus there is the possibility of both *intellectus archetypi* (on whose intuition the things themselves are grounded) and *intellectus ectypi* (which derives the data for its logical procedure from the sensible intuition of things) being at least understandable.

However, neither is our understanding through its representations the cause of the object (save in the case of moral ends), nor is the object the cause of the intellectual representations in the mind *(in sensu reali)*. Therefore the pure concepts of the understanding must not be abstracted from the sense perceptions, nor must they express the reception of representations through the senses; though they must have their origin in the nature of the soul, they are neither brought about by the objects nor do they create the object itself.

In the Dissertation I was content to explain the nature of intellectual representations in a merely negative way, namely, to state that they were not modifications of the soul brought about by the object. However, I silently 131 passed over the further question of how a representation which refers to an object without being in any way affected by it can be possible. I had said that the sensible representations present the things as they appear, the intellectual representations present them as they are.

By what means, then, are these things given to us, if not by the way in which they affect us? And if such intellectual representations depend on our inner activity, whence comes the agreement which they are supposed to have with objects — objects which are nevertheless not possibly produced by our act? And the axioms of pure reason about these objects — how do they agree with these objects without the agreement having been reached with the aid of experience?

In mathematics this is possible, because the objects before us are only quantities and can be represented as quantities, due to the fact that it is possible for us to produce the mathematical representations by taking a numerical unit a given number of times. Hence the concepts of quantities can be spontaneous and their axioms can be determined a priori.

But in the case of relationships involving qualities — as to how my understanding may form for itself completely a priori concepts of things (with which the things must necessarily agree), and as to how my understanding may formulate exact axioms about the possibility to such concepts (with which experience must be in exact agreement and which nevertheless are independent of experience) — this question, of how the faculty of understanding achieves this conformity with things themselves, is still left in a state of obscurity.

Plato assumed a previous intuition of Divinity as the primary source of the pure concepts of the understanding and of first principles. Mallebranche *(sic)* believed in a still effective eternal intuition of this Primary Being. Various moralists have accepted precisely this view with respect to basic moral laws. Crusius believed in certain implanted rules for the purpose of forming judgments, together with the concepts which God — to the extent to which they are necessary to harmonize with things — implanted into the human soul. Of these systems, one may call the former *influxum hyperphysicum,* and the latter the *harmoniam praestabilitam intellectualem.* But the *deus ex machina* in the determination of the origin and validity of our knowledge is the greatest absurdity one could hit upon and has — besides its deceptive circle in the series of inferences from our human perceptions — also the additional disadvantage that it provokes all sorts of fancy ideas and every pious and speculative sort of brainstorm.

While I was searching in such ways for the sources of intellectual knowl- 132 edge (without which one cannot determine the nature and limits of metaphysics), I divided this science into its natural distinct parts, and sought to reduce transcendental philosophy (that is to say, all concepts belonging to completely pure reason) to a certain number of categories, but not like Aristotle, who, in his ten predicaments, placed them side by side as he found them, in a purely chance juxtaposition. On the contrary, I arranged them according to the way they divide themselves in classes following a few fundamental laws of the understanding.

Without going into details here about the whole series of investigations that has continued right up to the final goal, I can say that so far as my essential purpose is concerned, I have succeeded, and that now I am in a position to bring out a *Critique of Pure Reason*[1] which will deal with the nature of theoretical as well as practical knowledge insofar as the latter is purely intellectual. Of this, I will first work out the first part, which will deal with the sources of metaphysics, its methods and limits. After that I will work out the pure principles of morality. With respect to the first part, I should be in a position to publish it within three months.

In mental operations of such delicate nature, nothing is more of a hindrance than to be occupied with thoughts that lie outside the scope of the field. Even though the mind is not always exerting itself, it must still, in its relaxed and happy moments, remain uninterruptedly open to any chance suggestion that may present itself. Encouragements and diversion must serve to maintain the mind's powers of flexibility and mobility, whereby one is kept in readiness to view the subject matter from other sides all the time and to widen his horizon from a microscopic observation to a universal outlook in order that he may take up all conceivable positions so that views from one may verify those from another. There has been no other reason than this, my worthy friend, which has delayed my answers to your pleasant letters — for you have no desire that I should write you empty words.

With respect to your discerning and deeply thoughtful little work [*Observations Drawn from Speculative Philosophy,* 1771], several parts have exceeded my expectations. However, for reasons already mentioned, I cannot let myself go into the details.

---

[1] This is Kant's first use of the expression *critique of pure reason,* but it is not possible to determine whether at this time he meant it as the title of the book he was working on, or as a general name for the entire intellectual project in which he was engaged.

133   But, my friend, the effect which an undertaking of this kind has with respect to the status of the sciences among the educated public is such that if, due to the indisposition that threatens to interrupt its execution, I begin to feel anxious about this project (which I regard as my most important work, the greater part of which I have already before me), then I am frequently comforted by the thought that my work will be just as lost to public usefulness if it were published as it would be if it remained forever unknown. For it takes a literary man with more reputation and eloquence than I possess to stimulate the readers in such a way that they exert themselves to meditate on his writings. . . .

But enough of this. It appears that one doesn't obtain a hearing by stating only negative propositions. One must rebuild on the plot where one has torn down, or, at least, if one has cleared away fancy ideas he must make the pure insights of the understanding dogmatically intelligible and delineate their limits. With this I am now occupied, and this is the reason why, often contrary to my intention to answer friendly letters, I withhold from such tasks what free time my very frail constitution allows me for contemplation, and give myself over to the natural bent of my thoughts. And though you find me so negligent in replying, you should give up the idea of paying me in kind and suffering me to go without your letters. Even so, I would count on your constant affection and friendship towards me, just as you may remain always assured of mine. If you will be satisfied with short answers then you shall have them in the future. Between us the assurance of the honest sympathy which we have with each other must take the place of empty formalities.

I await your next delightful letter as a token of your sincere conciliation. And please fill it up with such accounts as you must have aplenty, living as you do at the very seat of the sciences, and please excuse my taking the liberty of asking for this. Greet Mr. Mendelssohn and Mr. Lambert, likewise Mr. Sulzer, and convey my apologies to these gentlemen for similar reasons.

Do remain forever my friend, just as I am yours.

I. Kant

Königsberg
February 21, 1772

IV

Critique of Pure Reason

Editor's Introduction

The book which Kant told Marcus Herz he would publish later in 1772 did not appear until 1781. It was composed, he says, in a period of a few months toward the end of what has become known as Kant's "silent decade," during which he had presumably published little, but had written many manuscripts which he now collated and combined just before publishing the book. In 1787 he published a second edition, in which he made an effort to respond to some of the reviewer's problems with the first edition and correct some of their misunderstandings. Though much Kant scholarship has been devoted to discovering inconsistencies (or proving their nonexistence), and though it does require considerable intellectual effort to understand the details and to master all the parts of the *Critique*, the main contents of the work are unmistakable and not very difficult to understand. Patience, however, and slow reading are necessary. On first reading, at least, one can use the *Prolegomena* as a guide through what Kant himself called "the thorny paths" of the *Critique*.

In the Inaugural Dissertation, Kant had said that pure intellectual concepts (now called categories) give us knowledge of things as they are (i.e., things in themselves, as objects of reason = noumena), and in the letter to Herz he asked how an intellectual concept can refer to an object which did not, through the senses, cause that concept to arise in the mind. How Kant would have answered that question in 1772 we do not know, but presumably he had some answer to it else he would not have been so confident that the *Critique* would soon be ready for publication. Apparently soon after his letter to Herz he was awakened from his "dogmatic slumber"[1] by Hume, who asked a still more fundamental question, which gave Kant's "investigations in the field of speculative philosophy a quite new direction."

Hume's question concerned the origin and validity of judgments of cause and effect, especially the principle that every event has a cause. This principle is an example of what Kant regarded as an a priori synthetic judgment—a priori because a necessary truth not learned from experience, and synthetic because its necessity is not logical necessity. In generalizing Hume's problem Kant saw that mathematical and

[1] *Prolegomena*, below, pp. 157–159. The whole autobiographical Introduction to the *Prolegomena* should be read, as it describes the birth of the *Critique of Pure Reason*.

metaphysical judgments were likewise a priori and synthetic. Thus the problem of the *Critique* (and *Prolegomena* too) is: How are synthetic judgments a priori possible?[2]

Kant's answer to this question undercuts the question he had raised in his letter to Herz. In giving his theory of how synthetic judgments are a priori possible, he shows that we do not have any knowledge of noumena and things in themselves; synthetic a priori knowledge is confined to knowledge of objects of the senses, so the question he put to Herz does not arise. We must now see how Kant arrived at this conclusion.

A. Preface and Introduction

In *The Copernican Revolution*,[3] the first selection, from the Preface to the Second Edition, Kant draws a memorable analogy between his new theory of knowledge and Copernicus' astronomy. Copernicus taught that the apparent motions of the stars depend on the real motion of the earthly observer. By analogy, Kant says objects of experience (which are appearances of unknown things in themselves) conform to the operations of the mind, whereas hitherto it had been thought that the operations of the mind had to conform things. We can know this conformity a priori, logically prior to having experience of the appearances.

From this we see that Kant had already, in the Inaugural Dissertation, carried through part of the Copernican Revolution. What Kant had said there about the mental origin of the spatial and temporal form of objects of sense experience he now extends to the pure intellectual concepts (categories) which, in the Dissertation, were supposed to represent, by pure thought, things as they are. In the letter to Herz he did not understand how the forms of thought could correspond a priori to things as they are; now he sees that they do not, for our a priori conceptual knowledge applies *only* to the structures of objects of experience.

In a theory first designed to answer Hume's skeptical questions about our knowledge of objects of experience, Kant affirms Hume's skepticism of metaphysical knowledge of intelligible reality. If there is to be any metaphysics of supersensible reality, it cannot consist in knowledge of things in themselves; at most it can be based on rational faith. Thus the

---

[2] In the question: "How are synthetic judgments a priori possible?" the position of the words *a priori* indicates that *a priori* is an adverb modifying *possible*, so the question means: "How, without experience, is it possible for us to make a true synthetic judgment?" But often Kant, and almost invariably writers on Kant, read the question as if *a priori* were an adjective modifying *judgments*. Then the question reads: "How are synthetic a priori judgments possible?" Perhaps no great harm is done by this simpler locution provided it is remembered that *synthetic* refers to a kind of judgment (one which is not a substitution-instance of a logical truth), and *a priori* refers to our way of knowing it to be true (i.e., knowing it without recourse to experience).

[3] Kant himself did not use the expression "Copernican Revolution" even though he compared his "revolution in thinking" to that of Copernicus. It was Schopenhauer, apparently, who coined the name "Copernican Revolution."

first selection in this book appropriately ends with Kant's statement, "I had to deny *knowledge* in order to make room for *faith*." The full meaning of this statement will become clearer as one goes more deeply into Kant's philosophy as a whole.

The Origin of our Knowledge is from the Introduction to the second edition. It reminds us of Leibniz' aphorism: "There is nothing in the intellect that was not first in the senses, except the intellect itself." Kant states that all our knowledge begins with experience and that without sensation we would know nothing. But given sensations, we know *more* than sensation alone teaches, for our mind operates on the data of the senses to produce the experience of organized and synthesized knowledge of objects. The *Critique* has the task of detecting and justifying the mind's contribution of this *more*.[4]

B. Transcendental Aesthetic

The four selections that follow come from the Transcendental Aesthetic. First, a word about the title. The word *transcendental* refers to whatever is a ground for a priori knowledge; thus the forms of space and time, for example, are transcendental. Kant does not use the word in some highfalutin quasi-mystical sense as some philosophers and pseudophilosophers do. The word *aesthetic* as used in the *Critique of Pure Reason* has nothing to do with art or the beautiful. It is derived from the Greek *aisthesis*, which means sensation, and it refers here to the kind of sensible knowledge already described in the Inaugural Dissertation. Transcendental Aesthetic, then, is the part of the *Critique* concerned with the sensory conditions which make a priori knowledge possible. The selections are as follows:

Intuition. Intuition is direct acquaintance with an object, and for human beings this occurs through the senses. Kant never uses the word to refer to some mysterious, quasi-mystical apprehension of arcane truths; intuition is ordinarily what we call sense perception, which involves having a sensation caused by an object and interpreting this sensation as a sign of the presence and kind of object which affected us. Intuition that is accompanied by sensation is called, by Kant, *empirical intuition* and *sense perception*, these expressions being synonymous. But besides empirical intuition, Kant thinks that there can be *pure intuition*, i.e., intuition not accompanied by sensation. For example, in "seeing" a geometrical construction "with the mind's eye," we do not consider the sensations (if we have any) of the figures on the blackboard; rather, we "see" structures

---

[4] At this point, one who is reading Kant for the first time is advised to read next the Preamble to the *Prolegomena* (pp. 162–167). Much of it was included in the Introduction to the second edition of the *Critique of Pure Reason*, and there is no reason to print it twice. From it the reader will learn some of the technical terms he uses in the *Critique*.

of the space which may or may not be occupied by physical objects. We do not have a very good English word for this kind of mental process which Kant calls pure intuition, but the mental activity it names is well known.

Intuition is the source of all content of human knowledge, the content being (at least according to this beginning part of the *Critique*) passively received by our senses.

Whatever is an object of an empirical intuition (i.e., an intuition with sensation = sense perception) is an *appearance*. We do not intuit objects as they are in themselves, but only as they appear to minds like ours.

Space and Time (two sections). Space and time are objects of pure intuition and the a priori forms of empirical intuition. In these sections Kant largely repeats the teachings of the Inaugural Dissertation (Sections 14–15) and he will repeat them in *Prolegomena*, Sections 9–10.

Space, Time, and Mathematics. Kant compares his theory of space and time with those of Newton and Leibniz, and holds that only his theory that space is a subjective form of sensory experience is capable of explaining how we can know a priori that geometrical truths apply to objects of experience.

Appearance and Illusion. This is one of several answers Kant gave to his critics who interpreted his statement that things in space are only appearances of things in themselves to mean that it is an illusion that there are things in space. He attributes the latter view to Berkeley, and argues against identifying appearance and illusion. There are other attacks on "illusionism," also called "empirical idealism," in later parts of the *Critique* and *Prolegomena* (pp. 109, 178–179).

C. Transcendental Logic: The Analytic of Concepts

As a counterpart to Transcendental Aesthetic, the other major division in the main body of the *Critique* is Transcendental Logic. It deals with thought (concepts and judgments) in contrast to, but also applied to, the sensible intuitions, which are the subject matter of the concepts and judgments established by Transcendental Logic. Both the aesthetical and the logical are essential to knowledge. In one of Kant's most famous statements (often, however, misquoted) he says: "Thoughts [i.e., concepts] without content [i.e., intuitions] are empty, intuitions without concepts are blind . . . . The understanding can intuit nothing, the senses can think nothing" (A 51 = B 75).

In the Inaugural Dissertation Sec. 5 Kant had distinguished between the *logical use* of reason and the *real use*. The former was concerned with the formal logical relations between concepts, judgments, and inferences, and reason prescribed the rules for valid logical operations. It was independent of the meanings of the terms; in modern language, the logical use of the intellect operated with uninterpreted variables, which could be interpreted as data of intuition. The *real use* of the intellect had to do with reason as a source (and not just as a logical manipulator) of a priori concepts and judgments. By present-day usage this is not a logic at all but only a theory of knowledge. In the *Critique* Kant calls it transcendental logic, preserving the name *logic* because of a close connection he thought it had with general (or, as we would now say, formal) logic. In the next selection we shall see what this connection was.

The Metaphysical Deduction of the Categories, the first selection, shows how from the table of judgments contained in general (i.e., formal) logic there can be derived a table of pure concepts of the understanding, or categories. The gist of the rather complicated argument is this: a category is a concept which serves as a rule for synthesizing intuitions into a pattern reflected in one of the standard forms of judgments, and thus a category is a rule for the use, in cognition, of one of the standard logical forms of judgment. For each form of judgment there is a category, and the category has no use except in organizing experience and reporting it in the form of judgments. (Thus, for instance, the category of causation is a rule for the use of the hypothetical judgment.)

The Transcendental Deduction of the Categories. Whereas the Metaphysical Deduction was designed to show what concepts are necessary for our knowledge, it is the task of the Transcendental Deduction[5] to show that these categories can actually do the job of imposing an a priori conceptual structure on our experience of objects of intuition.

Unfortunately the Transcendental Deduction is the most difficult and obscure section of the entire *Critique*. Kant calls it "the most difficult task that could ever have been undertaken in the service of metaphysics" (*Prolegomena*, p. 160). The difficulties of the Transcendental Deduction are not made any less, or any less visible, by an effort to shorten it. But the woods of the Transcendental Deduction can be appreciated without identifying every tree in it. To give an overall view without too many difficulties and complications, I have chosen two texts which Kant refers to as "preliminary" and "transitional."

D. Transcendental Logic: The Analytic of Principles

Having established to his satisfaction the necessity and sufficiency of his categories as pure concepts serving as rules for the synthesis of our intuitions, Kant's next task is to show that they explain how synthetic judgments a priori are possible. This is the subject matter of the Analytic of Principles.

Of the Supreme Principle of All Synthetical Judgments repeats, now on a

---

[5] Note that *Deduction* in the expression *Transcendental Deduction* does not mean derivation from premises. It is a legal term, used metaphorically by Kant, referring to that part of a legal brief devoted to establishing the legitimacy of a claim to nobility.

less metaphorical level, the argument of the Copernican Revolution. Its conclusion might, indeed, serve as a motto for the entire book: "The conditions of the possibility of experience are at the same time conditions of the possibility of the objects of experience."

A list of all the principles is included in the *Prolegomena*, p. 188. Kant's treatment of the causal and the modal principles is given in the next two Sections.

The Second Analogy of Experience is Kant's answer to the specific question raised by Hume, which, when generalized, led to the main question of the *Critique*. Hume had argued that the causal principle is neither a priori nor based upon experience; rather, it expresses a *"custom* or *habit"* in the mind which carries our thoughts from one event to another, making us suppose a causal necessity and power to lie in the things we perceive. Kant's reply, in brief, is that we cannot know in what temporal order events occur without conceiving the earlier to be or to contain a causal condition of the later. The only way we can know specifically what caused some particular event is by induction from observations, and Hume is correct that this knowledge is a posteriori; but in the process of induction to discover specific causes of particular events, the causal principle already functions in determining which of the two events is the earlier, so that we can infer which of the two may be called the cause of the other.

The Postulates of all Empirical Thinking Whatsoever. This selection is a discussion of the modal categories (possibility, actuality, necessity). Kant argues that they are not objective, but refer to the specific mental context or faculty (intuition, understanding, or reason) in which an object or state of affairs is considered. The explanation of these distinctions becomes exceedingly important for an understanding of the refutation of the ontological argument (pp. 137–141) and for an understanding of the *Critique of the Faculty of Teleological Judgment*, Section 76 (p. 397).

Kant interrupts this discussion by inserting in the second edition *The Refutation of Idealism*. This is an argument against Descartes' teaching that we are directly certain only of our own existence, and that knowledge of the existence of other things (except God) is based on uncertain inference. Kant argues, on the contrary, that one's knowledge of oneself as determined in time is dependent upon one's direct, not inferential, knowledge of the existence of things in space.

E. Transcendental Logic: Transcendental Dialectic

The last major division of Transcendental Logic is the Dialectic. The word "dialectic" in classical general logic referred to the formulation, detection, and refutation of fallacies. Transcendental Dialectic, accordingly, deals with the fallacies which occur when the categories and forms of intuition are employed to give a specious knowledge of transcendent[6] things (things in themselves, noumena, the soul, the world as a whole, and God).

It is worthwhile to compare the Dialectic with Section 5 of the Inaugural Dissertation. There it was argued that when a spatial or temporal intuitive element infected intellectual concepts, it kept them from their normal function of giving knowledge of things as they are. In the *Critique*, on the other hand, Kant argues that the categories in the *absence* of intuition give no knowledge, because without intuition all true judgments are analytical; yet when sensible intuition surreptitiously enters into thought of the transcendent, it generates only spurious and sophistical knowledge. It is the task of Transcendental Dialectic to expose the illusion that we can in *any* way know what is beyond possible experience.

The *Introduction*, briefly and metaphorically, shows what the Dialectic is about.

Transcendental Idealism and Empirical Realism, a selection from the first edition, argues that transcendental idealism, Kant's theory that appearances are representations in the mind, is compatible with empirical realism, which asserts the existence of objects in space. It was no doubt this section in the first edition which brought on the charges that Kant was a Berkeleyan idealist, the reply to which he gave in the *Prolegomena*, and in the selection on Appearance and Illusion in the second edition (pp. 109 and 177–178).

The next three selections are from the chapter entitled, "The Antithetic of Pure Reason".

Introduction to the Antithetic. Kant explains how it is possible, and he thinks inevitable, that each of a pair of contradictory propositions in speculative metaphysics can be supported by equally good arguments; yet being contradictories, only one of each pair of them can presumably be true. Such a pair of provable contradictories is called an antinomy. (There are four antinomies of pure reason; see *Prolegomena* pp. 210–211. Each of the other two *Critiques* has its own antinomy.)

Third Antinomy of Pure Reason. In the thesis it is proved that there is freedom, and in the antithesis that everything is causally necessitated. These appear to be contradictories, and therefore, it seems, one of them must be false; but there are equally cogent arguments for both.

Explanation of the Cosmological Idea of Freedom. The thesis and antithesis, however, are not in fact contradictory if the thesis is interpreted as applicable to things in themselves and the antithesis to phenomena of the senses. Kant argues that the very same human behavior may be regarded

---

[6] "Transcendent" must be distinguished from "transcendental." The former refers to anything beyond the boundary of possible experience, and its opposite is "immanent"; the latter refers to a necessary condition of our knowledge, and its opposite is "empirical." Unfortunately Kant sometimes confused these pairs and erroneously contrasted "transcendent knowledge" to "empirical knowledge."

as a part of nature under causal necessitation and as a noumenal act uncaused by antecedent conditions and therefore free.

Kant at the end says, perhaps disingenuously, that he has not tried to prove the actuality, or even the real possibility, of freedom; he has merely showed that it is not to be judged *impossible* because it appears, erroneously, to be excluded by the conception of natural necessity. It will be the task of the ethical works to fill out this possibility and to give arguments for the actuality of freedom of the will. They will not be able to produce *knowledge* of free causality, but make it an object of rational faith for the sake of which, Kant says, he denied knowledge of the transcendent.

The Critique of Rational Theology examines the claims that the existence of God can be proved. It is in three selections.

Of the Impossibility of an Ontological Proof of the Existence of God shows that any judgment attributing existence to something is a synthetical judgment, and that existence is not an analytical predicate of anything, even of a perfect or most real being.

The two remaining sections refute the validity of the cosmological (causal) and the physico-theological arguments for the existence of God by showing that they tacitly make use of the ontological argument, and since it falls they also fall with it. Kant has commendatory things to say about the physico-theological argument, though it is invalid as a proof of the existence of God; the proper function of this argument will be taken up again in the *Critique of the Faculty of Judgment.*

The translation is by F. Max Müller (London: Macmillan, 1896), thoroughly revised and modernized by the present editor.

On the marginal pagination of the Critique, see above, p. 23.

SUGGESTIONS FOR FURTHER READING

Ewing, A. C. *A Short Commentary on Kant's Critique of Pure Reason.* University of Chicago Press, 1950.

Kemp Smith, Norman. *A Commentary on Kant's Critique of Pure Reason.* Humanities Press, 1950.

Paton, H. J., *Kant's Metaphysic of Experience.* New York, Macmillan, 1951. 2 volumes.

Walsh, W. H. *Kant's Criticism of Metaphysics.* Edinburgh University Press, 1982.

Watson, John. *The Philosophy of Kant Explained.* (1908). Reprint Garland Publishing Inc., 1976.

Critique of Pure Reason

A
PREFACE AND INTRODUCTION

The Copernican Revolution in Metaphysics

Whether the treatment of the kind of knowledge with which reason is B vii occupied follows the secure method of a science or not can easily be determined by the result. If, after repeated preparations, it comes to a standstill as soon as its real goal is approached; or, if, in order to reach it, it is obliged to retrace its steps again and again; or if it is impossible to produce unanimity among those who are engaged in the work, about the manner in which their common object should be obtained, we may be convinced that such a study is far from having attained the secure method of a science, and is only groping in the dark. In that case we confer a great benefit upon reason if only we find out the right method, though many things should have to be surrendered as useless which were comprehended in the original aim that had been chosen without sufficient reflection.

That logic, from the earliest times, has followed that secure method may viii be seen from the fact that since Aristotle it has not had to retrace a single step, unless we choose to consider as improvements the removal of some unnecessary subtleties or the clearer definition of its subject matter, both of which pertain to the elegance rather than the certainty of the science. It is remarkable also that to the present day it has not been able to make one step in advance, so that to all appearance it may be considered completed and perfect. If some modern philosophers thought to enlarge it by introducing psychological chapters on the different faculties of knowledge (of imagination, wit, etc.), or metaphysical chapters on the origin of knowledge, or the different degrees of certainty according to the difference of objects (idealism, skepticism, etc.), or lastly, anthropological chapters on prejudices, their causes and remedies, this could only arise from ignorance of the peculiar nature of logical science. We do not enlarge the boundaries of the sciences but only disfigure them if we allow their bounds to be confounded: and the boundary of logic is definitely fixed by the fact that it is a science which does nothing but fully exhibit and strictly prove all formal rules of thought (whether it be a priori or empirical, whatever be its origin or its object, and ix whatever be the impediments, accidental or natural, that it has to encounter in the human mind).

That logic should in this respect have been so successful is due entirely to its limitation, whereby it has not only the right but the duty to abstract from all the objects of knowledge and their differences, so that the understanding has to deal with nothing beyond itself and its own forms. It was, of course, far more difficult for reason to enter on the secure method of science when it had to deal not with itself only but also with objects. Logic, therefore, as a kind of preparation (propaedeutic), forms, as it were, the vestibule of the sciences only, and where real knowledge is concerned, a logic is presupposed for its critical evaluation only, while the acquisition of knowledge must be sought in what are properly and objectively called "the sciences."

If there is to be in those sciences an element of reason, something in them must be known a priori, and knowledge may stand in a twofold relation to its object, either simply determining it and its concept (which must be supplied from elsewhere) or making its object actual also. The former is theoretical, the latter practical rational knowledge. In both the *pure* part, namely, that in which reason determines its object entirely a priori (whether it contain much or little), must be treated first, without mixing up with it what comes from other sources; for it is bad economy to spend blindly whatever comes in and not to be able to determine, when there is a stoppage, what part of the income can bear the expenditure, and where reductions must be made.

Mathematics and physics are the two theoretical rational sciences which have to determine their objects a priori; the former quite purely, the latter in part so, and in part from other sources of knowledge than reason.

Mathematics, from the earliest time to which the history of human reason can reach, followed among that wonderful people, the Greeks, the safe path of a science. But it must not be supposed that it was as easy for mathematics as for logic, in which reason is concerned with itself alone, to find or rather to make for itself that royal road. I believe, on the contrary, that there was a long period of tentative work (chiefly among the Egyptians), and that the change is to be ascribed to a *revolution*, produced by the happy thought of a single man, whose experiment pointed unmistakably to the path that had to be followed, and opened and traced out for the most distant times the safe way of a science. The history of that intellectual revolution, which was far more important than the discovery of the passage around the celebrated Cape of Good Hope, and the name of its fortunate author, have not been preserved to us. But the story preserved by Diogenes Laertius, who names the reputed author of the smallest elements of ordinary geometrical demonstration (even of such as, according to general opinion, do not require to be proved), shows at all events that the memory of the revolution produced by the very first traces of the discovery of a new method appeared extremely important to the mathematicians, and thus remained unforgotten. A new light flashed on the first man who demonstrated the properties of the isosceles triangle, for he xii found that he had not to investigate what he saw in the figure or the mere concept of that figure and thus to learn its properties; but that he had to produce (by construction)[7] what he had himself, according to a priori concepts, placed into that figure and represented in it, so that, in order to know anything with certainty a priori, he must not attribute to that figure anything beyond what necessarily follows from what he has himself placed in it in accordance with the concept.

It took a much longer time before physics entered on the highway of science; no more than a century and a half has elapsed since Bacon's ingenious proposal partly initiated that discovery, partly gave a new impetus to it as others were already on the right track — a discovery which, like the former, can be explained only by a rapid intellectual revolution. In what I have to say I shall confine myself to natural science so far as it is founded on empirical principles.

When Galileo let balls of a particular weight, which he had measured, roll down an inclined plain; or Torricelli made the air carry a weight which he had previously determined to be equal to that of a definite volume of water; or when, in later time, Stahl* changed metal into calx and calx again into metal by withdrawing and restoring something, a new light flashed on all students of nature. They comprehended that reason has insight only into that which xiii she herself produces on her own plan, and that she must move forward with the principles of her judgments according to a fixed law and compel nature to answer her questions, but not let herself be led by nature, as it were in leading strings, because accidental observations made on no previously fixed plan will never converge towards a necessary law, which is the only thing reason seeks and requires. Reason, holding in one hand its principles according to which concordant appearances alone can be admitted as laws of nature, and in the other hand the experiment which she has devised according to these principles, must approach nature in order to be taught by it: but not in the character of a pupil who agrees to everything the master likes, but as an appointed judge who compels the witnesses to answer the question which he himself proposes. Therefore even the science of physics owes the beneficial revolution in its character entirely to the happy thought that we ought to seek in nature (and not import into it by means of fiction) whatever reason has to learn from nature and could not know by itself, and that we must do this in accordance with what reason itself has originally placed in nature. Thus only has the study of nature entered on the secure method of a science, after having for many centuries done nothing but grope in the dark.

Metaphysics, a completely separated and speculative rational science of reason which declines all teaching of experience and rests on concepts only (not on their application to intuition, as occurs in mathematics), a science in

---

[7] For a fuller account of what Kant takes to be the essential method of mathematical reasoning, see Prize Essay, above, pp. 29–34.

*I am not closely following the course of the history of the experimental method, nor are the first beginnings of it very well known.

which reason, therefore, is meant to be her own pupil, has hitherto not been so fortunate as to enter upon the secure path of science, although it is older than all other sciences and would remain even if all the rest were swallowed up in the abyss of an all-destroying barbarism. In metaphysics, reason, even if it tries only to understand a priori (as it pretends to do) those laws which are confirmed by the commonest experience, is constantly brought to a stand-still, and we are obliged again and again to retrace our steps because they do not lead us where we want to go; while as to any unanimity among those who

xv   are engaged in the same work, there is so little of it in metaphysics that it has become rather an arena specially destined, it would seem, for those who wish to exercise themselves in mock fights, and where no combatant has as yet succeeded in gaining an inch of ground that he could call permanently his own. It cannot be denied therefore, that the method of metaphysics has consisted in groping only and, what is the worst, in groping among mere concepts.

What then can be the reason that hitherto no secure method of the science has been discovered? Shall we say that it is impossible? Then why should nature have visited our reason with restless aspiration to look for it, as if it were reason's most important concern? Nay more, how little should we be justified in trusting our reason if, with regard to one of the most important objects we wish to know, it not only abandons us, but lures us on by vain hopes, and in the end betrays us! Or, if hitherto we have failed only to come upon the right path, what indications are there to make us hope that, if we renew our researches, we shall be more successful than others before us?

The examples of mathematics and natural science, which by one revolu-
xvi   tion have become what they now are, seem to me sufficiently remarkable to induce us to consider what may have been the essential element in that intellectual revolution which has proved so beneficial to them, and at least to make the experiment of imitating them so far as the analogy between them (as rational sciences) and metaphysics permits.

Hitherto it has been supposed that all our knowledge must conform to objects; but under that supposition all attempts to establish anything about them a priori by means of concepts, and thus to enlarge our knowledge, have come to nothing. The experiment ought therefore to be made whether we might not succeed better with the problems of metaphysics by assuming that objects must conform to our mode of cognition, for this would better agree with the required possibility of an a priori knowledge of them, which is to settle something about the objects before they are given us. We have here the same case as with the first thought of Copernicus, who, not being able to get on with the explanation of the movements of the heavenly bodies as long as he assumed that all the stars turned round the spectator, tried to ascertain whether he could not better succeed by assuming the spectator to be turning round and the stars to be at rest. A similar experiment may be tried in
xvii   metaphysics so far as the intuition of objects is concerned. If the intuition had

to conform to the constitution of objects, I do not see how we could know anything of it a priori, but if the object, as an object of the senses, conforms to the constitution of our faculty of intuition, I can very well conceive of such a possibility. As, however, I cannot rest in these intuitions if they are to become knowledge, but have to refer them as representations to something as their object, and must determine that object by them, I have the choice of admitting either that the concepts by which I carry out that determination conform to the object, being then again in the same perplexity on account of the manner in which I can know anything about the object a priori; or that objects, or — what is the same — the experience in which alone they are known as given objects, must conform to these concepts. In the latter case, the solution becomes easy because experience, as a kind of knowledge, requires understanding, and I must therefore, even before objects are given to me, presuppose the rules of the understanding as existing within me a priori, these rules being expressed in concepts a priori to which all objects of experience must necessarily conform and with which they must agree. With regard to objects, so far as they are conceived by reason only and conceived as   xviii necessary, which can never be given in experience (at least in that form in which they are conceived by reason), we shall find that the attempts at conceiving them (for they must admit to being conceived) will furnish an excellent test of our new mode of thought, according to which we do not know of things anything a priori except what we ourselves put into them.*

This experiment succeeds as well as we could desire, and promises to metaphysics in its first part, which deals with a priori concepts to which corresponding objects may be given in experience, the secure method of a science. For by thus changing our point of view, the possibility of a priori   xix knowledge can well be explained and, what is still more, the laws which lie a priori at the foundation of nature as the sum total of the objects of experience may be supplied with satisfactory proofs, neither of which was possible with the procedure hitherto adopted. But there arises from this deduction of our faculty of knowing a priori, as given in the first part of metaphysics, a somewhat startling result, apparently most detrimental to the objects of metaphysics that have to be treated in the second part: namely, the impossibility of

---

*This method, borrowed from the student of nature, consists in our looking for the elements of pure reason in that which can be confirmed or refuted by experiments. Now it is impossible, in order to test the propositions of pure reason, particularly if they venture beyond all the bounds of possible experience, to make any experiment with their objects (as in natural science); we can therefore only try with concepts and propositions which we admit a priori, by so contriving that the same objects may be considered on one side as objects of the senses and of the understanding in experience, and on the other side as objects which are only objects thought by the isolated [pure] reason which strives to go beyond all the bounds of experience. This gives us two sides to be looked at; and if we find that, by looking on things from that twofold point of view there is agreement with the principle of pure reason, while by admitting one point of view only there arises an inevitable conflict with reason, then the experiment decides in favor of the correctness of that distinction.

xx   going with it beyond the frontier of possible experience, which is precisely the most essential purpose of metaphysical science. But here we have exactly the experiment which, by disproving the opposite, establishes the truth of our first estimate of the a priori knowledge of reason, namely, that it can refer to appearances only, and must leave the thing in itself unknown to us, though existing by itself. For that which impels us by necessity to go beyond the boundary of experience and all appearances is the unconditioned, which reason must rightly postulate in all things in themselves for everything conditioned, so that the series of conditions should thus become complete. [Now for the experiment.] Assume that our experience conforms to objects as things in themselves; we find that the unconditioned cannot be conceived without contradiction. Assume that our representations of things as they are given to us do not conform to things in themselves but rather that the objects [of experience] conform to our mode of representation; we find that the contradiction vanishes. From this it follows that the unconditioned must not be looked for in things so far as we know them (i.e., insofar as they are given to us [in experience]) but only in them so far as we do *not* know them (i.e., as things in themselves). Seeing this, we clearly perceive that what we at first assumed only tentatively is fully confirmed.*

xxi   But, after all progress in the field of the supersensible has thus been denied to speculative reason, it is still open to us to see whether in the practical knowledge of reason *data* may not be found which enable us to determine the transcendent concept of the unconditioned which is demanded by reason, in order thus, according to the wish of metaphysics, to get beyond the boundary of all possible experience by means of our a priori knowledge which is possible to us for practical purposes only. In this case, speculative reason has at least gained for us room for such an extension of knowledge, though it had to leave it empty, so that we are not only at liberty, but are really called upon, xxii to fill it up, if we are able, by practical data of reason.†

---

*This experiment of pure reason has a great similarity to that of the chemists, which they sometimes call the experiment of reduction, or the synthetical process in general. The analysis of the metaphysicians divided pure a priori knowledge into two very heterogeneous elements, the knowledge of things as appearance and the knowledge of things as things in themselves. Dialectic combines these two again, to bring them into harmony with reason's necessary Idea of the unconditioned, and then finds that this harmony can never be obtained except through the above distinction, which therefore must be supposed to be true.

†In the same manner the laws of gravity, determining the movements of the heavenly bodies, imparted the character of established certainty to what Copernicus had assumed at first as an hypothesis only, and proved at the same time the invisible force (Newtonian attraction) which holds the universe together, which would have remained forever undiscovered if Copernicus had not dared, by an hypothesis, which though contradicting the senses was yet true, to seek the observed movements, not in the heavenly bodies, but in the spectator. As an hypothesis only I also propose in this preface my own view of metaphysics, which has so many analogies with the Copernican hypothesis, though in the *Critique* itself it is proved by means of our representations of space and time and the elementary concepts of the understanding, not hypothetically but apodictically; for I wish that people should observe the first attempts at such a change, which must always be hypothetical.

The very object of the critique of pure speculative reason consists in this attempt at changing the old procedure of metaphysics and imparting to it the secure method of a science, after having completely revolutionized it following the example of geometry and physical science. The *Critique* is a treatise on method (*Traité de la méthode*), not a system of science itself, but it marks out, nevertheless, the whole plan of that science, both its boundaries and its internal organization. For pure speculative reason has this advantage that it is xxiii able, nay, bound to measure its own powers, according to the different ways in which it chooses its own objects and completely enumerates the different ways of choosing problems, and thus traces a complete outline of a system of metaphysics. This is due to the fact that, with regard to the first point, nothing can be attributed to objects in knowledge a priori except what the thinking subject takes from within itself; while, with regard to the second point, reason, so far as its principles of cognition are concerned, forms a separate and independent unity, in which, as in an organic body, every member exists for the sake of all the others, and all others exist for the sake of the one, so that no principle can be safely applied in one relation unless it has been carefully examined in all its relations to the whole employment of pure reason. Hence, too, metaphysics has this singular advantage which it cannot share with any other science in which reason has to deal with objects (for logic deals only with the form of thought in general): if metaphysics has once attained, by means of this critique, to the secure method of a science, it can completely comprehend the whole field of knowledge pertaining to it, and thus finish its work and leave it to posterity as a capital that can never be added to, because it has to deal only with principles and the limits of their xxiv employment, which are fixed by these principles themselves. And this completeness becomes indeed an obligation, if it is to be a fundamental science of which we must be able to say *nihil actum reputans, si quid superesset agendum* ("believing nothing done if anything remained to be done").

But, it will be asked, what kind of treasure is it which we mean to bequeath to posterity in this metaphysics of ours, after it has been purified by criticism and thereby brought to a stable condition? After a superficial view of this work it may seem that its advantage is *negative* only, warning us against venturing with speculative reason beyond the boundaries of experience. Such is no doubt its primary use; but it becomes positive when we perceive that the principles with which speculative reason ventures beyond its bounds lead inevitably not to an extension but, if carefully considered, to a narrowing xxv of the employment of reason, because, by infinitely extending the boundaries of sensibility to which they properly belong, they threaten to supplant the pure (practical) employment of reason. Hence our *Critique*, by limiting sensibility to its proper sphere, is no doubt negative; but by removing an impediment, which threatened to narrow or even entirely to destroy its practical employment, it is in reality of very important *positive* use, if only we are convinced that there is an absolutely necessary practical use of pure reason (the moral use) in which reason must inevitably go beyond the boundaries of sensibility; practical reason, though not requiring for this purpose the assistance of speculative reason, must at all events be assured against its opposition, lest reason be brought into conflict with itself. To deny that this service rendered by criticism is a positive advantage would be the same as to argue that the police confer upon us no positive advantage, their principal occupation being to prevent violence which citizens would have to apprehend from each other so that each may pursue his vocation in peace and security.

We have established in the analytical part of our *Critique* the following points: First, that space and time are only forms of sensible intuition, therefore conditions of the existence of things as appearances only; second, that we have no concepts of the understanding, and therefore nothing whereby we xxvi can arrive at a knowledge of things, except insofar as an intuition corresponding to these concepts can be given, and that consequently we cannot have knowledge of any object as a thing in itself, but only insofar as it is an object of sensible intuition, that is, as appearance. This proves no doubt that all theoretical knowledge of reason is limited to objects of experience; but it should be carefully borne in mind that this leaves it perfectly open to us to *think* the same objects as things in themselves, though we cannot *know* them.*
For otherwise we should arrive at the absurd conclusion that there is appearxxvii ance without something that appears.

Let us suppose that the necessary distinction, established in our *Critique*, between things as objects of experience and the same things in themselves, had not been made. In that case, the principle of causality, and with it the mechanism of nature as determined by it, would apply to all things without exception as efficient causes. I should then not be able to say of one and the same thing, for instance of the human soul, that its will is free and at the same time subject to the necessity of nature, that is, not free, without involving myself in a palpable contradiction: and this because in the two propositions, I had taken the soul in one and the same sense, namely as a thing in general (as something in itself), for without previous criticism I could not but take it so. If, however, our *Critique* is true in teaching us to take an object in two senses, namely either as an appearance or as a thing in itself, and if the deduction of our concepts of the understanding is correct, and the principle of causality applies to things only if they are taken in the first sense, namely so far as they are objects of experience, but not to things taken in the second sense [as

---

*In order to *know* an object, I must be able to prove its possibility, either from its actuality, as attested by experience, or *a priori* by means of reason. But I can *think* whatever I please, provided only I do not contradict myself, that is, provided my conception is a possible thought, though I may be unable to answer for the existence of a corresponding object in the sum total of all possibilities. Before I can attribute to such a concept objective reality (real possibility, as distinguished from the former, which is purely logical), something more is required. This something more, however, need not be sought for just in the sources of theoretical knowledge, for it may be found in those of practical knowledge also.

things in themselves], we can without contradiction think the same will when in appearance (in visible actions) as necessarily conforming to the law of xviii nature and so far not free, and yet on the other hand when belonging to a thing in itself as not subject to that law of nature, and therefore free. Now it is quite true that I may not *know* my soul as a thing in itself by means of speculative reason (and still less through empirical observation), and consequently may not know freedom as the quality of a being to which I attribute effects in the world of sense, because in order to do this I should have to know such a being as determined in its existence and yet as not determined in time (which, as I cannot provide my concept with any intuition, is impossible). This does not, however, prevent me from *thinking* freedom; that is, my representation of it contains at least no contradiction within itself, if only our critical distinction between the two modes of representation (the sensible and the intelligible) and the consequent limitation of the concepts of the pure understanding and of the principles based upon them have been properly carried out. If, then, morality necessarily presupposes freedom (in the strictest sense) as a property of our will, producing as a priori *data* its practical principles belonging originally to our reason, which principles, without freedom, would be absolutely impossible, while speculative reason had proved xxix that such freedom cannot be even thought, the former supposition, i.e., the moral one, would necessarily have to yield to the other, whose denial involves a palpable contradiction, so that freedom, and with it morality would have to give way to the mechanism of nature, which contains no contradiction unless freedom is presupposed. Now, however, as morality requires nothing but that freedom should only not contradict itself, and that, though unable to understand it we should at least be able to think it, there being no reason why freedom should interfere with the natural mechanism of the same act if only taken in a different sense, the doctrine of morality may well hold its place, and the doctrine of nature may hold its place too. This would have been impossible if our critical examination had not previously taught us our inevitable ignorance with regard to things in themselves, and limited everything that we can know theoretically to mere appearances.

The same discussion as to the positive advantage to be derived from the critical principles of pure reason might be repeated with regard to the concept of God and of the simple nature of our soul; but for the sake of brevity I shall pass this by. I am not allowed even to assume God, freedom, and immortality for the sake of the necessary practical employment of my reason, if I cannot deprive speculative reason of its pretensions of transcendent insights, because reason, in order to arrive at these, must use principles which are intended originally for objects of possible experience only. If, in spite of this, these principles are applied to what cannot be an object of experience, it really changes this into an appearance and thus renders all practical extension of pure reason impossible. I had therefore to deny *knowledge* in order to make room for *faith*. For the dogmatism of metaphysics, that is, the pre-

sumption that it is possible to achieve anything in metaphysics without a
antecedent critique of pure reason, is the source of all that unbelief, itself
always very dogmatical, which wars against all morality. . . .

The Origin of Our Knowledge

1   That all our knowledge begins with experience there can be no doubt. For
how should the faculty of knowledge be called into activity, if not by objects
which affect our senses and which, on the one hand, produce representations
by themselves or on the other, rouse the activity of our understanding to
compare, connect, or separate them and thus to convert the raw material of
our sensible impressions into knowledge of objects, which we call experience? With respect to time, therefore, no knowledge within us is antecedent
to experience, but all knowledge begins with it.

But though all our knowledge begins with experience, it does not follow
that it all arises from experience. For it is quite possible that even our
empirical knowledge is a compound of that which we perceive through
impressions, and of that which our own faculty of knowledge (incited by
sense impressions) supplies from itself, a supplement which we do not
distinguish from that raw material until long practice has stimulated our
2   attention and rendered us capable of separating one from the other.

It is therefore a question which deserves at least closer investigation and
cannot be disposed of at first sight: Whether there is any knowledge independent of all experience and even of all impressions of the senses? Such
knowledge is called *a priori*[8] and is distinguished from empirical knowledge,
which has its source *a posteriori*, that is, in experience. . . .

B
TRANSCENDENTAL AESTHETIC

Intuition

33   Whatever the way and the means may be by which a cognition may relate to
objects, there is one cognition that relates to them directly, and to which all
thought as a means is directed. This is *intuition*. Intuition is possible only
when the object is given, and the object can be given at least to human beings
only by affecting the mind in a certain way. The ability (receptivity) to
receive representations through the way in which we are affected by objects is
called sensibility.

Objects, therefore, are given to us through our sensibility. Sensibility
alone supplies us with intuitions. These intuitions are thought by the understanding, from which arise concepts. All thought, therefore, must directly or,

[8]One who is reading the *Critique* for the time is advised now to read the *Prolegomena*, pp.
162–167 for explanation of the distinctions between *a priori* and *a posteriori*, *analytic* and *synthetic*.

by means of certain common characteristics, indirectly relate to intuitions, i.e., to our sensibility, for in no other way can objects be given to us. The 34 effect produced by an object upon the faculty of representations, so far as we are affected by it, is called sensation. An intuition of an object by means of sensation is called empirical. The undetermined object[9] of an empirical intuition is called appearance.

In an appearance I call that which corresponds to the sensation its *matter;* that which brings it about that the manifold matter of the appearance is to be perceived as arranged in a certain order, I call its *form.* Now it is clear that it cannot be sensation through which sensations are arranged and put in certain forms. Only the matter of appearances is given us a posteriori, but their form must lie ready for them in the mind a priori, and must therefore be capable of being considered as separate from all sensations.

I call all representations in which there is nothing that belongs to sensation *pure* (in a transcendental sense). The pure form, therefore, of all sensible intuitions, that form in which the manifold elements of the appearances are seen in a certain order, must be found in the mind a priori. And this pure form of sensibility may be called pure intuition. 35

Thus, if we take away from the representation of a body what the understanding thinks of it (viz., the concepts of substance, force, divisibility, etc.), and likewise what in it belongs to sensation (viz., impenetrability, hardness, color, etc.) there still remains for me something of that empirical intuition, namely extension and figure. These belong to pure intuition, which, a priori and even without a real object of the senses of sensation, exists in the mind as a mere form of sensibility.

Space

   a. Space does not represent any quality of any things in themselves or of 42 objects in their relation to one another; space does not represent any determination which is inherent in objects themselves and which would remain even if all subjective conditions of intuition were removed. For no determinations of objects, whether belonging to them absolutely or in their relation to others, can be intuited before the existence of the things themselves; that is to say, they can never be intuited a priori.

   b. Space is nothing but the form of all appearances of the external senses; it is the subjective condition of our sensibility, without which no external intuition is possible to us. If, then, we consider that the receptivity of the subject, its capacity to be affected by objects, must necessarily precede all intuition of objects, we shall understand how the form of all appearances may be given before all real perceptions, how it may be, in fact, a priori in the mind, and

---

[9] *Der unbestimmte Gegenstand.* Kant will later use the word *appearance* to refer to *any* object of the senses, but will argue that reference to an object requires conceptual determination (*Bestimmung*) of an empirical intuition.

may, as pure intuition by which all objects must be determined, contain, priori to all experience, principles regulating their relations.

It is therefore from the human standpoint only that we can speak of space, extended objects, etc. If we drop the subjective conditions under which alone we can gain external intuition, that is, so far as we ourselves may be affected by objects, the representation of space means nothing. For this predicate is

43 applied to objects only insofar as they appear to us and are objects of our senses. The constant form of this receptivity, which we call sensibility, is a necessary condition of all relations in which objects as outside us can be perceived. When abstraction is made of these objects, what remains is pure intuition which we call space. As the peculiar conditions of our sensibility cannot be looked upon as conditions of the possibility of objects themselves, but only of their appearance to us, we may say indeed that space comprehends all things which may appear to us externally, but not all things in themselves, whether perceived by us or not, or by any subject whatsoever. We cannot judge whether the intuitions of other thinking beings function under the same conditions which determine our intuition and which for us are universally binding. If we add the limitation of the judgment to the concept of the subject, the judgment gains absolute validity. The proposition: All things are beside each other in space, is valid only under the limitation that things are taken as objects of our sensible intuition. If I add that condition to the concept and say: All things, as outer appearances, are beside each other in space, the rule obtains universal and unlimited validity.

44 Our discussions, therefore, teach the reality (i.e., the objective validity) of space with regard to all that can come to us as an object, but likewise they teach the ideality of space with regard to things when they are considered in themselves by our reason, without regard to the nature of our sensibility. We maintain the *empirical reality* of space, so far as every possible experience is concerned, but at the same time affirm its *transcendental ideality*. That is to say, we maintain that space is nothing if we leave out of consideration the condition of all possible experience, and assume it as something on which things in themselves are in any way dependent.

Time

49 *a.* Time is not something existing by itself or inherent in things as an objective determination of them, something that might remain when abstraction is made of all subjective conditions of intuition. For in the former case it would be something real, without being a real object. In the latter case it could not, as a determination or order inherent in things themselves, be antecedent to things as their condition and be intuited and known by means of synthetical propositions a priori. All this is perfectly possible if time is nothing but a subjective condition under which alone intuitions take place

within us. For in that case this form of internal intuition can be represented prior to the objects themselves, that is, a priori.

b. Time is nothing but the form of the inner sense, that is, of our intuition of ourselves and of our internal state. Time cannot be a determination peculiar to external appearances. It refers neither to their shape nor to their position. It determines only the relation of representations in our internal state. And 50 precisely because this internal intuition supplies no shape, we try to make good this deficiency by means of analogies. We represent the succession of time by a line progressing to infinity, in which the manifold constitutes a series of one dimension only, and we infer from the properties of this line all the properties of time with one exception (i.e., that the parts of the line are simultaneous and those of time are successive). From this it becomes clear also that the representation of time is itself an intuition, because all its relations can be expressed by means of an external intuition.

c. Time is the formal condition a priori of all appearances whatsoever. Space, as the pure form of all external intuition, is an a priori condition of outer appearances only. But as all representations, whether they have for their objects external things or not, belong in themselves, as determinations of the mind, to our inner state, and as this inner state falls under the formal conditions of inner intuition, and therefore of time, time is an a priori condition of all appearances whatsoever, and is so directly as a condition of internal appearances of our mind and thereby indirectly a condition of external ap- 51 pearances also. If I am able to say a priori that all external appearances are in space and are determined a priori according to the relation of space, I can, according to the principle of the internal sense, make the general assertion that all appearances, that is, all objects of the senses, are in time and necessarily stand in temporal relations to each other.

If we drop our manner of inwardly intuiting ourselves and of comprehending by means of that intuition all external intuitions which are within our power of representation, and thus take objects as they may be in themselves, then time is nothing. Time has objective validity with reference to appearance only, because these are themselves things which we accept as objects of our senses; but time is no longer objective if we abstract from the sensible character of our intuitions, that is to say, that mode of representation which is peculiar to ourselves, and speak of things in general. Time is therefore simply a subjective condition of our (human) intuition (which is always sensible, so far as we are affected by objects), but by itself, apart from the subject, nothing. Nevertheless with respect to all appearances, that is, all things which can come within our experience, time is necessarily objective.

Space, Time, and Mathematics

Time and space are therefore sources of knowledge from which various a 55 priori synthetical cognitions can be derived. Of this, pure mathematics gives a

splendid example in the case of our cognitions of space and its various
56 relations. As they are both pure forms of all sensible intuition, they render
synthetical propositions a priori possible. But these sources of a priori knowledge, being conditions of sensibility only, fix their own boundaries, in that
they can refer to objects only insofar as they are considered as appearances,
but cannot represent things in themselves. Appearance is the only field in
which they are valid; beyond it, they have no objective application. This
ideality[10] of space and time, however, leaves the truthfulness of our experience quite untouched, because we are equally sure of it whether these forms
are inherent in things in themselves or necessarily attach only to our intuition
of them.

Those who, on the contrary, maintain the absolute reality of space and
time, whether as subsistent or only as inherent, must come into conflict with
the principles of experience itself. For if they admit space and time as
subsisting (which is generally the view held by mathematical students of
nature [e.g., Newton]), they have to admit two eternal infinite and self-subsisting nonentities ([absolute] space and time) which, without there being
anything actual, exist only in order to comprehend all that is actual. If they
take the second view (held by some metaphysical students of nature [e.g.,
Leibniz]) and look upon space and time as relations of appearances, simulta-
57 neous or successive, abstracted from experience and represented confusedly
in their abstracted form, they are obliged to deny to mathematical propositions their a priori validity with regard to actual things (for instance, things in
space), or at all events to deny their apodictic certainty, which cannot arise a
posteriori while the a priori concepts of space and time are, according to their
opinion, creations of the imagination only. Their source, they hold, must be
looked for in experience, imagination framing out of the relations abstracted
from experience something which contains the universal character of these
relations but which cannot exist without the restrictions which nature has
imposed upon them.

The mathematical students of nature accomplish at least this, that they
keep the sphere of appearances free for mathematical propositions, but as
soon as the understanding endeavors to transcend that sphere they become
bewildered by these very conditions. The metaphysical students of nature
have the advantage that the representations of space and time do not stand in
their way when they wish to form judgments of objects not as appearances but
only as considered by the understanding; but they can neither account for the
possibility of mathematical knowledge a priori (there being, for them, no true
and objectively valid intuition a priori), nor bring the laws of experience into
true harmony with the a priori doctrines of mathematics. According to our

[10] Kant wrote *reality*, an obvious slip of the pen.

theory of the true character of these original forms of sensibility, both diffi-culties vanish.

Appearance and Illusion

If I say that the intuition of external objects and the self-intuitions of the   69
mind represent both the objects and the mind in space and time [respec-tively] as they affect our senses (i.e., as they appear), I do not mean that they are mere *illusion*. For the objects, and even the properties which we attribute to them, are always looked upon as something actually given in appearance, and all we do is to distinguish the object as appearance from itself as an object in itself, since their character [as given] depends only on the manner of intuition on the part of the subject in relation to a given object. Thus if I assert that the quality of space and time, according to which as a condition of their existence I accept both external objects and my own soul, lies in my manner of intuition and not in these objects by themselves, I do not mean to say that bodies only *seem* to exist outside me, or that my soul only *seems* to be given in my self-consciousness. It would be my own fault if I changed that which ought to count as appearance into mere illusion.*

This cannot happen, however, according to our principle of the ideality of   70
all sensible intuitions. On the contrary, it is only when we attribute *objective reality* to these forms of intuition that everything is changed inevitably into mere illusion. For if we take space and time to be properties that, if they exist at all, would have to be found in things in themselves; and if we then survey the absurdities in which we should be involved in having to admit that, even if all existing things were removed, there would remain two infinite things which are neither substances nor inherent in substances yet which exist and are necessary conditions of the existence of all things, then we really cannot blame the good Berkeley for degrading bodies to mere illusion. Nay, it would follow that even our own existence, which would thus be made dependent on the independent reality of such a nonentity as time, must itself become a mere illusion, an absurdity which hitherto no one has been guilty of.

---

*Predicates of appearance can be attributed to the object in relation to our senses, for instance to the rose its red color and its scent. But what is merely illusion can never be attributed to the object as a predicate, for the simple reason that the illusion attributes to the object by itself something which belongs to it only in relation to the senses, or to a subject in general — as, for instance, the two handles which were formerly attributed to Saturn. That which is never to be found in the object itself, but always in its relation to a subject and is inseparable from its representation by a subject is appearance, and the predicates of space and time are therefore rightly attributed to objects of the senses, as such. In this there is no illusion. If, on the contrary, I were to attribute to the rose *in itself* redness, handles to Saturn, and extension to all external objects without restricting my judgment to the relation of these objects to a subject, we should have illusion.

C
TRANSCENDENTAL LOGIC: THE ANALYTIC OF CONCEPTS

Metaphysical Deduction of the Categories

102   General logic, as we have often said, takes no account of the contents of our
knowledge, but awaits the representations which will come from elsewhere
in order to be turned into concepts by an analytical process. Transcendental
logic, on the contrary, has before it the manifold contents of sensibility a
priori, supplied by transcendental aesthetic as the material for the concepts
of the pure understanding, without which those concepts would be devoid
of content, therefore entirely empty. Space and time contain a manifold of
pure intuition a priori, and they belong to the conditions of the receptivity of
our mind under which alone it can receive representations of objects, and
which therefore must also affect the concepts of them. The spontaneity of
thought requires that what is manifold in the pure intuition should be first
gone through, received, and connected, in order to produce from it a cognition. This act I call *synthesis.*

103   In its most general sense I understand synthesis to be the act of putting
different representations together, and of comprehending the manifold variety of representations under one cognition. Such a synthesis is pure if the
manifold is given not empirically but a priori (as space and time). Before we
can proceed to analyze our representations, they must first be given, and as
far as their contents are concerned, no concepts can arise analytically. Knowledge is first produced by the synthesis of what is manifold (whether given
empirically or a priori). That knowledge may at first be crude and confused
and in need of analysis, but it is synthesis which really collects the elements of
knowledge and unites them to form a certain content. Synthesis is therefore
the first thing which we have to consider if we want to give an account of the
first origin of our knowledge.

We shall see hereafter that synthesis in general is the mere result of what I
call the faculty of imagination, a blind but indispensable function of the soul
without which we should have no knowledge whatsoever, but of the existence of which we are scarcely ever conscious. To reduce this synthesis to
concepts is a function that belongs to the understanding, and by this synthesis
the understanding first supplies us with cognition properly so called.

104   Pure synthesis, taken in general, gives us the pure concept of the understanding. By this pure synthesis I mean that which rests on the foundation of
synthetical unity a priori. Thus our counting (as we best perceive when
dealing with larger numbers) is a synthesis according to concepts, because it
rests on a common ground of unity (as, for instance, the decade). The unity of
the synthesis of the manifold becomes necessary under this concept.

By means of analysis, which general logic deals with, different representations are brought under one concept[11]; but what transcendental logic teaches is how to bring, not the representations themselves, but the *pure synthesis* of representations to concepts. What must first be given us a priori for the sake of knowledge of any object is the manifold in pure intuition. The second is the synthesis of the manifold by means of imagination. But this does not yet produce true knowledge. The concepts which impart unity to this pure synthesis and which consist entirely in the representation of their necessary synthetical unity, add the third contribution towards knowledge of a given object, and these concepts rest on the understanding.

The same function which imparts unity to the various representations *in* 105 *one judgment* imparts unity likewise to the mere synthesis of various representations *in one intuition,* and this unity may be called the pure concept of the understanding. The same understanding, by the same operations by which in concepts it achieves, through analytical unity, the logical form of a judgment, introduces also, through the synthetical unity of the manifold in intuition in general, a transcendental content into its representations. These representations are therefore called pure concepts of the understanding, and they refer a priori to objects, a reference which cannot be established by general logic.

In this manner there arise exactly as many pure concepts of the understanding which refer a priori to objects of intuition in general, as in our table there were logical functions in all possible judgments,[12] because these functions are the only ones belonging to understanding and completely specifying its power. Borrowing a term from Aristotle, we shall call these concepts *categories,* our intention being originally the same as his, though widely diverging from it in execution.

[11]This is the "analytical unity" referred to in the middle of the next paragraph. It might be clearer to call it "abstract unity," singling out what is common to several empirical representations.

[12]For the logical table of judgments which guided Kant to the table of categories, see *Prolegomena*, Section 21 (below, pp. 187–8). Since Kant is arguing that the work of understanding is to judge, a judgment being a synthesis of representations according to a logical rule, it is not surprising that the table of categories, which are rules for the synthesis of representations, should conform to the logical table of judgments. Kant's table of judgments has been much criticized, but it provided what he called "a clue" to the discovery of the categories.

Table of Categories

    I. *Of Quantity*   II. *Of Quality*
       Unity.   Reality.
       Plurality.   Negation.
       Totality.   Limitation.

    III. *Of Relation*   IV. *Of Modality*
       Of Inherence and Subsistence   Possibility.—Impossibility.
       (*substantia et accidens*)   Existence.—Non-existence.
       Of Causality and Dependence   Necessity.—Contingency.
       (cause and effect)
       Of Community (reciprocity
       between the active and the
       passive).

    This, then, is a list of all original pure concepts of synthesis which belong to the understanding a priori, and for which alone it is called pure understanding; for it is by these concepts alone that it can understand anything in the manifold of intuition, and think an object of it. . . .

Transcendental Deduction of the Categories

    There are only two possible ways in which synthetical representations and their objects can fit together, refer to each other with necessity, and, so to
speak, meet each other. Either it is the object alone that makes the representation possible, or it is the representation alone that makes the object possible. In the former case their relation is empirical only, and the representation is therefore never possible a priori. This applies to appearances with reference to whatever in them belongs to sensation. In the latter case, though the representation by itself (for we do not speak here of its causality by means of the will) cannot produce its object so far as its existence is concerned, nevertheless the representation determines the object a priori if through it alone it is possible to know it as an object. To know a thing as an object is possible only under two conditions. First, there must be intuition by which the object is given us, though as appearance only; secondly, there must be a concept by which an object is thought to correspond to that intuition. From what we have said before it is clear that the first condition, namely, that under which alone objects can be intuited, exists (as the form of intuition) in the mind a priori. All appearances therefore must conform to that formal conditions of sensibility, because it is through sensibility alone that they appear, that is, that they are given and empirically intuited.

    Now the question arises whether there are not also antecedent concepts a priori, which form conditions under which alone something can be, if not intuited, yet thought as an object of whatever kind it may be; for in that case all empirical knowledge of objects would necessarily conform to such concepts, it being impossible that anything should become an object of experi-   126 ence without them. All experience contains, besides the intuition of the senses by which something is given, a concept of the object which is given (i.e., which appears in intuition). Such concepts of objects in general therefore must form conditions a priori of all knowledge produced by experience, and the objective validity of the categories, as such concepts a priori, rests on this very fact that by these categeories alone, so far as the form of thought is concerned, experience becomes possible. If by these categories alone it is possible to think any object of experience, it follows that they refer by necessity and a priori to all objects of experience.

There is therefore a principle for the transcendental deduction of all concepts a priori which must guide the whole of our investigation, namely, that they must be recognized as conditions a priori of the possibility of experience, whether of the intuition which is found in it, or of the thought. Concepts which supply the objective ground of the possibility of experience are for that very reason necessary. . . .

There is but one experience in which all perceptions are represented in   A110 thoroughgoing and lawlike connection, as there is but one space and one time in which all the forms of appearances and all relations of being or not-being take place. If we speak of different experiences, we mean only different perceptions so far as they belong to one and the same general experience. It is the permanent and synthetical unity of perceptions that constitutes the form of experience, and experience is nothing but the synthetical unity of appearance according to concepts.

Unless these concepts were founded on a transcendental ground of unity,   A111 unity of synthesis according to empirical concepts would be purely accidental and a whole crowd of appearances might rush into our soul and be such that no experience could be formed from them. All relation between our knowledge and its objects would be lost, because knowledge would no longer be held together by general and necessary laws; it would therefore become thoughtless intuition, never knowledge, and would be to us the same as nothing.

The conditions a priori of any possible experience in general are at the same time conditions of the possibility of any objects of our experience. Now I maintain that the categories of which we are speaking are nothing but the conditions of thought which make experience possible, just as space and time contain the conditions of that intuition for the same experience. These categories, therefore, are also fundamental concepts by which we think objects in general for the appearances, and have therefore a priori objective validity. This is exactly what we wished to prove.

The possibility, nay the necessity, of these categories rests on the relation

between our sensibility, and therefore all possible appearances, and that original apperception[13] in which everything must be necessarily subject to the conditions of the permanent unity of self-consciousness, that is, must
A112   submit to the general functions of that synthesis which we call synthesis according to concepts, by which our apperception can show its permanent and necessary identity a priori. Thus the concept of cause is nothing but a synthesis of that which follows in temporal succession with other appearances, but it is a synthesis according to concepts. Without such a unity which rests on an a priori rule and subjects all appearances to itself, no permanent and general, and therefore no necessary, unity of consciousness would be formed in the manifold of our perceptions. Such perceptions would then belong to no experience at all, they would be without object, a blind play of representations, less even than a dream.

All attempts therefore at deriving these pure concepts of the understanding from experience and ascribing to them a purely empirical origin are perfectly vain and useless. I shall not dwell here on the fact that a concept of cause, for instance, contains an element of necessity which no experience can ever supply, because experience, though it teaches us that after one appearance something else follows habitually, can never teach us that it follows necessarily, nor that we could a priori, without any limitation, derive from it as condition any conclusion as to what must follow. And thus I ask with reference to that empirical rule of association, which must always be admitted if we say that everything in the succession of events is so entirely subject to rules that nothing ever happens without something preceding it on which it
113   always follows: What does it rest on, if it is a law of nature, nay, how is that very association itself possible? You call the ground for the possibility of the association of the manifold, so far as it is contained in the objects themselves, the *affinity* of the manifold. I ask, therefore, how do you make that comprehensive affinity in which appearances stand, nay must stand, under permanent laws, conceivable to yourselves?

According to my principles, it is easily conceivable. All possible appearances belong, as representations, to the whole of our possible self-consciousness. From this, as a transcendental representation, numerical identity is inseparable and a priori certain, because nothing can become knowledge except by means of that original apperception. As this identity must necessarily enter into the synthesis of the whole of the manifold of appearances, if that synthesis is to become empirical knowledge, it follows that the appearances are subject to conditions a priori to which their synthesis (in apprehension) must always conform. The representation of a general condition according to which something manifold *can* be arranged (in a uniform manner) is called a

[13]The "original synthetic unity of apperception" is expressed by the proposition: "The *I think* must be able to accompany all my representations" (B 131). Since to think is to judge, and to judge is to relate representations under the rules of the categories, all representations must be capable of being united in one single system of experience (consciousness in general). See p. 186.

rule and if it *must* be so arranged, a *law*. All appearances therefore stand in a permanent connection according to necessary laws, and possess that *tran-* A114 *scendental affinity* of which the *empirical affinity* is a mere consequence.

It sounds no doubt very strange and absurd that nature should have to conform to our subjective ground of apperception, nay, be dependent upon it with respect to her laws. But if we consider that what we call nature is nothing else than a whole of appearances, not a thing in itself but a number of representations in our mind, we shall no longer be surprised that we see her only through the fundamental faculty of our knowledge, namely transcendental apperception, and in that unity without which it could not be called the object (or the whole) of all possible experience, that is, nature. We shall thus also understand why we can recognize this unity a priori, and therefore as necessary, which would be perfectly impossible if it were given in itself and independent of the first sources of our own thinking. In that case I could not tell whence we should take the synthetical propositions of such general unity of nature. They would have to be taken from the objects of nature themselves, and as this could be done only empirically, we could derive in this way none but an accidental unity, which is very different from that necessary connection which we mean when we speak of nature.

D
TRANSCENDENTAL LOGIC: THE ANALYTIC OF PRINCIPLES

Of the Highest Principle of all Synthetical Judgments 193

The explanation of the possibility of synthetical judgments is a subject of which general logic knows nothing, not even its name, while in a transcendental logic it is the most important task of all, indeed the only one when we have to consider the possibility of synthetical judgments a priori, their conditions and the extent of their validity, for when that task is accomplished, the object of transcendental logic, namely, to determine the extent and limits of the pure understanding, will have been fully accomplished.

In forming an analytical judgment I remain within a given concept, and seek to extract something from it. If what I predicate of that concept is affirmative, I predicate of that concept only what is already thought in it; if it is negative, I only exclude from it the opposite of it. In forming synthetical judgments, on the contrary, I have to go beyond the given concept in order to bring something together with it which is totally different from what is thought in it. Here we have neither the relation of identity nor that of contradiction, and nothing in the judgment itself by which we can discover its truth or its falsity. 194

Granted, then, that if we must go beyond the given concept in order to compare it synthetically with another, a third thing is necessary in which the synthesis of the two concepts becomes possible. What then is that third, the medium of all synthetical judgments? It can be only that in which all our concepts are contained, namely inner sense and its a priori form, time. The synthesis of representations depends upon the imagination, but their synthetical unity, which is necessary for forming a judgment, depends upon the unity of apperception. It is here, therefore, that the possibility of synthetical judgments and (since inner sense, imagination, and apperception contain the sources of representations a priori) the possibility of *pure* synthetical judgments also will have to be discovered. Indeed, they will on these grounds be necessary if any knowledge of objects is to be obtained that rests entirely on a synthesis of representations.

If knowledge is to have objective reality, that is, is to refer to an object and receive by means of it any sense and meaning, the object must necessarily be given in some way. Without that, all concepts are empty. We have thought of them, but we have not by this thinking arrived at any knowledge of them; we 195 have only played with representations. For an object to be given (if by this is meant not mediately given only, but exhibited directly in intuition), it is necessary to refer the representation by which the object is thought to actual or possible experience. Even space and time, however pure these concepts may be of all that is empirical, and however certain it is that they are represented in the mind purely a priori, would nevertheless lack all objective validity, all sense and meaning, if we could not show the necessity of their use with reference to objects of experience. Their representation is a mere schema, always referring to that reproductive imagination which calls up the objects of experience, without which objects they would be meaningless. The same applies to all concepts whatsoever.

It is therefore the *possibility of experience* which alone gives objective reality to all our cognitions a priori. Experience depends on the synthetical unity of appearances, that is, on a synthesis according to concepts of the object of appearances in general. Without it, experience would not even be knowledge, but only a rhapsody of perceptions which would never grow into a connected text according to rules of an altogether coherent (possible) consciousness, nor into a transcendental and necessary unity of apperception. 196 Experience depends, therefore, on a priori principles for its form, that is, on general rules of unity in the synthesis of appearances, and the objective reality of these rules can always be shown by their being necessary conditions in all experience and even in the possibility of all experience. Without such a relation synthetical propositions a priori would be quite impossible, because they would have no third medium, that is, no object, in which the synthetical unity of their concepts could prove their objective reality.

Without requiring for it any experience, we know a great deal a priori in synthetical judgments about space in general, and about the figures which productive imagination traces in it. But this our knowledge would be nothing but a playing with the cobwebs of the brain if space were not considered as the condition of appearances which supply the material for outer experience.

Those pure synthetical judgments therefore refer always, though only indirectly, to possible experience or rather to the possibility of experience on which alone the objective validity of their synthesis is founded.

As, therefore, experience, being an empirical synthesis, is in its possibility the only kind of knowledge that imparts reality to every other [i.e., pure] synthesis, this other [pure] synthesis as knowledge a priori possesses truth (agreement with its object) on this condition only: it contains nothing beyond what is necessary for the synthetical unity of experience in general.   197

The highest principle of all synthetical judgments is therefore this: Every object is subject to the necessary conditions of the synthetical unity of the manifold of intuition in a possible experience.

Thus synthetical judgments a priori are possible if we relate the formal conditions of intuition a priori, the synthesis of imagination, and the necessary unity of it in transcendental apperception, to possible empirical knowledge in general; and if we say: the conditions of the *possibility of experience* in general are at the same time conditions of the *possibility of objects of experience* themselves, and thus possess objective validity in a synthetical judgment a priori.

The Second Analogy of Experience: The Law of Causation

Everything that happens (begins to be) presupposes something on
   which it follows according to a rule. [First edition]
All changes take place according to the law of connection between   232
   cause and effect. [Second edition]

Proof

   . . . The apprehension of the manifold of appearance is always succes- 234
sive. The representations of the parts follow one upon another. Whether they also follow one upon the other in the object is a second point for reflection not covered by the first sentence. We may indeed call everything, even every representation so far as we are conscious of it, an object, but it requires a profounder investigation to discover what this word may mean with regard to appearances, not insofar as they (as representations) are objects, but insofar 235 as they only stand for an object. So far as appearances, as representations only, are at the same time objects of consciousness, they cannot be distinguished from our apprehension of them, that is, from their being received in the synthesis of our imagination, and we must therefore say that the manifold of appearances is always produced in the mind successively. If appearances were things in themselves, the succession of the representations of their manifold would never enable us to judge how that manifold was connected in the object, for we always have to deal only with our representations; how things may be in themselves, without reference to the representations by which they affect us, is completely beyond the sphere of our knowledge. Since appear-

ances are not things in themselves, and are yet the only thing that can be given to us to know, I am therefore asked to say what kind of connection in time belongs to the manifold of the appearance itself when the representation of it in our apprehension is always successive. Thus, for instance, the apprehension of the manifold in the appearance of a house that stands before me is successive. The question then arises, whether the manifold of the house itself is in itself successive, which of course no one will admit. When I raise my
236 concepts of an object to their transcendental meaning, I find that a house is not a thing in itself but an appearance only, that is, a representation whose transcendental object is unknown. What then can be the meaning of the question, how the manifold in the appearance itself (which is not a thing in itself) may be connected? Here that which is contained in our successive apprehension is considered as representation [only] and the given appearance, though it is nothing but the complex of these representations, is considered as the object with which my concept, drawn from the representations which I apprehend, is to accord. As the accord between knowledge and its object is truth, it is easily seen that we can ask here only for the formal conditions of empirical truth, and that the appearance in contradistinction to the apprehended representations can be represented as an object different from them only if [the apprehension of it] is subject to a rule distinguishing it from every other apprehension and necessitating some one kind of conjunction of the manifold. That in the appearance which contains the condition of this necessary rule of apprehension is *the object*.

Let us now proceed to our task. That something happens, that is, that something or some state which did not exist before begins to exist, cannot be
237 perceived empirically unless there exists antecedently an appearance which did not contain that state; for a reality following on empty time, that is, a beginning of existence preceded by no state of things, can be apprehended as little as empty time itself. Every apprehension of an event is therefore a perception following on another perception. But as this is true of all synthesis of apprehension, as I showed above in the appearance of a house, the apprehension [of an event] would not thereby be different from any other apprehension. But if in an appearance which contains an event I call the antecedent state of perception A and the subsequent state B, I observe that B can only follow A in my apprehension, while the perception A cannot follow B but can only precede it. I see, for instance, a ship moving down a stream. My perception of its place below follows my perception of its place higher up in the course of the stream, and it is impossible that in the apprehension of *this*[14] appearance that the ship should be perceived first below and then higher up. We see therefore that the order in the succession of perceptions in our apprehension is determined, and our apprehension is regulated by that order.

---

[14] Emphasis added. Kant is not saying that we cannot see a ship go upstream. (He has been accused of this silliness.)

In the example of a house, my perceptions could begin in the apprehension at the roof and end in the basement, or begin below and end above; they could 238 apprehend the manifold of the empirical intuition from right to left or from left to right. There was no determined order in the succession of these perceptions, fixing the point where I had to begin in apprehension in order to connect the manifold empirically; but in the apprehension of an event there is always a rule which makes the order of the successive perceptions in the apprehension of this appearance necessary.

In our case, therefore, we shall have to derive the *subjective succession* in our apprehension from the *objective succession* in the appearance, because otherwise the order of apprehension of the former would be entirely undetermined and would not enable us to distinguish one [kind of] appearance from another. The subjective order of the apprehension alone proves nothing as to the connection of the manifold in the object, because it is quite arbitrary. The objective succession must therefore consist in the order of the manifold in an appearance, according to which the apprehension of what is happening follows the apprehension of what has happened, *in conformity with a rule.* Thus only can I be justified in saying not only of my apprehension but of the appearance itself, that there exists in it a succession. This is the same as to say that I cannot arrange the apprehension otherwise than in that very succession.

In conformity with this, there must exist in that which ever precedes an event the condition of a rule by which this event follows at all times, and 239 necessarily; but I cannot go back from the event and determine by apprehension that which went before. For no appearance goes back from the succeeding to the preceding point of time, although it is related to some preceding point of time, while the progress from a given time to a determined following time is necessary. Therefore, as there certainly is something that follows, I must necessarily refer it to something else which precedes, and upon which it follows by rule, that is, by necessity, so that the event, as conditional, affords a safe indication *of some kind of preceding condition,* and this condition itself is what determines the event.

If we suppose that nothing precedes an event upon which that event must follow according to rule, all succession of perception would then exist in apprehension only, that is, only subjectively. But it would not permit us to determine objectively what would have to be the really preceding and what the following among the perceptions. We should thus have a mere play of representations unconnected with any object, that is, no appearance would by our perception be distinguished in time from any other appearance because the succession in apprehension would always be one and the same and there would be nothing in the appearance to determine the succession so as to render a certain sequence objectively necessary. I could not say, therefore, 240 that [one state] follows another in an appearance, but only that one apprehension follows another. This is purely subjective, does not determine any object, and cannot be considered to be knowledge of any object (even in appearance).

If, therefore, experience teaches us that something happens, we always suppose that something precedes it which it follows by rule. Otherwise I could not say of the object that it follows, because its following in my apprehension only without being determined by rule in reference to what precedes would not justify us in admitting there to be a sequence in the object. It is always with reference to a rule by which appearances as they follow (that is, as they happen) are determined by an antecedent state, that I can give an objective character to my subjective synthesis of apprehension; it is under this supposition alone that an experience of anything that happens becomes possible.

It might seem indeed as if this were in contradiction to all that has been said on the procedure of the human understanding, it having been supposed that only by perception and comparison of many events repeatedly and uniformly following preceding appearances are we led to the discovery of a
241 rule according to which certain events always follow certain appearances, and that thus only are we enabled to form for ourselves the concept of cause. If this were so, that concept would be empirical only, and the rule which it supplies, that everything that happens must have a cause, would be as contingent as the experience on which it is based. The universality and necessity of that rule would then be fictitious only and devoid of any true and universal validity; it would not be a priori, but founded on induction only. The case is the same with other pure representations a priori (for instance, space and time), of which we are able to extract clear concepts from experience only because we have put them first into experience, and because experience is rendered possible only by them. It is true, no doubt, that the logical clearness of this representation of a rule determining the succession of events, as a concept of a cause, becomes possible only when we have used it in experience; but as the condition of the synthetical unity of appearances in time, it was the foundation of all experience, and consequently preceded it a priori.

The Postulates of all Empirical Thinking Whatsoever, and the Refutation of Idealism

265 1. What agrees with the formal conditions of experience (conditions of intuition and concepts) is *possible*.
2. What is connected with the material conditions of experience (sensation) is *actual*.
3. That which, in its connection with the actual, is determined by universal conditions of experience is (exists as) *necessary*.

267 The postulate of the possibility of things demands that the concept of the things should agree with the formal conditions of experience in general. This (the objective form of experience in general) contains all synthesis which is required for a knowledge of objects. A concept is to be considered empty and

as referring to no object if the synthesis which it comprehends does not belong to experience. If it belongs to experience, it is either borrowed from experience (in which case the concept is empirical), or it is a synthesis on which, as an a priori condition, experience in general (the form of experience) is based (in which case it is a pure concept). A concept, even though pure, can belong to experience if its object can be found only in experience. For whence could the character of possibility of an object, which can be conceived by a synthetical concept a priori, be derived, except from the synthesis which constitutes the form of empirical knowledge of objects? It is a necessary logical condition that 268 such a concept must contain nothing contradictory, but this is by no means sufficient to establish the objective reality of a concept, that is, the possibility of an object conceived by the concept. Thus in the concept of a figure to be enclosed between two straight lines, there is nothing contradictory, because the concepts of two straight lines and their intersecting contain no negation of a figure. The impossibility depends, not on the concept itself, but on its construction in space, that is, the conditions of space and its properties, and it is these that have objective reality or apply to possible things, because they contain a priori in themselves the form of experience in general. . . .

The postulates concerning our knowledge of the actuality of things re- 272 quire perception, therefore sensation and consciousness of it, not indeed direct perception of the object itself whose existence is to be known, but of a connection between it and some actual perception according to the Analogies of Experience, which determine in general all real connection in experience.

In the mere concept of a thing no sign of its existence can be discovered. For though the concept be ever so perfect, so that nothing should be wanting in it to enable us to conceive the thing with all its properties, existence has nothing to do with all this. It depends only on the question whether such a thing be given us, so that its perception could even precede its concept. A concept preceding experience implies only its possibility, while perception, 273 which supplies the material of a concept, is the only indication of its actuality. It is possible, however, even before perceiving a thing, and therefore in a certain sense a priori, to know its existence, provided it hang together with some other perceptions according to the principles of their empirical connection (the Analogies). For in that case the existence of a thing hangs together at least with our perceptions in a possible experience, and guided by our Analogies, starting from our actual perception, we can arrive at the thing in the series of possible perceptions. Thus we know the existence of some magnetic matter pervading all bodies, from the perception of attracted iron filings; though our organs are not so constituted as to render a direct perception of that matter possible according to the laws of sensibility and the texture of our perceptions, we would arrive in our experience at a direct empirical intuition of that magnetic matter if only our senses were more acute. (Their actual obtuseness does not concern the form of possible experience.) Wherever, therefore, perception and its advance can reach according to empirical laws,

274   there our knowledge also of the existence of things can reach. But if we do not begin with experience, or do not proceed according to the laws of the empirical connection of appearances, our guessing or inquiring into the existence of anything will be only a vain display. A serious objection, however, against these rules for proving existence indirectly is brought forward by idealism, and this is the proper place for its refutation.

Refutation of Idealism

Idealism (I mean *material* idealism) is the theory which declares the existence of objects in space outside us to be either doubtful and not demonstrable, or false and impossible. The former is the *problematical* idealism of Descartes, who declares one empirical assertion only to be undoubted, namely that *I am.* The latter is the *dogmatic* idealism of Berkeley, who declares space and all things to which it belongs as an inseparable condition, to be something impossible in itself and, therefore, things in space to be mere imaginations. Dogmatic idealism is inevitable if we look upon space as a property belonging to things in themselves, for in that case space and everything of which it is a condition would be a nonentity. The ground on which that idealism rests has been removed by us in the Transcendental Aesthetic. Problematic idealism, which asserts nothing but only pleads our inability to prove any existence except our own by means of immediate experience, is

275   reasonable and in accordance with a sound philosophical way of thinking, which permits no decisive judgment before a sufficient proof of it has been found. The required proof will have to demonstrate that we may have not only imagination, but also experience, of external things, and this it seems can hardly be effected in any other way than by proving that even our inner experience, which Descartes considers to be undoubted, is possible only under the supposition of outer experience.

Theorem
The bare, but empirically determined, consciousness of my own existence proves the existence of objects in space outside me.

Proof

I am conscious of my own existence as determined in time, and all determination in time presupposes something *permanent* in perception.[15] That permanent, however, cannot be an intuition in me, because all the grounds which determined my existence so far as they can be found in me are representations, and, as representations, they themselves require something permanent, different from them, in reference to which their change must be

---

[15] Kant gives a proof of the first sentence in the First Analogy of Experience (A 182 = B 224). The second sentence was changed by Kant after the type had been set, and the translation follows his revision as he inserted it into his Preface.

determined. The perception of this permanent, therefore, is possible only through a *thing* outside me, and not through the mere *representation* of a thing outside me, and the determination of my existence in time is, consequently, possible only by the existence of actual things which I perceive outside me. As the consciousness [of my existence] in time is necessarily connected with 276 the consciousness of the possibility of that determination of time, it is also necessarily connected with the existence of things outside me as the condition of the determination of time. In other words, consciousness of my own existence is, at the same time, an immediate consciousness of the existence of other things outside me.

Note 1. It will have been observed that in the foregoing proof the trick played by idealism has been turned against itself, and with greater justice. Idealism assumed that the only immediate experience is inner experience, and that from it we can do no more than infer external things and do this only in an untrustworthy manner, as always happens if from given effects we infer definite causes, it being quite possible that the cause of the representations which is ascribed by us, it may be wrongly, to external things may lie within ourselves. We have proved, however, that outer experience is really immediate* and that only by means of it, not the consciousness of my own existence, 277 yet its determination in time, that is, inner experience, becomes possible. No doubt the representation of *I am*, which expresses the consciousness that can accompany all thought, is that which immediately includes the existence of a subject; but it does not include a *knowledge* of the subject, and therefore no empirical knowledge, that is, experience of it. For experience requires, in addition to the thought of something existing, also intuition, and in this case inner intuition in respect to which (that is, in respect to time) the subject must be determined. For that purpose external objects are absolutely necessary, so that inner experience itself is possible only mediately, though outer experience.

Note 2. This view is fully confirmed by the empirical use of our faculty of knowledge as applied to the determination of time. Not only are we unable to perceive any determination of time except through a change in external relations (motion) of what is permanent in space (for instance the movement 278 of the sun with respect to terrestrial objects), but we really have nothing permanent to which we could refer the concept of a substance, as an intuition, except *matter* only, and even its permanence is not derived from exter-

---

*The *immediate* consciousness of the existence of external things is not simply assumed in the preceding theorem, but proved, whether we can understand the possibility of this consciousness or not. The question with regard to that possibility would come to this: whether we have an inner sense only and no outer sense but merely an outer imagination. It is clear, however, that, even in order only to imagine something as outer, that is to represent it to the senses in intuition, we must have an outer sense and thus distinguish immediately the mere receptivity of an outer intuition from the spontaneity which characterizes every act of imagination. For merely to imagine an outer sense would really be to destroy the faculty of intuition, which is to be determined by the faculty of imagination.

nal experience but is presupposed a priori as a necessary condition of all determination of time, and therefore also of the inner sense with respect to my own existence through the existence of external things. The consciousness of myself, in the representation of the ego, is not an intuition, but a merely intellectual representation of the spontaneity of the thinking subject. Hence that ego has not the slightest predicate derived from intuition which, as a permanent predicate, might serve as the correlate of the determination of time in inner sense (such as is, for instance, impenetrability in matter as an empirical intuition).

Note 3. From the fact that the existence of external objects is required for the possibility of a definite consciousness of ourselves, it does not follow that every intuitive representation of external things involves their existence, for such a representation may well be the mere effect of the faculty of imagination (in dreams as well as madness); but it can be such an effect only through the reproduction of former external perceptions which, as we have shown, is impossible without the actuality of external objects. What we wanted to prove here was that inner experience in general is possible only through outer experience in general. Whether this or that supposed experience by purely 279 imaginary must be settled according to its own particular properties and relations, and through a comparison with the criteria of all actual experience.

With reference to the third postulate we find that it refers to material necessity in existence, and not to merely formal and logical necessity in the connection of concepts. As it is impossible that the existence of the objects of the senses should ever be known entirely a priori, though it may be known to a certain extent a priori with reference to another already given existence, and as even in that case we can arrive only at such an existence as must somewhere be contained in the whole of experience of which the given perception forms a part, it follows that the necessity of existence can never be known from concepts, but always only from the connection with what is actually perceived according to the general rules of experience. There is no existence that can be known as necessary under the condition of other given appearances, except the existence of effects from given causes, according to the laws of causality. It is not therefore the existence of things (substances) but the existence of their state of which alone we can know the necessity, and we know this only from other states which are given in perception, according 280 to the empirical laws of causality. Hence it follows that the criterion of necessity can be found only in the law of possible experience, viz., that everything that happens is determined a priori by its cause in appearance. We therefore know in nature the necessity only of those effects of which the causes are given, and the character of necessity in existence never goes beyond the field of possible experience, and even there it does not apply to the existence of things as substances, because such substances can never be looked upon as empirical effects or as something that happens and arises.

Necessity, therefore, affects only the relations of appearances according to the dynamical law of causality, and the possibility, dependent upon it, of concluding a priori from a given existence (of a cause) to another existence (that of an effect). Thus the principle that everything that happens is hypothetically necessary subjects all the changes in the world to a law, that is, to a rule of necessary existence, without which there would not even be such a thing as nature. Hence the proposition that nothing happens by blind chance (*in mundo non datur casus*) is an a priori law of nature, and so is likewise the other proposition that no necessity in nature is a blind, but always a conditional and therefore an intelligible necessity (*non datur fatum*). Both these 281 are laws by which the mere play of changes is rendered subject to a *nature of things* (as appearances), or, what is the same, to that unity of the understanding in which alone they can belong to experience as the synthetical unity of appearances. . . .

E
TRANSCENDENTAL LOGIC: TRANSCENDENTAL DIALECTIC

Introduction

We have now not only traversed the whole domain of the pure understand- 294 ing, and carefully examined each part of it, but we have also measured its extent, and assigned to everything in it its proper place. This domain, however, is an island and enclosed by nature itself within limits that can never be changed. It is the country of truth (a very attractive name), but surrounded by a wide and stormy ocean, the true home of illusion, where many a fog bank 295 and ice that soon melts away tempt us to believe in new lands, while constantly deceiving the adventurous mariner with vain hopes, and involving him in adventures which he can never leave, and yet can never bring to an end.

There exists a natural and inevitable dialectic of pure reason, not one in 354 which a mere bungler might get entangled from want of knowledge, or which a sophist might artfully devise to confuse rational people, but one which is inherent in and inseparable from human reason, and which, even after its illusion has been exposed, will never cease to fascinate our reason, and to precipitate it into momentary errors, such as require to be removed again and again.

Transcendental Idealism and Empirical Realism[16]

. . . We must distinguish two kinds of idealism, the transcendental and A369 the empirical. Transcendental idealism teaches that all appearances are representations only, not things in themselves, and that space and time

---

[16]This criticism of empirical idealism is from the first edition of the *Critique*, omitted from the second. It should be compared with the Refutation of Idealism in the second edition, above pp. 122–124.

therefore are only sensible forms of our intuition, not determinations given independently by themselves or conditions of objects as things in themselves. Opposed to this transcendental idealism is transcendental realism, which considers space and time as something given in itself, independent of our sensibility. Thus the transcendental realist represents all external appearances (admitting their reality) as things in themselves existing outside us —the expression "outside us" being interpreted according to the pure concepts of the understanding [to mean "independent of us"]. It is this transcendental realist who afterwards acts the empirical idealist, and who, after wrongly supposing that the objects of the senses, if they are to be external, must have an existence by themselves and without our senses, yet from this point of view considers all our sensible representations insufficient to render certain the reality of their objects.

A370   The transcendental idealist, on the contrary, may well be an empirical realist, or, as he is called, a dualist. That is, he may admit the existence of matter without taking a step beyond mere self-consciousness, or admitting more than the certainty of representations in me and therewith the *cogito ergo sum*. For, as he considers matter and even its internal possibility as an appearance only, which if separated from our sensibility is nothing, matter with him is only a class of representations (intuition) which are external, not as if they referred to objects external in themselves, but because they refer perceptions to space, in which everything is outside everything else, while space itself is inside us.

We have declared ourselves from the very beginning in favor of this transcendental idealism. In our system, therefore, we need not hesitate to admit the existence of matter on the testimony of mere self-consciousness, and to consider it as established by its testimony in the same manner as the existence of myself as a thinking being. I am conscious of my representations, and hence they exist as well as myself who has these representations. External objects (bodies), however, are appearances only, therefore nothing but a class of my representations, the objects of which are something by means of these representations only, and apart from them are nothing. External things,

A371   therefore, exist by the same right as I myself, both on the immediate testimony of my self-consciousness, with this difference only, that the representation of myself, as a thinking subject, is referred to the internal sense only, while the representations which indicate extended beings are referred to the outer sense also. With reference to the reality of external objects, I need as little trust to inference, as with reference to the reality of the object of my internal sense (my thoughts), both being nothing but representations, the immediate perception (consciousness) of which is at the same time a sufficient proof of their reality.

The transcendental idealist therefore is an empirical realist, and allows to matter, as appearance, a reality which need not be inferred but may be immediately perceived. Transcendental realism, on the contrary, is necessarily left in doubt and sees itself obliged to give way to empirical idealism, because it considers the objects of the external senses as something different from the senses themselves, taking mere appearances as independent beings existing outside us. Even with the very best consciousness of our representation of these things, however, it is far from certain that, if a representation exists, its corresponding object must exist also. But it is clear that in our system external things, that is, matter in all its shapes and changes, are nothing but mere appearances, that is, representations, within us, of the A372 reality of which we are immediately conscious.

The Antithetic of Pure Reason
Introduction

. . . The Transcendental Antithetic is an investigation of the antinomy of 448 pure reason, its causes and results. If we apply our reason not to objects of experience in order to make use of the principles of the understanding, but venture to extend reason beyond the boundary of experience, there arise 449 pseudorational propositions which can neither hope for conformation by nor fear refutation from experience. For every one of them is not only in itself free from contradiction, but can point to conditions of its necessity in the nature of reason itself—unfortunately, however, its opposite can produce equally valid and necessary grounds for *its* support.

The questions which naturally arise in such a dialectic of pure reason are the following:

1. In what propositions is pure reason inevitably subject to an antinomy?[17]
2. On what grounds does this antinomy depend?
3. Whether, and in what way, reason may, in spite of this contradiction, find a way to certainty?

A dialectical proposition of pure reason must have the following characteristics to distinguish it from all purely sophistical propositions. First, it does not refer to a gratuitous question, but to one which human reason in its natural progress must necessarily encounter. Secondly, it, as well as its opposite, carries within itself not a merely artificial illusion which disappears when once seen through, but a natural and inevitable illusion which always remains even when it no longer deceives us and which, though rendered harmless, cannot be annihilated. 450

This dialectical doctrine will not refer to the unity of the understanding in concepts of experience, but to the unity of reason in mere Ideas.[18] The condition of this unity of reason in mere Ideas is meant to agree with the

[17] A complete list of the antinomies of pure theoretical reason is given in *Prolegomena*, below, pp. 210–211.

[18] *Idee* is a pure concept of the faculty of reason, a concept to which no intuition can be given. It is, however, unlike a Platonic idea, in that it is not an object of knowledge, and has no known ontological status. It serves, however, *regulatively* in leading understanding and will (asymptotically) to complete systematic unity. When Kant uses this word in its technical sense, it is translated *Idea* (with capital I) to distinguish it from *idea* which is sometimes used colloquially to translate *Vorstellung*. See p. 32 n.

understanding as a synthesis according to rules. But as the absolute unity of that synthesis, it must agree with reason. Consequently, if the synthesis is adequate to the unity of reason, it must be too great for the understanding; and if suited to the understanding it is too small for reason. Hence a conflict must arise which cannot, do what we will, be avoided.

These apparently rational but really sophistical assertions open a dialectical battlefield, where victory always comes to that side which is allowed to make the attack, and where those who are obliged to keep on the defensive must certainly succumb. Hence doughty knights, whether fighting for the good or the bad cause, are sure to win their laurels if only they take care that they have the right to make the last attack and are not obliged to stand a new onslaught from the enemy. We can easily imagine that this arena has often been entered and many victories have been won by both sides, the last 451 decisive victory being always gained by the defender of a right good cause maintaining his place, his opponent forbidden ever to carry arms again. As impartial judges we must take no account of which is the good and which the bad cause that the two champions defend. It is best to let them fight it out between themselves in the hope that, after they have rather tired out than injured each other, they may themselves perceive the uselessness of their quarrel, and part as good friends.

This method of watching or even provoking such a conflict of assertions, not in order to decide in favor of one or the other side, but in order to find out whether the object of the struggle be not a mere illusion which everybody tries in vain to grasp and which can never be of use to anyone even if no resistance were made to him — this method, I say, may be called the *skeptical method.* It is totally different from *skepticism,* or that artful and scientific ignorance which undermines the foundations of all knowledge in order, if possible, to leave nothing trustworthy and certain anywhere. The skeptical 452 method, on the contrary, aims at certainty, because while watching a contest carried out honestly and intelligently on both sides, it tries to discover the point at which the misunderstanding arises in order to do what is done by wise legislators, namely to derive from the embarrassments of judges in lawsuits information as to what is imperfectly or not quite accurately determined in their laws. The antinomy which shows itself in the application of laws is, considering our limited wisdom, the best criterion of the original legislation (nomothetic), and helps attract the attention of reason, which in abstract speculations does not easily become aware of its errors, to important points in the determination of its principles. . . .

The Third Antinomy: Freedom and Natural Law

472   *Thesis*

Causality according to the laws of nature is not the only causality from which all the appearances of the world can be derived. In order to account for these appearances it is necessary to admit also another kind of causality, that of freedom.

Proof

Let us assume that there is no other causality than that according to the laws of nature. In that case everything that takes place presupposes an anterior state on which it follows inevitably according to a rule. But that anterior state must itself be something which has taken place (which has come to be in time and did not exist before), because had it always existed, its effect too would not have only just arisen, but would have existed always. The causality of a cause, therefore, through which something takes place is itself an event which, again according to the law of nature, presupposes an anterior state and its causality, and this again an anterior state, and so on. If, therefore, everything takes place only according to laws of nature, there will always be a 474 secondary beginning but never a first beginning, and therefore no completeness of the series on the side of successive causes. But the law of nature consists in this: that nothing takes place without a cause sufficiently determined a priori. Therefore the proposition that all causality is possible according to the laws of nature contradicts itself if taken in unlimited generality, and it is impossible, therefore, to maintain that [natural] causality is the only one.

We must therefore admit another causality, through which something takes place without its cause being further determined according to necessary laws by a preceding state. That is, we must admit an *absolute spontaneity of causes,* by which a series of appearances, moving forward according to natural laws, begins of itself. We must consequently admit transcendental freedom, without which, even in the course of nature, the series of appearances on the side of causes can never be complete.

Antithesis 473

There is no freedom, but everything in the world takes place entirely according to the laws of nature.

Proof

If we admit that there is freedom in the transcendental sense as a particular kind of causality according to which events in the world could take place, that is, a faculty of absolutely originating a state and with it a series of consequences, it would follow that not only would a series have its absolute beginning through this spontaneity, but that the determination of that spontaneity, itself to produce the series, that is, its causality, would have an absolute beginning, nothing preceding it by which this act is determined according to constant laws. Every beginning of an act, however, presupposes a state in which the cause is not yet active, and a dynamically primary beginning of an act presupposes a state which has no causal connection with the preceding state of that cause, that is, in no wise follows from it. Transcendental freedom is therefore opposed to the law of causality, and represents such a connection of successive states of efficient causes that no unity of experience is possible 475 with it. It is therefore an empty fiction of the mind, and is not to be met with in any experience.

We have, therefore, nothing but nature, in which we must try to find the connection and order of cosmical events. Freedom (independence) from the laws of nature is no doubt a deliverance from restraint, but also from the guidance of all rules. One cannot say that, instead of the laws of nature, laws of freedom may enter into the causality of the course of the world, for if determined by laws it would not be freedom but nothing else than nature. Nature, therefore, and transcendental freedom differ from each other as lawfulness and lawlessness. The former, no doubt, imposes upon the understanding the difficult task of looking higher and higher for the origin of events in the series of causes, because their causality is always conditioned. In return for this, however, it promises a complete and well-ordered unity of experience; while, on the other side, the fiction of freedom promises, no doubt, to the inquiring mind, rest in the chain of causes, leading the mind up to an unconditioned causality which begins to act of itself, but which, as it is itself blind, tears the thread of rules by which alone a complete and coherent experience is possible.

Explanation of the Cosmological Idea of Freedom

. . . The law of nature, that everything that happens has a cause, and that
570 the causality of that cause, i.e., its activity (since the cause is anterior in time and, in relation to an effect which has arisen, cannot itself have always existed but must itself have happened at some time), must have its cause among the appearances by which it is determined, and that therefore all events in the order of nature are empirically determined—this law, I say, through which alone appearances become nature and objects of experience, is a law of the understanding which can on no account be surrendered and from which no single appearance can be exempted; because in doing this we should place it outside all possible experience, separate it from all objects of possible experience, and change it into a mere figment of the mind or cobweb of the brain. . . . The question is whether, if we recognize in the whole series of events nothing but natural necessity, we may yet regard the same event which on one side is an effect of nature only, on the other side as an effect of freedom; or whether there is a direct contradiction between these two kinds of causality.

There can certainly be nothing among the causes in appearance that could originate a series absolutely and by itself. Every action, as appearance, so far as it produces an event, is itself an event and presupposes another state in which its cause can be discovered; and thus everything that happens is only a continuation of the series, and no beginning, happening by itself, is possible in it. Actions of natural causes in the succession of time are therefore them-
572 selves effects which in their turn presuppose causes in the series of time. A spontaneous and original action by which something takes place which did not exist before cannot be expected in the causal nexus of appearances.

But is it really necessary that, if effects are appearances, the causality of their cause, which cause itself is appearance, could be nothing but empirical? Although every effect in appearance requires a connection with its cause according to the laws of empirical causality, is it not possible that empirical causality itself could nevertheless without in the least breaking its connection with natural causes, be an effect of a nonempirical, intelligible causality? That is, could it not be the effect of a caused action which was original with respect to appearances and thus itself not appearance, but intelligible with respect to its causality while, as a link in the chain of nature, it is to be regarded as belonging entirely to the world of sense?

We require the principle of the causality of appearances among themselves in order to be able to look for and to produce natural conditions, that is, causes of natural events in appearance. If this is admitted and not weakened by any exceptions, the understanding, which in its empirical employment 573 justly recognizes in all events nothing but nature, has really all it can demand, and physical explanations may proceed without let or hindrance. The understanding would not be wronged in the least, if we assumed, though it be a mere fiction, that some among natural causes have a power which is intelligible only, whose determination to activity does not rest on empirical conditions but on mere grounds of the intellect, provided only that activity in appearance of that cause be in accordance with all the laws of empirical causality. For in this way the active subject, as *causa phaenomenon* would be joined with nature through the indissoluble dependence of all its action, and only the noumenon[19] of that subject (with all its causality in appearance) would contain certain conditions which, if we want to ascend from the empirical to the transcendental object, would have to be considered as intelligible only. For, if only we follow the rule of nature in that which may be the cause among appearances, it is indifferent to us what kind of ground of these appearances and of their connection may be conceived to exist in the transcendental subject which is empirically unknown to us. This intelligible ground does not touch the empirical questions; it would concern only, it seems, thought in the pure understanding. Although the effects of that 574 thought and action of the pure understanding may be discovered in the appearances, these must nevertheless be completely explicable from the cause in appearance according to the laws of nature, taking their empirical character as the highest ground of explanation, and ignoring the intelligible character which is the transcendental ground of the empirical character, its sensible sign.

Let us apply this to experience. Man is one of the appearances in the world of sense, and in so far one of the natural causes the causality of which must be subject to empirical laws. As such he must, like all other objects in nature, have an empirical character. We perceive it through the forces and faculties which he shows in his actions and effects. In lifeless or merely animal nature, we see no ground for admitting any faculty not sensuously conditioned. Man, however, who knows all the rest of nature through his senses only, knows

---

[19] Kant wrote *phaenomenon*, a slip of the pen.

himself also through pure apperception, and this in actions and internal decisions which he cannot ascribe to the impressions of sense. Man is thus to himself partly a phenomenon, partly, however (with reference to certain

575 faculties) a purely intelligible object, because the actions of these faculties cannot be ascribed to the receptivity of sensibility. We call these faculties understanding and reason. It is the latter, in particular, which is entirely distinguished from all empirically conditioned forces or faculties, because it weighs its objects according to Ideas, and determines the understanding accordingly, which then makes an empirical use of its concepts (however pure they be).

That our reason possesses causality, or that we at least think there is such a causality in it, is clear from the imperatives which, in all practical matters, we impose as rules on our executive powers. The *ought* expresses a kind of necessity and connection with causes which we do not find elsewhere in the whole of nature. The understanding can know in nature only what is present, past, or future. It is impossible that anything in it ought to be different from what it is in fact, in all these temporal relations. If we look only at the course of nature, the *ought* has no meaning whatever. We cannot ask what ought to be in nature, as little as we can ask what qualities a circle ought to possess. We can ask only what happens in nature, and what are the properties of that which happens.

The *ought* expresses a possible action the ground of which cannot be anything but a bare concept, while in every merely natural action the ground

576 must always be an appearance. Now it is quite true that while the action to which the *ought* applies must be possible under natural conditions, these natural conditions do not affect the determination of the will itself but only its effects and results among appearances. There may be ever so many natural grounds which impel me to will and ever so many sensuous temptations, but they can never produce an *ought;* they can produce only a willing which is always conditioned but by no means necessary, and to which the *ought,* pronounced by reason, opposes measure, prohibition, and authority. Whether it be an object of the senses only (the pleasant) or an object of pure reason (the good), reason does not yield to the empirically given impulse, and does not follow the order of things as they present themselves as appearances, but frames for itself, with perfect spontaneity, a new order according to Ideas to which it adapts the empirical conditions and according to which it declares actions to be necessary even though they have not taken place and, maybe, never will take place. Yet it is presupposed that reason may have causality with respect to these actions, for otherwise no effects in experience could be expected to result from these Ideas.

Let us take our stand here and assume as at least possible that reason

577 actually possesses causality with reference to appearances. In that case, reason though it be, it must nevertheless show an empirical character, because every cause presupposes a rule according to which certain appearances

follow as effects, and every rule requires in the effects a uniformity on which the concept of cause (as a power) is founded. This, so far as it is derived from mere appearances, may be called the *empirical character*. This is permanent, while the effects according to a diversity of concomitant and in part restraining conditions appear in changeable forms.

Every man therefore has an empirical character of his arbitrary will (*Willkür*), which is nothing but a certain causality of his reason. It exhibits in its actions and effects in appearance a rule according to which one may infer the motives of reason and its actions, both in kind and degree, and judge of the subjective principles of his will. As that empirical character itself must be inferred from appearances as an effect, and from their rule which is supplied by experience, all the acts of a man in [the realm of] appearance are determined from his empirical character and from the other concomitant causes according to the order of nature, and if we could investigate all the manifes- 578 tations of his will to the very bottom, there would be not a single human action which we could not predict with certainty and recognize as necessary from its preceding conditions. There is no freedom therefore with reference to this empirical character, and yet it is only with reference to it that we can consider man, when we are merely observing and, as is the case in anthropology, trying to investigate physiologically the motive causes of his actions.

If, however, we consider the same actions with reference to reason, not with reference to speculative [i.e., theoretical] reason in an effort to *explain* their origin, but solely so far as reason is the cause which *produces* them — in a word, if we compare actions with [practical] reason — we find a rule and order totally different from the order of nature. For from this point of view it may be that everything *ought not to have happened* which, according to the course of nature, *has happened*, and because of its empirical grounds had to happen. And sometimes we find, or at least believe that we find, that the Ideas of reason have really proved their causality with reference to human actions as appearances, and that these actions have taken place not because they were determined by empirical causes, but by grounds of reason.

Now supposing one could say that reason possesses causality in reference 579 to appearances, could the action of reason be called free in that case, as it is precisely determined by the empirical character (the sensuous mode) and rendered necessary by it? That character again is determined by the intelligible character (the mode of thinking). We do not know the latter, however, but signify it by appearances which give us direct knowledge only of the sensuous mode (the empirical character).* An action, so far as it is to be attributed to the mode of thinking as its cause, does not result from the mode

---

*The true morality of actions (merit or guilt), even that of our own conduct, remains therefore entirely hidden. Our imputations can refer to the empirical character only. How much of that may be the pure effect of freedom, how much is to be ascribed to nature only and to the faults of temperament for which man is not responsible, or to his happy constitution (*merito fortunae*) no one can discover, and no one can judge with perfect justice.

of thinking according to empirical laws; that is, it is not *preceded* by the conditions of pure reason, but preceded only by the effects of these conditions on the appearances of the inner sense. Pure reason, as a simple intelligible faculty, is not subject to the form of time or to the conditions of succession in time. The causality of reason in its intelligible character does not arise or begin to be at a certain time in order to produce an effect; for in that case it would be subject to the natural law of appearances, which determines all causal series in time, and its causality would then be nature and not freedom. What we can say, therefore, is that if reason can possess causality with reference to appearances, it is a faculty through which the sensuous condition of an empirical series of effects first begins. For the condition that lies in reason is not sensuous, and therefore does not itself begin. Thus we get what we missed in all empirical series, namely, that the condition of a series of events should itself be empirically unconditioned. For here the condition is really *outside* the series of appearances, in the intelligible, and is therefore not subject to any sensuous condition nor to any temporal determination through preceding causes.

Nevertheless, the same cause belongs also, in another respect, to the series of appearances. Man himself is an appearance. His will has an empirical character, which is the empirical cause of all his actions. There is no condition determining man according to this character which is not contained in the series of natural effects and subject to their law according to which there can be no empirically unconditioned causality of anything which happens in time. No given action, therefore, since it can be perceived as appearance only, can begin absolutely by itself. Of pure reason, however, we cannot say that the state in which it determines the will is preceded by another state in which that state is itself determined, for as reason itself is not an appearance and not subject to any of the conditions of sensibility, there exists in it, even in reference to its causality, no succession in time, and the dynamical law of nature which determines the succession of time according to rules cannot be applied to it.

Reason is therefore the constant condition of all voluntary actions by which man appears. Every one of them is determined beforehand in his empirical character before it becomes actual. With regard to the intelligible character, however, of which the empirical is only the sensible schema, there is neither before nor after; and every action, without regard to the temporal relations which connect it with other appearances, is the immediate effect of the intelligible character of pure reason. Reason, therefore, acts freely, without being determined dynamically in the chain of natural causes by external or internal conditions earlier in time. That freedom must then not only be regarded negatively, as independence of empirical conditions (for in that case the faculty of reason would cease to be a cause of appearances), but should be defined positively also, as the power of beginning spontaneously a series of events. Hence in reason itself nothing begins, and since it is itself the unconditioned condition of every free action, reason admits of no higher condition antecedent in time, while nevertheless its effect takes its beginning in the series of appearances, though it can never constitute in that series an absolute first beginning.

In order to illustrate the regulative principle of reason by an example of its empirical application, not in order to confirm it (for such arguments are useless for transcendental propositions), let us take a voluntary action, for example, a malicious lie by which a man has produced a certain confusion in society. We first try to find out the motives for it and afterwards try to decide how far it and its consequences may be imputed to the offender. With regard to the first point, one has first to follow up his empirical character to its very sources, which are to be found in wrong education, bad company, in part also in the viciousness of a natural disposition and a nature insensible to shame, or ascribed to frivolity and heedlessness, not omitting the occasioning causes at the time of the lie. In all this the procedure is exactly the same as in the investigation of a series of determining causes of a given natural effect. But 583 though one believes that the act was thus determined, one nevertheless blames the offender, not on account of his unhappy natural disposition, not on account of influencing circumstances, not even on account of his former course of life, but because one supposes that one might leave entirely out of account what that course of life may have been, and consider the past series of conditions as having never existed, and the act itself as totally unconditioned by previous states, as if the offender had with it begun a new series of effects, quite by himself. This blame is founded on a law of reason, reason being considered as a cause which, independent of all the before-mentioned empirical conditions, would and should have determined the man to have behaved otherwise. We do not regard the causality of reason as a concurrent agency only, but as complete in itself, even though the sensuous motives did not favor, but even opposed it. The action is imputed to the man's intelligible character. At the moment when he tells the lie, the guilt is entirely his; that is, we regard reason, in spite of all empirical conditions of the act, as completely free, and the lie has to be imputed entirely to it.

Such an imputation shows that we think that reason is not at all affected by the influences of sense, and that it does not change (although its appearances, that is, the mode in which it shows itself by its effects, do change); that 584 in it no state precedes as determining a following state; and that reason does not belong to the series of sensuous conditions which render appearances necessary according to the law of nature. Reason, it is supposed, is present in all the actions of man and in all circumstances of time, and is always the same; but it is itself never in time, never in a new state in which it was not before; it is *determining*, not *determined*. We cannot ask, therefore, why reason has not determined itself differently, but only why it has not differently determined the appearances by its causality. And here no answer is really possible. For a different intelligible character would have given a different empirical character, and if we say that in spite of the whole of his previous course of life the offender could have avoided the lie, this means only that it was in the power of reason, and that reason in its causality is subject to no conditions of appearance and the passage of time; it means, lastly, that the difference of time, though it makes a great difference in appearances and their relation to each other, can, as the appearances are neither things nor causes in themselves, produce no difference of action in reference to reason.

585   We thus see that, in judging of voluntary actions, so far as their causality is concerned, we can get only so far as the intelligible cause, but not beyond. We can see that that cause is free, that it determines independently of sensibility, and therefore is capable of being the sensuously unconditioned condition of appearances. To explain why that intelligible character should under present circumstances give rise to these appearances and this empirical character and no other exceeds all the powers of our reason, indeed all its right of questioning, as if we were to ask why the transcendental object to our external sensible intuition gives us intuition in space only and in no other form. But the problem which we have to solve does not require us to ask or answer such questions. Our problem was whether freedom is contradictory to natural necessity in one and the same action. This we have sufficiently answered by showing that freedom may have relation to a very different kind of condition from those of nature, so that the law of the latter does not affect the former, and each may exist independent of, and undisturbed by, the other.

It should be clearly understood that, in what we have said, we had no intention of establishing the *actuality* of freedom as one of the powers which
586 contain the cause of appearances in our world of sense. For not only would this have been no transcendental consideration at all, which is concerned with concepts only, but it could never have succeeded, because from experience we can never infer anything but what must be represented in thought according to the laws of experience. It was not even our intention to prove the *possibility* of freedom, for in that also we should not have succeeded, because from a priori concepts alone we can never know the possibility of any real ground or any causality. We have here treated freedom as a transcendental Idea only, which leads reason to think that it can absolutely begin the series of conditions in [the realm of] appearance by what is sensuously unconditioned. By this, reason becomes involved in an antinomy of its own laws which it had prescribed to the empirical use of the understanding. That this antinomy rests on a mere illusion, and that nature does not contradict the causality of freedom, was the only thing we could prove, or cared to prove.

Critique of Rational Theology

618   There are only three kinds of proofs of the existence of God by speculative [i.e., theoretical] reason.

All the paths that can be followed to this end begin either from the definite experience and peculiar nature of the world of sense known to us through experience, and ascend from it, following the laws of causality, to the highest cause existing outside the world; or they rest on an indefinite experience only, that is, on any existence which is empirically given; or lastly, they leave all experience out of account, and infer entirely a priori from mere concepts the existence of a supreme cause. The first proof is the physico-theological, the second the cosmological, the third the ontological. There are no more, 619 and there can be no more.

I shall show that neither on the one path, the empirical, nor on the other, the transcendental, can reason achieve anything, and that it stretches its wings in vain when it tries to soar beyond the world of sense by the power of mere speculation. But the order in which these three arguments should be examined will be the reverse of that followed by reason in its gradual development, which is the same as the order in which they have been placed above. For we shall be able to show that although experience gave the first impulse, it is the transcendental concept only that guides reason in its endeavors and fixes the final goal which reason wishes to attain. I shall therefore begin with the examination of the transcendental proof, and see afterwards how far it may be strengthened by the addition of empirical elements.

Of the Impossibility of an Ontological Proof of the Existence of God

It is easily perceived from what has been said before that the concept of an 620 absolutely necessary Being is a concept of pure reason, that is, a mere Idea the objective reality of which is by no means proved by the fact that reason requires it. That Idea does no more than point to a certain but unattainable completeness, and serves rather to limit the understanding than to extend its sphere. It seems strange and absurd, however, that an inference to an absolutely necessary existence from a given existence in general should seem urgent and correct, and yet that all the conditions under which the understanding can form a concept of such a necessity should be entirely against us.

People have in all ages talked of an *absolutely necessary* Being, but they have tried not so much to understand whether and how a thing of that kind could even be conceived as rather to prove its existence. No doubt a verbal definition of that concept is quite easy, if we say that it is something the nonexistence of which is impossible. This, however, does not make us much wiser with reference to the conditions that make it necessary to consider the 621 nonexistence of a thing as absolutely inconceivable. It is these conditions which we want to know, and whether by that concept we are thinking anything or not. For to use the word *unconditioned* in order to get rid of all the conditions which the understanding always requires when wishing to conceive something as necessary, does not render it in the least clear to us whether, after all, we are still thinking anything or perhaps nothing by the concept of the unconditionally necessary.

Nay, more than this, people have imagined that by a number of examples they had explained this concept, at first risked at haphazard but afterwards become quite familiar, and that therefore all further inquiry about its intelligibility was unnecessary. It was said that every proposition of geometry, such as, for instance, that a triangle has three angles, is absolutely necessary, and people began to talk of an object entirely outside the sphere of our understanding as if they knew perfectly well what, by that concept, they wished to say of it.

But all these pretended examples are taken without exception from *judgments* only, not from *things* and their existence. Now the unconditioned necessity of judgments is not the same as an absolute necessity of things. The absolute necessity of a judgment is only a conditioned necessity of the thing or of the predicate in the judgment. The proposition did not say that three angles were absolutely necessary, but that under the condition of the existence of a triangle, three angles are given in it of necessity. Nevertheless, this pure logical necessity has exerted so powerful an illusion that, after having formed of a thing an a priori concept so constituted that it seemed to include existence in its sphere, people thought that they could conclude with certainty that, because existence necessarily belongs to the object of that concept provided that I posit the thing as given (as existing), its existence also must necessarily be posited (according to the rule of identity) and that the being therefore must itself be absolutely necessary because its existence is implied in a concept which is freely accepted and under the condition that I posit the object of it.

If in an identical judgment I reject the predicate and retain the subject, there arises a contradiction, and hence I say that the former belongs to the latter necessarily. But if I reject the subject as well as the predicate, there is no contradiction, because there is nothing left that can be contradicted. To accept a triangle and yet to reject its three angles is contradictory; but there is no contradiction at all in admitting the nonexistence of the triangle and of its three angles. The same applies to the concept of an absolutely necessary being. Remove its existence, and you remove the thing itself with all its predicates, so that a contradiction becomes impossible. There is nothing external to which a contradiction could apply, because the thing is not meant to be externally necessary; nor is there anything internal that could be contradicted, for in removing the thing out of existence you have removed at the same time all its internal properties. If you say, *God is almighty,* that is a necessary judgment because almightiness cannot be removed if you posit a deity, that is an infinite Being, with the concept of which the other concept of almightiness is identical. But if you say, *God is not,* then neither His almightiness nor any other of His predicates is given; they are all, together with the subject, removed out of existence, and therefore there is not the slightest contradiction in that sentence.

We have seen, therefore, that if I remove the predicate of a judgment together with its subject, there can never be an internal contradiction whatever that predicate may be. The only way of evading that conclusion would be to say that there are subjects which cannot be removed out of existence, but must always remain. But this would be the same as to say that there exist absolutely necessary subjects, an assumption the correctness of which I have called into question and the possibility of which you had undertaken to prove. For I cannot form the least concept of a thing which, if it had been removed together with all its predicates, would leave behind a contradiction; and except contradiction, I have no other test of impossibility by pure concepts a priori. Against all these general arguments (which no one can object to) you challenge me with a case which you represent as a proof by a fact, namely, that there is one concept, and this one concept only, in which the nonexistence or the removal of its object would be self-contradictory, namely, the concept of the most real being (*ens realissimum*). You say that it possesses all reality, and you are no doubt justified in accepting such a being as possible. This for the present I may admit, though the absence of self-contradictoriness in a concept is far from proving the possibility of its object.* Now [the argument proceeds], the whole of reality comprehends existence, and therefore existence is contained in the concept of a thing which is possible. If that thing is negated the internal possibility of the thing would be negated, and that is self-contradictory.

I answer: Even in introducing into the concept of a thing, which you wish to think in its possibility only, the concept of existence under whatever disguise it may be, you have been guilty of a contradiction. If you were allowed to do this, you would apparently have carried your point, but in reality you have achieved nothing but only committed a tautology. I simply ask you, whether the proposition that *this* or *that thing* (which, whatever it may be, I grant you as possible) *exists*, is an analytical or a synthetical proposition? If the former, then by its existence you add nothing to your thought of the thing, but in that case either the thought within you would be the thing itself, or you would have presupposed existence as belonging to possibility and (according to your own showing) deduced existence from internal possibility, which is nothing but a miserable tautology. The mere word *reality*, which in the concept of a thing sounds different from *existence* in the concept of the predicate, can make no difference. For if you call all positing (without determining what it is that is posited) reality, you have placed a thing with all its predicates within the concept of the subject, and assumed it as real, and you do nothing but repeat it in the predicate. If, on the contrary, you admit, as every sensible man must do, that every proposition involving existence is synthetical, how can you say that the predicate of existence does not admit of removal without contradiction, a distinguishing property which is peculiar to analytical propositions only, the distinctive character of which depends on it?

*A concept is always possible if it is not self-contradictory. This is the logical characteristic of possibility, and by it the object of the concept is distinguished from the *nihil negativum*. But it may nevertheless be an empty concept, unless the objective reality of the synthesis by which the concept is generated has been distinctly shown. This, however, as shown above, must always rest on principles of possible experience, and not on the principle of analysis (the principle of contradiction). This is a warning against inferring directly from the possibility of concepts (logical) the possibility of things (real).

I might have hoped to put an end to this subtle argumentation without many words and simply by an accurate definition of the concept of existence, if I had not seen that the illusion in mistaking a logical predicate for a real one (that is, a predicate which determines a thing) resists all correction. Everything can become a *logical predicate,* even the subject itself may be predicated of itself, because logic takes no account of any contents. *Determination,* however, is a predicate added to the concept of the subject and enlarging it, and it must not therefore already be contained in it.

Being is evidently not a real predicate or a concept of something that could be added to the concept of a thing. It is merely the positing of a thing and of certain determinations in it. Logically, it is merely the copula of a judgment. The proposition, *God is almighty,* contains two concepts, each having its

627 object, namely God and almightiness. The small word *is* is not an additional predicate, but only serves to put the predicate in relation to the subject. If, then, I take the subject (God) with all its predicates (including that of almightiness) and say, *God is* or *There is a God,* I do not attach a new predicate to the concept of God, but only posit the subject in itself, with all its predicates, and indeed the object, in relation to my concept. The content of both must be the same, and nothing can have been added to the concept, which expresses only possibility, by my thinking its object as simply given and saying *It is.* And thus the real does not contain more than the possible. A hundred real dollars do not contain a penny more than a hundred possible dollars. For as the possible dollars signify the concept and the real dollars signify the object and the positing of it in itself, it is clear that, in case the former contained more than the latter, my concept would not express the whole object and would not, therefore, be its adequate concept. In my financial position no doubt there exists more by one hundred real dollars than by their concept only (their possibility) because in reality the object is not just contained analytically in my concept but is added to my concept (which is a determination of my state) synthetically; but the conceived hundred dollars are not in the least increased through the existence which is outside my concept.

628   By whatever and by however many predicates I may think a thing (even if I completely determine it), nothing is added to it if I add that the thing exists. If this were not so, it would not be the same that I had thought in the concept to exist, but something more, and I could not say that the exact object of my concept existed. Nay, even if I were to think in a thing every reality except one, that missing reality would not be supplied by my saying that so defective a thing exists, for it would exist with the same defect with which I had thought it; otherwise what exists would be something different from what I thought. If, then, I try to conceive a being as the highest reality (without any defect) the question still remains whether it exists or not. For though in my concept there may be wanting nothing of the possible real content of a thing in general, something still is wanting in its relation to my whole state of thinking, namely that the knowledge of that object should be possible also a

posteriori. And here we perceive the cause of our difficulty. If we were concerned with an object of our sense, I could not mistake the existence of a thing for the mere concept of it; for by the concept the object is thought to be in harmony only with the general conditions of a possible empirical knowl- 629 edge, while by its existence it is thought to be contained in the whole content of experience. Through this connection with the content of the whole of experience, the concept of an object is not in the least increased; our thought has only received through it one more possible perception. If, however, we are thinking existence through the pure category alone, we need not wonder that we cannot find any characteristic to distinguish it from mere possibility.

Whatever our concept of an object may contain, therefore, we must always step outside it in order to attribute existence to it. With objects of the senses, this takes place through their connection with any one of my perceptions according to empirical laws; with objects of pure thought, however , there is no means of knowing their existence, because it would have to be known entirely a priori, while our consciousness of every kind of existence, whether by direct perception or by inferences which connect something with perception, belongs entirely to the unity of experience, and any existence outside that field, though it cannot be declared to be absolutely impossible, is a presupposition that cannot be justified by anything.

The concept of a Supreme Being, in many respects, is a very useful Idea, but being an Idea only it is quite incapable of increasing by itself alone our knowledge with regard to what exists. It cannot even do so much as to inform 630 us any further as to the possibility of any existence beyond what is known in and through experience. The analytical mark of possibility, which consists in the absence of contradiction in mere positings (realities), cannot be denied to it; but the connection of all real properties in one and the same thing is a synthesis the possibility of which we cannot judge a priori because these realities are not given to us as such, and because, even if they were given, no judgment whatever would take place, it being necessary to look for the mark of the possibility of synthetical knowledge in experience only, to which the object of an Idea can never belong. Thus we see that the celebrated Leibniz is far from having achieved what he thought he had, namely to understand a priori the possibility of so sublime an ideal Being.

Time and labor therefore are lost on the famous ontological (Cartesian) proof of the existence of a Supreme Being from mere concepts; and a man might as well imagine that he could become richer in knowledge by mere Ideas, as a merchant in capital, if, in order to improve his position, he were to add a few naughts to his cash account.

Of the Impossibility of a Cosmological Proof of the Existence of God

. . . The cosmological proof, which we have now to examine, retains the 632 connection of absolute necessity with the highest reality, but instead of reasoning, like the ontological argument, from the highest reality to necessity in existence, it reasons only from the already given unconditioned necessity of any being to its unlimited reality. It thus brings everything into the groove of an at least natural (whether rational or pseudorational) syllogism which carries the greatest conviction for both the common and the speculative understanding. The cosmological proof has evidently drawn the first outline of all proofs of natural theology which have been followed at all times and will be followed in the future also, however they may be hidden and disguised. We shall now proceed to exhibit and examine this cosmological proof which Leibniz calls the proof *a contingentia mundi* [argument from the contingency of the world].

It runs as follows: If there exists anything, there must exist also an absolutely necessary being. Now I, at least, exist; therefore there exists an abso-
633   lutely necessary being. The minor premise contains an experience, the major the inference from experience in general to the existence of the necessary being.* This proof therefore beings with experience, and is not entirely a priori or ontological; and, as the object of all possible experience is called the world, this proof is called the cosmological proof. As it takes no account of any peculiar property of the objects of experience by which this world of ours may differ from any other possible world, it is distinguished, also in name, from the physico-theological proof, which argues from observations of the peculiar property of this our world of sense.

The proof then proceeds as follows. The necessary being can be determined in one way only, that is, by one only [of each pair] of all possible opposite predicates; it must therefore be determined completely by its own concept. Now there can be only one concept of a thing which completely determines it a priori, namely the concept of the *ens realissimum* [most real
634   being]. It follows, therefore, that the concept of the *ens realissimum* is the only one by which a necessary being can be thought, and therefore it is concluded that a highest being exists by necessity.

There are so many sophistical propositions in this cosmological argument that it really seems as if speculative reason had spent all its dialectical skill in order to produce the greatest possible transcendental illusion. Before examining it, we shall draw up a list of them by which reason has put forward an old argument disguised as a new one in order to appeal to the agreement of two witnesses, one supplied by pure reason, the other by experience. In reality, however, there is only one witness, namely the first, who changes his dress and voice in order to be taken for a second witness. In order to have a secure foundation, this proof takes its stand on experience, and pretends to be different from the ontological proof which places its whole confidence only in pure concepts a priori. The cosmological proof, however, uses that experi-

*This inference is too well known to require detailed exposition. It rests on the apparently transcendental law of causality in nature, that everything contingent has its cause, which, if in turn contingent, must likewise have a cause, till the series of subordinate causes ends in an absolutely necessary cause, without which the series of causes could not be complete.

ence only in order to take one step, namely the step to the existence of a necessary being in general. What properties that being may have can never be learnt from the empirical argument, and for that purpose reason takes leave of it altogether, and tries to find out from concepts only what properties 635 an absolutely necessary being must possess (i.e., which among all possible things contains in itself the requisite conditions — *requisita* — of absolute necessity). These requisites are believed by reason to exist in the concept of an *ens realissimum* only, and reason concludes at once that this must be the absolutely necessary being. In this conclusion it is simply assumed that the concept of a being of the highest reality is perfectly adequate to the concept of absolute necessity in existence, so that the latter might be inferred from the former. But this is the same proposition as that maintained in the ontological argument and is simply taken over into the cosmological proof, nay, made its foundation, although the intention was to avoid it. For it is clear that absolute necessity is an existence from mere concepts. If, then, I say that the concept of the *ens realissimum* is such a concept, and is the only concept adequate to necessary existence, I am bound to admit that necessary existence may be inferred from this concept. The whole conclusive strength of the so-called cosmological argument rests, therefore, in fact on the ontological proof from mere concepts, while the appeal to experience is quite superfluous, and though it may lead us on to the concept of an absolute necessity it cannot demonstrate it as belonging to any definite object. For as soon as we intend to demonstrate this, we must at once abandon all experience and try to 636 find out which among the pure concepts may contain the conditions of the possibility of an absolutely necessary being. But if in this way we can understand only the possibility of such a being, also its existence is proved. This really means that among all possible things there is one which carries with it absolute necessity, that is, this one being exists with absolute necessity.

Sophisms in arguments are most easily discovered if they are put forward in a correct scholastic form. This we shall now proceed to do.

If the proposition is right that every absolutely necessary being is the most real being (and this is the *nervus probandi* of the cosmological proof), it must, like all affirmative judgments, be capable of conversion at least *per accidens*. This would give us the proposition: some *entia realissima* are absolutely necessary beings. One *ens realissimum*, however, does not differ from any other on any point, and what applies to one applies to all. In this case, therefore, I may apply absolute conversion to the proposition, and say that every *ens realissimum* is a necessary being. As this proposition is determined by its concepts a priori only, it follows that the mere concept of the *ens realissimum* must carry with it its absolute necessity. This, which was maintained by the ontological argument and not recognized by the cosmological, in fact forms the foundation of the conclusion of the cosmological argument, though in a disguised form. . . .

I said before that a whole nest of dialectical assumptions lay hidden in the 637 cosmological proof and that transcendental criticism might easily detect and destroy it. I shall only enumerate them leaving it to the experience of the reader to follow up the fallacies and remove them.

We find, first, the transcendental principle of inferring a cause from the contingent. The principle that everything contingent must have a cause is valid only in the world of sense and has not even a meaning outside it. For the purely intellectual concept of the contingent cannot produce a synthetical proposition like that of causality, and the principle of causality has no meaning and no criterion of use except in the world of sense.

Secondly, the inference of a first cause, based on the impossibility of an infinite ascending series of given causes in the world of senses, is an inference which the principles of the use of reason do not allow us to draw even in experience, while here that principle is extended beyond experience, whither that series can never be prolonged.

Thirdly, the false self-satisfaction of reason with regard to the completion of that series, brought about by removing in the end every kind of condition without which, nevertheless, no concept of necessity is possible; and, when any definite concepts have become impossible, then accepting this as a completion of the concept.

Fourthly, mistaking the logical possibility (absence of internal contradiction) of a concept of an all-united reality for the transcendental possibility which requires a principle for the execution of such a synthesis, the principle being applicable, however, only in the field of possible experience. *Et caetera.*

Of the Impossibility of the Physico-Theological Proof

648   Since neither the concept of things in general nor the experience of any existence in general can satisfy our demands, there still remains one way open, namely, to ask whether any *definite* experience, and consequently experience of things in the world as it is, its constitution and disposition, may supply a proof which could give us the certain conviction of the existence of a Supreme Being. Such a proof we should call physico-theological. If that proof too should prove impossible, then it is clear that no satisfactory proof whatever is possible from purely speculative reason in support of the existence of a being corresponding to our transcendental Idea.

649   After what has been said it will be readily understood that we may expect an easy and complete [negative] answer to this question. For how could there ever be an experience adequate to an Idea? It is the very nature of an Idea that no experience can ever be adequate to it. The transcendental Idea of a necessary and all-sufficient original being is so overwhelming, so high above everything empirical, which is always conditioned, that we can never find in experience enough material to fill such a concept, and can only grope about among things conditioned, looking in vain for the unconditioned, of which no rule of any empirical synthesis can ever give us an example or even show the way towards it.

If the highest being should itself stand in that chain of conditions, it would be a link in the series and would, exactly like the lower links above which it is placed, require further investigation with regard to its own still higher cause. If, on the contrary, we mean to separate it from that chain and not include it as a purely intelligible being in the series of natural causes, what bridge is then open by which reason could reach it, considering that all rules determining the transition from effect to cause, nay, all synthesis and extension of our knowledge in general, refer to nothing but possible experience, and there- 650 fore to the objects of the world of sense only, and are valid nowhere else?

This present world presents us so immeasurable a stage of variety, order, fitness, and beauty, whether we follow it up in the infinity of space or in its unlimited division, that even with the little knowledge which our poor understanding has been able to gather, all language about so many and such inconceivable wonders loses its vigor, all numbers their power of measuring, and all our thoughts their necessary determination, so that our judgment on the whole is lost in a speechless but all the more eloquent astonishment. Everywhere we see a chain of causes and effects, of means and ends, of order in birth and death; and as nothing has entered by itself into the state in which we find it, everything points to another thing as its cause. As that cause requires the same further enquiry, the whole universe would be lost in the abyss of nothing unless we admitted something original and independent which, existing by itself outside the chain of infinite contingencies, should support it and, as the cause of its origin, secure to it at the same time its permanence. Looking at all things in the world, what greatness shall we attribute to that highest cause! We do not know the whole contents of the world, still less can we measure its magnitude by a comparison with all that is 651 possible. But, since when we think of the causation [of the world] we cannot do without an ultimate and highest being, what hinders us from fixing the degree of its perfection beyond everything else that is possible? This we can easily do, though only in the faint outline of an abstract concept, if we think of all possible perfections united in it as in one substance. Such a concept would agree with the demand of our reason which requires parsimony in the number of principles; it would have no contradictions in itself; it would be favorable to the extension of the employment of reason in the midst of experience by guiding it towards order and system; and, lastly, it would never be decidedly opposed to any experience.

This proof will always deserve to be treated with respect. It is the oldest and clearest, and most in conformity with human reason. It gives life to the study of nature, deriving its own existence from it, and thus constantly acquiring a new vigor. It reveals aims and intentions where our own observation by itself would not have discovered them, and enlarges our knowledge of 652 nature by leading us towards that peculiar unity the principle of which exists outside nature. This knowledge rests again on its cause, namely, the transcendental Idea, and thus raises the belief in a Supreme Author to an irresistable conviction. It would therefore be not only extremely sad but utterly vain to attempt to diminish the authority of this proof. Reason, constantly strengthened by the powerful arguments that come to hand by themselves, though they are no doubt empirical only, cannot be discouraged by any doubts of subtle and abstract speculation. Roused from every inquisitive indecision as from a dream, by one glance at the wonders of nature and the majesty of the cosmos reason soars from height to height till it reaches the highest, from the conditioned to conditions, till it reaches the supreme and unconditioned Author of all.

Although we have nothing to say against the reasonableness and utility of this line of argument, but wish on the contrary to commend and encourage it, we cannot approve the claims which this proof advances to apodictic certainty; nor can we ratify its claims to approval on its own merits, requiring no favor and no help from any other quarter. It cannot injure the good cause if the dogmatical language of the overweening sophist is toned down to the

653   moderate and modest statements of a faith which does not require unconditioned submission, yet is sufficient to give rest and comfort. I therefore maintain that the physico-theological proof can never by itself alone establish the existence of a Supreme Being, but must always leave it to the ontological proof, to which it serves only as an introduction, to supply its deficiency; so that, after all, it is the ontological proof which contains *the only possible argument* (supposing always that any speculative proof is possible), and human reason can never do without it.

The principal points of the physico-theological proof are the following. First. There are everywhere in the world clear indications or an intentional arrangement carried out with great wisdom, and forming a whole indescribably various in its contents and infinite in its extent.

Secondly. The fitness of this arrangement is entirely foreign to the things existing in the world, and belongs to them only contingently. That is, the nature of different things could never spontaneously, by the combination of so many means, cooperate towards definite aims, if these means had not been selected and arranged on purpose by a rational disposing principle according to certain fundamental Ideas.

Thirdly. There exists, therefore, a sublime and wise cause (or many) which must be the cause of the world, not only as a blind all-powerful nature, by means of unconscious *fecundity,* but as an intelligence, by *freedom.*

Fourthly. The unity of that cause may be inferred with certainty from the

654   unity of the reciprocal action of the parts of the world, as portions of a skillful edifice, so far as our experience reaches, and beyond it, with plausibility, according to the principles of analogy.

I do not wish, for the sake of mere argument, to criticize natural reason because, from the analogy between certain products of nature and certain works of human art (houses, ships, watches) by which man does violence to nature and forces it to adapt itself to our aims and not to follow its own, it concludes that a similar causality (namely understanding and will) must be at the basis of nature. Nor do I argue with it in deriving the internal possibility of a self-acting nature (which may render all human art and even human reason possible) from another, though superhuman, art, even if it is a kind of reasoning which probably could not stand the severest test of transcendental criticism. Still one must admit that if we have to name such a cause, we cannot do better than to follow the analogy of such products of human design, which are the only ones of which we know fully both cause and effect. There would be no excuse for reason to surrender the causality which it knows and have recourse to obscure and indemonstrable principles of explanation which it does not know.

According to this argument, the fitness and harmony existing in so many works of nature might prove the contingency of the form but not the matter, 655 that is, not the substance in the world, because for the latter purpose it would be necessary to prove in addition that the things of the world would be in themselves incapable of such order and harmony according to general laws, unless even in their substance they were products of a supreme wisdom. For this purpose, very different arguments would be required from those derived from the analogy to human art. The utmost, therefore, that could be established by such a proof would be an *architect of the world*, always very much hampered by the quality of the material with which he has to work, not a *creator* to whose Idea everything is subject. This would by no means suffice for the intended aim of proving an all-sufficient original being. If we wished to prove the contingency of matter itself, we would have to have recourse to a transcendental argument, and this is the very thing which was to be avoided [by the physico-theological argument].

The inference, therefore, really proceeds from the order and design that can be observed everywhere in the world, as an entirely contingent arrangement, to the existence of a cause proportionate to it. The concept of that cause must therefore teach us something quite definite about it, and can therefore be no other concept but that of a being which possesses all might, 656 wisdom, etc., in one word, all perfection of an all-sufficient being. The predicates of a very great, of an astounding, of an immeasurable might and virtue give us no definite concept, and can never tell us really what the thing is in itself. They are only relative representations of the magnitude of an object which the observer of the world compares with himself and his own power of comprehension, and which would be equally grand whether we magnify the object or reduce the observing subject to smaller proportions in reference to it. Where we are concerned with the magnitude of the perfection of a thing in general, there exists no definite concept except that which comprehends all possible perfection, and only the all (*omnitudo*) of reality is thoroughly determined in the concept.

Now I hope that no one would profess to comprehend the relation of that part of the world which he has observed (in its extent as well as in its contents) to omnipotence, the relation of the order of the world to the highest wisdom, and the relation of the unity of the world to the absolute unity of its author, etc. Physico-theology, therefore, can never give a definite concept of the highest cause of the world, and is insufficient, therefore, as a principle of theology, which is itself to form the basis of religion.

657 The step leading to absolute totality is entirely impossible on the empirical road. Nevertheless, that step is taken in the physico-theological proof. How then has this broad abyss been bridged over?

The fact is that, after having reached the stage of admiration of the greatness, the wisdom, the power, etc. of the Author of the world, and seeing no farther advance possible, one suddenly leaves the argument carried on by empirical proofs and lays hold of that contingency which from the very first was inferred from the order and design of the world. The next step from that contingency leads, by means of transcendental concepts only, to the existence of something absolutely necessary, and another step from the absolute necessity of the first cause to its completely determined or determining concept, namely, that of an all-embracing reality. Thus we see that the physico-theological proof, baffled in its own undertaking, takes sudden refuge in the cosmological proof, and as this is only the ontological proof in disguise, it really carries out its original intention by means of pure reason only, though it so strongly disclaimed in the beginning all connection with it, and professed to base everything on clear proofs from experience. . . .

658 Thus we have seen that the physico-theological proof rests on the cosmological, and the cosmological on the ontological proof of the existence of one original being as the Supreme Being; and, as besides these three there is no other path open to speculative reason, the ontological proof, based exclusively on pure concepts of reason, is the only possible one, always supposing, of course, that any proof of a proposition so far transcending the empirical use of the understanding is possible at all.

V

Prolegomena to Any Future Metaphysics Which Will Be Able to Come Forth as a Science

Editor's Introduction

First a word about the title of this book. *Prolegomena* is a Greek word for prefatory remarks or an introduction. *Science* (in German: *Wissenschaft*) does not have the restricted meaning which this word ordinarily conveys in English, where "science" without some qualifying adjective generally means natural science. In German, however, the word ordinarily (and not just in Kant's writings) means any systematic body of knowledge possessing a recognized technical vocabulary and methodology, usually associated with the existence of a guild of scholars devoted to advancing and teaching this knowledge.

Thus, when Kant thinks of metaphysics as becoming a science, two things are involved: what his predecessors like Descartes and Leibniz called metaphysics was not a science, and the metaphysics to which this book is introductory will be a science. The two kinds of metaphysics differ not only in scientific status, but also in subject matter. The earlier nonscientific metaphysics was speculative (it went beyond experience and so could not be tested) and dogmatic (it proceeded without a prior examination of the capacity of human reason to achieve speculative knowledge). The scientific metaphysics for which Kant is preparing the way will consist of a system of fundamental principles that are synthetic and are known a priori. As we have learned from the *Critique of Pure Reason*, such propositions are valid only as organizing principles for sensory experience and do not reach supersensible realities, things in themselves and noumena. The new science, therefore, will be metaphysics, but a *metaphysics of experience:* a science of the necessary conditions and a priori features of knowledge of the sensible world, but not extending beyond or above it.

Soon after publishing the first edition of the *Critique of Pure Reason*, Kant began work on a small book which he referred to as a book of selections, a textbook, a book of readings, finally as *prolegomena*. In the first sentence of the book Kant says that it is for the use of future teachers of the new philosophy, not for those who are only learners. Many generations of both teachers and students have in fact used this book as a guide in understanding and explaining the longer and more difficult *Critique*. It is well suited to this role, the organization of the material being congruent in both works:

Prolegomena	*Critique of Pure Reason*
Preamble, §§1–5	Introduction. (In second edition, Introduction is in part identical with Preamble.)
How is Pure Mathematics Possible? §§6–13	Transcendental Aesthetic
How is Pure Science of Nature Possible?	
§§14–22	Analytic of Concepts
§§23–26, 32–35	Analytic of Principles
How is Metaphysics in General Possible? §§40–56	Transcendental Dialetic

The Conclusion of the *Prolegomena* and the section entitled "How is Metaphysics Possible as a Science?" do not correspond directly to any single parts of the *Critique*, but the material in both is closely related to that of the Dialectic.

It should be noticed that not all parts of the *Prolegomena* fit into our table of parallels and they seem to interrupt the continuity of Kant's explication of the *Critique*. The reason for these sections is probably to be found in an anonymous review of the *Critique* published in 1782 just when Kant was about to publish the *Prolegomena*. From the review he learned that he had not made himself clear to readers; since the review misinterpreted some things and complained of the difficulty of the book, he tried to make difficult matters easier to understand. More significantly, the review accused Kant of being a Berkeleian idealist, an interpretation Kant sharply rejected. Just before publication of the book comprising the passages listed in the table above, Kant wrote responses to the review, interlarded them in the almost finished book, and published the *Prolegomena* as we now have it before us. Though the book would be neater without them, we have included these replies to the review with the exception of an Appendix with the spiteful title: "A Specimen of a Judgment of the *Critique* made Prior to its Examination."

Since it is so much like the *Critique* in content and organization, a detailed section-by-section Introduction with the scope of the Editor's Introduction to the *Critique* is not called for. But there are four distinct and important differences between the two books, and these must be explained in some detail.

(1) *The analytic and the synthetic methods.* These are not to be confused with analytic and synthetic judgments. In the Prize Essay Kant had argued that the proper method of mathematics was the synthetical, while philosophy can employ only the analytical method. He must have changed his mind about this, because he now says that the *Critique* was written

from the standpoint of the synthetical method. That is, it begins with the fundamental conditions of knowledge (forms of intuition, categories, irreducible faculties of the mind, etc.) and derives from them the existence, truth, and validity of a priori synthetic principles such as the causal law. The *Prolegomena,* on the other hand, presupposes what the *Critique* was meant to have demonstrated (viz., the possibility of pure mathematics and of the pure science of nature), and makes a regress upon their necessary conditions in the intuitions, concepts, and cognitive processes of the knowing mind.

On the whole we can perhaps agree that this difference exists between the first edition of the *Critique* and the *Prolegomena.* It breaks down, however, when applied to the second edition, because Kant in the Introduction to that edition took over, bodily, the questions raised in the *Prolegomena* (how pure mathematics and science of nature are possible) as the starting point for the method of the rest of the book. Many critics of Kant have concluded from this that the argument of the *Critique* is a vicious circle: by mixing the analytical and the synthetical method and their different starting points, he presupposes what he should have demonstrated. An extensive secondary literature has grown up around the question of the propriety of Kant's writing the *Critique of Pure Reason* from an equivocal starting point.

Actually the distinction between the analytic and the synthetic method is not as sharp as definitions make it appear. Probably Kant is right, in the Prize Essay, in describing the working of the philosopher's mind along the lines of the analytic method, regardless of whether he expounds his teachings in the analytic or the synthetic mode. The distinction between the two methods is perhaps more a matter of style of exposition than a matter of fundamental logical or methodological importance.

Certainly, however, the analytical mode of exposition as practiced in the *Prolegomena* makes for far greater clarity and easier comprehensibility.

(2) *A greater emphasis upon realism.* What most disturbed Kant in the review was the accusation that he was a follower of Berkeley's idealism. Berkeley was not mentioned in the first edition of the *Critique,* but this did not deter his reviewers from seeing Berkeley's thought and influence in such sections as the one entitled, "Transcendental Idealism and Empirical Realism" (this book, above, pp. 125–127). They were sharply rebuked by Kant for this, and Kant both here and in the second edition of the *Critique* tried to distance himself from "the good Berkeley," as he contemptuously refers to the Bishop. Again, a vast secondary literature, much of it singularly ill-tempered, has been published about the true relations of Kant's philosophy to that of Berkeley.

The *Prolegomena* makes a strong and clear case against interpreting Kant as a Berkeleian, by emphasising one important and obvious difference between them. Kant thinks the existence of an unknowable thing in itself is incompatible with Berkeley's denial of material substance as an unknown cause or substratum of ideas. Thus the thing in itself, which plays a relatively minor role in the first edition (and in much of the second edition) of the *Critique* receives repeated and explicit treatment in the *Prolegomena.*

(3) *The neglect of the transcendental unity of apperception in the Prolegomena.* One of the principal topics in the Transcendental Deduction of the Categories in the *Critique* concerns what Kant calls the transcendental unity of apperception, which refers to the necessary fact that all my representations are synthesized in *one* consciousness, as a condition of their being synthesized together into concepts and judgments of objects. Its principle is: "The 'I think' must be able to accompany all my representations" (B 16). Since "I think" means "I judge," the transcendental unity means that all my representations can be connected by judgments into one systematic whole, and the unity of self-consciousness is the transcendental ground of the unity of knowledge of experience.

Kant calls this principle the highest point of transcendental philosophy —but it is hardly mentioned in the *Prolegomena!* Since the selections from the *Critique* in this present volume do not include full discussions of the transcendental unity, the reader of this text may not notice the absence or feel the lack of this principle in the *Prolegomena.* Nevertheless the reader may wish or need to know *why* it is absent.

There seem to be two reasons for it. (a) Some of the most difficult writing, in both editions of the *Critique,* is about the transcendental unity of apperception; it is a subject which Kant *could* not simplify, however much he may have tried. He wanted the *Prolegomena* to be as simple and as "popular" as possible; therefore he tried to make a detour around this most difficult obstacle. (b) He had a replacement for it which he called *consciousness in general.* He believed it could do the work of the transcendental unity of apperception if he had a different and simpler Transcendental Deduction of the Categories.

(4) *A new deduction of the categories.* Kant was dissatisfied with the Transcendental Deduction of the Categories in the first edition of the *Critique,* and in the second edition he replaced it with an almost wholly new version though he said, perhaps not quite accurately, that it was substantially the same in substance and differed only in style. Between the first and second editions he wrote the *Prolegomena,* Sections 18–22 of which give a Deduction which is quite different from those of both the first and the second editions of the *Critique.*

The new Deduction is based on applying the analytical method to two kinds of judgments. There are *judgments of perception,* which refer only to one's own subjective states of mind and mental events, and *judgments of experience,* which, if correct, can be confirmed by other people. Judgments of experience, Kant says, are not limited to describing what is in *my consciousness* (e.g., my pleasure in a fragrance) but hold for *consciousness in general* or what all qualified observers can agree upon (e.g., that it is the fragrance of a rose). Consciousness in general is an ideal consciousness, what my and your consciousnesses have in common when abstraction is made from your and my peculiarities and idiosyncrasies. Kant is the inventor of the doctrine of the mutual entailment of *objectivity* and *intersubjectivity*. The difference between a judgment of perception valid only for me and a judgment of experience valid for me and any competent observer is the difference between a judgment which refers only to my state of mind or my mental events and a judgment that refers to an object knowable both to me and to others; it is the distinction between a judgment based on and referrable to my consciousness only and a judgment based on and referrable to consciousness in general (*Bewusstsein Überhaupt*).

Kant explains the difference between the scope and validity of the two kinds of judgment by the absence of categorial concepts in judgments of perception, and their presence in judgments of experience. You and I cannot have the same sensations, but we can follow the same rules (categories) in making judgments of what we perceive, and when we follow the same rules we produce judgments upon which, at least in principle, we can agree. We explain our agreement by saying that our judgments refer not to me or to you, but to objects of experience accessible to both of us, or to consciousness in general.

The argument is exceedingly simple: the categories give the rules for the judgment of consciousness in general; consciousness in general is consciousness of objects; therefore categories apply to objects of experience, or objects of experience conform to the conceptual conditions of our judgment upon them.

This deduction of the categories has the advantage of simplicity and lucidity. Unfortunately, however, it is vulnerable to a very simple but effective objection: even judgments of perception make use of (though they do not mention) categorial concepts. Perhaps Kant himself saw this weakness because, for some reason, he abandoned this argument when he rewrote the Transcendental Deduction of the Categories in the second edition of the *Critique of Pure Reason*. Some philosophers have attempted to reformulate the *Prolegomena* Deduction so as to avoid the error of supposing that there are category-free judgments. There is a considerable secondary literature on this topic, and in recent years debate about it has been very lively.

For additional further reading, see the books listed above p. 94.

This translation is the second revision I have made of the original translation by Paul Carus (1902). The first revision was published by The Liberal Arts Press in 1951. I have here made still further revisions for the present edition. The translation printed here is complete except for Sections 3, 39, 54, and 55, the Appendix, and part of Section 13.

Prolegomena to Any Future Metaphysics Which Will Be Able to Come forth as a Science

INTRODUCTION

These *Prolegomena* are for the use not of mere learners but of future teachers, and even the latter should not expect that they will be serviceable for the systematic exposition of a ready-made science, but merely for the discovery of the science itself.

There are scholars to whom the history of philosophy both ancient and modern is philosophy itself; for them, the present *Prolegomena* are not written. They must wait till those who endeavor to draw from the fountain of reason itself have completed their work; it will then be the turn of these scholars to inform the world of what has been done. Unfortunately, nothing can be said which, in their opinion, has not been said before, and truly the same prophecy applies to all future time; for since the human reason has for many centuries speculated about innumerable subjects in various ways, it is hardly to be expected that we should not be able to discover analogies for every new idea among the old sayings of past ages.

My purpose is to persuade all those who think metaphysics worth studying that it is absolutely necessary to pause a moment and, regarding all that has been done as though undone, to propose first the preliminary question: Whether such a thing as metaphysics be even possible at all?

If it be a science, how is it that it cannot, like other sciences, obtain universal and lasting recognition? If not, how can it maintain its pretensions and keep the human understanding in suspense with hopes never ceasing, yet never fulfilled? Whether then we demonstrate our knowledge or our ignorance in this field, we must come once and for all to a definite conclusion concerning the nature of this so-called science, which cannot possibly remain on its present footing. It seems almost ridiculous, that while every other science is continually advancing, in this, which pretends to be wisdom incarnate, whose oracle everyone consults, we should constantly move round the same spot without gaining a single step. And so its votaries having melted away, we do not find people confident of their ability to shine in other sciences risking their reputation here, where everybody, however ignorant on other matters, presumes to deliver a final verdict, because in this domain there is actually as yet no standard weight and measure to distinguish sound knowledge from shallow talk.

After all, it is nothing extraordinary in the elaboration of a science that, when people begin to wonder how far it has advanced, the question should at last occur whether and how such a science is possible at all. Human reason so delights in building that it has several times built up a tower and then razed it to see how the foundation was laid. It is never too late to become reasonable and wise; but if the knowledge comes late, there is always more difficulty in starting a reform.

The question whether a science is possible presupposes a doubt as to its actuality. But such a doubt offends everyone whose whole fortune consists in this supposed jewel; hence he who raises the doubt must expect opposition from all sides. Some, in proud consciousness of possessions which are ancient and therefore considered legitimate, will take their metaphysical compendia in their hands and look down on him with contempt. Others, who never see anything except it be identical with what they have seen elsewhere before, will not understand him, and everything will remain for a time as if nothing had happened to excite the concern or raise the hope for an impending change.

Nevertheless, I venture to predict that the independent reader of these prolegomena will not only doubt his previous science, but ultimately will be 257 fully persuaded that it cannot exist unless the demands here stated on which its possibility depends be satisfied; and, as this has never happened, that there is, as yet, no such thing as metaphysics. But as it can never cease to be in demand*— since the interests of common sense are so intimately interwoven with it — he must confess that a radical reform, or rather a new birth of the science after a new plan, is unavoidable however men may struggle against it for a while.

Since the *Essays* of Locke and Leibniz, or rather since the origin of metaphysics so far as we know its history, nothing has ever happened which could have been more decisive to its fate than the attack made upon it by David Hume. He threw no light on this species of knowledge, but he certainly struck a spark by which light might have been kindled had it caught some inflammable substance, and had its smouldering fire been carefully nursed and developed.

Hume started from a single but important concept in metaphysics, namely that of the connection of cause and effect (including its derivatives force and action, and so on). He challenged reason, which pretends to have generated this concept in her own womb, to answer by what right she thinks anything could be so constituted that if that thing be posited, something else must necessarily be posited (for this is the meaning of the concept of cause). He demonstrated irrefutably that it was perfectly impossible for reason to think a priori and by means of concepts such a combination, for it implies necessity,

---

* *Rusticus exspectat, dum defluat amnis, at ille Labitur et labetur in omne volubilis aevum.*
—Horace.
(The peasant waits on the shore for the river to flow by, but it flows on and will roll on forever.)

and we cannot at all see why, in consequence of the existence of one thing, another must necessarily exist, or how the concept of such a combination can arise a priori. From this he inferred that reason was altogether deluded with reference to this concept, which she erroneously considered as her own child, whereas in reality it was nothing but a bastard of imagination impregnated by experience, which subsumed certain representations under the law of association and mistook a subjective necessity (custom) for an objective necessity arising from insight. Hence he inferred that reason had no power to think such combinations, even in general, because her concepts would then be purely fictitious and all her pretended a priori cognitions nothing but common experience marked with a false stamp. In plain language, this means that there is not and cannot be any such thing as metaphysics at all.*

However hasty and mistaken Hume's inference may appear, it was at least founded upon investigation, and this investigation deserved the concentrated attention of the brighter spirits of his day as well as determined efforts on their part to discover, if possible, a happier solution to the problem in the sense proposed by him, all of which would have speedily resulted in a complete reform of the science.

But Hume suffered the usual misfortune of metaphysicians, of not being understood. It is positively painful to see how utterly his opponents, Reid, Oswald, Beattie, and lastly even Priestley, missed the point of the problem; for while they were ever taking for granted that which he doubted, and demonstrating with zeal and often with impudence that which he never thought of doubting, they so misconstrued his valuable suggestion that everything remained in its old state, as if nothing had happened. The question was not whether the concept of cause was right, useful, and even indispensable for our knowledge of nature, for this Hume had never doubted; but whether
259 that concept could be thought by reason a priori, and consequently whether it possessed an inner truth, independent of experience, implying a perhaps more extended use not restricted exclusively to objects of experience. This was Hume's problem. It was solely a question concerning the origin, not concerning the indispensable need of using the concept. Were the former decided, the conditions of the use and the sphere of its valid application would have been determined as a matter of course.

But to satisfy the conditions of the problem, the opponents of the great thinker should have penetrated very deeply into the nature of reason, so far as

---

*Nevertheless Hume called this destructive science metaphysics and attached to it great value. "Metaphysics and morals," he declares, "are the most considerable branches of science. Mathematics and natural philosophy are not half so valuable" ["Of the Rise and Progress of the Arts and Sciences," *Essays Moral, Political, and Literary*, XIV (edited by Green and Grose, I, 187)]. But the acute man merely regarded the negative use arising from the moderation of extravagant claims of speculative reason, and the complete settlement of the many endless and troublesome controversies that mislead mankind. He overlooked the positive injury which results if reason be deprived of its most important prospects, which can alone supply to the will the highest aim for all its endeavors.

it is concerned with pure thinking — a task which did not suit them. They found a more convenient method of being defiant without insight, namely, the appeal to *common sense*. It is indeed a great gift of heaven to possess a right or (as they now call it) plain common sense. But this common sense must be shown in action by well-considered and reasonable thoughts and words, not by appealing to it as an oracle when no rational justification for one's position can be advanced. To appeal to common sense when insight and science fail, and no sooner — this is one of the subtle discoveries of modern times, by means of which the most superficial ranter can safely enter the lists with the most thorough thinker and hold his own. But as long as a particle of insight remains, no one would think of having recourse to such a subterfuge. Seen clearly, it is but an appeal to the opinion of the multitude, at whose applause the philosopher blushes, while the popular charlatan glories and boasts in it. I should think that Hume might fairly have laid as much claim to common sense as Beattie and, in addition, to a critical reason (such as the latter did not possess) which keeps common sense in check and prevents it from speculating, or, if speculations are under discussion, restrains the desire to decide because it cannot satisfy itself concerning its own premises. By this means alone can common sense remain sound. Chisels and hammers may suffice to work a piece of wood, but for etching we require an etcher's needle. Thus common sense and speculative understanding are each serviceable, but each 260 in its own way; the former in judgments which apply immediately to experience; the latter when we judge universally from concepts alone, as in metaphysics, where that which calls itself (in spite of the inappropriateness of the name) sound common sense has no right to judge at all.

I openly confess that a reminder by David Hume was the very thing which many years ago first interrupted my dogmatic slumber and gave my investigations in the field of speculative philosophy quite a new direction. I was far from following him in the conclusions at which he arrived by regarding only a part of his problem, not the whole, without reference to which reason can give us no insight. But if we start from a well-founded though undeveloped thought which another has bequeathed to us, we may well hope by continued reflection to advance farther than the acute man to whom we owe the first spark of light.

I therefore first tried whether Hume's objection could be put into a general form, and soon found that the concept of the connection of cause and effect was by no means the only concept by which the understanding thinks the connection of things a priori, but rather that metaphysics consists altogether of such concepts. I sought to ascertain their number, and when I had satisfactorily succeeded in this I proceeded to the deduction of these concepts, which I was now certain were not derived from experience, as Hume had attempted to derive them, but sprang from the pure understanding. This deduction (which seemed impossible to my acute predecessor, and which had never even occurred to anyone else, though no one had hesitated to use the con-

cepts without investigating the basis of their objective validity) was the most difficult task which ever could have been undertaken in the service of metaphysics; and the worst was that metaphysics, such as it is, could not assist me in the least, because this deduction alone can render metaphysics possible. But as soon as I had succeeded in solving Hume's problem, not merely in a particular case, but with respect to the whole faculty of pure reason, I could
261   proceed safely, though slowly, to determine the whole sphere of pure reason completely and from universal principles, in its boundaries as well as in its contents. This was required for metaphysics in order to construct its system according to a safe plan.

But I fear that the execution of Hume's problem in its widest extent (namely, my *Critique of Pure Reason*) will fare as the problem itself fared when first proposed. It will be misjudged because it is misunderstood, and misunderstood because men choose to skim through the book and not to think through it — a disagreeable task because the work is dry, obscure, opposed to all ordinary notions, and, moreover, long-winded. I confess, however, that I did not expect to hear from philosophers complaints about want of popularity, entertainment, and facility when the existence of highly prized and indispensable knowledge is at stake, which cannot be established except by the strictest rules of scholastic precision. Popular appeal may follow, but is inadmissable at the beginning. Yet as regards a certain obscurity, arising partly from the intricacy of the plan, owing to which the principal points of the investigation are easily lost sight of, the complaint is just, and I intend to remove it by the present *Prolegomena*.

The *Critique*, which discusses the pure faculty of reason in its whole compass and bounds, will remain the foundation to which the *Prolegomena*, as a preliminary exercise, refers; for critique as a science must first be established as complete and perfect before we can think of letting metaphysics appear on the scene or even have the most distant hope of attaining it.

We have long been accustomed to seeing antiquated knowledge produced as new by taking it out of its former context and fitting it into a systematic garment of any fancy pattern with new titles. Most readers will set out by expecting nothing else from the *Critique*, but these *Prolegomena* may per-
262   suade them that it is a perfectly new science, of which no one has ever even thought, the very idea of which was unknown, and for which nothing hitherto accomplished can be of the smallest use, except it be the suggestion of Hume's doubts. Yet even he suspected nothing of such a formal science, but ran his ship ashore for safety's sake, landing on skepticism, there to let it lie and rot; whereas my object is to give it a pilot who, by means of safe principles of navigation drawn from a knowledge of the globe, and provided with a complete chart and compass, may steer the ship whither he listeth.

If in a new science which is wholly isolated and unique in its kind we started with the prejudice that we could judge of things by means of supposed knowledge previously acquired — though this is precisely what has first to be called into question — we should fancy we saw everywhere only what we had already come to know because the expressions used in both have a similar sound. But everything would appear utterly metamorphosed, senseless, and unintelligible because we should have as foundation our own thoughts, made by long habit into second nature, instead of the author's thoughts. But the long-windedness of the work (so far as it depends upon the subject and not the execution), its consequent unavoidable dryness and scholastic precision, are qualities which can only benefit the science though they may discredit the book.

Few writers are gifted with the subtlety and, at the same time, with the grace of David Hume, or with the depth, as well as the elegance, of Moses Mendelssohn. Yet I flatter myself I might have made my own exposition popular, had my object been merely to sketch out a plan and leave its completion to others, instead of having my heart in the welfare of the science to which I had so long devoted myself; in truth, it required no little constancy and even self-denial to defer the sweets of immediate [popular] success to the prospect of a slower but more lasting reputation.

Making plans is often the occupation of an opulent and boastful mind, 263 which thus obtains the reputation of creative genius by demanding what it cannot itself supply, by censuring what it cannot improve, and by proposing what it knows not where to find. And yet something more should belong to a sound plan of a general critique of pure reason than mere conjectures if the plan is to be other than the usual declamation of pious aspirations. But pure reason is a sphere so separate and self-contained that we cannot touch a part without affecting all the rest. We can do nothing without first determining the position of each part and its relation to the rest; for, as our judgment within this sphere cannot be corrected by anything outside it, the validity and use of every part depends upon the relation in which it stands to all the rest within the domain of reason. As in the structure of an organized body, the purpose of each member can be derived only from the full conception of the whole. It may, then, be said of such a critique, that it is never trustworthy except it be perfectly complete down to the most minute elements of pure reason. In the sphere of this faculty you can determine and define either everything or nothing.

But although a mere sketch preceding the *Critique of Pure Reason* would be unintelligible, unreliable, and useless, it is all the more useful as a sequel. It enables us to grasp the whole, to examine in detail the chief points of importance in the science, and to improve in many respects our exposition as compared with the first execution of the work.

With that work complete, I offer here a sketch based on an *analytical* method, while the *Critique* itself had to be executed in the *synthetical* style, in order that the science may present all its articulations as the structure of a very distinctive cognitive faculty in their natural combination. But should any reader find this sketch, which I publish as the *Prolegomena to Any Future*

Metaphysics, still obscure, let him consider that not everyone is bound to study metaphysics; that many minds will succeed very well in the basic and even in deep sciences more closely allied to the empirical (*Anschauung*), while they cannot succeed in investigations dealing exclusively with abstract concepts.

264   In such cases men should apply their talents to other subjects. But he who undertakes to judge or, still more, to construct a system of metaphysics must satisfy the demands made here, either by adopting my solution or by thoroughly refuting it and substituting another. To evade it is impossible.

In conclusion, let it be remembered that this much-abused obscurity (frequently serving as a mere pretext under which people hide their own indolence or dullness) has its uses, since all who in other sciences observe a judicious silence speak authoritatively in metaphysics and make bold pronouncements because their ignorance here does not stand out against others' knowledge. Still, their ignorance does stand out against sound critical principles, which we may therefore commend in the words of Vergil: *Ignavum, fucos, pecus a praesepibus arcent* (They defend the hives against the slothful drones).

PREAMBLE ON THE DISTINCTIVE CHARACTERISTICS OF ALL METAPHYSICAL KNOWLEDGE

Section 1. Of the Sources of Metaphysics

265   If it becomes desirable to expound any knowledge as a science, it will be necessary first to determine accurately those features which no other science has in common with it, constituting its distinctive character. Otherwise the boundaries of all the sciences become confused, and none of them can be treated thoroughly according to its nature.

The peculiar characteristic of a science may consist in a simple difference of object, or in the sources of knowledge, or in the kind of knowledge, or perhaps in all three conjointly. On these, therefore, depends the idea of a possible science and its territory.

First, as concerns the sources of metaphysical knowledge, its very concept implies that they cannot be empirical. Its principles (including not only its fundamental principles but also its basic concepts) must never be derived from experience. It must not be physical but metaphysical knowledge, namely, knowledge lying beyond experience. It can have therefore for its basis neither external experience, which is the source of physics proper, nor

266   internal, which is the basis of empirical psychology. It is therefore a priori knowledge, coming from pure understanding and pure reason.

But so far metaphysics would not be distinguishable from pure mathematics; it must therefore be called pure *philosophical* knowledge; and for the meaning of this term I refer the reader to the *Critique of Pure Reason**, where

---

* *Critique of Pure Reason* A 712 = B 741. [See also *Prize Essay,* this volume, pp. 40–41.—Ed.]

the distinction between these two employments of reason is sufficiently explained. So far concerning the sources of metaphysical knowledge.

Section 2. Concerning the Kind of Knowledge Which Can Alone be Called Metaphysical
a. On the Distinction between Analytical and Synthetical Judgments in General

The peculiarity of its sources demands that metaphysical knowledge must consist of nothing but a priori judgments. But whatever be their origin or logical form, there is a distinction in judgments as to their content, by which they are either merely *explicative*, adding nothing to the content of knowledge, or *ampliative*, augmenting the given knowledge. The former may be called *analytical*, the latter *synthetical*, judgments.

Analytical judgments express nothing in the predicate but what has already been actually thought in the concept of the subject, though not so clearly or with the same full consciousness. When I say, "All bodies are extended," I have not in the least amplified my concept of body but have only analyzed it, for extension was actually thought to belong to that concept before the judgment was made, though it was not expressed. This judgment is therefore analytical. On the contrary, the judgment, "Some bodies have weight," contains in its predicate something not actually thought in the universal concept of body; it amplifies my knowledge by adding something to 267 my concept, and must therefore be called synthetical.

b. The Common Principle of All Analytical Judgments is the Law of Contradiction

All analytical judgments depend wholly on the law of contradiction, and are in their nature a priori cognitions whether the concepts that supply them with matter be empirical or not. For the predicate of an affirmative analytical judgment is already contained in the concept of the subject, of which it cannot be denied without contradiction. In the same way its opposite is necessarily denied of the subject in an analytical negative judgment, by the same law of contradiction. Such is the nature of the judgments: "Every body is extended," and "No body is unextended."

For this reason all analytical judgments are a priori even when the concepts are empirical, as, for example, "Gold is a yellow metal"; for to know this I require no experience beyond my concept of gold as a yellow metal. It constitutes, in fact, the very concept, and I need only analyze it without looking beyond it.

c. Synthetical Judgments Require a Different Principle from the Law of Contradiction

There are synthetical a posteriori judgments of empirical origin; but there are also others which are certain a priori, and which spring from pure understanding and reason. Yet they both agree in this, that they cannot possibly spring from the principle of analysis, namely, the law of contradiction, alone. They require a quite different principle from which they may be deduced, subject of course always to the law of contradiction, which must never be violated even though everything cannot be deduced from it. I shall first classify synthetical judgments.

268
1. *Judgments of Experience are always synthetical.* For it would be absurd to base an analytical judgment on experience, as our concept suffices for the purpose without requiring any testimony of experience. That a body is extended is a judgment established a priori, and not an empirical judgment. For before appealing to experience, we have already all the conditions of the judgment in the concept, from which we have but to elicit the predicate according to the law of contradiction, and thereby to become conscious of the necessity of the judgment, which experience could not in the least teach us.

2. *Mathematical judgments are all synthetical.* This fact seems hitherto to have altogether escaped the observation of those who have analyzed human reason; it seems even directly opposed to all their conjectures, though it is incontestably certain and most important in its consequences. For as it was found that the conclusions of mathematicians all proceed according to the law of contradiction (as is demanded by apodictic certainty), men persuaded themselves that the fundamental principles were known by the same law. This was a great mistake, for a synthetical proposition can indeed be established by the law of contradiction, but only by presupposing another synthetical proposition from which it follows, but never by itself alone.

First of all we must observe that all strictly mathematical judgments are a priori and not empirical, because they carry with them necessity, which cannot be obtained from experience. But if this be not conceded to me, very good; I shall confine my assertion to *pure* mathematics, the very notion of which implies that it contains pure a priori and not empirical knowledge.

It might at first be thought that the proposition $7 + 5 = 12$ is a mere analytical judgment, following from the concept of the sum of seven and five according to the law of contradiction. But on closer examination it appears that the concept of the sum of $7 + 5$ contains merely their union in a single number, without its being at all thought what the particular number is which unites them. The concept of twelve is by no means thought by merely thinking of the combination of seven and five; analyze my concept of such a

269
sum as we may I shall not discover twelve in it. We must go beyond these concepts, by calling to our aid some intuition which corresponds to one of the concepts — that is, either our five fingers or five points (as Segner has it in his *Arithmetic*) — and we must add successively the units of the five given in the intuition to the concept of seven. Hence our concept is really amplified by the proposition $7 + 5 = 12$, and we add to the first concept a second concept not thought in it. Arithmetical propositions are therefore synthetical. This is seen the more plainly when we take larger numbers, for in such cases it is clear

that, however closely we analyze our concepts without calling intuition to our aid, we can never find the sum by such mere dissection.

Just as little is any principle of geometry analytical. That a straight line is the shortest path between two points is a synthetical proposition. The concept "shortest" is therefore altogether additional and cannot be obtained by analysis of the concept "straight line." Here, too, intuition must come to aid us. It alone makes the synthesis possible.[1] What usually makes us believe that the predicate of such apodictic judgments is already contained in our concept, and that the judgment is therefore analytical, is the ambiguity of the expression. We are required to join in thought a certain predicate to a given concept, and this necessity indeed belongs to the concepts. But the question is not what we are required to join in thought *to* a given concept but what we actually think together with and *in* it, though obscurely; and so it appears indeed that the predicate belongs to this concept necessarily yet not directly, but indirectly by means of an intuition which must be present.

Some other principles assumed by geometers are indeed actually analytical, and depend on the law of contradiction, but as analytical propositions they serve only as a method of concatenation and not as principles — for example, $a = a$, the whole is equal to itself, or $a + b > a$, the whole is greater than its part. And yet even these, though they are recognized as valid from mere concepts, are admitted in mathematics only because they can be represented in some intuition.

The essential and distinguishing feature of pure mathematics among all 272 other a priori knowledge is that it cannot at all proceed from concepts but only by means of the construction of concepts.* As therefore in its propositions it must proceed beyond the concept to that which its corresponding intuition contains, these propositions neither can, nor ought to, arise analytically by dissection of the concept, but are all synthetical.

I cannot refrain from pointing out the disadvantage resulting to philosophy from the neglect of this easy and apparently insignificant observation. Hume being prompted to cast his eye over the whole field of a priori cognitions in which human understanding claims such mighty possessions (a calling he felt worthy of a philosopher) heedlessly severed from it a whole, and indeed its most valuable, province, namely pure mathematics; for he imagined that its nature or, so to speak, the state constitution of this empire depended on totally different principles, namely on the law of contradiction alone; and although he did not divide judgments in this manner formally and universally as I have done, what he said was equivalent to this: that mathematics contains

---

[1] The text of the remainder of this section is arranged differently from that of the original and of the Akademie editions. This is indicated by discontinuities in the side pagination. On internal grounds it has been shown (by Vaihinger) that Kant's proof sheets must have become disarranged before final printing.

* *Critique of Pure Reason* A713 = B741. [See also *Prize Essay,* this volume, p. 31].

only analytical, but metaphysics synthetical a priori propositions. In this, however, he was greatly mistaken, and the mistake had a decidedly injurious effect upon his whole conception. But for this, he would have extended his question concerning the origin of our synthetical judgments far beyond the metaphysical concept of causality and included in it the possibility of mathematics a priori also, for this latter he would have had to assume to be equally

273 synthetical. And then he could not have based his metaphysical propositions on mere experience without subjecting the axioms of pure mathematics equally to experience, a thing he was far too acute to do. The good company into which metaphysics would thus have been brought would have saved it from the danger of contemptuous ill-treatment, for the thrust intended for it would necessarily have reached mathematics, and this was not and could not have been Hume's intention. Thus that acute man would have been led into considerations which must needs be similar to those which now occupy us, but which would have gained inestimably by his inimitably elegant style.

3. *Metaphysical Judgments,* properly so called, are all synthetical. We must distinguish judgments pertaining to metaphysics from metaphysical judgments properly so called. Many of the former are analytical, but they afford only the means for metaphysical judgments which are the whole end of the science and which are always synthetical. For if there are concepts pertaining to metaphysics, the judgments springing from simple analysis of them (as, for example, substance is that which exists only as subject, etc.) also pertain to metaphysics, and by means of several such analytical judgments we seek to approach the definition of the concepts. But as the analysis of a pure concept of the understanding (the kind of concept pertaining to metaphysics) does not proceed in any different manner from the dissection of any other, even any empirical, concepts not belonging to metaphysics (such as, air is an elastic fluid, the elasticity of which is not destroyed by any degree of cold), it follows that the concept, but not the analytical judgment, is properly metaphysical. This science has something distinctive and peculiar to it in the production of its a priori cognitions, which must be distinguished from the features it has in common with other rational knowledge. Thus the judgment that all the substance in things is permanent is a synthetical and properly metaphysical judgment.

If the a priori concepts which constitute the materials and tools of metaphysics have first been collected according to fixed principles, then their analysis will be of great value. It might be taught as a particular part (as a

274 *philosophia definitiva*), containing nothing but analytical judgments pertaining to metaphysics, and could be treated separately from the synthetical, which constitutes metaphysics proper. For indeed these analyses are not of much value except in metaphysics, that is, as regards the synthetical judgments which are to be generated by these previously analyzed concepts.

The conclusion drawn in this section then is that metaphysics is properly concerned with synthetical propositions a priori, and these alone constitute its purpose. For this, it indeed requires various dissections of its concepts and consequently analytical judgments, but in this respect the procedure in metaphysics is not different from that in any other kind of knowledge in which we merely seek to render our concepts distinct by analysis. But the generation of a priori knowledge by both intuitions and concepts, in fine, the generation of synthetical propositions a priori, especially in philosophical knowledge, constitutes the essential subject matter of metaphysics.[2]

Section 4. The General Question of the Prolegomena: Is Metaphysics Possible at All?

271

If a metaphysics which could maintain its place as a science were really in existence, we could say: "Here is metaphysics; learn it, and it will convince you irresistibly and irrevocably of its truth." This general question of the *Prolegomena* would then be useless, and there would remain only that other question (which would rather be a test of our acuteness than a proof of the existence of the thing itself): "How is metaphysics possible, and how does reason come to attain it?"

But human reason has not been so fortunate. There is no single book to which you can point as you do to Euclid and say, "This is metaphysics; here you may find the noblest objects of this science, the knowledge of a Supreme Being and of a future existence, proved from principles of pure reason." We can be shown many propositions, demonstrably certain and never questioned; but these are all analytical and concern the materials and the scaffolding for metaphysics rather than the extension of knowledge, which is our proper object in studying it (Section 2). Even supposing you produce synthetical judgments (such as the law of sufficient reason, which though we gladly concede its truth you have not proved, as you ought to do, from pure reason a priori); when you try to employ them for your principal purpose you lapse into such doubtful assertions that in all ages one metaphysics has contradicted another, either in its assertions or their proofs, and thus has itself destroyed its own claim to lasting assent. Indeed, the very attempts to set up such a science are the main cause of the early appearance of skepticism, a mental attitude in which reason treats itself with such violence that it could never have arisen save from complete despair of ever satisfying its most important aspirations. For long before men began to inquire into nature 272 methodically, they consulted abstract reason, which had to some extent been exercised in ordinary experience; for reason is ever present, while the laws of nature must usually be laboriously discovered. So metaphysics floated to the surface, like foam, which dissolved the moment it was scooped off. But immediately there appeared a new supply on the surface, to be eagerly gathered up by some, while others, instead of seeking in the depths the cause

[2] In Section 3 (omitted) Kant calls attention to Locke's anticipation of his distinction between analytic and synthetic judgment.

of the illusion, thought they showed their wisdom by ridiculing the idle labor
of their neighbors.

274   Weary therefore of dogmatism which teaches us nothing, and of skepticism
which does not even promise us anything, not even the quiet state of contented ignorance; disquieted by the importance of knowledge so much
needed; and rendered suspicious by long experience of all knowledge which
we believe we possess or which offers itself in the name of pure reason, there
remains but one critical question on the answer to which our future procedure depends, namely: Is metaphysics at all possible? But this question must
be answered not by skeptical objections to the asseverations of some actual
system of metaphysics (for we do not as yet admit such a thing to exist), but
from the conception, as yet only problematical, of a science of this sort.

In the *Critique of Pure Reason* I have treated this question synthetically, by
making inquiries into pure reason itself and endeavoring in this source to
determine the elements as well as the laws of its pure use according to
principles. The task is difficult and requires a resolute reader to penetrate by
degrees into a system based on no data except reason itself, which therefore
seeks, without resting on any fact, to unfold knowledge from its original
germs. The *Prolegomena,* however, are designed for preparatory exercises;
they are intended to point out what we have to do in order to make a science
actual if it is possible, rather than to propound the science itself. The *Prolego-*
275 *mena* must therefore rest upon something already known as trustworthy,
from which we can set out with confidence and ascend to sources as yet
unknown, the discovery of which will not only explain to us what we knew but
exhibit a sphere of many cognitions which all spring from the same sources.
The method of prolegomena, especially of those designed as a preparation
for future metaphysics, is consequently analytical.

But it happens, fortunately, that though we cannot assume metaphysics to
be an actual science, we can say with confidence that there are actually given
certain pure a priori synthetical cognitions, namely pure mathematics and
pure physics; both contain propositions which are unanimously recognized,
partly apodictically certain by reason alone, partly by general consent arising
from experience yet independent of experience. We therefore have at least
some uncontested synthetical knowledge a priori and need not ask *whether* it
be possible but *how* it is possible, in order that we may derive from the
principle which makes the given knowledge possible the possibility of all the
rest.

Section 5. The General Problem: How is Knowledge from Pure Reason Possible?

We have already learned the significant distinction between analytical and
synthetical judgments. The possibility of analytical propositions was easily
comprehended, being entirely founded on the law of contradiction. The

possibility of synthetic a posteriori judgments, or those which are gathered from experience, also requires no particular explanation, for experience is nothing but a continued synthesis of perceptions. There remain therefore only synthetical propositions a priori, of which the possibility must be sought or investigated, because they must depend upon other principles than the law of contradiction.

But here we need not first question the possibility of such propositions or ask whether they are possible. For there are enough of them of undoubted certainty; and, as our present method is analytical, we shall start from the fact that such synthetical but purely rational knowledge actually exists. But we must then inquire into the ground of this possibility and ask how such knowledge is possible, in order that we may be enabled to determine from the principles of its possibility the conditions of its use, its sphere and boundaries. The real problem upon which all depends, when expressed with scholastic precision, is therefore: How are synthetical propositions a priori possible?

For the sake of popular understanding I have expressed the problem somewhat differently, as an inquiry into purely rational knowledge, which I could do for once without detriment to the desired insight, because, as we have only to do here with metaphysics and its sources, the reader will, I hope, after the foregoing reminders keep in mind that when we speak of knowledge of pure reason we do not mean analytical but synthetical knowledge.*

Metaphysics stands or falls with the solution of this problem; its very existence depends on it. Let anyone make metaphysical assertions with ever so much plausibility, let him overwhelm us with conclusions; but if he has not previously proved himself able to answer this question satisfactorily, I have a right to say: This is all vain, baseless philosophy and false wisdom. You speak through pure reason and claim, as it were, to create cognitions a priori not only by dissecting given concepts, but also by asserting connections which do not rest upon the law of contradiction, and which you claim to conceive quite independently of all experience; how do you arrive at this, and how will you justify such pretensions? An appeal to the consent of the common sense of mankind cannot be allowed, for that is a witness whose authority depends merely upon rumor. Horace says: *Quodcumque ostendis mihi sic, incredulus odi* (Whatever you show me in this way, I despise and disbelieve).

---

*It is unavoidable that, as knowledge advances, certain expressions which have become classical after having been used since the infancy of science will be found inadequate and unsuitable, and a newer and more appropriate application of the terms will give rise to confusion. [This is the case with the term "analytical."] The analytical method, so far as it is opposed to the synthetical, is very different from one that consists of analytical propositions; it signifies only that we start from what is sought, as if it were given, and ascend to the only conditions under which it is possible. In this method we often use nothing but synthetical propositions, as in mathematical analysis, and it were better to term it the *regressive* method, in contradistinction to the *synthetic* or *progressive*. A principal part of logic too is distinguished by the name of analytic, which here signifies the logic of truth to contrast to dialectic, without considering whether the cognitions belonging to it are analytical or synthetical.

The answer to this question is as indispensable as it is difficult; and although the principal reason that it was not sought long ago is that the possibility of the question never occurred to anybody, there is yet another reason, namely, that a satisfactory answer to this one question requires a much more persistent, profound, and painstaking reflection than the most diffuse work on metaphysics, which on its first appearance promised immortal fame to its author. And every intelligent reader, when he carefully reflects what this problem requires, must at first be struck with its difficulty, and would regard it as insoluble and even impossible did there not actually exist pure synthetical cognitions a priori. This actually happened to David Hume, though he did not conceive the question in its entire generality as is done here and as must be done if the answer is to be decisive for all metaphysics. For how is it possible, said that acute man, that when a concept is given me I can go beyond it and connect with it another concept which is not contained in it, in such a manner as if the latter *necessarily* belonged to the former? Nothing but experience can furnish us with such connections (thus he concluded from the difficulty which he took to be impossibility), and all that vaunted necessity or, what is the same thing, knowledge assumed to be a priori, is nothing but a long habit of accepting something as true and hence of mistaking subjective necessity for objective.

278   Should my reader complain of the difficulty and trouble which I shall occasion him in the solution of this problem, he is at liberty to solve it himself in an easier way. Perhaps he will then feel obliged to the person who has undertaken for him a labor of such profound research and will rather feel some surprise at the facility with which, considering the nature of the subject, the solution has been attained. Yet it has cost years of work to solve the problem in its complete generality (using the term in the mathematical sense, for that which is sufficient in all cases), and finally to exhibit it in the analytical form that the reader will find here.

All metaphysicians are therefore solemnly and legally suspended from their occupations till they shall have fully answered the questions: How are synthetical cognitions a priori possible? For the answer contains the only credentials which they must show when they have anything to offer us in the name of pure reason. But if they do not possess these credentials, they can expect nothing else of reasonable people, who have been so often deceived, than to be dismissed without further inquiry.

If, on the other hand, they desire to carry on their business not as a science, but as an art of wholesome persuasion suitable to the common sense of man, this calling cannot in justice be denied them. They will then speak the modest language of rational belief; they will grant that they are not allowed even to conjecture, far less to know, anything which lies beyond the bounds of all possible experience, but only to assume (not for speculative use, which they must abandon, but for practical use only) the existence of something possible and even indispensable for the guidance of the understanding and of the will in life. In this manner alone can they be called useful and wise men, and the more so as they renounce the title of metaphysicians. For the latter profess to be speculative philosophers; and since, when judgments a priori are under discussion, poor probabilities cannot be admitted (for what is declared to be known a priori is thereby declared as necessary), such men cannot be permitted to play with conjectures, but their assertion must be 279 either science or nothing at all.

It may be said that the entire transcendental philosophy, which necessarily precedes all metaphysics, is nothing but the complete solution of the problem here propounded, in systematic order and completeness, and hence we have hitherto never had any transcendental philosophy. For what goes by its name is properly a part of metaphysics, whereas it is intended only to constitute the possibility of metaphysics and must therefore precede it. And it is not surprising that when a whole science, deprived of all help from other sciences and consequently in itself quite new, is required to answer a single question satisfactorily, we should find the answer troublesome, difficult, and shrouded in obscurity.

As we now proceed to this solution according to the analytical method, in which we assume that such cognitions from pure reason actually exist, we can appeal to only two sciences of theoretical knowledge (which alone is under consideration here), namely pure mathematics and pure natural science. For these alone can exhibit to us objects in intuition, and consequently (if there should occur in them a cognition a priori) can show the truth or conformity of the cognition to the object *in concreto,* that is, its actuality, from which we could proceed to the ground of its possibility by the analytical method. This facilitates our work greatly, for here universal considerations are not only applied to facts, but even start from them, while in a synthetical procedure they must be derived strictly *in abstracto* from concepts.

But in order to rise from these actual and, at the same time well-grounded, pure cognitions a priori to a possible knowledge of the kind we are seeking, namely to metaphysics as a science, we must comprehend that which occasions it — I mean the only natural, but in respect of its truth the still suspect, cognition a priori which lies at the basis of that science, the elaboration of which without any critical investigation of its possibility is commonly called metaphysics. In a word, we must comprehend the natural conditions of such a science as a part of our inquiry, and thus the transcendental problem will be 280 gradually answered by a division into four questions:

1. How is pure mathematics possible?
2. How is pure natural science possible?
3. How is metaphysics in general possible?
4. How is metaphysics as a science possible?

It may be seen that the solution of these problems, though chiefly designed to exhibit the essential matter of the *Critique,* has yet something peculiar which for itself alone deserves attention. This is the search for the sources of the given sciences in reason itself, so that its faculty of knowing something a priori may be investigated and measured by its own accomplishment. By this procedure these sciences gain, if not with respect to their contents, still in what concerns their proper use; and while they throw light on the higher question concerning their common origin, they give, at the same time, an occasion to explain their own nature better.

FIRST PART OF THE MAIN TRANSCENDENTAL PROBLEM
HOW IS PURE MATHEMATICS POSSIBLE?

Section 6

Here is a great and established branch of knowledge, encompassing even now a wonderfully large domain and promising an unlimited extension in the future, yet carrying with it thoroughly apodictic certainty, that is, absolute necessity, and therefore resting on no empirical grounds. Consequently it is a pure product of reason and, moreover, thoroughly synthetical. [Hence the question arises]: How then is it possible for human reason to produce such knowledge entirely a priori?

Does not this faculty [which produces mathematical knowledge], as it neither is nor can be based upon experience, presuppose some ground of knowledge a priori which lies deeply hidden, but which might reveal itself by these its effects if their first beginnings were but diligently ferreted out?

Section 7

281   We find that all mathematical cognition has this peculiarity: it must first exhibit its concept in intuition and indeed a priori, therefore in an intuition which is not empirical but pure.[3] Without this, mathematics cannot take a single step; hence its judgments are always *intuitive*, while philosophy must be satisfied with *discursive* judgments from mere concepts, and though philosophy may illustrate its teachings through an intuition, it can never derive them from it. This observation on the nature of mathematics gives us a clue to the first and highest condition of its possibility, which is that some pure intuition must form its basis, in which all its concepts can be exhibited or constructed *in concreto* yet a priori. If we can uncover this pure intuition and its possibility, we may thence easily explain how synthetical propositions a priori are possible in pure mathematics, and consequently how this science itself is possible. For just as empirical intuition [sense perception] enables us without difficulty to enlarge the concept which we frame of an object of intuition by new predicates which intuition itself presents synthetically in experience, so also pure intuition does likewise, only with this difference:

[3] On Kant's contrast between mathematical and philosophical method, see above pp. 29–40. For what Kant means by intuition and pure intuition, see above, p. 105.

when the intuition is pure, the synthetical judgment is a priori certain and apodictic, but when the intuition is empirical the judgment is a posteriori and only empirically certain. This is because the latter judgment contains only that which occurs in contingent empirical intuition, but the former contains that which must necessarily be discovered in pure intuition. Here intuition, being an intuition a priori, is inseparably joined with the concept prior to all experience or any particular perception.

Section 8

But with this step our perplexity seems rather to increase than to lessen. For the question now is: How is it possible to intuit anything a priori? An intuition is such a representation as would directly depend upon the presence of the object. Hence it seems impossible to intuit spontaneously a priori, because intuition would in that event have to take place without either a previous or a present object to refer to, and in consequence could not be 282 intuition. Concepts indeed are such that we can easily form some of them a priori, namely such as contain nothing but the thought of an object in general for instance, the concept of quantity, of cause, etc., without our finding ourselves in an immediate relation to an object. In order to be meaningful and significant, even these require a certain concrete use, that is, an application to some intuition by which an object of these concepts is given to us. But how can the intuition of the object precede the object itself?

Section 9

If our intuition were of such a nature as to represent things as they are in themselves, there would not be any intuition a priori, but intuition would be always empirical. For I can know only what is contained in the object in itself if it is present and given to me. It is indeed even then incomprehensible how the intuition of a present thing should make me know this thing as it is in itself, as its properties cannot migrate into my faculty of representation. But even granting this possibility, an intuition of that sort would not take place a priori, that is, before the object was presented to me; for without this latter fact no ground of a relation of my representation to the object can be imagined, unless it depend upon a direct inspiration.

Therefore in one way only can my intuition anticipate the actuality of the object, and be a cognition a priori, namely: if my intuition contains nothing but the form of sensibility, antedating in my mind all the actual impressions through which I am affected by objects.

For I can know a priori that objects of sense can be intuited only according to this form of sensibility. Hence it follows that propositions which concern this form of sensible intuition are possible and valid only for objects of the senses; also, conversely, that intuitions which are possible a priori can never concern any other things than objects of our senses.

Section 10

283   Accordingly, it is only the form of sensible intuition through which we can intuit things a priori, but through which we can know objects only as they appear to us (to our senses), not as they are in themselves; and this assumption is absolutely necessary if synthetical propositions a priori are to be granted as possible or if, in case they actually occur, their possibility is to be comprehended and determined beforehand.

Now, the intuitions which pure mathematics lays at the foundation of all its cognitions and judgments which come forth as apodictic and necessary are space and time. For mathematics must first present all its concepts in intuition, and pure mathematics in pure intuition; that is, it must construct them. If it proceeded in any other way, it would be impossible to take a single step; for mathematics proceeds, not analytically by dissecting concepts, but synthetically, and if pure intuition be wanting, there is nothing in which the matter for synthetical judgments a priori can be given. Geometry is based upon pure intuition of space. Arithmetic achieves its concept of number by the successive addition of units in time, and pure mechanics cannot attain its concepts of motion without employing the representation of time. Both representations, however, are only intuitions; for if we omit from the empirical intuitions of bodies and their alterations (motion) everything empirical, that is, everything belonging to sensation, space and time still remain, and these are therefore pure intuitions which lie a priori at the basis of the empirical. Hence they can never be omitted; but at the same time, by their being pure intuitions a priori, they prove that they are mere forms of our sensibility which must precede all empirical intuition, that is, all perception of actual objects, and conformably to which objects can be known a priori, but only as they appear to us.

Section 11

The problem of the present section is therefore solved. Pure mathematics, as synthetical knowledge a priori, is possible because it refers to no other objects than those of the senses. At the basis of their empirical intuition lies a
284   pure intuition (of space and of time) which is a priori because pure intuition is nothing but the form of our sensibility, which precedes the actual appearance of the objects, since in fact it makes it possible. Yet this faculty of intuiting a priori concerns not the matter of the appearance (that is, the sensation in it, for this constitutes what is empirical in it), but its form, namely, space and time. Should anyone venture to doubt that these are determinations adhering not to things in themselves but to their relations to our sensibility, I should be glad to know how he can find it possible to know a priori how their intuition will be characterized before we have any acquaintance with the things and before they are presented to us. Such, however, is the case with space and time. But this is quite comprehensible as soon as both count for

nothing more than formal conditions of our sensibility, while the objects count merely as appearances; for then the form of the appearance, that is, pure intuition, can certainly be represented as proceeding from ourselves, that is, a priori.

Section 12

In order to add something by way of illustration and conformation, we need only observe the ordinary and unavoidable procedure of geometers. All proofs of the complete congruence of two given figures (where the one can in every respect be substituted for the other) come ultimately to this, that they may be made to coincide, which is evidently nothing else than a synthetical proposition resting upon immediate intuition; and this intuition must be pure or given a priori, otherwise the proposition could not rank as apodictically certain but would have empirical certainty only. In that case it could be said only that it is always found to be so and holds good only as far as our perception has reached. That everywhere space (which [in its entirety] is itself no longer the boundary of another space) has three dimensions and that space cannot in any way have more is based on the proposition that not more than three lines can intersect at right angles in one point; but this proposition cannot be shown in any way from concepts, but rests immediately on intuition and indeed on pure and a priori intuition because it is apodictically 285 certain. That we can require a line to be drawn to infinity (*in indefinitum*) or that a series of changes (for example, spaces traversed by motion) shall be infinitely continued presupposes a representation of space and time which, in so far as it is bounded by nothing, can depend only on intuition, for from concepts alone this could never be inferred. Consequently the basis of mathematics is actually pure intuition a priori, which makes its synthetical and apodictically valid propositions possible. Hence our transcendental deduction of the concepts of space and time [in the Transcendental Aesthetic] explains at the same time the possibility of pure mathematics. Without such a deduction and the assumption that everything which can be given to our senses (to the external senses in space, to the internal one in time) is intuited by us as it appears to us, not as it is in itself, the truth of pure mathematics might be granted, but its existence could by no means be understood.

Section 13. Remark I. (The Objective Validity of Mathematics)[4]   287

Pure mathematics and especially pure geometry can have objective reality only on condition that they refer merely to objects of sense. But in regard to the latter, the principle holds good that our sensible representation is not a

---

[4] Section 13 begins by repeating the argument from the Inaugural Dissertation (pp. 62–63) that the paradox of incongruent counterparts shows that space is an object of intuition. This part of Section 13 is omitted, but the following Remarks are attached to Section 13. On the objective validity of mathematics, see *Critique of Pure Reason*, above, pp. 107–109.

representation of things in themselves, but of the way in which they appear to us. Hence it follows that the propositions of geometry are not the results of a mere creation of our poetic fancy which could not be referred with assurance to actual objects; but rather that they are necessarily valid of space and consequently of all that may be found in space, because space is nothing other than the form of all external appearances, and it is this form alone in which objects of sense can be given to us. Sensibility, the form of which is the basis of geometry, is that upon which the possibility of external appearance depends. Therefore these appearances can never contain anything but what geometry prescribes to them.

It would be quite otherwise if the senses were so constituted as to represent objects as they are in themselves. For then it would not by any means follow from the representation of space which, with all its properties, serves the geometer as an a priori foundation, that this foundation and everything which is thence inferred would have to be so in nature. The space of the geometer would be considered a mere fiction, and it would not be credited with objective validity because we could not see how things would of necessity have to agree with an image of them which we make spontaneously and previous to our acquaintance with them. But if this image, or rather this formal intuition, is the essential property of our sensibility by means of which alone objects are given to us, and if this sensibility represents not things in themselves but their appearances, then we easily comprehend and at the same time indisputably prove that all external objects of our world of sense must necessarily conform in the most rigorous way to the propositions of geometry; because sensibility, by means of its form of external intuition (space) with which the geometer is occupied, makes those objects possible as mere appearances.

It will always remain a remarkable phenomenon in the history of philosophy that there was a time when even mathematicians who were at the same time philosophers began to doubt, not the accuracy of their geometrical propositions so far as they concerned space, but their objective validity and the applicability to nature of the concept of space itself and all its geometrical properties. They showed much concern whether a line in nature might not consist of physical points, and consequently whether true space in the object might consist of simple parts, while the space which the geometer has in mind cannot be such. They did not recognize that physical space is not at all a property of things in themselves but only a form of our faculty of sensible representation. Nor did they see that all objects in space are only appearances, i.e., not things in themselves, but representations of our sensible intuition. Since the space which the geometer thinks is precisely the form of sensible intuition which we find a priori in us and contains the ground of the possibility of the form of all external appearances, the form of all external appearances must necessarily and most rigorously agree with the propositions which the geometer infers not from any fictitious concept but from the subjective basis of all external appearances, which is sensibility itself. In this and in no other way can geometry be made secure as to the undoubted objective reality of its propositions against all the intrigues of a shallow metaphysics, to which the propositions of geometry seem strange because it has not traced them to the sources of their concepts.

Section 13. Remark II. (Refutation of Idealism)[5]

Whatever is given us as object must be given us in intuition. All our intuition takes place by means of sense only; the understanding intuits nothing, but only reflects. And as we have just shown that the senses never and in no manner enable us to know things in themselves, but only their appearances which are mere representations of the sensibility, we concluded that "all bodies, together with the space in which they are, must be considered nothing but mere representations in us, and exist nowhere but in our thoughts." Is not this manifest idealism?

Idealism consists in the assertion that there are none but thinking beings, all other things which we believe to be perceived in intuition being nothing but representations in thinking beings, to which no object external to them in fact corresponds. I, on the contrary, say that things as objects of our senses existing outside us are given, but we know nothing of what they may be in themselves, since we know only their appearances, that is, the representations which they cause in us by affecting our senses. Consequently I grant by all means that there are bodies without us, that is, things which, though quite unknown to us as to what they are in themselves, we yet know by the representations which their influence on our sensibility procures us. These representations we call "bodies", a term signifying the appearance of the thing unknown to us, but not therefore less actual. Can this be termed idealism? It is the very contrary.

Long before Locke's time, but assuredly since him, it has been generally assumed and granted without detriment to the actual existence of external things that many of their predicates may be said to belong not to the things in themselves but to their appearances, and to have no proper existence outside our representation. Heat, color, and taste, for instance, are of this kind. Now, if I go farther and, for weighty reasons, rank as mere appearances the remaining qualities of bodies also, which are called primary qualities — such as extension, place, and, in general, space with all that belongs to it (impenetrability or materiality, shape, etc.) — no one in the least can adduce the reason of its being inadmissible. As little as the man who admits colors not to be properties of the object in itself but only modifications of the sense of sight, should on the account be called an idealist, so little can my thesis be

289

---

[5] See the Refutations of Idealism in the *Critique of Pure Reason*, pp. 122–124 and 125–127.

named idealistic merely because I find that more, nay all the properties which constitute the intuition of a body belong to its appearance only.

The existence of the thing that appears is not thereby destroyed, as in genuine idealism, but it is shown only that we cannot possibly know it by the senses, as it is in itself.

I should be glad to know what my assertions must be in order to avoid all idealism. Undoubtedly I would have to say that the representation of space is not only perfectly conformable to the relation which our sensibility has to objects — that I have said — but that it is quite similar to the object — an assertion in which I can find as little meaning as if I said that the sensation of red has a similarity to the property of cinnabar which excites this sensation in me.

290

Section 13. Remark III. (Appearance and Illusion)[6]

Hence we may at once dismiss an easily foreseen but futile objection: *That by admitting the ideality of space and of time the whole sensible world would be turned into mere sham.* After all philosophical insight into the nature of sensible cognition was spoiled by making the sensibility merely a confused mode of representation according to which we still know things as they are but without being able to reduce everything in this our representation to a clear consciousness, I proved that sensibility consists not in this logical distinction of clearness and obscurity but in a genetic distinction concerning the origin of knowledge itself. For sensible knowledge represents things not at all as they are, but only the mode in which they affect our senses; and consequently by the senses only appearances and not things in themselves are given to the understanding for reflection. After this necessary correction, an objection arises from an unpardonable and almost intentional misconception, as if my doctrine turned all the things of the world of sense into mere illusion.

When an appearance is given us, we are still quite free as to how we shall from the appearance judge the thing. The appearance depends upon the senses but the judgment upon the understanding; and the only question is whether the determination of the object is true or not. But the difference between truth and dreaming is not ascertained by the nature of those representations which are referred to objects (for they are the same in truth and in dreaming), but by their connection according to the rules which determine the coherence of the representations in the concept of an object, and by ascertaining whether they can subsist in one experience or not. And it is not the fault of the appearances if our cognition takes illusion for truth, that is, if the intuition by which an object is given us is considered a concept of the thing or even of its existence, which only the understanding can think. The senses represent to us the course of the planets as now progressive, now retrogressive, and herein is neither truth nor falsity, because as long as we

291

---

[6] See the corresponding section in *Critique of Pure Reason*, above, p. 109.

hold this to be nothing but appearance we do not judge of the objective character of their motion. But as a false judgment may easily arise when the understanding is not on its guard against considering this subjective mode of representation as objective, we say they they appear to move backward, it is not the senses which must be charged with the illusion [that they move backwards] but the understanding, whose province alone it is to make an objective judgment from appearance.

Thus, even if we did not at all reflect on the origin of our representations, whenever we connect our sensible intuitions (whatever they may contain) in space and time according to the rules of coherence of all knowledge in an experience, illusion or truth will arise according to whether we are negligent or careful. It is merely a question of the use of sensible representations in the understanding, and not of their origin. In the same way, if I consider all the representations of the senses, together with their form, space and time, to be nothing but appearances, and space and time to be a mere form of the sensibility which is not to be met with in objects outside it, and if I make use of these representations in reference to possible experience only, there is nothing in my regarding them as appearances that can lead astray or cause illusion. In spite of being mere appearances, they can correctly cohere according to rules of truth in experience. Thus all the propositions of geometry are true of space as well as of all the objects of the [outer] senses, and consequently of all possible experience, whether I consider space as a mere form of sensibility or as something cleaving to the things themselves. In the former cause, however, I comprehend how I can know a priori these propositions concerning all the objects of external intuition. Otherwise, everything else as regards all possible experience remains just as if I had not departed from the common view.

But if I venture to go beyond all possible experience with my concepts of space and time, which I cannot refrain from doing if I proclaim them charac- 292 ters inherent in things in themselves (for what should prevent me from letting them hold good of the same things, even though my senses might be different and unsuited to them?), then a grave error may arise owing to an illusion in which I proclaim to be universally valid what is merely a subjective condition of the intuition of things and certain only for all objects of senses and thus for all possible experience; for I would refer this condition of intuition to things in themselves, and not limit it to the conditions of experience.

My doctrine of the ideality of space and time, therefore, far from reducing the whole sensible world to mere illusion, is the only means of securing the application of one of the most important kinds of knowledge (which mathematics propounds a priori) to actual objects and of preventing its being regarded as mere illusion. For without this observation it would be quite impossible to make out whether the intuitions of space and time, which we borrow from no experience and which lie in our representation *a priori*, are mere phantasms of our brain to which objects do not correspond, at least not adequately, and thus whether geometry is a mere illusion. On the contrary, we have been able to show the unquestionable validity of geometry with regard to all the objects of the sensible world just because they are mere appearances.

Secondly, though these my principles make appearances out of the representations of the senses, they are so far from turning the truth of experience into mere illusion that they are rather the only means of preventing the transcendental illusion by which metaphysics has hitherto been deceived and been led to the childish endeavor of catching at bubbles because appearances, which are mere representations, were taken for things in themselves. Here originated the remarkable occurrence of the antinomy of reason which I shall mention later, and which is solved by the single observation that appearance, as long as it is employed in experience, produces truth, but the moment it transgresses the boundary of experience and consequently becomes transcendent, produces nothing but illusion.

Inasmuch as I leave the actuality of things as we represent them by the senses, this is no sweeping illusion invented for nature by me. For I limit our sensible intuition of these things to this: that sensible intuition, even the pure 293 intuitions of space and time, represents in no respect anything more than the mere appearance of those things and never their constitution in themselves. My protestation, too, against all charges of idealism is so valid and clear as to seem even superfluous were there not incompetent judges who, while they would like to have an old name for every deviation from their perverse though common opinion and never judge of the spirit of philosophic nomenclature but cling to the letter only, are ready to put their own conceits in place of well-defined concepts, and thereby deform and distort them. I have myself given my theory the name of transcendental idealism, but that cannot authorize anyone to confound it either with the empirical idealism of Descartes (indeed, his was only an insoluble problem, owing to which he thought everyone at liberty to deny the existence of the corporeal world because it could never be proved satisfactorily), or with the mystical and visionary idealism of Berkeley, against which and other similar phantasms our *Critique* contains the proper antidote. My idealism concerns not the existence of things (the doubting of which constitutes idealism in the ordinary sense), since it never came into my head to doubt it, but it concerns the sensible representation of things to which space and time especially belong. Of these [namely, space and time] and consequently of all appearances in general, I have shown only that they are neither things (but mere modes of representation) nor determinations belonging to things in themselves. But the word "transcendental", which with me never means a reference of our knowledge to things, but only the reference of our knowledge to the cognitive faculty, was meant to obviate this misconception. Yet rather than give further occasion to it by this word, I now retract it and desire this idealism of mine to be called "critical." But if it be really an objectionable idealism to convert actual things (not appearances) into mere representations, by what name shall we call him who conversely makes mere representations things? It may, I think, be called "dreaming idealism," in contradiction to the former, which may be called "visionary," both of which are to be refuted by my transcendental or, better, *critical* idealism.

SECOND PART OF THE MAIN TRANSCENDENTAL PROBLEM HOW IS PURE SCIENCE OF NATURE POSSIBLE?

294

Section 14

Nature is the existence of things so far as it is determined according to universal laws. If nature signified the existence of things in themselves, we could never know it either a priori or a posteriori. Not a priori, for how can we know what belongs to things in themselves, since this can never come to pass by the dissection of our concepts in analytical propositions? For I do not want to know what is contained in my concept of a thing, since that belongs to its logical essence; I want to know what in the actuality of the thing is superadded to my concept, by which a thing itself is determined in its existence apart from my concept. My understanding and the conditions on which alone it can connect the determinations of things in their existence do not prescribe any rule to the things themselves; these do not conform to my understanding, but my understanding would have to conform itself to the things. [For this to be possible,] the things would have to be first given me in order for me to take these determinations from them, and they would thus not be known a priori.

But knowledge of the nature of things in themselves a posteriori would be equally impossible. For if experience is to teach us laws to which the existence of things is subject, these laws, if they refer to things in themselves, would have to hold of necessity even outside our experience. But experience teaches us what exists and how it exists, but never that it must necessarily exist so and not otherwise. Experience therefore can never teach us the nature of things in themselves.

Section 15

We nevertheless actually possess a pure science of nature, in which are propounded a priori, and with all the necessity requisite to apodictical propo- 295 sitions, laws to which nature is subject. I need only call to witness the propaedeutic of natural science which, under the title of the universal science of nature, precedes all physics, which is founded upon empirical principles. In it we have mathematics applied to appearances, and also merely discursive principles (principles derived from concepts) which constitute the philosophical part of the pure knowledge of nature. But there are several things in it which are not quite pure and independent of empirical sources, such as the concept of motion, of impenetrability (upon which the empirical concept of matter rests), inertia, and many others, which prevent its being called a perfectly pure science of nature. Besides, it refers only to objects of the outer sense, and therefore does not give an example of a strictly universal science of nature, for such a science must bring nature in general, whether it regards the object of the outer or that of the inner sense (the object of physics as well as that of psychology), under universal laws. But among the principles of this universal physics there are a few which actually have the required universality; for instance, the propositions that "Substance is permanent," that "Every event is determined by a cause according to constant laws," etc.: These are actually universal laws of nature, which hold completely a priori. There is then in fact a pure science of nature, and the question arises: How is it possible?

Section 16

The word *nature* assumes yet another meaning which defines the object, whereas in the former sense it only denoted the conformity to law of the determinations of the existence of things generally. If we consider it *materialiter*, nature is the complex of all objects of experience. And with this only are we concerned, for things which can never be objects of experience, if they had to be known as to their nature, would oblige us to have recourse to concepts whose meaning could never be given *in concreto* by any example of possible experience.

Consequently we would have to form for ourselves empty concepts of their nature, the reality of which could never be determined. That is, we could never learn whether they actually referred to objects or were mere creations 296 of thought. The knowledge of what cannot be an object of experience would be hyperphysical, and with things hyperphysical we are not here concerned, but only with the knowledge of nature, the actuality of which can be confirmed by experience, though this knowledge is possible a priori and precedes all experience.

Section 17

The formal aspect of nature in this narrower sense is therefore the conformity to law of all objects of experience, and, so far as it is known a priori, their necessary conformity. But it has just been shown that the laws of nature can never be known a priori to apply to objects so far as they are considered as things in themselves and not in reference to possible experience. Our enquiry here extends not to things in themselves as objects (the properties of which we pass by) but to things as objects of possible experience, and the complex of these is what we here properly designate as nature. And now I ask, when the possibility of knowledge of nature a priori is in question, whether it is better to formulate the problem thus: How can we know a priori that things as objects of experience necessarily conform to law? or thus: How is it possible to know a priori the necessary conformity to law of experience itself as regards its objects generally?

Closely considered, the solution of the problem presented in either way amounts entirely to the same thing with regard to the pure knowledge of nature (which is the point of the question at issue). For the subjective laws, under which alone an empirical knowledge of things is possible, hold good of these things as objects of possible experience (not as things in themselves, which are not considered here). It is all the same whether I say: "A judgment of perception can never rank as experience without the law that, whenever an event is observed, it is always referred to some antecedent which it follows according to a universal rule," or: "Everything of which experience teaches that it happens must have a cause."

It is, however, more suitable to choose the first formula. For we can, a 297 priori and prior to all given objects, have knowledge of those conditions on which alone experience of them is possible, but never of the laws to which, without reference to possible experience, things may in themselves be subject. We cannot, therefore, study the nature of things a priori other than by investigating the conditions and the universal (though subjective) laws under which alone such a cognition as experience (as to mere form) is possible; it is in this way that we determine the possibility of things as objects of experience. For if I should choose the second formula and seek the a priori conditions under which nature as an object of experience is possible, I might easily fall into error and fancy that I was speaking of nature as a thing in itself, and then move around in endless circles in a vain search for laws concerning things of which nothing is given me.

Accordingly, we shall here be concerned with experience only and the universal conditions of its possibility, which are given a priori. Thence we shall define nature as the whole object of all possible experience. I think it will be understood that I here do not mean rules of the observation of a nature that is already given, for these already presuppose experience. Thus I do not mean how, through experience, we can study the laws of nature, for such laws would not then be laws a priori and would yield us no pure science of nature. Rather, [I mean to ask] how the conditions a priori of the possibility of experience are at the same time the sources from which all universal laws of nature must be derived.

Section 18

In the first place we must state that, while all judgments of experience are empirical, that is, have their ground in immediate sense-perception, not all empirical judgments are judgments of experience. For besides the empirical, and in general besides what is given to sensible intuition, special concepts must be superadded — concepts which have their origin wholly a priori in the pure understanding, and under which every perception must first of all be subsumed and then by their means changed into experience.

298 Empirical judgments, so far as they have objective validity, are *judgments of experience*, but those which are only subjectively valid I name mere *judgments of perception*. The latter require no pure concept of the understanding, but only the logical connection of perceptions in a thinking subject. But the former always require, besides the representations of sensible intuition, special concepts originally begotten in the understanding, which make it possible that the judgment of experience be objectively valid.

All our judgments are at first merely judgments of perception; they hold good only for us (for our own subject), and we do not until afterwards give them a new reference (to an object) and intend that they shall always hold good for us and in the same way for everybody else; for when a judgment agrees with an object, all judgments concerning the same object must likewise agree among themselves, and thus the objective validity of the judgment of experience signifies nothing else than its necessary universal validity. And conversely, when we have ground for considering a judgment as necessarily having universal validity (which never depends upon perception, but upon the pure concept of the understanding under which the perception is subsumed), we must consider that it is objective also — that is, that it expresses not merely a reference of a perception to a subject, but a characteristic of the object. For there would be no reason for judgments of other men to necessarily agree with mine if it were not the unity of the object to which they all refer and with which they accord; hence they must all agree with one another.

Section 19

Therefore objective validity and necessary universal validity (validity for everybody) are equivalent terms, and though we do not know the object in itself, yet when we consider a judgment as universally valid and hence as necessary, we thereby understand it to have objective validity. By this judgment we know the object (though it remains unknown as it is in itself) by the universally valid and necessary connection of the given perceptions. As this is the case with all objects of sense, judgments of experience borrow their 299 objective validity not from immediate knowledge of the object (which is impossible) but from the condition of universal validity of empirical judgments, which, as already said, never rests upon empirical or, in short, sensible conditions, but upon a pure concept of the understanding. The object always remains in itself unknown; but when by the concept of the understanding the connection of the representations that the object gives to our sensibility is determined as universally valid, the object is determined by this relation, and the judgment is objective.

To illustrate the matter: when we say, "The room is warm, sugar sweet, and wormwood bitter,"* we have only subjectively valid judgments. I do not expect that I or any other person shall always find it as I now do; each of these sentences expresses only a relation of two sensations in the same subject (myself), and in me only in my present state of perception; consequently they do not hold of the object. Such are judgments of perception. Judgments of experience are of quite a different nature. What experience teaches me under certain circumstances, it must always teach me and everybody; its validity is not limited to the subject nor to my state at a particular time. Hence I pronounce all such judgments objectively valid. For instance, when I say air is elastic, this judgment is as yet a judgment of perception only; I do nothing but relate two sensations to each other in my senses. But if I would have it called a judgment of experience, I require this connection to stand under a condition which makes it universally valid. I will therefore that I and everybody else should always connect necessarily the same perceptions under the same circumstances.

Section 20

300

We must consequently analyze experience in general in order to see what is contained in this product of the senses and understanding, and how the judgment of experience itself is possible. The foundation is the intuition of which I become conscious, that is, perception (*perceptio*), which pertains merely to the senses. But in the next place, there is judging, which belongs only to the understanding. But this judging may be twofold: first, I may merely compare perceptions and combine them in a consciousness of my particular state; or, second, I may combine them in a consciousness in general. The former judgment is merely a judgment of perception, and hence of subjective validity only; it is merely a connection of perceptions in my mental state, without reference to the object. Hence it does not, as is commonly imagined, suffice for experience that perceptions be compared and connected in consciousness through an act of judging; for from that arises no universal validity and necessity by virtue of which alone a judgment can be objectively valid, that is, can be called experience.

Quite another judgment is therefore required before perception can become experience. The given intuition must be subsumed under a concept which determines in general the form of judging the intuition, connects

---

*I freely grant that these examples do not represent such judgments of perception as ever could become judgments of experience, even if a concept of the understanding were superadded, because they refer merely to feeling, which everybody knows to be merely subjective and which of course can never be attributed to the object, and consequently can never become objective. I only wished to give here an example of a judgment that is merely subjectively valid, containing no ground for necessary universal validity and thereby for a relation to the object. An example of the judgments of perception which become judgments of experience by superadded concepts of the understanding will be given in the next note.

empirical consciousness of the intuition in a consciousness in general, and thereby procures universal validity for the empirical judgments. A concept of this nature is a pure a priori concept of the understanding, which does nothing but determine for an intuition the general way in which it can serve in judgments. If the concept be that of cause, it determines the intuition which is subsumed under it (for example, the intuition of air) relative to judging in general. Thus the concept of air in respect to its expansion serves in the relation of antecedent to consequent in a hypothetical judgment. The concept of cause accordingly is a pure concept of the understanding, which is totally different from any possible perception and serves only to determine the representation subsumed under it with respect to judging in general. Thus a pure concept of the understanding makes a universally valid judgment possible.

301   Before a judgment of perception can become a judgment of experience, it is required that the perceptions should be subsumed under some such concept of the understanding; for instance, air belongs under the concept of cause, which determines our judgment about it as hypothetical in respect to its expansion.* Thereby the expansion of the air is represented, not as belonging merely to the perception of the air in my present state or in several states of mine, or in the perceptual state of others, but as belonging to it necessarily. The judgment, "Air is elastic," becomes universally valid and a judgment of experience only because certain judgments precede it which subsume the intuition of air under the concept of cause and effect; and they thereby determine the perceptions not merely with respect to one another in me but with respect to the form of judging in general (which is here hypothetical), and in this way render the empirical judgment universally valid.

If all our synthetical judgments are analyzed so far as they are objectively valid, it will be found that they never consist of mere intuitions connected only (as is commonly believed) by comparison in a judgment; but that they would be impossible were not a pure concept of the understanding superadded to the concepts abstracted from intuition, under which concept these latter are subsumed and only in this manner combined into an objectively valid judgment. Even the judgments of pure mathematics in their simplest axioms are not exempt from this condition. The principle, "A straight line is the shortest distance between two points," presupposes that the line is subsumed under the concept of magnitude, which certainly is no mere intuition, but has its seat in the understanding alone and serves to determine the intuition of the line with regard to judgments which may be made about it in

---

*As an easier example, we may take the following: "When the sun shines on the stone, it grows warm." This judgment, however often I and others may have perceived this, is a mere judgment of perception and contains no necessity; perceptions are only as a matter of course conjoined in this way. But if I say, "The sun warms the stone," I add to the perception a concept of the understanding, namely that of cause, which necessarily connects with the concept of sunshine that of heat, and the synthetical judgment becomes of necessity universally valid (i.e., objective) and is converted from a perception into experience.

respect to their quantity, that is, in this case plurality (as *judicia plurativa*).[7]
For under a judgment of this kind it is understood that in a given intuition 302
there is contained a plurality of homogeneous parts.

Section 21

To prove, then, the possibility of experience as far as it rests upon pure
concepts of the understanding a priori, we must first represent in a complete
table what belongs to judging in general and the various functions (*Momente*)
of the understanding in making these judgments.[8] For the pure concepts of
the understanding must run parallel to these functions, since these concepts
are nothing more than concepts of intuition in general so far as these concepts
are determined by one or other of these functions of judging in themselves,
that is, necessarily and universally determined. In such a complete table also
the a priori principles of the possibility of all experience as objectively valid
empirical knowledge will be precisely determined, for they are nothing but
propositions which subsume all perceptions — given certain universal conditions of intuition — under these pure concepts of the understanding.

Logical Table of Judgments

1 *As to Quantity*	2 *As to Quality*
Universal	Affirmative
Particular	Negative
Singular	Infinite

3 *As to Relation*	4 *As to Modality* 303
Categorical	Problematic
Hypothetical	Assertoric
Disjunctive	Apodictic

[7] Footnote by Kant omitted.
[8] See *Critique of Pure Reason*, above pp. 110–111.

Transcendental Table of the Concepts of the Understanding

1	2
As to Quantity	*As to Quality*
Unity (Measure)	Reality
Plurality (Magnitude)	Negation
Totality (Whole)	Limitation

3	4
As to Relation	*As to Modality*
Substance	Possibility
Cause	Existence
Community	Necessity

PURE PHYSIOLOGICAL[9] TABLE OF THE UNIVERSAL PRINCIPLES OF THE SCIENCE OF NATURE

1	2
Axioms of Intuition	Anticipations of Perception

3	4
Analogies of Experience	Postulates of All Empirical Thinking Whatsoever

Section 21 *a*

304   In order to comprise the whole matter in one concept, it is first necessary to remind the reader that we are discussing not the origin of experience but that which lies in experience. The former pertains to empirical psychology and would even then never be adequately explained without the latter, which belongs to the critique of knowledge and particularly to the critique of the understanding.

Experience consists of intuitions, which belong to the sensibility, and of judgments, which are entirely the work of the understanding. But the judgments which the understanding forms solely from sensible intuitions are far from being judgments of experience. For in the one case the judgment connects only the perceptions as they are given in sensible intuition, while in the other the judgments must express what experience in general and not what the mere perception (which possesses only subjective validity) contains. The judgment of experience must therefore add to the sensible intuition and its logical connection in a judgment (after they have been rendered universal by comparison) something that determines the synthetical judgment as necessary and therefore as universally valid. This can be nothing else than that concept which represents the intuition as determined in itself with regard to one form of judgment rather than another, namely, a concept of that

---

[9] Kant here uses the word *physiological* in its etymological meaning as pertaining to nature (Gk. *phusis*), not as we use the term now as pertaining to the functions of the living body.

synthetical unity of intuitions which can be represented only by a given logical function of judgment.

Section 22

The sum of the matter is this: the business of the senses is to intuit, that of the understanding is to think. But thinking is uniting representations in one consciousness. This union originates either merely relative to the subject and is accidental and subjective, or it takes place absolutely and is necessary or objective. The union of representations in one consciousness is judgment. Thinking, therefore, is the same as judging or referring representations to judgments in general. Hence judgments are either merely subjective, when representations are referred to the consciousness of one subject only and united in it, or objective, when they are united in consciousness in general, that is, necessarily. The logical forms of all judgments are but various possi- 305 ble modes of uniting representations in a consciousness. But if they serve as concepts, they are concepts of the necessary union of representations in [any] consciousness, and so are principles of objectively valid judgments. This union of representations in consciousness is either analytical, by identity, or synthetical, by the combination and addition of various representations one to another. Experience consists in the synthetical connection of appearances (perceptions) in consciousness so far as that connection is necessary. Hence the pure concepts of the understanding are those under which all perceptions must be subsumed ere they can serve in judgments of experience, in which the synthetical unity of the perceptions is represented as necessary and universally valid.*

Section 23

Judgments, when considered merely as the condition of the union of given representations in consciousness, are rules. These rules, so far as they represent the union of representations as necessary, are rules a priori, and, insofar as they cannot be deduced from higher rules, are principles. But in regard to the possibility of all experience, merely in relation to the form of thinking in it, no conditions of judgments of experience are higher than those which

---

*But how does the proposition that judgments of experience contain necessity in the synthesis of perceptions agree with my statement so often before inculcated that experience as cognition a posteriori can afford contingent judgments only? When I say that experience teaches me something, I always mean only the perception that lies in experience — for example, the perception that heat always follows the shining of the sun on a stone. To this extent the proposition of experience is always accidental. That this heat necessarily follows from the illumination by the sun is contained indeed in the judgment of experience (by means of the concept of cause), but this is not itself a fact learned by experience; for, on the contrary, experience is first of all generated by this addition of the concept of the understanding (cause) to perception. How perception attains this addition may be seen by referring in the *Critique* to the [first] section of the "Transcendental Faculty of Judgment," [the chapter on Schematism, not included in this volume].

bring the appearances, according to the various form of their intuition, under
306 pure concepts of the understanding, which render the empirical judgment
objectively valid. These are therefore the a priori principles of possible
experience.

I he principles of possible experience are then at the same time universal
laws of nature, which can be known a priori. And thus the problem of our
second question: How is pure science of nature possible? is solved. For the
systematic structure which is required for the form of a science is to be met
with in perfection here, because, beyond the above-mentioned formal conditions of all judgments whatsoever (and hence of all rules in general) offered
in logic, no others are possible, and these constitute a logical system. The
concepts grounded thereupon, which contain the a priori conditions of all
synthetical and necessary judgments, accordingly constitute a transcendental system. Finally, the principles by means of which all appearances are
subsumed under these concepts, constitute a physiological [i.e., physical]
system, that is, a system of nature which precedes all empirical knowledge of
nature and makes it possible. It may therefore in strictness be denominated
the genuinely universal and pure science of nature.

Section 24

The first of the physiological [i.e., physical] principles subsumes all appearances as intuitions in space and time under the concept of quantity, and
is thus a principle of the application of mathematics to experience. The
second one does not subsume the strictly empirical element, namely sensation (which denotes what is real in intuition), directly under the concept of
magnitude, since sensation is not an intuition that contains either space or
time though it posits the object corresponding to it in space and time. But
there is between reality (sense-representation) and the zero or total void of
intuition a difference in time, which does have a magnitude. For between any
given degree of light and darkness, between any degree of heat and absolute
307 cold, and between any degree of occupancy of space and totally void space,
diminishing degrees can be conceived just as in like manner between consciousness and total unconsciousness (psychological darkness) ever diminishing degrees obtain.

Hence there is no perception that can prove an absolute absence; for
instance, no psychological darkness that cannot be considered as consciousness which is only outbalanced by a stronger consciousness. This occurs in all
cases of sensation, and so the understanding can anticipate even sensations,
which constitute the peculiar quality of empirical representations (appearances), by means of the principle that they all have degree (and consequently
that what is real in all appearance has degree). Here is the second application
of mathematics (*mathesis intensorum*) to the science of nature.

Section 25

The determination of the relation of appearances solely with regard to their existence is not mathematical but dynamical. It can never be objectively valid, and consequently never fit for experience, if it does not come under a priori principles by which empirical knowledge of appearances first becomes possible. Hence appearances must be subsumed under the concept of substance, which as a concept of a thing is the foundation of all determinations of existence; or, secondly — so far as a succession is found among appearances, that is, an event — under the concept of an effect with reference to a cause; or lastly — so far as coexistence is to be known objectively, that is, by a judgment of experience — under the concept of community (action and reaction). Thus a priori principles form the basis of objectively valid, though empirical, judgments — that is, of the possibility of experience so far as it must connect objects as existing in nature. These principles are the real laws of nature, which may be termed *dynamical.*

Finally knowledge of the agreement and connection, not only of appearances among themselves in experience, but of their relation to experience in general, belongs to the judgments of experience. This relation contains either their agreement with the formal conditions which the understanding recognizes, or their coherence with the material of the senses and perception, or combines both into one concept. Consequently their relation to experi- 308 ence in general entails possibility, actuality, and necessity according to universal laws of nature.[10] This would constitute the physiological [i.e., physical] doctrine of method for distinguishing truth from hypothesis and for determining the limits and certainty of hypothesis.

Section 26

The third table of principles, drawn by the critical method from the nature of the understanding itself shows an inherent perfection which raises it far above every other table which has hitherto, though in vain, been tried or may yet be tried by dogmatically analyzing objects themselves. It exhibits all synthetical a priori principles completely and according to a single principle, namely, the faculty of judging in general, constituting the essence of experience as regards the understanding; hence we can be certain that there are no more such principles. This affords a satisfaction which can never be reached by the dogmatic method. Yet this is not all — there is still greater merit in it.

We must carefully bear in mind the premise which shows the possibility of knowledge a priori and, at the same time, limits all such principles to a condition which must never be lost sight of if we desire it not to be misunderstood and extended in use beyond the original sense which the understand-

[10] See "Postulates of all Empirical Thinking Whatsoever" in *Critique of Pure Reason*, above, pp. 120–125.

ing attached to it. This limit is that they contain nothing but the conditions of possible experience in general so far as it is subjected to laws a priori. Consequently, I do not say that *things in themselves* possess a magnitude, that their reality possesses a degree, their existence a connection of accidents in a substance, etc. This nobody can prove, because such a synthetical connection from mere concepts without any reference to sensible intuition on the one side or connection of it in a possible experience on the other is absolutely impossible. The essential limitation of the concepts in these principles is that all *things as objects of experience,* and only these, stand necessarily a priori under the aforementioned conditions.

Hence there follows, secondly, a specifically peculiar mode of proof of these principles: they are not related directly to appearances and their rela-
309 tion, but to the possibility of experience, of which appearances constitute the matter only, not the form. Thus they are related to objectively and universally valid synthetical propositions which we distinguish as judgments of experience from those of perception. This takes place because appearances, as mere intuitions which *do* occupy a part of space and time, come under the concept of quantity, which synthetically unites the manifold of these intuitions according to rules. Insofar as the perception contains (in addition to intuition) sensation, between which and zero (that is, the total disappearance of sensation) there is an ever-decreasing transition, it is apparent that what is real in appearances must have a degree to the extent that sensation itself does *not* occupy any part of space or time.* Still the transition to this real from empty time or empty space is possible only in time. Consequently, although sensation, as the quality of an empirical intuition specifically differentiating it from other sensations, can never be known a priori, yet it can, in a possible experience in general, as magnitude of perception be intensively distinguished from every other similar perception. Hence the application of mathematics to nature, with respect to the sensible intuition by which nature is given to us, thus becomes possible and definite.

Above all, the reader must pay attention to the mode of proof of the principles which occur under the title of Analogies of Experience. For these do not refer to the genesis of intuitions, as do the principles of applying mathematics to natural science in general, but to the connection of their
310 existence in an experience; and this can be nothing but the determination of their existence in time according to necessary laws, under which alone the

---

*Heat and light are in a small space just as large, as to degree, as in a large one; in like manner internal representations, pain, and consciousness itself are not less in degree whether they last a short or a long time. Hence the quantity is here in a point and in a moment just as great as in any space or time, however great. Degrees are quantities not in intuition, but in mere sensation (or the quantity of the content [*Grundes*] of an intuition). Hence they can only be estimated quantitatively by the relation of 1 to 0, namely by their capability of decreasing by infinite intermediate degrees to disappearance, or of increasing from naught through infinite gradations to a determinate sensation in a certain time. *Quantitas qualitatis est gradus.* (The quantity of quality is degree.)

connection is objectively valid and thus experience. The proof, therefore, does not turn on the synthetical unity in the connection of things in themselves, but merely of the synthetical unity of perceptions, and of these not in regard to their matter but to the determination of time and of the relation of their existence in it according to universal laws. If the empirical determination in relative time is to be objectively valid (that is, to be experience), these universal laws must contain the necessary determination of existence in time generally (namely, according to a rule of the understanding a priori).

As these are *prolegomena* I cannot here further descant on the subject, but I recommend to my reader (who has probably been long accustomed to consider experience a mere empirical compounding of perceptions, and hence has not considered that it goes much beyond perceptions since it imputes to empirical judgments universal validity, and for that purpose requires a pure and a priori unity of the understanding) that he pay special attention to this distinction between experience and a mere aggregate of perceptions and that he judge the mode of proof from this point of view.

Section 27

We are now prepared to remove Hume's doubt. He justly maintains that we cannot comprehend by reason the possibility of causality, that is, of the reference of the existence of one thing to the existence of another which is necessitated by the former. I add that we comprehend just as little the concept of subsistence, that is, the necessity that at the foundation of the existence of things there lies a subject which cannot itself be the predicate of any other thing; nay, we cannot even form a concept of the possibility of such a thing (though we can point out examples of its use in experience). The very same incomprehensibility affects the community of things, as we cannot comprehend how from the state of one thing an inference to the state of quite another thing outside it can be drawn, and vice versa, and how substances which have each its own separate existence should depend upon one another necessarily. But I am far from holding these concepts to be derived merely from experience, and the necessity represented in them to be imaginary and 311 a mere illusion produced in us by long habit. On the contrary, I have amply shown that they and the principles derived from them are firmly established a priori before all experience, and have undoubted objective rightness, though only in regard to experience.

Section 28

Although I have not the least concept of such a connection of things in themselves, how they can either exist as substances or act as causes or stand in community with others as part of a whole, and I can just as little conceive such properties in appearances as such (because these concepts contain nothing that lies in the appearances, but only what the understanding alone must think), we nevertheless have a concept of such a connection of representations in our understanding and in judgments in general. This concept is: that representations appear, in one set of judgments, as subject in relation to predicates; in another, as ground in relation to consequent; in a third, as parts which constitute together a total possible cognition. Furthermore, we know a priori that without considering the representation of an object as determined in one or the other of these respects, we can have no valid knowledge of the object; and if we should occupy ourselves with the object in itself, there is not a single possible attribute by which I could know that it is determined under any of these aspects, that is, under the concept of either substance, cause, or (in relation to other substances) community, for I have no concept of the possibility of such a connection of existence. But the question is not how things in themselves are determined, but how the empirical knowledge of things is determined as regards the forms of judgments in general; that is, how things, as objects of experience, can and must be subsumed under these concepts of the understanding. And then it is clear that I completely comprehend not only the possibility but also the necessity of subsuming all appearances under these concepts — that is, of using them for principles of the possibility of experience.

312 ## Section 29

In order to test Hume's problematical concept (his *crux metaphysicorum*), the concept of cause, we are first given a priori by means of logic the form of a conditional judgment in general; that is, we have one cognition given as antecedent and another as consequent. It is possible that in perception we may meet with a rule of relation which runs thus: that a certain appearance is constantly followed by another, though not conversely; and this is a case for me to use the hypothetical judgment and say, for instance, that if the sun shines long enough upon a body it grows warm. Here there is indeed as yet no necessity of connection or concept of cause. But I proceed and say that, if this proposition, which is merely a subjective connection of perceptions, is to be a proposition of experience, it must be seen as necessary and universally valid. Such a proposition would be that the sun is by its light the cause of heat. The empirical rule is now considered as a law, and not as valid merely of appearances but valid of them for the purposes of a possible experience which requires universal and hence necessarily valid rules. I therefore easily comprehend the concept of cause as a concept necessarily belonging to the mere form of experience, and its possibility as that of a synthetical union of perceptions in consciousness in general; but I do not at all comprehend the possibility of a thing in general as a cause, because the concept of cause denotes a condition not at all belonging to things but only to experience. For experience can be nothing but objectively valid knowledge of appearances and their succession, so far as the earlier can be conjoined with the later according to the rule of hypothetical judgments.

Section 30

Hence even if the pure concepts of the understanding are thought to go beyond objects of experience to things in themselves (noumena), they have no meaning whatever. They serve, as it were, only to spell out appearances that we may be able to read them as experience. The principles which arise 313 from their reference to the sensible world serve our understanding only for empirical use. Beyond this they are arbitrary combinations without objective reality, and we can neither know their possibility a priori nor verify — nor even render intelligible by examples — their reference to objects; because examples can only be borrowed from some possible experience, and consequently the objects of these concepts can be found nowhere but in a possible experience.

This complete solution of Hume's problem (though unexpected by its originator) preserves for the pure concepts of the understanding their a priori origin and for the universal laws of nature their validity as laws of the understanding, yet in such a way as to limit their use to experience, because their possibility depends solely on the relation of the understanding to experience, but with a completely reversed mode of connection which never occurred to Hume — they do not derive from experience, but experience derives from them.

This is, therefore, the result of all our foregoing inquiries: *All synthetical principles a priori are nothing more than principles of possible experience.* They can never be related to things in themselves, but only to appearances as objects of experience. And hence pure mathematics as well as pure science of nature can never refer to anything more than appearances, and can only represent either that which makes experience in general possible, or else that which, as it is derived from these principles, must always be capable of being represented in some possible experience.

Section 31

And thus we have at last something definite on which to stand in all metaphysical enterprises, which have hitherto, boldly enough but blindly, attempted everything without discrimination. That the goal of their exertions should be so near struck neither the dogmatic thinkers or those who, confident in their supposed sound common sense, started with concepts and principles of pure reason (which though legitimate and natural were destined for mere empirical use) in quest of insights to which they neither knew nor could know any definite bounds, because they had never reflected nor were able to reflect on the nature or even the possibility of such a pure 314 understanding.

Many a naturalist of pure reason (by which I mean the man who believes he can decide in matters of metaphysics without any science) may pretend that, long ago, by the prophetic spirit of his sound sense, he not only suspected but knew and comprehended what is here propounded with so much ado, or, if he likes, with prolix and pedantic pomp: "that with all our reason we can never reach beyond the field of experience." But when he is questioned about his rational principles individually, he must grant that there are many of them which he has not taken from experience and which are therefore independent of it and valid a priori. How then, and on what grounds, will he restrain both himself and the dogmatist, who makes use of these concepts and principles beyond all possible experience because they are recognized to be independent of it? And even he, this adept in sound sense, in spite of his assumed and cheaply acquired wisdom, is not exempt from wandering inadvertently beyond objects of experience into the field of chimeras. He is often deeply enough involved in them; though, in announcing everything as mere probability, rational conjecture, or analogy, he gives by his popular language a color to his groundless pretensions.

Section 32

Since the oldest days of philosophy, inquirers into pure reason have conceived, besides the things of sense or appearances (phenomena) which make up the sensible world, certain beings of the understanding (noumena) which should constitute an intelligible world. And as appearances and illusion were by those men identified (a thing which we may well excuse in an undeveloped epoch), actuality was conceded only to the beings of the understanding.

Rightly considering objects of sense as mere appearances, we confess thereby that they are based upon a thing in itself, though we do not know this thing as it is in itself but only its appearances, namely, the way in which our senses are affected by this unknown something. The understanding, therefore, in assuming appearances, grants the existence of things in themselves also; and to this extent we may say that the thought of such things as are the basis of appearances, consequently of mere beings of the understanding, is not only admissable but also unavoidable.

Our critical deduction by no means excludes things of that sort (noumena), but rather limits the principles of the Transcendental Aesthetic to this, that they are not to extend to all things — as everything would then be turned into mere appearance — but are to hold good only of objects of possible experience. Beings of the understanding are hereby granted, but with the inculcation of this rule which admits of no exception: that we neither know nor can know anything at all definite of these pure beings of the understanding because our pure concepts of the understanding as well as our pure intuitions extend to nothing but objects of possible experience, consequently to mere things of sense; and as soon as we leave this sphere, these concepts retain no meaning whatsoever.

Section 33

There is indeed something seductive in our pure concepts of the understanding which tempts us to a transcendent use, a use which goes beyond all possible experience. Not only are our concepts of substance, power, action, reality, and others quite independent of experience, containing nothing of sense appearance and so apparently applicable to things in themselves (noumena), but, what strengthens this conjecture, they contain a necessity of determination in themselves, which experience never attains. The concept of cause implies a rule according to which one state follows another necessarily; but experience can show us only that one state of things often or, at most, commonly follows another, and therefore affords neither strict universality nor necessity.

Hence the concepts of the understanding seem to have a deeper meaning and import than can be exhausted by their merely empirical use, and so the understanding inadvertently adds for itself to the house of experience a much 316 more extensive wing, which it fills with nothing but beings of thought, without ever observing that it has transgressed with its otherwise legitimate concepts the bounds of their use.

Section 34

Two important and even indispensable, though very dry, investigations therefore were required in the *Critique of Pure Reason* [namely, the chapters on "The Schematism of the Pure Concepts of the Understanding" and "On the Ground of the Distinction of all Objects as Phenomena and Noumena"]. In the former it is shown that the senses furnish not the pure concepts of the understanding *in concreto,* but only the schema for their use, and that the object conformable to the schema occurs only in experience as the product of the understanding from materials of the sensibility. In the latter it is shown that, although our pure concepts of the understanding and our principles are independent of experience, and despite the apparently greater sphere of their use, still nothing whatever can be thought by them beyond the field of experience, because they can do nothing but determine merely the logical form of the judgment relatively to given intuitions. But as there is no intuition at all beyond the field of sensibility, these pure concepts, as they cannot possibly be exhibited *in concreto,* are void of all meaning; consequently all these noumena, together with their complex, the intelligible world,* are

---

*We speak of the "intelligible world", not (as the usual expression is) the "intellectual world". For cognitions are intellectual through the understanding and refer to our world of sense also; but objects, in so far as they can be represented merely by the understanding, and to which none of our sensible intuitions can refer, are termed "intelligible". But as some possible intuition must correspond to every object, we would have to assume an understanding that intuits things immediately; but of such we have not the least concept, nor have we any concept of the beings of the understanding to which it should be applied.

nothing but representations of a problem, of which the object is in itself possible but of which the solution, because of the nature of our understanding, is totally impossible. For our understanding is not a faculty of intuition, but of the connection of given intuitions in one experience. Experience must therefore contain all the objects for our concepts; beyond it no concepts have 317   any significance, as there is no intuition which might offer them a foundation.

Section 35

The imagination may perhaps be forgiven for occasional vagaries and for not keeping carefully within the limits of experience, since it gains life and vigor by such flights and since it is always easier to moderate its boldness than to stimulate its languor. But the understanding which ought to *think* can never be forgiven for indulging in vagaries; for we depend upon it alone for assistance to set bounds, when necessary, to the vagaries of the imagination.

But the understanding begins its aberrations very innocently and modestly. It first brings to light the elementary cognitions which inhere in it prior to all experience, but which yet must always have their application in experience. It gradually drops these limits — and what is there to prevent it, as it has quite freely derived its principles from itself? It then proceeds first to newly imagined powers in nature, then to beings outside nature — in short, to a world for whose construction the materials cannot be wanting because fertile fiction offers them abundantly, and though not confirmed it is never refuted by experience. This is the reason that young thinkers are so partial to metaphysics constructed in a truly dogmatic manner, and often sacrifice to it their time and talents which might be better employed otherwise.

But there is no use in trying to moderate these fruitless endeavors of pure reason by all manner of cautions about the difficulties of solving questions so occult, by complaints of the limits of our reason, and by degrading our assertions into mere conjectures. For if their impossibility is not distinctly shown, and reason's knowledge of itself does not become a true science in which the field of its right use is distinguished, so to say, with geometrical certainty from that of its worthless and idle employment, these fruitless efforts will never be wholly abandoned.

Section 36

How is nature itself possible? This question — the highest that transcenden-318   tal philosophy can ever reach and to which, as its boundary and completion it must proceed — really contains two questions.

First: How is nature in the material sense, that is, as to intuition, or considered as the totality of appearances, possible; how are space, time, and that which fills both — the object of sensation — possible at all? The answer is: by means of the constitution of our sensibility, according to which it is in its own way affected by objects which are in themselves unknown to it and totally different from those appearances. This answer is given in the *Critique* itself in the Transcendental Aesthetic, and in the *Prolegomena* by the solution to the first main problem.

Second: How is nature possible in the formal sense, as the totality of the rules under which all appearances must come in order to be thought as connected in experience? The answer must be this: it is possible only by means of the constitution of our understanding, according to which all the representations of sensibility are necessarily referred to a consciousness and by which the peculiar way in which we think (namely, by rules) and have experience also is possible; but this must be clearly distinguished from an insight into the objects themselves. This answer is given in the *Critique* in the Transcendental Logic and in the *Prolegomena* in the course of the solution of the second main problem.

But how can there be this peculiar property of our sensibility or understanding and of the necessary apperception which lies at the basis of the understanding and all thought? This question cannot be further resolved and answered, because it is of them that we are in need for all our answers and for all our thinking about objects.

There are many laws of nature which we can know only by experience; but conformity to law in the connection of appearances, that is, in nature in general, we cannot discover by any experience because experience itself requires laws which are a priori the ground of its possibility.

319

The possibility of experience in general is therefore at the same time the universal law of nature, and the principles of experience are themselves the very laws of nature. For we know nature only as the totality of appearances, that is, of representations in us; and hence we can derive the laws of their connection only from the principles of their connection in us, that is, from the conditions of their necessary union in one consciousness which constitutes the possibility of experience.

Even the main proposition expounded throughout this section — that the universal laws of nature can be known a priori — leads naturally to the proposition that the prescription of the highest laws of nature must lie in ourselves, that is, in our understanding; and that we must not seek the universal laws of nature in nature by means of experience, but conversely must seek nature, as to its universal conformity to law, in the conditions of the possibility of experience which lie in our sensibility and understanding. For how were it otherwise possible to know these laws a priori, as they are not rules of analytical knowledge but truly synthetical extensions of it?

Such a necessary agreement of the principles of possible experience with the laws of the possibility of nature can proceed from one or two causes: either these laws are drawn from nature by means of experience, or conversely nature is derived from the laws of the possibility of experience in general and is quite the same as the strict universal conformity to law by experience. The former is self-contradictory, for the universal laws of nature can and must be known a priori (that is, independently of all experience) and can and must be the foundation of all empirical use of the understanding; the latter alternative therefore alone remains.*

320   But we must distinguish the empirical laws of nature, which always presuppose particular perceptions, from the pure or universal laws of nature, which, without being based on particular perceptions, contain merely the conditions of their necessary unity in experience. In relation to the latter, nature and possible experience are quite the same; and as the conformity to law in possible experience depends upon the necessary connection of appearances in experience (without which we cannot know any object whatsoever in the sensible world), consequently upon the original laws of the understanding, it seems at first strange but is not the less certain to say: *The understanding does not derive its laws a priori from, but prescribes them to, nature.*

Section 37

We shall illustrate this seemingly bold proposition by an example, which will show that laws which we discover in objects of sensible intuition (especially when these laws are known as necessary) are commonly held by us to be such as have been placed there by the understanding, in spite of their being similar in all points to the laws of nature which we ascribe to experience.

Section 38

If we consider the properties of the circle, by which this figure combines in itself so many apparently unrelated determinations of space in a single universal rule, we cannot avoid attributing a constitution (*Natur*) to this geometrical thing. Two straight lines, for example, which intersect each other and the circle, howsoever they may be drawn, are always divided so that the rectangle constructed with the segments of the one is equal to that constructed with the segments of the other. The question now is: Does this law lie in the circle or in the understanding? That is, does this figure, independently of the understanding, contain in itself the ground of the law, or does the understanding, having constructed the figure itself, according to its concepts (of the equality of the radii), introduce into the figure this law

321   that the chords intersect in geometrical proportion? When we follow the proofs of this law, we soon perceive that it can be derived only from the

---

*Crusius alone thought of a compromise: that a spirit, who can neither err nor deceive, implanted these laws in us originally. But since false principles often intrude themselves, as indeed the very system of this man shows in not a few instances, we are involved in difficulties as to the use of such a principle in the absence of sure criteria to distinguish the genuine origin from the spurious, since we can never know certainly what the spirit of truth or the father of lies may have instilled in us.

condition on which the understanding founds the construction of this figure, namely the concept of the equality of the radii. But if we enlarge this concept to pursue further the unity of various properties of geometrical figures under common laws and consider the circle as a conic section, which of course is subject to the same fundamental conditions of construction as other conic sections, we shall find that all the chords which intersect within the ellipse, parabola, and hyperbola always intersect so that the rectangles of their segments are not indeed equal but always bear a constant ratio to one another. If we proceed still farther to the fundamental teachings of physical astronomy, we find a physical law of reciprocal attraction applicable to all material nature, the rule of which is that it decreases inversely as the square of the distance from each attracting point, that is, as the spherical surfaces increase over which this force spreads. This law seems to be necessarily inherent in the very nature of things, and hence is usually propounded as knowable a priori. Simple as the sources for this law are, resting merely upon the relation of spherical surfaces of different radii, its consequences are so rich with regard to the variety and simplicity of their agreement that not only are all possible orbits of the celestial bodies conic sections, but such a relation of these orbits to one another results that no other law of attraction than that of the inverse square of the distance can be imagined as fit for a cosmical system.

Here accordingly is nature, which rests upon laws that the understanding knows a priori and chiefly from the universal principles of the determination of space. Now I ask: Do the laws of nature lie in space, and does the understanding learn them by merely endeavoring to find out the enormous wealth of meaning that lies in space; or do they inhere in the understanding and in the way by which it determines space according to the conditions of the synthetical unity in which its concepts are all centered?

Space is something so uniform and so indeterminate in all its particular properties that we should certainly not seek a store of laws of nature from it, whereas that which determines space to assume the form of a circle or the figures of a cone and a sphere is the understanding, so far as it contains the 322 ground of the unity of their constructions.

The mere universal form of intuition, called space, must therefore be the substratum of all intuitions referrable to particular objects; and in it, of course, lies the condition of the possibility and of the variety of these intuitions. But the unity of the objects is entirely determined by the understanding and on conditions which lie in its own nature; and thus the understanding is the origin of the universal order of nature, in that it comprehends all appearances under its own laws and thereby produces, in an a priori manner, the form of the experience, by means of which whatever is to be known only by experience is necessarily subjected to its laws. For we are not concerned with the nature of things in themselves, which is independent of the conditions both of our sensibility and of our understanding, but with nature as an object of possible experience. The understanding, since it makes experience possible, hereby insists that the sensible world is either not an object of experience at all, or that it is a [system of] nature.[11]

THIRD PART OF THE MAIN TRANSCENDENTAL PROBLEM
HOW IS METAPHYSICS IN GENERAL POSSIBLE?

Section 40.

327   Pure mathematics and the pure science of nature had, for their own safety and certainty, no need for such a deduction as we have made of both. For the former rests upon its own evidence, and the latter (though sprung from pure sources of the understanding) rests upon experience and thorough confirmation by it. The pure science of nature cannot altogether refuse and dispense with the testimony of experience, because with all its certainty it can never, as philosophy, rival mathematics. Both sciences therefore, stood in need of this inquiry not for themselves but for the sake of another science: metaphysics.

Metaphysics has to do not only with concepts of nature, which always find application in experience, but also with pure rational concepts, which can never be given in any possible experience whatever. Consequently it deals with concepts whose objective reality (namely that they are not mere chimeras) and with assertions whose truth or falsity cannot be discovered or confirmed by any experience. This part of metaphysics, however, is precisely what constitutes its essential end, to which the rest is only means, and thus this science is in need of a deduction for its own sake. The third question now proposed relates therefore as it were to the root and peculiarity of metaphysics, that is, the occupation of reason merely with itself and the supposed knowledge of objects arising directly from this brooding over its own concepts, without requiring or indeed being able to reach that knowledge through experience.*

328   Without solving this problem, reason can never satisfy itself. The empirical use to which reason limits the pure understanding does not fully satisfy the proper calling of reason. Every single experience is only a part of the whole sphere of its domain, but the absolute totality of all possible experience is itself not experience. Yet it is a necessary problem for reason, the mere representation of which requires concepts quite different from the pure concepts of the understanding, whose use is only *immanent,* or refers to experience, so far as it can be given. But since the concepts of reason aim at

---

[11] Section 39, "Of the System of the Categories" omitted.

*If we can say that a science is actual, at least in the mind [*Idee*] of all men, as soon as it appears that the problems which lead to it are proposed to everybody by the nature of human reason, and that therefore many (though faulty) endeavors are unavoidably made in its behalf, then we are bound to say that metaphysics is subjectively (and indeed necessarily) actual, and therefore, we justly ask, how is it (objectively) possible?

the completeness, that is, the collective unity of all possible experience, they thereby transcend every given experience, and thus become *transcendent*.

As the understanding is in need of categories for experience, reason contains in itself the source of Ideas,[12] by which I mean necessary concepts whose objects cannot be given in any experience. Ideas are inherent in the nature of reason, as the categories are in that of the understanding. While categories carry with them an illusion likely to mislead, the illusion of the Ideas is inevitable though it certainly can be kept from misleading us.

Since all illusion consists in holding the subjective grounds of our judgments to be objective, a self-knowledge of pure reason in its transcendent (presumptuous) use is the sole preservative from the aberrations into which reason falls when it mistakes its calling and transcendently ascribes to the object that which concerns only its own subject and its guidance in all immanent use.

Section 41

The distinction of Ideas (pure concepts of reason) from categories (pure concepts of the understanding) as cognitions of quite distinct species, origin, and use is so important a point in founding a science which is to contain the system of all these a priori cognitions that, without this distinction, metaphysics is absolutely impossible or is at best a random, bungling attempt to build a 329 castle in the air without a knowledge of the materials or of their fitness for this or any purpose. Had the *Critique of Pure Reason* done nothing but first point out this distinction, it would thereby have contributed more to clear up our conception of, and to guide our inquiry into, the field of metaphysics than all the vain efforts which had hitherto been made to satisfy the transcendent problems of pure reason, but which had never surmised that we were in quite another field than that of the understanding, and which therefore classed concepts of the understanding and those of reason together as if they were the same kind.

Section 42

All pure cognitions of the understanding have this feature, that their concepts present themselves in experience, and their principle can be confirmed by it; whereas the transcendent cognitions of reason cannot, as Ideas, either appear in experience or, as propositions, ever be confirmed or refuted by it. Hence whatever errors may slip in unawares can be discovered only by pure reason itself—a discovery of much difficulty, because this very reason naturally becomes dialectical by means of its Ideas; and this unavoidable illusion cannot be limited by any objective and dogmatic researches into

[12] On Kant's uses of the word *Idee*, see *Critique of Pure Reason*, above, p. 127 n.

things, but only by a subjective investigation of reason itself as a source of Ideas.

Section 43

In the *Critique of Pure Reason* it was always my greatest care to endeavor, not only to carefully distinguish the several species of knowledge, but to derive from their common source concepts belonging to each one of them. I did this in order that, by knowing whence they originated, I might with assurance determine their use and might also have the unanticipated but invaluable advantage of knowing, according to certain principles, the com-
330   pleteness of my enumeration, classification, and specification of concepts a priori. Without this, metaphysics is a mere rhapsody, in which no one knows whether he has enough or whether and where something is still wanting. We can indeed have this advantage only in pure philosophy, but of pure philosophy it constitutes the very essence.

As I had found the origin of the categories in the four logical forms of all judgments of the understanding, it was quite natural to seek the origin of the Ideas in the three kinds of syllogisms. For as soon as these pure concepts of reason (the transcendental Ideas) are given, they could hardly, unless they be held innate, be found anywhere else than in the same activity of reason which, so far as it regards form, constitutes the logical element of syllogisms; but, so far as this activity presents judgments of the understanding as determined with respect to one or another [syllogistic] form a priori, it constitutes the transcendental concepts of pure reason.

The formal distinction of syllogisms entails their division into categorical, hypothetical, and disjunctive. The concepts of reason founded on them contain, therefore, first, the Idea of the complete subject (the substantial); second, the Idea of the complete series of conditions; third, the determination of all concepts in the Idea of a complete complex of that which is possible.* The first Idea is psychological, the second cosmological, the third theological; and as all three give occasion to dialectic, each in its own way, the division of the whole Dialectic of Pure Reason into its Paralogism, its Antinomy, and its Ideal was arranged accordingly. Through this deduction we may feel assured that all the claims of pure reason are completely represented and that none can be wanting, because the faculty of reason itself, whence they all take their origin, is thereby completely surveyed.

---

*In disjunctive judgments, we consider all possibility as divided in respect to a particular concept. By the ontological principle of the universal determination of a thing in general, I understand the principle that either the one or the other of all possible contradictory predicates must be assigned to any object. This is, at the same time, the principle of all disjunctive judgments, constituting the foundation of a complete whole of possibility, and in it the possibility of every object in general is considered as determined. This may serve as a slight explanation of the above propositions: that the activity of reason in disjunctive syllogisms is formally the same as that by which it fashions the Idea of a complete whole of all reality, containing in itself that which is positive in all pairs of contradictory predicates.

Section 44

In these general considerations it is remarkable that the Ideas of reason, unlike the categories, are of no service to the use of our understanding in experience, but quite dispensable and become even an impediment to the maxims of a rational knowledge of nature. Yet in another aspect still to be determined, they are necessary. Whether the soul is or is not a simple substance is of no consequence to us in the explanation of its appearances, for we cannot render the concept of a simple being sensible and thus concretely intelligible by any possible experience. The concept is therefore quite void as regards all hoped-for insight into the cause of appearances and cannot at all serve as a principle of explanation of that which inner and outer experience supplies. Similarly the cosmological Ideas of the beginning of the world or of its eternity (*a parte ante*) cannot be of any service to us for the explanation of any event in the world itself. And finally, according to a correct maxim of the philosophy of nature, we must refrain from explaining the design of nature as drawn from the will of a Supreme Being, because this would not be natural philosophy but a confession that we have come to the end of it. The use of these Ideas, therefore, is quite different from that of those categories by which (and by the principles built upon them) experience itself first becomes possible. But our laborious Analytic of the understanding would be superfluous if we had nothing else in view than the mere knowledge of nature as it can be given in experience; for reason does its work, both in mathematics and in the science of nature, quite safely and well without any of this subtle deduction. Therefore our critical examination of the understanding combines with the Ideas of pure reason for a purpose which lies beyond the empirical use of the understanding; but such an extended use of the understanding we have already declared to be totally inadmissable and without any object or meaning. Yet there must be a harmony between the nature of reason and that of the understanding, and the former must contribute to the perfection of the latter and cannot possibly upset it.

The answer to this question is as follows. Pure reason does not in its Ideas point to particular objects which lie beyond the field of experience, but only requires completeness of the use of the understanding in the system of experience. But this completeness can be completeness of principles only, not of intuiting and objects. In order, however, to represent the Ideas definitely, reason conceives of them after the fashion of the knowledge of an object. This knowledge is, as far as these rules are concerned, completely determined; but the object is only an Idea for the purpose of bringing the knowledge of the understanding as near as possible to the completeness indicated by that Idea.

Section 45. Prefatory Remark to the Dialectic of Pure Reason

We have shown in Sections 33 and 34 that the purity of the categories from all mixture of sensible determinations may mislead reason into extending their use beyond all experience to things in themselves; for though these categories themselves find no intuition which can give them meaning or sense *in concreto,* as mere logical functions they can represent a thing in general but by themselves alone give no determinate concept of anything. Such hyperbolical objects are distinguished by the appellation of *noumena,* or pure beings of the understanding (or better, beings of thought). Examples are substance, but conceived without permanent in time, and cause, but not acting in time. Here predicates that only serve to make the lawfulness of experience possible are applied to these concepts, and yet they are deprived of all conditions of intuition on which alone experience is possible, and so these concepts lose all significance.

There is no danger, however, of the understanding spontaneously making an excursion so wantonly beyond its own bounds into the field of mere beings of thought unless it is impelled by laws not its own. But when reason, which cannot be fully satisfied with any empirical use of the rules of the under-standing because this is always conditioned, requires a completion of the chain of conditions, the understanding is forced outside its proper sphere. And then it partly represents objects of experience in a series so extended that no experience can grasp it; partly even (with a view to completing the series) it seeks entirely beyond it for noumena, to which it can attach that 333 chain; and so, having at last escaped from the conditions of experience, it makes its stand as it were final. These then are the transcendental Ideas, which, in accord with the true but hidden ends of the natural destiny of our reason, aim not at extravagant concepts but at an unbounded extension of their empirical use, yet seduce the understanding by an unavoidable illusion to a transcendent use, which, though deceitful, cannot be restrained within the limits of experience by our making a resolve, but only by scientific instruction, and with much difficulty.

I.
THE PSYCHOLOGICAL IDEAS*

Section 46.

People have long since observed that in all substances the subject proper, that which remains after all the accidents (as predicates) are abstracted, consequently *the substantial,* remains unknown, and various complaints have been made concerning these limits of our knowledge. But it will be well to consider that the human understanding is not to be blamed for its inability to know the substance of things — that is, to determine it by itself — but rather for demanding definitely to know substance, which is only an Idea, as though it were a given object. Pure reason requires us to seek for every predicate of a

---

*See *Critique of Pure Reason,* "The Paralogisms of Pure Reason."

thing its own subject, and for this subject, which is itself necessarily nothing but a predicate, its subject, and so on indefinitely (or as far as we can reach). But it follows from this that we must not hold anything at which we can arrive to be an ultimate subject, and that the substantial itself can never be thought by our understanding, however deeply we may penetrate, even if all nature were unveiled to us. For the specific nature of our understanding consists in thinking everything discursively, that is, by concepts, and so by mere predicates to which, therefore, the absolute subject must always be wanting. Hence all the real properties by which we know bodies are mere accidents, not excepting even impenetrability, which we can only think as the effect of a   334 power of which the subject is unknown to us.

Now it appears as if we have this substance in the consciousness of ourselves (in the thinking subject), and indeed that we have it in an immediate intuition. For all the predicates of an internal sense refer to the ego as a subject, and I cannot conceive of myself as the predicate of any other subject. Hence completeness in the reference of the given concepts as predicates to a subject — not merely the Idea, but an object (the absolute subject itself) — seems to be given in experience. But this expectation is disappointed. For the ego is not a concept* but only the indication of the object of the inner sense, so far as we know it by no further predicate. Consequently it cannot itself be a predicate of any other thing, but just as little can it be a definite concept of an absolute subject; it is, as in all other cases, only the reference of the inner appearances to their unknown subject. Yet this Idea (which serves very well, as a regulative principle, to destroy totally all materialistic explanations of the internal appearances of the soul) occasions by a very natural misunderstanding a very specious argument which infers the nature of our thinking being from the supposed knowledge of the substantial element of our thinking being. This is specious so far as this supposed knowledge of it falls quite outside the scope of experience.

Section 47

But though we may call this thinking self (the soul) substance, it being the ultimate subject of thinking which cannot be further represented as the predicate of another thing, it remains quite empty and without significance if permanence — the quality which renders the concept of substances in experience fruitful — cannot be proved of it.

But permanence can never be proved of the concept of a substance as a   335 thing in itself; it is proved for the purposes of experience only. This is sufficiently shown by the first Analogy of Experience [in the *Critique of Pure Reason*], and whoever will not yield to this proof may try for himself whether

*Were the representation of the apperception (the ego) a concept, by which anything whatever could be thought, it could be used as a predicate of other things or contain predicates in itself. But it is nothing more than feeling of an existence without the least concept and is only the representation of that to which all thinking stands in relation (*relatione accidentis*).

he can succeed in proving, from the concept of a subject which does not itself exist as the predicate of another thing, that its existence is absolutely permanent and that it cannot originate or be annihilated either by itself or by any natural cause. Synthetical a priori judgments of this kind can never be proved in themselves, but only in reference to things as objects of a possible experience.

Section 48

If, therefore, from the concept of the soul as a substance we would infer its permanence, this inference is valid of it as regards possible experience only, but is not valid of the soul as a thing in itself and beyond all possible experience; consequently we can infer the permanence of the soul in life only, for the death of a man is the end of all experience which concerns the soul as an object of experience — unless the contrary be proved, which is the very question in hand. The permanence of the soul can therefore be proved only during the life of man (and no one cares to do that) but not, as we desire to prove, after death. The reason for this is that the concept of substance, so far as it is to be considered necessarily combined with the concept of permanence, can be so combined only according to the principles of possible experience, and therefore for the purposes of experience only.*

336 ## Section 49

That there is something real outside us which not only corresponds but must correspond to our outer perceptions can likewise never be proved to be a connection of things in themselves, but can well be proved for the sake of experience. This means that there is something empirical, that is, some appearance in space without us, that admits of a satisfactory proof; for we have nothing to do with other objects than those which belong to possible experience, because objects which cannot be given us in any experience are

---

*It is indeed very remarkable how carelessly metaphysicians have always passed over the principle of the permanence of substances without ever attempting a proof of it; doubtless because they found themselves abandoned by all proofs as soon as they began to deal with the concept of substance. Common sense, which felt distinctly that without this presupposition no 336 union of perceptions in experience is possible, supplied the want by a postulate. From experience itself it never could derive such a principle, partly because material things (substances) cannot be so traced in all their alterations and dissolutions that the matter can always be found undiminished, partly because the principle contains necessity, which is always the sign of an a priori principle. People then boldly applied this postulate to the concept of soul as a substance, and concluded a necessary continuance of the soul after the death of man (especially as the simplicity of this substance, which is inferred from the indivisibility of consciousness, secured it from destruction by dissolution). Had they found the genuine source of this principle — a discovery which requires deeper researches than they were ever inclined to make — they would have seen that the law of the permanence of substances arises for the purposes of experience only, and hence can hold good of things so far as they are to be known and conjoined with others in experience, but never independently of all possible experience, and consequently cannot hold good of the soul after death.

nothing for us. Empirically outside me is that which is intuited in space; and space, together with all the appearances it contains, belongs to the representations whose connection, according to laws of experience, proves their objective truth, just as the connection of the appearances of the inner sense proves the actuality of my soul as an object of the inner sense. By means of outer experience I am conscious of the actuality of bodies as external appearances in space, in the same manner as by means of inner experience I am conscious of the existence of my soul in time; but this soul is known only as an object of the inner sense by appearances that constitute an inner state of which the being in itself, which forms the basis of these appearances, is unknown. Cartesian idealism therefore does nothing but distinguish outer experience from a dream and the conformity to law (as a criterion of its truth) 337 of the former from the irregularity and false illusion of the latter. In both it presupposes space and time as conditions of the existence of objects, and it only inquires whether the objects of the outer sense which we, when awake, put in space, are as actually to be found in it as the object of the inner sense (the soul) is in time, that is, whether experience carries with it sure criteria to distinguish it from imagination. This doubt, however, may easily be disposed of, and we always dispose of it in common life by investigating the connection of appearances in space and time according to universal laws of experience. When the representation of external things thoroughly agrees with the universal laws of experience, we cannot doubt that they constitute true experience.

Since appearances are regarded as appearances only in accordance with their connection in experience, material idealism is easily refuted, and it is just as sure an experience that bodies exist outside us in space as that I myself exist according to the representation of the inner sense in time, for the concept "outside us" signifies only existence in space. However, just as the ego in the proposition "I am" means not only the object of inner intuition in time but the subject of consciousness, so also body means not only [the object of] outer intuition in space but the thing in itself which is the basis of this experience. Then the question whether bodies (as appearances of the outer sense) exist as bodies in nature apart from my thoughts may without hesitation be denied. The question whether I myself as an appearance of the inner sense (the soul, according to empirical psychology) exist apart from my faculty of representation in time is an exactly similar one and must likewise be answered in the negative. And in this manner, everything when it is reduced to its true meaning is decided and certain. The formal (which I have also called the transcendental) abolishes the material, or Cartesian, idealism. For if space be nothing but a form of my sensibility, it is as a representation in me just as actual as I myself am, and nothing but the empirical truth of the appearances in it remains for consideration. But if this is not the case, if space and the appearances in it are something existing outside us, then all the criteria of experience outside our perception can never prove the actuality of those objects outside us.

II
THE COSMOLOGICAL IDEAS*

Section 50

338   This product of pure reason in its transcendent use is its most remarkable phenomenon. It serves as a very powerful agent to rouse philosophy from its dogmatic slumber and to stimulate it to the arduous task of undertaking a critical examination of reason itself.

I term this Idea cosmological because it always takes its object only in the sensible world and does not need any other world than the one whose object is given in sense; consequently it remains in this respect in its native home, does not become transcendent, and is therefore so far not an Idea; whereas to conceive the soul as simple substance, on the contrary, means to conceive an object (the simple) which cannot be presented to the senses. Yet in spite of this, the cosmological Idea extends the connection of the conditioned with its condition (whether mathematical or dynamical) so far that experience can never keep up with it. It is therefore with regard to this point always an Idea, whose object can never be adequately given in experience.

Section 51

In the first place, the use of a system of categories becomes here so obvious and unmistakable that, even if there were not several other proofs of it, this alone would sufficiently prove it indispensable in the system of pure reason. There are only four such transcendent Ideas, as many as there are classes of categories; in each of which they refer only to the absolute completeness of the series of the conditions for a given condition. In accordance with these cosmological Ideas, there are only four kinds of dialectical assertions of pure reason itself. This antinomy, not arbitrarily invented but founded in the spurious principles of pure reason, a contradictory assertion stands opposed. As all metaphysical art of the most subtle distinction cannot prevent this opposition, it compels the philosopher to recur to the first sources of pure 339 reason itself. This antinomy, not arbitrarily invented but founded in the nature of human reason, hence unavoidable and never ceasing, contains the four following theses together with their antitheses:

1
Thesis: The world has, as to time and space, a beginning (a boundary).
Antithesis: The world is, as to time and space, infinite.

2
Thesis: Everything in the world consists of [elements that are] simple.
Antithesis: There is nothing simple, but everything is composite.

---

*Cf. *Critique of Pure Reason*, "The Antinomy of Pure Reason" [pp.127–130].

3

Thesis: There are in the world causes through freedom.
Antithesis: There is no freedom, but all is nature.

4

Thesis: In the series of world-causes there is some necessary being.
Antithesis: There is nothing necessary in this series, but in it all is contingent.

Section 52 *a*

Here is the most singular phenomenon of human reason, no other instance of which can be shown in any other use of reason. If, as is commonly done, we think of the appearances of the sensible world as things in themselves, if we assume the principles of their combination as principles universally valid of things in themselves and not merely of experience, as is usually, nay without our *Critique* unavoidably, done, there arises an unexpected conflict which can 340 never be removed in the common dogmatic way; because the thesis as well as the antithesis can be shown by equally clear, evident, and irresistible proofs —for I pledge myself as to the correctness of these proofs—and reason therefore perceives that it is divided against itself, a state at which the skeptic rejoices, but which must make the critical philosopher pause and feel ill at ease.

Section 52 *b*

We may blunder in various ways in metaphysics without fear of being detected in falsehood. If we but avoid self-contradiction, which in synthetical though fictitious propositions is quite possible, then whenever the concepts which we connect are mere Ideas that cannot, in their whole content, be given in experience, we cannot be refuted by experience. For how can we make out by experience whether the world exists from eternity or had a beginning, whether matter is infinitely divisible or consists of simple parts? Such concepts cannot be given in any experience however extensive, and consequently the falsehood of either the affirmative or the negative proposition cannot be discovered by the touchstone of experience.

The only possible case in which reason could unintentionally reveal its secret dialectic, falsely announced as its dogmatics, would be when it grounded an assertion upon a universally admitted principle and deduced, by a most accurate inference, the exact opposite of another assertion which is equally granted. This is what actually occurs here with regard to four natural Ideas of reason, whence four assertions on the one side and as many counter-assertions on the other arise, each consistently following from universally acknowledged principles. Thus by the use of these principles they reveal the dialectical illusion of pure reason, which would otherwise remain forever concealed.

It is therefore a decisive experiment, which must necessarily expose any
341 error lying hidden in the assumptions of reason.* Contradictory propositions
cannot both be false unless the concept on which each is founded is self-contradictory; for example, the propositions "A square circle is round" and "A
square circle is not round" are both false. For, as to the former, it is false that
the circle is round because it is quadrangular; and it is likewise false that it is
not round, that is, angular, because it is a circle. For the logical criterion of the
impossibility of a concept consists in this, that if we presuppose it, two
contradictory propositions both become false; consequently, as no medium
between them is conceivable, nothing at all is thought by that concept.

Section 52 c

The first two antinomies, which I call mathematical because they are
concerned with the addition or division of the homogeneous, are founded on
such a contradictory concept; and from this I explain how it happens that both
the thesis and the antithesis of the two are false.

When I speak of objects in space and in time, I do not speak of things in
themselves, of which I know nothing, but of things in appearance, that is, I
speak of experience, the particular way of knowing objects which is alone
afforded to man. I must not say of what I think in time or in space that, in itself
and independently of these my thoughts, it exists in time and in space, for in
that case I should contradict myself, because space and time, together with
the appearances in them, are nothing existing in themselves and outside my
representations, but are themselves only modes of representation, and it is
palpably contradictory to say that a mere mode of representation exists
342 without our representations. Objects of the senses therefore exist only in
experience, whereas to give them a self-subsisting existence apart from, or
prior to, experience is merely to think that there is experience without
experience, or before it.

Now if I enquire into the spatial and temporal magnitude of the world, it is
equally impossible, as regards both my concepts, to declare it infinite or to
declare it finite. For neither its finitude nor its infinitude can be contained in
experience, because experience either of an infinite space or of an infinite
elapsed time, or again, of the boundary of the world by an empty space or by
an antecedent empty time, is impossible; these are mere Ideas. The magnitude of the world, decided either way, would therefore have to exist in the

---

*I therefore would be pleased to have the critical reader devote to this antinomy of pure
reason his chief attention, because nature itself seems to have established it with a view to
stagger reason in its daring pretensions and to force it to self-examination. For every proof which
I have given of both thesis and antithesis I undertake to be responsible, and thereby to show the
certainty of the inevitable antinomy of reason. When the reader is brought by this curious
phenomenon to fall back upon the proof of the presumption upon which it rests, he will feel
himself obliged to investigate more thoroughly with me the ultimate foundation of all knowledge by pure reason.

world itself apart from all experience. But this contradicts the concept of a world of sense, which is merely a complex of appearance whose existence and connection occur only in representation, that is, in experience; for the world is not an object in itself; it is nothing except a mode of representation. Hence it follows that, as the concept of an absolutely existing world of sense is self-contradictory, a solution of the problem concerning its magnitude is always false, whether it is affirmative or negative.

The same holds of the second antinomy, which relates to the division of appearances. For these are mere representations, and the parts exist merely in representation; consequently the parts exist only in the division — that is, in a possible experience in which they are given — and the division reaches only as far as possible experience reaches. To assume that an appearance, for example, that of body, contains in itself before all experience all the parts which any possible experience can ever reach is to impute to a mere appearance, which can exist only in experience, an existence prior to experience. In other words, it would mean that mere representations exist before they are found in our faculty of representation. Such as assertion is self-contradictory, as is also every solution of the misunderstood problem, whether one maintains that bodies in themselves consist of infinitely many parts or of a finite number of simple parts.

Section 53

In the first (the mathematical) class of antinomies the falsehood of the presupposition consists in representing in one concept something self-contradictory as if it were consistent (that is, it represents an appearance as a thing in itself). But in the second (dynamical) class of antinomies, the falsehood of the presupposition consists in representing as contradictory what is in fact consistent. Whereas in the former case the opposed assertions were both false, in this case, on the other hand, where the presuppositions are opposed to one another by mere misunderstanding, they may both be true. 343

Any mathematical connection necessarily presupposes homogeneity of what is connected in the concept of magnitude, while the dynamical connection by no means requires this. When we have to deal with extensive magnitudes all the parts must be homogeneous with one another and with the whole, whereas in the connection of cause and effect homogeneity may be found, but is not necessary, for the concept of causality (by means of which something is posited through something else quite different from it) does not in the least require homogeneity.

If the objects of the world of sense are taken for things in themselves and the laws of nature for laws of things in themselves, the contradiction would be just as unavoidable; for the same predicate would be at once affirmed and denied of the same kind of object in the same sense. But if natural necessity belongs only to appearances and freedom only to things in themselves, no contradiction arises if we at the same time assume or admit both kinds of causality, however difficult or impossible it may be to make the latter kind of causality conceivable.

In appearance every effect is an event or something that happens in time; it must, according to the universal law of nature, be preceded by a determination of the causal act of its cause — this determination being a state of the cause — which it follows according to a constant law. But this determination of the cause to a causal act must likewise be something that takes place or happens; the cause must have begun to act, otherwise no succession between it and the effect could be conceived, and the effect, as well as the causal act of the cause, would have always existed. Therefore the determination of the cause to act must also have originated among appearances, and must consequently, like its effect, be an event which must in turn have its cause, and so on; hence natural necessity must be the condition on which efficient causes are determined. But if freedom is to be a property of certain causes of appearances, it must, as regards these appearances, which are events, be a faculty of starting them spontaneously. That is, it would not require that the causal act of the cause should itself begin [in time] and hence it would not require any other ground to determine it to start. But then the cause in relation to its causal act could not rank under time-determinations of its state; that is, it could not be an appearance, but would have to be considered a thing in itself, while only its effects would be appearance.* If without contradiction we can think of the beings of the understanding as exercising such an influence on appearances, then natural necessity will attach to all conditions of cause and effect in the sensible world; while on the other hand freedom can be granted to the cause which is itself not an appearance but the foundation of appearance. Nature and freedom therefore can without contradiction be attributed to the very same thing, but in different relations — on one side as an appearance, on the other as a thing in itself.

We have in us a faculty which not which only stands in connection with its subjective determining grounds [motives] which are natural causes of its action and is so far the faculty of the being that itself belongs to appearances, but is also related to objective grounds which are only Ideas so far as they can

*The Idea of freedom occurs only in the relation of the intellectual, as cause, to the appearance, as effect. Hence we cannot attribute freedom to matter in regard to the incessant action by which it fills its space, though this action takes place from an internal principle. We can likewise find no concept of freedom suitable to purely rational beings, for instance, to God, so far as His action is immanent. For His action, though independent of external determining causes, is determined in His eternal reason, that is, in the divine nature. It is only if something is to start by an action, so that the effect occurs in the sequence of time or in the world of sense (for example, the beginning of the world), that we can pose the question whether the causal act of the cause must in its turn have been started or whether the cause can originate an effect without its causal act itself having a beginning. In the former case, the concept of this activity is a concept of natural necessity; in the latter, that of freedom. From this the reader will see that as I explained freedom to be the power of starting an event spontaneously, I have exactly hit the concept which is the problem of metaphysics.

determine this faculty. This connection is expressed by the word *ought.* This faculty is called reason, and, so far as we consider a being (man) entirely according to this objectively determinable reason, he cannot be considered as a being of sense; this property is a property of a thing in itself, a property whose possibility we cannot comprehend. I mean we cannot comprehend how the *ought* should determine (even if it never has determined) its activity and become the cause of actions whose effect is an appearance in the sensible world. Yet the causality of reason would be freedom with regard to the effects in the sensible world, so far as we can consider objective grounds, which are themselves Ideas, as their determinants. For its action in that case would not depend upon subjective conditions, consequently not upon conditions of time, and of course not upon the law of nature which serves to determine the temporal conditions, because grounds of reason give the rule universally to actions, according to principles and without influence of the circumstances of time or place.

What I adduce here is meant merely as an example to make the state of affairs understandable and is not essential to our problem; for the problem must be decided from concepts alone, independently of the properties [of things] which we find in the actual world.

Now I may say without contradiction that all the actions of rational beings (so far as they are appearances met with in any experience) are subject to the necessity of nature, but the very same actions as regards merely the rational subject and its faculty of acting according to reason alone are free. For what is required for the necessity of nature? Nothing more than the determinability of every event in the world of sense according to unchanging laws, that is, a reference to a cause in the [world of] appearance; in such determination, the underlying thing in itself and its causality remain unknown. But, I say, the law of nature remains [in force] regardless of whether the rational being is the cause of the effects in the sensible world by its reason (that is, through freedom) or whether it does not determine them on grounds of reason. For if the former is the case, the action is performed according to maxims, the effect of which as appearance is always conformable to constant laws; if the latter is the case, and the action is not performed on principles of reason, the action [itself] is subjected to the empirical laws of sensibility, and in both cases the 346 effects are connected according to unchanging laws; more than this we do not require or know concerning natural necessity. But in the former case reason is the cause of these laws of nature, and is therefore free; in the latter, the effects follow according to the natural laws of sensibility alone, because reason does not influence it. But reason itself is not determined on that account by the sensibility (which is impossible), and is therefore free in this case too. Freedom is therefore no hindrance to natural law in appearances, nor does natural law abrogate the freedom of the practical use of reason which is connected with things in themselves as determining grounds.

Thus practical freedom (i.e., freedom in which reason possesses causality

according to objectively determining grounds) is rescued while natural necessity is not in the least curtailed with regard to the very same effects as appearances. The same remarks will serve to explain what we had to say concerning transcendental freedom and its compatibility with natural necessity in the same subject, but not taken in the same context. For, as to this, every beginning of an action of a being from objective causes regarded as determining grounds is always a *first beginning*, though the same action in the series of appearances is only a *subordinate beginning* which must be preceded by a state of the cause which determines it and which is itself determined in the same manner by another cause immediately preceding it. Thus we are able to attribute a faculty of beginning of themselves a series of states to rational beings or to any beings so far as their causality is determined in them as things in themselves, and do so without falling into contradiction with the laws of nature. For the relation of an action to objective grounds of reason is not a time-relation, and that which determines the causality does not precede the action in time, because such determining grounds do not represent a relation of objects to sense (to causes in the [world of] appearances) but to determining causes as things in themselves, which do not stand under the conditions of time. And in this way the action, with regard to the causality of
347 reason, can be considered as a first beginning, while as appearance it can be seen as merely a subordinate beginning. We may therefore without contradiction consider it in the former aspect as free, but in the latter (as it is merely appearance) as subject to natural causality.

As to the fourth antinomy, it is solved in the same way as the conflict of reason with itself in the third. For, providing the cause *in* appearance is distinguished from the cause *of* appearance (so far as it can be thought as a thing in itself), the two propositions are perfectly reconcilable; the one, that there is nowhere in the sensible world a cause (under similar laws of causality) whose existence is absolutely necessary; the other, that this world is nevertheless connected with a necessary being as its cause (but of another kind and according to another law). The incompatibility of these propositions rests entirely upon the mistake of extending what is valid merely of appearances to things in themselves and in confusing both in one concept.[13]

348 ## Section 56. General Remark on the Transcendental Ideas

The objects which are given us by experience are in many respects incomprehensible, and many questions to which the law of nature leads us when carried beyond a certain point (though still in complete conformity to the
349 laws of nature) admit of no answer. An example is the question: Why do

---

[13] Sections 54 and 55 omitted because redundant. Section 55 is hardly more than a reference to the refutations of arguments for the existence of God in the *Critique*, pp. 136–148 above.

material things attract one another? But if we entirely quit nature or, in pursuing its combinations, exceed all possible experience, and so enter the realm of mere Ideas, we cannot then say that the object is incomprehensible and that the nature of things proposes to us insoluble problems. For we are not then concerned with nature or even with given objects, but with mere concepts which have their origin solely in our reason, and with mere beings of thought; and all problems that arise from our concepts of them must be solved, because reason can and must give a full account of its own procedure* As the psychological, cosmological, and theological Ideas are nothing but pure concepts of reason which cannot be given in any experience, the questions which reason asks us about them are put to us, not by the objects, but by the maxims of our reason for the sake of its own satisfaction. They must all be capable of satisfactory answers, which are given by showing that they are principles which bring our use of the understanding into thorough agreement, completeness, and synthetical unity, and that they thus are valid of experience only, but of experience as a whole.

Although an absolute whole of experience is impossible, the Idea of a whole of knowledge according to principles must impart to our knowledge a peculiar kind of unity, that of a system, without which it is nothing but piecework and cannot be used for proving the existence of a highest purpose (which can only be the general system of all purposes). I do not here refer 350 only to the practical use, but also to the highest purpose of the speculative use, of reason.

The transcendental Ideas therefore express the peculiar function of reason as a principle of systematic unity in the use of the understanding. Yet if we assume this unity of the mode of knowledge to pertain to the object of knowledge, if we think that which is merely *regulative* to be *constitutive,* and if we persuade ourselves that we can by means of these Ideas widen our knowledge transcendently far beyond all possible experience, though it serves only to render experience within itself as nearly complete as possible, that is, to limit its progress by nothing that cannot belong to experience — if we do this, I say — we suffer from a mere misunderstanding in judging the proper role of our reason and its principles, and a dialectic arises which both confuses the empirical use of reason and sets reason at variance with itself.

---

*Herr Platner, in his *Aphorismen,* acutely says (Sections 728, 729), "If reason be a criterion, no concept which is incomprehensible to human reason can be possible. Incomprehensibility has place in what is actual only. Here incomprehensibility arises from the insufficiency of acquired ideas." It sounds paradoxical, but is otherwise not strange to say that in nature there is much that is incomprehensible (for example the faculty of reproduction); but if we mount still higher and go even beyond nature, everything again becomes comprehensible. For we then quit entirely the objects which can be given us and occupy ourselves exclusively with Ideas, in which occupation we can easily comprehend the law that reason prescribes by them to the understanding for its use in experience, because the law is reason's own product.

CONCLUSION

Section 57. On the Determination of the Bounds of Pure Reason

Having advanced the clearest proofs, it would be absurd for us to hope that we can know more of any object than belongs to the possible experience of it or lay claim to the least knowledge of anything not assumed to be an object of possible experience, which would determine it according to the constitution it has in itself. For how could we determine anything in this way, since time, space, and all the concepts of the understanding and still more all the concepts formed by empirical intuition (perception) in the physical world have and can have no other use than to make experience possible? For if this condition is omitted from the pure concepts of the understanding, they do not determine any object and have no meaning whatever.

But it would be, on the other hand, a still greater absurdity if we conceded no things in themselves, or set up our experience as the only possible way of 351 knowing things, our intuition of them in space and in time for the only possible intuition, and our discursive understanding for the archetype of every possible understanding; for this would be to wish to consider the principles of the possibility of experience as universal conditions of things in themselves.

Our principles, which limit the use of reason to possible experience, might in this way become transcendent and the limits of our reason be set up as limits of the possibility of things in themselves (as Hume's *Dialogues* may illustrate) if a careful critique did not guard the bounds of our reason with respect to its empirical use and set a term to its pretensions. Skepticism originally arose from metaphysics and its anarchic dialectic. At first, merely to favor the empirical use of reason, it might denounce everything that transcends this use as worthless and deceitful; but by and by, when it was perceived that the very same principles that are used in experience led insensibly and apparently with the same right still farther than experience extends, one began to doubt even the principles of experience. But there is no danger, for common sense will doubtless always assert its rights. A certain confusion, however, arose in science, which cannot determine how far reason is to be trusted, and why only so far and no farther; and this confusion can be cleared up and all future relapses obviated only by a formal determination, on principle, of the boundary of the use of our reason.

We cannot indeed, beyond all possible experience, form a definite concept of what things in themselves may be. Yet we are not at liberty to abstain entirely from inquiring into them; for experience never fully satisfies reason, but in answering our questions refers us farther and farther back and leaves us dissatisfied with their incomplete solution. This everyone may gather from the dialectic of pure reason, which therefore has its good subjective grounds. Having acquired, as regards the nature of our soul, a clear conception of the subject, and having come to the conviction that its manifestations cannot be explained materialistically, who can refrain from asking what the soul really 352 is, and, if no concept of experience suffices for the purpose, from accounting for it by a concept of reason (that of a simple immaterial being) even though we cannot by any means prove its objective reality? Who can satisfy himself with mere empirical knowledge in all the cosmological questions of the duration and magnitude of the world, of freedom or natural necessity, since every answer given on principles of experience begets a fresh question, which likewise requires its answer and thereby clearly shows the insufficiency of all physical modes of explanation to satisfy reason? Finally, who does not see in the thoroughgoing contingency and dependence of all his thoughts and assumptions on principles of experience the impossibility of stopping there? And who does not feel himself compelled, notwithstanding all interdictions against losing himself in transcendent Ideas, to seek rest and contentment, beyond all concepts which he can vindicate by experience, in the concept of a Being of which the Idea is such that its possibility cannot be understood, but at the same time cannot be refuted, because it relates to a mere being of the understanding, but without which reason must needs remain forever dissatisfied?

Bounds (in extended beings) always presuppose a space existing outside a certain definite place and inclosing it; limits do not require this, but are only negations which affect a quantity so far as it is not absolutely completed. But our reason, as it were, sees in its surroundings a space for knowledge of things in themselves, though we can never have definite concepts of them and are limited to appearances only.

As long as the knowledge of reason is homogeneous, definite bounds to it are inconceivable. In mathematics and in natural philosophy, human reason admits of limits but not of bounds. That is, it admits that something lies without it at which it can never arrive, but not that it will at any point find completion in its internal progress. The enlarging of our insights in mathematics and the possibility of new discoveries are infinite; and the same is the case with the discovery of new properties of nature, of new powers and laws, by continued experience and its rational combination. But nonetheless we need to acknowledge limits here, for mathematics refers to appearances only, and what cannot be an object of sensible intuition, such as the concepts of 353 metaphysics and of morals, lies entirely outside its sphere; it can never lead to them, but neither does it require them. There is, therefore, no continual progress and approximation towards these sciences, and there is not, as it were, any point or line of contact. Natural science will never reveal to us the internal constitution of things which, though not appearance, can serve as the ultimate ground for explaining appearances. Nor does natural science require this for its physical explanations. Nay, even if such grounds should be offered from other sources (for instance, through the influence of immaterial beings), they must be rejected and not used in the course of its explanations. For these explanations must be grounded only upon that which as an object of sense can belong to experience, and which can be brought into connection with our actual perceptions and empirical laws.

But metaphysics leads us towards bounds in the dialectical attempts of pure reason (not undertaken arbitrarily and wantonly, but stimulated by the nature of reason itself). And the transcendent Ideas, as they do not admit of evasion but are never capable of realization, serve to point out to us actually not only the bounds of the pure use of reason, but also the way to determine these bounds. Such is the end and the use of this natural predisposition of our reason, which has brought forth metaphysics as its favorite child, whose generation, like every other in the world, is not to be ascribed to blind chance, but to an original germ, wisely organized for great ends. For metaphysics, in its fundamental features, perhaps more than any other science, is placed in us by nature itself and cannot be considered the production of an arbitrary choice or a casual enlargement in the progress of experience, from which it is quite disparate.

Reason through all its concepts and the laws of the understanding, which are sufficient to reason for empirical use, that is, use within the sensible world, finds in this use no satisfaction, because ever-recurring questions deprive it of all hope of their complete solution. The transcendental Ideas which have that completion in view are such problems of reason. But it sees 354 clearly that the sensible world cannot contain this completion; neither, consequently, can all the concepts which serve merely for understanding the world of sense (space, time, and what we have adduced under the name of pure concepts of the understanding). The sensible world is nothing but a chain of appearances connected according to universal laws; it has therefore no subsistence by itself; it is not a thing in itself, and consequently must point to that which contains the basis of this appearance (i.e., to beings which cannot be known merely as appearance, but as things in themselves). In the knowledge of them alone can reason hope to satisfy its desire for completeness in proceeding from the conditioned to its conditions.

We have above (Sections 33 and 34) indicated the limits of reason with regard to all knowledge of mere beings of thought. Now, since the transcendental Ideas have made it necessary to approach them and have thus led us, as it were, to the spot where the occupied space (i.e., experience) touches the void (that of which we know nothing, i.e., noumena), we can determine the bounds of pure reason. For in all bounds there is something positive (for example, a surface is the boundary of corporeal space, and is therefore itself a space; a line is a space, which is the boundary of a surface, a point the boundary of a line, but yet always a place in space), but limits contain mere negations. The limits pointed out in those paragraphs are not enough after we have discovered that beyond them there still lies something (though we can never know what it is in itself). For the question now is: What is the attitude of our reason in this connection of what we know with what we do not and never shall know? This is an actual connection of a known thing with one quite unknown (and one which will always remain unknown), and though what is unknown should not become in the least more known — which we cannot even hope — yet the concept of this connection must be definite and capable of being rendered distinct.

We must, therefore, think an immaterial being, an intelligible world, and a Supreme Being (all mere noumena) because in them only, as things in themselves, does reason find that completion and satisfaction which it can never hope for in deriving appearances from their homogeneous grounds, 355 and because these appearances actually refer to something distinct from them (and totally heterogeneous) inasmuch as appearances always presuppose an object in itself and therefore suggest its existence, whether we can know more of it or not.

But as we can never know these beings of the understanding [noumena] as they are in themselves, that is, as definite, yet must assume them as regards the sensible world and connect them with it by reason, we are at least able to think this connection by means of concepts which express their relation to the world of sense. If we think a being of the understanding by nothing but pure concepts of the understanding, we then indeed represent nothing definite to ourselves and consequently our concept has no significance; but if we think of it by properties borrowed from the sensible world, it is no longer a being of the understanding, but is thought as one of the phenomena and as belonging to the sensible world. Let us take as an example the concept of the Supreme Being.

The deistic concept is a quite pure concept of reason, but represents only a thing containing all reality, without being able to determine any one reality [in it]; in order to do that, an example must be taken from the world of sense, in which case I should have an object of sense only, not something quite heterogeneous which can never be an object of sense. Suppose I attribute to the Supreme Being understanding, for instance; I have no concept of an understanding other than my own, one that must receive its intuitions by the senses and which is occupied in bringing them under rules of the unity of consciousness. Then the elements of my concept would always lie in the appearance; I should, however, because of the insufficiency of the appearance have to go beyond it to the concept of a being which neither depends upon appearances nor is bound up with them as conditions of its determination. But if I separate understanding from sensibility to obtain a pure understanding, then nothing remains but the mere form of thinking without intuition, by which alone I can know nothing definite and, consequently, no object. For that purpose, I should have to conceive another understanding, one which would intuit its objects; but of this I have not the least concept, because the human understanding is discursive and can know only by means of general concepts. The very same difficulties arise if we attribute a will to 356 the Supreme Being, for I have this concept only by drawing it from my inner experience, and therefore from my dependence for satisfaction upon objects whose existence I require, and so the concept of will rests upon sensibility, which is absolutely incompatible with the pure concept of the Supreme Being.

Hume's objections to deism are weak, and affect only the proofs and not the deistic assertion itself. But as regards theism, which depends on a stricter determination of the concept of the Supreme Being, which in deism is merely transcendent, Hume's objections are very strong and, according to how this concept is formulated, in certain (in fact, in all common) cases irrefutable. Hume always insists that by the mere concept of an original being to which we apply only ontological predicates (eternity, omnipresence, omnipotence) we think nothing definite, and that properties which could yield a concept *in concreto* would have to be superadded. He further insists that it is not enough to say it is a cause, but we must explain the nature of its causality, for example, that it is the causality of a being with understanding and will. He then begins his attack on the essential point, that is, theism itself. (He had previously directed his battery only against the proofs of deism, an attack which was not very dangerous in its consequences.) His dangerous arguments refer to anthropomorphism, which he holds to be inseparable from theism and to make it contradictory in itself; and if anthropomorphism be abandoned, theism must vanish with it and nothing remain but deism, of which nothing can come, which is of no value, and which cannot serve as foundation for religion or morals. If this anthropomorphism were really unavoidable, no proofs whatever for the existence of a Supreme Being, even were they all granted, could determine for us the concept of this Being without involving us in contradictions.

If we connect with the command to avoid all transcendent judgments of pure reason the command (which apparently conflicts with it) to proceed to concepts that lie beyond the field of its immanent (empirical) use, we discover that both can subsist together, but only at the boundary of the permitted use of reason. For this boundary belongs to the field of experience as well as to that of the beings of thought, and we are thereby taught how these so 357 remarkable Ideas serve merely for marking the boundaries of human reason. On the one hand, they give warning not boundlessly to extend knowledge of experience, as if nothing but world remained for us to know, and yet, on the other hand, not to transgress the bounds of experience and not to wish to think of judging about things beyond them as things in themselves.

But we stop at this boundary if we limit our judgment solely to the relation which the world may have to a Being whose very concept lies beyond all the knowledge which we can attain within the world. For we then do not attribute to the Supreme Being any of the properties in themselves by which we represent objects of experience, and we thereby avoid *dogmatic* anthropomorphism; but we attribute them to the relation of this Being to the world and allow ourselves a *symbolical* anthropomorphism, which in fact concerns language only and not the object itself. If I say we are compelled to consider the world *as if* it were the work of a Supreme Understanding and Will, I really say nothing more than that a watch, a ship, a regiment bears the same relation to the watchmaker, the shipbuilder, and commanding officer as the world of sense (or whatever constitutes the foundation of this complex of appearances) does to the unknown, which I do not know as it is in itself but as it is for me, that is, in relation to the world of which I am a part.

Section 58

Such a cognition is one of analogy, which does not signify (as is commonly understood) an imperfect similarity of two things, but a perfect similarity of relations between two quite dissimilar things.* By means of this analogy, 358 however, there remains a concept of the Supreme Being sufficiently determined *for us*, though we have left out everything that could determine it absolutely or *in itself*; for we determine it as regards the world and hence as regards ourselves, and more we do not require. The attacks which Hume makes upon those who would determine this concept absolutely, by taking the materials for doing so from themselves and the world, do not affect us; and he cannot object to us that we have nothing left if we give up the objective anthropomorphism of the concept of the Supreme Being.

For let us assume at the outset (as Hume in his *Dialogues* makes Philo grant Cleanthes), as a necessary hypothesis, the deistic concept of the First Being, in which this Being is thought by exclusively ontological predicates of substance, cause, and so on. This must be done because reason, actuated in the sensible world by conditions which are themselves always conditional, cannot otherwise have any satisfaction; and it therefore can be done without falling into anthropomorphism (which transfers predicates from the world of sense to a Being quite distinct from the world) because those predicates are pure categories which, though they do not give a determinate concept of that Being, yet give a concept not limited to any conditions of sensibility. Thus nothing can prevent our predicating of this Being a causality through reason with regard to the world, and thus passing to theism, without being obliged to attribute to this Being itself this kind of reason as a property inherent in it. For as to the former, the only possible way of forcing the use of reason (as 359

---

*There is, for example, an analogy between the juridical relation of human actions and the mechanical relation of moving forces. I never can do anything to another man without giving him a right to do the same to me on the same conditions; just as no mass can act with its moving forces on another mass without thereby occasioning the other to react equally against it. Here right and moving force are quite dissimilar things, but in their relation there is complete similarity. By means of such an analogy, I can obtain a notion of the relation of things which absolutely are unknown to me. For instance, as the promotion of the welfare of children (= a) is to the love of parents (= b), so the welfare of the human species (= c) is to that unknown character in God (= x) which we call love; not as if it had the least similarity to any human inclination, but because we can suppose its relation to the world to be similar to that which things in the world bear one another. But the concept of relation in this case is a mere category, namely, the concept of cause, which has nothing to do with sensibility.

regards all possible experience in complete harmony with itself) in the world of sense to the highest point is to assume a supreme reason as a cause of all the connections in the world. Such a principle must be quite advantageous to reason and can hurt it nowhere in its application to nature. As to the latter, reason is not thereby transferred as a property to the First Being in itself, but only to its relation to the world of sense, and so anthropomorphism is entirely avoided. For nothing is considered here but the cause of the form of reason which is perceived elsewhere in the world, and reason is indeed attributed to the Supreme Being so far as it contains the ground of this form of reason in the world, but according to analogy only — that is, so far as this expression shows merely the relation which the Supreme Being, unknown to us, has to the world in order to determine everything in it conformably to reason in the highest degree. We are thereby kept from using reason as an attribute for the purpose of conceiving God, but not from conceiving the world in such a manner as is necessary to have the greatest possible use of reason within it according to principle. We thereby acknowledge that the Supreme Being is quite inscrutable and even unthinkable in any definite way as to what it is in itself. We are thereby kept, on the one hand, from making a transcendent use of the concepts which we have of reason as an efficient cause (by means of will) in order to determine the Divine Nature by properties which are only borrowed from human nature, and from losing ourselves in gross and extravagant concepts; and, on the other hand, we are kept from deluging the contemplation of the world with hyperphysical modes of explanation according to our conceptions of human reason which we transfer to God, and so from losing for this contemplation its proper role, according to which it should be a rational study of nature alone, and not a presumptuous derivation of its appearances from a supreme reason. The expression suited to our feeble concepts is: we conceive the world *as if* it came, in its existence and internal plan, from a Supreme Reason. By this on the other hand, we know the constitution which belongs to the world itself without pretending to determine the nature of its cause in itself; and, on the other hand, we transfer the ground of this constitution (of the form of reason in the world) upon the

360　relation of the Supreme Cause to the world, without finding the world by itself sufficient for that purpose.*

Thus the difficulties which seem to oppose theism disappear by combining Hume's principle: "not to carry the use of reason dogmatically beyond the field of all possible experience," with this other principle, which he quite overlooked: "not to consider the field of experience as one which bounds

---

*I may say that the causality of the Supreme Cause holds the same place with regard to the world that human reason does with regard to its products. Here the nature of the Supreme Cause itself remains unknown to me; I only compare its effects (the order of the world), which I know, and their conformity to reason to the effects of human reason, which I also know; and hence I term the former "reason" without attributing to it on that account what I understand in man by this term, or attaching to it anything else known to me as its property.

itself in the eyes of our reason." The *Critique of Pure Reason*, here points out the true mean between dogmatism, which Hume combats, and skepticism, which he would substitute for it — a mean which is not like others that we find advisable to decide on for ourselves (as it were, by mechanically adopting something from one side and something from the other) and by which nobody is taught a better way. The *Critique* indicates a true mean which can be precisely determined on principles.

Section 59

At the beginning of this note I made use of the metaphor of a boundary, in order to establish the limits of reason in regard to its appropriate use. The world of sense contains merely appearances, which are not things in themselves; but the understanding, because it recognizes that the objects of experience are mere appearances, must assume that there are things in themselves, namely noumena. In our reason both are comprehended, and the question is: How does reason proceed to set boundaries to the understanding between the two fields? Experience, which contains all that belongs to the sensible world, does not bound itself; it only proceeds in every case from the conditioned to some other equally conditioned object. That which bounds it must lie quite outside it, and this is the field of pure beings of the understanding. But this field, so far as the determination of the nature of 361 these beings is concerned, is an empty space for us; and when it is a question of dogmatically defined concepts we cannot pass beyond the field of possible experience. But as a boundary itself is something positive, which belongs to that which lies within as well as to the space that lies without the given content, it is still an actual positive cognition which reason acquires only by enlarging itself to this boundary without attempting to pass it, because it there finds itself in the presence of an empty space in which it can think forms for things, but not things themselves. But the setting of a boundary to the field of the understanding by something which is otherwise unknown to it is still a cognition which belongs to reason even at this point, by which it is neither confined within the sensible nor strays beyond it, but only limits itself, as befits the knowledge of a boundary, to the relation between that which lies beyond it and that which is contained within it.

Natural theology is such a concept at the boundary of human reason, being constrained to look beyond this boundary to the Idea of a Supreme Being (and, for practical purposes, to that of an intelligible world also), not in order to determine anything about this pure being of the understanding, and thus to determine something that lies beyond the world of sense, but in order to guide the use of reason within the world of sense according to principles of the greatest possible theoretical as well as practical unity. For this purpose it makes use of the reference of the world of sense to an independent reason as the cause of all its connections. Thereby it does not just invent a being, but since beyond the sensible world there must be something that can be thought only by the pure understanding, it determines that something in this particular way, though only of course by analogy.

And thus there remains our original proposition, which is the result of the whole *Critique:* "Reason by all its a priori principles never teaches us anything more than objects of possible experience, and even of these nothing more than can be known by experience." But this limitation does not prevent reason from leading us to the objective boundary of experience, namely, to the relation to something which is not itself an object of experience but is the ground of all experience. Reason does not, however, teach us anything concerning this same something in itself; it instructs us only as regards its own complete and highest use in the field of possible experience. But this is all that can be reasonably desired in the present case, and with it we have cause to be satisfied.

362

Section 60

Thus we have fully exhibited metaphysics, in its subjective possibility, as it is actually given in the natural predisposition of human reason and in that which constitutes the essential end of its pursuit. Though we have found that this merely natural use of such a predisposition of our reason, if no discipline (which can arise only from a scientific critique) bridles and sets limits to it, involves it in transcendent inferences, in part specious and in part dialectically conflicting, and though we have found also that this fallacious metaphysics is not only unnecessary to the promotion of our knowledge of nature but even disadvantageous to it, there still remains a problem worthy of investigation, which is to find out the natural ends intended by this disposition of our nature to transcendent concepts, because everything that lies in nature must have been laid down originally for some useful purpose.

Such an inquiry is of a doubtful nature, and I acknowledge that what I can say about it is conjecture only, like every speculation about the ultimate ends of nature. Such a conjecture may be allowed me here, for the question does not concern the objective validity of metaphysical judgments but our natural predisposition to them, and therefore does not belong to the system of metaphysics, but to anthropology.

When I [combine] all the transcendental Ideas, the totality of which constitutes the proper problem of natural pure reason, compelling it to quit the mere contemplation of nature, to transcend all possible experience, and in this endeavor to produce the thing (be it knowledge or fiction) called metaphysics, I think I perceive that the aim of this natural tendency is to free our concepts from the fetters of experience and from the limits of the bare contemplation of nature so far at least as to open to us a field containing objects only for the pure understanding which no sensibility can reach, it opens this field of objects not for the purpose of speculatively occupying

ourselves with them (for there we can find no ground to stand on), but in   363
order that practical principles [may be assumed as at least possible] [14]; for
practical purposes, unless they find scope for their necessary expression and
hopè, could not expand to the universality which reason inexorably requires
from a moral point of view.

So I find that the psychological Idea (however little it may reveal to me the
nature of the human soul, which transcends all concepts of experience)
shows the insufficiency of those concepts plainly enough and thereby deters
me from materialism, a psychological concept which is unfit for any explanation of nature and which moreover confines reason in practical response. The
cosmological Ideas, by the obvious insufficiency of all possible knowledge of
nature to satisfy reason in its legitimate inquiry, serve in the same manner to
keep us from naturalism, which asserts nature to be sufficient for itself.
Finally, all natural necessity in the sensible world is conditional, as it always
presupposes the dependence of things upon others, and unconditional necessity must be sought only in the unity of a cause different from the world of
sense. But since the causality of this cause, if it were merely nature, could in
its turn never render the existence of the contingent (as its consequent)
comprehensible, reason frees itself by means of the theological Idea from
fatalism (both as blind natural necessity in the complex of nature itself
conceived without a first principle, and as a blind causality of this principle
itself) and leads to the concept of a cause possessing freedom, the concept of
a Supreme Intelligence. Thus the transcendental Ideas serve, if not to in-
struct us positively, at least to destroy the narrowing assertions of materialism, naturalism, and fatalism and thus to afford scope for moral Ideas beyond
the field of speculation. These considerations, I should think, explain in
some measure the natural predisposition of which I spoke. •

The practical value, which a merely speculative science may have, lies
outside the bounds of this science itself, and can therefore be considered as a
mere scholium, and like all scholia it does not form part of the science itself.
This application, however, surely lies within the bounds of philosophy, especially of philosophy drawn from the pure sources of reason where its specula-   364
tive use in metaphysics must necessarily be at one with its practical use in
morals. Hence the unavoidable dialectic of pure reason, considered in metaphysics as a natural disposition, deserves to be explained not merely as an
illusion to be removed, but also, if possible, as a natural provision as regards
its end. The task of giving this explanation, a work of supererogation, cannot
justly be assigned to metaphysics proper.

The solutions of the questions which are treated in the *Critique of Pure
Reason** should be considered a second scholium, but one which has a greater
affinity with the subject of metaphysics. For there, certain rational principles
are expounded which determine a priori the order of nature or rather of the

[14] Kant's sentence is incomplete; the emendation is conjectural.
* *Critique of Pure Reason*, "Regulative Use of the Ideas of Pure Reason."

understanding which seeks nature's laws through experience. They seem to be constitutive and legislative with regard to experience though they spring from pure reason, which cannot be considered, like the understanding, as a principle of possible experience. Now whether or not this harmony rests upon the fact that, just as nature does not inhere in appearances or in their source (sensibility) itself but only in the relation of the appearances to the understanding, a thorough unity in applying the understanding to bring about an entirety of all possible experience (in a system) can only belong to the understanding when it is in relation to reason, with the consequence that experience is in this way indirectly subordinate to the legislation of reason — this question may be discussed by those who desire to trace the nature of reason even beyond its use in metaphysics, into the general principles which will make a history of nature in general systematic. I have presented this as an important task, but have not attempted its solution in the book itself.[15]

365   And thus I conclude the analytical solution of the main question which I proposed: "How is metaphysics in general possible?" by ascending from the data of its actual use, as shown in its consequences, to the grounds of its possibility.

SOLUTION OF THE GENERAL PROBLEM OF THE *PROLEGOMENA* HOW IS METAPHYSICS POSSIBLE AS SCIENCE?

Metaphysics, as a natural disposition of reason, is actual; but if considered by itself alone (as the analytical solution of the third principal question showed), it is dialectical and illusory. If we think of taking principles from it, and using them to follow the natural, but on that account not less false, illusion, we can never produce science but only a vain dialectical art, in which one school may outdo another but in which none can ever acquire a just and lasting approbation.

In order that as a science metaphysics may be entitled to claim not mere fallacious plausibility but insight and conviction, a critique of reason itself must exhibit the whole stock of a priori concepts, their division according to their various sources (in sensibility, understanding, and reason), together with a complete table of them, the analysis of all these concepts with all their consequences and especially the possibility of synthetical knowledge a priori by means of a deduction of these concepts, the principles and bounds of their application — all of this in a complete system. Critique, therefore, and critique alone contains in itself the whole well-proved and well-tested plan, and even all the means required to establish metaphysics as a science; by other ways and means it is impossible. The question here, therefore, is not so much how this achievement is possible as how to set it going and how to induce men

---

[15]Kant's footnote here omitted. The problem he says he did not attempt to solve in the *Critique of Pure Reason* is solved to his satisfaction in the *Critique of the Faculty of Judgment*, below, pp. 345–349.

with clear heads to quit their hitherto perverted and fruitless occupation for one that will not deceive, and how such a union for the common end may best be directed.

This much is certain: that whoever has once tasted critique will be ever 366 after disgusted with all dogmatic twaddle which he formerly had to put up with because his reason had to have something, and could find nothing better for its support.

Critique stands in the same relation to the common metaphysics of the schools as chemistry does to alchemy, or as astronomy to the astrology of the fortune teller. I pledge myself that nobody who has thought through and grasped the principles of critique, even in these *Prolegomena* only, will ever return to that old and sophistical pseudoscience, but will rather with a certain delight look forward to metaphysics, which is now in his power, requiring no more preparatory discoveries and at last affording permanent satisfaction to reason. For here is an advantage upon which, of all possible sciences, metaphysics alone can with certainty reckon: that it can be brought to such completion and fixity as to be in need of no further change or be subject to any augmentation by new discoveries. This is because reason here has the sources of its knowledge in itself, not in objects and their observation by which its stock of knowledge could be further increased. When, therefore, it has exhibited the fundamental laws of its faculty completely and so definitely as to avoid all misunderstanding, there remains nothing further which pure reason could know a priori; nay, there is no ground even to raise further questions. The sure prospect of knowledge so definite and so compact has a peculiar charm, even if we should set aside all its uses, of which I shall hereafter speak.

All false art, all vain wisdom, lasts its time but finally destroys itself, and its highest culture is also the epoch of its decay. That this time is come for metaphysics appears from the state into which it has fallen among all learned nations, despite the zeal with which other sciences of every kind are prosecuted. The old arrangement of our university studies still preserves the shadow of metaphysics. Now and then an academy of science tempts men by offering prizes to write some essay on it, but it is no longer numbered among the rigorous sciences; and let anyone judge for himself how a sophisticated man, if he were called a great metaphysician, would receive the compliment, which may have been well meant but is scarcely coveted by anybody.

Yet, though the period of the downfall of all dogmatic metaphysics has 367 undoubtedly arrived, we are still far from being able to say that the period of its regeneration is come by means of a complete and thorough critique of reason. All transitions from one tendency to its contrary pass through the stage of indifference, and this moment is the most dangerous for an author, but in my opinion the most favorable for the science. For when party spirit has died out by a total dissolution of former connections, minds are in the best state to listen to several proposals for an organization according to a new plan.

When I say that I hope these *Prolegomena* will excite investigation in the field of critique and afford a new and promising object to sustain the general spirit of philosophy which seems on its speculative side to want sustenance, I can imagine beforehand that everyone whom the thorny paths of my *Critique* have tired and put out of humor will ask me upon what I found this hope. My answer is: upon the irresistible law of necessity.

That the human mind will ever give up metaphysical researches is as little to be expected as that, to avoid inhaling impure air, we should prefer to give up breathing altogether. There will, therefore, always be metaphysics in the world; everyone, especially every reflective man, will have it and, for want of a recognized standard, will shape it for himself, after his own pattern. What has hitherto been called metaphysics cannot satisfy any critical mind, but to forego it is impossible; therefore a critique of pure reason itself must now be attempted or, if one exists, investigated and brought to the full test, because there is no other means of supplying this pressing want which is something more than mere thirst for knowledge.

Ever since I have come to know critique, whenever I finish reading a book of metaphysics which, by the preciseness of its concepts and by the variety, order, and easy style, was not only entertaining but also helpful, I cannot help 368 asking, "Has this author really advanced metaphysics a single step?" The learned man whose works have been useful to me in other respects and always contributed to the cultivation of my metal powers will, I hope, forgive me for saying that I have never been able to find either their essays or my own less important ones (though vanity may speak in their favor) to have advanced the science of metaphysics in the least.

There is a very obvious reason for this: metaphysics did not then exist as a science, nor can it be gathered piecemeal, but its germ must be fully preformed in critique. But in order to prevent all misconception, we must remember what has already been said — that by the analytical treatment of our concepts the understanding gains a great deal, but the science of metaphysics is not thereby in the least advanced, because these dissections of concepts are nothing but the materials from which we intend to carpenter our science. Let the concepts of substance and of accident be ever so well dissected and defined; all this is very well as a preparation for some future use. But if we cannot prove that in all that exists the substance endures and only the accidents vary, our science is not the least advanced by all our analysis.

Metaphysics has hitherto never been able to prove a priori either this proposition or that of sufficient reason, still less any more complex theorem such as belongs to psychology or cosmology, or indeed any synthetical proposition. By all its analyzing, therefore, nothing is effected, nothing obtained or forwarded; and the science, after all the bustle and noise, still remains as it was in the days of Aristotle, though there were far better preparations for it than of old if only the clue to synthetical cognitions had been discovered.

If anyone thinks himself offended, he is at liberty to refute my charge by producing a single synthetical proposition belonging to metaphysics which he would volunteer to prove dogmatically a priori. Until he has actually performed this feat, I shall not grant that he has truly advanced the science, even if this proposition be sufficiently confirmed by common experience. No demand can be more moderate or more equitable and, in the (inevitably certain) event of its nonperformance, no assertion more just than that hitherto metaphysics has never existed as a science. 369

But if this challenge be accepted, there are two things which I must deprecate: first, trifling about probability and conjecture, which are as little suited to metaphysics as to geometry; and second, deciding by means of the divining rod of so-called common sense, which does not dip for everyone but accommodates itself to personal peculiarities.

As to the former, nothing can be more absurd than in metaphysics, a philosophy from pure reason, to think of grounding our judgments upon probability and conjecture. Everything that is to be known a priori is proclaimed to be apodictically certain, and must therefore be apodictically proved. We might as well think of grounding geometry or arithmetic upon conjecture. As to the calculus of probabilities in arithmetic, it does not contain probable but perfectly certain judgments concerning the degree of possibility of certain cases under given uniform conditions, which in the sum of all possible cases must infallibly happen according to rule, even though the rule is not sufficiently definite with respect to any single instance. Conjectures (by means of induction and analogy) can be suffered in an empirical science of nature, yet even there at least the possibility of what we assume must be quite certain.

The appeal to sound common sense[16] is even more absurd — if anything more absurd can be imagined — when it is a question of concepts and principles claimed to be valid not [merely] insofar as they hold with regard to experience, but [even] beyond the conditions of experience. For what is sound common sense? It is common understanding, so far as it judges correctly. And what is common understanding? It is the capacity of knowing and using rules *in concreto*, as distinguished from the theoretical understanding, which is the faculty of knowing rules *in abstracto*. Common sense can hardly understand the rule that every event is determined by its cause, and can never comprehend this rule in its generality. It therefore demands an example from experience; and when it hears that this rule means nothing but what it always thought when a window pane was broken or a kitchen utensil 370 missing, it then understands the principle and grants it. Common sense,

---

[16] "Sound common sense" (*gesunder Menschenverstand*) is not, of course, a *sense* at all; the senses do not judge (p. 189). Kant contrasts the *sound* or *common* human understanding to theoretical (*spekulativer*) understanding. Kant here uses the word "speculative" where "theoretical" is meant; it does not refer solely to thinking transcendently, and has as its antonym not "empirical" but "practical."

therefore, is of use only so far as it can see its rules confirmed by experience (though they are actually a priori); consequently to comprehend them a priori or independently of experience belongs to the speculative [theoretical] understanding and lies quite beyond the horizon of common sense. But the province of metaphysics is entirely confined to the kind of knowledge produced by speculative understanding, and it is certainly a poor sign of common sense to appeal to it as a witness, for it cannot in metaphysics form any opinion whatsoever, and one looks down upon it with contempt until one is in straits and can find in speculation neither advice nor help.

It is a common subterfuge of those false friends of common sense (who occasionally prize it highly, but usually despise it) to say that there must surely in all events be some propositions which are immediately certain and of which there is no occasion to give any proof or even any account at all, because we otherwise could never stop inquiring into the grounds of our judgments. But if we except the principle of contradiction, which is not sufficient to show the truth of synthetical judgments, they can never adduce, in proof of this privilege, anything else indubitable which they can ascribe directly to common sense, except mathematical propositions such as twice two make four, between two points there is but one straight line, etc. But these judgments are radically different from those of metaphysics. For in mathematics I can, by thinking, construct whatever I represent to myself as possible by a concept. I add to the first two the other two, one by one, and make the concept four; or I draw in thought from one point to another all manner of lines, equal as well as unequal, yet I can draw only one which is like in all its parts. But I cannot, by all my power of thinking, extract from the concept of a thing the concept of something else whose existence is necessarily connected with it. For this I must call in experience. And though my understanding furnishes me a priori (but only in reference to possible experience) with the concept of such a connection (causation), I cannot exhibit it, as I can the concepts of mathematics, by intuiting it a priori, and so show its
371 possibility a priori. This concept, together with the principles of its application, always requires, if it hold a priori as is requisite in metaphysics, a justification and deduction of its possibility, because we cannot otherwise know how far it holds good and whether it can be used in experience only or also beyond it.

Therefore in metaphysics, as a speculative science of pure reason, we can never appeal to common sense; we may do so only when we are forced to surrender metaphysics and renounce all pure speculative knowledge which must always be theoretical knowledge. In these circumstances we may have to forego metaphysics itself and its teachings for the sake of adopting a rational faith which alone may remain possible for us, sufficient to our needs, and perhaps even more salutary than knowledge itself. In this case, the state of affairs is quite altered. Metaphysics must be a science, not only as a whole but in all its parts; if it is not, it is nothing at all, since, as the speculation of pure reason, it would find support in nothing but common-sense beliefs. Outside the field of metaphysics, however, probability and common sense may be used justly and with advantage, but on quite special principles, the importance of which always depends upon their reference to the practical.

This is what I hold myself justified in requiring for the possibility of metaphysics as a science.[17]

[17] *Appendix: On What Can be Done to Make Metaphysics as a Science Actual,* omitted. The first thing which should be done, he implies, is to carefully read the *Critique of Pure Reason,* and he replies to a review which he says has written without an understanding of the book.

VI
Foundations of the Metaphysics of Morals

Editor's Introduction

Foundations of the Metaphysics of Morals, published in 1785, is the best-known and most widely read of all Kant's works. There are two reasons for this. It is, first and simply, a classic. It ranks high among the greatest classics of moral philosophy. Second, it can be understood without any previous knowledge of Kant's other books and is, in fact, itself a good introduction to his whole philosophy. For these reasons it is extensively used as a text in courses in ethics, history of philosophy, and Kant's philosophy, while its simple style makes it understandable also to those who are not students of philosophy.

It is necessary, as always with Kant's books, first to understand the title. It is a book on *foundations* of the metaphysics of morals; it is not itself a metaphysics of morals. The metaphysics of morals proper is a complete system of all the a priori synthetic judgments applicable to the human condition and belonging to morals; it is the subject matter of his book entitled *Metaphysics of Morals,* published in 1797. The *Foundations,* on the other hand, contains what Kant calls "a pure moral philosophy . . . completely free from everything which may be only empirical and thus belong to anthropology" (p. 245). The subject matter of the *Foundations* is the ethics of purely rational beings. The only rational beings we know are human beings, so his illustrations are necessarily drawn from human affairs, but the principles are not derived from human nature. This may seem to some to be rather far-fetched, but Kant tries in the Introduction to show the importance, both in theory and practice, of separating the pure a priori part of the theory of morals from the applied or empirical part of it. Much of the *Foundations* therefore belongs in what is now known as "meta-ethics."

FIRST SECTION

In the opening sentence Kant says that there is nothing in or out of the world (i.e., either human or divine) that is good without qualification (good in all circumstances) except a *good will.* However much people may desire happiness and value traits of character and gifts of fortune which help them in their pursuit of happiness, they do not count happiness and successful ways of attaining it as good without qualification; an impartial observer cannot approve of "a being adorned with no feature of a pure and good will enjoying uninterrupted prosperity." Though being good is not the cause of happiness, it is a condition of *worthiness* to be happy. This belief is an essential part of the whole Judaic, Platonic, Stoic, and Christian moral tradition. The care for one's own soul and the striving for "purity of heart" are absolute obligations of human beings.

The ordinary person is well aware of the difference between being good and being clever, and though by nature we desire to be happy, we do not ordinarily think of morality as *merely* a means to happiness even if we think that being moral is likely in the long run to lead to our happiness. It is sometimes said that Kant believed that a moral act cannot be one we want to do or one that would make us happy if we did it. This, however, is subtly different from what Kant says. He insists merely that in deciding what we morally ought to do, or in deciding whether to do what we know we morally ought to do, our private, subjective, emotional desires, whether they favor or oppose the act we morally ought to do, have nothing to do with the case; they may determine how we do behave, and even how in many situations it would be appropriate to behave, but they have nothing legitimate to say when it is a question of what is morally right, of what we *morally* ought to do. In saying this, Kant is neither an ascetic nor a Pharisee; he is, he believes, merely describing "the common moral consciousness" not yet corrupted or misled by the sophistical opinion that morality is only enlightened self-interest or an illusory veneer put upon our subconscious impulses.

From some simple examples[1] Kant elicits the pure moral principles stated on p. 268. An action is not truly moral, no matter how otherwise right and proper it is, unless it is done in the belief that, and *because* of the belief that, it is one's duty. Such an act is done out of respect for the moral law which makes it a duty; it is not sufficient that the act merely conform to what the law in fact requires though it be done out of some other motive than respect for the law. An act which conforms to the law

---

[1] Kant's examples here and in the next section, far from clarifying matters, have been often, perhaps generally, misunderstood to mean that in morality one must always go against one's inclinations and desires. These examples refer to human beings who have to go against their desires in order to do right, and they are often interpreted as evidence that Kant thought one cannot do right except when subduing his desires and going against his wishes. But this is not what the examples mean; they are not examples for emulation, but examples to elicit the moral element in action from a context in which there might be other values which would obscure its uniqueness. In *all* action Kant admits there is some object of desire, and the satisfaction of some of these desires is often regarded by others as being the root of the moral value. So Kant devised examples in which the object of desire was in *conflict* with the moral motive, in order that the values of desire should not be identified or confused with the moral value. Failure to understand the reason for the singularly unattractive examples has led to misinterpretations of Kant as a proponent of sour virtue. There is an immense literature on the examples, but most of it is worthless because authors often fail to see what they are examples *of*.

but is not done because of the law is said to be *legal*, not *moral* (but not immoral either).

About these basic principles, the poet Schiller, in agreement with Kant, said, "Only philosophers disagree, but men have always been unanimous." Still, this agreement is not sufficient to procure agreement about what the moral law *specifically* requires of one person or another. We cannot just act out of respect for the law; we cannot just do our duty because it is our duty—we have to do *something* which is our duty because it, specifically, is our duty. The derivation of what duty is from the concept of acting out of respect for the law occupies Kant in the next section, though even there he still deals mostly with abstract principles, saving the doctrine of *specific* duties here and now for the *Metaphysics of Morals*.

SECOND SECTION

The derivation of duties from the maxim of respect for the law runs from pp. 261–269. We may divide the derivation into six stages.

(1) The will is practical reason. While all things in nature work according to law, a rational being is one which can govern its behavior by its *conception* of the law. Will is the name generally (and not just by Kant) given to this ground of action. The conception or principle to which we refer in deciding on our actions is an imperative, which is an expression of an *ought*.

(2) An imperative is hypothetical if it has an if-clause (i.e., if it states (or suggests) that some action ought to be done as a means to some specific end). Such an imperative says, "If you would accomplish such and such a goal, do so and so." An imperative of this kind comes from our experience of the ways in which that goal may be achieved and of the most effective ways of getting what we want; such an imperative does not come from pure reason, but from practical reason in its empirical function, working upon the teachings of experience for the guidance of future behavior. Hence such an imperative does not *command*, as a law does; it only *counsels* us to act in a certain way. It cannot be a law because it is not universal, i.e., does not apply to all human beings; it applies at most to those human beings who have that one specific end in view, which cannot be supposed to be the end in view of everyone, or even of oneself at different times.

(3) If, however, the goal is happiness, which we may correctly suppose to be desired by everyone, we still cannot formulate any universal hypothetical imperative, for "happiness" is a word of such variable and changing meaning, differing from person to person and from time to time, that I cannot establish that everyone should act in the same way in order to reach it. Obviously, then, such hypothetical imperatives (which Kant

calls "pragmatic imperatives") as we do assert — often in the words of proverbial wisdom — have not the status of peremptory and inexorable moral laws that are to be *respected*. If there is a binding universal moral law, it cannot correspond to hypothetical imperatives.

(4) A moral imperative is unconditional (i.e., categorical). An imperative which is involved in the moral consciousness that we ought to do our duty whatever our inclinations cannot be derived from our inclinations themselves and their purposes. If there is such an imperative, it must come from pure reason, which is, in Kant's philosophy, always the only source of pure a priori and universal judgments. Because no specific goal or condition is stated under which and because of which the action ought to be done (as is necessarily the case with a *categorical* imperative) we must find the formula of the "ought" from the pure concept of ought. That is, the concept of ought must itself give a criterion for deciding what duty is.

A moral imperative commands unconditional conformity of our subjective maxim to a law, while the law contains no reference to a specific goal to which the maxim might be directed. The content of the maxim must be derived, therefore, not from the things we desire, but from the requirement which the categorical imperative places upon any maxim of desire whatever. The maxim, if moral, should contain no conditions (no reference to specific desires and purposes) which would prevent it from being itself a law. But no maxim could be itself a moral law unless it could be universally imperative (i.e., valid for all persons as rational beings, regardless of their specific desires). Thus we have a test for deciding whether a maxim is morally admissable or not; we ask: is it a maxim which *any* rational being could consistently will to be a maxim for *all* rational beings? The categorical imperative is the meta-ethical criterion for deciding whether a *maxim* is moral or not. Indirectly and with the addition of empirical information about conditions and circumstances, the categorical imperative is a criterion for determining which *actions* are moral.[2]

(5) There follows a derivation of other formulae for the categorical

---

[2]Kant is misunderstood on this point when it is said that for him the categorical imperative commands that I do only what I can will that all others should do. When "do" means "do some specific act" (such as: "eat at a certain restaurant at 6 P.M."), the absurdity is obvious. The categorical imperative commands that we act only on a universalizable *maxim*, and the very same maxim may be followed in very many different ways depending upon circumstance. What is important is that the maxim be such that each one can will that all act upon it, though one does one thing and another something else. Kant defines a maxim as a principle that has *rules* under itself, but sometimes he writes, inconsistently, as if the maxim were itself a rule for a specific action; this error is always made by those who misinterpret him on this point. For good modern discussions of this widespread error, see Marcus G. Singer, *Generalization in Ethics* (New York, 1961) and Onora Nell, *Acting on Principle* (New York, 1975).

imperative, all of which are said to be only different formulations of one and the same imperative. The most significant of them is the one (p. 273) that is based on the fact that all actions, including moral actions, have purposes (a fact which Kant is sometimes accused of not admitting). He asks, then, if there are any ends which we ought to project as obligatory both for ourselves and others, regardless of the specific personal purposes each of us has. The answer is that humanity is an end in itself, and a maxim which does not respect humanity both in oneself and in others cannot be a law valid for all people. The imperative requires us not to use other people merely as means to our own ends, but requires that we treat and respect them also as ends in themselves. It also implies that no person should use himself, or permit others to use him, solely as a means to some end.

(6) From these formulae there arise two important new conceptions: the autonomy of the will, and the dignity of man (pp. 276–277). In all previous attempts to discover the moral law, it was assumed that there had to be some *quid pro quo* (happiness or misery, heaven or hell) for morality; hence all moral imperatives were regarded as hypothetical. How can the categorical imperative motivate obedience, seeing that it promises nothing by way of reward?

Kant says that the moral law can obligate unconditionally only if it is given by the being who is to obey it, so that there is a direct interest in exacting obedience instead of merely an indirect interest in obeying it as a way of avoiding punishment. The conception that man is free only when he obeys a law he himself has participated in making originated with Rousseau; it is analogous to Kant's Copernican Revolution in his theory of knowledge (the law issues from the mind, not from the object).[3] Man is a member of two worlds: he is sovereign in the realm of ends (by virtue of being an end in himself), and he is subject in the realm of phenomena, causally determined but constrained by the imperative issued by his "other self."

Man has an absolute value (dignity) as a lawgiver and end in himself. Unlike a slavish subject who reluctantly obeys a command given by his master, the moral agent spontaneously (though not without struggle) obeys laws of which he, as a rational being, is author. A person who takes the law from some other source obeys it out of hope or fear; he is not free, not autonomous but heteronomous, not truly moral, because his maxims are hypothetical and he does not act out of respect for a universal law binding on him *because* he wills it to be binding on all rational beings.

---

[3] Kant develops the political consequences of this conception of law and freedom in his political writings, especially *Perpetual Peace,* and in *Idea for a Universal History,* below, pp. 413–457.

THIRD SECTION

In spite of its title, the Third Section deals with questions which are
likely nowadays to be considered metaphysical (e.g., the freedom of the
will and the relation of appearance to reality). Kant has admitted (p. 258)
that in all history no moral action may ever have taken place, but he has
asked: "What is morality, such that we could say that an action having
such and such characteristics would be morally right?" This is very
different from the new question: "*Can* such an action be performed? Or
are we acting under an illusion when we think we can act out of respect for
a law of pure practical reason?"

The new questions raise the question: is the will of man free? If it is
not, morality is impossible, because in that case the will would be
determined by something foreign to it — heredity, environment,
physiological and psychological impulses, etc., — and action would not be
autonomous but only a reaction to causes. To show that ethics is more
than a figment of our imagination, therefore, Kant must show that the will
is free.

Since morality and autonomy are correlative concepts (i.e., concepts
mutually implicative of each other), we cannot use one to establish the
reality of the other. Any argument that "we must be free because we are
morally obligated" is a *petitio principii* because "morally obligated" means
"subject to the categorical imperative" and "free" means (in this context,
at least) autonomous or "determined by no impulses of sense."

The way out of this vicious circle can be found only if there is an
independent ground for asserting the freedom of the will (i.e., a *nonmoral*
argument for freedom). The argument is in two stages. First, there is the
argument from the Third Antinomy in the *Critique of Pure Reason,* which
showed freedom to be *not impossible.* Now the argument on p. 286 shows
that freedom must be presupposed practically in *any* rational act of
choice, whether it be a moral choice, a pragmatic choice, or the choice,
say of evidence, involved in an act of reasoning. Kant has showed that
freedom is possible; now he shows that it is, in practice (but not solely in
moral practice) necessary.

Thus Kant begins to integrate his moral philosophy into the general
system of philosophy established in the first *Critique.* All that we perceive
is only the appearances of things. Behind the appearances there are
realities which we do not know, and behind the appearance of a human
being there is "something else as its basis, namely, his ego as it is in
itself." A person ascribes to this ego whatever is "pure activity" in
himself, whether it be the spontaneity of thought in cognition or the
spontaneity of a moral action; one can ascribe this freedom to the
transcendental ego because it, being in the intelligible world, is free from
the causal determination of the world of nature. The spontaneity involved

both in thought and moral action is a power of reason; hence as a reasonable being man presumes himself to be free, though as a sensuous being he appears under the mechanism of nature.

But—again in keeping with the *Critique of Pure Reason*—philosophy cannot establish any theoretical knowledge of the supersensible intelligible world in which we are free. Philosophy's task is to show that freedom is possible, and to mark out a region which fatalistic and materialistic speculations cannot occupy so as to destroy the foundations of morality (p. 297). This is "the outermost boundary of all moral inquiry"; it cannot explain freedom, but it can explain its inexplicability. In the words of the *Critique*, Kant found it necessary to deny knowledge (of the supersensible) in order to make room for the rational belief in freedom.

The translation (complete) by the Editor was first published by the University of Chicago Press, 1949, and in a revised edition by Liberal Arts Press, 1959. For the present edition it has again been still further revised.

SUGGESTIONS FOR FURTHER READING

Acton, Harold B. *Kant's Moral Philosophy*. St. Martin's Press, 1970.

Duncan, A.R.C. *Practical Reason and Morality. A Study of Kant's Foundations for the Metaphysics of Morals*. Thomas Nelson and Sons, 1957.

Paton, H.J. *The Categorical Imperative. A Study in Kant's Moral Philosophy*. University of Chicago Press, 1948.

Wolff, Robert Paul. *The Autonomy of Reason. A Commentary on Kant's Groundwork*. Harper and Row, 1974.

————, ed. *Kant's Foundations of the Metaphysics of Morals, with Critical Essays*. Bobbs Merrill, 1969.

Foundations of the
Metaphysics of Morals

PREFACE

Ancient Greek philosophy was divided into three sciences: physics, ethics, and logic. This division conforms perfectly to the nature of the subject, and one need improve on it perhaps only by supplying its principle in order both to insure its exhaustiveness and to define correctly the necessary subdivisions.

All rational knowledge is either material, and concerns some object, or formal, and is occupied only with the form of understanding and reason itself and with the universal rules of thinking, without regard to distinctions among objects. Formal philosophy is called logic. Material philosophy, however, which has to do with definite objects and the laws to which they are subject, is divided into two parts. This is because these laws are either laws of nature or laws of freedom. The science of the former is called physics, and that of the latter ethics. The former is also called theory of nature and the latter theory of morals.

Logic can have no empirical part — a part in which universal and necessary laws of thinking would rest upon grounds taken from experience. For in that case it would not be logic (i.e., a canon for understanding or reason which is valid for all thinking and which must be demonstrated). Natural and moral philosophy, on the other hand, can each have its empirical part. The former must do so, for it must determine the laws of nature as an object of experience, and the latter must do so because it must determine the human will so
far as it is affected by nature. The laws of the former are laws according to which everything happens; those of the latter are laws according to which everything ought to happen, but allow for conditions under which what ought to happen often does not.

All philosophy, so far as it is based on experience, may be called empirical; but, so far as it presents its doctrines solely on the basis of a priori principles, it may be called pure philosophy. Pure philosophy, when formal only, is logic; when limited to definite objects of the understanding, it is metaphysics.

In this way there arises the idea of a two-fold metaphysics — a metaphysics of nature and a metaphysics of morals. Physics, therefore, will have an empirical part and also a rational part, and ethics likewise. In ethics, however, the empirical part may be called more specifically practical anthropology; the rational part, morals proper.

All crafts, handiworks, and arts have gained by the division of labor, for when one person does not do everything but each limits himself to a particular job which is distinguished from all the others by the treatment it requires, he can do it with greater perfection and more facility. Where work is not thus differentiated and divided, where everyone is a jack-of-all-trades, the crafts remain at a primitive level. It might be worth considering whether pure philosophy in each of its parts does not require a man particularly devoted to it, and whether it would not be better for the learned profession as a whole to warn those who are in the habit of catering to the taste of the public by mixing up the empirical with the rational in all sorts of proportions which they themselves do not know — a warning to those who call themselves independent thinkers and who give the name of speculator to those who apply themselves exclusively to the rational part of philosophy. This warning would be that they should not, at one and the same time, carry on two employments which differ widely in the treatment they require, and for each of which perhaps a special talent is required, since the combination of these talents in one person produces only bunglers. I only ask whether the nature of the science does not require that a careful separation of the empirical from the rational part be made, with a metaphysics of nature put before real (empirical) physics and a metaphysics of morals before practical anthropology. Each branch of metaphysics must be carefully purified of everything empirical so that we can know how much pure reason can accomplish in each case and from what sources it creates its a priori teaching, whether the latter inquiry be 389 conducted by all moralists (whose name is legion) or only by some who feel a calling to it.

Since my purpose here is directed to moral philosophy, I narrow my proposed question to this: Is it not of the utmost necessity to construct a pure moral philosophy which is completely freed from everything which may be only empirical and thus belong to anthropology? That there must be such a philosophy is self-evident from the common idea of duty and moral laws. Everyone must admit that a law, if it is to hold morally (i.e., as a ground of obligation), must imply absolute necessity; he must admit that the command: Thou shalt not lie, does not apply to men only as if other rational beings had no need to observe it. The same is true for all other moral laws properly so called. He must concede that the ground of obligation here must not be sought in the nature of man or in the circumstances in which he is placed but a priori solely in the concepts of pure reason, and that every precept which rests on principles of mere experience, even a precept which is in certain respects universal, so far as it leans in the least on empirical grounds (perhaps only in regard to the motive involved) may be called a practical rule but never a moral law.

Thus not only are moral laws together with their principles essentially different from all practical knowledge in which there is anything empirical, but all moral philosophy rests solely on its pure part. Applied to man, it borrows nothing from knowledge of him (anthropology) but gives him, as a rational being, a priori laws. No doubt these laws require a power of judgment sharpened by experience partly in order to decide in which cases they apply and partly to procure for them access to man's will and to provide an impetus to their practice. For man is affected by so many inclinations that, though he is capable of the idea of a practical pure reason, he is not so easily able to make it concretely effective in the conduct of his life.

390   A metaphysics of morals is therefore indispensable, not merely because of motives to speculation on the source of the a priori practical principles which lie in our reason, but also because morals themselves remain subject to all kinds of corruption so long as the guide and supreme norm for their correct estimation is lacking. For it is not sufficient to that which should be morally good that it conform to the law; it must be done for the sake of the law. Otherwise its conformity is merely contingent and spurious because, though the unmoral ground may indeed now and then produce lawful actions, more often it brings forth unlawful ones. But the moral law can be found in its purity and genuineness (which is the central concern in the practical) nowhere else than in a pure philosophy; therefore metaphysics must lead the way, and without it there can be no moral philosophy. Philosophy which mixes pure principles with empirical ones does not deserve the name, for what distinguishes philosophy from common rational knowledge is its treatment in separate sciences of what is confusedly apprehended in such knowledge. Much less does it deserve the name of moral philosophy, since by this confusion it spoils the purity of morals themselves, and works contrary to its own end.

It should not be thought that what is here required is already present in the celebrated Wolff's propaedeutic to his moral philosophy (i.e., in what he calls universal practical philosophy) and that it is not an entirely new field which is to be opened. Precisely because his work was to be universal practical philosophy, it contained no will of any particular kind, such as one determined without any empirical motives by a priori principles; in a word, it had nothing which could be called a pure will, since it considered only volition in general with all the actions and conditions which pertain to it in this general sense. Thus his propaedeutic differs from a metaphysic of morals in the same way that general logic is distinguished from transcendental philosophy, the former expounding the actions and rules of thinking in general, and the latter presenting the actions and rules of pure thinking (i.e., of thinking by which objects are known completely a priori). For the metaphysics of morals is meant to investigate the idea and principles of a possible pure will and not the actions and conditions of human volition as such, which for the most part are drawn from psychology.

391   That general practical philosophy discussed (though improperly) laws and

duty is no objection to my assertion. For the authors of this science remain even here true to their idea of it. They do not distinguish the motives which are presented completely a priori by reason alone and which are thus moral in the proper sense of the world, from empirical motives which the understanding raises to universal concepts by comparing experiences. Rather, they consider motives without regard to the difference in their source but only with reference to their larger or smaller number (as they are considered to be all of the same kind); they thus formulate their concept of obligation, which is anything but moral, but which is all that can be desired in a philosophy which does not decide whether the origin of all possible practical concepts is a priori or a posteriori.

As a preliminary to a *Metaphysics of Morals* which I intend to publish someday, I issue these *Foundations.* There is, to be sure, no other foundation for such a metaphysics than a critical examination of pure practical reason, just as there is no other foundation for metaphysics than the already published critical examination of pure speculative reason. But, in the first place, a critical examination of pure practical reason is not of such extreme importance as that of the speculative reason, because human reason, even in the commonest mind, can easily be brought to a high degree of correctness and completeness in moral matters while, on the other hand, in its theoretical but pure use it is wholly dialectical. In the second place, I require of a critical examination of pure practical reason, if it is to be complete, that its unity with the speculative be subject to presentation under a common principle, because in the final analysis there can be but one and the same reason which must be different only in application. But I could not bring this to such a completeness without bringing in observations of an altogether different kind and without thereby confusing the reader. For these reasons I have employed the title, *Foundations of the Metaphysics of Morals,* instead of *Critique of Pure Practical Reason.*

Because, in the third place, a *Metaphysics of Morals,* in spite of its forbidding title, is capable of a high degree of popularity and adaptation to common understanding, I find it useful to separate this preliminary work of laying the foundation, in order not to have to introduce unavoidable subtleties into the 392 latter, more comprehensible work.

The present foundations, however, are nothing more than the search for and establishment of the supreme principle of morality. This constitutes a task altogether complete in design and one which should be kept separate from all other moral inquiry. My conclusions concerning this important question, which has not yet been discussed nearly enough, would, of course, be clarified by application of the principle to the whole system of morality, and it would receive much confirmation by the adequacy which it would everywhere show. But I must forego this advantage which would be, in the final analysis, more personally gratifying than commonly useful, because ease of use and apparent adequacy of a principle are not any sure proof of correctness, but rather awaken a certain partiality which prevents a rigorous investigation and evaluation of it for itself without regard to consequences.

I have adopted in this writing the method which is, I think, most suitable if one wishes to proceed analytically from common knowledge to the determination of its supreme principle, and then synthetically from the examination of this principle and its sources back to common knowledge where it finds its application. The division is therefore as follows:

1. First Section. Transition from Commonsense Knowledge of Morals to the Philosophical
2. Second Section. Transition from Popular Moral Philosophy to the Metaphysics of Morals
3. Third Section. Final Step from the Metaphysics of Morals to the Critical Examination of Pure Practical Reason

FIRST SECTION
TRANSITION FROM COMMON SENSE[1] KNOWLEDGE OF MORALS TO THE PHILOSOPHICAL

393   Nothing in the world — indeed nothing even beyond the world — can possibly be conceived which could be called good without qualification except a *GOOD WILL.* Intelligence, wit, judgment, and other talents of the mind however they may be named, or courage, resoluteness, and perseverence as qualities of temperament, are doubtless in many respects good and desirable; but they can become extremely bad and harmful if the will, which is to make use of these gifts of nature and which in its special constitution is called character, is not good. It is the same with gifts of fortune. Power, riches, honor, even health, general well-being and the contentment with one's condition which is called happiness make for pride and even arrogance if there is not a good will to correct their influence on the mind and on its principle of action, so as to make it generally fitting to its entire end. It need hardly be mentioned that the sight of a being adorned with no feature of a pure and good will yet enjoying uninterrupted good fortune can never give pleasure to an impartial rational observer. Thus the good will seems to constitute the indispensable condition even of worthiness to be happy.

Some qualities seem to be conducive to this good will and can facilitate its

---

[1] *gemeine Vernunfterkenntnis* (common rational knowledge) is one of several expressions Kant uses which may sometimes best be translated as "common sense." See pp. 259, 314, 369. Kant is very strict in his censure of those who appeal to common sense as an arbiter in philosophical disputes, yet he accepts it as a starting point, especially in ethics, where he says that the man of common sense has at least as much chance to be right as the philosopher (p. 256). In this title "common sense" is not being used as a technical term; it just means "what everyone knows" about morality.

action, but in spite of that they have no intrinsic unconditional worth. They rather presuppose a good will, which limits the high esteem which one 394 otherwise rightly has for them and prevents their being held to be absolutely good. Moderation in emotions and passions, self-control, and calm deliberation not only are good in many respects but seem even to constitute part of the inner worth of the person. But however unconditionally they were esteemed by the ancients, they are far from being good without qualification, for without the principles of a good will they can become extremely bad, and the coolness of a villain makes him not only far more dangerous but also more directly abominable in our eyes than he would have seemed without it.

The good will is not good because of what it effects or accomplishes or because of its competence to achieve some intended end; it is good only because of its willing (i.e., it is good in itself). And, regarded for itself, it is to be esteemed as incomparably higher than anything which could be brought about by it in favor of any inclination or even of the sum total of all inclinations. Even if it should happen that, by a particularly unfortunate fate or by the niggardly provision of a stepmotherly nature, this will should be wholly lacking in power to accomplish its purpose, and if even the greatest effort should not avail it to achieve anything of its end, and if there remained only the good will — not as a mere wish, but as the summoning of all the means in our power — it would sparkle like a jewel all by itself, as something that had its full worth in itself. Usefulness or fruitlessness can neither diminish nor augment this worth. Its usefulness would be only its setting, as it were, so as to enable us to handle it more conveniently in commerce or to attract the attention of those who are not yet connoisseurs, but not to recommend it to those who are experts or to determine its worth.

But there is something so strange in this idea of the absolute worth of the will alone, in which no account is taken of any use, that, notwithstanding the agreement even of common sense, the suspicion must arise that perhaps only high-flown fancy is its hidden basis, and that we may have misunderstood the 395 purpose of nature in appointing reason as the ruler of our will. We shall therefore examine this idea from this point of view.

In the natural constitution of an organized being (i.e., one suitably adapted to life), we assume as an axiom that no organ will be found for any purpose which is not the fittest and best adapted to that purpose. Now if its preservation, its welfare, in a word its happiness, were the real end of nature in a being having reason and will, then nature would have hit upon a very poor arrangement in appointing the reason of the creature to be the executor of this purpose. For all the actions which the creature has to perform with this intention of nature, and the entire rule of his conduct, would be dictated much more exactly by instinct, and the end would be far more certainly attained by instinct than it ever could be by reason. And if, over and above this, reason should have been granted to the favored creature, it would have served only to let him contemplate the happy constitution of his nature, to admire it, to rejoice in it, and to be grateful for it to its beneficent cause. But reason would not have been given in order that the being should subject his faculty of desire to that weak and delusive guidance and to meddle with the purpose of nature. In a word, nature would have taken care that reason did not break forth into practical use nor have the presumption, with its weak insight, to think out for itself the plan of happiness and the means of attaining it. Nature would have taken over the choice not only of ends but also of the means, and with wise foresight she would have entrusted both to instinct alone.

And, in fact, we find that the more a cultivated reason deliberately devotes itself to the enjoyment of life and happiness, the more the man falls short of true contentment. From this fact there arises in many persons, if only they are candid enough to admit it, a certain degree of misology, hatred of reason. This is particularly the case with those who are most experienced in its use. After counting all the advantages which they draw — I will not say from the invention of the arts of common luxury — from the sciences (which in the end seem to them to be also a luxury of the understanding), they nevertheless find that they have actually brought more trouble on their shoulders instead of gaining in happiness; they finally envy, rather than despise, the common run of men who are better guided by merely natural instinct and who do not permit their reason much influence on their conduct. And we must at least admit that a morose attitude or ingratitude to the goodness with which the world is governed is by no means found always among those who temper or refute the boasting eulogies which are given of the advantages of happiness and contentment with which reason is supposed to supply us. Rather, their judgment is based on the Idea of another and far more worthy purpose of their existence for which, instead of happiness, their reason is properly intended; this purpose, therefore, being the supreme condition to which the private purposes of men must, for the most part, defer.

Since reason is not competent to guide the will safely with regard to its objects and the satisfaction of all our needs (which it in part multiplies), to this end an innate instinct would have led with far more certainty. But reason is given to us as a practical faculty (i.e., one which is meant to have an influence on the will). As nature has elsewhere distributed capacities suitable to the functions they are to perform, reason's proper function must be to produce a will good in itself and not one good merely as a means, since for the former, reason is absolutely essential. This will need not be the sole and complete good, yet it must be the condition of all others, even of the desire for happiness. In this case it is entirely compatible with the wisdom of nature that the cultivation of reason, which is required for the former unconditional purpose, at least in this life restricts in many ways — indeed, can reduce to less than nothing — the achievement of the latter conditional purpose, happiness. For one perceives that nature here does not proceed unsuitably to its purpose, because reason, which recognizes its highest practical vocation in the establishment of a good will, is capable of a contentment of its own kind (i.e., one that springs from the attainment of a purpose determined by reason), even though this injures the ends of inclination.

We have, then, to develop the concept of a will which is to be esteemed as good in itself without regard to anything else. It dwells already in the natural and sound understanding and does not need so much to be taught as only to be brought to light. In the estimation of the total worth of our actions it always takes first place and is the condition of everything else. In order to show this, we shall take the concept of duty. It contains the concept of a good will, though with certain subjective restrictions and hindrances, but these are far from concealing it and making it unrecognizable, for they rather bring it out by contrast and make it shine forth all the more brightly. 397

I here omit all actions which are recognized as opposed to duty, even though they may be useful in one respect or another, for with these the question does not arise as to whether they may be done *from* duty, since they conflict with it. I also pass over actions which are really in accord with duty and to which one has no direct inclination, rather doing them because impelled to do so by another inclination. For it is easily decided whether an action in accord with duty is done from duty or for some selfish purpose. It is far more difficult to note this difference when the action is in accord with duty and, in addition, the subject has a direct inclination to do it. For example, it is in accord with duty that a dealer should not overcharge an inexperienced customer, and wherever there is much trade the prudent merchant does not do so, but has a fixed price for everyone so that a child may buy from him as cheaply as any other. Thus the customer is honestly served, but this is far from sufficient to warrant the belief that the merchant has behaved in this way from duty and principles of honesty. His own advantage required this behavior, but it cannot be assumed that over and above that he had a direct inclination to his customers and that, out of love, as it were, he gave none an advantage in price over another. The action was done neither from duty nor from direct inclination but only for a selfish purpose.

On the other hand, it is a duty to preserve one's life, and moreover everyone has a direct inclination to do so. But for that reason, the often anxious care which most men take of it has no intrinsic worth, and the maxim of doing so has no moral import. They preserve their lives according to duty, but not from 398 duty. But if adversities and hopeless sorrow completely take away the relish for life; if an unfortunate man, strong in soul, is indignant rather than despondent or dejected over his fate and wishes for death, and yet preserves his life without loving it and from neither inclination nor fear but from duty — then his maxim has a moral content.

To be kind where one can is a duty, and there are, moreover, many persons so sympathetically constituted that without any motive of vanity or selfishness they find an inner satisfaction in spreading joy and rejoice in the contentment of others which they have made possible. But I say that, however dutiful and however amiable it may be, that kind of action has no true moral worth. It is on a level with [actions done from] other inclinations, such as the inclination to honor, which, if fortunately directed to what in fact accords with duty and is generally useful and thus honorable, deserve praise and encouragement, but no esteem. For the maxim lacks the moral import of an action done not from inclination but from duty. But assume that the mind of that friend to mankind was clouded by a sorrow of his own which extinguished all sympathy with the lot of others, and though he still had the power to benefit others in distress their need left him untouched because he was preoccupied with his own. Now suppose him to tear himself, unsolicited by inclination, out of his dead insensibility and to do this action only from duty and without any inclination — then for the first time his action has genuine moral worth. Furthermore, if nature has put little sympathy into the heart of a man, and if he, though an honest man, is by temperament cold and indifferent to the sufferings of others perhaps because he is provided with special gifts of patience and fortitude and expects and even requires that others should have them too — and such a man would certainly not be the meanest product of nature — would not he find in himself a source from which to give himself a far higher worth than he could have got by having a good-natured temperament? This is unquestionably true even though nature did not make him philanthropic, for it is just here that the worth of character is brought out, 399 which is morally the incomparably highest of all: he is beneficent not from inclination, but from duty.

To secure one's own happiness is at least indirectly a duty, for discontent with one's condition under pressure from many cares and amid unsatisfied wants could easily become a great temptation to transgress against duties. But, without any view to duty, all men have the strongest and deepest inclination to happiness, because in this Idea all inclinations are summed up. But the precept of happiness is often so formulated that it definitely thwarts some inclinations, and men can make no definite and certain concept of the sum of satisfaction of all inclinations, which goes under the name of happiness. It is not to be wondered at, therefore, that a single inclination, definite as to what it promises and as to the time at which it can be satisfied, can outweigh a fluctuating idea and that, for example, a man with the gout can choose to enjoy what he likes and to suffer what he may, because according to his calculations at least on this occasion he has not sacrificed the enjoyment of the present moment to a perhaps groundless expectation of a happiness supposed to lie in health. But even in this case if the universal inclination to happiness did not determine his will, and if health were not at least for him a necessary factor in these calculations, there would still remain, as in all other cases, a law that he ought to promote his happiness not from inclination but from duty. Only from this law could his conduct have true moral worth.

It is in this way, undoubtedly, that we should understand those passages of Scripture which command us to love our neighbor and even our enemy, for love as an inclination cannot be commanded. But beneficence from duty, even when no inclination impels it and even when it is opposed by a natural and unconquerable aversion, is practical love, not pathological[2] love; it resides in the will and not in the propensities of feeling, in principles of action and not in tender sympathy; and it alone can be commanded.

[Thus the first proposition of morality is that to have genuine moral worth, an action must be done from duty.] The second proposition is: An action done from duty does not have its moral worth in the purpose which is to be achieved through it but in the maxim whereby it is determined. Its moral value, therefore, does not depend upon the realization of the object of the   400 action but merely on the principle of the volition by which the action is done irrespective of the objects of the faculty of desire. From the preceding discussion it is clear that the purposes we may have for our actions and their effects as ends and incentives of the will cannot give the actions any unconditional and moral worth. Wherein, then, can this worth lie, if it is not in the will in its relation to its hoped-for effect? It can lie nowhere else than in the principle of the will irrespective of the ends which can be realized by such action. For the will stands, as it were, at the crossroads halfway between its a priori principle which is formal and its a posteriori incentive which is material. Since it must be determined by something, if it is done from duty it must be determined by the formal principle of volition as such, since every material principle has been withdrawn from it.

The third principle, as a consequence of the two preceding, I would express as follows: Duty is the necessity of an action done from respect for law. I can certainly have an inclination to an object as an effect of the proposed action, but I can never have respect for it precisely because it is a mere effect and not an activity of a will. Similarly, I can have no respect for any inclination whatsoever, whether my own or that of another; in the former case I can at most approve of it and in the latter I can even love it (i.e., see it as favorable to my own advantage). But that which is connected with my will merely as ground and not as consequence, that which does not serve my inclination but overpowers it or at least excludes it from being considered in making a choice — in a word, law itself — can be an object of respect and thus a command. Now as an act from duty wholly excludes the influence of inclination and therewith every object of the will, nothing remains which can determine the will objectively except law and subjectively except pure respect for this practical law. This subjective element is the maxim* that I should follow such a law even if it thwarts all my inclinations.   401

Thus the moral worth of an action does not lie in the effect which is

---

[2] Here as elsewhere Kant uses the word *pathological* to describe motives and actions arising from feeling or bodily impulses, with no suggestion of abnormality or disease.

*A maxim is a subjective principle of volition. The objective principle (i.e., that which would   400 serve all rational beings also subjectively as a practical principle if reason had full power over the faculty of desire) is the practical law.

expected from it or in any principle of action which has to borrow its motive from this expected effect. For all these effects (agreeableness of my own condition, indeed even the promotion of the happiness of others) could be brought about through other causes and would not require the will of a rational being, while the highest and unconditional good can be found only in such a will. Therefore the preeminent good can consist only in the conception of law in itself (which can be present only in a rational being) so far as this conception and not the hoped-for effect is the determining ground of the will. This preeminent good, which we call moral, is already present in the person who acts according to this conception, and we do not have to look for it first in the result.*

402   But what kind of law can that be, the conception of which must determine the will without reference to the expected result? Under this condition alone can the will be called absolutely good without qualification. Since I have robbed the will of all impulses which could come to it from obedience to any law, nothing remains to serve as a principle of the will except universal conformity to law as such. That is, I ought never to act in such a way that I could not also will that my maxim should be a universal law. Strict conformity to law as such (without assuming any particular law applicable to certain actions) serves as the principle of the will, and it must serve as such a principle if duty is not to be a vain delusion and chimerical concept. The common sense of mankind (*gemeine Menschenvernunft*) in its practical judgments is in perfect agreement with this and has this principle constantly in view.

Let the question, for example, be: May I, when in distress, make a promise with the intention not to keep it? I easily distinguish the two meanings which the question can have, viz., whether it is prudent to make a false promise, or whether it conforms to duty. The former can undoubtedly be often the case, though I do see clearly that it is not sufficient merely to escape from the

---

401   *It might be objected that I seek to take refuge in an obscure feeling behind the word "respect," instead of clearly resolving the question with a concept of reason. But though respect is a feeling, it is not one received through any [outer] influence but is self-wrought by a rational concept; thus it differs specifically from all feelings of the former kind which may be referred to inclination or fear. What I recognize directly as a law for myself I recognize with respect, which means merely the consciousness of the submission of my will to a law without the intervention of other influences on my mind. The direct determination of the will by law and the consciousness of this determination is respect; thus respect can be regarded as the effect of the law on the subject and not as the cause of the law. Respect is properly the conception of a worth which thwarts my self-love. Thus it is regarded as an object neither of inclination nor of fear, though it has something analogous to both. The only object of respect is law, and indeed only the law which we impose on ourselves and yet recognize as necessary in itself. As a law we are subject to it without consulting self-love; as imposed on us by ourselves, it is a consequence of our will. In the former respect it is analogous to fear and in the latter to inclination. All respect for a person is only respect for the law (of righteousness, etc.) of which the person provides an example. Because we see the improvement of our talents as a duty, we think of a person of talent as the example of a law, as it were (the law that we should by practice become like him in his talents), and that constitutes our respect. All so-called moral interest consists solely in respect for the law.

present difficulty by this expedient, but that I must consider whether inconveniencies much greater than the present one may not later spring from this lie. Even with all my supposed cunning, the consequences cannot be so easily foreseen. Loss of credit might be far more disadvantageous than the misfortune I am now seeking to avoid, and it is hard to tell whether it might not be more prudent to act according to a universal maxim and to make it a habit not to promise anything without intending to fulfill it. But it is soon clear to me that such a maxim is based only on an apprehensive concern with consequences.

To be truthful from duty, however, is an entirely different thing from being truthful out of fear of untoward consequences, for in the former case the concept of the action itself contains a law for me, while in the latter I must first look about to see what results for me may be connected with it. To deviate from the principle of duty is certainly bad, but to be unfaithful to my maxim of prudence can sometimes be very advantageous to me, though it is 403 certainly safer to abide by it. The shortest but most infallible way to find the answer to the question as to whether a deceitful promise is consistent with duty is to ask myself: Would I be content that my maxim of extricating myself from difficulty by a false promise should hold as a universal law for myself as well as for others? And could I say to myself that everyone may make a false promise when he is in a difficulty from which he otherwise cannot escape? Immediately I see that I could will the lie but not a universal law to lie. For with such a law there would be no promises at all, inasmuch as it would be futile to make a pretense of my intention in regard to future actions to those who would not believe this pretense or — if they overhastily did so — would pay me back in my own coin. Thus my maxim would necessarily destroy itself as soon as it was made a universal law.

I do not, therefore, need any penetrating acuteness to discern what I have to do in order that my volition may be morally good. Inexperienced in the course of the world, incapable of being prepared for all its contingencies, I only ask myself: Can I will that my maxim become a universal law? If not, it must be rejected, not because of any disadvantage accruing to myself or even to others, but because it cannot enter as a principle into a possible enactment of universal law, and reason extorts from me an immediate respect for such legislation. I do not as yet discern on what it is grounded (this is a question the philosopher may investigate), but I at least understand that it is an estimation of a worth which far outweighs all the worth of whatever is recommended by the inclinations, and that the necessity that I act from pure respect for the practical law constitutes my duty. To duty every other motive must give place, because duty is the condition of a will good in itself, whose worth transcends everything.

Thus within the moral knowledge of ordinary human reason (*gemeine Menschenvernunft*) we have attained its principle. To be sure, ordinary human reason does not think this principle abstractly in such a universal form, but it

always has the principle in view and uses it as the standard for its judgments.
404 It would be easy to show how ordinary human reason, with this compass, knows well how to distinguish what is good, what is bad, and what is consistent or inconsistent with duty. Without in the least teaching common reason anything new, we need only to draw its attention to its own principle (in the manner of Socrates), thus showing that neither science nor philosophy is needed in order to know what one has to do in order to be honest and good, and even wise and virtuous. We might have conjectured beforehand that the knowledge of what everyone is obliged to do and thus also to know would be within the reach of everyone, even of the most ordinary man. Here we cannot but admire the great advantages which the practical faculty of judgment has over the theoretical in ordinary human understanding. In the theoretical, if ordinary reason ventures to go beyond the laws of experience and perceptions of the senses, it falls into sheer inconceivabilities and self-contradictions, or at least into a chaos of uncertainty, obscurity, and instability. In the practical, on the other hand, the power of judgment first shows itself to advantage when common understanding excludes all sensuous incentives from practical laws. It then even becomes subtle, quibbling with its own conscience or with other claims to what should be called right, or wishing to determine accurately, for its own instruction, the worth of certain actions. But the most remarkable thing about ordinary human understanding in its practical concern is that it may have as much hope as any philosopher of hitting the mark. In fact, it is almost more certain to do so than the philosopher, for while he has no principle which common understanding lacks, his judgment is easily confused by a mass of irrelevant considerations so that it easily turns aside from the correct way. Would it not, therefore, be wiser in moral matters to acquiesce in ordinary reasonable judgment and at most to call in philosophy in order to make the system of morals more complete and comprehensible and its rules more convenient for use (especially in disputation), than to steer the ordinary understanding from its happy simplicity in practical matters and to lead it through philosophy into a new path of inquiry and instruction?

Innocence is indeed a glorious thing, but it is very sad that it cannot well
405 maintain itself, being easily led astray. For this reason, even wisdom — which consists more in acting than in knowing — needs science, not so as to learn from it but to secure admission and permanence to its precepts. Man feels in himself a powerful counterpoise against all commands of duty which reason presents to him as so deserving of respect. This counterpoise is his needs and inclinations, the complete satisfaction of which he sums up under the name of happiness. Now reason issues inexorable commands without promising anything to the inclinations. It disregards, as it were, and holds in contempt those claims which are so impetuous and yet so plausible, and which refuse to be suppressed by any command. From this a natural dialectic arises, i.e., a propensity to argue against the stern laws of duty and their validity, or at least

to place their purity and strictness in doubt and, where possible, to make them more accordant with our wishes and inclinations. This is equivalent to corrupting them in their very foundations and destroying their dignity — a thing which even ordinary practical reason cannot finally call good.

In this way ordinary human reason is impelled to go outside its sphere and to take a step into the field of practical philosophy. But it is forced to do so not by any speculative need, which never occurs to it so long as it is satisfied to remain merely healthy reason; rather, it is impelled on practical grounds to obtain information and clear instruction respecting the source of its principle and the correct definition of this principle in its opposition to the maxims based on need and inclination. It seeks this information in order to escape from the perplexity of opposing claims and to avoid the danger of losing all genuine moral principles through the equivocation in which it is easily involved. Thus when ordinary practical reason cultivates itself, a dialectic surreptitiously ensues which forces it to seek aid in philosophy, just as the same thing happens in the theoretical use of reason. Ordinary practical reason, like theoretical reason, will find rest only in a complete critical examination of our reason.

SECOND SECTION
TRANSITION FROM POPULAR MORAL PHILOSOPHY
TO THE METAPHYSICS OF MORALS

Although we have derived our earlier concept of duty from the ordinary use 406
of our practical reason, it is by no means to be inferred that we have treated it as an empirical concept. On the contrary, if we attend to our experience of the way men act, we meet frequent and, as we must confess, justified complaints that we cannot cite a single sure example of the disposition to act from pure duty. There are also justified complaints that, though much may be done that accords with what duty commands, it is nevertheless always doubtful whether it is done from duty and thus whether it has moral worth. There have always been philosophers who for this reason have absolutely denied the reality of this disposition in human actions, attributing everything to more or less refined self-love. They have done so without questioning the correctness of the concept of morality. Rather they spoke with sincere regret of the frailty and corruption of human nature, which is noble enough to take as its precept an Idea so worthy of respect but which at the same time is too weak to follow it, employing reason, which should give laws for human nature, only to provide for the interest of the inclinations either singly or, at best, in their greatest possible harmony with one another.

It is, in fact, absolutely impossible by experience to discern with complete 407
certainty a single case in which the maxim of an action, however much it might conform to duty, rested solely on moral grounds and on the conception

of one's duty. It sometimes happens that in the most searching self-examination we can find nothing except the moral ground of duty which could have been powerful enough to move us to this or that good action and to such great sacrifice. But from this we cannot by any means conclude with certainty that a secret impulse of self-love, falsely appearing as the Idea of duty, was not actually the true determining cause of the will. For we like to flatter ourselves with a pretended nobler motive, while in fact even the strictest examination can never lead us entirely behind the secret incentives, for when moral worth is in question it is not a matter of actions which one sees but of their inner principles which one does not see.

Moreover, one cannot better serve the wishes of those who ridicule all morality as a mere phantom of human imagination overreaching itself through self-conceit than by conceding that the concepts of duty must be derived only from experience (for they are ready, from indolence, to believe that this is true of all other concepts too). For, by this concession, a sure triumph is prepared for them. Out of love for humanity I am willing to admit that most of our actions are in accord with duty; but if we look more closely at our thoughts and aspirations, we come everywhere upon the dear self, which is always turning up, and it is this instead of the stern command of duty (which would often require self-denial) which supports our plans. One need not be an enemy of virtue, but only a cool observer who does not confuse even the liveliest aspiration for the good with its actuality, to be sometimes doubtful whether true virtue can really be found anywhere in the world. This is especially true as one's years increase and the power of judgment is made wiser by experience and more acute in observation. This being so, nothing can secure us against the complete abandonment of our ideas of duty and preserve in us a well-founded respect for its law except the conviction that, even if there never were actions springing from such pure sources, our 408 concern is not whether this or that was done, but that reason of itself and independently of all appearances commanded what ought to be done. Our concern is with actions of which perhaps the world has never had an example, with actions whose feasibility might be seriously doubted by those who base everything on experience, and yet with actions inexorably commanded by reason. For example, pure sincerity in friendship can be demanded of every man, and this demand is not in the least diminished if a sincere friend has never existed, because this duty, as duty in general, prior to all experience lies in the Idea of reason which determines the will on a priori grounds.

No experience, it is clear, can give occasion for inferring the possibility of such apodictic laws. This is especially clear when we add that, unless we wish to deny all truth to the concept of morality and renounce its application to any possible object, we cannot refuse to admit that the law is of such broad significance that it holds not merely for men but for all rational beings as such; we must grant that it must be valid with absolute necessity, and not merely under contingent conditions and with exceptions. For with what right could we bring into unlimited respect something that might be valid only under contingent human conditions? And how could laws of the determination of our will be held to be laws of the determination of the will of any rational being whatever and of ourselves in so far as we are rational beings, if they were merely empirical and did not have their origin completely a priori in pure, but practical, reason?

Nor could one given poorer counsel to morality than to attempt to derive it from examples. For each example of morality which is exhibited must itself have been previously judged according principles of morality to see whether it was worthy to serve as an original example or model. By no means could it authoritatively furnish the concept of morality. Even the Holy One of the Gospel must be compared with our ideal of moral perfection before He is recognized as such; even He says of Himself, "Why call ye Me (Whom you see) good? None is good (the archetype of the good) except God only (Whom you do not see)." But whence do we have the concept of God as the highest 409 good? Solely from the Idea of moral perfection which reason formulates a priori and which it inseparably connects with the concept of a free will. Imitation has no place in moral matters, and examples serve only for encouragement. That is, they put beyond question the possibility of performing what the law commands, and they make visible that which the practical rule expresses more generally. But they can never justify our guiding ourselves by examples and our setting aside their true original, which lies in reason.

If there is thus no genuine supreme principle of morality which does not rest on pure reason alone independent of all possible experience, I do not believe it is necessary even to ask whether it is well to exhibit these concepts generally (*in abstracto*), which, together with the principles belonging to them, are established a priori. At any rate, the question need not be asked if knowledge of them is to be distinguished from ordinary knowledge and called philosophical. But in our times this question may be necessary. For if we collected votes as to whether pure rational knowledge separated from all experience (i.e., a metaphysics of morals) or popular practical philosophy is to be preferred, it is easily guessed on which side the majority would stand.

This condescension to popular notions is certainly very commendable once the ascent to the principles of pure reason has been satisfactorily accomplished. That would mean the prior establishment of the doctrine of morals on metaphysics and then, when it is established, procuring a hearing for it through popularization. But it is extremely absurd to want to achieve popularity in the first investigation, where everything depends on the correctness of the fundamental principles. Not only can this procedure never make claim to that rarest merit of true philosophical popularity, since there is really no art in being generally comprehensible if one thereby renounces all basic insight; but it produces a disgusting jumble of patched-up observations and half-reasoned principles. Shallow pates enjoy this, for it is very useful in everyday chitchat, while the more sensible feel confused and dissatisfied and

avert their eyes without being able to help themselves. But philosophers, who see through this delusion, get little hearing when they call people away
410 from this would-be popularity so that they may be genuinely popular once they have gained a definite understanding.

One need only look at the essays on morality favored by popular taste. One will sometimes meet with the particular vocation of human nature (but occasionally with the idea of a rational nature in general), sometimes perfection and sometimes happiness, here moral feeling, there fear of God, a little of this and a little of that in a marvelous mixture. It never occurs to the authors, however, to ask whether the principles of morality are, after all, to be sought anywhere in knowledge of human nature (which we can derive only from experience). And if this is not the case, if the principles are a priori, free from everything empirical, and found exclusively in pure rational concepts and not at all in any other place, they never ask whether they should undertake this investigation as a separate inquiry (i.e., as pure practical philosophy) or (if one may use a name so decried) a metaphysics* of morals. They never think of dealing with it alone and bringing it by itself to completeness and of requiring the public, which desires popularization, to await the outcome of this undertaking.

But a completely isolated metaphysics of morals, mixed with no anthropology, no theology, no physics or hyperphysics, and even less with occult qualities (which might be called hypophysical), is not only an indispensable substrate of all theoretically sound and definite knowledge of duties; it is also a desideratum of the highest importance to the actual fulfilment of its pre-
411 cepts. For the thought of duty and of the moral law generally, with no admixture of empirical inducements, has an influence on the human heart so much more powerful than all other incentives† which may be derived from the empirical field that reason, in the consciousness of its dignity, despises them and gradually becomes master over them. It has this influence only

---

*If one wishes, the pure philosophy of morals (metaphysics) can be distinguished from the applied (i.e., applied to human nature), just as pure mathematics and pure logic are distinguished from applied mathematics and applied logic. By this designation one is immediately reminded that moral principles are not founded on the peculiarities of human nature but must stand of themselves a priori, and that from such principles practical rules for every rational nature, and accordingly for man, must be derivable.

†I have a letter from the late excellent Sulzer in which he asks me why the theories of virtue accomplish so little even though they contain so much that is convincing to reason. My answer was delayed in order that I might make it complete. The answer is only that the teachers themselves have not completely clarified their concepts, and when they wish to make up for this by hunting in every quarter for motives to the morally good so as to make their physic right strong, they spoil it. For the commonest observation shows that if we imagine an act of honesty performed with a steadfast soul and sundered from all view to any advantage in this or another world and even under the greatest temptations of need or allurement, it far surpasses and eclipses any similar action which was affected in the least by any foreign incentive; it elevates the soul and arouses the wish to be able to act in this way. Even moderately young children feel this impression, and one should never represent duties to them in any other way.

through reason alone, which thereby first realizes that it can of itself be practical. A mixed theory of morals which is put together from incentives of feelings and inclinations and from rational concepts must, on the other hand, make the mind vacillate between motives which cannot be brought together under any principle and which can lead only accidentally to the good, and frequently lead to the bad.

From what has been said it is clear that all moral concepts have their seat and origin entirely a priori in reason. This is just as much the case in the most ordinary reason as in the reason which is speculative to the highest degree. It is obvious that they can be abstracted from no empirical and hence merely contingent cognitions. In the purity of origin lies their worthiness to serve us as supreme practical principles, and to the extent that something empirical is added to them, just this much is subtracted from their genuine influence and from the unqualified worth of actions. Furthermore, it is evident that it is not only of the greatest necessity from a theoretical point of view when it is a question of speculation but also of the utmost practical importance to derive the concepts and laws of morals from pure reason and to present them pure and unmixed, and to determine the scope of this entire practical but pure rational knowledge (the entire faculty of pure practical reason) without making the principles depend upon the particular nature of human reason, as speculative philosophy may permit and even find necessary. But since moral 412 laws should hold for every rational being as such, the principles must be derived from the universal concept of a rational being in general. In this manner all morals, which need anthropology for their application to men, must be completely developed first as pure philosophy (i.e., metaphysics), independently of anthropology (a thing easily done in such distinct fields of knowledge). For we know well that if we are not in possession of such a metaphysics, it is not merely futile [to try to] define accurately for the purposes of speculative judgment the moral element of duty in all actions which accord with duty, but impossible to base morals on legitimate principles for even ordinary practical use, especially in moral instruction; and it is only in this manner that pure moral dispositions can be produced and engrafted on men's minds for the purpose of the highest good in the world.

In this study we do not advance merely from the common moral judgment (which here is very worthy of respect) to the philosophical, as this has already been done; but we advance by natural stages from popular philosophy (which goes no farther than it can grope by means of examples) to metaphysics (which is not held back by anything empirical and which, as it must measure out the entire scope of rational knowledge of this kind, reaches even Ideas, where examples fail us). In order to make this advance, we must follow and clearly present the practical faculty of reason from its universal rules of determination to the point where the concept of duty arises from it.

Everything in nature works according to laws. Only a rational being has the capacity of acting according to the *conception* of laws (i.e., according to principles). This capacity is the will. Since reason is required for the derivation of actions from laws, will is nothing less than practical reason. If reason infallibly determines the will, the actions which such a being recognizes as objectively necessary are also subjectively necessary. That is, the will is a faculty of choosing only that which reason, independently of inclination, recognizes as practically necessary (i.e., as good). But if reason of itself does not sufficiently determine the will, and if the will is subjugated to subjective conditions 413 (certain incentives) which do not always agree with the objective conditions —in a word, if the will is not of itself in complete accord with reason (which is the actual case with men), then the actions which are recognized as objectively necessary are subjectively contingent, and the determination of such a will according to objective laws is a constraint. That is, the relation of objective laws to a will which is not completely good is conceived as the determination of the will of a rational being by principles of reason to which this will is not by its nature necessarily obedient.

The conception of an objective principle, so far as it constrains a will, is a command (of reason), and the formula of this command is called an *imperative*.

All imperatives are expressed by an "ought" and thereby indicate the relation of an objective law of reason to a will which is not in its subjective constitution necessarily determined by this law. This relation is that of constraint. Imperatives say that it would be good to do or to refrain from doing something, but they say it to a will which does not always do something simply because the thing is presented to it as good to do. Practical good is what determines the will by means of the conception of reason and hence not by subjective causes but objectively, on grounds which are valid for every rational being as such. It is distinguished from the pleasant, as that which has an influence on the will only by means of a sensation from purely subjective causes, which hold for the senses only of this or that person and not as a principle of reason which holds for everyone.*

414   A perfectly good will, therefore, would be equally subject to objective laws of the good, but it could not be conceived as constrained by them to accord with them, because it can be determined to act by its own subjective consti-

---

413   *The dependence of the faculty of desire on sensations is called inclination, and inclination always indicates a need. The dependence of a contingently determinable will on principles of reason, however, is called interest. An interest is present only in a dependent will which is not of itself always in accord with reason; in the divine will we cannot conceive of an interest. But even the human will can take an interest in something without thereby acting from interest. The former means the practical interest in the action; the latter, the pathological interest in the object of the action. The former indicates only the dependence of the will on principles of reason in themselves, while the latter indicates dependence on the principles of reason for the purpose of inclination, since reason gives only the practical rule by which the needs of inclination are to be aided. In the former case the action interests me, and in the latter the object of the action (so far as it is pleasant for me) interests me. In the First Section we have seen that, in the case of an action done from duty, no regard must be given to the interest in the object, but merely to the action itself and its principle in reason (i.e., the law).

tution only through the conception of the good. Thus no imperatives hold for the divine will or, more generally, for a holy will. The "ought" here is out of place, for the volition of itself is necessarily in unison with the law. Therefore imperatives are only formulas expressing the relation of objective laws of volition in general to the subjective imperfection of the will of this or that rational being, for example, the human will.

All imperatives command either *hypothetically* or *categorically*. The former present the practical necessity of a possible action as a means to achieving something else which one desires (or which one may possibly desire). The categorical imperative would be one which presented an action as of itself objectively necessary, without regard to any other end.

Since every practical law presents a possible action as good and thus as necessary for a subject practically determinable by reason, all imperatives are formulas of the determination of action which is necessary by the principle of a will which is in any way good. If the action is good only as a means to something else, the imperative is hypothetical; but if it is thought of as good in itself, and hence as necessary in a will which of itself conforms to reason as the principle of this will, the imperative is categorical.

The imperative thus says what action possible for me would be good, and it presents the practical rule in relation to a will which does not forthwith perform an action simply because it is good, in part because the subject does not always know that the action is good, and in part (when he does know it) because his maxims can still be opposed to the objective principles of practical reason.

The hypothetical imperative, therefore, says only that the action is good to some purpose, possible or actual. In the former case, it is a problematical, in the latter an assertorical, practical principle. The categorical imperative, 415 which declares the action to be of itself objectively necessary without making any reference to any end in view (i.e., without having any other purpose), holds as an apodictical practical principle.

We can think of what is possible only through the powers of some rational being as a possible end in view of any will. As a consequence, the principles of action thought of as necessary to attain a possible end in view which can be achieved by them, are in reality infinitely numerous. All sciences have some practical part consisting of problems which presuppose some purpose as well as imperatives directing how it can be reached. These imperatives can therefore be called, generally, imperatives of skill. Whether the purpose is reasonable and good is not in question at all, for the question concerns only what must be done in order to attain it. The precepts to be followed by a physician in order to cure his patient and by a poisoner to bring about certain death are of equal value in so far as each does that which will perfectly accomplish his purpose. Since in early youth we do not know what purposes we may have in the course of our life, parents seek to let their children learn a great many things and provide for skill in the use of means to all sorts of ends which they might choose, among which they cannot determine whether any one of them will become their child's actual purpose, though it may be that someday he may have it as his actual purpose. And this anxiety is so great that they commonly neglect to form and correct their children's judgment on the worth of the things which they may make their ends.

There is one end, however, which we may presuppose as actual in all rational beings so far as imperatives apply to them, that is, so far as they are dependent beings. There is one purpose which they not only *can* have but which we can presuppose that they all *do* have by a necessity of nature. This purpose is happiness. The hypothetical imperative which represents the practical necessity of an action as means to the promotion of happiness is an assertorical imperative. We may not expound it as necessary to a merely uncertain and only possible purpose, but as necessary to a purpose which we
416 can a priori and with assurance assume for everyone because it belongs to his essence. Skill in the choice of means to one's own highest well-being can be called prudence* in the narrowest sense. Thus the imperative which refers to the choice of means to one's own happiness (i.e., the precept of prudence), is still only hypothetical, and the action is not commanded absolutely but commanded only as a means to another end in view.

Finally, there is one imperative which directly commands certain conduct without making its condition some purpose to be reached by it. This imperative is categorical. It concerns not the material of the action and its intended result, but the form and principle from which it originates. What is essentially good in it consists in the mental disposition, the result being what it may. This imperative may be called the imperative of morality.

Volition according to these three principles is plainly distinguished by the dissimilarity in the constraints by which they subject the will. In order to clarify this dissimilarity, I believe that they are most suitably named if one says that they are either rules of sill, counsels of prudence, or commands (laws) of morality, respectively. For law alone implies the concept of an unconditional and objective and hence universally valid necessity, and commands are laws which must be obeyed even against inclination. Counsels do indeed involve necessity, but a necessity that can hold only under a subjectively contingent condition (i.e., whether this or that man counts this or that as part of his happiness). The categorical imperative, on the other hand, is restricted by no condition. As absolutely, though practically, necessary it can be called a command in the strict sense. We could also call the first impera-

---

*The word "prudence" may be taken in two senses, and it may bear the name of prudence with reference to things of the world and private prudence. The former sense means the skill of a man in having an influence on others so as to use them for his own purposes. The latter is the ability to unite all these purposes to his own lasting advantage. The worth of the first is finally reduced to the latter, and of one who is prudent in the former sense but not in the latter we might better say that he is clever and cunning yet, on the whole, imprudent.

tives *technical* (belonging to art), the second *pragmatic** (belonging to well-   417
being), and the third *moral* (belonging to free conduct as such, i.e., to
morals).

The question now arises: How are all these imperatives possible? This
question does not require an answer as to how the action which the imperative commands can be performed, but only an answer as to how the constraint
of the will, which the imperative expresses in setting the problem, can be
conceived. How an imperative of skill is possible requires no particular
discussion. Whoever wills the end, so far as reason has decisive influence on
his action, wills also the indispensably necessary steps to it that he can take.
This proposition, in what concerns the will, is analytical; for, in the willing of
an object as an effect, my causality, as an acting cause of this effect shown in
my use of the means to it, is already thought, and the imperative derives the
concept of actions necessary to this purpose from the concept of willing this
purpose. Synthethical propositions undoubtedly are necessary for determining the means to a proposed end, but they do not concern the ground, the act
of the will, but only the way to achieve the object. Mathematics teaches, by
synthetical propositions only, that in order to bisect a line according to an
infallible principle, I must make two intersecting arcs from each of its ex-
tremities; but if I know the proposed result can be obtained only by such an
action, then it is an analytical proposition that, if I fully will the effect, I must
also will the action necessary to produce it. For it is one and the same thing to
conceive of something as an effect which is in a certain way possible through
me, and to conceive of myself as acting in this way.

If it were only easy to give a definite concept of happiness, the imperatives
of prudence would perfectly correspond to those of skill and would likewise
be analytical. For it could then be said in this case as well as in the former that
whoever wills the end wills also (necessarily according to reason) the only
means to it which are in his power. But it is a misfortune that the concept of   418
happiness is so indefinite that, although each person wishes to attain it, he
can never definitely and self-consistently state what it is that he really wishes
and wills. The reason for this is that all elements which belong to the concept
of happiness are empirical (i.e., they must be taken from experience), while
for the Idea of happiness an absolute whole, a maximum, of well-being is
needed in my present and in every future condition. Now it is impossible for
even a most clear-sighted and most capable but finite being to form here a
definite concept of that which he really wills. If he wills riches, how much
anxiety, envy, and intrigues might he not thereby draw upon his shoulders! If

---

*It seems to me that the proper meaning of the word "pragmatic" could be most accurately
defined in this way. For sanctions which properly flow not from the law of states as necessary
statutes but from provision for the general welfare are called pragmatic. A history is pragmatically composed when it teaches prudence (i.e., instructs the world how it could provide for its
interest better than, or at least as well as, has been done in the past).

he wills much knowledge and vision, perhaps it might become only an eye that much sharper to show him as more dreadful the evils which are now hidden from him and which are yet unavoidable; or it might be to burden his desires — which already sufficiently engage him — with even more needs! If he wills long life, who guarantees that it will not be long misery? If he wills at least health, how often has not the discomfort of his body restrained him from excesses into which perfect health would have led him? In short, he is not capable, on any principle and with complete certainty, of ascertaining what would make him truly happy; omniscience would be needed for this. He cannot, therefore, act according to definite principles so as to be happy, but only according to empirical counsels (e.g., those of diet, economy, courtesy, restraint, etc.) which are shown by experience best to promote well-being on the average. Hence the imperatives of prudence cannot, in the strict sense, command (i.e., present actions objectively as practically necessary); thus they are to be taken as counsels (*consilia*) rather than as commands (*praecepta*) of reason, and the task of determining infallibly and universally what action will promote the happiness of a rational being is completely unsolvable. There can be no imperative which would, in the strict sense, command us to do what makes for happiness, because happiness is an ideal not of reason but of imagination, depending only on empirical grounds which one would 419 expect in vain to determine an action through which the totality of consequences — which in fact is infinite — could be achieved. Assuming that the means to happiness could be infallibly stated, this imperative of prudence would be an analytically practical proposition for it differs from the imperative of skill only in that its purpose is given, while in the imperative of skill it is merely a possible purpose. Since both, however, command the means to that which one presupposes as a willed purpose, the imperative which commands the willing of the means to him who wills the end is in both cases analytical. There is, consequently, no difficulty in seeing the possibility of such an imperative.

To see how the imperative of morality is possible, then, is without doubt the only question needing an answer. It is not hypothetical, and thus the objectively conceived necessity cannot be supported by any presupposed purpose, as was the case with the hypothetical imperatives. But it must not be overlooked that it cannot be shown by any example (i.e., it cannot be empirically shown) that there is such an imperative. Rather, it is to be suspected that all imperatives which appear to be categorical are tacitly hypothetical. For instance, when it is said, "Thou shalt not make a false promise," we assume that the necessity of this prohibition is not a mere counsel for the sake of escaping some other evil, so that it would read: "Thou shalt not make a false promise, lest, if it comes to light, thou ruinest thy credit." [In so doing] we assume that an action of this kind must be regarded as in itself bad and that the imperative prohibiting it is categorical, but we cannot show with

.

certainty by any example that the will is here determined by the law alone without any other incentives, although it appears to be so. For it is always possible that secretly fear of disgrace, and perhaps also obscure apprehension of other dangers, may have had an influence on the will. Who can prove by experience the nonexistence of a cause when experience shows us only that we do not perceive the cause? In such a case the so-called moral imperative, which as such appears to be categorical and unconditional, would be actually only a pragmatic precept which makes us attentive to our own advantage and teaches us to consider it.

Thus we shall have to investigate purely a priori the possibility of a categor-   420
ical imperative, for we do not have the advantage that experience would show us the reality of this imperative so that the [demonstration of its] possibility would be necessary only for its explanation, and not for its establishment. In the meantime, this much at least may be seen: the categorical imperative alone can be taken as a practical *law*, while all other imperatives may be called principles of the will but not laws. This is because what is necessary merely for the attainment of some chosen end can be regarded as itself contingent and we get rid of the precept once we give up the end in view, whereas the unconditional command leaves the will no freedom to choose the opposite. Thus it alone implies the necessity which we require of a law.

Secondly, in the case of the categorical imperative or law of morality, the cause of the difficulty in discerning its possibility is very weighty. This imperative is an a priori synthetical practical proposition* and since to discern the possibility of propositions of this sort is so difficult in theroetical knowl-edge it may well be gathered that it will be no less difficult in practical knowledge.

In attacking this problem, we will first inquire whether the mere concept of a categorical imperative does not also furnish the formula containing the proposition which alone can be a categorical imperative. For even when we know the formula of the imperative, to learn how such an absolute command is possible will require difficult and special labors which we shall postpone to the last section.

If I think of a hypothetical imperative as such, I do not know what it will contain until the condition is stated [under which it is an imperative]. But if I think of a categorical imperative, I know immediately what it will contain. For since the imperative contains, besides the law, only the necessity of the

---

*I connect a priori, and hence necessarily, the action with the will without supposing as a condition that there is any inclination [to the action] (though I do so only objectively, i.e., under the Idea of a reason which would have complete power over all subjective motives). This is, therefore, a practical proposition which does not analytically derive the willing of an action from some other volition already presupposed (for we do not have such a perfect will); it rather connects it directly with the concept of the will of a rational being as something which is not contained within it.

maxim* of acting in accordance with the law, while the law contains no
421 condition to which it is restricted, nothing remains except the universality of
law as such to which the maxim of the action should conform; and this
conformity alone is what is represented as necessary by the imperative.

There is, therefore, only one categorical imperative. It is: Act only according to that maxim by which you can at the same time will that it should
become a universal law.

Now if all imperatives of duty can be derived from this one imperative as a
principle, we can at least show what we understand by the concept of duty
and what it means, even though it remain undecided whether that which is
called duty is an empty concept or not.

The universality of law according to which effects are produced constitutes
what is properly called nature in the most general sense (as to form) (i.e., the
existence of things so far as it is determined by universal laws). [By analogy],
then, the universal imperative of duty can be expressed as follows: Act as
though the maxim of your action were by your will to become a universal law
of nature.

We shall now enumerate some duties, adopting the usual division of them
into duties to ourselves and to others and into perfect and imperfect duties.†

422 1. A man who is reduced to despair by a series of evils feels a weariness with
life but is still in possession of his reason sufficiently to ask whether it would
not be contrary to his duty to himself to take his own life. Now he asks
whether the maxim of his action could become a universal law of nature. His
maxim, however is: For love of myself, I make it my principle to shorten my
life when by a longer duration it threatens more evil than satisfaction. But it is
questionable whether this principle of self-love could become a universal law
of nature. One immediately sees a contradiction in a system of nature, whose
law would be to destroy life by the feeling whose special office is to impel the
improvement of life. In this case it would not exist as nature; hence that
maxim cannot obtain as a law of nature, and thus it wholly contradicts the
supreme principle of all duty.

2. Another man finds himself forced by need to borrow money. He well
knows that he will not be able to repay it, but he also sees that nothing will be
lent him if he does not firmly promise to repay it at a certain time. He desires

---

*A maxim is the subjective principle of acting and must be distinguished from the objective
principle (i.e., the practical law). The former contains the practical rule which reason determines according to the conditions of the subject (often its ignorance or inclinations) and is thus
the principle according to which the subject acts. The law, on the other hand, is the objective
principle valid for every rational being, and the principle by which it ought to act, i.e., an
imperative.

†It must be noted here that I reserve the division of duties for a future *Metaphysics of Morals*
and that the division here stands as only an arbitrary one (chosen in order to arrange my
examples). For the rest, by a perfect duty I here understand a duty which permits no exception
in the interest of inclination; thus I have not merely outer but also inner perfect duties. This runs
contrary to the usage adopted in the schools, but I am not disposed to defend it here because it is
all one to my purpose whether this is conceded or not.

to make such a promise, but he has enough conscience to ask himself whether it is not improper and opposed to duty to relieve his distress in such a way. Now, assuming he does decide to do so, the maxim of his action would be as follows: When I believe myself to be in need of money, I will borrow money and promise to repay it, although I know I shall never do so. Now this principle of self-love or of his own benefit may very well be compatible with his whole future welfare, but the question is whether it is right. He changes the pretension of self-love into a universal law and then puts the question: How would it be if my maxim became a universal law? He immediately sees that it could never hold as a universal law of nature and be consistent with itself; rather it must necessarily contradict itself. For the universality of a law which says that anyone who believes himself to be in need could promise what he pleased with the intention of not fulfilling it would make the promise itself and the end to be accomplished by it impossible; no one would believe what was promised to him but would only laugh at any such assertion as vain pretense.

3. A third finds in himself a talent which could, by means of some cultiva- 423 tion, make him in many respects a useful man. But he finds himself in comfortable circumstances and prefers indulgence in pleasure to troubling himself with broadening and improving his fortunate natural gifts. Now, however, let him ask whether his maxim of neglecting his gifts, besides agreeing with his propensity to idle amusement, agrees also with what is called duty. He sees that a system of nature could indeed exist in accordance with such a law, even though man (like the inhabitants of the South Sea Islands) should let his talents rust and resolve to devote his life merely to idleness, indulgence, and propagation — in a word, to pleasure. But he cannot possibly will that this should become a universal law of nature or that it should be implanted in us by a natural instinct. For, as a rational being, he necessarily wills that all his faculties should be developed, inasmuch as they are given him and serve him for all sorts of purposes.

4. A fourth man, for whom things are going well, sees that others (whom he could help) have to struggle with great hardships, and he asks, "What concern of mine is it? Let each one be as happy as heaven wills, or as he can make himself; I will not take anything from him or even envy him; but to his welfare or to his assistance in time of need I have no desire to contribute." If such a way of thinking were a universal law of nature, certainly the human race could exist, and without doubt even better than in a state where everyone talks of sympathy and good will or even exerts himself occasionally to practice them while, on the other hand, he cheats when he can and betrays or otherwise violates the right of man. Now although it is possible that a universal law of nature according to that maxim could exist, it is nevertheless impossible to will that such a principle should hold everywhere as a law of nature. For a will which resolved this would conflict with itself, since instances can often arise in which he would need the love and sympathy of

others, and in which he would have robbed himself, by such a law of nature springing from his own will, of all hope of the aid he desires.

The foregoing are a few of the many actual duties, or at least of duties we hold to be actual, whose derivation from the one stated principle is clear. We 424 must be able to will that a maxim of our action become a universal law; this is the canon of the moral estimation of our action generally. Some actions are of such a nature that their maxim cannot even be *thought* as a universal law of nature without contradiction, far from it being possible that one could will that it should be such. In others this internal impossibility is not found, though it is still impossible to *will* that that maxim should be raised to the universality of a law of nature, because such a will would contradict itself. We easily see that a maxim of the first kind conflicts with stricter or narrower (imprescriptable) duty, that of the latter with broader (meritorious) duty. Thus all duties, so far as the kind of obligation (not the object of their action) is concerned, have been completely exhibited by these examples in their dependence upon the same principle.

When we observe ourselves in any transgression of a duty, we find that we do not actually will that our maxim should become a universal law. That is impossible for us; rather, the contrary of this maxim should remain as a law generally, and we only take the liberty of making an exception to it for ourselves or for the sake of our inclination, and for this one occasion. Consequently, if we weighed everything from one and the same standpoint, namely, reason, we would come upon a contradiction in our own will, viz., that a certain principle is objectively necessary as a universal law and yet subjectively does not hold universally but rather admits exceptions. However, since we regard our action at one time from the point of view of a will wholly conformable to reason and then from that of a will affected by inclinations, there is actually no contradiction, but rather an opposition of inclination to the precept of reason *(antagonismus)*. In this the universality of the principle *(universalitas)* is changed into mere generality *(generalitas)*, whereby the practical principle of reason meets the maxim halfway. Although this cannot be justified in our own impartial judgment, it does show that we actually acknowledge the validity of the categorical imperative and allow ourselves (with all respect to it) only a few exceptions which seem to us to be unimportant and forced upon us.

425   We have thus at least established that if duty is a concept which is to have significance and actual law-giving authority for our actions, it can be expressed only in categorical imperatives and not at all in hypothetical ones. For every application of it we have also clearly exhibited the content of the categorical imperative which must contain the principle of all duty (if there is such). This is itself very much. But we are not yet advanced far enough to prove a priori that that kind of imperative really exists, that there is a practical law which of itself commands absolutely and without any incentives, and that obedience to this law is duty.

.

With a view to attaining this, it is extremely important to remember that we must not let ourselves think that the reality of this principle can be derived from the particular constitution of human nature. For duty is practical unconditional necessity of action; it must, therefore, hold for all rational beings (to which alone an imperative can apply), and only for that reason can it be a law for all human wills. Whatever is derived from the particular natural situation of man as such, or from certain feelings and propensities, or even from a particular tendency of the human reason which might not hold necessarily for the will of every rational being (if such a tendency is possible), can give a maxim valid for us but not a law; that is, it can give a subjective principle by which we might act if only we have the propensity and inclination, but not an objective principle by which we would be directed to act even if all our propensity, inclination, and natural tendency were opposed to it. This is so far the case that the sublimity and intrinsic worth of the command is the better shown in a duty the fewer subjective causes there are for it and the more they are against it; the latter do not weaken the constraint of the law or diminish its validity.

Here we see philosophy brought to what is, in fact, a precarious position, which should be made fast even though it is supported by nothing in either heaven or earth. Here philosophy must show its purity, as the absolute sustainer of its laws, and not as the herald of those which an implanted sense or who knows what tutelary nature whispers to it. Those may be better than nothing at all, but they can never afford fundamental principles, which reason alone dictates. These fundamental principles must originate entirely 426 a priori and thereby obtain their commanding authority; they can expect nothing from the inclination of men but everything from the supremacy of the law and due respect for it. Otherwise they condemn man to self-contempt and inner abhorrence.

Thus everything empirical is not only wholly unworthy to be an ingredient in the principle of morality but is even highly prejudicial to the purity of moral practices themselves. For, in morals, the proper and inestimable worth of an absolutely good will consists precisely in the freedom of the principle of action from all influences from contingent grounds which only experience can furnish. We cannot too much or too often warn against the lax or even base manner of thought which seeks its principles among empirical motives and laws, for human reason in its weariness is glad to rest on this pillow. In a dream of sweet illusions (in which it embraces not Juno but a cloud), it substitutes for morality a bastard patched up from limbs of very different parentage, which looks like anything one wishes to see in it, but not like virtue to anyone who has ever beheld her in her true form.*

*To behold virtue in her proper form is nothing else than to exhibit morality stripped of all admixture of sensuous things and of every spurious adornment of reward or self-love. How much she then eclipses everything which appears charming to the senses can easily be seen by everyone with the least effort of his reason, if it be not spoiled for all abstraction.

The question then is: Is it a necessary law for all rational beings that they should always judge their actions by such maxims as they themselves could will to serve as universal laws? If there is a such a law, it must be connected wholly a priori with the concept of the will of a rational being as such. But in order to discover this connection, we must, however reluctantly, take a step into metaphysics, although in a region of it different from speculative philos-
427 ophy, namely into the metaphysics of morals. In a practical philosophy it is not a question of assuming grounds for what happens but of assuming laws of what ought to happen even though it may never happen (that is to say, we assume objective practical laws). Hence in practical philosophy we need not inquire into the reasons why something pleases or displeases, how the pleasure of mere feeling differs from taste, and whether this is distinct from a general satisfaction of reason. Nor need we ask on what the feeling of pleasure or displeasure rests, how desires and inclinations arise, and how, finally, maxims arise from desires and inclination under the co-operation of reason. For all these matters belong to empirical psychology, which would be the second part of physics if we consider it as philosophy of nature so far as it rests on empirical laws. But here it is a question of objectively practical laws and thus of the relation of a will to itself so far as it determines itself only by reason, for everything which has a relation to the empirical automatically falls away, because if reason of itself alone determines conduct, it must necessarily do so a priori. The possibility of reason thus determining conduct must now be investigated.

The will is thought of as a faculty of determining itself to action in accordance with the conception of certain laws. Such a faculty can be found only in rational beings. That which serves the will as the objective ground of its self-determination is a purpose, and if it is given by reason alone it must hold alike for all rational beings. On the other hand, that which contains the ground of the possibility of the action, whose result is an end, is called the means. The subjective ground of desire is the incentive (*Triebfeder*) while the objective ground of volition is the motive (*Bewegungsgrund*). Thus arises the distinction between subjective purposes, which rest on incentives, and objective purposes, which depend on motives valid for every rational being. Practical principles are formal when they disregard all subjective purposes; they are material when they have subjective purposes and thus certain incentives as their basis. The purposes that a rational being holds before himself by choice as consequences of his action are material purposes and are without exception only relative, for only their relation to a particularly constituted faculty of desire in the subject gives them their worth. And this worth cannot afford any universal principles for all rational beings or any principles valid
428 and necessary for every volition. That is, they cannot give rise to any practical laws. All these relative purposes, therefore, are grounds for hypothetical imperatives only.

But suppose that there were something the existence of which in itself had absolute worth, something which, as an end in itself, could be a ground of definite laws. In it and only in it could lie the ground of a possible categorical imperative (i.e., of a practical law).

Now, I say, man and, in general, every rational being exists as an end in himself and not merely as a means to be arbitrarily used by this or that will. In all his actions, whether they are directed toward himself or toward other rational beings, he must always be regarded at the same time as an end. All objects of inclination have only conditional worth, for if the inclinations and needs founded on them did not exist, their object would be worthless. The inclinations themselves as the sources of needs, however, are so lacking in absolute worth that the universal wish of every rational being must be indeed to free himself completely from them. Therefore, the worth of any objects to be obtained by our actions is at all times conditional. Beings whose existence does not depend on our will but on nature, if they are not rational beings, have only relative worth as means, and are therefore called "things"; rational beings, on the other hand, are designated "persons" because their nature indicates that they are ends in themselves (i.e., things which may not be used merely as means). Such a being is thus an object of respect, and as such restricts all [arbitrary] choice. Such beings are not merely subjective ends whose existence as a result of our action has a worth for us, but are objective ends (i.e., beings whose existence is an end in itself). Such an end is one in the place of which no other end, to which these beings should serve merely as means, can be put. Without them, nothing of absolute worth could be found, and if all worth is conditional and thus contingent, no supreme practical principle for reason could be found anywhere.

Thus if there is to be a supreme practical principle and a categorical imperative for the human will, it must be one that forms an objective principle of the will from the conception of that which is necessarily an end for everyone because it is an end in itself. Hence this objective principle can serve as a universal law. The ground of this principle is: rational nature exists 429 as an end in itself. Man necessarily thinks of his own existence in this way, and thus far it is a subjective principle of human actions. Also every other rational being thinks of his existence on the same rational ground which holds also for myself*; thus it is at the same time an objective principle from which, as a supreme practical ground, it must be possible to derive all laws of the will. The practical imperative, therefore, is the following: Act so that you treat humanity, whether in your own person or in that of another, always as an end and never as a means only. Let us now see whether this can be achieved. To return to our previous examples:

First, according to the concept of necessary duty to oneself, he who contemplates suicide will ask himself whether his action can be consistent with

---

*Here I present this proposition as a postulate, but in the last section grounds for it will be found.

the idea of humanity as an end in itself. If in order to escape from burdensome circumstances he destroys himself, he uses a person merely as a means to maintain a tolerable condition up to the end of life. Man, however, is not a thing, and thus not something to be used merely as a means; he must always be regarded in all his actions as an end in himself. Therefore I cannot dispose of man in my own person so as to mutilate, corrupt, or kill him. (It belongs to ethics proper to define more accurately this basic principle so as to avoid all misunderstanding, e.g., as to amputating limbs in order to preserve myself, or to exposing my life to danger in order to save it; I must therefore omit them here.)

Second, as concerns necessary or obligatory duties to others, he who intends a deceitful promise to others sees immediately that he intends to use another man merely as a means, without the latter at the same time containing the end in himself. For he whom I want to use for my own purposes by 430 means of such a promise cannot possibly assent to my mode of acting against him and thus share in the purpose of this action. This conflict with the principle of other men is even clearer if we cite examples of attacks on their freedom and property, for then it is clear that he who violates the rights of men intends to make use of the person of others merely as means, without considering that, as rational beings, they must always be esteemed at the same time as ends (i.e., only as beings who must be able to embody in themselves the purpose of the very same action).*

Thirdly, with regard to contingent (meritorious) duty to oneself, it is not sufficient that the action not conflict with humanity in our person as an end in itself; it must also harmonize with it. In humanity there are capacities for greater perfection which belong to the purpose of nature with respect to humanity in our own person, and to neglect these might perhaps be consistent with the preservation of humanity as an end in itself, but not with the furtherance of that end.

Fourthly, with regard to meritorious duty to others, the natural purpose that all men have is their own happiness. Humanity might indeed exist if no one contributed to the happiness of others, provided he did not intentionally detract from it, but this harmony with humanity as an end in itself is only negative, not positive, if everyone does not also endeavor, as far as he can, to further the purposes of others. For the ends of any person, who is an end in himself, must as far as possible be also my ends, if that conception of an end in itself is to have its full effect on me.

431   This principle of humanity, and in general of every rational creature an end

---

*Let it not be thought that the banal "what you do not wish to be done to you . . . " could here serve as guide or principle, for it is only derived from the principle and is restricted by various limitations. It cannot be a universal law, because it contains the ground neither of duties to one's self nor of the benevolent duties to others (for many a man would gladly consent that others should not benefit him, provided only that he might be excused from showing benevolence to them). Nor does it contain the ground of obligatory duties to another, for the criminal would argue on this ground against the judge who sentences him. And so on.

in itself, is the supreme limiting condition on the freedom of action of each man. It is not borrowed from experience, first, because of its universality, since it applies to all rational beings generally, and experience does not suffice to determine anything about them; and secondly, because in experience humanity is not thought of (subjectively) as the purpose of men (i.e., as an object which we of ourselves really make our purpose). Rather it is thought of as the objective end which ought to constitute the supreme limiting condition of all subjective ends whatever they may be. Thus this principle must arise from pure reason. Objectively the ground of all practical legislation lies (according to the first principle) in the rule and form of universality, which makes it capable of being a law (at least a natural law); subjectively it lies in the end. But the subject of all ends is every rational being as an end in itself (by the second principle); from this there follows the third practical principle of the will as the supreme condition of its harmony with universal practical reason, viz, the Idea of the will of every rational being as making universal law.

By this principle all maxims are rejected which are not consistent with the will's giving universal law. The will is not only subject to the law, but subject in such a way that it must be conceived also as itself prescribing the law, of which reason can hold itself to be the author; it is on this ground alone that the will is regarded as subject to the law.

By the very fact that the imperatives are thought of as categorical, either way of conceiving them — as imperatives demanding the lawfulness of actions, resembling the lawfulness of the natural order; or as imperatives of the universal prerogative of the purposes of rational beings as such — excludes from their sovereign authority all admixture of any interest as an incentive to obedience. But we have been *assuming* the imperatives to be categorical, for that was necessary if we wished to explain the concept of duty; that there are practical propositions which command categorically could not of itself be proved independently, just as little as it can be proved anywhere in this section. One thing, however could have been done: to indicate in the imperative itself, by some determination inherent in it, that in willing from duty the renunciation of all interest is the specific mark of the categorical imperative, distinguishing it from the hypothetical. And this is now done in the third 432 formulation of the principle, viz., in the Idea of the will of every rational being as a will giving universal law. A will which is subject to laws can be bound to them by an interest, but a will giving the supreme law cannot possibly depend upon any interest, for such a dependent will would itself need still another law which would restrict the interest of its self-love to the condition that its [maxim] should be valid as a universal law.

Thus the principle of every human will as a will giving universal law in all its maxims* is very well adapted to being a categorical imperative, provided it

---

*I may be excused from citing examples to elucidate this principle, for those that have already illustrated the categorical imperative and its formula can here serve the same purpose.

is otherwise correct. Because of the Idea of giving universal law, it is based on no interest; and thus of all possible imperatives, it alone can be unconditional. Or, better, converting the proposition: if there is a categorical imperative (a law for the will of every rational being), it can command only that everything be done from the maxim of its will as one which could have as its object only itself considered as giving universal law. For only in this case are the practical principle and the imperative which the will obeys unconditional, because the will can have no interest as its foundation.

If now we look back upon all previous attempts which have ever been undertaken to discover the principle of morality, it is not to be wondered at that they all had to fail. Man was seen to be bound to laws by his duty, but it was not seen that he is subject to his own, but still universal, legislation, and that he is bound to act only in accordance with his own will, which is, however, designed by nature to be a will giving universal law. For if one thought of him as only subject to a law (whatever it may be), this necessarily implied some 433 interest as a stimulus or compulsion to obedience because the law did not arise from his will. Rather, his will had to be constrained by something else to act in a certain way. By this strictly necessary consequence, however, all the labor of finding a supreme ground for duty was irrevocably lost, and one never arrived at duty but only at the necessity of acting from a certain interest. This might be his own interest or that of another, but in either case the imperative always had to be conditional, and could not at all serve as a moral command. The moral principle I will call the principle of *autonomy* of the will in contrast to all other principles which I accordingly count under *heteronomy*.

The concept of any rational being as a being that must regard itself as giving universal law through all the maxims of its will, so that it may judge itself and its actions from this standpoint, leads to a very fruitful concept, namely that of a *realm of ends*.

By *realm* I understand the systematic union of different rational beings through common laws. Because laws determine which ends have universal validity, if we abstract from personal differences of rational beings, and thus from all content of their private purposes, we can think of a whole of all ends in systematic connection, a whole of rational beings as ends in themselves as well as a whole of particular purposes which each may set for himself. This is a realm of ends, which is possible on the principles stated above. For all rational beings stand under the law that each of them should treat himself and all others never merely as means, but in every case at the same time as an end in himself. Thus there arises a systematic union of rational beings through common objective laws. This is a realm which may be called a realm of ends (certainly only an ideal) because what these laws have in view is just the relation of these beings to each other as ends and means.

434   A rational being belongs to the realm of ends as a member when he gives universal laws in it while also himself subject to these laws. He belongs to it as

sovereign when, as legislating, he is subject to the will of no other. The rational being must regard himself always as legislative in a realm of ends possible through the freedom of the will whether he belongs to it as member or as sovereign. He cannot maintain his position as sovereign merely through the maxims of his will, but only when he is a completely independent being without need and with unlimited power adequate to his will.

Morality, therefore, consists in the relation of every action to the legislation through which alone a realm of ends is possible. This legislation must be found in every rational being. It must be able to arise from his will, whose principle then is to do no action according to any maxim which would be inconsistent with its being a universal law, and thus to act only so that the will through its maxims could regard itself at the same time as giving universal law. If the maxims do not by their nature already necessarily conform to this objective principle of rational beings as giving universal law, the necessity of acting according to that principle is called practical constraint, which is to say: duty. Duty pertains not to the sovereign of the realm of ends, but rather to each member and to each in the same degree.

The practical necessity of acting according to this principle (duty) does not rest at all on feelings, impulses, and inclinations; it rests solely on the relation of rational beings to one another, in which the will of a rational being must always be regarded as legislative, for otherwise it could not be thought of as an end in itself. Reason, therefore, relates every maxim of the will as giving universal laws to every other will and also to every action towards itself; it does not do so for the sake of any other practical motive or future advantage but rather from the Idea of the dignity of a rational being who obeys no law except one which he himself also gives.

In the realm of ends everything has either a *price* or a *dignity*. Whatever has a price can be replaced by something else as its equivalent; on the other hand, whatever is above all price and therefore admits of no equivalent, has dignity.

That which is related to general human inclinations and needs has a *market price*. That which, without presupposing any need, accords with a certain 435 taste (i.e., with pleasure in the purposeless play of our faculties) has a *fancy price*. But that which constitutes the condition under which alone something can be an end in itself does not have mere relative worth (price) but an intrinsic worth (*dignity*).

Morality is the condition under which alone a rational being can be an end in itself, because only through it is it possible to be a lawgiving member in the realm of ends. Thus morality, and humanity so far as it is capable of morality, alone have dignity. Skill and diligence in work have a market value; wit, lively imagination, and humor have a fancy price; but fidelity in promises and benevolence on principle (not benevolence from instinct) have intrinsic worth. Nature and likewise art contain nothing which could make up for their lack, for their worth consists not in the effects which flow from them nor in any advantage and utility which they procure; it consists only in mental dispositions, maxims of the will, which are ready to reveal themselves in this manner through actions even though success does not favor them. These actions need no recommendation from my subjective disposition or taste in order that they may be looked upon with immediate favor and satisfaction, nor do they have need of any direct propensity or feeling directed to them. They exhibit the will which performs them as the object of an immediate respect, since nothing but reason is required in order to impose them upon the will. The will is not to be cajoled into them, for this, in the case of duties, would be a contradiction. This esteem lets the worth of such a turn of mind be recognized as dignity and puts it infinitely beyond any price; with things of price it cannot in the least be brought into any competition or comparison without, as it were, violating its holiness.

And what is it that justifies the morally good disposition or virtue in making such lofty claims? It is nothing less that the participation it affords the rational being in giving universal laws. He is thus fitted to be a member in a possible realm of ends, to which his own nature already destined him. For, as an end in himself, he is destined to be a lawgiver in the realm of ends, free from all laws of nature and obedient only to those laws which he himself gives. Accordingly, his maxims can belong to a universal legislation to which he is at the 436   same time subject. A thing has no worth other than that determined for it by the law. The lawgiving which determines all worth must therefore have a dignity (i.e., an unconditional and incomparable worth). For the esteem which a rational being must have for it, only the word "respect"[3] is suitable. Autonomy is thus the basis of the dignity of both human nature and every rational nature.

The three aforementioned ways of presenting the principle of morality are fundamentally only so many formulas of the very same law, and each of them unites the others in itself. There is, nevertheless, a difference between them, but the difference is more subjectively than objectively practical, for the difference is intended to bring an Idea of reason closer to intuition (by means of a certain analogy) and thus nearer to feeling. All maxims have:

1. A form, which consists in universality, and in this respect the formula of the moral imperative requires that maxims be chosen as though they should hold as universal laws of nature.
2. A material (i.e., an end), and in this respect the formula says that the rational being, as by its nature an end and thus as an end in itself, must serve in every maxim as the condition restricting all merely relative and arbitrary ends.

[3]H.J. Paton, in his translation of this text, prefers to translate the German word *Achtung* as *reverence*. There are religious overtones of awe before the sublimity of the moral law which speak in favor of Paton's choice.

3. A complete determination of all maxims by the formula that all maxims which stem from autonomous legislation ought to harmonize with a possible realm of ends as with a realm of nature.*

There is a progression here like that through the categories of the unity of the form of the will (its universality), the plurality of material (the objects, ends), to the all-comprehensiveness or totality of the system of ends. But it is better in moral valuation to follow the rigorous method and to make the universal formula of the categorical imperative the basis: Act according to the 437 maxim which can at the same time make itself a universal law. But if one wishes to gain a hearing for the moral law, it is very useful to bring one and the same action under the three stated principles and thus, so far as possible, bring it nearer to intuition.

We can now end where we started, with the concept of an unconditionally good will. That will is absolutely good which cannot be bad, and thus it is a will whose maxims, when made universal law, can never conflict with itself. Thus this principle is also its supreme law: Always act according to that maxim whose universality as law you can at the same time will. This is the only condition under which a will can never come into conflict with itself, and such an imperative is categorical. Because the validity of the will as a universal law for possible actions has an analogy with the universal connection of the existence of things under universal laws, which is the formal element of nature in general, the categorical imperative can be expressed also as follows: Act on those maxims which can at the same time have themselves as universal laws of nature as their object. Such, then, is the formula of an absolutely good will.

Rational nature is distinguished from others in that it proposes an end to itself. This end would be the material of every good will. Since, however, in the Idea of an absolutely good will without the limiting condition that this or that end be achieved, we must abstract from every end to be actually effected (as any particular end would make each will only relatively good), we must conceive the end here not as one to be brought about, but as a self-existent end, and thus merely negatively, as that which must never be acted against and which consequently must never be valued merely as a means but in every volition also as an end. Now this end can never be other than the subject of all possible ends themselves, because this is at the same time the subject of a possible will which is absolutely good, for the latter cannot without contradiction be made secondary to any other object. The principle: Act with reference to every rational being (whether yourself or another) so that in your

---

*Teleology considers nature as a realm of ends; morals regards a possible realm of ends as a realm of nature. In the former the realm of ends is a theoretical Idea for the explanation of what actually is. In the latter it is a practical Idea for bringing about that which does not exist but which can become actual though our conduct and for making it conform with this Idea.

maxim it is an end in itself, is thus basically identical with the principle: Act by a maxim which involves its own universal validity for every rational being.

That in the use of means to any end I should restrict my maxim to the condition of its universal validity as a law for every subject is tantamount to saying that the subject of ends (i.e., the rational being itself) must be made the basis of all maxims of actions and thus be treated never as a mere means but as the supreme limiting condition in the use of all means (i.e., as at the same time an end).

It follows incontestably that every rational being must be able to regard himself as an end in himself with reference to all laws to which he may be subject whatever they may be, and thus see himself as giving universal laws. For it is just the fitness of his maxims to universal legislation that indicates that he is an end in himself. It also follows that his dignity (his prerogative) over all merely natural beings entails that he must take his maxims from the point of view that regards himself, and hence also every other rational being, as legislative. Rational beings are, on this account, called persons. In this way, a world of rational beings (*mundus intelligibilis*) is possible as a realm of ends, because of the legislation belonging to all persons as members. Consequently every rational being must act as if by his maxims he were at all times a legislative member of the universal realm of ends. The formal principle of these maxims is: So act as if your maxims should serve at the same time as universal law (for all rational beings).

A realm of ends is thus possible only by analogy with a realm of nature. The former is possible only by maxims (i.e., self-imposed rules), while the latter is possible by laws of efficient causes of things externally necessitated. Regardless of this difference, by analogy we call the natural whole a realm of nature so far as it is related to rational beings as its end; we do so even though the natural whole is looked upon as a machine. Such a realm of ends would actually be realized through maxims whose rule is prescribed to all rational beings by the categorical imperative, if they were universally obeyed. But a rational being, though he scrupulously follow this maxim, cannot for that reason expect every other rational being to be true to it, not can he expect the realm of nature and its orderly design to harmonize with him as a fitting member of a realm of ends which is possible through himself. That is, he cannot count on its favoring his expectation of happiness. Still the law: Act according to the maxim of a member of a merely potential realm of ends who gives universal law, remains in full force because it commands categorically. And just in this lies the paradox that simply the dignity of humanity as rational nature without any end or advantage to be gained by it, and thus respect for a mere Idea, should serve as the inflexible precept of the will. There is the further paradox that the sublimity of the maxims and the worthiness of every rational subject to be a law-giving member in the realm of ends consist precisely in the independence of his maxims from all such incentives. Otherwise he would have to be viewed as subject only the natural law of his needs. Although the realm of nature as well as that of ends would be thought of as united under a sovereign, so that the latter would no longer remain a mere Idea but would receive true reality, the realm of ends would undoubtedly gain a strong urge in its favor though its intrinsic worth would not be augmented. Regardless of this, even the one and only absolute legislator would still have to be conceived as judging the worth of rational beings only by the disinterested conduct which they prescribe to themselves merely from the Idea. The essence of things is not changed by their external relations, and without reference to these relations a man must be judged only by what constitutes his absolute worth, and this is true whoever his judge may be, even if it be the Supreme Being. Morality is thus the relation of actions to the autonomy of the will (i.e., to the possible giving of universal law by the maxims of the will). The action which can be compatible with the autonomy of the will is permitted; that which does not agree with it is prohibited. The will whose whose maxims are necessarily in harmony with the laws of autonomy is a holy will or an absolutely good will. The dependence of a will not absolutely good on the principle of autonomy (moral constraint) is *obligation*. Hence obligation cannot be predicated of a holy will. The objective necessity of an action from obligation is called *duty*.

From what has just been said, it can easily be explained how it happens that, although in the concept of duty we think of subjection to law, we do nevertheless at the same time ascribe a certain sublimity and dignity to the 440 person who fulfills all his duties. For though there is no sublimity in him in so far as he is subject to the moral law, yet he is sublime in so far as he is a giver of the law and subject to it for this reason only. We have also shown above how neither fear of nor inclination to the law is the incentive which can give moral worth to action; only respect for it can do so. Our own will, so far as it would act only under the condition of a universal legislation rendered possible by its maxims — this will ideally possible for us — is the proper object of respect, and the dignity of humanity consists just in its capacity to give universal laws under the condition that it is itself subject to this same legislation.

The Autonomy of the Will as the Supreme Principle of Morality

Autonomy of the will is that property of it by which it is a law to itself independent of any property of the objects of its volition. Hence the principle of autonomy is: Never choose except in such a way that the maxims of the choice are comprehended as universal law in the same volition. That this practical rule is an imperative, that is, that the will of every rational being is necessarily bound to it as a condition, cannot be proved by a mere analysis of the concepts occurring in it, because it is a synthetical proposition. To prove it, we would have to go beyond the knowledge of objects to a critical examination of the subject (i.e., to a critique of pure practical reason), for this synthetical proposition which commands apodictically must be susceptible of being known a priori. This matter, however, does not belong in the present section. But that the principle of autonomy, which is now in question, is the sole principle of morals can be readily shown by mere analysis of the concepts of morality; for by this analysis we find that its principle must be a categorical imperative and that the imperative commands neither more nor less than this very autonomy.

441 The Heteronomy of the Will as the Source of All Spurious Principles of Morality

If the will seeks the law which is to determine it elsewhere than in the fitness of its maxims to be given as universal law, and if thus it goes outside itself and seeks the law in the property of any of its objects, heteronomy always results. For then the will does not give itself the law, but the object through its relation to the will gives the law to it. This relation, whether it rests on inclination or on conceptions of reason, admits of only hypothetical imperatives: I should do something for the reason that I will something else. The moral (categorical) imperative, on the other hand, says that I should act in this or that way even though I have not willed anything else. For example, the former says that I should not lie if I wish to keep my good name. The latter says I should not lie even though it would not cause me the least injury. The latter, therefore, must disregard every object to such an extent that it has absolutely no influence on the will; it must so disregard it that practical reason (will) may not just minister to any interest not its own but rather show its commanding authority as the supreme legislation. Thus, for instance, I should seek to further the happiness of others, not as though its realization were of consequence to me (because of a direct inclination or some satisfaction related to it indirectly through reason); I should do so solely because the maxim which excludes it from my duty cannot be comprehended as a universal law in one and the same volition.

Classification of All Possible Principles of Morality Following from the Assumed Principle of Heteronomy

Here as everywhere in the pure use of reason so long as a critical examination of it is lacking, human reason tries all possible wrong ways before it succeeds in finding the one true way.

All principles which can be taken from this point of view are either empiri-
442 cal or rational. The former, drawn from the principle of happiness, are based on physical or moral feeling; the latter, drawn from the principle of perfection, are based either on the rational concept of perfection as a possible result or on the concept of an independent perfection (the will of God) as the determining ground of the will.

Empirical principles are not at all suited to serve as the basis of moral laws. For if the basis of the universality by which they should be valid for all rational beings without distinction (the unconditional practical necessity which is thereby imposed upon them) is derived from a particular tendency of human nature or the accidental circumstance in which it is found, that universality is lost. But the principle of one's own happiness is the most objectionable of the empirical principles. This is not merely because it is false and because experience contradicts the supposition that well-being is always proportional to good conduct, nor yet because this principle contributes nothing to the establishment of morality inasmuch as it is a very different thing to make a man happy from making him good, and to make him prudent and farsighted for his own advantage is far from making him virtuous. Rather, it is because this principle supports morality with incentives which undermine it and destroy all its sublimity, for it puts the motives to virtue and those to vice in the same class, teaching us only to make a better calculation while obliterating the specific difference between them. On the other hand, there is the alleged special sense,* the moral feeling. The appeal to it is superficial, since those who cannot think expect help from feeling, even with respect to that which concerns universal laws; they do so even though feelings naturally differ so infinitely in degree that they are incapable of furnishing a uniform standard of the good and bad, and also in spite of the fact that one cannot validly judge for others by means of his own feeling. Nevertheless, the moral feeling is nearer to morality and its dignity, inasmuch as it pays virtue the honor of ascribing the satisfaction and esteem for her directly to morality, and does not, as it were, say to her face that it is not her beauty but only our advantage which attaches us to her. 443

Among the rational principles of morality, there is the ontological concept of perfection. It is empty, indefinite, and consequently useless for finding in the immeasurable field of possible reality the greatest possible sum which is suitable to us; and, in specifically distinguishing the reality which is here in question from all other reality, it inevitably tends to move in a circle and cannot avoid tacitly presupposing the morality which it ought to explain. Nevertheless, it is better than the theological concept, which derives morality from a most perfect divine will. It is better not merely because we cannot intuit the perfection of the divine will, having rather to derive it only from our own concepts of which morality itself is foremost, but also because if we do not so derive it (and to do so would involve a most flagrant circle in explanation), the only remaining concept of the divine will is made up of the attributes of desire for glory and dominion combined with the awful conceptions of might and vengeance, and any system of ethics based on them would be directly opposed to morality.

---

*I count the principle of moral feeling under that of happiness, because every empirical interest promises to contribute to our well-being by the agreeableness that a thing affords, either directly and without a view to future advantage or with a view to it. We must likewise, with Hutcheson, count the principle of sympathy with the happiness of others under the moral sense which he assumed.

But if I had to choose between the concept of the moral sense and that of perfection in general (neither of which at any rate weakens morality, though they are not capable of serving as its foundation), I would decide for the latter, because it preserves the indefinite Idea of a will good in itself and free from corruption until it can be more narrowly defined. It at least withdraws the decision on the question from the realm of sensibility and brings it to the court of pure reason, although it does not even there decide the question.

For the rest, I think I may be excused from a lengthy refutation of all these doctrines. It is so easy, and presumably so well understood even by those whose office requires them to decide for one of these theories (since their students would not tolerate suspension of judgment), that such a refutation would be superfluous. What interests us more, however, is to know that all these principles set up nothing other than heteronomy of the will as the first ground of morality, and thus they necessarily miss their goal.

444   In every case in which the object of the will must be assumed as prescribing the rule which is to determine the will, the rule is nothing else than heteronomy. The imperative in this case is conditional, stating that if or because one wills such and such an object, one ought to act thus or so. Therefore the imperative can never command morally, that is, categorically. The object may determine the will by means of inclination, as in the principle of one's own happiness, or by means of reason directed to objects of our possible volition in general, as in the principle of perfection; but the will in these cases never determines itself directly by the conception of the action itself but only by the incentive which the foreseen result of the action incites in the will—that is: I ought to do something because I will something else. And here still another law must be assumed in me as the basis for this imperative; it would be a law by which I would necessarily will that other thing; but this law would in its turn require an imperative to restrict this maxim. Since the conception of a result to be obtained by one's own powers incites in the will an impulse which depends upon the natural characteristic of the subject, either of his sensibility (inclination and taste) or understanding and reason; and since these faculties according to the particular constitution of their nature find satisfaction in exercising themselves on the result of the voluntary action, it follows that it would really be nature which would give the law [to the action]. This law, as a law of nature, would have to be known and proved by experience, and as in itself contingent it would be unfit to be an apodictical practical rule such as the moral rule must be. Such a law always represents heteronomy of the will: the will does not give itself the law, but an external impulse gives the law to the will according to nature of the subject which is susceptible to receive it.

The absolutely good will, the principle of which must be a categorical imperative, is thus undetermined with reference to any object. It contains only the form of volition in general, and this form is autonomy. That is, the capability of the maxims of every good will to make themselves universal laws is itself the sole law which the will of every rational being imposes on himself, and it does not need to support this by any incentive or interest.

How such a synthetical practical a priori proposition is possible and why it is necessary is a problem whose solution does not lie within the boundaries of the metaphysics of morals. Moreover, we have not here affirmed its truth, and even less professed to command a proof of it. We showed only through the 445 development of the generally received concept of morals that autonomy of the will is unavoidably connected with it, or rather that it is its foundation. Whoever, therefore, holds morality to be something real and not a chimerical idea without truth must also concede its principle which has been derived here. Consequently, this section, like the first, was merely analytical. To prove that morality is not a mere phantom of the mind — and if the categorical imperative, and with it the autonomy of the will, is true and absolutely necessary as an a priori proposition, it follows that it is no phantom — requires that a synthetical use of pure practical reason be possible. But we must not venture on this use without first making a critical examination of this faculty of reason. In the last section we shall give the principal features of such an examination that will be sufficient for our purpose.

THIRD SECTION
TRANSITION FROM THE METAPHYSICS OF MORALS TO THE CRITICAL EXAMINATION OF PURE PRACTICAL REASON[4]

The Concept of Freedom is the Key to the Explanation of the Autonomy of the Will

As will is a kind of causality of living beings so far as they are rational, 446 freedom would be that property of this causality by which it can be effective independent of foreign causes determining it, just as natural necessity is the property of the causality of all irrational beings by which they are determined to activity by the influence of foreign causes.

The preceding definition of freedom is negative and therefore affords no insight into its essence. But a positive concept of freedom flows from it which is so much the richer and more fruitful. Since the concept of a causality entails that of laws according to which something (i.e., the effect) must be established through something else which we call cause, it follows that freedom is by no means lawless even though it is not a property of the will according to laws of nature. Rather, it must be a causality of a peculiar kind according to immutable laws. Otherwise a free will would be an absurdity. Natural necessity is, as we have seen, a heteronomy of efficient causes, for

---

[4]*Kritik der reinen praktischen Vernunft*. These words do not refer to the book, *Critique of Practical Reason*. At the time Kant wrote the *Foundations of the Metaphysics of Morals* he did not anticipate writing a second *Critique* but planned to go directly to the composition of the *Metaphysics of Morals* (first published in 1797).

every effect is possible only according to the law that something else deter-
447   mines the efficient cause to its causality. What else, then, can the freedom of
the will be but autonomy (i.e., the property of the will to be a law to itself)?
The proposition that the will is a law to itself in all its actions, however, only
expresses the principle that we should act according to no other maxim than
that which can also have itself as a universal law for its object. And this is just
the formula of the categorical imperative and the principle of morality.
Therefore a free will and a will under moral laws are identical.

Thus if freedom of the will is presupposed, morality together with its
principle follows from it by the mere analysis of its concepts. But the principle: An absolutely good will is one whose maxim can always include itself as a
universal law, is nevertheless a synthetical proposition. It is synthetical because by analysis of the concept of an absolutely good will that property of the
maxim cannot be found it it. Such synthetical propositions, however, are
made possible only by the fact that the two cognitions are connected with
each other through their union with a third in which both are to be found. The
positive concept of freedom furnishes this third cognition, which cannot be,
as in the case of physical causes, the sensible world of nature, in the concept
of which we find conjoined the concepts of something as cause in relation to
something else as effect. We cannot yet show directly what this third cognition is to which freedom directs us and of which we have an a priori Idea, nor
can we yet explain the deduction of the concept of freedom from pure
practical reason, and therewith the possibility of a categorical imperative. For
this, some further preparation is needed.

Freedom Must be Presupposed as the Property of the Will of all Rational Beings

It is not enough to ascribe freedom to our will, on whatever grounds, if we
do not also have sufficient grounds for attributing it to all rational beings. For
since morality serves as a law for us only as rational beings, it must hold for all
rational beings, and since it must be derived exclusively from the property of
freedom, freedom as a property of the will of all rational beings must be
448   demonstrated. And it does not suffice to prove it from certain alleged experiences of human nature (which is indeed impossible, as it can be proved only a
priori), but we must prove it as belonging universally to the activity of rational
beings endowed with a will. Now I say that every being which cannot act
otherwise than under the Idea of freedom is thereby really free in a practical
respect. That is to say, all laws which are inseparably bound with freedom
hold for it just as if its will were proved free in itself by theoretical philosophy.* Now I affirm that we must necessarily grant that every rational being

---

*I propose this argument as sufficient to our purpose: Freedom as an Idea is posited by all
rational beings as the basis for their actions. I do so in order to avoid having to prove freedom also
in its theoretical aspect. For even if the latter is left unproved, the laws which would obligate a
being who was really free would hold for a being who cannot act except under the Idea of his own
freedom. Thus we escape the onus which has been pressed on theory.

who has a will also has the Idea of freedom and that it acts only under this Idea. For in such a being we think of a reason which is practical (i.e., a reason which has causality with respect to its object). Now we cannot conceive of a reason which, in making its judgments, consciously responds to a bidding from the outside, for then the subject would attribute the determination of its power of judgment not to reason but to an impulse. Reason must regard itself as the author of its principles, independently of alien influences; consequently as practical reason or as the will of a rational being it must regard itself as free. That is to say, the will of a rational being can be a will of its own only under the Idea of freedom, and therefore from a practical point of view such a will must be ascribed to all rational beings.

Of the Interest Attaching to the Ideas of Morality

We have finally reduced the definite concept of morality to the Idea of freedom, but we could not prove freedom to be actual in ourselves and in human nature. We saw only that we must presuppose it if we would think of a 449
being as rational and conscious of its causality with respect to actions, that is, as endowed with a will; and so we find that on the very same grounds we must ascribe to each being endowed with reason and will the property of determining itself to action under the Idea of its freedom.

From presupposing this Idea [of freedom] there followed also the consciousness of a law of action: that the subjective principles of actions (i.e., maxims) must in every instance be so chosen that they can hold also as objective (i.e., universal) principles, and can thus serve as principles for our giving universal laws. But why should I, as a rational being, and why should all other beings endowed with reason, subject ourselves to this law? I will admit that no interest impels me to do so, for that would then give no categorical imperative. But I must nevertheless take an interest in it and see how it comes about, for this *ought* is properly a *would* that is valid for every rational being provided reason were practical for it without hindrance [i.e., exclusively determined its action]. For beings who, like ourselves, are affected by the senses as incentives different from reason, and who do not always do that which reason by itself alone would have done, that necessity of action is expressed as only an *ought*. The subjective necessity is thus distinguished from the objective.

It therefore seems that we have only presupposed the moral law, the principle of the autonomy of the will in the Idea of freedom, as if we could not prove its reality and objective necessity by itself. Even if that were so, we would still have gained something because we would at least have defined the genuine principle more accurately than had been done before; but with regard to its validity and the practical necessity of subjection to it, we would not have advanced a single step, for we could give no satisfactory answer to anyone who asked us why the universal validity of our maxim as a law had to be the restricting condition of our action. We could not tell on what is based the worth which we ascribe to actions of this kind — a worth so great that there can be no higher interest — nor could we tell how it happens that man believes that it is only through this that he feels his own personal worth, in 450 contrast to which the worth of a pleasant or unpleasant state is to be regarded as nothing.

We do find sometimes that we can take an interest in a personal quality which involves no [personal] interest in any [external] condition, provided only that the [possession of] this quality makes us fit to participate in the [desired] condition in case reason were to effect the allotment of this condition. That is, being worthy of happiness, even without the motive of partaking in happiness, can interest of itself. But this judgment is in fact only the effect of the importance already ascribed to moral laws (if by the Idea of freedom we detach ourselves from every empirical interest). But that we ought so to detach ourselves from every empirical interest, to regard ourselves as free in acting and yet as subject to certain laws, in order to find a worth wholly in our person which would compensate for the loss of everything which could make our situation desirable — how this is possible and hence on what grounds the moral law obligates us still cannot be seen in this way.

We must openly confess that there is a kind of circle here from which it seems that there is no escape. We assume that we are free in the order of efficient causes so that we can conceive of ourselves as subject to moral laws in the order of ends. And then we think of ourselves subject to these laws because we have ascribed freedom of the will to ourselves. This is circular because freedom and self-legislation of the will are both autonomy and thus are reciprocal concepts, and for that reason one of them cannot be used to explain the other and to furnish a ground for it. At most they can be used for the logical purpose of bringing apparently different conceptions of the same object under a single concept (as we reduce different fractions of the same value to the lowest common terms).

One recourse, however, remains open to us, namely, to inquire whether we do not assume a different standpoint when we think of ourselves as causes a priori efficient through freedom from that which we occupy when we conceive of ourselves in the light of our actions as effects which we see before our eyes.

The following remark requires no subtle reflection, and we may suppose that even the commonest understanding can make it, though it does so, after 451 its fashion, by an obscure discernment of judgment which it calls feeling: all conceptions, like those of the senses, which come to us without our choice enable us to know objects only as they affect us, while what they are in themselves remains unknown to us; therefore, as regards this kind of conception, even with the closest attention and clearness which understanding may ever bring to them we can attain only a knowledge of appearances and never a knowledge of things in themselves. As soon as this distinction is once made (perhaps merely because of a difference noticed between conceptions which are given to us from somewhere else and to which we are passive, and those which we produce from ourselves only and in which we show our own activity), it follows of itself that we must admit and assume behind the appearances something else which is not appearance, namely, things in themselves; we do so although we must admit that we cannot approach them more closely and can never know what they are in themselves, since they can never be known by us except as they affect us. This must furnish a distinction, though a crude one, between a world of sense and a world of understanding. The former, by differences in our sensible faculties, can be very different to various observers, while the latter, which is its foundation, remains always the same. A man may not presume to know even himself as he really is by knowing himself through inner sensation. For since he does not, as it were, produce himself or derive his concept of himself a priori but only empirically, it is natural that he obtain his knowledge of himself through inner sense and consequently only through the appearance of his nature and the way in which his consciousness is affected. But beyond the characteristic of his own subject which is compounded of these mere appearances, he necessarily assumes something else as its basis, namely, his ego as it is in itself. Thus in respect to mere perception and receptivity to sensations he must count himself as belonging to the world of sense; but in respect to that which may be pure activity in himself (i.e., in respect to that which reaches consciousness directly and not by affecting the senses) he must reckon himself as belonging to the intellectual world. But he has no further knowledge of that world.

To such a conclusion the thinking man must come with respect to all things 452 which may present themselves to him. Presumably it is to be met with in the commonest understanding which, as is well known, is very much inclined to expect behind the objects of the senses something else invisible and acting of itself. But common understanding soon spoils it by trying to make the invisible again sensible (i.e., to make it an object of intuition). Thus the common understanding becomes not in the least wiser.

Now man really finds in himself a faculty by which he distinguishes himself from all other things, even from himself so far as he is affected by objects. This faculty is reason. As a pure, spontaneous activity it is elevated even above understanding. For though the latter is also a spontaneous activity and does not, like sense, which is passive, merely contain representations which arise only when one is affected by things, it cannot produce by its activity any other concepts than those which serve to bring the sensible representations under rules and thereby to unite them in one consciousness. Without this use of sensibility it would think nothing at all; on the other hand, reason shows such a pure spontaneity in the case of Ideas that it far transcends anything that sensibility can give to consciousness, and shows its chief occupation in distinguishing the world of sense from the world of understanding, thereby prescribing limits to the understanding itself.

For this reason a rational being must regard itself *qua* intelligence (and not from the side of his lower faculties) as belonging to the world of understanding and not to that of the senses. Thus it has two standpoints from which it can consider itself and recognize the laws [governing] the employment of its powers and all its actions: first, as belonging to the world of sense, under the laws of nature (heteronomy), and, second, as belonging to the intelligible world under laws which, independent of nature, are not empirical but founded on reason alone.

As a rational being and thus as belonging to the intelligible world, man cannot think of the causality of his own will except under the Idea of freedom, for independence from the determining causes of the world of sense (an independence which reason must always ascribe to itself) is freedom. The concept of autonomy is inseparably connected with the Idea of freedom, and with the former there is inseparably bound the universal principle of morality, which is the ground in Idea of all actions of rational beings, just as natural law is the ground of all appearances.

We have now removed the suspicion which we raised that there might be a hidden circle in our reasoning from freedom to autonomy and from the latter to the moral law. This suspicion was that we laid down the Idea of freedom for the sake of the moral law in order later to derive the law from freedom, and that we were thus unable to give any basis for the law, presenting it only as a *petitio principii* which well-disposed minds might gladly allow us, but which we could never advance as a demonstrable proposition. But we now see that, if we think of ourselves as free, we transport ourselves into the intelligible world as members of it and know the autonomy of the will together with its consequence, morality; while if we think of ourselves as obligated, we consider ourselves as belonging both to the world of sense and at the same time to the intelligible world.

How Is a Categorical Imperative Possible?

The rational being counts himself, *qua* intelligence, as belonging to the intelligible world, and only as an efficient cause belonging to it does he call his causality will. On the other side, however, he is conscious of himself as a part of the world of sense in which his actions are found as mere appearances of that causality. But we do not discern how they are possible on the basis of that causality which we do not know; rather, those actions must be regarded as determined by other appearances, namely, desires and inclinations belonging to the world of sense. As a member of the intelligible world only, all my actions would completely accord with the principle of the autonomy of the pure will, and as a part only of the world of sense would they have to be assumed to conform wholly to the natural law of desires and inclinations and thus to the heteronomy of nature. (The former actions would rest on the supreme principle of morality, and the latter on that of happiness.) But since the intelligible world contains the ground of the world of sense and hence of its laws, the intelligible world is (and must be conceived as) directly legislative for my will, which belongs wholly to the intelligible world. Therefore I 454 recognize myself *qua* intelligence as subject to the law of the world of understanding and to the autonomy of the will. That is, I recognize myself as subject to the law of reason which contains in the Idea of freedom the law of the intelligible world, while at the same time I must acknowledge that I am a being which belongs to the world of sense. Therefore I must regard the laws of the intelligible world as imperatives for me, and actions in accord with this principle as duties.

Thus categorical imperatives are possible because the Idea of freedom makes me a member of an intelligible world. Consequently, if I were a member of that world only, all my actions *would* always be in accordance with the autonomy of the will. But since I intuit myself at the same time as a member of the world of sense, my actions *ought* to conform to it, and this categorical "ought" presents a synthetic a priori proposition, since besides my will affected by my sensuous desires there is added the Idea of exactly the same will as pure, practical of itself, and belonging to the intelligible world, which according to reason contains the supreme condition of the sensuously affected will. It is similar to the manner in which concepts of the understanding, which of themselves mean nothing but lawful form in general, are added to the intuitions of the sensible world, thus rendering possible a priori synthetic propositions on which all knowledge of a system of nature rests.

The practical use of ordinary human reason confirms the correctness of this deduction. When we present examples of honesty of purpose, of steadfastness in following good maxims, and of sympathy and general benevolence even with great sacrifices of advantage and comfort, there is no man, not even the most malicious villain (provided he is otherwise accustomed to using his reason), who does not wish that he also might have these qualities, but because of his inclinations and impulses cannot bring this about, yet at the same time wishes to be free from such inclinations which are burdensome even to him. He thus proves that with a will free from all impulses of sensibility, he in thought transfers himself into an order of things altogether different from that of his desires in the field of sensibility. He cannot expect to obtain by that wish any gratification of desires or any state which would satisfy his actual or even imagined inclinations, for the Idea itself, which elicits this wish from him, would lose its preeminence if he had any such 455 expectation. He imagines himself to be this better person when he transfers himself to the standpoint of a member of the intelligible world to which he is involuntarily impelled by the Idea of freedom (i.e., of independence from the determining causes in the world of sense); and from this standpoint he is conscious of a good will, which on his own confession constitutes the law for his bad will as a member of the world of sense. He acknowledges the authority of the law even while he transgresses it. The moral "ought" is therefore his own volition as a member of the intelligible world, and it is conceived by him as an "ought" only insofar as he regards himself at the same time as a member of the world of sense.

On the Extreme Boundary of all Practical Philosophy

In respect to their will, all men think of themselves as free. Hence arise all judgments of acts as being such as ought to have been done, although they were not done. But this freedom is not an empirical concept and cannot be such, for it continues to hold even though experience shows the contrary of the demands which are necessarily conceived to be consequences of the supposition of freedom. On the other hand it is equally necessary that everything that happens should be inexorably determined by natural laws, and this natural necessity is likewise no empirical concept because it implies the concept of necessity and thus of a priori knowledge. But this concept of a system of nature is confirmed by experience, and it is inevitably presupposed if experience, which is knowledge of the objects of the senses interconnected by universal laws, is to be possible. Therefore freedom is only an Idea of reason whose objective reality in itself is doubtful, while nature is a concept of the understanding which shows and must necessarily show its reality by examples of experience.

There now arises a dialectic of reason, since the freedom ascribed to the will seems to stand in contradiction to natural necessity. At this parting of the ways reason in its speculative aspect finds the path of natural necessity more well-beaten and usable than that of freedom, but in its practical aspect the path of freedom is the only one on which it is possible to make use of reason in our conduct. Hence it is as impossible for the subtlest philosophy as for the commonest reasoning to argue freedom away. Philosophy must therefore assume that no true contradiction will be found between freedom and natural necessity in the same human actions, for it cannot give up the concept of nature any more than that of freedom.

Hence if we should never be able to conceive how freedom is possible, at least this apparent contradiction must be convincingly eradicated. For if even the thought of freedom contradicted itself or nature, it would have to be surrendered in competition with natural necessity.

But it would be impossible to escape this contradiction if the subject, who seems to himself to be free, thought of himself in the same sense or in the same relationship when he calls himself free as when he assumes that in the same action he is subject to natural law. Therefore it is an inescapable task of speculative philosophy to show at least that its illusion of contradiction rests on the fact that we [do not] think of man in a different sense and relationship when we call him free from that in which we consider him as part of nature and subject to its laws. It must show not only that they can very well coexist but also that they must be thought of as necessarily united in one and the same subject; for otherwise no ground could be given as to why we should burden reason with an Idea which, though it may without contradiction be united with another that is sufficiently established, nevertheless involves us in a perplexity which sorely embarrasses reason in its theoretical use. This duty is imposed only on theoretical philosophy, so that it may clear the way for practical philosophy. Thus the philosopher has no choice as to whether he will remove the apparent contradiction or leave it untouched, for in the latter case the theory of it would be unoccupied land, into the possession of which the fatalist could rightly enter and drive all morality from its alleged property as occupying it without title.

Yet we cannot say here that we have reached the boundary of practical philosophy. For the settlement of the controversy does not belong to practical philosophy, as the latter only demands from theoretical reason that it put an 457 end to the discord in which it entangles itself in theoretical questions, so that practical reason may have rest and security from outward attacks which could dispute it the ground on which it desires to erect its edifice.

The title to freedom of the will claimed by ordinary reason is based on the consciousness and the conceded presupposition of the independence of reason from merely subjectively determining causes which together constitute what belongs only to sensation and is included under the general name of sensibility. Man, who in this way regards himself as intelligence, puts himself in a different order of things and in a relationship to determining grounds of an altogether different kind when he thinks of himself as intelligence with a will and thus as endowed with causality, compared with that other order of things and that other set of determining grounds which become relevant when he perceives himself as a phenomenon in the world of sense (as he really is also) and submits his causality to external determination according to natural laws. Now he soon realizes that both can subsist together— indeed, that they must. For there is not the least contradiction between a thing in appearance (as belonging to the world of sense) being subject to certain laws from which, as a thing or being in itself, it is independent. That he must think of himself in this twofold manner rests, with regard to the first, on the consciousness of himself as an object affected through the senses, and, with regard to what is required by the second, on the consciousness of himself as intelligence (i.e., as independent of sensible impressions in the use of reason), and thus as belonging to the intelligible world.

This is why man claims to possess a will which does not make him accountable for what belongs only to his desires and inclinations, but thinks of actions which can be done only by disregarding all his desires and sensuous attractions as possible and indeed as necessary for him. The causality of these actions lies in him as an intelligence and in effects and actions in accordance with principles of an intelligible world, of which he knows only that reason alone, and indeed pure reason independent of sensibility, gives the law in it. Moreover, since it is only as intelligence that he is his proper self (as man he is only appearance of himself), he knows that those laws apply to him directly and categorically, so that that to which inclinations and impulses and hence the entire nature of the world of sense incite him cannot in the least impair the laws of his volition as an intelligence. He does not even hold himself responsible for these inclinations and impulses or attribute them to his 458 proper self (i.e., his will), though he does impute to his will the indulgence which he may grant to them when he permits them to influence his maxims to the detriment of the rational laws of his will.

When practical reason thinks itself into an intelligible world, it does in no way transcend its boundaries. It would do so, however, if it tried to intuit or feel itself into it. The intelligible world is only a negative thought with respect to the world of sense, which does not give reason any laws for determining the will. It is positive only in the single point that freedom as negative determination is at the same time connected with a positive power and even a causality of reason. This causality we call a will to act so that the principle of actions will accord with the essential characteristic of a rational cause (i.e., with the condition of universal validity of a maxim as law). But if it were to borrow an object of the will (i.e., a motive) from the intelligible world, it would overstep its boundaries and pretend to be acquainted with something of which it knows nothing. The concept of a world of understanding is therefore only a standpoint from which reason sees itself forced to take outside appearances, in order to think of itself as practical. If the influences of sensibility were determining for man, this would not be possible; but it is necessary unless he is to be denied the consciousness of himself as an intelligence, and thus as a rational and rationally active cause (i.e., a cause acting in freedom). This thought certainly implies the Idea of an order and legislation different from that of natural mechanism, which apply to the world of sense; and it makes necessary the concept of an intelligible world, the whole of rational beings as things in themselves. But it does not give us the least occasion to think of it otherwise than according to its formal condition only (i.e., the universality of the maxim of the will as law and thus the autonomy of the will), which alone is consistent with freedom. All laws, on the other hand, which are directed to an object make for heteronomy, which belongs only to natural laws and which can apply only to the world of sense.

But reason would overstep its bounds if it undertook to explain how pure 459 reason can be practical, which is the same problem as explaining how freedom is possible.

We can explain nothing but what we can reduce to laws whose object can be given in some possible experience. But freedom is only an Idea, the objective reality which can in no way be shown to accord with natural laws or to be in any possible experience. Since no example in accordance with any analogy can support it, it can never be comprehended or even imagined. It holds only as the necessary presupposition of reason in a being who believes himself conscious of a will (i.e., of a faculty different from the mere faculty of desire, or a faculty of determining himself to act as an intelligence and thus according to laws of reason independently of natural instincts. But where determination according to natural laws comes to an end, there too all explanation ceases, and nothing remains but defence (i.e., refutation of the objections from those who pretend to have seen more deeply into the essence of things and who boldly declare freedom to be impossible). We can show them only that the supposed contradiction they have discovered lies nowhere else than in their necessarily regarding man [only] as appearance in order to make natural law valid with respect to human actions, and now when we require them to think of man *qua* intelligence as a thing in itself, they still persist in considering him as appearance [only]. Obviously, then, the detachment of his causality (his will) from all natural laws of the world of sense in one and the same subject is a contradiction, but this disappears when they reconsider and confess, as is reasonable, that behind the appearances things in themselves must stand as their hidden ground, and that we cannot expect the laws of the activity of these grounds to be the same as those under which their appearances stand.

The subjective impossibility of explaining the freedom of the will is the same as the impossibility of discovering and explaining an interest* which man can take in moral laws. Nevertheless, he does actually take an interest in them, and the foundation of this interest in us we call the moral feeling. This 460 moral feeling has been erroneously construed by some as the standard for our moral judgment, whereas it must be regarded rather as the subjective effect which the law has upon the will to which reason alone gives objective grounds.

In order to will an action which reason alone prescribes to the sensuously affected rational being as the action which he ought to will, there is certainly required a power of will to instil a feeling of pleasure of satisfaction in the fulfilment of duty, and hence there must be a causality of reason to determine sensibility in accordance with its own principles. But it is wholly impossible to discern, i.e., to make a priori conceivable, how a mere thought containing nothing sensuous is able to produce a sensation of pleasure or displeasure. For that is a particular kind of causality of which, as of all causality, we cannot determine anything a priori but must consult experience only. But since experience can exemplify the relation of cause to effect only as subsisting

*Interest is that by which reason becomes practical (i.e., a cause determining the will). We 459 therefore say only of a rational being that he takes an interest in something; irrational creatures feel only sensuous impulses. A direct interest in the action is taken by reason only if the universal validity of its maxim is a sufficient determining ground of the will. Only such an interest is pure. 460 But if reason can determine the will only by means of another object of desire or under the presupposition of a particular feeling of the subject, reason takes merely an indirect interest in the action, and since reason for itself alone without experience can discover neither objects of the will nor a particular feeling which lies at its root, that indirect interest would be only empirical and not a pure interest of reason. The logical interest of reason in advancing its insights is never direct but rather presupposes purposes for which they are to be used.

between two objects of experience, while here pure reason by mere Ideas (which furnish no object for experience) is to be the cause of an effect which does lie within experience, an explanation of how and why the universality of the maxim as law (and hence morality) interests us is completely impossible for us men. Only this much is certain: that it is valid for us not because it interests us (for that is heteronomy and dependence of practical reason on sensibility, i.e., on a basic feeling; and thus it could never be morally legislating); but that it interests us because it is valid for us as men, inasmuch as it has arisen from our will as intelligence and hence from our proper self; but what belongs to mere appearance is necessarily subordinated to the character of the thing in itself.

461

Thus the question *How is a categorical imperative possible?* can be answered to this extent: We can cite the only presupposition under which it is possible. This is the Idea of freedom, and we can have have insight into the necessity of this presupposition which is sufficient to the practical use of reason (i.e., to the conviction of the validity of this imperative and hence also of the moral law). But how this presupposition itself is possible can never be discerned by any human reason. However, on the presupposition of freedom of the will as an intelligence, its autonomy as the formal condition under which alone it can be determined is a necessary consequence. To presuppose the freedom of the will is not only quite possible, as speculative philosophy itself can prove, for it does not involve itself in a contradiction with the principle of natural necessity in the interconnection of appearances in the world of sense. But it is also unconditionally necessary that a rational being conscious of its causality through reason, and thus conscious of a will different from desires, should practically presuppose freedom (i.e., presuppose it in the Idea as the fundamental condition of all his voluntary acts). Yet how pure reason, without any other incentives whencesoever derived, can by itself be practical (i.e., how the simple principle of the universal validity of its maxims as laws — which would certainly be the form of a pure practical reason — without any material (object) of the will in which we might in advance take some interest), can itself furnish an incentive and produce an interest which would be called purely moral; or, in other words, *how pure reason can be practical* — to explain this, all human reason is wholly incompetent, and all the pain and work of seeking an explanation of it are wasted.

462

It is just the same as if I sought to find out how freedom itself as the causality of a will is possible, for in so doing I would leave the philosophical basis of explanation behind, and I have no other. Certainly I could revel in the intelligible world, the world of intelligences, which still remains to me; but although I have a well-founded Idea of it, still I do not have the least knowledge of it, nor can I ever attain knowledge of it by all the exertions of my natural faculty of reason. This intelligible world signifies only a something which remains when I have excluded from the determining grounds of my will everything belonging to the world of sense, in order to isolate the principle of motives from the field of sensibility. I do so by limiting it and showing that it does not contain absolutely everything in itself but that outside it there is still more; but this more I do not know. After banishing all material (i.e., knowledge of objects), from pure reason which formulates this ideal, there remain to me only the form, the practical law of the universal validity of maxims, and, in accordance with this, reason in relation to a pure intelligible world as a possible efficient cause determining the will. Any incentive must here be totally absent unless this Idea of an intelligible world or that in which reason directly takes an interest be the incentive. But to make this conceivable is precisely the problem we cannot solve.

Here, then, is the outermost boundary of all moral inquiry. To define it is very important, both in order that reason may not seek around, on the one hand, in the world of sense, in a way harmful to morals, for the supreme motive and for a comprehensible but empirical interest; and so that it will not, on the other hand, impotently flap its wings in the space (for it, an empty space) of transcendent concepts which we call the intelligible world, without being able to move from its starting point and so losing itself amid phantoms. Furthermore, the Idea of a pure intelligible world as a whole of all intelligences to which we ourselves belong as rational beings (though on the other side we are at the same time members of the world of sense) is always a useful and permissible Idea for the purpose of a rational faith. This is so even though all knowledge terminates at its boundary, for the glorious ideal of a universal realm of ends in themselves (rational beings) can awaken in us a lively interest in the moral law. To that realm we can belong as members only when 463 we scrupulously conduct ourselves by maxims of freedom as if they were laws of nature.

Concluding Remark

The speculative use of reason with respect to nature leads to the absolute necessity of some supreme cause of the world. The practical use of reason with respect to feedom leads also to an absolute necessity, but to the necessity only of laws of actions of a rational being as such. Now it is an essential principle of all use of reason to push its knowledge to an awareness of its necessity, for otherwise it would not be rational knowledge. But it is also an equally essential restriction of this very same reason that it cannot discern the necessity of what is or of what occurs or of what ought to be done unless a condition under which it is or occurs or ought to be done is presupposed. In this way, however, the satisfaction of reason is only postponed further and further by the unceasing search for the condition. Reason, therefore, restlessly seeking the unconditionally necessary, sees itself compelled to assume it though it has no means by which to make it comprehensible; it is happy enough if it can discover only the concept which is compatible with this presupposition. It is, therefore, no objection to our deduction of the supreme principle of morality, but a reproach that we must make to human reason generally, that it cannot render comprehensible the absolute necessity of an unconditional practical law (such as the categorical imperative must be). Reason cannot be blamed for being unwilling to explain it by a condition (i.e., by making some interest its basis), for then the law would cease to be moral and would no longer be the supreme law of freedom. And so we do not indeed comprehend the unconditional practical necessity of the moral imperative; yet we do comprehend its incomprehensibility, which is all that can fairly be demanded of a philosophy which in its principles strives to reach the boundary of human reason.

VII

Critique of Practical Reason

Editor's Introduction

The *Critique of Practical Reason,* published in 1787, grew out of revisions Kant was making for the second edition of the *Critique of Pure Reason,* published in the same year. In the *Foundations of the Metaphysics of Morals* he had made the "transition" to a critique of pure practical reason, but at that time he did not foresee the publication of a book with that title. In expanding the *Critique of Pure Reason,* however, he found it expedient to make no revisions in the few parts concerning moral philosophy, and made a new beginning, as it were, in a separate *Critique.* It is related to the *Foundations* as the first *Critique* is to the *Prolegomena.* The selections from the *Critique of Practical Reason* are from chapters which have no counterpart in the *Foundations;* the whole of the *Foundations* and the selections chosen from the second *Critique* together provide the most important parts of Kant's moral philosophy.

First, a word about the title of the book. *Practical reason,* a term originated by Aristotle and used throughout the history of philosophy, is one of the names of what is ordinarily called *the will.* It is reason in its role of guiding intentional behavior, and is contrasted with *theoretical reason* (sometimes called by Kant *speculative reason*) which guides and organizes our search for knowledge. But out of the asymmetry in the titles of the first two *Critiques* a common misunderstanding arises in the minds of many. Because one is called the critique of *pure* reason and the other the critique of *practical* reason, it is erroneously thought that there is a contrast between pure and practical reason. That is false. The purpose of the second *Critique* is precisely the opposite of this: it is to show that *pure* reason can be practical (i.e., that there are a priori rational components in will). Everyone from Aristotle to Hume had believed that there is practical reason; Kant was almost the first to argue that pure reason can be, and in ethical conduct is, practical.

A
THE HIGHEST GOOD AND THE
ANTINOMY OF PRACTICAL REASON

The highest good *(summum bonum)* consists in the exercise of perfect virtue accompanied by the just degree of happiness. It is an object of desire to every rational being, and it is our duty to try to achieve it. Virtue and happiness conjoined in the highest good are related to each other conditionally (i.e., one must be a condition of the other). Virtue is not, however, a condition of happiness; it makes one *worthy* of happiness, but it does not bring one happiness as a regular thing. Happiness and the desire for happiness, on the other hand, do not produce virtue but may, in fact, be the principal obstacles in the way to virtue.

Thus arises an antinomy. The furthering of the highest good is a duty of man, but for the reasons just given the highest good is impossible. Hence the moral law, which requires of man that he do all in his power to achieve the highest good, is null, void, and inherently false.

Kant resolves this antinomy in much the same way as he resolved the antinomy of pure theoretical reason (see above, pp. 128–130). He distinguished between the phenomenal and the noumenal realms, between what is actual in the world of experience and what is possible in the realm of reason. The highest good, impossible in the realm of nature (because virtue does not cause happiness, nor happiness virtue), may yet be possible in the supersensible world. The highest good is possible in the noumenal world under two conditions: (a) the soul is immortal, so that it may progress endlessly towards a state of perfect virtue, and (b) God exists as the moral governor of the world, rewarding virtue with happiness.

Thus Kant *postulates* the immortality of the soul and the existence of God. In postulating these, Kant does not claim to establish their truth but only to establish the moral necessity of believing them (having a rational faith in them).

Not to believe in them is, in effect, to reject the possibility of the highest good, and to reject this is to reject also a clear dictate of the moral law that we should earnestly seek it. Rejecting the possibility of the highest good does not exempt one from obedience to the moral law, but it does involve one in the inconsistency of believing one is obligated to do something while at the same time believing that it is impossible to do it.

At most, then, Kant's argument is an argument for *believing in* the immortality of the soul and the existence of God; it is not an argument to show that the soul is immortal or that God actually exists. Toward the end of this chapter Kant considers the relation of morality to religion (the relation of "What ought I do?" to "What may I hope?"). Religion, for Kant, is based on morality, not morality on religion.

B
OF THE WISE ADAPTATION OF MAN'S COGNITIVE FACULTIES TO HIS PRACTICAL VOCATION

This, the concluding section of the Dialectic, is Kant's most succinct justification for "denying knowledge in order to make room for faith" (p. 103).

C
MORAL EDUCATION

This selection is a treatise on moral education. Kant holds that, in spite of being considered stern and severe, "pedantic, Prussian, and Puritan," his ethical principles have an immediate appeal to the innocent mind of a child because they are imbedded in the common moral consciousness of mankind (p. 319). He thinks eudaemonism and popular moral philosophy not only fail to educate the child in genuine morality, but may lead him away from the true path of virtue and may even corrupt him into thinking that virtue is to be practiced for the sake of future happiness. He warns against inflating the child's mind with illusions of heroic and supererogatory virtue. There is nothing sentimental, indulgent, or compromising in Kant's portrayal of human nature. The dignity, austerity, and nobility of Kant's conception is further developed in the next section.

D
THE STARRY HEAVENS ABOVE ME AND
THE MORAL LAW WITHIN ME

This is the Conclusion of the *Critique*. It is included because of the memorable first sentence and for the manner in which he works out the contrast between man as a trivial part of visible nature and as a lawgiver in the realm of ends. From this there is an easy transition to the more difficult introductory material from the third *Critique*, which immediately follows.

––––––––––––––––

The translation by the Editor was first published by the University of Chicago Press, 1949, and in a revised version by Liberal Arts Press 1956. It has been revised again for the present edition by the Editor.

SUGGESTIONS FOR FURTHER READING

Beck, Lewis White. *A Commentary of Kant's Critique of Practical Reason.* University of Chicago press, 1960.
Wood, Allen W. *Kant's Moral Religion.* Cornell University Press, 1970.
See also the books listed on p. 243.

Critique of Practical Reason

A
THE DIALECTIC OF PURE PRACTICAL REASON

The concept of the "highest" contains an ambiguity which, if not attended to, can occasion unnecessary disputes. It can mean the "supreme" *(supremum)* or the "perfect" *(consummatum)*. The former is the unconditional condition, i.e., the condition which is subordinate to no other *(originarium);* the latter is that whole which is no part of a yet larger whole of the same kind *(perfectissimum)*. That virtue (as the worthiness to be happy) is the supreme condition of whatever appears to us to be desirable and thus of all our pursuit of happiness, and that it is consequently the supreme good have been proved in the Analytic. But from this it does not follow that virtue is the entire and perfect good as the object of the faculty of desire of rational finite beings. For the perfect good, happiness is also required — required not merely in the partial eyes of the person who makes himself his end but also in the judgment of an impartial reason which disinterestedly regards that person as an end in himself. For to be in need of happiness and also to be worthy of it and yet not to partake of it could not be in accordance with the perfect volition of an omnipotent rational being, if we assume such only for the sake of the argument. Inasmuch as virtue and happiness together constitute the possession of the highest good for one person, and happiness in exact proportion to moral-
111 ity (as the worth of a person and his worthiness to be happy) constitutes that of a possible world, the highest good means the whole, the perfect good, wherein virtue is always the supreme good, being the condition having no condition superior to it, while happiness, though something always pleasant to him who possesses it, is not of itself absolutely good in every respect but always presupposes conduct in accordance with the moral law as its condition.

Two terms necessarily combined in one concept must be related as ground and consequent, and this unity must be regarded either as analytic (logical connection) according to the law of identity or a synthetic (real connection) according to the law of causality. The connection of virtue with happiness can, therefore, be understood in one of two ways. Either the endeavor to be virtuous and the rational pursuit of happiness are not two different actions but absolutely identical; in this case no maxim is needed as a ground of the former other than that needed for the latter. Or that connection is predicated upon virtue's producing happiness as something different from the consciousness of virtue, as a cause produces an effect.

304

Of the ancient Greek schools, there were only two opposing each other on this issue. But so far as the definition of the concept of the highest good is concerned, they followed one and the same method, since neither held virtue and happiness to be two different elements of the highest good, but both sought the unity of principle under the rule of identity. But again they differed in that each selected a different principle as the fundamental one. The Epicurean said: To be conscious of one's maxims as leading to happiness is virtue. The Stoic said: To be conscious of one's virtue is happiness. To the former, prudence amounted to morality; to the latter, who chose a higher term for virtue, morality alone was true wisdom.

We cannot but regret that these men (whom we must nevertheless admire since they so early attempted all the conceivable ways of extending philosophy's conquest) unfortunately applied their acuteness to digging up an identity between such extremely heterogeneous concepts as those of happiness and virtue. But it fit the dialectical spirit of their times (and still sometimes leads subtle minds astray) to overcome essential differences in principle, which can never be united, by seeking to translate them into a conflict of words and thus to devise an apparent unity of concepts with other terms. This commonly occurs in cases where the unification of heterogenous principles 112 lies either so high or so deep, or would require so thorough a revolution of doctrines otherwise accepted in a philosophical system, that men fear to go deeply into the real difference and prefer to treat it as a mere diversity in formulas.

While both schools tried to ferret out the sameness of the practical principles of virtue and happiness, they were not for that reason agreed as to the way in which to force out this identity; rather they became widely separated from each other, as the one sought its principle on the sensuous and the other on the logical side, one putting it in the consciousness of sensuous need and the other in the independence of practical reason from all sensuous grounds of determination. The concept of virtue, according to the Epicurean, lay already in the maxim of furthering one's own happiness; the feeling of happiness, for the Stoic, was, on the contrary, already contained in the consciousness of his virtue. Whatever is contained in another concept, however, is the same as one of its parts but not the same as the whole, and two wholes can, moreover, be specifically different from each other though they consist of the same content if their parts are combined in different ways. The Stoic asserted virtue to be the entire highest good, and happiness was only the consciousness of this possession belonging to the state of the subject. The Epicurean stated that happiness was the entire highest good and that virtue was only the form of the maxim by which it could be procured through the rational use of means to it.

But it is clear from the Analytic that the maxims of virtue and those of one's own happiness are wholly heterogeneous and far removed from being at one in respect to their supreme practical principle; and even though they belong

to a highest good, which they jointly make possible, they strongly limit and check each other in the same subject. Thus the question, "How is the highest good practically possible?" remains an unsolved problem in spite of all previous attempts at conciliation. That which makes it so difficult a problem is shown in the Analytic: happiness and morality are two specifically different
113 elements of the highest good and therefore their combination cannot be known analytically (as if a person who sought his happiness found himself virtuous merely through solving his problem, or one who followed virtue found himself *ipso facto* happy in the consciousness of this conduct). The highest good is a *synthesis* of concepts. Since, however, this combination is known as a priori and thus as practically necessary, and not derivable from experience, and since the possibility of the highest good therefore rests on no empirical principles, the deduction of this concept must be transcendental. It is a priori (morally) necessary to bring forth the highest good through the freedom of the will; the condition of its possibility, therefore, must rest solely on a priori grounds of knowledge.

I. The Antinomy of Practical Reason

In the highest good which is practical for us (i.e., one which is to be made real by our will), virtue and happiness are thought of as necessarily combined, so that the one cannot be assumed by practical reason without the other belonging to it. Now this combination is, like every other, either analytic or synthetic. Since it cannot be analytic, as has been shown, it must be thought synthetically and, more particularly, as the connection of cause and effect, for it concerns a practical good (i.e., one that is possible through action). Therefore the desire for happiness must be the motive to maxims of virtue, or the maxim of virtue must be the efficient cause of happiness. The first is absolutely impossible, because (as has been proved in the Analytic) maxims which put the determining ground of the will in the desire for one's happiness are not moral at all and can serve as ground for no virtue. The second however, is, also impossible, since every practical connection of causes and effects in the world, as a result of the determination of the will, is dependent not on the moral dispositions of the will but on knowledge of natural laws and the physical capacity of using them to its purposes; consequently, no necessary connection, sufficient to the highest good, between happiness and virtue in the world can be expected from the most meticulous
114 observance of the moral law. Since, now, the furthering of the highest good, which contains this connection in its concept, is an a priori necessary object of our will and is inseparably related to the moral law, the impossibility of the highest good must prove the falsity of the moral law also. If, therefore, the highest good is impossible according to practical rules, then the moral law which commands that it be furthered must be fantastic, directed to empty imaginary ends, and consequently inherently false.

II. Critical Resolution of the Antinomy of Practical Reason

In the antinomy of pure speculative reason there is a similar conflict between natural necessity and freedom in the causation of events in the world. It was resolved by showing that there is no true conflict if the events and even the world in which they occur are regarded as only appearances (as they should be). This is because one and the same acting being as appearance (even to his own inner sense) has a causality in the sensuous world always in accord with the mechanism of nature; while with respect to the same event, so far as the acting person regards himself as noumenon (as pure intelligence, existing without temporal determination), he can contain a determining ground of that causality according to natural laws, and this determining ground of natural causality itself is free from every natural law.

It is just the same with the present antinomy of pure practical reason. The first of the two propositions, viz., that striving for happiness produces a ground for a virtuous disposition, is absolutely false; the second, viz., that a virtuous disposition necessarily produces happiness, is not, however, *absolutely* false but false only in so far as this disposition is regarded as the form of causality in the world of sense. Consequently, it is false only if I assume existence in this world to be the only mode of existence of a rational being, and therefore it is only *conditionally* false. But not only since I am justified in thinking of my existence as that of a noumenon in an intelligible world but also since I have in the moral law a pure intellectual determining ground of my causality (in the sensible world), it is not impossible that the morality of 115 disposition should have a necessary relation as cause to happiness as effect in the sensible world, though this relation be indirect, mediated by an intelligent Author of nature. In a system of nature which is the object of the senses only, however, this combination can occur only contingently, and as such it is not sufficient to the highest good.

Thus, in spite of this apparent conflict of a practical reason with itself, the highest good is the necessary highest end of a morally determined will and a true object thereof; for it is practically possible, and the maxims of this will, which refer to it by their material, have objective reality. At first this objective reality was called in question by the antinomy in the combination of morality with happiness according to a general law; but this difficulty arose only from a misconception, because the relationship between appearances was held to be a relationship of things in themselves to these appearances.

When we see ourselves obliged to seek at such distance — namely, in the context of an intelligible world — the possibility of the highest good which reason presents to all rational beings as the goal of all their moral wishes, it must appear strange that philosophers of both ancient and modern times have been able to find happiness in very just proportion to virtue in *this* life (in the world of sense) or at least have been able to convince themselves of it. For Epicurus as well as the Stoics extolled happiness springing from the consciousness of virtuous living above everything else, and he was not so base in his practical precepts as one might conclude from the principles of his theory, which he used for explanation and not for action, or from the principles as interpreted by many who were misled by his use of the term "pleasure" for "contentment." He, on the contrary, reckoned the most disinterested practice of the good among the ways of experiencing the most intimate joy; and moderation and control of the inclinations, as these might have been required by the strictest moral philosopher, belonged in his scheme for enjoyment, whereby he understood constant cheerfulness. He diverged from the Stoics chiefly by placing the *motive* in this enjoyment, which the Stoics correctly refused to do. For the virtuous Epicurus, like even now many morally well-meaning persons who do not give deep enough consideration to their principles, fell into the error of presupposing the virtuous disposition to be already in the persons to whom he wished to provide incentives to virtue. It is true that the upright man cannot be happy if he is not conscious of his righteousness, since with such a character the moral self-condemnation to which his own way of thinking would force him in case of any transgression would rob him of all enjoyment of the pleasantness which his condition might otherwise entail. But the only question is, "How is such a character and turn of mind in estimating the worth of his existence even possible?" For prior to this no feeling for any moral worth can be found in a subject. A man, if he is virtuous, will certainly not enjoy life without being conscious of his righteousness in each action, however favorable fortune may be to him in the physical circumstances of life; but can one make him virtuous before he has so high an estimation of the moral worth of his existence merely by commending to him the contentment of spirit which will arise from the consciousness of righteousness for which he as yet has no sense?

But, on the other hand, there is always here an occasion for a subreption *(vitium subreptionis)* and, as it were, for an optical illusion in the self-consciousness of what one does in contradistinction to what one feels, which even the most experienced person cannot entirely avoid. The moral disposition is necessarily connected with a consciousness of the determination of the will directly by a law. Now the consciousness of a determination of the faculty of desire is always a ground for satisfaction in the resulting action; but this pleasure, this satisfaction with one's self, is not the determining ground of the action; on the contrary, the determination of the will directly by reason alone is the ground of the feeling of pleasure, and this remains a pure practical determination of the faculty of desire, not a sensuous one. Since this determination produces the same inward effect, (i.e., an impulse to activity), as does a feeling of agreeableness which is expected from the desired action, we see that what we ourselves do may easily be looked upon as something which we merely passively feel, the moral motive being held to be a sensuous impulse, as always occurs in so-called illusions of the senses (and here we have such an illusion of the inner sense). It is a very sublime thing in human nature to be determined to actions directly by a pure law of reason, and even the illusion wherein the subjective element of this intellectual determinability of the will is held to be sensuous and an effect of a particular sensuous feeling (an "intellectual feeling" being self-contradictory) partakes of this sublimity. It is of great importance to point out this quality of our personality and to cultivate so far as possible the effect of reason on this feeling. But we must, nevertheless, be on guard against degrading and deforming the real and authentic incentive, the law itself, by awarding spurious praise to the moral ground of determination as incentive as though it were based on feelings of particular joys, thus setting it, as it were, against a false foil; for these joys are only its consequences. Respect, in contrast to the enjoyment or gratification of happiness, is something for which there can be no feeling basic and prior to reason, for such a feeling would always be sensuous and pathological. Respect as the consciousness of the direct constraint of the will through law is hardly analogous to the feeling of pleasure, although in relation to the faculty of desire it produces exactly the same effect, but from different sources. But only through this mode of conception can one achieve what is sought, namely, that actions be done not merely according to duty (as a consequence of pleasant feelings) but from duty, which must be the true goal of all moral cultivation.

Do we not have a word to denote a satisfaction with existence, an analogue of happiness which necessarily accompanies the consciousness of virtue, and which does not indicate a gratification, as "happiness" does? We do, and this word is "self-contentment," which in its real meaning refers only to negative satisfaction with existence in which one is conscious of needing nothing. Freedom and the consciousness of freedom, as a capacity for following the moral law with an unyielding disposition, is independence from inclinations, at least from them as motives determining (though not as affecting) our desiring; and, so far as I am conscious of freedom in obeying my moral maxims, it is the exclusive source of an unchanging contentment necessarily connected with it and resting on no particular feeling. This may be called 118 intellectual contentment. Sensuous contentment (improperly so called) which rests on the satisfaction of inclinations, however refined they may be, can never be adequate to that which is conceived under contentment. For inclinations vary; they grow with the indulgence we allow them, and they leave behind a greater void than the one we intended to fill. They are consequently always burdensome to a rational being, and, though he cannot put them aside, they nevertheless elicit from him the wish to be free of them. Even an inclination to do that which accords with duty (e.g., to do beneficent acts) can at most facilitate the effectiveness of moral maxims but not produce such maxims. For in such maxims, everything must be directed to the thought of the law as the determining ground if the action is not to contain mere legality but also morality. Inclination, be it good-natured or otherwise, is blind and slavish; reason, when it is a question of morality, must not play the part of mere guardian of the inclinations, but, without regard to them, as pure practical reason it must care for its own interest to the exclusion of all else. Even the feeling of sympathy and warmhearted fellow-feeling, when preceding the consideration of what is duty and serving as a determining ground, is burdensome even to right-thinking persons, confusing their considered maxims and creating the wish to be free from them and subject only to law-giving reason.

Thus we can understand how the consciousness of this capacity of a pure practical reason through a deed (virtue) can produce a consciousness of mastery over inclinations and thus of independence from them and from the discontentment which always accompanies them, bringing forth a negative satisfaction with one's condition (i.e., contentment), whose source is contentment with one's own person. Freedom itself thus becomes in this indirect way capable of enjoyment. This cannot be called happiness, since it does not depend upon a positive participation of feeling; nor can it be called bliss, because it does not include complete independence from inclinations and desires. It does nevertheless resemble the latter so far at least as the determination of the will which it involves can be held to be free from their influence, and thus, at least in its origin, it is analogous to the self-sufficiency which can be ascribed only to the Supreme Being.

119   From this solution of the antinomy of practical pure reason, it follows that in practical principles a natural and necessary connection between the consciousness of morality and the expectation of proportionate happiness as its consequence may be thought at least possible, though it is by no means known or understood. On the other hand, it is seen that principles for the pursuit of happiness cannot possibly produce morality and that therefore the supreme good (as the first condition of the highest good) is morality; and that happiness, though it indeed constitutes the second element of the highest good, does so only as the morally conditioned but necessary consequence of the former. Only with this subordination is the highest good the entire object of pure practical reason, which pure practical reason must necessarily think as possible because reason commands us to contribute everything possible to its realization. But the possibility of such a connection of the conditioned with its condition belongs wholly to the supersensible relations of things, and cannot be given under the laws of the world of sense, even though the practical consequence of this Idea, the actions which are devoted to the highest good, do belong to this world. Therefore we shall seek to establish the grounds of that possibility primarily with respect to that which is directly in our power but which reason holds out to us as the supplement to our impotence to [realize] the possibility of the highest good, which practical principles hold to be necessary.

IV. The Immortality of the Soul as a Postulate
of Pure Practical Reason

The achievement of the highest good in the world is the necessary object of a will determinable by the moral law. In such a will, however, the perfect fitness of moral dispositions to the moral law is the supreme condition of the highest good. This fitness, therefore, must be just as possible as its object, because it is contained in the command that requires us to promote the highest good. But the perfect fitness of the will to the moral law is holiness, which is a perfection of which no rational being in the world of sense is at any time capable. But since it is required as practically necessary, it can be found only in an endless progress to that perfect fitness; on principles of pure practical reason it is necessary to assume such a practical progress as the real object of our will.

This infinite progress is possible, however, only under the presupposition of an infinitely enduring existence and personality of the same rational being; this is called the immortality of the soul. Thus the highest good is practically possible only under the supposition of the immortality of the soul, and the latter, as inseparably bound to the moral law, is a postulate of pure practical reason. By a postulate of pure practical reason I understand a theoretical proposition which is not as such demonstrable, but which is an inseparable corollary of an a priori unconditionally valid practical law. . . .

V. The Existence of God as a Postulate of Pure Practical Reason

In the foregoing analysis the moral law led to a practical task which is assigned solely by pure reason and without any concurrence of sensuous incentives. It is the task of perfecting the first and principal part of the highest good, viz., morality. Since this task can be executed only in eternity, it led to the postulate of immortality. The same law must lead us to affirm the possibility of the second element of the highest good (i.e., happiness proportional to that morality); and it must do so just as disinterestedly as before, by a purely impartial reason. This it can do on the supposition of the existence of a cause adequate to that effect. It must postulate the existence of God as necessarily belonging to the possibility of the highest good (the object of our will which is necessarily connected with the moral legislation of pure reason). We now proceed to exhibit this connection in a convincing manner.

Happiness is the condition of a rational being in the world in whose whole existence everything goes according to wish and will. It rests on the harmony of nature with his whole end and with the essential determining ground of his will. But the moral law as a law of freedom commands through motives wholly independent of nature and independent of its harmony with our faculty of desire (as incentives). Still, the rational being acting in the world is not at the same time the cause of the world and of nature itself. Hence there is not the slightest ground in the moral law for a necessary connection between the morality and the proportionate happiness of a being who belongs to the world as one of its parts and thus as dependent upon it. Not being nature's cause, his will cannot by its own strength bring nature, as it touches on his happiness, into complete harmony with his practical principles. Nevertheless, in the practical task of pure reason (i.e., in the necessary endeavor after the highest good), such a connection is posited as necessary: we *ought* to seek to further the highest good (which therefore must be at least possible). Therefore the existence is postulated also of a cause of the whole of nature, itself distinct from nature, which contains the ground for the exact coincidence of happiness with morality. The supreme cause, however, must contain the ground of the agreement of nature not only with a law of the will of rational beings, but with the Idea of this law so far as they make it the supreme ground of determination of the will. Thus it contains the ground of the agreement of nature not merely with actions moral in their form but also with their morality as motives to such actions (i.e., the agreement of nature with their moral disposition). Therefore the highest good is possible in the world only on the supposition of a supreme cause of nature which has a causality corresponding to the moral disposition. Now a being which is capable of actions by the idea *(Vorstellung)* of laws is an intelligence, a rational being, and the causality of such a being according to this idea of laws is his will. Therefore the supreme cause of nature, in so far as it must be presupposed for the highest good, is a being which is the cause (and consequently the author) of nature through understanding and will (i.e., God). As a consequence, the postulate of the possibility of the highest derivative good (the best world) is at the same time the postulate of the reality of the highest original good, namely, the postulate of the existence of God. Now it was our duty to promote the highest good, and it is not merely our privilege but a necessity connected with duty as a requisite to presuppose the possibility of this highest good. The highest good stands only under the condition of the existence of God, and this condition inseparably connects this supposition with duty. Therefore it is morally necessary to assume the existence of God.

It is well to notice here that this moral necessity is subjective, a need, and not objective, duty itself. For there cannot be a duty to assume the existence of anything, because such a supposition concerns only the theoretical use of reason. It is also not to be understood that the assumption of the existence of God is necessary as a ground of all obligation in general (for this rests, as has been fully shown, solely on the autonomy of reason itself). All that belongs to duty is the endeavor to produce and to further the highest good in the world, the possibility of which may thus be postulated though our reason can conceive it only by presupposing a highest intelligence. To assume its existence is thus connected with the consciousness of our duty, though this assumption itself belongs to the realm of theoretical reason. Considered only in reference to the latter, it is a hypothesis (i.e., a ground of explanation). But in reference to the comprehensibility of an object (the highest good) placed before us by the moral law, and thus as a practical need, it can be called *faith* and even pure *rational faith*, because pure reason alone (by its theoretical as well as practical employment) is the source from which it springs.

From this deduction it now becomes clear why the Greek schools could never succeed in solving their problem of the practical possibility of the highest good. It was because they made the rule of the use which the human will makes of its freedom the sole and self-sufficient ground of its possibility, thinking that they had no need of the existence of God for this purpose. They were certainly correct in establishing the principle of morals by itself, independently of this postulate and merely from the relation of reason to the will, thus making the principle of morality the *supreme* practical condition of the highest good; but this principle was not the *entire* condition of its possibility. The Epicureans had indeed raised a wholly false principle of morality (i.e., that of happiness) into the supreme one, and for law had substituted a maxim of voluntary choice of each according to his inclination. But they proceeded consistently enough, in that they degraded their highest good in proportion to the baseness of their principle and expected no greater happiness than that which could be attained through human prudence (wherein both temperance and the moderation of inclinations belong), though everyone knows prudence to be scarce enough and to produce diverse results according to circumstances, not to mention the exceptions which their maxims continually had to admit and which made them worthless as laws. The Stoics, on the other hand, had chosen their supreme practical principle, virtue, quite correctly as the condition of the highest good. But as they imagined the degree of virtue which is required for its pure law as completely attainable in this life,   127 they not only exaggerated the moral capacity of man, under the name of "sage," beyond all the limits of his nature, making it into something which is contradicted by all our knowledge of men; they also refused to accept the second component of the highest good (i.e., happiness) as a special object of human desire. Rather, they made their sage, like a god in the consciousness of the excellence of his person, wholly independent of nature (as regards his own contentment), exposing him to the evils of life but not subjecting him to them. (They also represented him as free from everything morally evil.) Thus they really left out the highest good the second element (personal happiness), since they placed the highest good only in acting and in contentment with one's own personal worth, including it in the consciousness of moral character. But the voice of their own nature could have sufficiently refuted this.

The doctrine of Christianity,* even when not regarded as a religious
128   doctrine, gives at this point a concept of the highest good (the Kingdom of
God) which alone is sufficient to the strictest demand of practical reason. The
moral law is holy (unyielding) and demands holiness of morals, although all
the moral perfection to which man can attain is only virtue; that is, a law-
abiding disposition resulting from respect for the law and thus implying
consciousness of a continuous propensity to transgress it, or at least to defile-
ment consisting in an admixture of many spurious (not moral) motives to
obedience to the law; consequently man can achieve only a self-esteem
combined with humility. And thus with respect to the holiness required by
the Christian law, nothing remains to the creature but endless progress,
though for the same reason the hope for endless duration is justified. The
worth of a character completely accordant with the moral law is infinite,
because all possible happiness, in the judgment of a wise and omnipotent
dispenser of happiness, has no other limits than the lack of fitness of rational
beings to their duty. But the moral law does not of itself promise happiness,
for happiness is not, according to concepts of any natural order, necessarily
connected with obedience to the law. Christian ethics supplies this defect of
the second indispensable component of the highest good by presenting a
world wherein reasonable beings single-mindedly devote themselves to the
moral law; this is the Kingdom of God, in which nature and morality come
into a harmony, foreign to each as such, through a holy Author of the world,
129   who makes possible the derivative highest good. The holiness of morals is
prescribed to them even in this life as a guide to conduct, but the well-being
proportionate to this, which is bliss, is thought of as attainable only in eternity. This is due to the fact that the former must always be the archetype of
their conduct in every state, and progressing toward it is possible and necessary even in this life, whereas the latter, under the name of happiness, cannot
(as far as our own capacity is concerned) be reached in this life and is
therefore made an object of hope only. Nevertheless, the Christian principle
of morality is not theological and thus heteronomous, being rather the autonomy of pure practical reason itself, because it does not make the knowledge
of God and His will the basis of these laws but makes such knowledge the

---

*The view is commonly held that the Christian precept of morals has no advantage over the
moral concept of the Stoics in respect to its purity; but the difference between them is nevertheless obvious. The Stoic system makes the consciousness of strength of mind the pivot around
which all moral intentions should turn; and, if the followers of this system spoke of duties and
even defined them accurately, they nevertheless placed the incentives and the real determining
ground of the will in an elevation of character above the base incentives of the senses which have
their power only through weakness of the mind. Virtue was, therefore, for them a certain
heroism of the sage who, raising himself above the animal nature of man, was sufficient to
himself, subject to no temptation to transgress the moral law, and elevated above duties though
he propounded duties to others. But all this they could not have done had they conceived this law
in the same purity and rigor as does the precept of the Gospel. If I understand by "Idea" a
perfection to which the senses can give nothing adequate, the moral Ideas are not transcendent
(i.e., of such a kind that we cannot even sufficiently define the concept of which we are uncertain
whether there is a corresponding object, as are the Ideas of speculative reason); rather, they serve

basis only of succeeding to the highest good on condition of obedience to these laws; it places the real incentive for obedience to the law not in the desired consequences of obedience but in the conception of duty alone, in true observance of which the worthiness to attain the latter alone consists.

In this manner, through the concept of the highest good as the object and final end of pure practical reason, the moral law leads to religion. Religion is the recognition of all duties as divine commands, not as sanctions (i.e., arbitrary and contingent ordinances of a foreign will), but as essential laws of any free will as such. Even as such, they must be regarded as commands of the Supreme Being because we can hope for the highest good (to strive for which is our duty under the moral law) only from a morally perfect (holy and beneficent) and omnipotent will; and, therefore, we can hope to attain it only through harmony with this will. But here again everything remains disinterested and based only on duty, without being based on fear or hope as incentives, which, if they became principles, would destroy the entire moral worth of the actions. The moral law commands us to make the highest possible good in a world the final object of all our conduct. This I cannot hope to effect except through the agreement of my will with that of a holy and beneficent Author of the world. And although my own happiness is included in the concept of the highest good as a whole wherein the greatest happiness is thought of as connected in exact proportion to the highest degree of moral 130 perfection possible to creatures, still it is not happiness but the moral law (which, in fact, sternly places restricting conditions upon my boundless longing for happiness) which is proved to be the ground determining the will to further the highest good.

Therefore, morals is not really the doctrine of how to make ourselves happy but of how we are to be *worthy* of happiness. Only if religion is added to it can the hope arise of someday participating in happiness in proportion as we endeavored not to be unworthy of it.

One is worthy of possessing a thing or a state when his possession is harmonious with the highest good. We can easily see now that all worthiness is a matter of moral conduct, because this constitutes the condition of everything else (which pertains to one's state) in the concept of the highest good (i.e., participation in happiness). From this there follows that one must never

---

as models of practical perfection, as an indispensable rule of moral conduct, and as a standard for comparison. If I now regard Christian morals from their philosophical side, it appears in comparison with the ideas of the Greek schools as follows: the ideas of the Cynics, Epicureans, Stoics, and Christians are, respectively, the simplicity of nature, prudence, wisdom, and holiness. In respect to the way they achieve them, the Greek schools differ in that the Cynics found common 128 sense sufficient, while the others found it in the path of science, and thus all held it to lie in the use of man's merely natural powers. Christian ethics, because it formulated its precept as pure and uncompromising (as befits a moral precept), destroyed man's confidence of being wholly adequate to it, at least in this life; but it reestablished it by enabling us to hope that, if we act as well as lies in our power, what is not in our power will come to our aid from another source, whether we know in what way or not. Aristotle and Plato differed only as to the origin of our moral concepts.

consider morals itself as a doctrine of happiness (i.e., as an instruction in how to achieve happiness). For morals has to do only with the rational condition *(conditio sine qua non)* of happiness and not with means of achieving it. But when morals (which imposes only duties instead of providing rules for selfish wishes) is completely expounded, and a moral wish has been awakened to promote the highest good (to bring the Kingdom of God to us),which is a wish based on law and one to which no selfish mind could have aspired, and when for the sake of this wish the step to religion has been taken — then only can ethics be called a doctrine of happiness, because the *hope* for it first arises with religion.

From this it can also be seen that, if we inquire into God's final end in creating the world, we must name not the happiness of rational beings in the world but the highest good, which adds further condition to the wish of rational beings to be happy, viz., the condition of being worthy of happiness, which is the morality of these beings, for this alone contains the standard by which they can hope to participate in happiness at the hand of a *wise* creator. For since wisdom, theoretically regarded, means the knowledge of the high-

131 est good and, practically, the conformity of the will to the highest good, one cannot ascribe to a supreme independent wisdom an end based only on benevolence. For we cannot conceive the action of this benevolence (with respect to the happiness of rational beings) except as conformable to the restrictive conditions of harmony with the holiness* of His will as the highest original good. Then perhaps those who have placed the end of creation in the glory of God, provided this is not thought of anthropomorphically as an inclination to be esteemed, have found the best term. For nothing glorifies God more than what is the most estimable thing in the world, namely, respect for His command, the observance of sacred duty which His law imposes on us, when there is added to this His glorious plan of crowning such an excellent order with corresponding happiness. If the latter, to speak in human terms, makes Him worthy of love, by the former He is an object of worship (adoration). Human beings can win love by doing good, but by this alone even they never win respect; the greatest well-doing does them honor only by being exercised according to worthiness.

It follows of itself that, in the order of ends, man (and every rational being) is an end in himself (i.e., he is never to be used merely as a means for

---

*Incidentally, and in order to make the peculiarity of this concept clear, I make the following remark. While we ascribe various attributes to God, whose quality we find suitable also to creatures (e.g., power, knowledge, presence, goodness, etc.), though in God they are present in a higher degree under such names as omnipotence, omniscience, omnipresence, and perfect goodness, etc., there are three which exclusively and without qualification of magnitude are ascribed to God, and they are all moral. He is the only holy, the only blessed, and the only wise being, because these concepts of themselves imply unlimitedness. By the arrangements of these He is thus the holy lawgiver (and creator), the beneficent ruler (and sustainer), and the just judge. These three attributes contain everything whereby God is the object of religion, and in conformity to them the metaphysical perfections of themselves arise in reason.

someone — even for God — without at the same time being himself an end, and that thus the humanity in our person must itself be holy to us, because man is subject to the moral law and therefore subject to that which is of itself holy, and it is only on account of this and in agreement with this that anything 132 can be called holy. For this moral law is founded on the autonomy of his will as a free will, which by its universal laws must necessarily be able to agree with that to which it subjects itself.

Of the Wise Adaptation of Man's Cognitive Faculties to His Practical Vocation[1]

If human nature is called upon to strive for the highest good, the measure 146 of its cognitive faculties and especially their relation to one another must be assumed to be suitable to this end. But the critique of pure speculative reason demonstrates the utter insufficiency of speculative reason to solve the most weighty problems which are presented to it in a way satisfactory to its end; but that critique did not ignore the natural and unmistakable hints of the same reason or the great steps that it can take in approaching this great goal which is set before it but which it can never of itself reach even with the aid of the greatest knowledge of nature. Thus nature here seems to have provided us only in a stepmotherly fashion with a faculty needed for our end.

Now assuming that it had here indulged our wish and had provided us with that power of insight or enlightenment which we would like to possess or which some erroneously believe they do possess, what would be the consequence so far as we can discern it? In so far as our whole nature was not changed at the same time, the inclinations (which under any condition have the first word) would first strive for their satisfaction and, conjoined with 147 reasonable consideration, for the greatest possible and most lasting satisfaction under the name of happiness. The moral law would afterward speak in order to hold them within their proper limits and even to subject them all to a higher end which has no regard to inclination. But instead of the conflict which now the moral disposition has to wage with inclinations and in which, after some defeats, moral strength of mind may be gradually won, God and eternity in their awful majesty would stand unceasingly before our eyes (for that which we can completely prove is as certain as that which we can ascertain by sight). Transgression of the law would indeed be shunned, and the commanded would be performed. But because the disposition from which actions should be done cannot be instilled by any command, and because the spur to action would in this case be always present and external, reason would have no need to endeavor to gather its strength to resist the inclinations by a vivid idea of the dignity of the law. Thus most actions conforming to the law would be done from fear, few would be done from

---

[1]The concluding section of the Dialectic.

hope, none from duty. The moral worth of actions, on which alone the worth of the person and even of the world depends in the eyes of supreme wisdom, would not exist at all. The conduct of man, so long as his nature remained as it now is, would be changed into mere mechanism, where, as in a puppet show, everything would gesticulate well but no life would be found in the figures.

But it is quite otherwise with us. With all the exertion of our reason we have only a very obscure and ambiguous view into the future; the Governor of the world allows us only to conjecture His existence and majesty, not to behold or clearly prove them; the moral law in us, without promising or threatening us with anything certain, demands of us a disinterested respect; finally, only when this respect has become active and dominating, it allows us a view into the realm of the supersensuous, though only a glimpse. Thus only can there be a truly moral character dedicated directly to the law and thus only can the rational creature become worthy of participating in the highest good corresponding to the moral worth of his person and not merely to his
148 actions. Thus what the study of nature and of man has sufficiently shown elsewhere may well be true here, viz., that the inscrutable wisdom through which we exist is not less worthy of veneration in respect to what it denies us than in what it has granted.

MORAL EDUCATION[2]

151   It is clear that the grounds of determination of the will — the direct thought of the law and objective obedience to it as duty — which alone make the maxims really moral and give them a moral worth, must be thought of as the real incentives of actions, for otherwise legality of actions but not morality of dispositions would result. But it is not so clear — in fact, it must appear highly improbable at first glance — that subjectively the exhibition of pure virtue can have more power over the human mind, giving a far stronger incentive to effectuate even that legality and to bring forward more powerful resolves to prefer the law to everything else solely out of respect for it, than all allurements arising from enjoyment and everything which may be counted as
152 happiness or from all threats of pain and harm. But it is really so, and if human nature were not so constituted, no way of presenting the law by circumlocutions and indirect recommendations could ever produce morality of dispositions. Everything would be mere cant; the law would be hated or even perhaps despised, though nevertheless followed for the sake of one's own advantage. The letter of the law (legality) would be met with in our actions, but the spirit of the law (morality) would not be found in our dispositions. Since with all our efforts we cannot completely free ourselves from reason in judging, we would inevitably appear in our own eyes as worthless and depraved, even if we sought to compensate ourselves for this mortification

---

[2]From the part entitled, "Methodology of Pure Practical Reason."

before the inner tribunal by indulging in all the enjoyments which a supposed natural or divine law might be thought, in our delusion, to have connected with legality by means of a kind of police machinery regulating its operations by what we do without troubling itself about our motives for doing it.

Certainly it cannot be denied that in order to bring either an as yet uneducated or a degraded mind into the path of the morally good, some preparatory guidance is needed to attract it by a view to its own advantage or to frighten it by fear of harm. As soon as this machinery, these leading strings, have had some effect, the pure moral motive must be brought to mind. This is not only because it is the sole ground of character (a consistent practical habit of mind according to unchangeable maxims) but also because, in teaching a man to feel his own worth, it gives his mind a power, unexpected even by himself, to pull himself loose from all sensuous attachments (so far as they would fain dominate him) and, in the independence of his intelligible nature and in the greatness of soul to which he sees himself called, to find himself richly compensated for the sacrifice he makes. We should prove, by observations which anyone can make, that this property of our minds, this receptivity to a pure moral interest and the moving force in the pure thought of virtue when properly commended to the human heart, is the strongest incentive to the good and indeed the only one when it is a question of continual and 153 meticulous obedience to moral maxims. It must be remembered, however, that if these observations show only the reality of such a feeling but no moral improvement resulting from it, that is no argument against what is the only method by which the objectively practical laws of pure reason can be made subjectively practical through the mere thought of duty, nor does it show that this thought is an empty fantasy. For since this method has never yet been widely used, experience can tell us nothing of its results; one can ask only for proofs of the receptivity to such motives, which I shall briefly present and then in few words outline the method of founding and cultivating genuine moral dispositions.

If we attend to the course of conversation in mixed companies consisting not merely of scholars and subtle reasoners but also of business people or women, we notice that besides storytelling and jesting they have another entertainment, namely, arguing; for storytelling, if it is to have novelty and interest, soon exhausts itself, while jesting easily becomes insipid. Now of all arguments there are none which excite more readily participation by those who are otherwise soon bored with all subtle thinking, or which are more likely to bring a certain liveliness into the company, than one about the moral worth of this or that action from which the character of some person is to be made out. Those who otherwise find everything which is subtle and minute in theoretical questions dry and vexing soon take part when it is a question of the moral import of a good or bad act that is recounted; and they are exacting, meticulous, and subtle in excogitating everything which lessens or even casts suspicion on the purity of purpose and thus on the degree of virtue to an extent we do not expect of them on any other subject of speculation. One can often see the character of the person who judges others revealed in his judgments. Some of them as they exercise their judicial office especially upon the dead, appear to be chiefly inclined to defend the good that is related of this or that deed against all injurious charges of insincerity, finally protecting the entire moral worth of the person against the reproach of dissimulation and secret wickedness. Others, on the contrary, incline more to attacking this worth by accusations and fault-finding. But we cannot always ascribe to the

154 latter the wish to argue away virtue from all human examples in order to reduce it to an empty name; often it is rather a well-meaning strictness in the definition of genuine moral import according to an uncompromising law, in comparison with which (in contrast to comparison with examples) self-conceit in moral matters is very much reduced, and humility is not merely taught but also felt by each in a penetrating self-examination. Nevertheless, we can often see, in the defenders of purity of purpose in given examples, that where there is a presumption of righteousness they would gladly remove the least spot; and they do so lest, if all examples be disputed and all human virtue be denied its purity, the latter be held to be a mere phantom and all effort to attain it be deprecated as vain affectation and delusory conceit.

I do not know why the educators of youth have not long since made use of this propensity of reason to enter with pleasure upon the most subtle examination of practical questions put to them, and why, after laying the foundation in a purely moral catechism, they have not searched through biographies of ancient and modern times with the purpose of having examples at hand of the duties they lay down, so that, by comparing similar actions under various circumstances, they could begin to exercise the moral judgment of their pupils in marking the greater or lesser moral significance of the actions. They would find that even very young people, who are not yet ready for speculation of other kinds, would soon become very acute and not a little interested, since they would feel the progress of their power of judgment; what is most important, they could confidently hope that frequent practice in recognizing and approving of good conduct in all its purity, and in noting even the least deviation from it with sorrow or contempt, would leave a lasting impression of esteem for the one and disgust for the other, even though this practice is pursued only as a game of judgment in which children could compete with one another. By the mere habit of frequently looking upon actions as praise-

155 worthy or blameworthy, a good foundation would be laid for righteousness in the future course of life. But I wish they would spare them examples of so-called noble (supermeritorious) actions, which so fill our sentimental writings, and would refer everything to duty only and the worth which a man can and must give himself in his own eyes through the consciousness of not having transgressed his duty, since whatever runs up into empty wishes and longings for unattainable perfection produces mere heroes of romance, who, while priding themselves on their feeling of transcendent greatness, release

themselves from observing common and everyday responsibility as petty and insignificant.*

If one asks, however, what pure morality really is, by which, as the touch-stone, the moral import of each action must be tested, I must confess that only philosophers can put the decision on this question in doubt. For by common sense it is long since decided, not by abstract general formulas but rather by habitual use, like the difference between the right and the left hand. We will therefore first show the distinctive mark of pure virtue in an example and, imagining that we have put it before, say, a ten-year-old boy for his judgment, see whether he must necessarily judge so by himself without being guided by the teacher.

Tell him the story of an honest man whom someone wishes to induce to join the calumniators of an innocent but powerless person (say, Anne Boleyn accused by Henry VIII of England). He is offered advantages (e.g., great gifts or high rank); he rejects them. This will cause only applause and approval in 156 the mind of the hearer, because they represent mere gain. Now come threats of loss. Among the slanderers there are his best friends who now renounce his friendship; near-relatives who threaten him (who is without fortune) with disinheritance; powerful persons who can persecute and harass him in all places and in every circumstance; a prince who threatens him with loss of freedom and even of life itself. But the measure of his suffering may be full, so that he may feel the pain which only the morally good heart can very deeply feel, let his family, which is threatened with extreme need and want, entreat him to yield; think of the man himself, who, though righteous, has feelings which are not insensible or hardened to either sympathy or his own needs, at the moment when he wishes never to have lived to see the day which brings him such unutterable pain — think of him without any wavering or even a doubt remaining true to his resolution to be honest. — Thus one can lead the young listener step by step from mere approval to admiration, and from admiration to marveling, and finally to the greatest veneration and a lively wish that he himself could be such a man (though certainly not in his circum-stances). Yet virtue is here worth so much only because it costs so much, not because it brings any profit. All the admiration and even the endeavor to be like this character rest here solely on the purity of the moral principle, which can be clearly shown only by removing from the incentive of the action

---

*It is entirely proper to extol actions which display a great, unselfishness, and sympathetic disposition and humanity. But in them we must attend not so much to the elevation of soul, which is very fleeting and ephemeral, as to the subjection of the heart to duty, from which a more lasting impression can be expected as it entails principles and not just ebullitions, as the former does. One need only to reflect a little to find an indebtedness which the vaunted hero has in some way incurred to the human race (even if it be only that, by the inequality of men under the civil constitution, he enjoys advantages on account of which others must be lacking to just that extent), which will prevent the thought of duty from being repressed by the self-complacent imagination of merit.

everything which men might count as a part of happiness. Thus morality must have more power over the human heart the more purely it is presented. From this it follows that, if the law of morals and the image of holiness and virtue are to exert any influence at all on our minds, they can do so only insofar as they are laid to heart in their purity as incentives unmixed with any view to well-being, because it is in suffering that they most notably show themselves. But a factor whose removal strengthens the effect of a moving force must have been a hindrance; consequently, all admixture of incentives which derive from one's own happiness are a hindrance to the influence of the moral law on the human heart.

157   I assert further that, if in the admired action the motive from which it was done was esteem for duty, this respect for the law and not any pretension to inner greatness of mind or noble and meritorious sentiment, is that which has the most power over the mind of the spectator. Consequently, duty, not merit, has not only the most definite influence but, when seen in the true light of its inviolability, also the most penetrating influence on the mind.

In our times, when one hopes to have more effect on the mind through yielding, soft-hearted feelings or high-flying, puffed-up pretensions, which wither instead of strengthen the heart, than through the dry and earnest Idea of duty which is more fitting to human imperfection and progress in goodness, attention to this method is more needed than ever. One defeats his purpose by setting actions called noble, magnanimous, and meritorious as models for children with the notion of captivating them by infusing an enthusiasm for these actions. For as they are considerably backward in the observance of the commonest duty and even in the correct estimation of it, this amounts to speedily making them fantastic romancers. Even among the instructed and experienced portion of mankind, this supposed incentive has, if not an injurious, at least no genuine moral, effect on the heart, which is what one hoped to produce by its means.

All feelings, and especially those which produce unusual exertions, must produce their effect in the moment when they are at their height and before they subside, else they have no effect at all. This is due to the fact that the heart naturally returns to its natural and moderate behavior and soon falls back into its previous languor because it has been brought into contact with something which stimulated it, not with something that strengthened it. Principles must be erected on concepts; on any other foundation there are only passing moods which give the person no moral worth and not even confidence in himself, without which the consciousness of his moral disposition and character, the highest good in man, cannot arise. These concepts, as they are to become subjectively practical, must not remain objective laws of morality which we merely admire and esteem in relation to mankind in general. Rather we must see the Idea of them in relation to man as an

158 individual, for then the law appears in a form deserving of high respect though not as pleasing as if it belonged to the element to which he is naturally

accustomed; on the contrary, it often compels him to leave this element, not without self-denial, and to give himself over to a higher element in which he can maintain himself only with effort and with unceasing apprehension of falling back into the former. In a word, the moral law demands obedience from duty, not from a predilection which cannot and should not be presupposed at all.

Let us now see in an example whether there is more subjective moving force of an incentive in the thought of an action as noble and magnanimous than when the action is thought of merely as duty in relation to the solemn moral law. The action by which someone with the greatest danger to his own life seeks to save others in a shipwreck and at last loses his own life will indeed be counted, on the one hand, as duty, but, on the other hand, even more as a meritorious action; but [in the latter case] our esteem for it will be weakened very much by the concept of his duty to himself, which here seems to have been infringed. More decisive is the magnanimous sacrifice of his life for the preservation of his country, and yet there still remain some scruples as to whether it is so perfect a duty to devote one's self spontaneously and unbidden to this purpose, and the action itself does not have the full force of a model and impulse to imitation. But if it is an inexorable duty, transgression against which by itself violates the moral law without respect to human welfare and, as it were, tramples on its holiness (the kind of duties which one usually calls duties to God, because we think of Him as the ideal of holiness in a substance), we give our most perfect esteem to pursuing it and sacrificing to it everything that ever had value for our dearest inclinations; and we find our soul strengthened and elevated by such an example when we convince ourselves, by contemplating it, that human nature is capable of such an elevation above everything that nature can present as an incentive in opposition to it. Juvenal describes such an example in a climax which makes the reader vividly feel the power of the incentive which lies in the pure law of duty as duty: "Be a stout soldier, a faithful guardian, and an incorruptible judge; if summoned to bear witness in some dubious and uncertain cause, 159 though Phalaris himself should bring up his bull and dictate to you a perjury, count it the greatest of all sins to prefer life to honor, and to lose, for the sake of living, all that makes life worth living."[3]

Whenever we bring any flattering thought of merit into our actions, the incentive is already mixed with self-love and thus has some assistance from the side of the sensuous. But to put everything else after the holiness of duty and to know that we *can* do it because our own reason acknowledges it as its law and says that we *ought* to do it — that is, as it were, to lift ourselves altogether out of the world of sense; this elevation is inseparably present in the consciousness of the law as an incentive of a faculty which rules over the

---

[3] Juvenal *Satire* viii. 79–84, trans. G.G. Ramsey. Phalaris was tyrant of Agrigentum, who had a brass ox constructed in which people were roasted to death.

sensuous, though not always effectively. But frequent concern with this incentive and the at first minor attempts at using it give hope of its effectiveness, so that gradually the greatest but still purely moral interest in it will be produced in us.

The method therefore takes the following course. The first step is to make judging according to moral laws a natural occupation which accompanies our own free actions as well as our observations of those of others, and to make it, as it were, a habit. We must sharpen these judgments by first asking whether the action is objectively in accordance with the moral law, and if so, with which one; by this, heed to the law which gives only a principle of obligation is distinguished from one which is in fact obligatory *(leges obligandi a legibus obligantibus)*. For instance, we distinguish between the law of that which the needs of men require of me from that which their rights demand, the latter prescribing essential duties while the former assigns nonessential duties. This teaches how to distinguish between the different duties which come together in an action. The second point to which attention must be directed is the question as to whether the action is done (subjectively) for the sake of the moral law, and thus not only is morally correct as a deed, but also has moral worth as a disposition because of the maxim from which it was done. Now there is no doubt that this exercise and the consciousness of cultivation of our reason which judges concerning the practical must gradually produce a certain interest even in its own law and thus in morally good actions. For we ultimately take a liking to that the observation of which makes us feel that our powers of knowledge are extended, and this extension is especially furthered by that wherein we find moral correctness, since reason, with its faculty of determining according to a priori principles what ought to occur, can find satisfaction only in such an order of things. Even an observer of nature finally likes objects which first offend his senses when he discovers in them the great design of their organization, so that his reason finds nourishment in observing them; Leibniz spared an insect which he had carefully examined under the microscope, and replaced it on its leaf, because he had been instructed by viewing it and, as it were, had received a benefit from it.

But this occupation of the faculty of judgment, which makes us feel our own powers of knowledge, is not yet interest in actions and their morality itself. It only enables one to entertain oneself with such judging and gives virtue or a turn of mind based on moral laws a form of beauty which is admired but not yet sought ("[Honesty] is praised, and starves").[4] It is the same with everything whose contemplation produces subjectively a consciousness of the harmony of our powers of representation by which we feel our entire cognitive faculty (understanding and imagination) strengthened; it produces a satisfaction that can be communicated to others, but the existence of its

160

---

[4] The allusion is to Juvenal *Satire* i.74. On the symbolic relation of beauty to morality, see *Critique of Faculty of Judgment* 59 (below, pp. 385–387).

object remains indifferent to us, as it is seen only as the occasion for our becoming aware of the store of our talents by which we are elevated above the mere animal level.

Now the second exercise begins its work. It lies in calling to notice the purity of will by a vivid exhibition of the moral disposition in examples. It is presented first only as negative perfection (i.e., indicating that no incentives of inclinations are the determining grounds influencing an action done as a duty). By this, the pupil's attention is held to the consciousness of his freedom; and, although this renunciation excites an initial feeling of pain, at the same time, by relieving him of the constraint even of his true needs, it frees him from the manifold discontent in which all these needs involve him and makes his mind receptive to the feeling of contentment from other sources. 161 The heart is freed from a burden which has secretly pressed upon it; it is lightened when in instances of pure moral resolutions there is revealed to man, who previously has not correctly known it, a power of inner freedom to release himself from the impetuous importunity of the inclinations, to such an extent that not even the dearest of them has an influence on a resolution for which he now makes use of his reason. In a case where I alone know that injustice lies in what I do, and where an open confession of it and an offer to make restitution is in direct conflict with vanity, selfishness, and an otherwise not illegitimate antipathy to the man whose rights I have impaired, if I can set aside all these considerations there is a consciousness of an independence from inclinations and circumstances and of the possibility of being sufficient to myself, which is salutary for me in yet other respects. The law of duty, through the positive worth which obedience to it makes us feel, finds easier access through the respect for ourselves in the consciousness of our freedom. If it is well established, so that a man fears nothing more than to find himself on self-examination to be worthless and contemptible in his own eyes, every moral disposition can be grafted on to this self-respect, for the consciousness of freedom is the best, indeed the only, guard that can keep ignoble and corrupting influences from bursting in upon the mind. . . .

THE STARRY HEAVENS ABOVE ME, THE MORAL LAW WITHIN ME[5]

Two things fill the mind with ever new and increasing wonder and awe, the oftener and the more steadily I reflect upon them: the starry heavens above me and the moral law within me. I do not merely conjecture them and seek them as if they were obscured in darkness or in the transcendent region beyond my horizon: I see them before me, and I connect them directly with 162 the consciousness of my own existence. The starry heavens begin at the place

[5] The Conclusion to the entire second *Critique*.

I occupy in the external world of sense, and they broaden the connection in which I stand into an unbounded magnitude of worlds beyond worlds and systems of systems and into the limitless times of their periodic motion, their beginning and duration. The latter begins at my invisible self, my personality, and exhibits me in a world which has true infinity but which only the understanding can trace — a world in which I recognize myself as existing in a universal and necessary (and not, as in the first case, only contingent) connection, and thereby also in connection with all those visible worlds. The former view of a countless multitude of worlds annihilates, as it were, my importance as an *animal creature* which must give back to the planet (a mere speck in the universe) the matter from which it came, matter which is for a little time endowed with vital force, we know not how. The latter, on the contrary, infinitely raises my worth as that of an *intelligence* by my being a person in whom the moral law reveals to me a life independent of all animality and even of the whole world of sense, at least so far as it may be inferred from the final destination assigned to my existence by this law, a destination which is not restricted to the conditions and boundaries of this life but reaches into the infinite.

But though admiration and respect can indeed excite to inquiry, they cannot supply the want of it. What, then, is to be done in order to set inquiry on foot in a useful way appropriate to the sublimity of its objects? Examples may serve for warnings here, but also for imitation. The observation of the world began from the noblest spectacle that was ever placed before the human senses and that our understanding can dare to follow in its vast expanse, and it ended in — astrology. Morals began with the noblest attribute of human nature, the development and cultivation of which promised infinite benefits, and it ended in — fanaticism or superstition. So it goes with all crude attempts in which the principal part of the business depends on the use of reason, a use which does not come of itself, like that of the feet, from frequent exercise, especially when it concerns attributes which cannot be so directly exhibited in common experience. Though late, when the maxim did come to prevail of carefully examining every step which reason had to take and not letting it proceed except on the path of a well-considered method, the study of the structure of the world took an entirely different direction and therewith attained an incomparably happier result. The fall of a stone and the motion of a sling, resolved into their elements and the forces manifested in them treated mathematically, finally brought that clear and henceforth unchangeable insight into the structure of the world which, as observations continue, we may hope to broaden but need not fear having to retract.

This example recommends to us the same path in treating of the moral capacities of our nature and gives hope of a similarly good issue. We have at hand examples of the morally judging reason. We may analyze them into their elementary concepts, adopting, in default of mathematics, a process similar to that of chemistry, i.e., we may, in repeated experiments on common sense, separate the empirical from the rational, exhibit each of them in a pure state, and show what each by itself can accomplish. Thus we shall avoid the error of a crude and unpracticed judgment and (which is far more important) the extravagances of genius, by which, as the adepts of the philosopher's stone, visionary treasures are promised and real treasures are squandered for lack of methodical study and knowledge of nature. In a word, science (critically sought and methodically directed) is the narrow gate that leads to the doctrine of wisdom, when by this is understood not merely what one ought to do but what should serve as a guide to teachers in laying out plainly and well the path to wisdom which everyone should follow, and in keeping others from going astray. It is a science of which philosophy must always remain the guardian; and though the public takes no interest in its subtle investigations, it may very well take an interest in the doctrines which such considerations first make clear to it.

VIII

Critique of the Faculty of Judgment

Editor's Introduction

Kant published the *Critique of the Faculty of Judgment* in 1790. Though most parts of it are both interesting and clear, it is not easy to comprehend the organization and the significance of the whole. This Introduction, therefore, is somewhat longer and more detailed than those provided the other selections. The difficulty lies in the fact that Kant deals with four topics which do not have any apparent connection with each other. They are, in fact, intimately related, but their relationship must be discovered without a great deal of help from Kant. The following is a brief statement of the topics.

(1) *The architectonic problem.* This is the first topic discussed in the Introduction, Sections II and III. Kant wanted to show how the realm of nature under causal, mechanical, laws can be subject also to the laws of freedom, so that the course of nature can be affected by the free acts of human beings. Nature is phenomena under the laws of the understanding; reason gives laws of what *ought* to occur in nature where, according to the first *Critique*, everything is as it *must be*. The realm of freedom and the realm of nature were separated in the first and second *Critiques*; now the task of the third *Critique* is to bring them together again under a supersensible condition. "Nature must be so thought that the conformity to law of its form at least harmonizes with the possibility of the purposes to be effected in it according to the laws of freedom" (p. 342). Kant's task is to show that pure practical and pure theoretical reason are "one and the same reason, which must differ only in application: (p. 247)

(2) *The problem of formal purposiveness.* This problem is discussed in Sections IV and V and part of VIII in the Introduction. Nature, though it is a realm of mathematical shapes and relations, causal laws and mechanical efficient causes, has a finer-grained structure than that determined by the a priori laws of the understanding. The very abstract laws given to nature by the understanding do not of themselves explain the simplicity, uniformity, and harmony of nature which make our inductive and analogical reasoning about it possible and fruitful. In spite of all the laws of the understanding, the a posteriori content of our perceptions might have been so complicated and various that we would be unable to perform any fruitful inductions or discover any predictable relations between brute facts. Nevertheless we do find nature amenable

to division into genera and species; there is a gradual continuity from one genus to another, without gaps, yet preserving the existence of natural kinds; some of the laws of physics are deducible from others; the same laws hold on our terrestrial globe and on the most distant heavenly bodies. Since the basic laws of nature are of the mind's own making, it is not surprising that nature as phenomena under law should exemplify such *basic* laws as that of causality and the conservation of substance; but it is less easily explained why nature seems to be so organized under *specific* laws not given a priori by the understanding that minds like ours can succeed in understanding the intricacies of nature. It is as if nature had been designed for the purpose of enabling minds like ours to understand it. This harmony of nature among all its parts is called by Kant "the formal purposiveness of nature,"[1] and if we think of nature as if it were designed for our cognitive benefit it will not seem as alien to our moral purposes as nature without this design does.

(3) *The aesthetic problem.* In carrying out his plan to unify, or at least to reconcile, nature and freedom, Kant uncovered a priori elements in our judgments of the beautiful and the sublime in nature and in art. In the course of answering the deeply systematic architectonic question about the relation of morality to nature, Kant — almost incidentally, it might seem — wrote one of the greatest treatises on aesthetics. Of course there was nothing incidental about it; Kant had intended to write a "Critique of Taste" even before he wrote the *Critique of Pure Reason*, but only the rest of the critical philosophy provided the context in which the experience of beauty and the sublime could be seen as having a bearing on the relation between them and the teleological organization of nature. This topic is the subject matter of the first Book, but it is discussed also in Sections VI and VII of his Introduction.

(4) *The biological problem.* This problem is raised in Section VIII of Kant's Introduction and occupies the major portion of the second Book. In the structures discovered by astronomy and physics, nature appears to be harmonious, and Kant interprets this to mean that nature has a formal purposiveness or fittingness to human cognitive processes. It would, however, be almost unintelligible to ask, in that context, what is the purpose of Saturn's rings or the Milky Way.[2] But there are things in

---

[1] "Purposiveness of nature" is almost synonymous with what other eighteenth-century writers called "harmony of nature."

[2] In the eighteenth century such questions did not appear to most philosophers to be unintelligible, for they regarded specific structures in the physical world as having purposes, and natural theology based its arguments for the existence of God on the purposes found, or imagined, to lie in natural objects of astronomy and geology, as well as in living beings. But when Kant, in his precritical writings, argued for the existence of God from what he thought was evidence of design in nature, he did not start from exceptional events or complicated structures in natural bodies, but from the orderly design of inorganic nature as a whole, especially from the simplicity of explanation by a few extremely general laws.

nature whose purpose we can intelligibly and fruitfully inquire into. For example, what is the purpose of the heart? The heart is somewhat like a pump which a human being could construct for his own purposes; it is not produced by man, but by nature; and it has a purpose in serving the life of the organism. An organism is called, by Kant, a natural purpose. Some philosophers and biologists believe — then and now — that organisms can be explained mechanically in terms of physics, chemistry, and efficient causes without our having to take notice of the function or purpose which its organs seem to serve; some do not. If Kant can show that teleological concepts are necessary for biological explanation — and specially if he can show that their use is not incompatible with mechanical explanation — he can better comprehend man in his dual role as a teleological being in nature and as a mechanical part of nature. Thus in dealing with an epistemological problem of biological methodology, Kant was still seeking for the relation between nature as the realm of mechanism and nature as the environment in which human freedom and purposes are to be realized.

In reading the *Critique* it is important both to isolate and to interrelate these four problems. At each stage, one should know which of the four problems is occupying Kant's central attention. Then by seeing each specific topic from the point of view of the first problem, the relationship among the remaining parts will become clear. Nevertheless, the *Critique* may still give the impression of being an aggregate of independent investigations, not a systematic whole of the kind Kant always insisted upon in the other *Critiques*. What, the reader may ask, does aesthetics have to do with disputes among biologists?

In our twentieth-century intellectual climate, the answer will very likely be: Nothing. Kant was not, however, alone in thinking he saw an intimate conceptual connection between them, and if we recall some of the intellectual background of both art and science in the eighteenth century, his juxtaposition of these two topics will no longer appear arbitrary. In the eighteenth century almost no one thought they were irrelevant to one another, and there were two philosophical conceptions which related them to each other. Both are to be found in Kant.

(1) *The artifactual conception of art and nature.* Given the Newtonian conception of nature as a vast machine under mechanical laws, it was assumed that it was created, organized (and, according to Newton and Descartes, sustained) by God. The analogy between the creation and organization of nature, on the one hand, and the works of human hands and minds, on the other, in the creation of artifacts (small clocks, for example, being likened to the great clock of the diurnal motion of the earth), constituted the subject matter of natural theology.[3] Nature as a

---

[3] For Kant's evaluation of the conception of nature as divine artistry, see above, pp. 144–148.

whole and in the details of its parts, preeminently in its *biological* parts, was itself the work of a Divine Artist, God.

(2) *The organic conception of art and nature.* Opposing this was another conception of nature, drawn from both neo-Platonic and Aristotelian sources. According to this, nature is not a work of divine art but is, or is like, a living whole molded by "plastic vital forces" instead of by mechanical impact and attraction.[4] Nature produces living beings and beautiful forms out of her infinite fecundity, and when human beings, themselves parts of nature, manifest the creative functions of nature in their self-consciousness, skill, and genius, they produce the fine arts.

The relation between art and biology in Kant's time was therefore much more intimate than it is in present-day aesthetics and philosophy of nature. It was quite natural for him to discuss them together, and given this historical background it is not hard to see why he did so.

With all these diverse purposes, the architectonic parallels which Kant liked to maintain between the structures of the *Critiques* begin to break down. Here one finds the rubrics *analytic, dialectic, antinomy, deduction,* and the like; but they give little guidance through the work, and can generally be ignored without loss.

A
INTRODUCTION

Section II (Section I is omitted) presents the well-known two-world theory of the realm of nature and the realm of freedom. Kant raises the question whether they can be regarded as parts of a single system.

Section III introduces a third faculty of the mind, which links reason (giving moral law) and understanding (giving natural law). This is the faculty of judgment. As both reason and understanding have a priori functions, it is plausible to assume that there may be a priori principles in the faculty of judgment too. Besides the triad of cognitive faculties (reason, understanding, judgment) there is also a triad of mental faculties in general: cognition, desire, and feeling (of pleasure and pain). Thinking analogically again, Kant suspects that there is more than a mere formal parallelism here, and that judgment and feeling are intimately related. If so, there may be a priori conditions for feelings.

Section IV describes the faculty of reflective judgment. Judgment in general is the ability to relate universals to particulars (as in syllogism), and if the particular is given for which the universal (or law) is to be

---

[4]This view was held by Kant's pupil Johann Gottfried Herder and by Goethe. The contrast between the two views is expressed in Hume's *Dialogues Concerning Natural Religion*, especially Part VI.

found, judgment is called *reflective*. (Otherwise it moves from a given universal to the particular and is called *determinant* judgment.)

Universal laws given by the understanding determine the broad structures of scientific knowledge and the principal properties of bodies. But nature presents to our observation a vast array of specific facts for which the understanding provides *only* the necessary a priori conditions. Yet we succeed in grouping these facts and subsuming them under contingent empirical universals and laws. The Copernican Revolution gives us *no* reason to expect this and *no* explanation for it. Rather it is as though nature in its detailed empirical properties and connections had been designed so that it could be understood by minds like ours.

Section V examines the concept of purposiveness, and argues that the purposiveness or harmony of nature (its fittingness for our understanding it) is an a priori regulative Idea. We do not know that nature has purposes, but assuming that it does makes the success of our explanatory efforts intelligible instead of surprising.

Section VI observes that human beings experience pleasure not only when their desires are satisfied or their senses gratified, but also when they achieve cognitive success, as, for example, when some new hypothesis is brilliantly confirmed or a complicated geometrical proposition is elegantly demonstrated. We also take pleasure in the mere perception of an object of nature or a work of art when there seems to be a fittingness of the object to our perceptive capacities. When the third is the source of our pleasure, we express it in an *aesthetical judgment of taste*.

Section VII gives a preliminary account of two kinds of aesthetical judgment: the judgment of the merely agreeable, and the judgment of taste. They are distinguished like judgments of perception and judgments of experience in *Prolegomena*, Section 18. What, then, is the a priori condition present in judgments of experience and judgments of taste, but absent from judgments of perception and judgments of mere agreeableness? That is the question which will occupy Kant in the *Critique of the Faculty of Aesthetical Judgment*.

Section VIII deals with purposiveness of nature in general, whereby it is understandable that it should be amenable to systematic explanation under a few a priori regulative principles. It also raises the problem of the apparent design of specific objects in nature that Kant calls natural purposes and to which most of the second Book is devoted.

The Introduction provides a good preview of what is to be expected in the *Critique* proper. It does not make clear, however, the manner in which the *Critique of the Faculty of Judgment* reconciles and integrates the first two *Critiques*, or the manner in which the faculty of judgment brings peace between understanding and reason. For Kant's definitive solution of these problems one must wait until Sections 59, 76, 77, and 78.

Unfortunately, these sections cannot be understood without an understanding of what leads up to them.

B
CRITIQUE OF THE FACULTY OF AESTHETICAL JUDGMENT

Kant first analyzes the experience of beauty, doing so through the rather artificial treatment of aesthetic judgments by adhering to the table of judgments in the first *Critique*. Aside from this unnecessary technicality, the analysis is interestingly and clearly written, and a brief introduction suffices.

Sections 1–5 describe the quality of aesthetic pleasure. They carefully distinguish the pleasure we take in beauty from that which we feel upon the satisfaction of a desire or the gratification of our senses. Taste is the ability to judge an object called beautiful because of a *disinterested pleasure* one feels in perceiving it.

Sections 6–9 point out that in making judgments of beauty we claim a *universal* validity for our judgment. In this the judgment of taste differs from a statement that something gives *me* pleasure by gratifying *my* sense or satisfying *my* desire.

Sections 10–17 say that objects are judged to be beautiful if they are perceived to be purposive (as if designed by an artist) without serving any *particular* purpose. Here Kant uses the famous expression, "purposiveness without purpose" (p. 364). It pleases through its effect upon our cognitive faculties, in being so adapted to their free and easy play that the object is perceived *as if* it had been designed to facilitate our mental activity.

Sections 18–22 deal with the modality of the aesthetic judgment of taste. The satisfaction we feel in perceiving a beautiful object is a *necessary pleasure* and a pleasure for all perceivers of it. Like any necessity (whether in morals or in cognition) this character of necessity requires a justification (deduction). The formal "Deduction of the Judgment of Taste" does not take place until Sections 36–38 (omitted from this volume because of their redundancy), but the substance of the Deduction is found here in Sections 20–22. In brief: the pleasure we have in the perception of a beautiful object arises from the harmonious play of our imagination and understanding. Since these cognitive faculties are common to all human beings who can communicate knowledge to each other, their *sensus communis*, the pleasure one feels in their harmonious activity can be ascribed, at least in principle, to all human beings, not in the sense that all human beings actually pass the same aesthetic judgment on the same object, but that they *ought* to and would do so if their taste were free from extraneous considerations.

Sections 23, 25, 26, and 27 give the substance of Kant's theory of the sublime. The two principal categories of aesthetics in the eighteenth century were the beautiful and the sublime, Whereas the beautiful was that which was perceived immediately as conformable to our cognitive faculties and thus as giving pleasure by its perception, the sublime was that which was disinterestedly perceived not as conforming to our cognitive capacity, but rather as overwhelming it by the magnitude or power of natural objects. Their threat to our comprehension or well-being is overcome by "man's unconquerable mind" which is itself the true original of sublimity, but we erroneously transfer this character to the things of nature. In the sublime, the aesthetic and moral experiences are more intimately related than in the beautiful, as Kant recounts it below in Section 59.

Section 44 distinguishes fine arts from the merely pleasing arts, and *Section 45* describes the experience of the products of fine arts as being like the experience of natural beauty. From this Kant moves, in *Section 46*, to the assertion that fine art is the product of genius, a kind of *natural force*, a natural gift which gives the rule to art.

As in all the *Critiques*, there is, of course, an antinomy. It arises from the conflict of two commonplaces: There is no disputing about taste, and taste may be contested. In *Section 56* it is expressed in a contradiction between "the judgment of taste is based upon concepts," and "the judgment of taste is not based upon concepts." *Section 57* resolves the antinomy by showing that "based upon concepts" is equivocal, and both the apparently contradictory principles are true.

Our selections from the first part of the *Critique* come to an end with *Section 59*, "Of Beauty as a Symbol of Morality." Kant points to many parallels between morals and taste, and suggests that both depend upon a common, but to us unknowable, supersensible condition. Thus finally, after a "detour" through one of the world's classics in aesthetics, we come back to the technical question of how the faculty of judgment, exercised on natural objects and the products of genius, points to a common source of morals and nature as well as to their reconciliation. It gives us no knowledge of the common metaphysical source of the diverse realms of our experience, but only a point of view from which the two worlds may be reconciled in our own minds.

C
CRITIQUE OF THE FACULTY OF TELEOLOGICAL JUDGMENT

A teleological judgment is one which explains something by reference to its purpose. Teleological judgments are made by the faculty of reflective judgment. Determinant judgment explains the beating of the heart, for instance, by reference to physico-chemical and physiological causes which apply also to many other processes; reflective judgment says it beats to pump blood to the rest of the body. What is the relation between these two kinds of explanations, and what bearing does this have on the fundamental problem of relating mechanism to freedom? To answer these questions is the task of the second part of the *Critique*.

Sections 64–66 distinguish human artifacts (made by human beings for human purposes) from natural purposes (organisms) by the reproduction, growth, self-repair, and mutual dependence of parts in living beings. In living beings each part is reciprocally means and end for the other parts of the same whole, and to explain the part one must refer to its function in the whole. The concept of an organized whole is not a constitutive concept or category for determinant judgment; it is only a regulative concept for reflective judgment, guiding its search for the efficient causes of biological states and occurrences.

Section 70 shows that there is an antinomy of teleological judgment, an at least apparent contradiction between the law of mechanical causation (Second Analogy of Experience, pp 117–120) and the teleological principle that every part of an organism is there because of the function it serves.

Sections 71 and 75 present Kant's resolution of the antinomy. He now interprets the Second Analogy of Experience as a regulative maxim on the same footing as the principle of teleology. We are to *look for*, and be dissatisfied until we find, mechanical explanations of the functions of an organ, but this search is to be *guided by* thoughts of the purpose an organ serves. We cannot succeed in the former without guidance from the latter, but we will never be satisfied with an explanation that stops with a statement merely of the purpose. Thus there is a division of labor, but not a conflict, between the two conceptions.

So much for the problem of biological methodology. We must not lose sight of the larger project of which the biological is only a part, namely Kant's project of reconciling the legislation of the understanding with that of reason, or freedom with the laws of nature. This larger and more difficult subject is treated in the next three sections. Unfortunately they are difficult, and as a climactic point in Kant's philosophy as a whole they warrant a somewhat fuller introduction.

Section 76, disingenuously entitled "Remark," returns to the topic dealt with in the "Postulates of All Empirical Thinking" (first *Critique*, pp. 120–125 above). There it was concluded that the modal distinctions between the possible, the actual, and the necessary are not ontological distinctions applicable to things in themselves, but are epistemological distinctions based upon which cognitive faculty is involved in a judgment. Here Kant extends that line of thought to cover the modal distinction between *ought* and *is*. He concludes that "it is due to the subjective constitution of our practical faculty [reason] that moral laws must be represented as commands [oughts]", and not as factual statements of what *is* (p. 399).

Sections 77 and 78 continue the investigation of the characteristic of the human mind (which might very well have been quite differently constituted) that makes it possible for us human beings to think of some things as natural purposes and not simply as consequences of antecedent causes.

Kant has already said that the whole of an organism is a condition of its parts and must be taken into account in giving an explanation of the organs of the body. Under the rule of efficient causes, however, each part is an antecedent and independent condition of the whole. The only way we human beings can understand a whole to be a condition of its parts is by thinking not the whole but the *concept of the whole* to be the cause of its parts. *A thing the concept of which is a cause of its existence is a purpose* (p. 345). Therefore we human beings interpret the dependence of the part on the whole as a case of purpose and not as a case of efficient causation.

It is, therefore, a peculiar limitation of the human mind which makes it possible, indeed necessary, to give a teleological explanation. We can, however, imagine a mind different in specifiable ways from the human mind, which would not find it possible or necessary to draw the distinction between whole-part and part-whole causal relations, and hence no distinction between teleological and efficient causes. Therefore it follows that we need not interpret the distinction as an ontological conflict between two kinds of causes, each effective in its own "world," but simply as a consequence of human cognitive limitations.

To make this plausible, however, Kant must specify what the peculiarity of the human mind is, and show that it is not necessarily present in other minds which we can conceive of (but, of course, not know). The peculiarity is that our intellect is discursive and moves from intuitive data to abstract concepts. Thus the particular given in empirical intuition is, *for us*, independent of concepts except when a concept is cause of the object, in which case the judgment is teleological, since the object whose cause is its concept is a purpose. But so far as we know there can be a nonhuman *intuitive intellect* which would move directly from having a concept to intuiting the existence of its object. Human beings do this only indirectly by an intervening bodily action which directly causes the existence of the object and thus we see the object as our purpose, since our concept of it was indirectly its cause. But for an intuitive intellect no intervening action would be necessary: to think of the thing and to bring it into existence as an object of intuition would be the same act. For such an intellect, there would be no difference between—in fact, there would no longer be—explanations in terms of efficient causes and explanations in terms of final causes. Efficient causality and final causality would be identical.

Kant is not asserting that there are beings with an intuitive intellect, to whom the thought of an object is the same as the intuition of its existence. (Sometimes in the history of philosophy such an intellect has been ascribed to God.) Kant is saying only that human beings must distinguish between two kinds of causal judgments, the mechanical and the teleological, and in doing so we create for ourselves the great problems of the *ought* and the *is*, of freedom and nature, of teleology and mechanism. It is only to minds like ours that they seem opposed. But we may believe (we cannot know) that the supersensible common ground of the realm of freedom and the realm of nature lies beyond the opposing modes of human explanation and the to us apparent opposition between two realms.

Section 84 (The reader may now relax). This section continues a line of thought introduced in the *Critique of Practical Reason* (above, pp. 312 – 317) which leads to the conception of the final purpose of the world, and concludes that it is man as a moral agent existing in a realm of ends.

The translation of the Critique of the Faculty of Judgment *is that of J.H. Bernard (London, 1892). It has been very extensively revised by the present Editor.*

SUGGESTIONS FOR FURTHER READING

Cassirer, Ernst. *Kant's Life and Thought.* Yale University Press, 1981. Chapter 6.
Cassirer, H.W. *A Commentary on Kant's Critique of Judgment.* Barnes and Noble, 1970.
Crawford, Donald W. *Kant's Aesthetic Theory.* University of Wisconsin Press, 1974.
MacMillan, R.A.C. *The Crowning Phase of the Critical Philosophy. A Study of Kant's Critique of Judgment.* (London 1912) reprint, Garland Publishing Inc., 1975.
McFarland, John. *Kant's Concept of Teleology.* University of Edinburgh Press, 1970.
Pluhar, Werner S. Translator's Introduction to Kant's *Critique of Judgment,* Hackett Publishing Company, 1987.
Zumbach, Clark. *The Transcendent Science. Kant's Conception of Biological Methodology.* Nijhoff, 1984.

Critique of the Faculty of Judgment

A. INTRODUCTION

II. Of the Realm[1] of Philosophy in General

Our whole cognitive faculty has two realms, that of natural concepts and that of the concept of freedom; through both it gives laws a priori. In accordance with this, philosophy is divided into theoretical and practical, but the territory to which its realm extends and in which its legislation is exercised is always only the complex of all objects of possible experience, so long as they are taken to be nothing more than appearances, for otherwise no legislation of the understanding with respect of them is possible.

Legislation through natural concepts is carried on by the understanding and is theoretical. Legislation through the concept of freedom is carried on by reason, and is only practical. It is in the practical sphere alone that reason can give laws; in theoretical knowledge (of nature), reason, knowing the law by means of the understanding, can merely deduce from these given laws consequences which always remain within [the boundaries of] nature. . . .

Understanding and reason, therefore, exercise two distinct legislations on one and the same territory of experience, and do so without prejudice to each other. The concept of freedom as little disturbs the legislation of nature as the natural concept influences legislation through reason. The possibility of at least thinking without contradiction the coexistence of the two legislations and of the corresponding faculties in the same subject has been shown in the *Critique of Pure Reason*, since it has annulled the objections to this [possibility] by exposing the dialectical illusion which they contain.[2]

These two different realms, then, do not limit each other in their legislation, though they incessantly do so in the effects they have world of sense. That they do not constitute *one* realm arises from this: that the natural concept represents its objects in intuition, not as things in themselves but as mere appearances; the concept of freedom, on the other hand, represents in its object a thing in itself, but not in intuition. Hence neither of them can

---

[1] In this Section Kant indulges his well known penchant for using political and legal metaphors in discussing the relations among the different mental faculties. The most important of the metaphors are: (a) field (*Feld*) — the scope of all objects to which the concepts of a faculty refer (example: the field of the supersensible); (b) territory (*Boden*) — that part of the field in which the concepts have cognitive validity (example: the territory of the sensible); (c) realm (*Gebiet*) —that part of the territory in which the faculty is a priori legislative (example: the realm of freedom and the realm of nature).

[2] Kant is referring especially to the third Antinomy in the *Critique of Pure Reason*; see above, pp. 129–131.

furnish theoretical knowledge of its object (or even of the thinking subject) as a thing in itself. This would be the supersensible, the Idea of which we must indeed make the basis of the possibility of all these objects of experience, but this Idea we can never extend or elevate into knowledge.

There is, then, an unbounded but also inaccessible field for our whole cognitive faculty — the field of the supersensible — wherein we find no territory [for knowledge] and therefore no realm for theoretical cognition by concepts either of understanding or of reason. This field we must indeed occupy with Ideas on behalf of the theoretical as well as the practical use of reason, but we can supply to them in reference to the laws arising from the concept of freedom no other than practical reality, by which our theoretical knowledge is not extended in the slightest degree toward the supersensible.

176 Now even if an immeasurable gulf is fixed between the sensible realm of the concept of nature and the supersensible realm of concept of freedom, so that no transition is possible from the first to the second (by means of the theoretical use of reason), just as if they were two different worlds of which the first could have no influence upon the second, yet the second is *meant* to have an influence upon the first. The concept of freedom is meant to actualize in the world of sense the purpose proposed by its laws, and consequently nature must be so thought that the conformity to law of its form at least harmonizes with the possibility of the purposes to be effected in it according to the laws of freedom. There must, therefore, be a ground of the unity of the supersensible which lies at the basis of nature, with that which the concept of freedom practically contains; and the concept of this ground, although it does not attain either theoretically or practically to a knowledge of the ground, and hence has no realm of its own, nevertheless makes possible the transition from the mode of thought according to the principles of the one to that according to the principles of the other.

III. Of the Critique of the Faculty of Judgment as a Means of Combining the Two Parts of Philosophy into a Whole

The critique of the cognitive faculties, as regards what they can accomplish a priori, has, properly speaking, no realm with respect to objects, because critique is not doctrine, but has only to investigate whether and how, in accordance with the state of these faculties, a doctrine is possible by their means. Its field extends to all their pretensions, in order to confine them within their legitimate bounds. But what cannot enter into the division of philosophy into theoretical and practical may yet enter into the critique of the pure faculty of cognition in general, even if it contains principles available neither for theoretical nor for practical use. The natural concepts, which contain the ground of all theoretical knowledge a priori, rest on the legislation of the understanding. The concept of freedom, which contains the ground of all sensuously unconditioned practical principles a priori, rests on the legislation of reason. Both faculties, therefore, besides being capable of applying their logical form to principles of whatever origin, have also as content their special legislations above which there is no other (a priori). 177 Hence the division of philosophy into theoretical and practical is justified.

But in the family of the higher cognitive faculties there is a middle term between understanding and reason. This is the faculty of judgment, of which we have cause for supposing (according to analogy) that it may contain in itself, if not the [power] of giving laws of its own, still a special principle of its own for seeking laws, though it be a merely subjective a priori principle. This principle, even if it have no field of objects as its realm, yet may have somewhere a territory with a certain character for which no other principle can be valid.

But besides (to judge by analogy) there is an additional ground for bringing the faculty of judgment into connection with another arrangement of our representative faculties, which seems to be of even greater importance than that of its relationship with the family of the cognitive faculties. For all faculties or capacities of the soul can be reduced to three, which cannot be any further derived from one common ground: the faculty of knowledge, the feeling of pleasure and pain, and the faculty of desire.[3] For the faculty of 178 knowledge, the understanding is alone legislative if (as must happen when it is concerned by itself without confusion with the faculty of desire) this faculty as the faculty of theoretical knowledge is referred to nature; for to nature (as appearance) alone is it possible for us to give laws by means of natural concepts a priori (i.e., by pure concepts of the understanding). For the faculty of desire, as a supreme faculty according to the concept of freedom, reason (in which alone this concept has a place) gives laws a priori. Between the faculties of knowledge and desire there is the feeling of pleasure, just as the faculty of judgment mediates between understanding and reason. We may therefore suppose provisionally that judgment likewise contains in itself an a priori principle. And as pleasure or pain is necessarily combined with the faculty of desire (either preceding this principle, as in the lower desires, or following it, as in the higher when desire is determined by the moral law), we may suppose that the faculty of judgment will bring about a transition from 179 the pure faculty of knowledge, the realm of natural concepts, to the realm of the concept of freedom, just as in its logical use the faculty of judgment makes possible the transition from understanding to reason.

Although, then, philosophy can be divided into only two main parts, the theoretical and the practical, and although all that we may be able to say of the special principles of the faculty of judgment must be counted as belonging to it in its theoretical part (i.e., to rational cognition in accordance with natural concepts), yet the critique of pure reason, which must decide all this as regards the possibility of the system before undertaking [to construct] it,

---

[3] A long footnote is omitted here.

consists of three parts: the critique of pure understanding, of the pure faculty of judgment, and of pure reason. These faculties are called pure because they give laws a priori.

IV. Of Judgment as a Faculty Giving Laws A Priori

Judgment in general is the faculty of thinking the particular as contained under the universal. If the universal (the rule, the principle, the law) be given, judgment which subsumes the particular under it (even if, as transcendental faculty of judgment, it furnishes a priori the conditions in conformity with which subsumption under that universal is alone possible) is *determinant*. But if only the particular is given, for which the universal has to be found, the faculty of judgment is only *reflective*.

The faculty of determinant judgment only subsumes under universal transcendental laws given by understanding; the law is marked out for it, a priori, and it has therefore no need to think out a law for itself in order to be able to subordinate the particular in nature to the universal. But the forms of nature are so manifold, and there are so many modifications of the universal transcendental natural concepts left undetermined by the laws given a priori by pure understanding—because these laws concern only the possibility of a nature in general (as an object of sense)—that there must be laws for these
180 [forms and modifications] also. These, as empirical, may be contingent from the point of view of *our* understanding; and yet, if they are to be called laws, (as the concept of a nature requires), they must be regarded as necessary in virtue of a principle of the unity of the manifold variety, though this principle be unknown to us. Reflective judgment, which is obliged to ascend from the particular in nature to the universal, requires on that account a principle that it cannot borrow from experience, because its function is to establish the unity of all empirical principles under higher ones, and hence to establish the possibility of their systematic subordination. Reflective judgment can only give such a transcendental principle as a law by and to itself. It cannot derive it from outside (for then it would be determinant judgment), nor can it prescribe it to nature, because reflection upon the laws of nature adjusts itself to nature, not nature to the conditions under which we attempt to arrive at a concept of it—a concept which is left wholly contingent by nature itself.

This principle can be no other than the following: As universal laws of nature have their ground in our understanding, which prescribes them to nature (although only according to the universal concept of it as nature), so particular empirical laws, in respect of what in them is left undetermined by these universal laws, must be considered in accordance with such a unity as they would have if an understanding (though not *our* understanding) had furnished them to our cognitive faculties, in such ways as to make possible a system of experience comprising the particular laws of nature. Not as if, in this way, such an understanding had to be assumed as actual (for it is only our reflective judgment to which this Idea serves as a principle—for reflecting, not for determining); but our faculty of reflective judgment through this [conception of such an understanding] gives a law only to itself, not to nature.

The concept of an object, so far as it contains the ground of the actuality of this object, is the *purpose* [of the object], and the agreement of a thing with that constitution of things which is possible only according to purposes is called the *purposiveness* of its form. Thus, the principle of [reflective] judgment in respect of the forms of things of nature under empirical laws generally is the *purposiveness of nature* in its variety. That is, nature is represented 181 by means of this concept as if an understanding contained the ground of the unity of the variety of its empirical laws.

The purposiveness of nature is therefore a particular concept a priori which has its origin solely in the faculty of reflective judgment. For we cannot ascribe to natural products anything like nature's relating them to purposes; we can use this concept only to reflect upon such products with regard to the connection of appearances given in them according to empirical laws. This concept is also quite different from that of practical purposiveness (in human art or in morals), though it is certainly thought by analogy to practical purposiveness.

V. The Principle of the Formal Purposiveness of Nature is a Transcendental Principle of the Faculty of Judgment

A transcendental principle is one in which is represented a priori the universal condition under which alone any thing whatsoever can be object of our knowledge. On the other hand, a principle is called metaphysical if it represents the a priori condition under which alone objects, whose concept must be empirically given, can be further determined a priori. Thus the principle of the cognition of bodies as substances and as changeable substances is transcendental if it asserts that their changes must have a cause; it is metaphysical if it asserts that their changes must have an external cause. For in the former case bodies need be thought only by means of ontological predicates (pure concepts of the understanding, e.g. substance), in order to know the proposition a priori; but in the latter case the empirical concept of a body (as a thing movable in space) must lie at the basis of the proposition, although once this basis has been laid down it may be seen completely a priori that this latter predicate (motion only by external causes) belongs to body. Thus, as I shall presently show, the principle of the purposiveness of nature (in the variety of its empirical laws) is a transcendental principle. For the concept of objects, so far as they are thought as standing under this principle, is only the pure concept of objects of possible empirical cognition in general, and contains nothing empirical. On the other hand, the principle of practical 182 purposiveness, which must be thought in the Idea of the determination of a free will, is a metaphysical principle, because the concept of a faculty of desire as a will must be given empirically (i.e, it does not belong among the transcendental predicates). Neither principle, however, is empirical; both are a priori, because for the combination of the predicate with the empirical concept of the subject of their judgments no further experience is needed, but it can be apprehended completely a priori.

That the concept of a purposiveness of nature belongs to transcendental principles can be sufficiently seen from the maxims of the faculty of judgment which lie at the basis of the investigation of nature a priori and yet do not go farther than the possibility of experience, and consequently no farther than the possibility of the knowledge of nature — not indeed of nature in general, but of [a] nature determined through a variety of particular laws. These maxims present themselves in the course of metaphysical wisdom whose necessity we cannot demonstrate from concepts. Nature takes the shortest way (*lex parsimoniae*); at the same time, it makes no leaps either in the course of its changes or in the juxtaposition of specifically different forms (*lex continui in natura*); its great variety in empirical laws is yet unity under a few principles (*principia praeter necessitatem non sunt multiplicanda* etc.)

If we propose to set forth the origin of these fundamental propositions and try it by the psychological method, we violate their sense. For they do not tell us what happens (i.e., by what rule our cognitive powers actually operate and how we judge, but how we ought to judge; and this logical objective necessity does not emerge if the principles are merely empirical. Hence that purposiveness of nature for our cognitive faculties and their use, which is plainly manifest from them, is a transcendental principle of judgments and requires therefore also a transcendental deduction, by means of which the ground for these judgments must be sought in the sources of cognition a priori.

We must find in the grounds of the possibility of an experience in the very
183 first place something necessary, viz., the universal laws without which nature in general (as an object of sense) cannot be thought; and these rest on the categories, applied to the formal conditions of all intuition possible for us, so far as it also is given a priori. Now under these laws the faculty of judgment is determinant, for it has nothing to do but subsume under the given laws. For example, the understanding says that every change has its cause (a universal law of nature); the transcendental faculty of judgment has nothing further to do than to supply a priori the condition of subsumption under the concept of the understanding placed before it, the condition of subsumption under this concept being the succession [in time] of the determinations of one and the same thing. For nature in general (as an object of possible experience), that law is known as absolutely necessary. But the objects of empirical knowledge are determined in many other ways than by that formal time-condition alone, or, at least so far as we can judge a priori, they are determinable in many other ways. Hence, specifically different natures can be causes in an infinite variety of ways, as well as in virtue of what they have in common as belonging to nature in general; and each of these modes must (in accordance with the concept of cause in general) have its rule, which is a law and therefore brings

necessity with it, although we do not, because of the constitution and limitations of our cognitive faculties, comprehend this necessity. We must therefore think in nature, in respect of its merely empirical laws, a possibility of infinitely various empirical laws which are contingent, so far as our insight goes (i.e., we cannot know them a priori), and because of this we judge the unity of nature according to empirical laws and the possibility of the unity of experience (as a system according to empirical laws) to be contingent. Still, such a unity must necessarily be presupposed and assumed, for otherwise there would be no thorough going connection of empirical cognitions in a whole of experience. The universal laws of nature no doubt furnish such a connection of things according to their kind, as natural beings as such, but not specifically as such particular natural beings. Hence the faculty of judgment must assume for its special use this principle a priori: that what in the particular (empirical) laws of nature is from the human point of view contin- 184 gent, contains a unity of laws in the combination of its manifold in possible experience — a unity of laws not to be fathomed by us, but yet thinkable by us.

This unity of the laws in a combination which we know as contingent in itself though conforming with a necessary intention (need) of understanding, is represented as the purposiveness of objects (here: objects of nature). So the faculty of judgment, which in respect of things under possible (not yet discovered) empirical laws is merely reflective, must think of nature in respect of these laws according to a principle of purposiveness for our cognitive faculty, which then is expressed in the above maxims of judgment. This transcendental concept of a purposiveness of nature is neither a natural concept nor a concept of freedom, because it ascribes nothing to the object (nature) but only represents the peculiar way in which we must proceed in reflecting upon the objects of nature in respect to a thoroughly connected experience, and is consequently a subjective principle (maxim) of the faculty of judgment. Hence, as if it were a lucky chance favoring our design, we are rejoiced (properly speaking, relieved of a want) when we meet with such systematic unity under merely empirical laws, although we had necessarily assumed that there was such a unity without our comprehending it or being able to prove it.

In order to convince ourselves of the correctness of this deduction of the concept before us and the necessity of assuming it as a transcendental principle of cognition, just consider the magnitude of the problem. The problem, which lies a priori in our understanding, is to make a connected experience out of given perceptions of a nature containing an infinite variety of empirical laws. The understanding is, no doubt, in possession a priori of universal laws of nature without which nature could not be an object of experience, but it needs in addition a certain order of nature in its particular rules, which can be known only empirically and which are, as regards the understanding, contingent. These rules, without which we could not proceed from the universal

analogy of a possible experience in general to the particular experience, must be thought by it as laws (i.e., as necessary), for otherwise they would not constitute an order of nature, although their necessity can never be known or
185 comprehended. Although, therefore, the understanding can determine nothing a priori in respect of [particular] objects, it must, in order to trace out these empirical so-called laws, place at the basis of all reflection upon objects an a priori principle, viz., that a knowable order of nature is possible in accordance with these [particular] laws.

The following propositions express some such principle. There is in nature a subordination of genera and species comprehensible by us. Each one approximates to some other according to a common principle, so that a transition from one to another and so on to a higher genus may be possible. Though it seems at the outset unavoidable for our understanding to assume different kinds of causality for the specific differences of natural operations, yet these different kinds may stand under a small number of principles, with the investigation of which we have to busy ourselves. This harmony of nature with our cognitive faculty is presupposed a priori by the faculty of judgment on behalf of its reflection upon nature and in accordance with nature's empirical laws, while the understanding at the same time recognizes it objectively as contingent, and it is only the faculty of judgment that ascribes it to nature as a transcendental purposiveness in relation to the cognitive faculty of the subject. For without this presupposition we should have no order of nature in accordance with empirical laws, and consequently no guiding thread for an experience ordered by these in all their variety, or for an investigation of them.

For it might easily be thought that, in spite of all the uniformity of natural things according to universal laws, without which we should not have the form of empirical cognition in general, the specific variety of the empirical laws of nature and their effects might yet be so great that it would be impossible for our understanding to detect in nature a comprehensible order; impossible to divide its products into genera and species so as to use the principles which explain and make intelligible the one for the explanation and comprehension of another; or, out of such confused material (strictly, we should say, out of material so infinitely various as not to be measured by our faculty of comprehension) impossible to make a connected experience.

The faculty of judgment has therefore in itself also a principle a priori of the possibility of nature, but only in a subjective aspect, by which it prescribes not to nature (autonomy) but to itself (heautonomy) a law for its
186 reflection upon nature. This we might call the *law of the specification of nature* in respect of its empirical laws. The faculty of judgment does not cognize this a priori in nature but assumes it on behalf of a natural order cognizable by our understanding in the distinction which it makes among the universal laws of nature when it wishes to subordinate to these the variety of particular [empirical] laws. If, then, we say that nature specifies its universal laws according to

the principle of purposiveness for our cognitive faculty (i.e., in accordance with the necessary business of the human understanding in finding the universal for the particular which perception offers it), and again in finding connection for the diverse (which, however,is a universal for each species) in the unity of a principle, we thus neither prescribe to nature a law, nor do we learn one from nature by observation (although such a principle may be confirmed by observation). For it is not a principle of determinant but merely of reflective judgment. We only require that, be nature disposed as it may as regards its universal laws, investigation into its empirical laws may be carried on in accordance with that principle and the maxims founded on it, because it is only so far as that holds that we can make any progress with the use of our understanding in experience or gain knowledge.

VI. Of the Combination of the Feeling of Pleasure with the Concept of the Purposiveness of Nature

The just-mentioned harmony of nature in the variety of its particular laws with our need of finding universality of principles for it must be judged as, by our insight, contingent; yet at the same time it must be judged to be indispensable for the needs of our understanding and consequently as a purposiveness by which nature is harmonized with our intention which has only knowledge for its aim. The universal laws of the understanding, which are at the same time laws of nature, though they arise from spontaneity, are just as necessary as the laws of the motion of matter. Their production presupposes no design on the part of our cognitive faculty, because it is only by means of these laws that we first attain a concept of what the knowledge of things of nature involves, and these laws hold necessarily of nature as the object of our 187 cognition in general. But, so far as we can see, it is contingent that the order of nature in its particular laws, in variety and heterogeneity possibly transcending our comprehension, should be actually conformable to our power of comprehension. The discovery of this [order in the contingent laws of nature] is the business of the understanding, which intentionally aims at a necessary purpose of its own, viz., bringing unity of principles into this order. The faculty of judgment must then ascribe this purpose to nature, because the understanding cannot here prescribe any [set of specific laws] to it.

The attainment of that design is bound up with the feeling of pleasure, and since the condition of this attainment is a representation a priori — principle for reflective judgment in general — the feeling of pleasure is determined by a ground a priori and is valid for every man, and that merely by reference to the cognitive faculty, the concept of purposiveness not having here the least reference to the faculty of desire. This purposiveness [in the organization of nature under contingent laws] is wholly different from all practical purposiveness of nature [i.e., usefulness to human beings]. . . .

188 ## VII. Of the Aesthetical Representation of
the Purposiveness of Nature

That which in the representation of an object is merely subjective (i.e., which constitutes its reference to the subject but not to the object), is its aesthetical character; that which serves or can be used for the determination of the object (for cognition) is its logical validity.[4] In the cognition of an object
189 of sense, both references are present. In the sense-representation of external things, the quality of space wherein we intuit them is the merely subjective element in my representation of them (by which it remains undecided what they may be as objects in themselves), on account of which relation the object is thought through the representation merely as appearance. But space, notwithstanding its merely subjective quality, is at the same time an ingredient in the cognition of things as appearances. Sensation (i.e., external sensation) expresses the merely subjective element of our representations of external things, but it is also the proper material (what is real) in them (by which something existing is given), just as space is the mere form a priori of the possibility of their intuition. Nevertheless, sensation is also employed in the knowledge of external objects.

But the subjective element in a representation, which *cannot* be an ingredient in cognition, is the pleasure or pain which is bound up with it. Through it I cognize nothing in the object of the representation although the pleasure or pain may be the effect of some cognition. Now the purposiveness of a thing, so far as it is represented in perception, is not characteristic of the object itself (for purposiveness cannot be perceived) although it may be inferred from a knowledge of things. The purposiveness, therefore, which precedes the cognition of an object and which, even without our wishing to use the representation of it for cognition is at the same time immediately bound up with it, is that subjective element which cannot be an ingredient in cognition. Hence the object is called purposive only when its representation is directly combined with the feeling of pleasure, and this very representation is an aesthetical representation of purposiveness.

If pleasure is bound up with the mere apprehension (*apprehensio*) of the form of an object of intuition, without reference to a concept for a definite cognition [of it], then the representation is thereby referred not to the object but simply to the subject, and the pleasure can express nothing else than its harmony with the cognitive faculties which come into play in reflective
190 judgment, and, to the extent that they are in play, the pleasure can only express a subjective formal purposiveness of the object. For that apprehension of forms in the imagination can never take place unless the faculty of reflective judgment, though unintentionally, at least compares it with its faculty of referring intuitions to concepts. If in this comparison the imagination (like the faculty of a priori intuitions) is placed by means of a given

---

[4] Kant's distinction here is analogous to that between judgments of perception and judgments of experience, in *Prolegomena* Sections 18–20 (above, pp. 184–186).

representation in agreement with the understanding (as the faculty of concepts), and thereby a feeling of pleasure is aroused, the object must then be regarded as purposive for reflective judgment. Such a judgment is an aesthetical judgment upon the purposiveness of the object which does not base itself upon any present concept of the object, nor does it furnish any such concept. In the case of an object whose form (not the matter of its representation, i.e., sensation), in the mere reflection upon it (without reference to any concept to be obtained of it), is judged to be the ground of a pleasure in the representation of such an object, this pleasure is judged to be bound up with the representation necessarily, and consequently not only for the subject who apprehends this form, but for every judging being whatever. The object is then called beautiful, and the faculty of judging by means of such a pleasure (and, consequently judging with universal validity) is called *taste*. For since the ground of the pleasure is placed exclusively in the form of the object for reflection in general — and, consequently, in no sensation of the object, and also without reference to any concept which anywhere involves design — it is only the conformity to law in the empirical use of the faculty of judgment in general (unity of the imagination with the understanding) in the subject with which the representation of the object harmonizes in reflection, the conditions of which are universally valid a priori. And since this harmony of the object with the faculties of the subject is [only] contingent, it brings about the representation of its purposiveness [only] in respect of the cognitive faculties of the subject.

Here, now, is a pleasure which, like all pleasure or displeasure that is not produced through the concept of freedom (i.e., through the preceding determination of the higher faculties of desire by pure reason) can never be comprehended from concepts as necessarily bound up with the representation of an object. It must always be cognized as combined with the representation only by means of reflective perception. Consequently, like all empirical judgments, it can declare no objective necessity and lay claim to no a priori 191 validity. But the judgment of taste claims also, as every other empirical judgment does, to be valid for all men, and in spite of its inner contingency this is always possible. The strange and irregular thing is that it is not an empirical concept but a feeling of pleasure (consequently, not a concept at all) which, by the judgment of taste, is attributed to everyone, just as if it were a predicate involved in the cognition of the object, a predicate connected with the representation of the object.

A singular judgment of experience (e.g., by one who perceives a movable drop of water in an ice crystal) may justly claim that every other person should find it the same because he has formed this judgment according to the universal conditions of the determinant faculty of judgment under the laws of a possible experience in general. Just in the same way, he who feels pleasure in mere reflection upon the form of an object without respect to any concept, although this judgment is empirical and singular, justly claims the agreement of all men because the ground of this pleasure is found in the universal though subjective condition of reflective judgments, viz., the purposive harmony of an object (whether a product of nature or of art) with the mutual relations of the cognitive faculties (imagination and understanding), a harmony required in every empirical cognition. The pleasure, therefore, in the judgment of taste is dependent on an empirical representation and cannot be bound up a priori with any concept. We cannot determine a priori what object is or is not according to taste; that we must find out by experiment. But the pleasure is the determining ground of this judgment only because we are conscious that it rests solely on reflection and on the universal, though only subjective, conditions of the harmony of that reflection with the cognition of objects in general, for which the form of the object is purposive.

Thus the reason why the possibility of judgments of taste is subject to a 192 critique is that they presuppose a principle a priori, although this principle is neither a cognitive one for the understanding nor a practical for the will, and therefore is not in any way determinant a priori.

Susceptibility to pleasure from reflection upon the forms of things (of nature as well as of art) indicates not only a purposiveness of the objects in relation to the reflective faculty of judgment, conformable to the concept of nature in the subject, but also conversely a purposiveness of the subject in respect of the objects according to their form, or even their formlessness, in virtue of the concept of freedom. Hence the aesthetical judgment is related as a judgment of taste not only to the beautiful, but also, as springing from a spiritual feeling, it is related to the sublime. Thus the "Critique of the Faculty of Aesthetical Judgment" must be divided into two corresponding sections.

VIII. Of the Logical Representation of the Purposiveness in Nature

Purposiveness may be represented in an object given in experience on a merely subjective ground as the harmony of its form — in the apprehension (*apprehensio*) of it prior to any concept — with the cognitive faculties, in order to unite the intuition with concepts to effect a cognition. Or it may be represented objectively as the harmony of the form of the object with the possibility of the thing itself, according to a concept of it which does precede and contain the ground of this form. We have seen that the representation of purposiveness of the first kind rests on the immediate pleasure in the form of the object which occurs in the mere reflection upon it. But the representation of purposiveness of the second kind, since it refers to the form of the object and not to the cognitive faculties of the subject in the apprehension of it, but to a definite cognition of the object under a given concept, has nothing to do with a feeling of pleasure in things, but only with the understanding in its judgment upon them. If the concept of an object is given, the business of the faculty of judgment using the concept for cognition consists in *presentation* (*exhibitio*) (i.e., in setting a corresponding intuition beside the concept). This 193 may take place either through our imagination, as in technique (*Kunst*) when we realize a preconceived concept of an object which is a purpose of ours, or through nature in its technique[5] (as in organized bodies) when we supply to it our concept of its purpose in order to judge of its products. In the latter case it is not merely the purposiveness of nature in the form of the thing that is represented, but this its product is represented as a *natural purpose*. Although our concept of a subjective purposiveness of nature in its forms according to empirical laws is not a concept of the object but only a principle of the faculty of judgment for furnishing itself with concepts amid the immense variety of nature (and thus for being able to ascertain its own position [in the world]); yet we thus ascribe to nature, as it were, a regard for our cognitive faculty according to the analogy of purpose. Thus we can regard *natural beauty* as the presentation of the concept of formal (merely subjective) purposiveness, and *natural purposes* as the presentation of the concept of a real (objective) purposiveness. The former of these we judge of by taste (aesthetical, by the medium of the feeling of pleasure); the latter, by understanding and reason (logical, according to concepts.)

On this is based the division of the *Critique of the Faculty of Judgment* into the critique of the *aesthetical* and of the *teleological* faculty of judgment. By the first we understand the faculty of judging of the formal purposiveness (otherwise called subjective) of nature by means of the feeling of pleasure or displeasure; by the second, the faculty of judging its real (objective) purposiveness by means of understanding and reason. . . .

CRITIQUE OF THE FACULTY OF AESTHETICAL JUDGMENT

Analytic of the Beautiful

First Moment:[6] On the Quality of the Judgment of Taste   203

Section 1. The Judgment of Taste* is Aesthetical

In order to decide whether anything is beautiful or not, we refer [its] representation by the imagination (perhaps in conjunction with the understanding) to the subject and its feeling of pleasure or displeasure; we do not,

---

[5] By "technique of nature," Kant means "the causality of nature in respect to the form of its products as purposes." It is the regulative Idea under which we investigate nature *as if* nature practiced a technique analogous to ours in the creation of artifacts. Note the connection between *an art* and *a technique.*

[6] *Moment* is a technical term from Kant's logic, meaning (among other things) a basic conceptual component in the sufficient condition of something. The four moments in the analysis of the judgment of the beautiful correspond to the four major categories of quantity, quality, relation, and modality.

*The definition of taste laid down here is that it is the faculty of judging of the beautiful. The analysis of judgments of taste must show what is required in order to call an object beautiful. The moments to which this judgment has regard in its reflection I have sought in accordance with the guidance of the logical functions of judgment, for in a judgment of taste a reference to the understanding is always involved. I consider the aspect of quality first, because the aesthetical judgment of beauty pays attention to it first.

by the understanding, refer the representation to the object in order to know it. The judgment of taste is therefore not a judgment of cognition, and is consequently not logical but aesthetical, by which we understand a judgment whose determining ground can be no other than subjective. With the exception of the reference to the feeling of pleasure or displeasure, every reference of representations may be objective; even the reference of sensations may be objective, signifying the real element of an empirical representation. But by the feeling of pleasure or displeasure nothing in the object is signified, but there is a feeling which the subject has of itself as it is affected by the representation of the object.

To apprehend a regular, suitable building by means of one's cognitive faculty (whether in a clear or a confused way of representation) is something quite different from being conscious of this representation as connected with the sensation of satisfaction. Here the representation is referred only to the subject and to its feeling of life, under the name of the feeling of pleasure or displeasure. This establishes a quite separate faculty of discrimination and of judging, adding nothing to cognition but only comparing the given representation in the subject with the whole faculty of representations of which the mind is conscious in the feeling of its state. Given representations in a judgment can be empirical (consequently, aesthetical); but the judgment which is formed by means of them is logical provided the judgment refers them to the object. Conversely, if the given representations are rational, but are referred in a judgment simply to the subject (to its feeling), the judgment is to that degree always aesthetical.

Section 2. The Satisfaction Which Determines the Judgment of Taste is Disinterested Satisfaction

The satisfaction which we associate with the representation of the existence of an object is called *interest*. Such satisfaction always has reference to the faculty of desire, either as its determining ground or as necessarily connected with its determining ground. But when the question is whether a thing is beautiful, we do not want to know whether anything depends or can depend upon its existence, either for myself or anyone else; but how we judge it by mere contemplation (intuition or reflection). If someone asks me if I find that palace beautiful which I see before me, I may answer: I do not like things of that kind which are made merely to be stared at. Or I can answer like that Iroquois Sachem, who was pleased in Paris by nothing more than by the cook shops. Or again, after the manner of Rousseau, I may rebuke the vanity of the great who waste the sweat of the people on such superfluous things. In fine, I could easily convince myself that if I found myself on an uninhabited island without hope of ever again coming among men, and could conjure up just such a beautiful building by my mere wish, I should not even give myself the trouble if I had a sufficiently comfortable hut. This may all be admitted and approved, but we are not now talking of this. We wish only to know if this mere representation of the object is accompanied in me with satisfaction, however indifferent I may be to the existence of the object of this representation. We easily see that, in saying it is beautiful and in showing that I have taste, I am concerned, not with any manner in which I depend on the existence of the object, but with that which I make out of this representation in myself, Everyone must admit that a judgment about beauty in which the least interest mingles is very partial, and is not a pure judgment of taste. We must not in the least be prejudiced in favor of the existence of the thing but be quite indifferent in this respect, in order to play the judge in things of taste.

We cannot, however, better elucidate this proposition, which is of capital importance, than by contrasting the pure disinterested* satisfaction in judgments of taste with the satisfaction which is connected with an interest, especially if we can at the same time be certain that there are no other kinds of interest than those which are now to be specified.

Section 3. The Satisfaction in the Pleasant
is Bound Up with Interest

That which pleases the senses in sensation is [the] *pleasant.* Here is the place for calling attention to, and censuring, a very common confusion in the two senses which the word "sensation" can have. All satisfaction (it is said or thought) is itself sensation (of a pleasure). Consequently everything that 206 pleases is pleasant just because it pleases (and according to its different degrees or relations to other pleasant sensations it is called agreeable, lovely, delightful, enjoyable, etc.) But if this be admitted, then impressions of sense which determine inclination, fundamental propositions of reason which determine the will, merely contemplated forms [in] intuition which determine the faculty of judgment, are quite the same as regards the effect upon the feeling of pleasure [i.e., they are all "pleasant"]. For their effect on the feeling of pleasure would be pleasantness in the sensation of one's state; and since in the end all the operations of our faculties must issue in the practical and unite in it as their goal, we could suppose no other way of estimating things and their worth than that which consists in the gratification of what they promise. [If this were the case] it would be of no consequence how this [satisfaction] was obtained, and since the choice of means alone would make a difference, men could blame one another for stupidity and indiscretion, but never for baseness and wickedness, for they all, each according to his own way of seeing things, seek one goal (i.e., gratification).

If a modification of the feeling of pleasure or displeasure is called sensation, this word signifies something quite different from what I mean when I

---

*A judgment upon an object of satisfaction may be quite *disinterested* but yet very *interesting,* i.e., not based upon an interest, but bringing interest with it. All pure moral judgments are of this kind. Judgments of taste, however, do not in themselves establish any interest. Only in society is it *interesting* to have taste. . . . [7]

[7] Kant alludes to Section 41 (not printed in this volume).

call sensation the representation of a thing by sense, as a receptivity belonging to the cognitive faculty. For in the latter case the representation is referred to the object, in the former simply to the subject. Referred to the subject, it is available for no cognition, not even for that by which the subject knows itself.

In the foregoing elucidation we understand by the word "sensation" an objective representation of sense; and in order to avoid misinterpretation, we shall call that which must always remain merely subjective and which can constitute absolutely no representation of an object by the ordinary term "feeling." The green color of the meadows belongs to *objective* sensation as a perception of an object of sense; its pleasantness belongs to *subjective* sensation which represents no object; that is, it is referred to feeling, by which the object is considered as an object of satisfaction (which is not cognition of it).

207   A judgment about an object by which I describe it as pleasant expresses an interest in it. This is plain from the fact that by sensation it excites a desire for objects of that kind; consequently the satisfaction presupposes not the mere judgment about it but the relation of its existence to my state so far as this is affected by such an object. Hence we do not say of the pleasant merely that it *pleases* but that it *gratifies*. I do more than assent to what gratifies; my inclination is aroused by it, and when it is pleasant in the most lively fashion, there is no judgment at all upon the character of the object, for those who always lay themselves out for enjoyment (for that is the word describing intense gratification) would fain dispense with all judgment.

209   ### Section 5. Comparison of the Three Specifically Different Kinds of Satisfaction

The pleasant and the good both have a relation to the faculty of desire. The former brings a satisfaction which is pathologically[7] conditioned (by impulse, *stimuli*), the latter a pure practical satisfaction which is determined not merely by the representation of the object but also by the represented connection of the subject with the existence of the object. It is not merely the object that pleases, but also its existence. On the other hand, the judgment of taste is merely *contemplative;* it is a judgment which, indifferent to the existence of an object, associates its character with the feeling of pleasure and displeasure. But this contemplation itself is not directed to concepts; for the judgment of taste is not a cognitive judgment (either theoretical or practical), and thus is not based on concepts, nor has it concepts as its goal.

210   The pleasant, the beautiful, and the good designate then three different relations of representations to the feeling of pleasure and displeasure, in reference to which we distinguish different objects and ways of representing them. The expressions corresponding to each, by which we mark our complacency in them, are not the same. That which *gratifies* a man is called *pleasant;* that which merely *pleases* him is *beautiful;* that which is *esteemed* or

[8]On Kant's use of the word *pathological*, see above, p. 253 n.

approved by him (i.e., that to which he accords an objective worth), is *good.* Pleasantness concerns irrational animals also, but beauty concerns only men (i.e., animal, but still rational, beings) — not merely *qua* rational (e.g., as spirits) but *qua* animal also — and good concerns every rational being whatsoever. This is a proposition which can be completely established and explained only in the sequel. We may say that, of all these three kinds of satisfaction, that of taste in the beautiful is alone a disinterested and free satisfaction; for no interest, either of sense or of reason, here forces our assent. Hence we may say of satisfaction that it is related in the three aforesaid cases to inclination, to favor, or to respect. Favor is the only free satisfaction. An object of inclination and one that is set before our desire by a law of reason leave us no freedom to turn anything into an object of pleasure, for all interest presupposes or generates a want, and, as the determining ground of assent to the object, leaves the judgment about the object no longer free.

As regards the interest of inclination in the case of the pleasant, everyone says that hunger is the best sauce, and everything that is edible is relished by people with a healthy appetite. Thus a satisfaction of this sort shows no choice directed by taste. It is only when the want is appeased that we can distinguish which man has or has not taste. In the same way there may be manners (conduct) without virtue, politeness without good will, decorum without honor, etc. For where the moral law speaks, there is no longer, objectively, a free choice as regards what is to be done, and to show taste in its execution (or in judging another's execution of it) is something quite different from manifesting the moral attitude of thought. For this includes a command and involves a need, while moral taste only plays with the objects of satisfaction, without attaching itself to any one of them.

Explanation of the Beautiful Resulting from the First Moment: Taste is the   211 faculty of judging an object or a way of representing it by an entirely disinterested satisfaction or dissatisfaction. The object of such satisfaction is called *beautiful.*

Second Moment: Of the Quantity of the Judgment of Taste

Section 6. The Beautiful is That Which Apart from Concepts is Represented as the Object of a Universal Satisfaction

This explanation of the beautiful can be derived from the preceding explanation of it as the object of an entirely disinterested satisfaction. For the fact of which everyone is conscious, that the satisfaction is for him quite disinterested, implies in his judgment a ground of satisfaction for all men. For since it does not rest on any inclination of the subject nor upon any other antecedent interest, and since the person who judges feels himself quite free as regards the satisfaction which he attaches to the object, he cannot find the ground of this satisfaction in any private conditions connected with himself, and hence he must regard it as grounded on what he can presuppose in every other person. Consequently he must believe that he has reason for attributing a similar satisfaction to everyone. He will therefore speak of the beautiful as if beauty were a characteristic of the object and the judgment were logical (constituting a cognition of the object by means of concepts of it), although it is only aesthetical and involves merely a relation of the representation of the object to the subject. For it has this similarity to a logical judgment: we can presuppose its validity for all men. But this universality cannot arise from concepts, for from concepts there is no transition to the feeling of pleasure or displeasure (except in pure practical laws, which bring an interest with them

212 which is absent from pure judgments of taste). Consequently the judgment of taste, accompanied with the consciousness of separation from all interest, must claim validity for every man, though this universality does not depend upon concepts. That is, there must be bound up with it a claim to subjective universality.

Section 7. Comparison of the Beautiful with the Pleasant and the Good with Respect to the Above Characteristic

As regards the pleasant, everyone is content that his judgment, which he bases upon private feeling and by which he says that an object pleases him, should be limited to his own person. Thus he is quite contented that when he says, "Canary wine is pleasant," another man may correct his expression and remind him that he ought to say, "It is pleasant *to me*." And this is the case not only with the taste of the tongue, the palate, and the throat, but for whatever is pleasant to anyone's eyes and ears. To one, violet color is soft and lovely; to another, it is washed out and dead. One man likes the tone of wind instruments, another that of strings. It would be folly to reprove as incorrect another man's judgment which is different from our own, as if these judgments were logically opposed. As regards the pleasant, therefore, the fundamental proposition is valid: *everyone has his own taste* (the taste of sense).

It is quite different with the beautiful. It would be laughable if a man who fancied his own taste thought to justify himself by saying, "This object (the house we see, the coat that person wears, the concert we hear, the poem submitted to our judgment) is beautiful *for me*." For he must not call it beautiful if it pleases only him. Many things may have for him charm and pleasantness — no one troubles himself about that — but if he gives out anything as beautiful he suppose in others the same satisfaction; he judges not merely for himself, but for everyone, and speaks of beauty as if it were a

213 property of things. Hence he says, "The *thing* is beautiful," and he does not just count on the agreement of others with this his judgment of satisfaction because he has found this agreement several times before; rather, he *demands* it of them. He blames them if they judge otherwise, and he denies them taste which he nevertheless requires of them. Here, then, we cannot say that each man has his own particular taste. For this would be as much as to say that

there is no taste whatever (i.e., no aesthetical judgment which can make a rightful claim upon the assent of everyone).

At the same time we find that there is an agreement among men in their judgments upon the pleasant, and by reference to this agreement we deny taste to some and attribute it to others; by taste here we mean not one of our organic senses, but a faculty of judging the pleasant generally. Thus we say of a man who knows how to entertain his guests with pleasures (of enjoyment by all the senses), so that they are all pleased: "He has taste." But here the universality is taken only comparatively, and there emerge rules which are only *general* (like all empirical ones) and not *universal,* which the judgment of taste upon the beautiful claims to be. The judgment just referred to has reference to sociability, so far as this rests upon empirical rules. In respect of the good it is true that judgments make rightful claim to validity for everyone; but the good is represented only *by means of a concept* as the object of a universal satisfaction, which is the case with neither the pleasant nor the beautiful.

Section 8. The Universality of the Satisfaction is Represented in a Judgment of Taste Only as Subjective

This particular property of the universality of an aesthetic judgment which is to be met with in a judgment of taste is noteworthy, not indeed for the logician but for the transcendental philosopher. It requires no small trouble to discover its origin, but in doing so we discover a property of our cognitive faculty which, without this analysis, would remain unknown.

First, we must be fully convinced of the fact that in a judgment of taste about the beautiful the satisfaction in the object is imputed to everyone 214 without being based upon a concept (for then it would be the good). Further, this claim to universal validity so essentially belongs to a judgment by which we describe anything as beautiful that, if this were not thought in it, it would never come into our thoughts to use the expression "beautiful" at all, for everything which pleases without a concept would be counted as pleasant. In respect of the pleasant, everyone has his own opinion, and no one assumes that another agrees with his judgment of taste, though this is always assumed in a judgment of taste about beauty. I may call the first the taste of sense, the second the taste of reflection, so far as the first makes mere private judgments and the second makes judgments supposed to be generally valid (public); but in both cases the judgments are aesthetical (not practical) judgments about an object merely in respect of the relation of its representation to the feeling of pleasure and displeasure. Now here is something strange. As regards the taste of sense, not only does experience show that its judgment (of pleasure or displeasure connected with anything) is not valid universally, but everyone is content not to impute agreement with it to others (although actually there is often found a very widespread concurrence in these judgments). On the other hand, the taste of reflection has its claim to the universal validity of its judgments about the beautiful rejected often enough, as experience teaches, although it may find it possible (as it actually does) to assert judgments which can demand this universal agreement. In fact, it imputes this to everyone for each of its judgments of taste, and the persons who judge do not dispute the possibility of such a claim, though in particular cases they cannot agree as to the correct application of this faculty.

Here we must remark that a universality which does not rest on concepts of objects (not even on empirical ones) is not logical but aesthetical; it involves no objective quantity of the judgment but only a quantity which is subjective. For I use the expression *general validity*, which signifies the validity of the reference of a representation not to the cognitive faculty, but to the feeling of pleasure and displeasure for every subject. (We can avail ourselves also of the same expression for the logical quantity of the judgment if only we prefix 215 *objective* to *universal validity*, to distinguish it from that which is merely subjective and aesthetical.)

A judgment with objective universal validity is also always valid subjectively (i.e., if the judgment holds for everything contained under a given concept, it holds also for everyone who represents an object by means of this concept). But from a subjective universal validity (i.e., aesthetical and resting on no concept, we cannot infer logical universal validity, because that kind of judgment does not extend to the object. Therefore the aesthetical universality which is ascribed to a judgment must be of a particular kind, because it does not unite the predicate of beauty with the concept of the object considered in its whole logical sphere, and yet extends it to the whole sphere of judging persons.

In respect of logical quantity, all judgments of taste are singular judgments. Because I must refer the object immediately to my feeling of pleasure and displeasure, and do that not by means of concepts, they cannot have the quantity of objective generally valid judgments. Nevertheless, if the singular representation of the object of the judgment of taste, in accordance with the conditions determining the object, were transformed by comparison[9] into a concept, a logically universal judgment could result. For example, I describe by a judgment of taste the rose that I see as beautiful. But the judgment which results from the comparison of several singular judgments, "Roses in general are beautiful," is no longer an aesthetical, but a logical judgment based on an aesthetical one. The judgment, "The rose is pleasant" (to smell) is, though aesthetical and singular, not a judgment of taste but a judgment of sense. It is distinguished from the former by the fact that the judgment of taste carries with it an aesthetic quantity of universality (i.e., of validity for everyone). This cannot be found in a judgment about the pleasant. It is only judgments about the good which, although they determine satisfaction in an

---

[9] Comparison is the first stage of concept formation, and is the likening of representations to one another in relation to the analytical unity of consciousness. — Kant's *Lectures on Logic*, 6.

object, have logical and not merely aesthetical universality, for they are valid of the object as cognitive of it, and thus are valid for everyone.

If we judge objects merely according to concepts, then all representation of beauty is lost. Thus there can be no rule according to which anyone is to be forced to recognize something as beautiful. We cannot press upon others with the help of any reasons or fundamental propositions our judgment that a coat, a house, or a flower is beautiful. People wish to submit the object to   216 their own eyes, as if the satisfaction in it depended upon sensation; and yet, if we then call the object beautiful, we believe that we speak with a universal voice, and we claim the assent of everyone, while private sensation can decide only for the observer himself and his own satisfaction.

We may see now that in the judgment of taste nothing is postulated but such a universal voice, in respect to satisfaction without intervention of concepts; and thus there is postulated the possibility of an aesthetical judgment that can, at the same time, be regarded as valid for everyone. The judgment of taste itself does not *postulate* the agreement of everyone (for that can be done only by a logically universal judgment, because it can adduce reasons); it only *imputes* this agreement to everyone, as a case of the rule in respect of which it expects not confirmation by concepts but assent from others. The universal voice is, therefore, only an Idea[10] (we do not yet inquire upon what it rests). It may be uncertain whether or not the man who believes that he is laying down a judgment of taste is, as a matter of fact, judging in conformity with that Idea; but that he refers his judgment to that Idea, and consequently that his judgment is intended to be a judgment of taste, he announces by using the expression "beauty". He can be quite certain of this for himself by the mere consciousness of separating off everything belonging to the pleasant and the good from the satisfaction which is left; and this is all on which he promises himself the agreement of everyone — a claim which would be justified under these conditions if only he did not often make mistakes, and lay down erroneous judgments of taste.

Section 9. Investigation of the Question: Whether in the Judgment of Taste the Feeling of Pleasure Precedes or Follows the Judging of the Object

The solution of this question is the key to the critique of taste, and so is worthy of all attention.

If the pleasure in the given object comes first, and it is only its universal   217 communicability that is to be acknowledged in the judgment of taste about the representation of the object, there would be a contradiction. For such pleasure would be no different from the mere pleasantness of sensation, and so in accordance with its nature could have only private validity, because it is directly dependent upon the representation through which the object is given.

---

[10] On the meaning of the word "Idea" see above, p. 127 n.

Hence it is the universal communicability of the mental state in the given representation which, as the subjective condition of the judgment of taste, must be fundamental and must have pleasure in the object as its consequence. But nothing can be universally communicated except cognition and representation so far as it belongs to cognition. For it is only thus that cognition can be objective, and only through this has it a universal point of reference, with which the representative power of everyone is compelled to harmonize. If the determining ground of our judgment as to this universal communicability of the representation is to be merely subjective (i.e., is conceived independently of any concept of the object), it can be nothing else than the state of mind which is to be met with in the relation of our representative powers to each other, so far as they refer a given representation to cognition in general.

The cognitive powers which are involved in this representation are here in free play, because no definite concept limits them to a definite rule of cognition. Hence the state of mind in this representation must be a feeling of the free play of the representative powers in a given representation with reference to a cognition in general. Now a representation by which an object is given, if it is to become a cognition, requires imagination for gathering together the manifold of intuition, and understanding for the unity of the concept uniting the representations.[11] This state of free play of the cognitive faculties in a representation by which an object is given must be universally communicable, because cognition, as the determination of the object with which given representations (in any subject whatsoever) are to agree, is the only kind of representation which is valid for everyone.

The subjective universal communicability of the mode of representation in a judgment of taste, since it is to be possible without presupposing a definite concept, can refer to nothing else than the state of mind in the free play of imagination and understanding (so far as they agree with each other, as is requisite for cognition in general). We are conscious that this subjective relation, suitable for cognition in general, must be valid for everyone, and thus must be universally communicable just as if it were a definite cognition, which always rests on that relation between understanding and imagination as its subjective condition.

This merely subjective (aesthetical) judging of the object, or the representation by which the object is given, precedes the pleasure in the object and is the ground of the pleasure in the harmony of the cognitive faculties. The universal subjective validity of the satisfaction bound up by us with the representation of the object which we call beautiful is based only on that universality of the subjective conditions for the judging of objects [in general]. That the power of communicating one's state of mind, even though

[11] On the relation of imagination to understanding in cognition, see above. *Critique of Pure Reason* p. 110 in this volume.

only in respect of the cognitive faculties, carries a pleasure with it, we can easily show from the natural propensity of man toward sociability (an empirical and psychological propensity). But this is not enough for our purposes here. The pleasure that we feel in a judgment of taste is necessarily imputed by us to everyone else, as if, when we call a thing beautiful, it is to be regarded as a characteristic of the object which is determined in it according to concepts, in spite of the fact that beauty without a reference to the feeling of the subject is nothing by itself. But we must reserve the examination of this question until we have answered that other question — if and how aesthetical judgments are possible a priori.

We now occupy ourselves with the easier question: In what way are we conscious of a mutual subjective harmony of the cognitive powers in the judgment of taste? Is it aesthetically by mere internal sense and sensation, or is it intellectually by the consciousness of our intentional activity, by which we bring them into play?

If the given representation which occasions the judgment of taste were a concept uniting understanding and imagination in the judging of the subject into a cognition of the object, the consciousness of this relation would be intellectual (as in the objective schematism of the faculty of judgment of which the *Critique of Pure Reason* treats[12]). But then the judgment would not refer to pleasure and displeasure, and consequently would not be a judgment 219 of taste. But the judgment of taste, independently of concepts, determines the object with regard to satisfaction and the predicate of beauty. Therefore that subjective unity of the relation between understanding and imagination can make itself known only by means of sensation. The excitement of both faculties to indeterminate but, through the stimulus of the given sensation, harmonious activity, which belongs to cognition in general, is the sensation whose universal communicability is postulated by the judgment of taste. An objective relation can only be thought, but so far as it is subjective by its conditions, it can be felt in its effect upon the mind; and of a relation based on no concept (like the relation of the representative powers to the cognitive faculty in general), no other consciousness is possible than that through the sensation of the effect, and this effect is the more lively play of both mental powers of imagination and understanding when animated by their mutual agreement. A representation which, as individual and apart from comparison with others, has an agreement with the conditions of universality which it is the business of the understanding to supply, brings the cognitive faculties into that proportionate accord which we require in all cognition, and which we regard as holding for everyone who is so constituted as to judge by means of understanding and sense in combination. That is, we regard it as holding for every man.

Explanation of the Beautiful Resulting from the Second Aspect: The beautiful is that which pleases universally without [requiring] a concept.

---

[12] Kant refers to *Critique of Pure Reason*, Analytic, Book II, ch. i (not included in this volume).

Third Moment: Of Judgments of Taste According to the Relation of the Purposes Which are Brought into Consideration in Them

Section 10. Of Purposiveness in General

If we wish to explain what a purpose is according to its transcendental determinations (without presupposing anything empirical, like the feeling of pleasure), [we say] purpose is the object of a concept insofar as the concept is regarded as the cause of the object (the real ground of its possibility); the causality of a concept in respect to its object is its purposiveness (*forma finalis*). Where, then, not merely the cognition of an object but the object itself (its form and existence) is thought as an effect possible only by means of the concept of the object, there we think a purpose. The representation of the effect is here the determining ground of its cause and precedes the effect. The consciousness of the causality of a representation in maintaining the subject in the same state is what we generally call pleasure, while displeasure is the representation which contains the ground for converting the state of representations into their opposite, by restraining or removing them.

The faculty of desire, so far as it is determinable to act only through concepts (i.e., in conformity with the representation of a purpose), is the will. An object, or a state of mind, or even an action, although its possibility does not necessary presuppose the representation of a purpose, is called purposive for this reason only: its possibility can be explained and conceived by us only as far as we assume for its ground a causality according to purposes (i.e., a will which would have ordered them according to the representation of a certain rule). There can be, then, purposiveness without purpose, so far as we do not place the causes of this form in a will but yet can make the explanation of its possibility intelligible to ourselves only by deriving it from a will. We are not always forced to regard from the point of view of reason the possibility of what we observe; hence we can observe at least the purposiveness of a form without basing it on a purpose as the material of the *nexus finalis*, and we can notice purposiveness in objects, though only by way of reflection.

Section 11. The Judgment of Taste Has Nothing at its Basis Except the Form of Purposiveness of an Object (or of its Mode of Representation)

Every purpose, if it be regarded as a ground of satisfaction, always carries with it an interest as the determining ground of the judgment about the object of pleasure. Therefore no subjective purpose can lie at the basis of the judgment of taste. Nor can the judgment of taste be determined by a representation of an objective purpose, that is, by any representation of the possibility of the object itself in accordance with principles of purposive combination; the judgment of taste consequently cannot be determined by the concept of the good, because it is an aesthetical and not a cognitive judgment. It therefore has to do with no concept of the character and internal or external possibility of the object through this or that cause, but merely with the relation of the representative powers to one another so far as they are determined by a representation.

This relation, in finding an object to be beautiful, is bound up with the feeling of pleasure which is declared by the judgment of taste to be valid for everyone. Hence a pleasantness [merely] accompanying the representation can as little contain the determining ground [of the judgment] as the representation of the perfection of the object and the concept of the good can determine it. The determining ground can be nothing else than the subjective purposiveness in the representation by which an object is given to us, so far as we are conscious of this purposiveness. It constitutes the satisfaction that we, without a concept, judge to be universally communicable, and consequently this is the determining ground of the judgment of taste.

Section 12. The Judgment of Taste Rests on A Priori Grounds

To establish a priori the connection of the feeling of pleasure or displeasure as an effect with any representation whatever (either sensation or concept) as its cause, is absolutely impossible, for that would be a particular causal relation which (in the case of objects of experience) can be known only 222 a posteriori and through the medium of experience itself. We have, indeed, in the *Critique of Practical Reason*, derived from universal moral concepts a priori the feeling of respect as a special and peculiar modification of feeling that will not strictly correspond either to the pleasure or the displeasure we get from empirical objects. But there we could go beyond the bounds of experience and call in a causality which rests on a supersensible attribute of the subject, namely freedom. And even there, properly speaking, it would not be this feeling which we derive from the Idea of the moral as cause, but merely the determination of the will. But the state of mind which accompanies any determination of the will is in itself a feeling of pleasure and identical with it, and therefore does not follow from it as its effect. This last would have to be assumed only if the concept of the moral as a good preceded the determination of the will by the law, for in that case the pleasure bound up with the concept of the good could not be derived from it as a mere cognition.

The case is similar with the pleasure in aesthetical judgments, only here the pleasure is merely contemplative and does not bring about an interest in the object, while in the moral judgment the pleasure is practical [inciting to action]. The consciousness of the exclusively formal purposiveness in the play of the subject's cognitive powers, in a representation through which an object is given, is the pleasure itself. This is because it contains a determining ground of the activity of the subject in exciting its cognitive powers, and therefore contains an inner purposive causality (in regard to cognition in general, not limited to any specific cognitions), and consequently it contains a mere form of the subjective purposiveness of a representation in an aesthetical judgment. This pleasure is in no way practical, neither like that arising from the pathological ground of pleasantness, nor that from the intellectual ground of the good of which we are conscious. But it still involves causality, maintaining without further design the state of the representation itself and the activity of the cognitive powers. We linger over the contemplation of the beautiful because this contemplation strengthens and reproduces itself; this is analogous to (though not of the same kind as) that lingering which takes place when a [physical] charm in the representation of the object repeatedly arouses the attention of a passive mind.

Section 13. The Pure Judgment of Taste is Independent of Charm and Emotion

223

Every interest spoils the judgment of taste and detracts from its impartiality, especially if the purposiveness is not (as with the interest of reason) placed before the feeling of pleasure but grounded on it. This always happens in an aesthetical judgment of anything so far as it gratifies or grieves us. Hence judgments so affected by interest can lay no claim to universally valid satisfaction, or at least so much the less claim the more there are sensations of this sort among the determining grounds of taste. Taste is always barbaric which needs a mixture of charms and emotions in order that there may be satisfaction, and still more so if it makes these the measure of approval.

Nevertheless, charms are often not only taken account of in the case of beauty (which properly speaking ought to be concerned solely with form) as contributory to the universal aesthetical satisfaction, but they are passed off as in themselves beauties and thus the matter of satisfaction is substituted for the form. This misconception, which like so many others has something true at its base, may be removed by a careful definition of these concepts.

A judgment of taste on which charm and emotion have no influence (even though they may be bound up with satisfaction in the beautiful) — a judgment which therefore has as its determining ground only the purposiveness of the form — is a *pure judgment of taste*.

Section 14. Elucidation by Examples

Aesthetical judgments can be divided, like theoretical (logical) judgments, into empirical and pure. The first assert pleasantness or unpleasantness; the second assert the beauty of an object or the manner of representing it. The former are judgments of sense (material aesthetic judgments); the latter alone, as formal, are strictly judgments of taste.

224

A judgment of taste is pure only so far as no merely empirical satisfaction is mingled with its determining ground. But this mingling always occurs if charm or emotion has any share in the judgment by which anything is to be described as beautiful.

Here many objections present themselves which fallaciously put forward charm not merely as a necessary ingredient of beauty, but as alone sufficient to justify a thing's being called beautiful. A mere color (e.g., the green of a grass plot), and a mere tone (as distinguished from sound and noise) like that of a violin, are by most people described as beautiful in themselves, although both seem to have at their basis merely the matter of representations (i.e., simply sensation), and therefore deserve to be called pleasant only. But we must at the same time remark that the sensations of colors and of tones have a right to be regarded as beautiful in so far as they are pure. This is a predicate which concerns their form and is the only [element] of these representations which certainly admits of universal communicability; for we cannot assume that the quality of sensations is the same for all subjects, and we can hardly say that the pleasantness of one color or the tone of one musical instrument is judged preferable to that of another in the same way by everyone.

If we assume with Euler that colors are isochronous vibrations (*pulsus*) of the aether, as sounds are of the air in a state of disturbance, and — what is most important — that the mind not only perceives by sense the effect of these in exciting the organ, but also perceives by reflection the regular play of impressions (and thus the form of the combination of different representations) — which I do not at all doubt[13] — then colors and tones cannot be reckoned as mere sensations, but must be held to be formal determinations of the unity of a manifold of sensations, and thus as beauties.

"Pure" in a simple mode of sensation means that its uniformity is troubled and interrupted by no foreign sensation; purity belongs only to form, because here we can abstract from the quality of the mode of sensation (that is, abstract from the colors and tone, if any, which sensation represents). Hence all simple colors, so far as they are pure, are regarded as beautiful; composite 225 colors have not this advantage because, since they are not simple, we have no standard for judging whether they should be called pure or not.

But as regards the beauty attributed to the object on account of its form, to suppose it to be capable of enhancement through the charm of the object is a common error, and one very prejudicial to genuine, uncorrupted, well-founded taste. We can doubtless add these charms to beauty and to the bare satisfaction we find in it, in order to evoke an interest in the representation of the object, and thus they may serve as an advocate of taste and its cultivation, especially when it is yet crude and unexercised. But they actually do injury to the judgment of taste if they draw attention to themselves as the grounds for judging of beauty. So far are they from adding to beauty that they must be admitted only by indulgence as aliens, and provided always that they do not disturb the beautiful form in cases where taste is still weak and unexercised.

In painting, sculpture, and in all the formative arts — in architecture and horticulture as far as they are fine arts — the delineation is the essential thing; and here it is not what gratifies in sensation but what pleases by its form that is fundamental for taste. The colors which light up the sketch belong to charm; they may indeed enliven the object for sensation, but they cannot make it worthy of contemplation and beautiful. In most cases they are rather limited by the requirements of beautiful form, and even where charm is permissible it is ennobled solely by form.

---

[13] First and second editions read: "very much doubt." Translation follows third edition, 1799.

Every form of the objects of sense (both of external sense and also indirectly of internal sense) is either *figure* or *play*. In play it is either play of figures (in space, as pantomime and dancing) or the play of mere sensations (in time). The charm of colors or of the pleasant tones of an instrument may be added, but the delineation in the first case, and the composition in the second, constitute the proper object of the pure judgment of taste. To say that the purity of colors and of tones, or their variety and contrast, seems to add to beauty does not mean that, because they are in themselves pleasant, they add something on a par with our satisfaction in the form; they add to
226 beauty because they make the form more exactly, definitely, and completely intuitable, and by their charm they excite the representation while they awaken and fix our attention on the object itself.

Even what we call ornaments (*parerga*) (i.e., those things which do not belong to the complete representation of the object internally as elements of it, but only externally as complements, and which augment the satisfaction of taste) do so only by their form, as, for example, the frames of pictures or the draperies of statues or the colonnades of palaces. But if the ornament does not itself consist in beautiful form, and if it is used as a golden frame is used merely to recommend the painting by its charm, it is then called finery, and injures genuine beauty.

Emotion, that is, a sensation in which pleasantness is produced by a momentary checking and a consequent more powerful overflow of the vital force, does not belong to beauty at all. But sublimity, with which the feeling of emotion is bound up, requires a different standard of judgment from that which is at the foundation of taste; and thus a pure judgment of taste has for its determining ground neither charm nor emotion — in a word, no sensation as the material of the aesthetical judgment.

229 ## Section 16. The Judgment of Taste by Which an Object is Declared to be Beautiful Under the Condition of a Definite Concept is Not a Pure Judgment of Taste

There are two kinds of beauty: free beauty (*pulchritudo vaga*) and merely dependent beauty (*pulchritudo adhaerens*). The former presupposes no concept of what the object is meant to be; the latter does presuppose such a concept, and [concerns] the perfection of the object in accordance with this concept.

The first is called the self-subsistent beauty of this or that thing; the second, as depending upon a concept (conditioned beauty), is ascribed to objects which stand under the concept of a particular purpose.

Flowers are free natural beauties. Hardly anyone but a botanist knows what sort of a thing a flower ought to be; and even he, though recognizing in the flower the reproductive organ of the plant, pays no regard to this natural purpose if he is passing judgment on the flower by taste. There is, then, at the basis of this judgment no perfection of any kind, no internal purposiveness to which the collection of the manifold is referred. Many birds (such as the parrot, the humming bird, the bird of paradise) and many sea shells are beauties in themselves which do not adhere to an object defined by concepts with respect to its purpose, but please freely and in themselves. So also delineations *à la grecque,* foliage for borders or wall papers, mean nothing in themselves; they represent nothing, no object under a definite concept, and are free beauties. What are called in music phantasies (i.e., pieces without a theme) and in fact all music without words belong in the class of free beauties.

In judging of a free beauty according to the mere form, the judgment of taste is pure. There is presupposed no concept of any purpose which the manifold of the given is to serve, and which therefore is to be represented in it, for by such a concept the freedom of the imagination which disports itself   230 in the contemplation of the figure would be only limited.

But human beauty (i.e., the beauty of a man, a woman, or a child), the beauty of a house, or a building (be it church, palace, arsenal, or summer house), presupposes a concept of the purpose which determines what the thing is to be, and consequently a concept of its perfection. It is therefore adherent beauty. Now as the combination of the pleasant (in sensation) with beauty, which properly is concerned only with form, is a hindrance to the purity of the judgment of taste, so also is its purity injured by the combination with beauty of the good (viz., that manifold which is good for the thing itself in accordance with its purpose).

We could add much to a building which would immediately please the eye — if only it were not to be a church. We could adorn a figure with all kinds of spirals and light but regular lines, as the New Zealanders do with their tattooing — if only it were not the body of a human being. And the figure of a human being could have much finer features and a more pleasing and gentle cast of countenance — provided it were not intended to represent a man, much less a warrior.

The satisfaction in the manifold of a thing in reference to the internal purpose which determines its possibility is a satisfaction grounded on a concept; but the satisfaction in beauty is such as presupposes no concept but is immediately bound up with the representation through which the object is *given* (not through which it is *thought*). If, now, the judgment of taste in respect of the beauty of a thing is made dependent on the purpose of the thing as judged by reason, and is thus limited, it is no longer a free and pure judgment of taste.

It is true that taste gains by this combination of aesthetical with intellectual satisfaction, inasmuch as it becomes fixed; and though it is not universal, yet in respect to certain purposively determined objects it becomes possible to prescribe rules for it. These, however, are not rules of taste, but merely rules for the unification of taste with reason (i.e., of the beautiful with the good), by which the beautiful becomes available as an instrument of design in

231 respect of the good. Thus the tone of mind which is self-maintaining and of
subjective universal validity is made to underlie the [moral] way of thinking
which can be maintained only by painful resolve, but is of objective universal
validity. Properly speaking, however, perfection gains nothing by beauty, nor
beauty by perfection; but when we by means of a concept compare the
representation by which an object is given to us with the object as regards
what it ought to be we cannot avoid considering along with it the sensations of
the subject, And thus when both states of mind are in harmony, our whole
faculty of representative power gains.

A judgment of taste, then, in respect of an object with a definite internal
purpose, can be pure only if the person judging either has no concept of this
purpose or else abstracts from it in his judgment. Such a person, although
forming an accurate judgment of taste in judging of the object as free beauty,
would be blamed and accused of bad taste by one who, looking to the purpose
of the object, considers the beauty in the object as only a dependent attribute. But both are right in their own way — the one in reference to what he
has before his eyes, the other in reference to what he has in his thought. By
means of this distinction we can settle many disputes about beauty between
judges of taste, by showing that the one is speaking of free and the other of
dependent beauty, and that the first is making a pure and the second an
applied judgment of taste.

Section 17. Of the Ideal[14] of Beauty

There can be no objective rule of taste which will determine by concepts
what is beautiful. For every judgment from this source of taste is aesthetical;
the feeling of the subject, not a concept of the object, is its determining
ground. To seek for a principle of taste which will furnish, by means of
definite concepts, a universal criterion of the beautiful is fruitless trouble,
because what is sought is impossible and self-contradictory. The universal
communicability of sensation without concepts (the sensation of satisfaction
or dissatisfaction), and the unanimity (so far as possible) of all times and all
232 peoples about this feeling in the representation of certain objects: these
constitute the empirical, though weak and hardly sufficient, criterion for the
derivation of taste, confirmed by examples, from grounds, deeply hidden in
but common to all men, of their unanimity in judging the forms under which
objects are given to them.

Hence we consider some products of taste as *exemplary*. Not that taste can
be acquired by imitating others, for it must be an original faculty. He who
imitates a model shows skill, no doubt, insofar as he attains to it; but he shows

---

[14]Kant defines Ideal: "The Idea, not merely *in concreto* but *in individuo,* that is, as an
individual thing, determinable or even determined by the Idea alone" (*Critique of Pure Reason* A
568 = B 596). When used in this technical sense, Ideal is always capitalized. On the use of the
word Idea and its capitalization, see above p. 127 n.

taste only insofar as he can judge of the model itself.* It follows that the highest model, the archetype of taste, is only an Idea, which everyone must produce in himself and according to which we must judge every object of taste, every example of judgment by taste, and even the taste of everyone. *Idea* properly means a concept of reason, and *Ideal* the representation of an individual being regarded as adequate to its Idea. Hence that archetype of taste, which certainly rests on the indeterminate Idea which reason has of a maximum, but which cannot be presented by concepts but only in an individual presentation, is better called the Ideal of the beautiful. Although we are not in possession of this, we yet strive to produce it in ourselves. But it can be an Ideal of the imagination only, because it rests on a exhibition and not on concepts, and the imagination is the faculty of exhibiting something. How do we arrive at such an Ideal of beauty? A priori, or empirically? Moreover, what species of the beautiful is capable of having an Ideal?

First, it is well to remark that the beauty for which an Ideal is to be sought cannot be *vague* [i.e., free and indeterminate] beauty, but is *fixed* by a concept of objective purposiveness, and thus it cannot be the object of a wholly pure judgment of taste, but of a judgment of taste which is in part 233 intellectual. That is, in whatever grounds of judgment an Ideal is to be found, an Idea of reason in accordance with definite concepts must lie at its basis, which determines a priori the purpose on which the internal possibility of the object rests. An Ideal of beautiful flowers, of a beautiful piece of furniture, or a beautiful view, is inconceivable. But neither can an Ideal be represented of a beauty dependent upon definite purposes, such as the beauty of a beautiful dwelling house, a beautiful tree, a beautiful garden, and the like; presumably because their purposes are not sufficiently determined and fixed by the concept, and thus their purposiveness is nearly as free as it is in the case of vague beauty. The only being which has the purpose of its existence in itself is *man*, who can determine his purposes by reason; or, where he must receive them from external perception, can compare them with essential and universal purposes and can judge their accordance with them aesthetically. Man is, then, alone of all objects in the world capable of an Ideal of beauty, as it is only humanity in his person, as an intelligence, that is subject to the Ideal of perfection.

But there are here two elements. First, there is the aesthetical *normal Idea*, which is an individual intuition (of the imagination), representing the standard of our judgment [upon man] as a thing belonging to a particular animal

---

*Models of taste as regards the arts of speech must be composed in a dead and learned language. The first in order that they may not suffer that change which inevitably comes over living languages, in which noble expressions become flat, common ones antiquated, and newly created ones have only a short circulation. The second because learned languages have a grammar which is subject to no wanton change of fashion, but the rules of which are preserved unchanged.

species. Second, there is the *rational Idea* which makes the purposes of humanity, so far as they cannot be sensibly represented, the principle for judging of a figure through which, as their effect in appearance, those purposes are revealed. The normal Idea of the figure of an animal of a particular race must take its elements from experience. But the greatest purposiveness in the construction of the figure that would be available for the universal standard of aesthetical judgment upon each individual of this species — the image on which nature's technique was as it were intentionally based and to which only the whole race and not any isolated individual is adequate — this lies merely in the Idea of the judging subject. And this, with its proportions as an aesthetical Idea, can be completely exhibited *in concreto* in a model. In order to make intelligible in some measure (for who can extract her whole secret from nature?) how this comes to pass, we shall attempt a psychological explanation.

234   We must remark that, in a way quite incomprehensible to us, the imagination cannot only recall on occasion the signs for concepts long past, but can also reproduce the image of the figure of the object out of a countless number of objects of different kinds or even of the same kind. Further, if the mind is concerned with comparisons, imagination can, in all probability, actually though unconsciously let one image glide into another; and thus, by the concurrence of several of the same kind, come by an average, which serves as the common measure of all. Everyone has seen a thousand full-grown men. If you wish to judge of their normal size, estimating it by means of comparison, the imagination (as I think) allows a great number of images (perhaps the whole thousand) to fall on one another. If I am allowed to apply here the analogy of optical presentation, it is in the space where most of them are combined and inside the contour where the place is illuminated with the most vivid colors, that the *average size* is cognizable, which, both in height and breadth, is equally far removed from the extremes of the greatest and smallest stature. And this is the stature of a beautiful man. (We could arrive at the same thing mechanically by adding together all thousand sizes, heights, breadths, and thicknesses, and dividing the sum by a thousand. But the imagination does this by means of a dynamical effect, which arises from the various impressions of the figures on the organ of internal sense.) If now, in a similar way, for this average man we seek the average head, for this head the average nose, etc., such figure is at the basis of the normal Idea in the country where the comparison is instituted. Thus necessarily under these empirical conditions a Negro must have a different normal Idea of the beauty of the [human figure] from a white man, a Chinaman a different normal Idea from a European, etc. And the same is the case with the model of a beautiful horse or dog of a certain breed. This normal Idea is not derived from proportions got from experience [and regarded as] definite rules, but it is in accordance with it that rules for judging become in the first instance possible. The normal Idea is the image for the whole race, which floats among all the variously different intuitions of individuals, which nature takes as archetype in her

productions of the same species, but which appears not to be fully reached in any individual case. It is by no means the whole archetype of beauty in the race, but only the form constituting the indispensable condition of all beauty, and thus merely correctness in the presentation of the race. It is, like the celebrated Doryphorus of Polycletus, the rule, (Myron's Cow might also be used thus for its kind.) It can therefore contain nothing specifically characteristic, for then it would not be the normal Idea for the race. Its presentation pleases, not by its beauty but merely because it contradicts no condition under which alone a thing of this kind can be beautiful. The presentation is merely [academically] correct.* 235

We must yet distinguish the normal Idea of the beautiful from the Ideal, which on grounds already put forward we can expect only in the human figure. In this the Ideal consists in the expression of the moral, without which the object would not please universally and thus positively (not, by being an accurate presentation, merely not displease). The visible expression of moral Ideas that rule men inwardly can indeed be got only from experience; but to make its connection with all which our reason unites with the morally good in the Idea of the highest purposiveness — goodness of heart, purity, strength, peace, etc. — visible as it were in bodily manifestation (as the effect of that which is internal) requires a union of pure Ideas of reason with great imaginative power even in him who wishes to judge of it, still more in him who wishes to present it. The correctness of such an Ideal of beauty is shown by its permitting no sensible charm to mingle with the satisfaction in the object, and yet allowing us to take a great interest in the object. This shows that a judgment in accordance with such a standard can never be purely aesthetical, and that a judgment in accordance with an Ideal of beauty is not a mere judgment of taste. 236

Explanation of the Beautiful Derived from the Third Moment: Beauty is the form of the purposiveness of an object so far as this is perceived in it without any representation of a purpose.†

---

*It will be found that a perfectly regular countenance, such as a painter might wish to have for a model, ordinarily tells us nothing because it contains nothing characteristic, and therefore rather expresses the Idea of the species than the specific [traits] of a person. The exaggeration of a characteristic of this kind (i.e. such as does violence to the normal Idea, for instance, of the purposiveness of the species) is called *caricature*. Experience also shows that these quite regular countenances commonly indicate internally only a mediocre man, presumably (if it may be assumed that external nature expresses the proportions of internal) because, if no mental disposition exceeds that proportion which is requisite to constitute a man free from faults, one can expect nothing of what is called *genius*, in which nature seems to depart from the ordinary relations of the mental powers on behalf of some special one.

†It might be objected to this explanation that there are things in which we see a purposive form without cognizing any purpose in them, like the stone implements often gotten from old sepulchral tumuli with a hole in them, as if for a handle. Although they plainly indicate by their shape a purposiveness of which we do not know the purpose, they are nevertheless not described as beautiful. But if we regard a thing as an artifact, that is enough to make us admit that its shape has reference to some design and definite purpose, and hence there is no direct satisfaction in the contemplation of it. On the other hand a flower (e.g. a tulip) is regarded as beautiful because in perceiving it we find a certain purposiveness which, in our judgment, is referred to no purpose at all.

Fourth Moment: Of the Judgment of Taste According to the Modality of the Satisfaction in the Object

Section 18. What Modality in a Judgment of Taste May Be

I can say of every representation that it is at least *possible* that, as a cognition, it should be bound up with a pleasure. Of a representation that I call pleasant I say that it *actually* excites pleasure in me. But the beautiful we think of as having a *necessary* reference to satisfaction. Now this necessity is of 237 a peculiar kind. It is not a theoretical objective necessity, for then it would be known a priori that everyone will feel this satisfaction in the object called beautiful by me. It is not a practical necessity, for then, by concepts of pure rational will serving as a rule for freely acting beings, the satisfaction would be the necessary result of an objective law, and would indicate only that we absolutely (without any further intention) ought to act in a certain way. But the necessity which is thought in an aesthetical judgment can be called only exemplary (i.e., a necessity of assent of all to a judgment which is regarded as the example of a universal rule which we cannot state). Since an aesthetical judgment is not an objective cognitive judgment, this necessity cannot be derived from definite concepts and is therefore not apodictic. Still less can it be inferred from the universality of experience of a complete agreement of judgments about the beauty of a certain object. For not only would experience hardly furnish sufficiently numerous vouchers for this, but also on empirical judgments we can base no concept of the necessity of these judgments.

Section 19. The Subjective Necessity Which we Ascribe to the Judgment of Taste is Unconditioned

The judgment of taste requires the agreement of everyone, and he who describes anything as beautiful claims that everyone *ought* to give his approval to the object in question and likewise describe it as beautiful. The *ought* in the aesthetical judgment is therefore pronounced in accordance with all the data which are required for judging, and yet is pronounced only conditionally. We ask for the agreement of everyone else, because we have for it a ground which is common to all; and we could count on this agreement provided we were always sure that we had correctly subsumed the case under that ground as rule of approval.

Section 20. The Condition of the Necessity Which a Judgment of Taste Asserts is the Idea of a Common Sense

If judgments of taste, like cognitive judgments, had a definite objective principle, then the person who makes them in accordance with this principle 238 would claim an unconditioned necessity for his judgment. If they lacked all principle, like judgments of mere taste of sense, we would not allow them any necessity whatever. Hence they must have a subjective principle which determines what pleases or displeases only by feeling and not by concepts, yet with universal validity. Such a principle could only be regarded as a *common sense*. It is essentially different from ordinary understanding which people sometimes call common sense (*sensus communis*); for ordinary understanding does not judge by feeling but always by concepts, though usually only by obscurely thought principles.

Hence it is only under the presupposition that there is a common sense (by which we do not mean an external sense, but the effect resulting from the free play of our cognitive faculties) that the judgment of taste can be made.

Section 21. Have We a Grounds for Presupposing a Common Sense?

Cognitions and judgments, along with the conviction that accompanies them, must admit of universal communicability; for otherwise there would be no harmony between them and the object, and they would be collectively a mere subjective play of the representation powers, exactly as skepticism desires. But if cognitions are to admit of communicability, so must also the state of mind. This state of mind is the accordance of the cognitive powers in general and that proportion among them which is requisite for a representation, by which an object is given to us, to be made into a cognition, for without this subjective condition of cognition, cognition as an effect would not arise. Cognition always takes place when a given object by sense excites the imagination to collect the manifold, and the imagination in its turn excites the understanding to bring about a unity of this manifold in concepts.[15] But this accordance of the cognitive powers has a different proportion according to the variety of the objects which are given. However, it must be such that this internal relation, through which one mental faculty is animated by another, will be generally the most beneficial for both faculties in the cognition of 239 given object; and this accordance can be determined only by feeling, and not by concepts. Since, now, this accordance itself must admit of universal communicability and consequently our feeling of it must be universally communicable, and since the universal communicability of a feeling presupposes a common sense, we have grounds for assuming that there is a common sense. This common sense is assumed without relying on psychological observations, but is assumed simply as the necessary condition of the universal communicability of our knowledge, which is presupposed in every logic and in every principle of knowledge which is not skeptical.

Section 22. The Necessity of the Universal Agreement that is Thought in a Judgment of Taste is a Subjective Necessity, Which is Represented as Objective Under the Presupposition of a Common Sense

In all judgments by which we describe anything as beautiful, we do not indulge anyone's being of a different opinion; but we do not ground our judgment on concepts, rather, only on our feeling, which we therefore place

---

[15] See *Critique of Pure Reason*, above, p. 110.

at its basis as a common, not private, feeling. This common sense cannot be grounded on experience, for it aims at justifying judgments which contain an *ought*. It does not say that everyone *will* agree with my judgment, but that he *ought*. And so common sense, as an example of whose judgment I here put forward my judgment of taste and on account of which I attribute to the latter an *exemplary* validity, is a mere ideal norm. Under the supposition of it I have the right to make into a rule for everyone both a judgment that accords with this norm, and the satisfaction in an object expressed in such judgment. For the principle which concerns the agreement of different judging persons, although only subjective, is yet assumed as subjectively universal (an Idea necessary for everyone), and thus can claim universal assent (as if it were objective) provided we are sure that we have correctly subsumed [the particular cases] under it.

This indeterminate norm of a common sense is actually presupposed by us, as is shown by our claim to make judgments of taste. Whether there is in 240 fact such a common sense as a constitutive principle of the possibility of experience, or whether a yet higher principle of reason makes it into merely a regulative principle for producing in us a common sense for higher purposes; whether, therefore, taste is an original and natural faculty or only the Idea of an artificial faculty yet to be acquired, so that a judgment of taste with its assumption of a universal assent is in fact only a requirement of reason for producing such a harmony of sentiment; whether the *ought* (i.e., the objective necessity of the confluence of the feeling of any man with that of every other) signifies only the possibility of our arriving at this accord, and the judgment of taste merely affords an example of the application of this [higher] principle —these questions we have neither the wish nor the power to investigate at this point. Our present task is only to resolve the faculty of taste into its elements in order to unite them at last in the Idea of a common sense.

Explanation of the Beautiful Resulting from the Fourth Moment: The beautiful is that which without any concept is known as the object of a necessary satisfaction.

Analytic of the Sublime

The Mathematical Sublime (Selections from Sections 23, 25, 26, 27)

244   The beautiful and the sublime agree in this: that both please in themselves. . . .

But there are remarkable differences between the two. The beautiful in nature is connected with the form of the object, which consists in having [definite] boundaries. The sublime, on the other hand, is to be found in a formless object, so far as in it or by occasion of it *boundlessness* is represented while yet its totality is also present to thought. Thus the beautiful seems to be regarded as the presentation of an indefinite concept of the understanding, the sublime as that of a like concept of reason. . . .

But the inner and most important distinction between the sublime and the beautiful is the following. . . . Natural beauty (which is independent) 245 brings with it a purposiveness in its form by which the object seems to be, as it were, pre-adapted to our faculty of judgment, and thus constitutes in itself an object of satisfaction. On the other hand, that which excites in us, without any reasoning about it but in the bare apprehension of it, the feeling of the sublime may appear, as regards its form, to violate purpose in respect of the faculty of judgment, to be unsuited to our representative faculty, and as it were to do violence to the imagination, and the more it does so, the more sublime it is judged to be. . . .

It is remarkable that, although we have no interest in some object (i.e., its 249 existence is a matter of indifference to us), yet its size alone, even if it is considered as formless, may bring a satisfaction with it that is universally communicable and that consequently involves the consciousness of a subjective purposiveness in the use of our cognitive faculty. This is not indeed a satisfaction in the object as in the case of the beautiful (because it may be formless), for in the beautiful the faculty of reflective judgment finds itself purposively determined in reference to cognition in general. In the sublime it is rather a satisfaction in the extension of the imagination by itself.

If, under the above limitation, we say simply of an object that it is great, this is no mathematically determinate judgment but only a judgment of reflection upon our representation of it, which is subjectively purposive for a certain use of our cognitive powers in the estimation of magnitude. . . . But if we call anything not only great, but absolutely great in every point of view 250 (great beyond all comparison) (i.e., if we call it sublime), we soon see that it is not permissable to seek for an adequate standard of this magnitude outside itself [to seek for some intuitive or arbitrary unit of size]; it can be sought only in itself. It is a magnitude which is like itself alone. . . . *The sublime is that in comparison with which everything else is small.* Here we easily see that nothing can be given in nature, however great it is judged by us to be, which could not, if considered in another relation, be reduced to the infinitely small; and conversely there is nothing so small that does not admit of extension by our imagination to the greatness of a world if compared with still smaller standards. Telescopes have furnished us with abundant material for the first remark, microscopes for the second. Nothing, therefore, which can be an object of the senses is, considered on this basis, to be called sublime. . . . *The sublime is that the mere ability to think which shows a faculty of the mind surpassing every standard of sense.*

Just as the faculty of aesthetical judgment in judging the beautiful refers 256 the imagination in its free play to the understanding, in order to harmonize it with concepts of the latter (in general, without determining any one of them), so does the same faculty, when judging a thing to be sublime, refer itself to reason in order that it may subjectively be in accordance with its Ideas, no matter what they are; it does so that it may produce a state of mind conformable to them and compatible with that brought about by the influ-

ence of definite (practical [i.e., moral]) Ideas upon our feeling. Hence we
see that true sublimity must be sought only in the mind of the judging
subject, not in the natural object the judgment upon which occasioned this
state. Who would call sublime shapeless mountain masses piled in wild
disarray upon one another with their pyramids of ice, or the gloomy, raging
sea? But the mind feels itself raised in its own estimation if, while contemplating them without reference to their form and abandoning itself to imagination and reason . . . it finds all the power of its imagination to be inade-
257   quate to its Ideas [of reason]. . . . This feeling of the sublime in nature is
respect for our own calling (*Bestimmung*), which by a certain subreption we
attribute to an object in nature, converting respect for the Idea of humanity in
our own person into respect for the object in nature.

The Dynamical Sublime (Selections from Section 28)

260   *Might* is that which is superior to great hindrances. It is called *dominion* if it
is superior to the resistance of that which itself possesses might. Nature,
considered in an aesthetical judgment as might that has no dominion over us,
is *dynamically sublime.*

If nature is to be judged by us as dynamically sublime, it must be represented as exciting fear. . . . That which we are driven to resist is an evil, and
if we do not find our powers a match for it, it is an object of fear. Hence nature
can be regarded by the faculty of aesthetical judgment as might, and consequently as dynamically sublime, only so far as it is considered an object of
fear.

But we can regard an object as fearful without being afraid of it, that is, if
we judge of it in such a way that we only think a case in which we would wish
261   to resist it and yet in which all resistance would be altogether vain. . . . He
who fears can form no judgment about the sublime in nature, just as he who is
seduced by inclination and appetite can form no judgment about the beautiful. The person who is afraid flies from the sight of the object which inspires
him with dread, and it is impossible to find satisfaction in a terror that is
seriously felt. . . .

Bold, overhanging, and as it were threatening rocks; clouds piled up in the
sky, moving with lightning flashes and peals of thunder; volcanoes in all their
violence of destruction; hurricanes with their track of devastation; the boundless ocean in a state of tumult; the lofty waterfall of a mighty river, and such
like — these reveal our power to resist them to be triflingly small in comparison with their might. But the sight of them is more attractive the more fearful
they are, provided only that we are secure; and we willingly call these objects
sublime because they raise the energies of the soul above their accustomed
height and reveal in us a power of resistance of a quite different kind, which
gives us courage to measure ourselves against the apparent almightiness of
nature.

But in the immensity of nature and in the insufficiency of our faculties to adapt a standard proportionate to the aesthetical estimation of the magnitude of its realm, we find our own limitation. In our rational faculty, however, we find at the same time a different, nonsensuous standard which has that infinity itself as the unit in comparison with which everything in nature is small; thus in our mind we find a superiority to nature even in its immensity. And so also the irresistibility of its might, while making us recognize our own physical impotence as beings of nature, discovers to us a faculty of judging independently of nature and a superiority over nature; on this is based a kind of self-preservation entirely different from that which external nature can attack and endanger. Thus humanity in our own person remains unhumiliated, though as mortal creatures we have to submit to the dominion of 262 nature. In this way nature, in our aesthetical judgments, is not judged to be sublime insofar as it excites fear, but because it calls up that power in us (which is not nature) of regarding as small the things about which we are solicitous (goods, health, life), and of regarding nature's might (to which we are certainly subjected with respect to these things) as without dominion over us and our personality; to it we do not bow when it is a question of asserting or forsaking our fundamental principles. Therefore nature is here called sublime merely because it elevates the imagination to a presentation of those cases in which the mind can feel the proper sublimity of its own calling, sublime even in comparison with nature itself. . . .

Sublimity, therefore, does not reside in anything in nature, but only in our 264 mind insofar as we can become conscious that we are superior to nature within us, and therefore also superior to nature without us so far as it has any influence on us. Everything that excites this feeling in us — the might of nature that calls forth our forces — is then called, although improperly, sublime. Only by supposing this Idea in ourselves and only in reference to it are we capable of attaining to the Idea of the sublimity of that being which produces an inner respect in us, not merely by the might that it displays in nature, but even more by means of the faculty which resides in us of judging it fearlessly and of regarding our calling as sublime over it.

Deduction[16] of Pure Aesthetical Judgments

Section 44. Of Fine Art[17]

. . . If an art, fitted with the knowledge of a possible object, performs the 305 actions necessary to make it actual, it is *mechanical art*. If, on the other hand, the direct intention is to produce the feeling of pleasure, it is called *aesthetical art*. The latter is either *pleasant art* or *fine art*. It is pleasant art if its purpose is

---

[16] This part of the book is misnamed, being a somewhat miscellaneous collection, the deduction (justification of the necessity) of aesthetical judgments of taste having been substantially completed in Sections 20–22 (but repeated in Sections 36–38, which are omitted from this edition).

[17] *schöne Kunst*, literally *beautiful art* or *beaux arts*.

that pleasure should accompany the representations as mere sensations; it is fine art if the pleasure is to accompany the representations as modes of cognition.

Pleasant arts are those that are directed merely to enjoyment. In this class are all those charming arts that can gratify a company at table (e.g., the art of telling stories in an entertaining way, of starting the company in frank and lively conversation, of raising them by jest and laugh to a certain pitch of merriment when, as people say, there may be a great deal of gossip at the feast but no one will be answerable for what he says, because everyone is concerned only with momentary entertainment and not with any permanent material for reflection or subsequent discussion. (Among the pleasant arts are to be reckoned also the way of arranging the table for enjoyment and, at great feasts, the management of the music. Music is a wonderful thing. Regarded solely as a pleasant noise, without anyone paying the least attention to its composition, it is meant to dispose the minds of the guests to gaiety, and it favors the free conversation of each with his neighbor.) To this class of art belong also all games which bring with them no further interest than that of making time pass imperceptibly.

306   Fine art, on the other hand, is a mode of representation which is purposive in itself and which, although devoid of [definite] purpose, furthers the culture of the mental powers to sociable communication. The universal communicability of a pleasure carries with it, in its very concept, that the pleasure is not one of enjoyment from mere sensation, but must be pleasure of reflection; thus aesthetical art as fine art has for its standard the faculty of reflective judgment, and not sensation.

Section 45. Fine Art is an Art So Far as it Appears also to be Nature

In a product of fine art, we must become conscious that it is art and not nature, but the purposiveness in its form must seem to be as free from all constraint of arbitrary rules as if it were a product of nature alone. On this feeling of freedom in the play of our cognitive faculties, which must at the same time be purposive, rests that pleasure which alone, without being based on concepts, is universally communicable. Nature is beautiful because it looks like art, and art can be called beautiful only if we are conscious of it as art while yet it looks like nature.

Whether we are dealing with the beauty of nature or the beauty of art, we in either case say: This is beautiful which pleases in the mere act of judging it (not in the sensation of it, or by means of a concept). Art has always a definite intention in producing something. But if this something were bare sensation, something merely subjective which is to be accompanied by pleasure, the product would please in the act of judging only by mediation of sensible feeling. And if the intention were directed to the production of a definite object, then if that object were produced by art the object would please only

through concepts. But in neither case would the art please in the mere act of 307
judging (i.e., it would not please as fine art, but only as mechanical art).

Hence the purposiveness in the product of fine art, although it is designed, must not seem to be designed; fine art must look like nature, though we are conscious of it as art. A product of art appears like nature when it punctiliously agrees with the rules according to which alone it can become what it ought to be; but this is not pedantic agreement, the form of the schools does not obtrude itself, and it shows no trace of the rule's having been before the eyes of the artist and having fettered his mental powers.

Section 46. Fine Art is the Art of Genius

Genius is the talent or natural gift which gives the rule to art. Since talent, as the innate productive faculty of the artist, itself belongs to nature, we may express the matter thus: Genius is the innate mental disposition (*ingenium*) through which nature gives the rule to art.

Whatever may be thought of this definition, whether it is merely arbitrary or is adequate to the concept that we are accustomed to combine with the word *genius* . . . we can prove in advance that, according to the signification of the word here adopted, fine arts must necessarily be considered as arts of genius.

For every art presupposes rules by means of which a product, if it is to be called artificial, is represented as possible. But the concept of fine art does not permit the judgment upon the beauty of a product to be derived from any rule which has a concept as its determining ground, and consequently it cannot be derived from any concept of the way in which the product may be possible. Therefore fine art cannot itself excogitate the rule according to which it can create its product. But since at the same time a product can never be called art unless there was some precedent rule, nature in the person of the artist must, by the disposition of his faculties, give the rule to art. That is, fine art is possible only as a product of genius.

We thus see

(1) that genius is a talent for producing that for which no definite rule can be given; it is not a mere aptitude for what can be learned by rule. Hence originality must be its first property.   308

(2) But since it can produce also original nonsense, its products must be models (i.e., exemplary); themselves not springing from imitation, they must serve as a standard or rule of judgment for others.

(3) It cannot describe or indicate scientifically how it brings about its products, but it gives a rule just as nature does. Hence the author of a product for which he is indebted to his genius does not himself know how he has come by his ideas; and he has not the power to devise the like at pleasure or in accordance with a plan and to communicate it to others in precepts that will enable them to

produce similar products. (Here it is probable that word *genius* is derived from [the Latin] *genius*, that peculiar guiding or guardian spirit given to a man at his birth, from whose suggestions these original ideas proceed.)

(4) Nature, by the medium of genius, does not prescribe rules to science but to art, and to it only insofar as it is fine art.

Dialectic of the Faculty of Aesthetical Judgment

Section 56. Exposition of the Antinomy of Taste

338 The first commonplace of taste is contained in the proposition by which every tasteless person proposes to avoid censure: *everyone has his own taste.* That is as much as to say that the determining ground of the [aesthetical] judgment is merely subjective (gratification or pain), and that the judgment has no claim on the necessary assent of others.

The second commonplace invoked even by those who concede to judgments of taste the right to speak with validity for everyone is: *there is no disputing about taste.* That is as much as to say that although the determining ground of a judgment of taste may even be objective, it cannot be reduced to definite concepts, and that consequently nothing about the judgment itself can be *decided* by proofs though much may be rightly *contested.* For *contesting* and *disputing* are doubtless at one in this: by means of mutual opposition of judgments they seek to produce agreement. But they differ in that disputing hopes to bring this about according to definite concepts as determining grounds, and consequently disputing assumes objective concepts as grounds of the judgment. Where objective grounds cannot be adduced, disputing is regarded as ineffective.

We easily see that, between these two commonplaces, there is a proposition wanting which, though it has not passed into proverb, is familiar to everyone: *taste may be contested* (though it may not be disputed). This proposition involves the contradictory of the first of the commonplaces, for wherever contesting is permissible, there must be hope of mutual reconciliation, and therefore in contesting a judgment we must count on grounds of our judgment that have not merely private validity, and are therefore not merely subjective. And to this, the proposition *everyone has his own taste* is directly opposed.

There emerges therefore in respect of the principle of taste the following antinomy:

(1) *Thesis.* The judgment of taste is not based upon concepts, for otherwise it would admit of dispute (i.e., would be determinable by argument).

(2) *Antithesis.* The judgment of taste is based on concepts, for
339 otherwise, despite its diversity, we could not contest it (could not claim for our judgment the necessary assent of others).

Section 57. Solution of the Antinomy of Taste

The conflict between these principles that underlie every judgment of taste (which are nothing else than the two peculiarities of the judgment of taste exhibited in the Analytic) cannot be removed except by showing that the concept to which we refer the object in this kind of judgment is not taken in the same sense in both maxims of the faculty of aesthetical judgment. This twofold sense or twofold point of view is necessary to our transcendental faculty of judgment, but the illusion which arises from the confusion of one with the other is natural and unavoidable.

The judgment of taste must refer to some concept. Otherwise it could make absolutely no claim to be necessarily valid for everyone. But it is not therefore capable of being proved *from* a concept, because a concept may be either determinable or in itself undetermined and undeterminable. The concepts of the understanding are of the former kind; they are determinable through predicates of sensible intuition which can correspond to them. But the transcendental rational concept of the supersensible which lies at the basis of all sensible intuition is of the latter kind, and therefore cannot be theoretically further determined.

The judgment of taste is applied to objects of sense, but not with a view to determining a concept of them for the understanding, for it is not a cognitive judgment. It is thus only a private judgment in which a singular representation intuitively perceived is referred to the feeling of pleasure, and so far would be limited in its validity to the individual judging. The object is for me an object of satisfaction; by others it may be regarded quite differently — everyone has his own taste.

Nevertheless there is undoubtedly contained in the judgment of taste a wider reference to the representation of the object (as well as of the subject) whereon we base an extension of judgments of this kind as necessary for everyone. At the basis of this there must necessarily be a concept somewhere, though a concept which cannot be determined through intuition. But through a concept of this sort we know nothing, and consequently it can 340 supply no proof for the judgment of taste. Such a concept is reason's bare pure concept of the supersensible which underlies the object (and also the subject judging it) [both] regarded as objects of sense and thus as appearance. For if we do not admit such a reference, the claim of the judgment of taste to universal validity would not hold good. If the concept on which it is based were only a mere confused concept of the understanding, like the concept of perfection, with which we could bring the sensible intuition of the beautiful into correspondence, it would be at least possible to base the judgment of taste on arguments, which contradicts the thesis.

But all contradiction disappears if I say: the judgment of taste is based on a concept (vis., the concept of the general ground of the subjective purposiveness of nature for the faculty of judgment) by which nothing can be known and proved in respect of the object, because the concept is in itself undeterminable and useless for knowledge. Yet at the same time and on that very account the judgment has validity for everyone (though, of course, for each only as a singular judgment directly accompanying his intuition) because its determining ground lies perhaps in the concept of that which may be regarded as the supersensible substrate of humanity.

The solution of an antinomy depends only on the possibility of showing that two apparently contradictory propositions do not in fact contradict each other, but that they may be consistent although the explanation of the possibility of their concept transcends our cognitive faculties. That this illusion is natural and unavoidable by human reason, and also why it is so and remains so even when it ceases to deceive after the analysis of the apparent contradiction, may be thus explained.

In the two contradictory judgments we take the concept on which the universal validity of a judgment must be based in the same sense, and yet we apply to it two opposite predicates. In the thesis we mean that the judgment of taste is not based upon *determinate* concepts, and in the antithesis that the
341 judgment of taste is based upon a concept, but an *indeterminate* one (viz., the concept of the supersensible substrate of appearances). Between these two there is no contradiction.

We can do nothing more than remove this conflict between the claims and counterclaims of taste. It is absolutely impossible to give a definite objective principle of taste in accordance with which its judgment could be derived, examined, and established, for then the judgment would not be a judgment of taste at all. The subjective principle, viz., the indefinite Idea of the supersensible in us, can only be put forward as the sole key to the puzzle of this faculty whose sources are hidden from us. It can be made no further intelligible.

The proper concept of taste, that it is a merely reflective faculty of aesthetical judgment, lies at the basis of the antinomy here exhibited and adjusted. Thus the two apparently contradictory principles are reconciled — *both can be true*, which is sufficient. If, on the other hand, we assume, as some do, pleasantness as the determining ground of taste (on account of the singularity of the representation which lies at the basis of the judgment of taste) or, as others will have it, the principle of perfection (on account of the universality of this predicate), and settle the definition of taste accordingly, then there arises an antinomy which it is absolutely impossible to adjust except by showing that *both* the contrary (not merely contradictory) *propositions are false*. This would prove that the concept on which they are based is self-contradictory. Hence we see that the removal of the antinomy of the faculty of aesthetical judgment takes a course similar to that pursued in the solution of the antinomies of pure theoretical reason. And thus here, as also in the *Critique of Practical Reason*, the antinomies force us against our will to look beyond the sensible and to seek in the supersensible the point of union of all our a priori faculties, because no other expedient is left to make our reason harmonious with itself.

Section 59. Of Beauty as the Symbol of Morality

Intuitions are always required to establish the reality of our concepts. If the 351
concepts are empirical, the intuitions are called *examples*. If they are pure
concepts of the understanding, the intuitions are called *schemata*. If, on behalf
of theoretical knowledge, we wish to establish the objective reality of concepts of reason (Ideas), we are asking for something impossible, because
absolutely no intuition can be given which will be adequate to them.* . . .

All intuitions which we supply to concepts a priori are therefore either 352
schemata or *symbols,* of which the former contain direct and the latter indirect
presentations of a concept. The former do this demonstratively; the latter by
means of an analogy (making use even of empirical intuitions) in which the
faculty of judgment exercises a double function, first applying the concept to
the object of a sensible intuition, and then applying the rule of reflection
made upon that intuition to a quite different object of which the first is only
the symbol. Thus a monarchical state is represented by a living body if it is
governed by laws native to the people, and by a mere machine (like a hand
mill) if governed by an individual absolute will; but in both cases only
symbolically. For between a despotic state and a hand mill there is certainly
no similarity, but there is a similarity in the rules according to which we
reflect upon these two things and their causality. This matter has not been
sufficiently analyzed before, however much it deserves a deeper investigation; but this is not the place to linger over it.

Our language is full of indirect presentations of this sort, in which the
expression does not contain the schema proper to a concept, but merely a
symbol of reflection. Thus the words *ground* (support, basis), *to depend* (to be
held up from above), to *flow* from something (instead of: to follow), *substance*
(as Locke expresses it: the support of accidents), and countless others are not
schematical but symbolical hypotyposes and expressions for concepts, not by
means of a direct intuition but only by analogy with it (i.e., by the transfer-
ence of reflection upon an object of intuition to a quite different concept to 353
which perhaps no intuition can ever directly correspond). If we are to give the
name of knowledge to a mere mode of representation (which is quite permissible if the representation is not a principle of theoretical determination of
what an object is in itself, but of the practical determination of what the Idea
of it should be for us and for its purposive use), then all our knowledge of God
is merely symbolical. One falls into anthropomorphism if one regards knowledge of God along with the properties of understanding, will, etc. (which
show their reality only in beings in this world) as schematical, just as he who
gives up every intuitive element falls into deism, by which nothing at all is
cognized, not even in a practical point of view.

Now I say the beautiful is the symbol of the morally good, and that it is only

---

*The intuitive in cognition must be contrasted to the discursive (not the symbolical). The
intuitive is either *schematical* by exhibition, or *symbolical,* as a representation in accordance with a
mere analogy.

in this respect (a reference which is natural to every man and which every man postulates in others as a duty) that it gives pleasure with a claim for the agreement of everyone else. By this the mind is made conscious of a certain ennoblement and elevation above mere passivity to pleasure received through sense, and the worth of others is estimated in accordance with a like maxim of their faculty of judgment. That is the *intelligible* to which . . . taste looks, with which our higher cognitive faculties are in accord, and without which a downright contradiction would arise between their nature and the claims made by taste. In this capacity the faculty of judgment does not see itself, as in empirical judging, subjected to a heteronomy of empirical· laws; it gives the law to itself in respect of the objects of so pure a satisfaction, just as reason does in respect of the faculty of desire. Hence, both on account of this inner possibility in the subject and of the external possibility of a nature that agrees with it, it finds itself to be referred to something within the subject as well as without him, something that is neither nature nor freedom, but which is connected with the supersensible ground of freedom. In this supersensible ground therefore, the theoretical faculty is bound together in unity with the practical in a way which, though common, is yet unknown. We shall indicate some points of this analogy, while at the same time we shall note the difference.

(1) The beautiful pleases immediately (but only in reflective intuition, not, like morality, in its concept).

354 (2) It pleases apart from any interest. (The morally good is indeed necessarily bound up with an interest, though not with one that precedes the judgment upon the satisfaction, but with one that is first of all produced by it.)

(3) The freedom of the imagination (and therefore of the sensibility of our faculty) is represented in judging the beautiful as harmonious with the conformity to law of the understanding. (In the moral judgment the freedom of the will is thought of as the harmony of the latter with itself, according to universal laws of reason).

(4) The subjective principle in judging the beautiful is represented as universal (i.e., as valid for every man), though not knowable through any universal concept. (The objective principle of morality is also expounded as universal — i.e., for every subject and for every action of the same subject — and thus as knowable by means of a universal concept). Hence the moral judgment is not only susceptible to definite constitutive principles, but is possible only by basing its maxims on these principles in their universality.

A reference to this analogy is usual even with the common understanding, and we often describe beautiful objects of nature or art by names that seem to put a moral appreciation at their base. We call buildings or trees majestic and magnificent, landscapes laughing and gay, even colors are called innocent, modest, tender, because they excite sensations which have something analogous to the consciousness of the state of mind brought about by moral judgments. Taste makes possible the transition, without any violent leap, from the charm of sense to habitual moral interest, as it represents the imagination in its freedom as capable of purposive determination for the understanding, and so teaches us to find even in objects of sense a free satisfaction apart from any charm of sense.

C
CRITIQUE OF THE FACULTY OF TELEOLOGICAL JUDGMENT

Analytic of the Faculty of Teleological Judgment

Section 64. Of the Distinguishing Marks of Things as Natural Purposes

In order to see that a thing is possible only as a purpose and that we are 369 forced to seek the causality of its origin not in the mechanism of nature but in a cause whose capability of acting is determined through concepts, it must 370 meet two conditions. First, its form cannot be possible according to mere natural laws (i.e., laws which we can know through the understanding alone applied to objects of the senses). Second, the empirical knowledge of its cause and effect presupposes concepts of reason. The contingency, with respect to reason, of its form under all empirical laws is a ground for regarding its causality as possible only through reason. For reason, which must know the necessity of any form of a natural product in order to discern the conditions of its genesis, cannot assume that this particular form is necessary [under the laws of nature]. The cause of its origin is then referred to a faculty of acting in accordance with purposes (a will), and the object which can be represented as possible only in this way is represented as a purpose.

In a seemingly uninhabited country suppose a man perceived a geometrical figure, say a regular hexagon, inscribed in the sand. Reflecting on the concept of the figure, his reason would make him aware (though dimly) of the unity of the principle of its construction, and would not regard the sand, or the neighboring sea, or the winds, or beasts with similar footprints, or any other irrational cause as a ground of the possibility of the shape. For the unlikelihood (*Zufälligkeit*) of the coincidence of the figure with such a concept—a coincidence which is possible only through reason—would seem to him to be so infinitely great that it would be just as if there were no natural law, no cause in the mere mechanical working of nature capable of producing it, but as if only the concept of such an object, as a concept which reason alone can supply and with which it can compare the thing, could contain the causality for such an effect. This, then, would be regarded as a purpose, but as a product of art, not as a natural purpose (*vestigium hominis video* [—Vitruvius, "I see the footprint of a man"]).

But in order to regard the thing known as a natural product also as a purpose — consequently as a natural purpose, if this is not a contradiction — something more is required. I would say provisionally: a thing exists as a natural purpose if it is, although in a double sense, both cause and effect of itself. For herein lies a causality the likes of which cannot be combined with the bare concept of a natural being without attributing to it a purpose. But though it can certainly be thought without contradiction, it cannot be really understood. We shall elucidate the determination of this Idea of a natural purpose by an example, before we analyze it completely.

In the first place, a tree generates another tree according to a known natural law. But the tree produced is of the same genus, and so it produces itself generically. On the one hand, as effect it is continually self-produced; on the other hand, as cause, it continually produces itself, and so perpetuates itself generically.

Second, a tree produces itself as an individual. This kind of effect we call growth, but it is quite different from any increase according to mechanical laws and is to be reckoned as generation, though under another name. The matter that the tree incorporates it first works up into a specifically peculiar quality, which natural mechanism external to it cannot supply, and thus it develops itself by aid of a material which, as compounded, is its own product. No doubt, as regards the constituent extracted from external nature, it must be regarded only as an educt; but in the separation and recombination of this raw material we see an originality in the separating and formative power of this kind of natural being which is infinitely beyond the reach of art, if it attempts to reconstruct such vegetable products out of the elements obtained from their analysis or out of material supplied by nature for their sustenance.

Third, each part of a tree generates itself in such a way that the maintenance of any one part depends reciprocally on the maintenance of the rest. A bud of one tree engrafted on the branch of another produces in the alien stock a plant of its own kind, and so also a scion engrafted on a foreign trunk. Hence we may regard each twig or leaf even of the same tree as merely engrafted upon or inoculated into it, and so as an independent tree attached to another and parasitically nourished by it. At the same time, while the leaves are products of the tree, they also in turn give support to it, for the repeated defoliation of a tree kills it, and its growth thus depends on the action of the leaves upon the trunk. The self-help of nature in case of injury in the vegetable creation, when the want of a part that is necessary for the maintenance of its neighbors is supplied by the remaining parts, and the abortions or malformations in growth, in which certain parts, on account of causal defects or hindrances, form themselves is a new way to maintain what exists, and so produce an anomalous creature, I shall only mention in passing, though they are among the most wonderful properties of organized creatures.

Section 65. Things Regarded as Natural Purposes are Organized
Beings [Organisms]

According to the characteristic presented in the preceding section, a thing
which, though a natural product, is to be known as possible only as a natural
purpose, must bear itself alternately as cause and as effect. This, however, is
a somewhat inexact and indeterminate expression which needs derivation
from a determinate concept.

Causal combination as thought solely by the understanding is a connection
constituting an ever progressing series of causes and effects, and things
which, as effects, presuppose others as causes cannot in turn be at the same
time causes of these. This sort of causal combination we call that of efficient
causes (*nexus effectivus*). But, on the other hand, a causal combination according to a concept of reason (a concept of purposes) can also be thought, which
regarded as a series would lead either forward or backward; in this the thing
that has been called the effect may with equal propriety be termed the cause
of that of which it is the effect. In the practice of human arts, we easily find
connections such as this. For example, a house is the cause of the money
received for rent, but also conversely the representation of this possible
income was the use of building the house. Such a causal connection we call
that of final causes (*nexus finalis*). We may perhaps suitably name the first the
connection of real causes, the second the connection of ideal causes. From 373
this nomenclature it is at once seen that there can be no more than these two
kinds of causality.

For a thing to be a natural purpose, it is requisite in the first place that its
parts (as regards their presence and their form) be possible only through their
reference to the whole. For the thing itself is a purpose, and so is comprehended under the concept or an Idea which must determine a priori all that is
to be contained in it. But so far as a thing is thought as possible merely in this
way, it is an artifact (i.e., a product of a rational cause distinct from the matter
of the parts whose causality in collecting and combining the parts is determined through its Idea of a whole possible by their means) and consequently
not possible through external nature.

But if a thing as a natural product is to involve in itself and in its internal
possibility a reference to purposes (i.e., to be possible only as a natural
purpose without the causality of the concepts of rational beings outside it),
then it is requisite, secondly, that its parts should so combine in the unity of a
whole that they are reciprocally cause and effect of each other's form. Only in
this way can the Idea of a whole conversely (reciprocally) determine the form
and combination of all the parts, not indeed as cause — for then it would be
an artificial product — but as the ground of cognition, for him who is judging
it, of the systematic unity and combination of all the manifold given material.

For a body, then, to be judged in itself and its internal possibility as a
natural purpose, it is requisite that its parts depend mutually upon one
another, both as to their form and their combination, and so produce a whole

by their own causality; while conversely in a being possessing a causality of concepts adequate to make such a product, the concept of the whole may be regarded as its cause according to a principle. In this case the connection of efficient causes may be judged as an effect through final causes.

In such a product of nature, every part not only exists *by means of* the other parts, but is thought as existing *for the sake* of the others and the whole. That is, every part exists as an instrument (organ). As such it might be an artificial 374 instrument, and so might be represented only as a purpose that is possible in general. But [in a natural purpose] its parts are all organs reciprocally producing one another, and this can never be the case with artificial instruments, but only with nature which supplies all the material for the instruments (even for those of art). Only a product of such a kind can be called a natural purpose and this because it is an organized and self-organizing being [an organism].

In a watch, one part is the instrument for moving the other parts, but the wheel is not the efficient cause of the production of the others. No doubt one part is there for the sake of the others, but it does not exist by their means. In this case the producing cause of the parts and of their form is not contained in the nature of the material, but is external to it in a being which can produce effects according to its ideas of a whole made possible by means of its causality. Hence a watch wheel does not produce other wheels, still less does one watch produce other watches, using and organizing foreign material for that purpose. It does not by itself replace parts of which it has been deprived, nor does it make good what is lacking by the addition of missing parts, nor if it has gone out of order does it repair itself. All of this we may expect from organized nature. An organized being is then not a mere machine, for that has merely moving power, but an organized being possesses in itself formative power of a self-propagating kind which it communicates to its materials though they have it not of themselves. It organizes them, and this cannot be explained by the mere mechanical faculty of motion.

We say of nature and its faculty in organized products far too little if we describe it as an *analogon of art,* for this suggests an artificer, a rational being outside it. Much rather, nature organizes itself and its organized products in every species, no doubt after one general pattern but with suitable deviations, which self-preservation demands according to circumstances. We perhaps approach near to this inscrutable property if we describe it as an *analogon of life,* but if we do, we must either endow matter as mere matter with a property which contradicts its very being (hylozoism) or associate with it an 375 alien principle standing in communion with it (a soul). But in the latter case, if such a product is to be a natural product, we must either presuppose organized matter as the instrument of that soul, which does not make the soul a whit more comprehensible, or regard the soul as artificer of this structure, and so remove the product from [the system of] corporeal nature. To speak strictly, then, the organization of nature has in it nothing analogous to any causality we know.* Beauty in nature can be rightly described as an analogon of art because it is ascribed to objects only in reference to reflection upon their external aspects, and consequently only on account of the form of their external surface. But internal natural perfection, as it belongs to those things which are possible only as natural purposes, and are therefore called organized beings, is not analogous to any physical (natural) power known to us. Nay, regarding ourselves as, in the widest sense, belonging to nature, it is not even thinkable or explicable by means of any exactly fitting analogy to human arts.

The concept of a thing as in itself a natural purpose is therefore no constitutive principle of understanding or of reason, but it can serve as a regulative concept for the faculty of reflective judgment, to guide our investigation of objects of this kind by distant analogy with our own causality according to purposes generally and as a basis of meditations upon their ultimate ground. This latter use, however, is not for the sake of knowledge of nature or its ultimate ground, but rather for the sake of our faculty of practical reason, by analogy with which we consider the cause of that purposiveness.

Organized beings are, then, the only things in nature which, considered in themselves and apart from any relation to other things, can be thought as possible only as purposes of nature. Hence they first afford objective reality 376 to the concept of a purpose of nature, as distinguished from a practical purpose, and so they give to the science of nature the basis for a teleology (i.e., a mode of judgment about natural objects according to a special principle which otherwise we should in no way be justified in introducing) because we cannot see a priori the possibility of this kind of causality.

Section 66. Of the Principle of Judging of Internal Purposiveness in Organized Beings

This principle, which is at the same time a definition, is as follows: *An organized product of nature is one in which every part is reciprocally purpose and means.* In it nothing is in vain, without purpose, or to be ascribed to a blind mechanism of nature.

In origin, the principle is no doubt derived from experience (i.e., from methodized experience called observation). But on account of the universality and necessity it ascribes to such purposiveness it cannot rest solely on empirical grounds, but must have as its basis an a priori principle, though it be

---

*We can conversely throw light upon a certain combination, much more often met with in Idea than in actuality, by means of an analogy to so-called immediate natural purposes. In a recent complete transformation of a great people into a state the word *organization* for the regulation of magistracies, etc., and even of the whole body politic, has often been fitly used. For in such a whole every member should surely be purpose as well as means, and, while all work together toward the possibility of the whole, each should be determined as regards place and function by means of the Idea of the whole. [Kant probably alludes here to the organization of the United States of America: *e pluribus unum.*]

merely regulative and though these purposes may lie only in the Idea of the judging subject and not in an efficient cause. We may therefore describe the principle as a maxim for judging of the internal purposiveness of organized beings.

It is an acknowledged fact that dissectors of plants and animals, in order to investigate their structure and find out the reasons why and for what end such parts, such a disposition and combination of parts, and just such an internal form have been given them, assume as indisputably necessary the maxim that nothing in such a creature is vain, just as they lay down the fundamental proposition of the universal science of nature that nothing happens by chance. In fact, they can as little free themselves from this teleological proposition as from the universal physical proposition; as without the latter we should have no experience at all, so without the former we should have no guiding thread for the observation of a species of natural beings which we have conceived teleologically under the concept of natural purposes.

377   Now this concept brings reason into a quite different order of things from that of the mere mechanism of nature, which is no longer satisfying here. An Idea is to be the ground of the possibility of the natural product. But because this Idea is an absolute unity of representation, while the material is a diversity of things that can by itself supply no definite unity of composition, if the unity of the Idea is to serve as the a priori ground of determination of a natural law of the causality of the form of composition [of the material], the purpose of nature must be extended to everything included in its product. For if we once refer action of this sort on the whole to any supersensible ground of determination beyond the blind mechanism of nature, we must judge of nature wholly according to this principle, and we have then no reason to regard the form of such a thing as partly dependent upon mechanism, for by such mixing up of disparate principles no certain rule of judging would be left.

For example, it may be that in an animal body many parts (such as the hide, bones, hair) can be conceived as concretions according to mere mechanical laws. And yet the cause which brings together the required matter, modifies it, forms it, and puts it in its appropriate place, must always be judged of teleologically, so that here everything must be considered as organized, and everything again in a certain relation to the thing itself as an organ.

Dialectic of the Faculty of Teleological Judgment

386   ### Section 70. Exposition of the Antinomy (of the Faculty of Teleological Judgment)

So far as reason has to do with nature as the complex of objects of external sense, it can base itself partly upon laws that the understanding prescribes a priori to nature, partly upon laws it can extend indefinitely by means of the empirical determinations found in experience. To apply the laws of the former kind (i.e., the universal laws of material nature in general, the faculty of judgment needs no special principle of reflection, since it is there determinant because an objective principle is given to it by the understanding. But as regards the particular laws that can only be made known through experience, there can be under them such a great variety and diversity that the faculty of judgment must serve as its own principle in investigating and searching into the appearances of nature in accordance with a law. Such a guiding thread is needed if we are to hope for a connected empirical cognition according to a thoroughgoing conformity of nature to law, even its unity under empirical laws. In this contingent unity of particular laws, it may well happen that the faculty of judgment in its reflection proceeds from two maxims. One of these is suggested to it a priori by the understanding, but the other is prompted by particular experiences which bring reason into play in order to form a judgment upon corporeal nature and its laws in accordance with a particular principle, [i.e., purposiveness]. Hence it comes about that these two kinds of maxims seem not to be capable of existing together, and consequently a dialectic arises which leads the faculty of judgment into confusion about the 387 principle of its reflection.

The first maxim of the faculty of judgment is the *proposition:* All production of material things and their forms must be judged to be possible according to merely mechanical laws.

The second maxim is the *counterproposition:* Some products of material nature cannot be judged to be possible according to merely mechanical laws. (To judge them requires a quite different law of causality, namely, that of final causes.)

If these regulative principles of investigation be converted into constitutive principles of the possibility of objects, they will run thus:

Proposition: All production of material things is possible according to merely mechanical laws.

Counterproposition: Some production of material things is not possible according to merely mechanical laws.

As constitutive principles, objective principles for the determinant judgment, they would contradict each other, and consequently one of the two propositions would necessarily be false. We should then, it is true, have an antinomy, but not an antinomy of the faculty of judgment; the conflict will be in the legislation of reason. Reason, however, can prove neither the one nor the other of these fundamental propositions, because we can have a priori no determinant principle of the possibility of things according to mere empirical laws of nature.

On the other hand, when seen as the first-mentioned maxims of reflective judgment, they involve no contradiction in fact. For if I say, I must judge, according to merely mechanical laws, of the possibility of all events in material nature, and consequently of all forms regarded as its products, I do not therefore say: *They are possible in this way alone* apart from any other kind of causality. All that is implied is: I must always reflect upon them according to the principle of the mechanism of nature, and consequently investigate this as far as I can, because unless this lies at the basis of the investigation there can be no proper knowledge of nature at all. But this does not prevent us, if opportunity offers, from following out the second maxim in the case of certain natural forms (and even at the instance of these, in the case of the whole of nature), in order to reflect upon them according to the principle of final

388 causes, which is quite a different thing from explaining them according to the mechanism of nature. Reflection in accordance with the first maxim is thus not suspended; on the contrary, we are told to follow it as far as we can. Nor is it said that these forms would not be possible in accordance with the mechanism of nature. It is asserted only that *human* reason, in following this maxim and this path could never find the least ground for that which constitutes the specific character of a natural purpose, though it would increase its knowledge of natural laws. Thus it is left undecided whether or not, in the unknown inner ground of nature, physico-mechanical and purposive combination in the same thing may be united in one principle. We only say that our reason is not in a position to unite them, and that therefore the faculty of judgment (as reflective, from subjective grounds, not as determinant, in consequence of an objective principle of the possibility of things in themselves)[18] is compelled to think a different principle from that of natural mechanism as the ground of the possibility of certain forms in nature.

Section 71. Preliminary to the Solution of the Above Antinomy

We can in no way prove the impossibility of the production of organized natural products by the mechanism of nature because we cannot see into the first inner ground of the infinite multiplicity of the particular laws of nature, which are contingent for us since they are known only empirically; and so we cannot arrive at the inner all-sufficient principle of the possibility of a [system of] nature, a principle which lies [not in nature but] in the supersensible. Whether, therefore, the productive power of nature is sufficient for that which we judge to be formed or combined in accordance with the Idea of purposes, as well as for that which we believe to require a merely mechanical system of nature; or whether there lies at the basis of things which we must necessarily judge as properly natural purposes a quite different kind of original causality which cannot be contained in material nature or in its

389 intelligible substrate, viz. an architectonic understanding — this is a question to which our reason, very narrowly limited in respect to the concept of causality if it is to be specified a priori, can give no answer whatever. But it is just as certain and beyond doubt that, in regard to our cognitive faculties, the mere mechanism of nature can furnish no ground of explanation of the production of organized beings. For the reflective power of judgment it is therefore a quite correct fundamental proposition that, for the connection of things according to final causes which is so plain, there must be thought a

---

[18]Kant wrote *things in themselves,* but probably meant *things themselves.*

causality distinct from that of mechanism, namely, the causality of an (intelligent) cause of the world acting in accordance with purposes; but for the determinant judgment this would be a hasty and unprovable proposition. In the first case it is a mere maxim of judgment, in which the concept of that causality is a mere Idea to which we by no means undertake to assign reality, but which we use as a guide to reflection, which remains thereby always open to mechanical grounds of explanation, and which does not withdraw itself from the world of sense. In the second case the proposition would be an objective principle prescribed by reason, to which the faculty of determinant judgment would have to subject itself; but in so doing it would withdraw itself beyond the world of sense into the transcendent, and perhaps would be led into error.

All appearance of an antinomy between the maxims of the proper physical (mechanical) and the teleological (technical)[19] methods of explanation rests therefore on this: we confuse a fundamental proposition of the reflective with one of the determinant faculty of judgment, and the *autonomy* of the first (which has only subjective validity for our use of reason in respect to particular empirical laws) with the *heteronomy* of the second, which must regulate itself according to laws, universal or particular, given to it by the understanding.

Section 75. The Concept of an Objective Purposiveness of Nature as a Critical Principle of Reason for the Faculty of Reflective Judgment

397

It is one thing to say: "The production of certain things in nature or of the whole of nature is possible only through a cause which determines itself to action according to design," and quite another say, "I cannot, because of the peculiar constitution of my cognitive faculties, judge concerning the possibility of these things and their production in any other fashion than by 398 conceiving for this a cause working according to design (i.e., a being which is productive in a way analogous to the causality of an intelligence)." In the former case, I wish to establish something concerning the object and am bound to establish the objective reality of an assumed concept; in the latter, reason determines only the use of my cognitive faculties, conformably to their peculiarities and to the essential conditions of their range and limits. Thus the former principle is an objective proposition for the determinant faculty of judgment, the latter merely a subjective proposition for the reflective judgment (i.e., a maxim which reason prescribes to it).

We are in fact necessarily obliged to ascribe the concept of design to nature if we wish to investigate it in its organized products by continued observation; and this concept is therefore an absolutely necessary maxim for the empirical use of our reason. It is plain that, once such a guiding thread for the study of nature is admitted and verified, we must at least try this maxim of judgment

---

[19] "Technical" in the sense of having to do with the "technique of nature"; see above, p. 353.

in the inquiry into nature as a whole, because in this way many of nature's laws might be discovered which on account of the limitation of our insight into its inner mechanism would otherwise remain hidden. But though in regard to this latter employment this maxim of judgment is certainly useful, it is not indispensable, for nature as a whole is not given as organized (in the narrow sense of the word indicated above). On the other hand, in regard to those natural products which must be judged of as designed and not formed otherwise, if we are to have empirical knowledge of their inner constitution, this maxim of the reflective judgment is absolutely necessary, because the very thought of them as organized beings is impossible without combining with it the thought of their designed production.

Now the concept of a thing whose existence or form we think possible under the condition of a purpose is inseparably bound up with the concept of its contingency according to natural laws. Hence the natural things that we find possible only as purposes supply the best proof of the contingency of the 399 world-whole; to the common understanding and to the philosopher alike they are the only valid ground of proof of its dependence on and origin from a Being existing outside the world — a Being who must also be intelligent for the sake of its purposive form. Teleology, then, finds the consummation of its investigations only in theology.

But what now in the end does the most complete teleology prove? Does it prove that there is such an intelligent Being? No. It proves only that, according to the constitution of our cognitive faculties and the consequent combination of experience with the highest principles of reason, we can form absolutely no concept of the possibility of such a world [as this], save by thinking a designedly working supreme cause of the world. Objectively we cannot therefore lay down the proposition that there is an intelligent original Being; but only subjectively for the use of our judgment in its reflection upon the purposes in nature, which can be thought of according to no other principle than that of a designing causality of a highest cause.

If we wished to establish on teleological grounds this proposition dogmatically, we should be beset with difficulties from which we could not extricate ourselves. For then the proposition would at bottom be reduced to the conclusion that the organized beings in the world are not otherwise possible than by a designedly working cause. And we should unavoidably have to assert that, because we can follow up these things in their causal combination only under the idea of purposes, and know them only according to their conformity to law, we are thereby justified in assuming the same as a condition necessary for every thinking and knowing being — a condition consequently attaching to the object and not merely to our subject. But we do not succeed in sustaining such an assertion. For since we do not, properly speaking, *observe* the purposes in nature as designed, but only in our reflection upon its products *think* this concept as a guiding thread for our faculty of judgment, purposes are not given to us through the object. It is quite impossible for us a priori to vindicate, as something to be assumed, the objective reality of such a concept. It remains therefore a proposition resting only upon subjective conditions of judgment reflecting in conformity with our cognitive faculties. If we expressed this proposition dogmatically and as objectively valid, it would be: There is a God. But we men are permitted only the limited formula: We cannot think and make comprehensible the purposiveness 400 which must lie at the ground of our knowledge of the internal possibility of many natural things except by representing it and the world in general as a product of an intelligent cause, a God.

Now, if this proposition, based on an inevitably necessary maxim of our judgment, is completely satisfactory from every *human* point of view for both the speculative and practical use of our reason, I should like to know what we lose by not being able to prove it as also valid for higher beings, from objective grounds (which, unfortunately, are beyond our faculties). It is indeed quite certain that we cannot adequately know, much less explain, organized beings and their internal possibility according to mere mechanical principles or nature, and we can say boldly it is alike certain that it is absurd for me to make any such attempt and to hope that another Newton will arise in the future who shall make comprehensible to us the production of even a blade of grass according to natural laws which no design has ordered. We must absolutely deny this insight to men.

But then how do we know that in nature, if we could penetrate to the principle by which it specifies the universal laws known to us, there cannot lie hidden in its mere mechanism a sufficient ground of the possibility of organized beings, without supposing there is any design in their production? Would it not be judged presumptuous of us to say this? Probabilities are here of no account when we have to do with judgments of pure reason. We cannot therefore judge objectively, either affirmatively or negatively, concerning the proposition: Does a being acting according to design lie at the basis of what we rightly call natural purposes, as the cause of the world, and consequently as its author? So much only is sure, that if we are to judge according to what is permitted us to see by our own proper nature (the conditions and limitations of our reason), we can place at the basis of the possibility of these natural purposes nothing other than an Intelligent Being. This alone is in conformity with the maxim of our reflective judgment and therefore with a ground which, though subjective, is inseparably attached to the human race.   401

Section 76. Remark [on the Modal Predicates][20]

. . . Reason is a faculty of principles and proceeds in its furthest reach to the unconditioned; understanding is at its service only under a certain condition which must be given. Without concepts of understanding, to which objective reality must be given, reason cannot judge objectively and syntheti-

[20] See the discussion of the same topic in *Critique of Pure Reason*, above, pp. 120–123, 124–125.

cally; as theoretical reason it contains in itself absolutely no constitutive but merely regulative principles. We soon see that where understanding cannot follow, reason is transcendent and distinguishes itself in Ideas established as regulative principles, but not in objectively valid concepts. But understanding, which cannot keep pace with reason, is requisite for the validity [of our knowledge] of objects, while it limits the validity of those Ideas to the subject, although it extends it generally to all human subjects. That is, understanding limits the validity of the Ideas to the condition that, because of the nature of our human cognitive faculties or, more generally, according to the concept *which we ourselves can make* of the faculty of a finite intelligent being in general, there can and must be no other way of thought; but this is not to assert that the ground of such a judgment lies in the object. We shall give some examples which, though they are too important and difficult to impose on the reader as proved propositions, yet will give him matter for thought and may serve to elucidate what we are here specifically concerned with.

It is indispensably necessary for the human understanding to distinguish between the possibility and the actuality of things. The ground of this lies in the subject and in the nature of our faculties. There would not be such a 402 distinction between the possible and the actual were there not requisite for knowledge two quite different elements, understanding for concepts, and sensible intuition for objects corresponding to them. If our understanding were intuitive, it would have no objects except those that are actual. Concepts, which concern merely the possibility of an object, and sensible intuitions, which give us something without enabling us to cognize it as an object, would both disappear. The whole of our distinction between the merely possible and the actual rests on this: the possible signifies only the positing of the representation of a thing in relation to our concept and, in general, in relation to the faculty of thought, while the actual signifies positing the thing in itself[19] outside the concept. The distinction, then, of possible things from actual things is one which has merely subjective validity for the human understanding, because we can always have a thing in our thought although it is [actually] nothing, or we can represent a thing as given although we have no concept of it. The propositions, therefore, that things can be possible without being actual, and that consequently no conclusion can be drawn as to actuality from mere possibility, are quite valid for human reason; but this does not prove that the distinction lies in things themselves. That this does not follow, and that consequently these propositions, though valid of objects insofar as our cognitive faculty as sensibly conditioned busies itself with objects of sense, do not hold for things in general, appears from the irrepressible demand of reason to assume something (the original ground) necessarily existing as unconditioned, in which possibility and actuality should no longer be distinguished, and for which Idea our understanding has absolutely no

---

[21] Kant wrote "thing in itself", but it suffices for his argument to say "thing itself."

concept (i.e., can find no way of representing such a thing and its manner of existence). For if the understanding thinks such a thing (which it may do at pleasure), the thing is represented merely as possible. If it is conscious of it as given in intuition, then it is actual, but nothing as to its possibility is thereby thought. Hence the concept of an absolutely necessary Being is no doubt an indispensable Idea of reason, but it is a problematical concept unattainable by human understanding. It is valid for the employment of our cognitive faculties in accordance with their peculiar constitution, but not valid of the object. Nor is it valid for every knowing being, because I cannot presuppose in every such being thought and intuition as two distinct conditions of the exercise of its cognitive faculties, and consequently as conditions of the possibility and actuality of things. An understanding into which this distinc- 403 tion did not enter might say: All objects that I know to exist, and the possibility of some which do not exist (their contingency, if they were to exist, would be distinguished from their necessity) might never come into the consciousness of such a being at all. But what makes it difficult for our understanding with its concepts to keep up with reason is merely this: what for it, as human understanding, is transcendent (i.e., impossible because of the subjective conditions of its knowledge) is made by reason into a principle appertaining to the object. Here the maxim always holds that all objects the cognition of which surpasses the faculty of understanding are thought by us according to the subjective conditions of the exercise of the faculties which necessarily attach to our human nature. If judgments laid down in this way (and there is no alternative in regard to transcendent concepts) cannot be constitutive principles determining the object as it is, they will remain regulative principles adapted to the human point of view, immanent in their exercise, and sure.

Just as reason in the theoretical consideration of nature must assume the Idea of an unconditioned necessity of its original ground, so also it presupposes in the practical sphere its own unconditioned causality in respect of nature (freedom) in that it is conscious of its own moral command. Here the objective necessity of the act, as a duty, is opposed to that necessity which it would have as an event if its ground lay in nature and not in freedom (i.e., in the causality of reason). The morally absolutely necessary act is regarded as physically quite contingent, since that which *ought* necessarily to happen often does not happen. It is clear, then, that it is owing to the subjective constitution of our practical faculty that moral laws must be represented as commands, and the actions conforming to them as duties; and that reason expresses this necessity, not by an *is* (*happens*) but by an *ought to be*. This would not be the case were reason considered in its causality independent of sensibility as the subjective condition of its application to the objects of nature, and so as cause in an intelligible world entirely in agreement with the moral law. For in such a world there would be no distinction between *ought to* 404 *do* and *does*, between a practical law of that which is possible through us and the theoretical laws of that which is actual through us. Though, therefore, an intelligible world in which everything would be actual merely because (as something good) it is possible, together with freedom as its formal condition, is for us a transcendent concept, not a constitutive principle able to determine an object and its objective reality, yet because of the constitution of our (in part) sensuous nature and faculty it is, so far as we can represent it in accordance with the constitution of our reason, for us and for all rational beings that have a connection with the world of sense, a universal regulative principle. This principle does not objectively determine the constitution of freedom as a form of causality, but it makes the rule of actions according to that Idea a command for everyone, with no less validity than if it did so determine it.

In the same way we may concede this much as regards the case in hand. Between natural mechanism and the technique of nature (i.e., its purposive connection) we should find no distinction were it not that our understanding is of the kind that must proceed from the universal to the particular. The faculty of judgment in respect of the particular can recognize no purposiveness and, consequently, can form no determinant judgments without having a universal law under which to subsume the particular. Now the particular, as such, contains something contingent in respect of the universal, while reason requires unity and conformity of the contingent to law in the combination of particular laws of nature. This conformity of the contingent to law is called purposiveness, and the derivation of particular laws from the universal as regards their contingent element is impossible a priori through the determination of the concept of the object. Hence the concept of the purposiveness of nature in its products is necessary for the human faculty of judgment in respect of nature, but has not to do with the determination of objects. It is, therefore, a subjective principle of reason for the faculty of judgment, which as regulative (not constitutive) is just as necessarily valid for our human faculty of judgment as if it were an objective principle.

405   ### Section 77. Of the Distinctive Characteristic of the Human Faculty of Understanding Because of Which the Concept of a Natural Purpose Becomes Possible for Us

We have brought forward in the "Remark" peculiarities of our cognitive faculties (even the higher ones) that we are easily led to transfer as objective predicates to things themselves. But they concern Ideas, no object adequate to which can be given in experience, and they could serve only as regulative principles in the pursuit of experience. This is the case with the concept of a natural purpose which concerns the cause of the possibility of such a predicate, which cause can lie only in the Idea. But the result corresponding to it (i.e., the product) is given in nature, and the concept of a causality of nature as of a being acting according to purposes seems to make the Idea of a natural purpose into a constitutive principle of the natural purpose; this Idea is therein different from all other Ideas.

This difference consists, however, in the fact that the Idea in question is not a principle for the understanding but for the faculty of judgment. It is, therefore, merely the application of an understanding in general to possible objects of experience, in cases where the faculty of judgment can be only reflective, not determinant, and where consequently the object, although given in experience, cannot be determinately judged in conformity with the Idea (certainly not with complete adequacy), but can only be reflected upon.

There emerges, therefore, a distinctive characteristic of our (human) understanding in respect of the faculty of judgment in its reflection upon things of nature. But if this be so, the Idea of a possible understanding different from the human must be fundamental here. (Just so in the *Critique of Pure Reason* we must have in our thoughts another possible [kind of] intuition if ours is to be regarded as a particular species for which objects hold only as appearances.) And so we are able to say: Certain natural products, because of the special constitution of our understanding, must be considered by us in regard to their possibility as if produced designedly and on purpose. But we do not thereby demand that there should be actually given a particular cause which 406 has the representation of a purpose as its determining ground, and we do not deny that an understanding different from (i.e., higher than) the human might find the ground of the possibility of such products of nature in the mechanism of nature (i.e., in a causal combination of which an understanding is not explicitly assumed as a cause).

We have now to do with the relation of *our* understanding to the faculty of judgment, viz., to seek for a certain contingency in the constitution of our understanding to which we may point as a peculiarity distinguishing it from other possible understandings.

This contingency is found, naturally enough, in the *particular,* which the faculty of judgment is to bring under the *universal* of the concepts of understanding. For the universal of our (human) understanding does not determine the particular, and it is contingent in how many ways different things that agree in a common characteristic may come before our perception. Our understanding is a faculty of concepts (i.e., a discursive understanding) for which it obviously must be contingent of what kind and how very different the particulars in nature may be that can be given to it and brought under its concepts. Intuition also belongs to knowledge, and a faculty of a *complete spontaneity of intuition* would be a cognitive faculty distinct from sensibility and quite independent of it. In other words, it would be an understanding in the most general sense. Thus we can think of an *intuitive* understanding (negatively, simply as not discursive) which does not proceed from the universal to the particular and so to the individual (through concepts). For it, that contingency of the conformity of nature in its products according to *particular* laws with the understanding would not be met with, and it is this contingency that makes it so hard for our understanding to reduce the multiplicity of nature to the unity of knowledge. Our understanding can accomplish this reduction only by bringing natural characteristics into agreement with our faculty of concepts — an agreement which is always highly contingent. An intuitive understanding would have no need for this procedure.

Our understanding has then this peculiarity as concerns the faculty of judgment: that, in cognition by the understanding, the particular is not determined by the universal and cannot therefore be derived from it alone, but at the same time this particular in the variety of nature must so accord 407 with the universal (by means of concepts and laws) that it is to be capable of being subsumed under it. The accordance in such circumstances must be highly contingent and, for the faculty of judgment, without a definite principle.

In order to be able at least to think the possibility of such an accordance of things in nature with our faculty of judgment (which accordance we think of as contingent and consequently as possible only because of a purpose directed to our faculty of understanding) we must at the same time think of another understanding, by reference to which and apart from any purpose ascribed to it, we may represent as necessary that accordance of natural laws with our faculty of judgment, which our understanding can think only through the medium of purposes.

Our understanding has the property of proceeding in its cognition (e.g., of the causes of a product) from the *analytical-universal* (concepts) to the particular (the given empirical intuition). As regards the manifold variety of the latter, it determines nothing but must await this determination by the faculty of judgment in subsuming the empirical intuition (if the object is a natural product) under the concept. We can, however, think of an understanding, not discursive like ours but intuitive, which proceeds from the *synthetical-universal* (the intuition of a whole as such) to the particular (i.e., from the whole to the parts). This intuitive understanding and its representation of the whole does not include in itself the contingency of the combination of the parts which our understanding requires in order to make a definite form of the whole possible. Our understanding must progress from [contingent] parts thought to be universal grounds to different possible forms [of the whole] subsumed under them as consequences. According to the constitution of our understanding, a real whole of nature is regarded only as the effect of the concurrent motive powers of the parts. Suppose then that we wish not to represent the possibility of the whole as dependent on that of the parts (after the manner of our discursive understanding), but according to the standard of the intuitive (original) understanding to represent the possibility of the parts (in their constitution and combination) as dependent on that of the whole. In accordance with the above peculiarity of our understanding, it cannot happen that the whole should contain the ground of the possibility of

the connection of the parts (which would be a contradiction in discursive   408
cognition), but only that the *representation* of a whole may contain the ground
of the possibility of its form and of the connection of the parts belonging to it.
Such a whole would be an effect (a product), the representation of which is
regarded as the *cause* of its possibility. The product of a cause whose determining ground is the representation of its effect is what we mean by purpose.
Hence it is merely a consequence of the particular constitution of our understanding that it represents products of nature as possible according to a
different kind of causality from that of the natural laws of matter, namely,
that of purposes and final causes.

This principle has not to do with the possibility of such things themselves
(even when considered as phenomena) according to the manner of their
production, but merely with the judgment which our understanding can pass
upon them. Here we see at once why it is that in natural science we are not
long contented with an explanation of the products of nature by a causality
according to purposes. For in such an explanation we desire to judge of
natural productions exclusively in a manner comfortable to our faculty of
judging (i.e., to the faculty of reflective judgment), and not [as in natural
science] in reference to things themselves on behalf of the faculty of determinant judgment. It is not at all necessary to prove here that such an *intellectus
archetypus* is possible, but only that we are led to the Idea of it—which
contains no contradiction—as a counterpart to our discursive understanding
(*intellectus ectypus*) which has need of images and to the contingency of this
feature of our cognitive faculty.

If we consider a material whole, according to its form, as a product of the
parts with their powers and faculties of combining with one another (as well
as bringing in foreign materials), we think a mechanical mode of production
of it. In this way no concept emerges of a whole as purpose, whose internal
possibility presupposes throughout the Idea of a whole on which depend the
constitution and mode of action of the parts, as we must think an organized
body. It does not indeed follow, as has been shown, that the mechanical
production of such a body is impossible. To say so would be to say that it
would be impossible, i.e., contradictory, for any understanding to think such
a unity in the connection of the manifold without the Idea of the unity being
at the same time its producing cause; this would be equivalent to saying that
the unity in the manifold could not arise without designed production. This,   409
however, would follow in fact if we were justified in regarding material beings
as things in themselves. For then the unity that constitutes the ground of the
possibility of natural formations would be simply the unity of space. But
space is no real ground for the generation of things, but only their formal
condition (though it has this similarity to the real ground we are seeking, that
in space no part can be determined except in relation to the whole, the
representation of which therefore lies at the ground of the possibility of the
parts [of space itself]). But now it is at least possible to consider the material

world as appearance only and to think as its substrate something as a thing in itself which is not appearance, and to attach to this a corresponding intellectual intuition (even though it is not ours). Although unknowable by us, there would be a supersensible real ground for nature, to which we ourselves belong. In nature regarded as an object of sense, what is necessary is judged according to mechanical laws. But the agreement between, and the unity of, the particular laws and their derivative forms, which are contingent according to mechanical laws, exist in nature as an object of reason. This object and the entire system of nature itself must be judged according to teleological laws. Thus we should judge nature according to two different kinds of principles without the mechanical way of explanation being shut out by the teleological, as it would be if they contradicted each other.

Though we could easily surmise what could only with difficulty be maintained with certainty and proved, from what has been said we are permitted to see that the principle of a mechanical derivation of purposive natural products is consistent with the teleological, but in no way enables us to dispense with it. In a thing that we must judge to be a natural purpose (an organized being), we can no doubt try all the known and yet to be discovered laws of mechanical production, and even hope to make good progress by doing so; but we can never get rid of the call for a quite different ground of production for the possibility of such a product, viz., causality by means of purposes. Absolutely no human reason (in fact, no finite reason in quality like ours, however much it may surpass it in degree) can hope to understand the production of even a blade of grass by mere mechanical causes. As regards the possibility of such an object, the teleological connection of causes and effects is quite indispensable for the faculty of judgment, even for studying it by the clue of experience. For external objects as appearances an adequate ground related to purposes cannot be met with; and though the ground lies in nature, it must be sought only in the supersensible substrate of nature, from all possible insight into which we are cut off. Hence it is absolutely impossible for us to produce from nature itself grounds of explanation of purposive combinations, and it is necessary, by the constitution of human cognitive faculties, to see the supreme ground of these purposive combinations in an original understanding as the cause of the world.

Section 78. Of the Union of the Principle of the Universal Mechanism of Matter with the Teleological Principle of the Technique of Nature

It is infinitely important for reason not to let slip the mechanism of nature in its products, and in their explanation not to pass it by, because without it no insight into the nature of things can be attained. Suppose it admitted that a supreme Architect created directly the forms of nature as they have been from the beginning, or that He predetermined those which, in the course of nature, continually form themselves on the same model. Our knowledge of nature is not thereby in the least furthered, because we cannot know the mode of action of that Being and the Ideas which are to contain the principles of the possibility of natural things, and we cannot by them explain nature as from above downward (a priori). And if, starting from the forms of the objects of experience, from below upward (a posteriori), we wish to explain the purposiveness which we believe we meet with in experience by appealing to a cause working in accordance with purposes, then our explanation is quite tautological, and we only mock reason with words. Indeed, when we lose ourselves in this way of explanation in the transcendent, whither natural knowledge cannot follow, reason is seduced into poetical extravagance, which it is its peculiar calling to avoid.

On the other hand, it is just as necessary a maxim of reason not to ignore 411 the principle of purposes in the products of nature. For although it does not make the mode of their origination any more comprehensible, it is a heuristic principle for investigating the particular laws of nature, even supposing that we wish to make no use of it for explaining nature itself. In explaining the products of nature, we always call them natural purposes even though they apparently exhibit a designed unity of purpose, that is, we do not seek the ground of the possibility of natural purposes beyond nature. But since we must in the end come to this latter question [of the ground of the possibility of natural purposes], it is just as necessary to think for natural purposes a special kind of causality which is not itself found in nature as it is to think a special kind of causality in the mechanism of natural causes. To the receptivity of forms different from those to which matter is susceptible by mechanism there must be added a spontaneity of a cause (which therefore cannot be matter) without which no ground can be assigned for those forms. No doubt reason, before it takes this additional step, must proceed with caution and not try to explain teleologically every technique of nature (i.e., every formative power of nature which displays — as in regularly constructed bodies — a purposiveness of figure for our mere apprehension); rather, it must always regard such productions as mechanically possible. But on that account to wish entirely to exclude the teleological principle and to follow simple mechanism only — in cases where, in the rational investigation of the possibility of natural forms through their causes, purposiveness shows itself quite undeniably as the relation to a different kind of causality — to do this must make reason fantastic and send it wandering among chimeras of unthinkable natural forces, just as an exclusively teleological mode of exploration which takes no account of natural mechanism makes it visionary (*schwärmerisch*).

In the same natural thing both principles cannot be connected as fundamental principles of explanation (deduction) of one from the other (i.e., they do not unite for the faculty of determinant judgment as dogmatical and constitutive principles of insight into nature). If I choose to regard a maggot as the product of the mere mechanism of nature (of the new formation that nature produces of itself, when its elements are set free by corruption), I

cannot derive the same product from the same matter as from a causality
412 acting according to purposes. Conversely, if I regard the same creature as a
natural purpose, I cannot count on any mechanical mode of its production
and regard this as the constitutive principle of my judgment upon its possibility, and so unite both principles. One method of explanation excludes the
other, even supposing that objectively both grounds of the possibility of such
a product rested on a single ground to which we did not have access. The
principle which should render possible the compatibility of both in judging of
nature must be placed in that which lies outside both (and consequently
outside the possible empirical representation of nature), but which contains
their ground. It must be placed in the supersensible, and each of the two
methods of explanation must be referred to it. Now of this we can give no
concept except the indeterminate concept of a ground which makes the
judging of nature by empirical laws possible, but which we cannot determine
more closely by any predicate. Hence the union of both principles cannot rest
upon a ground of explanation of the possibility of a product according to given
laws for the faculty of determinant judgment, but only upon a ground of its
exposition by reflective judgment. To explain is to derive from a principle,
which we must clearly know and of which we can give an account. No doubt
the principle of the mechanism of nature and that of its causality of purposes
in one and the same natural product must coalesce in a single higher principle
which is their common source, because otherwise they could not subsist side
by side in the observation of nature. But if this principle, objectively common
to the two, which therefore warrants the association of their respective
maxims of the investigation of nature, be such that though it can be pointed to
it cannot be determinately known nor clearly put forward for use in cases
which arise, then from such a principle we can draw no explanation (i.e., no
clear and determinate derivation of the possibility of a natural product in
accordance with these two diverse principles). But the principle common to
the mechanical and the teleological derivations is the supersensible which we
must place at the basis of nature regarded as phenomenon. And of this, in a
theoretical point of view, we cannot form the least determinate concept. It
cannot, therefore, in any way be explained according to it as principle, how
413 nature (in its particular laws) constitutes for us one system, which can be
known as possible either by the principle of physical generation or by the
principle of generation by final causes. If it happens that there are objects of
nature whose possibility cannot be thought by us according to the principle of
mechanism (which always has a claim on an explanation of a natural being)
without relying on teleological propositions, we can only make an hypothesis.
Namely, we suppose that we may hopefully investigate natural laws with
reference to both according to whether the possibility of the product is
knowable by our understanding in using the one or the other principle
without stumbling at the apparent contradiction which comes into view
between the principles by which they are judged. For at least the possibility is

assured that both may be united objectively in one principle, since they concern appearances which presuppose a common ground.

Mechanism, then, and the teleological (designed) technique of nature, in respect of the same product and its possibility, may stand under a common supreme principle of nature in its particular laws. But since this principle is transcendent, because of the limitation of our understanding, we cannot unite the two principles in the explanation of the same production of nature, even if the inner possibility of the product is intelligible only through a causality according to purposes (as is the case with organized matter). We revert then to the fundamental principle of teleology. According to the constitution of the human understanding, no other than designedly working causes can be assumed for the possibility of organized beings in nature; and the mere mechanism of nature cannot be adequate to the explanation of these products. But we do not attempt to decide anything by this fundamental proposition as to the possibility of such things themselves.

This is only a maxim of the reflective, not the determinant, faculty of judgment. Consequently it is valid only for us subjectively, not objectively for the possibility of things of this kind themselves (in which both kinds of production may well cohere in one and the same ground). Further, unless the concept of teleological generation were supplemented at the same time by a mechanism found in nature, this kind of production could not be judged as a natural product. Hence the above maxim leads to the necessity of a unifica- 414 tion of both principles in judging of things as natural purposes in themselves, but does not lead us to substitute one for the other either altogether or in part. For in the place of what is thought (at least by us) as possible only by design we cannot set mechanism, and in the place of what is cognized as mechanically necessary we cannot set contingency which would need a purpose as its determining ground; but we can only subordinate the one (mechanism) to the other (designed technique), which may quite well be the case, according to the transcendental principle of the purposiveness of nature. For where purposes are thought of as grounds of the possibility of certain things, we must assume a means to them whose law of working requires for itself nothing presupposing a purpose; this law can be mechanical and yet be a cause subordinated to designed effects. Considering the organic products of nature and impressed by their infinite number, we assume (a permissible hypothesis) design in the combination of natural causes following particular laws as a universal principle of the faculty of judgment reflecting on the world as a whole. Thus we can think of a great and indeed universal combination of mechanical with teleological laws in the productions of nature, without interchanging the principles by which they are judged, or putting one in place of the other. For in judging teleologically, matter under the mechanical laws of its nature can be subordinated as a means to the represented purpose, even if the form it assumes is judged to be possible only by design. But since the ground of this compatability lies in that which is neither one nor the other (neither mechanism nor purposive combination), but is the supersensible sustrate of nature of which we know nothing, the two ways of representing the possibility of such objects are not to be blended together by our (human) reason. However, we cannot judge of their possibility otherwise than by judging them as ultimately resting on a supreme understanding by the connection of final causes, and thus the teleological method of explanation is not eliminated.

415   Now it is quite indeterminate, and for our understanding always indeterminable, how much the mechanism of nature does as a means toward each designed end in nature. However, on account of the intelligible principle of the possibility of a nature in general, already mentioned, it may be assumed that it is possible throughout, under the two kinds of universally accordant laws (the physical and those of final causes), although we cannot see how this takes place. Hence we do not know how far the mechanical method of explanation which is possible for us may extend. So much only is certain that, so far as we can go in this direction, it must always be inadequate for things that we once recognize as natural purposes, and therefore, by the constitution of our understanding, we must subordinate these grounds collectively to a teleological principle.

On this is based a privilege and, on account of the importance which the study of nature by the principle of mechanism has for the theoretical use of our reason, also an appeal. We should explain all products and occurrences in nature, even the most purposive, by mechanism as far as it is in our power (the limits of which we cannot give an account of in this kind of investigation). But at the same time we are not to lose sight of the fact that those things which we cannot even put forward for investigation except under the concept of a purpose of reason, must in conformity with the essential constitution of our reason and notwithstanding those mechanical causes be subordinated by us finally to causality in accordance with ends.

Methodology of the Faculty of Teleological Judgment

434   *Section 84. Of the Final Purpose of the Existence of*
       a World, that is, of Creation Itself

A final purpose is that purpose which needs no other as a condition of its possibility.

If the mere mechanism of nature be assumed as the ground of the explanation of its purposiveness, we cannot ask: What are things there for? For according to such an idealistic[22] system it is only the physical possibility of things (for to think of them as purposes would be mere purposeless sophistry) that is under discussion, and whether we refer this [apparently purposive] form of things to chance or to blind necessity, in either case the

---

[22] "Idealistic" in the sense that the teleological connection does not exist in reality, but only in our idea of it.

question would be vain. If, however, we assume the purposive combination in the world to be real and to be [brought about] by a particular kind of causality, viz. that of a *designedly* working cause, we cannot stop at the question: Why have things in the world (organized beings) this or that form? Why are they placed by nature in this or that relation to one another? For once we conceive of an understanding that must be regarded as the cause of the possibility of such forms as are actually found in things, we must inquire into the objective ground which would have determined this productive 435 understanding to bring about an effect of this kind. This ground is then the final end in reference to which such things are there.

I have said above that the final end is not an end which nature would be competent to bring about and to produce in conformity with its Idea, because it is unconditioned. For there is nothing in nature, regarded as a sensible being, for which the determining ground present in it would not always in its turn be conditioned, and this holds not merely of external (material) nature but also of internal (thinking) nature — it being understood, of course, that I am here considering only that in myself which is nature. But a thing that is to exist necessarily on account of its objective constitution as the final purpose of an intelligent cause, must be of the kind that, in the order of purposes, it is dependent on no other condition than its Idea alone.

We have in the world only one kind of beings whose causality is teleological (directed to purposes) and are at the same time so constituted that the law according to which they have to determine purposes for themselves is represented as unconditioned and independent of natural conditions, yet as in itself necessary. The being of this kind is man, but man considered as noumenon, the only natural being in which we can recognize, from its own peculiar constitution, a supersensible faculty (freedom) and even the law of [its] causality together with the object which this faculty can propose to itself as the highest end (the highest good in the world).

Of man (and likewise of every rational creature in the world) as a moral being it can no longer be asked why (*quem in finem*) he exists. His existence has the highest end in itself, to which as far as is in his power he can subject the whole of nature, contrary to which at least he cannot regard himself as subject to any influence of nature. If now things of the world, as beings dependent in their existence, need a supreme cause acting according to purposes, man is the final purpose of creation, since without him the chain of successively subordinated purposes would not be completely grounded. Only in man, and in him only as subject of morality, do we meet with unconditioned law-giving in respect of purposes, which therefore alone renders him capable of being a final purpose, to which the whole of nature is 436 teleologically subordinated. . . .

IX

Idea for a Universal History
from a Cosmopolitan Point of View

Editor's Introduction

The occasion for writing this essay is explained by Kant in the footnote on p. 415. It was published in 1784, but it is placed here out of its proper chronological order because it is a fitting conclusion to the second and third *Critiques*, showing what concrete political progress mankind has made towards achieving the realm of ends, which is only abstractly presented in the *Critiques*. It is likewise a suitable introduction to the writings on politics which follow.

Kant was not just an abstruse metaphysician and epistemologist, or a moral philosopher distant from the urgent problems of his times. He was a learned student of history, and intellectually and emotionally very caught up in the stirring political issues of the late eighteenth century, especially the American and the French Revolutions.

The word *Idea* in the title is used in a slightly different sense from the technical one introduced in the *Critique of Pure Reason* (above, p. 127 n). The Idea here is a kind of a priori model or paradigm for writing history. The facts of history are questions for historical research by historians, but the long-range meaning of the facts and their significance for our understanding of human nature and destiny are not questions to be answered by empirical historical investigation. They are philosophical questions the answers to which, though conjectural, can guide research and give significance to the facts discovered by the historian. They may even affect, indirectly at least, the future history of mankind. Thus the Idea is a regulative concept.

In this short and well-written paper Kant develops his conception of history: the rise of civil society out of barbarism, the development of larger political communities and greater areas of peaceful intercourse among peoples, the origin of culture and morality, progress, and the future of mankind. The condemnation of war points forward to *Perpetual Peace*, published eleven years later.

The translation is by the Editor, and was first published in Kant on History *(Bobbs Merrill, 1959).*

SUGGESTIONS FOR FURTHER READING

Kant on History, edited by L.W. Beck. New York: Bobbs-Merrill, 1959. (Contains translations of all Kant's writings on the philosophy of history.)

Booth, William James. *Interpreting the World: Kant's Philosophy of History and Politics.* University of Toronto Press, 1986.

Despland, Michel. *Kant on History and Religion.* McGill-Queens University Press, 1973.

Galston, W.A. *Kant and the Problem of History.* University of Chicago Press, 1975.

Yovel, Yirmiahu. *Kant and the Philosophy of History.* Princeton University Press, 1980.

Idea for a Universal History from a Cosmopolitan Point of View*

Whatever concept one may hold from a metaphysical point of view con- cerning the freedom of the will, certainly its appearances, which are human actions, like every other natural event, are determined by universal laws. However obscure their causes, history, which is concerned with narrating these appearances, permits us to hope that if we attend to the play of freedom of the human will in the large, we may be able to discern a regular movement in it, and that what seems complex and chaotic in the single individual may be seen from the standpoint of the human race as a whole to be a steady and progressive though slow evolution of its original endowment. Since the free will of man has obvious influence upon marriages, births, and deaths, they seem to be subject to no rule by which the number of them could be reckoned in advance. Yet the annual tables of them in the major countries prove that they occur according to laws as stable as the unstable weather, which we likewise cannot determine in advance, but which, in the large, maintains the growth of plants, the flow of rivers, and other natural events in an unbroken, uniform course. Individuals and even whole peoples think little on this. Each, according to his own inclination, follows his own purpose, often in opposition to others; yet each individual and people, as if following some guiding thread, go toward a natural but to each of them unknown goal; all work toward furthering it, even if they would set little store by it if they did know it.

Since men in their endeavors behave, on the whole, not just instinctively, like the brutes, nor yet like rational citizens of the world according to some agreed-on plan, no history of man conceived according to a plan seems to be possible, as it might be possible to have such a history of bees or beavers. One cannot suppress a certain indignation when one sees men's actions on the great world-stage and finds, beside the wisdom that appears here and there 18 among individuals, everything in the large woven together from folly, child-

---

*A statement in the "Short Notices" of the twelfth number of the *Gothaische Gelehrte Zeitung* of this year [1784], which no doubt was based on my conversation with a scholar who was traveling through, occasions this essay, without which that statement could not be understood.

[The notice said: "A favorite idea of Professor Kant's is that the ultimate purpose of the human race is to achieve the most perfect civic constitution, and he wishes that a philosophical historian might undertake to give us a history of humanity from this point of view, and to show to what extent humanity in various ages has approached or drawn away from this final purpose, and what remains to be done in order to reach it."]

ish vanity, even from childish malice and destructiveness. In the end, one does not know what to think of the human race, so conceited in its gifts. Since the philosopher cannot presuppose any [conscious] individual purpose among men in their great drama, there is no other expedient for him except to try to see if he can discover a natural purpose in this idiotic course of things human. In keeping with this purpose, it might be possible to have a history with a definite natural plan for creatures who have no plan of their own.

We wish to see if we can succeed in finding a clue to such a history; we leave it to Nature to produce the man capable of composing it. Thus Nature produced Kepler, who subjected, in an unexpected way, the eccentric paths of the planets to definite laws; and she produced Newton, who explained these laws by a universal natural cause.

FIRST THESIS

All natural capacities of a creature are destined to evolve completely to their natural end.

Observation of both the outward form and inward structure of all animals confirms this of them. An organ that is of no use, an arrangement that does not achieve its purpose, are contradictions in the teleological theory of nature. If we give up this fundamental principle, we no longer have a lawful but an aimless course of nature, and blind chance takes the place of the guiding thread of reason.

SECOND THESIS

In man (as the only rational creature on earth) *those natural capacities which are directed to the use of his reason are to be fully developed only in the race, not in the individual.*

Reason in a creature is a faculty of widening the rules and purposes of the use of all its powers far beyond natural instinct; it acknowledges no limits to its projects. Reason itself does not work instinctively, but requires trial, practice, and instruction in order gradually to progress from one level of insight to another. Therefore a single man would have to live excessively long in order to learn to make full use of all his natural capacities. Since Nature has set only a short period for his life, she needs a perhaps unreckonable series of generations, each of which passes its own enlightenment to its successor in order finally to bring the seeds of enlightenment to that degree of development in our race which is completely suitable to Nature's purpose. This point of time must be, at least as an ideal, the goal of man's efforts, for otherwise his natural capacities would have to be counted as for the most part vain and aimless. This would destroy all practical principles, and Nature, whose wisdom must serve as the fundamental principle in judging all her other offspring, would thereby make man alone a contemptible plaything.

THIRD THESIS

Nature has willed that man should, by himself, produce everything that goes beyond the mechanical ordering of his animal existence, and that he should partake of no other happiness or perfection than that which he himself, independently of instinct, has created by his own reason.

Nature does nothing in vain, and in the use of means to her goals she is not prodigal. Her giving to man reason and the freedom of the will which depends upon it is clear indication of her purpose. Man accordingly was not to be guided by instinct, not nurtured and instructed with ready-made knowledge; rather, he should bring forth everything out of his own resources. Securing his own food, shelter, safety, and defense (for which Nature gave him neither the horns of the bull, nor the claws of the lion, nor the fangs of the dog, but hands only), all amusement which can make life pleasant, insight and intelligence, finally even goodness of heart — all this should be wholly his own work. In this, Nature seems to have moved with the strictest parsimony, and to have measured her animal gifts precisely to the most stringent needs of a begin- 20 ning existence, just as if she had willed that, if man ever did advance from the lowest barbarity to the highest skill and mental perfection and thereby worked himself up to happiness (so far as it is possible on earth), he alone should have the credit and should have only himself to thank — exactly as if she aimed more at his rational self-esteem than at his well-being. For along this march of human affairs, there was a host of troubles awaiting him. But it seems not to have concerned Nature that he should live well, but only that he should work himself upward so as to make himself, through his own actions, worthy of life and of well-being.

It remains strange that the earlier generations appear to carry through their toilsome labor only for the sake of the later, to prepare for them a foundation on which the later generations could erect the higher edifice which was Nature's goal, and yet that only the latest of the generations should have the good fortune to inhabit the building on which a long line of their ancestors had (unintentionally) labored without being permitted to partake of the fortune they had prepared. However puzzling this may be, it is necessary if one assumes that a species of animals should have reason, and, as a class of rational beings each of whom dies while the species is immortal, should develop their capacities to perfection.

FOURTH THESIS

The means employed by Nature to bring about the development of all the capacities of men is their antagonism in society, so far as this is, in the end, the cause of a lawful order among men.

By "antagonism" I mean the unsocial sociability of men i.e., their propensity to enter into society, bound with a mutual opposition which constantly

threatens to break up the society. Man has an inclination to associate with
21 others, because in society he feels himself to be more than man (i.e., as more
than the developed form of his natural capacities). But he also has a strong
propensity to isolate himself from others, because he finds in himself at the
same time the unsocial characteristic of wishing to have everything go according to his own wish. Thus he expects opposition on all sides because, in
knowing himself, he knows that he, on his own part, is inclined to oppose
others. This opposition it is which awakens all his powers, brings him to
conquer his inclination to laziness and, propelled by vainglory, lust for power,
and avarice, to achieve a rank among his fellows whom he cannot tolerate but
from whom he cannot withdraw. Thus are taken the first true steps from
barbarism to culture, which consists in the social worth of man; thence
gradually develop all talents, and taste is refined; through continued enlightenment the beginnings are laid for a way of thought which can in time convert
the coarse, natural disposition for moral discrimination into definite practical
principles, and thereby change a society of men driven together by their
natural feelings into a moral whole. Without those in themselves unamiable
characteristics of unsociability whence opposition springs — characteristics
each man must find in his own selfish pretensions — all talents would remain
hidden, unborn in an Arcadian shepherd's life, with all its concord, contentment, and mutual affection. Men, good-natured as the sheep they herd,
would hardly reach a higher worth than their beasts; they would not fill the
empty place in creation by achieving their end, which is rational nature.
Thanks be to Nature, then, for the incompatibility, for heartless competitive
vanity, for the insatiable desire to possess and to rule! Without them, all the
excellent natural capacities of humanity would forever sleep, undeveloped.
Man wishes concord; but Nature knows better what is good for the race; she
wills discord. He wishes to live comfortably and pleasantly; Nature wills that
he should be plunged from sloth and passive contentment into labor and
trouble, in order that he may find means of extricating himself from them.
The natural urges to this, the sources of unsociableness and mutual opposition from which so many evils arise, drive men to new exertions of their forces
22 and thus to the manifold development of their capacities. They thereby
perhaps show the ordering of a wise Creator and not the hand of an evil spirit
who bungled in his great work or spoiled it out of envy.

FIFTH THESIS

The greatest problem for the human race, to the solution of which Nature drives
man, is the achievement of a universal civic society which administers law among
men.

The highest purpose of Nature, which is the development of all the capacities which can be achieved by mankind, is attainable only in society, and more
specifically in the society with the greatest freedom. Such a society is one in

which there is mutual opposition among the members, together with the most exact definition of freedom and fixing of its limits so that it may be consistent with the freedom of others. Nature demands that humankind should itself achieve this goal like all its other destined goals. Thus a society in which freedom under external laws is associated in the highest degree with irresistible power (i.e., a perfectly just civic constitution), is the highest problem Nature assigns to the human race; for Nature can achieve her other purposes for mankind only upon the solution and completion of this assignment. Need forces men, so enamored otherwise of their boundless freedom, into this state of constraint. They are forced to it by the greatest of all needs, a need they themselves occasion inasmuch as their passions keep them from living long together in wild freedom. Once in such a preserve as a civic union, these same passions subsequently do the most good. It is just the same with trees in a forest: each needs the others, since each in seeking to take the air and sunlight from others must strive upward, and thereby each realizes a beautiful, straight stature, while those that live in isolated freedom put out branches at random and grow stunted, crooked, and twisted. All culture, art which adorns mankind, and the finest social order are fruits of unsociableness, which forces itself to discipline itself and so, by a contrived art, to develop the natural seeds to perfection.

SIXTH THESIS   23

This problem is the most difficult and the last to be solved by mankind.

The difficulty which the mere thought of this problem puts before our eyes is this. Man is an animal which, if he lives among others of his kind, requires a master. For he certainly abuses his freedom with respect to other men, and although as a reasonable being he wishes to have a law which limits the freedom of all, his selfish animal impulses tempt him, where possible, to exempt himself from them. He thus requires a master, who will break his will and force him to obey a will that is universally valid, under which each can be free. But whence does he get his master? Only from the human race. But then the master is himself an animal, and needs a master. Let him begin it as he will, it is not to be seen how he can procure a magistracy which can maintain public justice and which is itself just, whether it be a single person or a group of several elected persons. For each of them will always abuse his freedom if he has none above him to exercise force in accord with the laws. The highest master should be just in himself, and yet a man. This task is therefore the hardest of all; indeed, its complete solution is impossible, for from such crooked wood as man is made of, nothing perfectly straight can be built.*

*The role of man is very artificial. How it may be with the dwellers on other planets and their nature we do not know. If, however, we carry out well the mandate given us by Nature, we can perhaps flatter ourselves that we may claim among our neighbors in the cosmos no mean rank. Maybe among them each individual can perfectly attain his destiny in his own life. Among us, it is different; only the race can hope to attain it.

That it is the last problem to be solved follows also from this: it requires that there be a correct conception of a possible constitution, great experience gained in many paths of life, and — far beyond these — a good will ready to accept such a constitution. Three such things are very hard, and if they are ever to be found together it will be very late and after many vain attempts.

24   **SEVENTH THESIS**

   The problem of establishing a perfect civic constitution is dependent upon the problem of a lawful external relation among states and cannot be solved without a solution of the latter problem.

   What is the use of working toward a lawful civic constitution among individuals (i.e., toward the creation of a commonwealth)? The same unsociability which drives man to this causes any single commonwealth to stand in unrestricted freedom in relation to others; consequently, each of them must expect from another precisely the evil which oppressed individuals and forced them to enter into a lawful civic state. The friction among men, the inevitable antagonism, which is a mark of even the largest societies and political bodies, is used by Nature as a means to establish a condition of quiet and security. Through war, through the taxing and never-ending accumulation of armament, through the want which any state, even in peacetime, must suffer internally, Nature forces them to make at first inadequate and tentative attempts; finally, after devastations, revolutions, and even complete exhaustion, she brings them to that which reason could have told them at the beginning and with far less sad experience, to wit, to step from the lawless condition of savages into a league of nations. In a league of nations, even the smallest state could expect security and justice, not from its own power and by its own decrees, but only from this great league of nations (*Foedus Amphictyonum*[1]), from a united power acting according to decisions reached under the laws of their united will. However fantastical this idea may seem — and it was laughed at as fantastical when put forward by the Abbé de St. Pierre and by Rousseau, perhaps because they believed the realization of this idea was to be expected soon. — the necessary outcome of the destitution to which each man is brought by his fellows is to force the states to the same decision (hard though it be for them) that savage man also was reluctantly forced to take, namely, to give up brutish freedom and to seek quiet and security under a lawful constitution.

   All wars are accordingly so many attempts (not in the intention of man, but
25 in the intention of Nature) to establish new relations among states, and through the destruction or at least the dismemberment of all of them to create new political bodies, which, again, either internally or eternally, can-

   [1] An allusion to the Amphictyonic League, a league of Greek tribes originally for the protection of a religious shrine, which later gained considerable political power.

not maintain themselves and which must in turn suffer like revolutions; until finally, through the best possible civic constitution and common agreement and legislation in external affairs, a state is created which, like a civic commonwealth, can maintain itself automatically.

[There are three questions here which really come to one.] Would it be expected from an Epicurean concourse of efficient causes that states, like minute particles of matter in their chance contacts, should form all sorts of unions which in their turn are destroyed by new impacts, until once, finally, by chance a structure should arise which could maintain its existence — a fortunate accident that could hardly occur? Or are we not rather to suppose that Nature here follows a lawful course in gradually lifting our race from the lower levels of animality to the highest level of humanity, doing this by her own secret art, and developing in accord with her law all the original gifts of man in this apparently chaotic disorder? Or perhaps we should prefer to conclude that, from all these actions and counteractions of men in the large, absolutely nothing, at least nothing wise, is to issue? That everything should remain as it always was, that we cannot therefore tell but that discord, natural to our race, may not prepare for us a hell of evils however civilized we may now be, by annihilating civilization and all cultural progress through barbarous devastation? (This is the fate we may well have to suffer under the rule of blind chance — which is in fact identical with lawless freedom — if there is no secret wise guidance in Nature.) These three questions, I say, mean about the same as this: Is it reasonable to assume a purposiveness in all the parts of nature and to deny it to the whole?

Purposeless savagery held back the development of the capacities of our race; but finally, through the evil into which it plunged mankind, it forced our race to renounce this condition and to enter into a civic order in which those 26 capacities could be developed. The same is done by the barbaric freedom of established states. Through wasting the powers of the commonwealths in armaments to be used against each other, through devastation brought on by war, and even more by the necessity of holding themselves in constant readiness for war, they stunt the full development of human nature. But because of the evils which thus arise, our race is forced to find, above the (in itself healthy) opposition of states which is a consequence of their freedom, a law of equilibrium and a united power to give it effect. Thus it is forced to institute a cosmopolitan condition to secure the external safety of each state.

Such a condition is not unattended by the danger that the vitality of mankind may fall asleep; but it is at least not without a principle of balance among men's actions and counteractions, without which they might be altogether destroyed. Until this last step to a union of states is taken, which is the halfway mark in the development of mankind, human nature must suffer the cruelest hardships under the guise of external well-being; and Rousseau was not far wrong in preferring the state of savages, so long, that is, as the last stage to which the human race must climb is not attained.

To a high degree we are, through art and science, *cultured*. We are *civilized*—perhaps too much for our own good—in all sorts of social grace and decorum. But to consider ourselves as having reached *morality*—for that, much is lacking. The ideal of morality belongs to culture; its use for some simulacrum of morality in the love of honor and outward decorum constitutes mere civilization. So long as states waste their forces in vain and violent self-expansion, and thereby constantly thwart the slow efforts to improve the minds of their citizens by withdrawing even support from them, nothing in the way of a moral order is to be expected. For such an end, a long internal working of each political body toward the education of its citizens is required. Everything good that is not based on a morally good disposition, however, is nothing but pretense and glittering misery. In such a condition the human species will no doubt remain until, in the way I have described, it works its way out of the chaotic conditions of its international relations.

EIGHTH THESIS

27

The history of mankind can be seen, in the large, as the realization of Nature's secret plan to bring forth a perfectly constituted state as the only condition in which the capacities of mankind can be fully developed, and also bring forth that external relation among states which is perfectly adequate to this end.

This is a corollary to the preceding. Everyone can see that philosophy can have her belief in a millenium, but her millenarianism is not Utopian, since the Idea[2] can help, though only from afar, to bring the millenium to pass. The only question is: Does Nature reveal anything of a path to this end? And I say: She reveals something, but very little. This great revolution seems to require so long for its completion that the short period during which humanity has been following this course permits us to determine its path and the relation of the parts to the whole with as little certainty as we can determine, from all previous astronomical observation, the path of the sun and his host of satellites among the fixed stars. Yet, on the fundamental premise of the systematic structure of the cosmos and from the little that has been observed, we can confidently infer the reality of such a revolution.

Moreover, human nature is so constituted that we cannot be indifferent to the most remote epoch which our race may come to, if only we may expect it with certainty. Such indifference is even less possible for us, since it seems that our own intelligent action may hasten this happy time for our posterity. For that reason, even faint indications of approach to it are very important to us. At present, states are in such an artificial relation to each other that none of them can neglect its internal cultural development without losing power and influence among the others. Therefore the preservation of this natural end [culture], if not progress in it, is fairly well assured by the ambitions of

---

[2]Kant is here using the word *Idea* in his usual technical sense. See p. 127 n.

states. Furthermore, civic freedom can hardly be infringed without the evil consequences being felt in all walks of life, especially in commerce, where the effect is loss of power of the state in its foreign relations. But this freedom 28 spreads by degrees. When the citizen is hindered in seeking his own welfare in his own way so long as it is consistent with the freedom of others, the vitality of the entire enterprise is sapped, and therewith the powers of the whole are diminished. Therefore limitations on personal actions are step by step removed, and general religious freedom is permitted. Enlightenment comes gradually, with intermittent folly and caprice, as a great good which must finally save men from the selfish aggrandizement of their masters, always assuming that the latter know their own interest. This enlightenment, and with it a certain commitment of heart which the enlightened man cannot fail to make to the good he clearly understands, must step by step ascend the throne and influence the principles of government.

Although, for instance, our world rulers at present have no money left over the public education and for anything that concerns what is best in the world, since all they have is already committed to future wars, they will still find it to their own interest at least not to hinder the weak and slow independent efforts of their peoples in this work. In the end, war itself will be seen as not only so artificial, in outcome so uncertain for both sides, in aftereffects so painful in the form of an ever-growing war debt (a new invention) that cannot be met, that it will be regarded as a most dubious undertaking. The impact of any revolution on all states on our continent, so closely knit together through commerce, will be so obvious that the other states, driven by their own danger but without any legal basis, will offer themselves as arbiters, and thus they will prepare the way for a distant international government for which there is no precedent in world history. Although this political body at present exists only as a rough outline, nevertheless in all the members there is rising a feeling which each has for the preservation of the whole. This gives hope finally that after many reformative revolutions, a universal cosmopolitan condition, which Nature has as her ultimate purpose, will come into being as the womb wherein all the original capacities of the human race can develop.

NINTH THESIS 29

A philosophical attempt to work out a universal history according to a natural plan directed to achieving the civic union of the human race must be regarded as possible and, indeed, as contributing to this end of Nature.

It is strange and apparently silly to wish to write a history in accordance with an Idea of how the course of the world must be if it is to lead to certain rational ends. It seems that with such an Idea only a romance could be written. Nevertheless, if one may assume that Nature, even in the play of human freedom, works not without plan or purpose, this Idea could still be of use. Even if we are too blind to see the secret mechanism of its workings, this

Idea may still serve as a guiding thread for presenting as a system, at least in broad outlines, what would otherwise be a planless conglomeration of human actions. For if one starts with Greek history, through which every older or contemporaneous history has been handed down or at least certified;* if one follows the influence of Greek history on the construction and misconstruction of the Roman state which swallowed up the Greek, then the Roman influence on the barbarians who in turn destroyed it, and so on down to our times; if one adds episodes from the national histories of other peoples insofar as they are known from the history of the enlightened nations, one will discover a regular progress in the constitution of states on our continent (which will probably give law, eventually, to all the others). If, further, one concentrates on the civic constitutions and their laws and on the relations
30 among states, insofar as through the good they contained they served over long periods of time to elevate and adorn nations and their arts and sciences, while through the evil they contained they destroyed them, if only a germ of enlightenment was left to be further developed by this overthrow and a higher level was thus prepared — if, I say, one carries through this study, a guiding thread will be revealed. It can serve not only for clarifying the confused play of things human, and not only for the art of prophesying later political changes (a use which has already been made of history even when seen as the disconnected effect of lawless freedom), but for giving a consoling view of the future (which could not be reasonably hoped for without the presupposition of a natural plan) in which there will be exhibited in the distance how the human race finally achieves the condition in which all the seeds planted in it by Nature can fully develop and in which the destiny of the race can be fulfilled here on earth.

Such a justification of Nature — or, better, of Providence — is no unimportant reason for choosing a standpoint toward world history. For what is the good of esteeming the majesty and wisdom of Creation in the realm of brute nature and of recommending that we contemplate it, if that part of the great stage of supreme wisdom which contains the purpose of all the others — the history of mankind — must remain an unceasing reproach to it? If we are forced to turn our eyes from it in disgust, doubting that we can ever find a perfectly rational purpose in it and hoping for that only in another world?

That I would want to displace the work of practicing empirical historians with this Idea of world history, which is to some extent based upon an a priori principle, would be a misinterpretation of my intention. It is only a suggestion of what a philosophical mind (which would have to be well versed in

---

*Only a learned public, which has lasted from its beginning to our own day, can certify ancient history. Outside it, everything else is *terra incognita;* and the history of peoples outside it can only be begun when they come into contact with it. This happened with the Jews in the time of the Ptolemies through the translation of the Bible into Greek, without which we would give little credence to their isolated narratives. From this point, when once properly fixed, we can retrace their history. And so with all other peoples. The first page of Thucydides, says Hume, is the only beginning of all real history.

history) could essay from another point of view. Otherwise the notorious complexity of a history of our time must naturally lead to serious doubt as to how our descendants will begin to grasp the burden of the history we shall leave to them after a few centuries. They will naturally value the history of 31 earlier times, from which the documents may long since have disappeared, only from the point of view of what interests them (i.e., in answer to the question of what the various nations and governments have contributed to the goal of world citizenship and what they have done to damage it). To consider this, so as to direct the ambitions of sovereigns and their agents to the only means by which their fame can be spread to later ages: this can be a minor motive for attempting such a philosophical history.

X

Perpetual Peace:
A Philosophical Sketch

Editor's Introduction

The date of publication of this tractate (1795) is significant. It was Kant's first publication following the imposition of the ban on his theological writings, and this explains the somewhat sardonic tone in the Introduction and the "Secret Article" which allude to the dangers of political interference with scholarly work and publication. The year 1795 was historically important, for in that year King Frederick William II withdrew from the War of the First Coalition and made peace (the "Peace of Basel") with the revolutionary government in France. This, in Kant's opinion, promised well for the future government of France and the peace of Europe, since it was his conviction, expressed in this book, that a republican form of government is a prerequisite for peace among states, and "No state shall by force interfere with the constitution of another state" (p. 432).

The book is drawn up in mock-heroic style, in imitation of a treaty of peace, with definitive and secret articles and codicils. In no other work does Kant resemble less the common caricature of him as an unworldly idealist. Because he had held, in the *Idea for a Universal History*, that nature and history were moving men, even without moral aspiration, towards civil order and peace among states, he does not here build first upon moral theory, but upon quite specific steps that could be taken even "by a race of devils" towards the formation of a league of nations for preserving peace. Kant's distrust of human nature, however, secures him from the follies of Utopianism. Only towards the end of the book, when he argues for the hegemony of morality over politics, do we discern the connection between this political manifesto and the moral philosophy which underlies his project.

The translation is by the Editor; it was first published by the University of Chicago Press, 1949, reprinted by Liberal Arts Press, 1967, and revised for the present edition. It is complete except for the omission of six long footnotes.

SUGGESTIONS FOR FURTHER READING

Kant's Political Writings, ed. Hans Reiss. Cambridge University Press, 1970.
Friedrich, Carl Joachim. *Inevitable Peace.* Harvard University Press, 1948.
Riley, Patrick. *Kant's Political Philosophy.* Roman and Littlefield, 1983.
Williams, Howard. *Kant's Political Philosophy.* St. Martin's Press, 1986.

Perpetual Peace:
A Philosophical Sketch

INTRODUCTION

VIII, 343   Whether the satirical inscription "Eternal Peace" on a Dutch innkeeper's sign upon which a burial ground was painted had for its object mankind in general, or the rulers of states in particular, who are insatiable of war, or merely the philosophers who dream this sweet dream, it is not for us to decide. But one condition the author of this essay wishes to lay down. The practical politician assumes the attitude of looking down with great self-satisfication on the political theorist as a pedant whose empty ideas in no way threaten the security of the state, inasmuch as the state must proceed on empirical principles; so the theorist is allowed to play his game without interference from the worldly wise statesman. Such being his attitude, the practical politician — and this is my condition — should at least act consistently also in the case of a conflict and not suspect some danger to the state in the political theorist's opinions which are ventured and publicly expressed without any ulterior purpose. By this *clausula salvatoria* the author desires formally and emphatically to deprecate herewith any malevolent interpretation which might be placed on his words.

SECTION I
CONTAINING THE PRELIMINARY ARTICLES
FOR PERPETUAL PEACE AMONG STATES

1. "No Treaty of Peace Shall Be Held Valid in Which There Is Tacitly Reserved Matter for a Future War"

Otherwise a treaty would be only a truce, a suspension of hostilities but not peace, which means the end of all hostilities — so much so that even to attach the word "perpetual" to it is a dubious pleonasm. The causes for making future wars (which are perhaps unknown to the contracting parties) are without exception annihilated by the treaty of peace, even if they should be dug out of dusty documents by acute sleuthing. When one or both parties to a treaty of peace, being too exhausted to continue warring with each other, make a tacit reservation (*reservatio mentalis*) in regard to old claims to be elaborated only at some more favorable opportunity in the future, the treaty is made in bad faith, and we have an artifice worthy of the casuistry of a Jesuit. Considered by itself, it is beneath the dignity of a sovereign, just as the

344

readiness to indulge in this kind of reasoning is unworthy of the dignity of his minister.

But if, in consequence of enlightened concepts of statecraft, the glory of the state is placed in its continual aggrandizement by whatever means, my conclusion will appear merely academic and pedantic.

2. "No Independent States, Large or Small, Shall Come Under the Dominion of Another State by Inheritance, Exchange, Purchase, or Donation"

A state is not, like the ground which it occupies, a piece of property (*patrimonium*). It is a society of men whom no one else has any right to command or to dispose of except the state itself. It is a trunk with its own roots. But to incorporate it into another state like a graft is to destroy its existence as a moral person, reducing it to a thing; such incorporation thus contradicts the Idea of the original contract without which no right over a people can be conceived.* Everyone knows to what dangers Europe, the only part of the world where this manner of acquisition is known, has been brought, even down to the most recent times, by the presumption that states could espouse one another; it is in part a new kind of industry for gaining ascendancy by means of family alliances and without expenditure of forces and in part a way of extending one's domain. Also the hiring-out of troops by one state to another, so that they can be used against an enemy not common to both, is to be counted under this principle; for in this manner the subjects, as though they were things to be manipulated at pleasure, are used and also used up.

3. "Standing Armies (*miles perpetuus*) Shall in Time Be Totally Abolished"   345

For they incessantly menace other states by their readiness to appear at all times prepared for war; they incite them to compete with each other in the number of armed men, and there is no limit to this. For this reason, the cost of peace finally becomes more oppressive than that of a short war, and consequently a standing army is itself a cause of offensive war waged in order to relieve the state of this burden. Add to this that to pay men to kill or to be killed seems to entail using them as mere machines and tools in the hand of another (the state), and this is hardly compatible with the rights of mankind in our own person. But the periodic and voluntary military exercises of citizens who thereby secure themselves and their country against foreign aggression are entirely different.

The accumulation of treasure would have the same effect, for, of the three

---

*A hereditary kingdom is not a state which can be inherited by another state, but the right to govern it can be inherited by another physical person. The state thereby acquires a ruler, but he, as a ruler (i.e., as one already possessing another realm), does not acquire the state.

powers — the power of armies, of alliances, and of money — the third is perhaps the most dependable weapon. Such accumulation of treasure is regarded by other states as a threat of war, and if it were not for the difficulties in learning the amount, it would force the other state to make an early attack.

4. "National Debts Shall Not Be Contracted with a View to the External Friction of States"

This expedient of seeking aid within or without the state is above suspicion when the purpose is domestic economy (e.g., the improvement of roads, new settlements, establishment of stores against unfruitful years, etc.) But as an opposing machine in the antagonism of powers, a credit system which grows beyond sight and which is yet a safe debt for the present requirements — because all the creditors do not require payment at one time — constitutes a dangerous money-power. This ingenious invention of a commercial people in this century is dangerous because it is a war treasure which exceeds the treasures of all other states; it cannot be exhausted except by default of taxes which is inevitable, though it can be long delayed by the stimulus to trade which occurs through the reaction of credit on industry and commerce. This facility in making war, together with the inclination to do so on the part of rulers — an inclination which seems inborn in human nature — is thus a great 346 hindrance to perpetual peace. Therefore, to forbid this credit system must all the more be a preliminary article of perpetual peace, because it must eventually entangle many innocent states in the inevitable bankruptcy, and thus openly harm them. They are therefore justified in allying themselves against such a state and its measures.

5. "No State Shall by Force Interfere with the Constitution or Government of Another State"

For what is there to authorize it to do so? The offense perhaps which a state gives to the subjects of another state? Rather the example of the evil into which a state has fallen because of its lawlessness should serve as a warning. Moreover, the bad example which one free person affords another as a *scandalum acceptum* is not an infringement of his rights. But it would be quite different if a state, by internal rebellion, should fall into two parts, each of which pretended to be a separate state making claim to the whole. To lend assistance to one of these cannot be considered an interference in the constitution of the other state (for it is then in a state of anarchy). But so long as the internal dissension has not come to this critical point, such interference by foreign powers would infringe on the rights of an independent people struggling with its internal disease; hence it would itself be an offense and would render the autonomy of all states insecure.

6. "No State Shall, during War, Permit Such Acts of Hostility as Would Make Mutual Confidence in the Subsequent Peace Impossible: Such Are the Employment of Assassins (*percussores*), Poisoners (*venefici*), Breach of Capitulation, and Incitement to Treason (*perduellio*) in the Opposing State."

These are dishonorable stratagems. For some confidence in the character of the enemy must remain even in the midst of war, as otherwise no peace could be concluded and the hostilities would degenerate into a war of extermination (*bellum internecinum*). War, however, is only the sad recourse in the state of nature (where there is no tribunal which could judge with the force of law) by which each state asserts its right by violence and in which neither party can be adjudged unjust (for that would presuppose a juridical decision); in lieu of such a decision, the issue of the conflict (as if given by a so-called "judgment of God") decides on which side justice lies. But between states no punitive war (*bellum punitivum*) is conceivable, because there is no relation between them of master and servant.

It follows that a war of extermination, in which the destruction of both parties and of all justice can result, would permit perpetual peace only in the vast burial ground of the human race. Therefore, such a war and the use of *all* means leading to it must be absolutely forbidden. But that the means cited do inevitably lead to it is clear from the fact that these infernal arts, vile in themselves, when once used would not long be confined to the sphere of war. Take, for instance, the use of spies (*uti exploratoribus*). In this, one employs the infamy of others (which can never be entirely eradicated) only to encourage its persistence even into the state of peace, to the undoing of the very spirit of peace.

Although the laws stated objectively (i.e., as expressing the intention of the rulers), are prohibitions (*leges prohibitivae*), some of them are of that strict kind which hold regardless of circumstances (*leges strictae*) and which demand prompt execution. Such are Nos. 1, 5, and 6. Others, like Nos. 2, 3, and 4, while not exceptions from the rule of law, nevertheless are subjectively broader (*leges latae*) in respect to their observation, containing permission to delay their execution without, however, losing sight of the end. This permission does not authorize, under No. 2, for example, delaying until doomsday (or, as Augustus used to say, *ad calendas Graecas*) the reestablishment of the freedom of states which have been deprived of it (i.e., it does not permit us to fail to do it, but it allows a delay to prevent precipitation which might injure the goal striven for). For the prohibition concerns only the manner of acquisition which is no longer permitted, but does not prohibit possession, which, though not bearing a requisite title of right, has nevertheless been held lawful in all states by the public opinion of the time of the putative acquisition.

SECTION II
CONTAINING THE DEFINITIVE ARTICLES
FOR PERPETUAL PEACE AMONG STATES

348   The state of peace among men living side by side is not the natural state
(*status naturalis*); the natural state is one of war. This does not always mean
349 open hostilities, but at least an unceasing threat of war. A state of peace,
therefore, must be *established,* for in order to be secure against hostility it is
not sufficient that hostilities simply not be committed; and, unless this
security is pledged to each by his neighbor (a thing that can occur only in a
civil state), each may treat his neighbor, from whom he demands this security, as an enemy.

First Definitive Article for Perpetual Peace
"The Civil Constitution of Every State Shall Be Republican"

The only constitution which derives from the idea of the original compact,
350 and on which all juridical legislation of a people must be based, is the
republican. This constitution is established, firstly, by principles of the freedom of the members of a society (as human beings); secondly, by principles
of dependence of all upon a single common legislation (as subjects); and,
thirdly, by the law of their equality (as citizens). The republican constitution,
therefore, is, with respect to law, the one which is the original basis of every
form of civil constitution. The only question now is: Is it also the one which
alone can lead to perpetual peace?
351   The republican constitution, besides the purity of its origin (having sprung
from the pure source of the concept of law), also gives a favorable prospect for
the desired consequence (i.e., perpetual peace). The reason is this. If the
consent of the citizens is required in order to decide that war should be
declared (and in this constitution it cannot but be the case), nothing is more
natural than that they would be very cautious in commencing such a poor
game, decreeing for themselves all the calamities of war. Among the latter
would be: having to fight, having to pay the costs of war from their own
resources, having painfully to repair the devastation war leaves behind, and,
to fill up the measure of evils, load themselves with a heavy national debt that
would embitter peace itself and that can never be liquidated on account of
constant wars in the future. But, on the other hand, in a constitution which is
not republican, and under which the subjects are not citizens, a declaration of
war is the easiest thing in the world to decide upon, because war does not
require of the ruler, who is the proprietor and not a member of the state, the
least sacrifice of the pleasures of his table, the chase, his country houses, his
court functions, and the like. He may, therefore, resolve on war as on a
pleasure party for the most trivial reasons and with perfect indifference leave
the justification which decency requires to the diplomatic corps who are ever
ready to provide it.

In order not to confuse the republican constitution with the democratic (as is commonly done), the following should be noted. The forms of a state 352 (*civitas*) can be divided either according to the persons who possess the sovereign power or according to the mode of administration exercised over the people by the chief, whoever he may be. The first is properly called the form of sovereignty (*forma imperii*), and there are only three possible forms of it: autocracy, in which only one possesses sovereign power; aristocracy, in which some associated together possess sovereign power; or democracy, in which all those who constitute society possess sovereign power. They may be characterized, respectively, as the power of a monarch, of the nobility, or of the people. The second division is that by the form of government (*forma regiminis*) and is based on the way in which the state makes use of its power; this way is based on the constitution, which is the act of the general will through which the many persons become one nation. In this respect government is either republican or despotic. Republicanism is the political principle of the separation of the executive power (the administration) from the legislative; despotism is that of the arbitrary autonomous execution by the state of laws which it has itself decreed. Thus in a despotism the public will is administered by the ruler as his own will. Of the three forms of the state, that of democracy is, properly speaking, necessarily a despotism, because it establishes an executive power in which "all" decide for or even against one who does not agree; that is, "all," who are not quite all, decide, and this is a contradiction of the general will with itself and with freedom.

Every from of government which is not representative is, properly speaking, without form. The legislator can unite in one and the same person his function as legislative and as executor of his will just as little as the universal of the major premise in a syllogism can also be the particular subsumed under the universal in the minor. And even though the other two constitutions are always defective to the extent that they do leave room for this mode of administration, it is at least possible for them to assume a mode of government conforming to the spirit of a representative system (as when Frederick II at least *said* he was merely the first servant of the State).* On the other 353 hand, the democratic mode of government makes this impossible, since everyone wishes to be master. Therefore, we can say: the smaller the personnel of the government (the smaller the number of rulers), the greater is their representation and the more nearly the constitution approaches to the possibility of republicanism; thus the constitution may be expected by gradual

---

*The lofty epithets of "the Lord's anointed," "the executor of the divine will on earth," and "the vicar of God," which have been lavished on sovereigns, have been frequently censured as crude and intoxicating flatteries. But this seems to me without good reason. Far from inspiring a monarch with pride, they should rather render him humble, providing he possesses some intelligence (which we must assume). They should make him reflect that he has taken an office too great for man, an office which is the holiest God has ordained on earth, to be the trustee of the rights of men, and that he must always stand in dread of having in some way injured this "apple of God's eye."

reform finally to raise itself to republicanism. For these reasons it is more difficult for an aristocracy than for a monarchy to achieve the one perfectly juridical constitution, and it is impossible for a democracy to do so except by violent revolution.

The mode of government, however, is incomparably more important to the people than the form of sovereignty, although much depends on the greater or lesser suitability of the latter to the end of [good] government. To conform to the concept of law, however, government must have a representative form, and in this system only a republican mode of government is possible; without it, government is despotic and arbitrary whatever the constitution may be. None of the ancient so-called "republics" knew this system, and they all finally and inevitably degenerated into despotism under the sovereignty of one, which is the most bearable of all forms of despotism.

Second Definitive Article for a Perpetual Peace
"The Law of Nations Shall Be Founded
on a Federation of Free States"

354 Peoples, as states, like individuals, may be judged to injure one another merely by their coexistence in the state of nature (i.e., while independent of external laws). Each of them may and should for the sake of its own security demand that the others enter with it into a constitution similar to the civil constitution, for under such a constitution each can be secure in its right. This would be a league of nations, but it would not have to be an international state, a state consisting of nations. That would be contradictory, since a state implies the relation of a superior (legislating) to an inferior (obeying, i.e., the people[1]). But a number of nations in one state would constitute only one nation. This contradicts the presupposition, for here we have to weigh the rights of nations against each other so far as they are distinct states and not amalgamated into one.

When we see the attachment of savages to their lawless freedom, preferring ceaseless combat to subjection to a lawful constraint which they might establish, and thus preferring senseless freedom to rational freedom, we regard it with deep contempt as rudeness, barbarity, and a brutish degradation of humanity. Accordingly, one would think that civilized peoples (each united in a state) would hasten all the more to escape, the sooner the better, from such a depraved condition. But, instead, each state places its majesty (for it is absurd to speak of the majesty of the people) in being subject to no external juridical restraint, and the splendor of its sovereign consists in the fact that many thousands stand at his command to sacrifice themselves for something that does not concern them and without his needing to place

---

[1] *Volk.* Elsewhere in this paragraph it is necessary to translated *Volk* as *nation.*

himself in the least danger.* The chief difference between European and American savages lies in the fact that many tribes of the latter have been eaten up by their enemies, while the former know how to make better use of their conquered enemies than to dine off them; they know better how to use them to increase the number of their subjects and thus the quantity of 355 instruments for even more extensive wars.

When we consider the perverseness of human nature which is nakedly revealed in the uncontrolled relations between nations (a perverseness veiled in the state of civil law by the constraint exercised by government), we may well be astonished that the word "law" has not yet been banished from war politics as pedantic and that no state has yet been bold enough to advocate this point of view. Up to the present Hugo Grotius, Pufendorf, Wattel, and many other importune comforters have been cited in justification of war, though their code, philosophically or diplomatically formulated, has not and cannot have the least legal force, because states as such do not stand under a common external power. There is no instance on record that a state has ever been moved to desist from its purpose because of arguments backed up by the testimony of such great men. But the homage which each state pays (at least in words) to the concept of law proves that there is slumbering in man an even greater moral disposition to become master of the evil principle in himself (which he cannot disclaim) and to hope for the same from others. Otherwise the word "law" would never be pronounced by states which wish to war upon one another; it would be used only derisively, as a Gallic prince interpreted it when he said, "It is the prerogative which nature has given the stronger that the weaker should obey him."

States do not plead their cause before a tribunal; war alone is their way of bringing suit. But by war and its favorable issue in victory, right is not decided, and though by a treaty of peace a particular war is brought to an end, the state of war, of always finding a new pretext to hostilities, is not terminated. Nor can this be declared wrong, considering the fact that in the state of war each is the judge of his own case. But the obligation which men in a lawless condition have under the natural law which requires them to abandon the state of nature does not quite apply to states under the law of nations, for as states they already have an internal juridical constitution and have thus 356 outgrown compulsion from others to submit to a more extended lawful constitution according to their ideas of right. This is true in spite of the fact that reason from its throne of supreme morally legislating authority absolutely condemns war as a legal recourse and makes a state of peace a direct duty, even though peace cannot be established or secured except by a compact among nations.

---

*A Bulgarian prince gave the following answer to the Greek emperor who good-naturedly suggested that they settle their difference by a duel: "A smith who has tongs won't pluck the glowing iron from the fire with his bare hands."

For these reasons there must be a league of a particular kind, which can be called a league of peace (*foedus pacificum*), and which would be distinguished from a treaty of peace (*pactum pacis*) by the fact that the latter terminates only one war, while the former seeks to make an end to all wars forever. This league does not tend to any dominion over the power of the state but only to the maintenance and security of the freedom of the state itself and of other states in league with it, without there being any need for them to submit to civil laws and their coercion, as men in a state of nature must submit.

The practicability (objective reality) of this idea of federation, which should gradually spread to all states and thus lead to perpetual peace, can be proved. For if fortune directs that a powerful and enlightened people can make itself a republic, which by its nature must be inclined to perpetual peace, this gives a fulcrum to the federative unification of other states so that they may adhere to it and thus secure freedom under the Idea of the law of nations. By more and more such associations, the federation may be gradually extended.

We may readily conceive that a people should say, "There ought to be no war among us, for we want to make ourselves into a state; that is, we want to establish a supreme legislative, executive, and judiciary power which will reconcile our differences peaceably." But when this state says, "There ought to be no war between myself and other states, even though I acknowledge no supreme legislative power by which our rights are mutually guaranteed," it is not at all clear on what I can base my confidence in my own rights unless it is the free federation, the surrogate of the civil social order, which reason necessarily associates with the concept of the law of nations — assuming that something is really meant by the latter.

The concept of a law of nations as a right to make war does not really mean anything, because it is then a law of deciding what is right by unilateral 357 maxims through force and not by universally valid public laws which restrict the freedom of each one. The only conceivable meaning of such a law of nations might be that it serves men right who are so inclined that they destroy each other and thus find perpetual peace in the vast grave that swallows both the atrocities and their perpetrators. For states in their relation to each other, there cannot be any reasonable way out of the lawless condition which entails only war except that they, like individual men, should give up their savage (lawless) freedom, adjust themselves to the constraints of public law, and thus establish a continuously growing state consisting of various nations (*civitas gentium*), which will ultimately include all the nations of the world. But since, with their conception of the law of nations, they do not will this, and reject in practice what is correct in theory, then if all is not to be lost there can be, in place of the positive Idea of a world-republic, only a negative surrogate of an alliance which averts war. While it endures and spreads and restrains the hostile inclinations which fear the reign of law, it is in constant peril of their breaking loose again.**Furor impius intus* . . . *fremit horridus ore cruento* (Virgil).[2]

Third Definitive Article for a Perpetual Peace "The Law of World Citizenship Shall Be Limited to Conditions of Universal Hospitality"

Here, as in the preceding articles, it is not a question of philanthropy but of 358 right. Hospitality means the right of a stranger not to be treated as an enemy when he arrives in the land of another. One may refuse to receive him when this can be done without causing his destruction; but, so long as he peacefully occupies his place, one may not treat him with hostility. It is not a question of being received as a guest in one's house, as a particularly benevolent convention would be needed in order to give him a claim to be treated as a guest for a certain length of time. It is rather a right of visit, a right of demanding of others that they admit one to their society. This right all men have by virtue of their common possession of the surface of the earth, where, as on a spherical surface, they cannot infinitely disperse and hence must finally tolerate the presence of each other. Originally no one had more right than another to a particular part of the earth.

Uninhabitable parts of the earth, the sea, and deserts divide this community of all men, but the ship and the camel (the desert ship) enable them to approach each other across these unruled regions and to establish communication by using the common right to the face of the earth, which belongs to human beings generally. The inhospitality of the inhabitants of coasts (for instance, of the Barbary Coast) in robbing ships in neighboring seas or of enslaving stranded travelers, or the inhospitality of the inhabitants of the deserts (for instance, the Bedouin Arabs) who see approach to nomadic tribes as conferring the right to plunder them, is thus opposed to natural law, even though it extends the right of hospitality (i.e., the privilege of foreign arrivals) no further than to conditions permitting them to seek to communicate with the inhabitants. In this way distant parts of the world can come into

---

*It would not ill become a people that has just terminated a war to decree, besides a day of thanksgiving, also a day of fasting in order to ask heaven, in the name of the state, for forgiveness for the great iniquity which the human race still goes on to perpetuate in refusing to submit to a lawful constitution in their relation to other peoples, preferring, from pride in their independence, to make use of the barbarous means of war even though they are not able to attain what is sought, namely, the rights of a single state. The thanksgivings for victory won during the war, the hymns which are sung to the God of Hosts (in good Israelitic manner), stand in equally sharp contrast to the moral idea of the Father of Men. For they not only show a sad enough indifference to the way in which nations seek their rights, but in addition express a joy in having annihilated a multitude of men or their happiness.

[2] Within, impious Rage, sitting on savage arms, his hands fast bound behind with a hundred brazen knots, shall roar in the ghastliness of bloodstained lips" (*Aeneid* I, 294–96, trans. H. Rushton Fairclough [Loeb Classical Library]

peaceable relations with each other, and these are finally publicly established by law. Thus the human race can gradually be brought closer and closer to a constitution establishing world citizenship.

But to this perfection compare the inhospitable actions of the civilized and especially of the commercial states of our part of the world. The injustice which they show to lands and peoples they visit (which is equivalent to conquering them) is carried by them to terrifying lengths. America, the lands inhabited by the Negro, the Spice Islands, the Cape, etc., were at the time of their discovery considered by these civilized intruders as lands without owners, for they counted the inhabitants as nothing. In East India (Hindustan), under the pretense of establishing economic undertakings they 359 brought in foreign soldiers and used them to oppress the natives, excited widespread wars among the various states, spread famine, rebellion, perfidy, and the whole litany of evils which afflict mankind.

China and Japan (Nippon), who have had experience with such guests, have wisely refused them entry, the former permitting them to approach their shores but not to enter, while the latter permit this approach to only one European people, the Dutch, but treat them like prisoners, not allowing them any communication with the inhabitants. The worst of this (or, to speak with the moralist, the best) is that all these outrages profit them nothing, since all these commercial ventures stand on the verge of collapse, and the Sugar Islands, that place of the most refined and cruel slavery, produce no real revenue except indirectly, only serving a not very praiseworthy purpose of furnishing sailors for war fleets and thus for the conduct of war in Europe. This service is rendered to powers which make a great show of their piety, and, while they drink injustice like water, they regard themselves as the elect in point of orthodoxy.

360 Since the narrower or wider community of the peoples of the earth has developed so far that a violation of rights in one place is felt throughout the world, the idea of a law of world citizenship is no high-flown or exaggerated notion. It is a supplement to the unwritten code of the civil and international law, indispensable for the maintenance of the public human rights and hence also of perpetual peace. One cannot flatter himself into believing one can approach this peace except under the condition outlined here.

FIRST SUPPLEMENT
OF THE GUARANTEE FOR PERPETUAL PEACE

The guarantee of perpetual peace is nothing less than that great artist, nature (*natura daedala rerum*). In her mechanical course we see that her aim 361 is to produce a harmony among men, against their will and indeed through their discord. As a necessity working according to laws we do not know, we 362 call it fate. But, considering its design in world history, we call it providence, inasmuch as we discern in it the profound wisdom of a higher cause which predetermines the course of nature and directs it to the objective final end of the human race. We do not observe or infer this providence in the cunning contrivances of nature, but, as in questions of the relation of the form of things to ends in general, we can and must supply it from our own minds in order to conceive of its possibility by analogy to actions of human art. The Idea of the relationship and harmony between these actions and the end which reason directly assigns to us is transcendent from a theoretical point of view; from a practical standpoint, with respect, for example, to the ideal of perpetual peace, the concept is dogmatic and its reality is well established, and thus the mechanism of nature may be employed to that end. The use of the word "nature" is more fitting to the limits of human reason and more modest than an expression indicating a providence unknown to us. This is especially true when we are dealing with questions of theory and not of religion, as at present, for human reason in questions of the relation of effects to their causes must remain within the limits of possible experience. On the other hand, the use of the word "providence" here intimates the possession of wings like those of Icarus, conducting us toward the secret of its unfathomable purpose.

Before we more narrowly define the guarantee which nature gives, it is necessary to examine the situation in which she has placed her actors on her vast stage, a situation which finally assures peace among them. Then we shall see how she accomplishes the latter. Her preparatory arrangements are: 363

1. In every region of the world she has made it possible for men to live.
2. By war she has driven them even into the most inhospitable regions in order to populate them.
3. By the same means, she has forced them into more or less lawful relations with each other.

That in the cold wastes by the Arctic Ocean the moss grows which the reindeer dig from the snow in order to make itself the prey or the conveyance of the Ostyak or Samoyed; or that the saline sandy deserts are inhabited by the camel which appears created as it were in order that they might not go unused — that is already wonderful. Still clearer is the end when we see how besides the furry animals of the Arctic there are also the seal, the walrus, and the whale which afford the inhabitants food from their flesh and warmth from their blubber. But the care of nature excites the greatest wonder when we see how she brings wood (though the inhabitants do not know whence it comes) to these barren climates, without which they would have neither canoes, weapons, nor huts, and when we see how these natives are so occupied with their war against the animals that they live at peace with each other — but what drove them there was presumably nothing else than war.

The first instrument of war among the animals which man learned to tame and to domesticate was the horse (for the elephant belongs to later times, to the luxury of already established states). The art of cultivating certain types of plants (grain) whose original characteristics we do not know, and the increase and improvement of fruits by transplantation and grafting (in Europe perhaps only the crab apple and the wild pear), could arise only under conditions prevailing in already established states where property was secure. Before this could take place, it was necessary that men who had first subsisted in anarchic freedom by hunting,* fishing, and sheepherding should have been forced into an agricultural life. Then salt and iron were discovered. These were perhaps the first articles of commerce for the various peoples and were sought far and wide; in this way a peaceful traffic among nations was established, and thus understanding, conventions, and peaceable relations were established among the most distant peoples.

364

As nature saw to it that men *could* live everywhere in the world, she also despotically willed that they *should* do so, even against their inclination and without this *ought* being based on a concept of a duty to which they were bound by a moral law. She chose war as the means to this end. So we see peoples whose common language shows that they have a common origin. For instance, the Samoyeds on the Arctic Ocean and a people with a similar language a thousand miles away in the Altaian Mountains are separated by a Mongolian people adept at horsemanship and hence at war; the latter drove the former into the most inhospitable arctic regions where they certainly would not have spread of their own accord.† Again, it is the same with Finns who in the most northerly part of Europe are called Lapps; Goths and Sarmatians have separated them from the Hungarians to whom they are related in language. What can have driven the Eskimos, a race entirely distinct from all others in America and perhaps descended from primeval European adventurers, so far into the North, or the Pescherais as far south as Tierra del Fuego, if it were not war which nature uses to populate the whole earth? War itself requires no special motive but appears to be engrafted on human nature; it passes even for something noble, to which the love of glory impels men quite apart from any selfish urges. Thus among the American savages just as much as among those of Europe during the age of chivalry,

365

*Among all modes of life there is undoubtedly none more opposed to a civilized constitution than that of hunting, because families which must dwell separately soon become strangers and, scattered in extensive forests, also enemies, since each needs a great deal of space for obtaining food and clothing. The Noachic ban on blood (Genesis IX, 4–6) (which was imposed by the baptized Jews as a condition on the later Christians who were converted from heathenism, though in a different connection — see The Acts XV, 20; XXI, 25) seems to have been originally nothing more than a prohibition against the hunting life, because here raw flesh must often have been eaten; when the latter was forbidden, so also was the former.

†One could ask: If nature willed that these icy coasts should not remain uninhabited, what would become of the inhabitants if nature ever failed (as might be expected) to bring driftwood to them? For it is reasonable to believe that, in the progress of civilization, the occupants of the temperate zones would make better use of the wood along rivers than simply to let it fall into the water and be carried to the sea. I answer: If nature will first have compelled them to peace, the dwellers along the Ob, the Yenisei, or the Lena will bring it to them commercially, exchanging it for animal products in which the sea around the arctic coasts abounds.

military valor is held to be of great worth in itself, not only during war (which is natural) but in order that there should be war. Often war is waged only in order to show valor; thus an inner dignity is ascribed to war itself, and even some philosophers have praised it as an ennoblement of humanity, forgetting the pronouncement of the Greek who said, "War is an evil inasmuch as it produces more wicked men than it takes away." So much for the measures nature takes to lead the human race, considered as a class of animals, to her own end.

Now we come to the question concerning that which is most essential in the design of perpetual peace: What has nature done with regard to this end which man's own reason makes his duty? That is, what has nature done to favor man's moral purpose, and how has she guaranteed (by compulsion but without prejudice to his freedom), that he shall do that which he ought to but does not do under the laws of freedom? This question refers to all three phases of public law, namely, civil law, the law of nations, and the law of world citizenship. If I say of nature that she wills that this or that occur, I do not mean that she imposes a duty on us to do it, for this can be done only by free practical reason; rather I mean that she herself does it, whether we will or not (*fata volentem ducunt, nolentem trahunt.* – Seneca. [Fates lead the willing, drive the unwilling].)

1. Even if a people were not forced by internal discord to submit to public laws, war would compel them to do so, for we have already seen that nature has placed each people near another which presses upon it, and against this it must form itself into a state in order to defend itself. Now the republican   366
constitution is the only one entirely fitting to the rights of man. But it is the most difficult to establish and even harder to preserve, so that many say a republic would have to be a nation of angels, because men with their selfish inclinations are not capable of a constitution of such sublime form. But precisely with these inclinations nature comes to the aid of the general will established on reason, which is revered even though impotent in practice. Thus it is only a question of a good organization of the state (which does lie in man's power), whereby the powers of each selfish inclination are so arranged in oppostition that one moderates or destroys the ruinous effect of the other. The consequence for reason is the same as if none of them existed, and man is forced to be a good citizen even if not a morally good person.

The problem of organizing a state, however hard it may seem, can be solved even for a race of devils, if only they are intelligent. The problem is: "Given a multitude of rational beings requiring universal laws for their preservation, but each of whom is secretly inclined to exempt himself from them, to establish a constitution in such a way that, although their private intentions conflict, they check each other, with the result that their public conduct is the same as if they had no such intentions."

A problem like this must be capable of solution; it does not require that we know how to attain the moral improvement of men but only that we should

know the mechanism of nature in order to use it on men, organizing the
conflict of the hostile intentions present in a people in such a way that they
must compel themselves to submit to coercive laws. Thus a state of peace is
established in which laws have force. We can see, even in actual states, which
are far from perfectly organized, that in their foreign relations they approach
that which the idea of right prescribes. This is so in spite of the fact that the
intrinsic element of morality is certainly not the cause of it. (A good constitution is not to be expected from morality, but, conversely, a good moral culture
of a people is to be expected only under a good constitution.) Instead of
genuine morality, the mechanism of nature brings it to pass through selfish
inclinations, which naturally conflict outwardly but which can be used by
367 reason as a means for making room for its own end, the sovereignty of law,
and, as concerns the state, for promoting and securing internal and external
peace.

This, then, is the truth of the matter: Nature inexorably wills that the right
should finally triumph. What we neglect to do comes about by itself, though
with great inconveniences to us. "If you bend the reed too much, you break
it; and he who attempts too much attempts nothing" (Bouterwek).

2. The idea of international law presupposes the separate existence of
many independent but neighboring states. Although this condition is itself a
state of war (unless a federative union prevents the outbreak of hostilities),
this is rationally preferable to the amalgamation of states under one superior
power, as this would end in one universal monarchy, and laws always lose in
vigor what government gains in extent; hence a soulless despotism falls into
anarchy after stifling the seeds of the good. Nevertheless, every state, or its
ruler, desires to establish lasting peace in this way, aspiring if possible to rule
the whole world. But nature wills otherwise. She employs two means to
separate peoples and to prevent them from mixing: differences of language
and of religion.* These differences involve a tendency to mutual hatred and
pretexts for war, but the progress of civilization and men's gradual approach
to greater harmony in their principles finally lead to peaceful agreement.
This is not like that peace which despotism (in the burial ground of freedom)
produces through a weakening of all powers; it is, on the contrary, produced
and maintained by their equilibrium in liveliest competition.

368   3. Just as nature wisely separates nations, which the will of every state,
sanctioned by the principles of international law, would gladly unite by
artifice or force, nations which could not have secured themselves against
violence and war by means of the law of world citizenship unite because of

---

*Difference of religion—a singlular expression! It is precisely as if one spoke of different
moralities. There may very well be different kinds of historical faiths attached to different means
employed in the promotion of religion, and they belong merely in the field of learned investigation. Similarly there may be different religious texts (Zendavesta, the Veda, the Koran, etc.), but
such differences do not exist in religion, there being only one religion valid for all men and in all
ages. These can, therefore, be nothing else than the accidental vehicles of religion, thus changing with times and places.

mutual interest. The spirit of commerce, which is incompatible with war, sooner or later gains the upper hand in every state. As the power of money is perhaps the most dependable of all the powers (means) included under the state power, states see themselves forced, without any moral urge, to promote honorable peace and by mediation to prevent war wherever it threatens to break out. They do so exactly as if they stood in perpetual alliances, for great offensive alliances are in the nature of the case rare and even less often successful.

In this manner nature guarantees perpetual peace by the mechanism of human passions. Certainly she does not do so with sufficient certainty for us to predict the future in any theoretical sense, but adequately from a practical point of view, making it our duty to work toward this end, which is not just a chimerical one.

SECOND SUPPLEMENT
SECRET ARTICLE FOR PERPETUAL PEACE

A secret article in transactions under public law is objectively (i.e., from the standpoint of its content) a contradiction. Subjectively, however, a secret clause can be present in a transaction because the persons who dictate it might find it inconvenient to their dignity to declare openly that they are its authors.

The only article of this kind is contained in the statement: "The opinions of philosophers on the conditions of the possibility of public peace shall be consulted by those states armed for war."

But it appears humiliating to the legislative authority of a state, to whom we must naturally attribute the utmost wisdom, to seek instruction from subjects (the philosophers) on principles of conduct toward other states. It is, nevertheless, very advisable to do so. Therefore, the state tacitly and secretly 369 invites them to give their opinions, that is, the state will let them publicly and freely talk about the general maxims of warfare and of the establishment of peace (for they will do that of themselves, provided they are not forbidden to do so). It does not require a particular convention among states to see that this is done, since their agreement on this point lies in an obligation already established by universal human reason which is morally legislative.

I do not mean that the state should give the principles of philosophers any preference over the decisions of lawyers (the representatives of the state power); I only ask that they be given a hearing. The lawyer, who has made not only the scales of right but also the sword of justice his symbol, generally uses the latter not merely to keep back all foreign influences from the former; but if the scale does not sink the way he wishes, he also throws the sword into it (*vae victis*), a practice to which he often has the greatest temptation because he is not also a philosopher, even in morality. His office is only to apply positive laws, not to inquire whether they might not need improvement. The administrative function, which is the lower one in his faculty, he counts as the highest because it is invested with power (as is the case also with the other faculties [of medicine and theology]). The philosophical faculty occupies a very low rank against this allied power. Thus it is said of philosophy, for example, that she is the handmaiden to theology, and the other faculties claim as much. But one does not see distinctly whether she precedes her mistress with a flambeau or follows bearing her train.

That kings should philosophize or philosophers become kings is not to be expected. Nor is it to be wished, since the possession of power inevitably corrupts the untrammeled judgment of reason. But kings or kinglike peoples which rule themselves under laws of equality should not suffer the class of philosophers to disappear or to be silent, but should let them speak openly. This is indispensable to the enlightenment of the business of government, and, since the class of philosophers is by nature incapable of plotting and lobbying, it is above suspicion of being made up of propagandists.

APPENDIX I
ON THE OPPOSITION BETWEEN MORALITY AND POLITICS WITH RESPECT TO PERPETUAL PEACE

370   Taken objectively, morality is in itself practical, being the totality of unconditionally mandatory laws according to which we ought to act. It would obviously be absurd, after granting authority to the concept of duty, to pretend that we cannot do our duty, for in that case this concept would itself drop out of morality (*ultra posse nemo obligatur*—no one is obligated to do more than he can.) Consequently, there can be no conflict of politics, as a practical doctrine of right, with ethics, as a theoretical doctrine of right. That is to say, there is no conflict of practice with theory, unless by ethics we mean a general doctrine of prudence, which would be the same as a theory of the maxims for choosing the most fitting means to accomplish the purposes of self-interest. But to give this meaning to ethics is equivalent to denying that there is any such thing at all.

Politics says, "Be ye wise as serpents"; morality adds, as a limiting condition, "and guileless as doves." If these two injunctions are incompatible in a single command, then politics and morality are really in conflict; but if these two qualities ought always to be united, the thought of contrariety is absurd, and the question as to how the conflict between morals and politics is to be resolved cannot even be posed as a problem. Although the proposition, "Honesty is the best policy," implies a theory which practice unfortunately often refutes, the equally theoretical, "Honesty is better than any policy," is beyond refutation and is indeed the indispensable condition of policy.

The tutelary divinity of morality yields not to Jupiter, for this tutelary divinity of force still is subject to fate. That is, reason is not yet sufficiently enlightened to survey the entire series of predetermining causes, and such vision would be necessary for one to be able to foresee with certainty the happy or unhappy effects which follow human actions by the mechanism of nature (though we know enough to have hope that they will accord with our wishes). But what we have to do in order to remain in the path of duty (according to rules of wisdom) reason instructs us by her rules, and her teaching suffices for attaining the ultimate end.

Now the practical man, to whom morality is merely theory even though he 371 concedes that it can and should be followed, ruthlessly renounces our good-natured hope [that it will be followed]. He does so because he pretends to have seen in advance that man, by his nature, will never will what is required for realizing the end which leads him to perpetual peace. Certainly the will of each individual to live under a juridical constitution according to principles of freedom (i.e., the distributive unity of the will of all) is not sufficient to this end. That all together should will this condition (i.e., the collective unity of the united will) — a solution to this troublous problem — is also required. Thus a whole of civil society is formed. But since a uniting cause must supervene upon the variety of particular volitions in order to produce a common will from them, establishing this whole is something that no one individual in the group can perform; hence in the practical execution of this idea we can count on nothing but force to establish the juridical condition, on the compulsion of which public law will later be established. We can scarcely hope to find in the lawgiver a moral intention sufficient to induce him to commit to the general will the establishment of a legal constitution after he has formed the nation from a horde of savages; therefore, we cannot but expect (in practice) to find in execution wide deviations from this Idea (in theory).

It will then be said that he who once has power in his hands will not allow the people to prescribe laws for him; a state which once is able to stand under no external laws will not submit to the decision of other states questions of the way in which it seeks its rights against them; and one continent, which feels itself superior to another, even though the other does not interfere with it, will not neglect to increase its power by robbery or even conquest. Thus all theoretical plans of civil and international laws and laws of world citizenship vanish into empty and impractical ideas, while practice based on empirical principles of human nature, not blushing to draw its maxims from the usages of the world, can alone hope to find a sure ground for its political edifice.

If there is no freedom and no morality based on it, and everything which 372 occurs or can occur happens by the mere mechanism of nature, certainly politics (which is the art of using this mechanism for ruling men) is the whole of practical wisdom, and the concept of right is an empty thought. But if we find it necessary to connect the latter with politics, and even to raise it to a limiting condition thereon, the possibility of their being united must be conceded. I can easily conceive of a moral politician (i.e., one who so chooses political principles that they are consistent with those of morality); but I cannot conceive of a political moralist, one who forges a morality in such a way that it conforms to the statesman's advantage.

When a remediable defect is found in the constitution of the state or in its relations to others, the principle of the moral politician will be that it is a duty, especially of the rulers of the state, to inquire how it can be remedied as soon as possible in a way conforming to natural law as a model presented by reason; this he will do even if it costs self-sacrifice. But it would be absurd to demand that every defect be immediately and impetuously changed, since the disruption of the bonds of a civil society or a union of world citizens before a better constitution is ready to take its place is against all politics agreeing with morality. But it can be demanded that at least the maxim of the necessity of such a change should be taken to heart by those in power so that they may continuously approach the goal of the constitution that is best under laws of right. A state may exercise a republican rule, even though by its present constitution it has a despotic sovereignty; until gradually the people becomes susceptible to the influence simply of the idea of the authority of law (as if it possessed physical power) and thus is found fit to be its own legislator (as its own legislation is originally established on law). If a violent revolution, engendered by a bad constitution, introduces by illegal means a more legal constitution, to lead the people back to the earlier constitution would not be permitted; but, while the revolution lasted, each person who openly or covertly shared in it would have justly incurred the punishment due to those
373 who rebel. As to the external relations of states, a state cannot be expected to renounce its constitution even though it is a despotic one (which has the advantage of being stronger in relation to foreign enemies) so long as it is exposed to the danger of being swallowed up by other states. Thus even in the case of the intention to improve the constitution, postponement to a more propitious time may be permitted.*

It may be that despotizing moralists, in practice blundering, often violate rules of political prudence through measures they adopt or propose too precipitately; but experience will gradually retrieve them from their infringement of nature and lead them on to a better course. But the moralizing politician, by glossing over principles of politics which are opposed to the right with the pretext that human nature is not capable of the good as reason prescribes it, only makes reform impossible and perpetuates the violation of law.

*These are permissive laws of reason. Public law laden with injustice must be allowed to stand either until everything is of itself ripe for complete reform or until this maturity has been brought about by peaceable means; for a legal constitution, even though it be right to only a low degree, is better than none at all, the anarchic condition which would result from precipitate reform. Political wisdom, therefore, will make it a duty to introduce reforms which accord with the ideal of public law. But even when nature herself produces revolutions, political wisdom will not employ them to legitimize still greater oppression. On the contrary, it will use them as a call of nature for fundamental reforms to produce a lawful constitution founded upon principles of freedom, for only such a constitution is durable.

Instead of possessing the *practical science* they boast of, these politicians have only *practices;* they flatter the power which is then ruling so as not to be remiss in their private advantage, and they sacrifice the nation and, where possible, the whole world. This is the way of all professional lawyers (not legislators) when they go into politics. Their task is not to reason too nicely about the legislation but to execute the current commands on the statute books; consequently, the legal constitution in force at any time is to them the best, but when it is amended from above, this amendment always seems best too. Thus everything is preserved in its accustomed mechanical order. Their adroitness in fitting into all circumstances gives them the illusion of being 374 able to judge constitutional principles according to concepts of right (thus not empirically but a priori). They make a great show of understanding *men* (which is certainly something to be expected of them, since they have to deal with so many) without understanding *man* and what can be made of him, for they lack the higher point of view of anthropological observation which is needed for this. If with these ideas they go into civil and international law, as reason prescribes it, they take this step in a spirit of chicanery, for they still follow their accustomed mechanical routine of despotically imposed coercive laws in a field where only concepts of reason can establish a legal compulsion according to the principles of freedom, and where for the first time a justly durable constitution is possible. In this field the pretended practical man thinks he can solve the problem of establishing such a constitution without the rational Idea but solely from the experience he has had with what was previously the most lasting constitution — a constitution which in many cases was opposed to law.

The maxims which he makes use of (though he does not divulge them) are, roughly speaking, the following sophisms:

1. *Fac et excusa.* Seize every favorable opportunity for usurping the right of the state over its own people or over a neighboring people; the justification will be easier and more elegant *ex post facto*, and the power can be more easily glossed over especially when the supreme power in the state is also the legislative authority which must be obeyed without argument. It is much more difficult to do violence when one has first to wait upon the consideration of convincing arguments and to meet them with counterarguments. Boldness itself gives the appearance of inner conviction of the legitimacy of the deed, and the God of success is afterward the best advocate.

2. *Si fecisti, nega.* What you have committed, deny that it was your fault — for instance, that you have brought your people to despair and hence to rebellion. Rather assert that it was due to the obstinacy of your subjects; or, if you have conquered a neighboring nation, say that the fault lies in the nature 375 of man, who, if not met by force, can be counted on to make use of it to conquer you.

3. *Divide et impera.* That is, if there are certain privileged persons in your nation who have chosen you as their chief (*primus inter pares*), set them at variance with one another and embroil them with the people. Show the latter

visions of greater freedom, and all will soon depend on your untrammeled will. Or if it is foreign states that concern you, it is a pretty safe means to sow discord among them so that, by seeming to protect the weaker, you can conquer them one after another.

Certainly no one is now the dupe of these political maxims, for they are already universally known. Nor are they blushed at as if their injustice were too glaring, for great powers blush only at the judgment of other great powers but not at that of the common masses. It is not that they are ashamed of revealing such principles (for all of them are in the same boat with respect to the morality of their maxims); they are ashamed only when these maxims fail, for they still have political honor which cannot be disputed — and this honor is the aggrandizement of their power by whatever means.

All these twistings and turnings of an immoral doctrine of prudence in leading men from their natural state of war to a state of peace prove at least 376 that men in both their private and their public relationships cannot reject the concept of right or trust themselves openly to establish politics merely on the artifices of prudence. Nor do they refuse obedience to the concept of public law (this is especially conspicuous in the case of international law); on the contrary they give all due honor to it, even when they are inventing a hundred pretenses and subterfuges to escape from it in practice, imputing its authority, as the source and union of all laws, to crafty force. Let us put an end to this sophism, if not to the injustice it protects, and force the false representatives of power to confess that they do not plead in favor of the right but in favor of might. This is revealed in the imperious tone they assume as if they themselves could command the right. Let us remove the delusion by which they and others are duped, and discover the supreme principle from which the intention to perpetual peace stems. Let us show that everything evil which stands in its way derives from the fact that the political moralist begins where the moral politician would correctly leave off, and that, since he thus subordinates principles to the end (putting the cart before the horse), he vitiates his own purpose of bringing politics into agreement with morality.

To make practical philosophy self-consistent, it is necessary, first, to de- 377 cide the question: In problems of practical reason, must we begin from its material principles (i.e., the end as the object of choice)? Or should we begin from the formal principles of pure reason (i.e., from the principle which is concerned solely with freedom in outer relations and which reads, "So act that you can will that your maxim could become a universal law, regardless of the end")?

Without doubt it is the latter which has precedence, for as a principle of law it has unconditional necessity. On the other hand, the former is obligatory only if we presuppose the empirical conditions of the proposed end (i.e., its practicability). Thus if this end (in this case, perpetual peace) is a duty, it must be derived from the formal principle of the maxims of external actions. The first principle, that of the political moralist, pertaining to civil and international law and the law of world citizenship, is merely a problem of technique (*problema technicum*); the second, as the problem of the moral politician to whom it is an ethical problem (*problema morale*), is far removed from the other in its method of leading toward perpetual peace, which is wished for not merely as a material good but also as a condition issuing from an acknowledgment of duty.

For the solution of the former, the problem of political prudence, much knowledge of nature is required so that its mechanism may be employed toward the desired end; yet all this is uncertain in its results for perpetual peace, with whatever sphere of public law we are concerned. It is uncertain, for example, whether the people are better kept in obedience and maintained in prosperity by severity or by the charm of distinctions which flatter their vanity, by the power of one or the union of various chiefs, or perhaps merely by a serving nobility or by the power of the people. History furnishes us with contradictory examples from all governments (with the exception of the truly republican, which can alone appeal to the mind of a moral politician). Still more uncertain is an international law allegedly erected on the statutes of ministries. It is, in fact, a word without meaning, resting as it does on compacts which, in the very act of being concluded, contain secret reservations for their violation.

On the other hand, the solution of the second problem, that of political wisdom, presses itself upon us, as it were; it is clear to everyone and puts to shame all affectation. It leads directly to the end, but, remembering discretion, it does not precipitately hasten to do so by force; rather, it continuously 378 approaches it under the conditions offered by favorable circumstances.

Then it may be said, "Seek ye first the kingdom of pure practical reason and its righteousness, and your end (the blessing of perpetual peace) will necessarily follow." For it is the peculiarity of morals, especially with respect to its principles of public law and hence in relation to a politics known a priori, that the less it makes conduct depend on the proposed end (i.e., the intended material or moral advantage), the more it agrees with it in general. This is because it is the universal will given a priori (in a nation or in the relations among different nations) which determines the law among men, and if practice consistently follows it, this will can also, by the mechanism of nature, cause the desired result and make the concept of law effective. So, for instance, it is a principle of moral politics that a people should unite into a state according to juridical concepts of freedom and equality, and this principle is based not on prudence but on duty. Political moralists may argue as much as they wish about the natural mechanism of a mass of men forming a society, assuming a mechanism which would weaken those principles and vitiate their end; or they may seek to prove their assertions by examples of poorly organized constitutions of ancient and modern times (for instance, of democracies without representative systems). They deserve no hearing, particularly as such a pernicious theory may itself occasion the evil which it prophesies, throwing human beings into one class with all other living machines, differing from them only in their consciousness that they are not free, which makes them, in their own judgment, the most miserable of all beings in the world.

The true but somewhat boastful sentence which has become proverbial, *Fiat iustitia, pereat mundus* ("Let justice reign even if all the villains in the world should perish from it"), is a stout principle of right which cuts asunder the whole tissue of artifice or force. But it should not be misunderstood as a permission to use one's own right with extreme rigor (which would conflict with ethical duty); it should be understood as the obligation of those in power not to limit or to extend anyone's right through sympathy or disfavor for others. This requires, first, an internal constitution of the state erected on pure principles of right, and, second, a convention of the state with other near or distant states (analogous to a universal state) for the legal settlement of their differences. This implies only that political maxims must not be derived from the welfare or happiness which a single state expects from obedience to them, and thus not from the end which one of them proposes for itself. That is, they must not be deduced from volition as the supreme yet empirical principle of political wisdom, but rather from the pure concept of the duty of right, from the *ought* whose principle is given a priori by pure reason, regardless of what the physical consequences may be. The world will by no means perish by a diminution in the number of evil men. Moral evil has the inescapable property of being opposed to and destructive of its own purposes (especially in the relationships between evil men); thus it gives place to the moral principle of the good, though only through a slow progress.

Thus objectively, or in theory, there is no conflict between morals and politics. Subjectively, however, in the selfish propensity of men (which should not be called "practice" as this would imply that it rested on rational maxims), this conflict will always remain. Indeed, it should remain, because it serves as a whetstone of virtue, whose true courage (by the principle, *tu ne cede malis, sed contra audentior ito* — yield not to evils, but go against the stronger — Vergil) in the present case does not so much consist in defying with strong resolve evils and sacrifices which must be undertaken along with the conflict, but rather in detecting and conquering the crafty and far more dangerously deceitful and treasonable principle of evil in ourselves, which puts forward the weakness of human nature as justification for every transgression.

In fact, the political moralist may say: the ruler and people, or nation and nation, do each other no injustice when by violence or fraud they make war on each other, although they do commit injustice in general in that they refuse to respect the concept of right, which alone could establish perpetual peace. For since the one does transgress his duty against the other, who is likewise lawlessly disposed toward him, each gets what he deserves when they destroy each other. But enough of the race still remains to let this game continue into the remotest ages in order that posterity, someday, might take these perpetrators as a warning example. Hence Providence is justified in the history of the world, for the moral principle in man is never extinguished, while with advancing civilization reason grows pragmatically in its capacity to realize ideas of law. But at the same time the culpability for the transgressions also grows. If we assume that humanity never will or can be improved, the only thing which a theodicy seems unable to justify is creation itself, the fact that a race of such corrupt beings ever was on earth. But the point of view necessary for such an assumption is far too high for us, and we cannot theoretically support our philosophical concepts of the supreme power which is inscrutable to us.

To such dubious consequences we are inevitably driven if we do not assume that pure principles of right have objective reality (i.e., that they may be applied), and that the people in a state and, further, states themselves in their mutual relations should act according to them, whatever objections empirical politics may raise. Thus true politics can never take a step without rendering homage to morality. Though politics by itself is a difficult art, its union with morality is no art at all, for this union cuts the knot which politics could not untie when they were in conflict. The rights of men must be held sacred, however much sacrifice it may cost the ruling power. One cannot compromise here and seek the middle course of a pragmatic conditional law between the morally right and the expedient. All politics must bend its knee before the right. But by this it can hope slowly to reach the stage where it will shine with an immortal glory.

APPENDIX II
OF THE HARMONY WHICH THE TRANSCENDENTAL CONCEPT OF PUBLIC RIGHT ESTABLISHES BETWEEN MORALITY AND POLITICS

If, like the teacher of law, I abstract from all the material of public law (i.e., 381 abstract from the various empirically given relationships of men in the state or of states to each other), there remains only the form of publicity, the possibility of which is implied by every legal claim, since without it there can be no justice (which can only be conceived as publicly known) and thus no right, since it can be conferred only in accordance with justice. Every legal claim must be capable of publicity. Since it is easy to judge whether it is so in a particular case (i.e., whether it can be compatible with the principles of the agent), this gives an easily applied criterion found a priori in reason, by which the falsity (opposition to law) of the pretended claim (*praetensio iuris*) can, as it were, be immediately known by an experiment of pure reason.

Having set aside everything empirical in the concept of civil or international· law (such as the wickedness in human nature which necessitates coercion), we can call the following proposition the transcendental formula of public law: "All actions relating to the right of other men are unjust if their maxim is not consistent with publicity."

This principle is to be regarded not merely as ethical (as belonging to the doctrine of virtue) but also as juridical (concerning the right of man). A maxim which I cannot divulge without defeating my own purpose must be kept secret if it is to succeed; and, if I cannot publicly avow it without inevitably exciting universal opposition to my project, the necessary and universal opposition which can be foreseen a priori is due only to the injustice with which the maxim threatens everyone. This principle is, furthermore, only negative (i.e., it only serves for the recognition of what is not just to others). Like an axiom, it is indemonstrably certain and, as will be seen in the following examples of public law, easily applied.

1. In the law of the state (*ius civitatis*) or domestic law, there is a question which many hold to be difficult to answer, yet it is easily solved by the transcendental principle of publicity. The question is: "Is rebellion a legitimate means for a people to employ in throwing off the yoke of an alleged tyrant (*non titulo, sed exercitio talis*)?" The rights of the people are injured and no injustice befalls the tyrant when he is deposed. There can be no doubt on this point. Nevertheless, it is in the highest degree illegitimate for the subjects to seek their rights in this way. If they fail in the struggle and are then subjected to severest punishment, they cannot complain about injustice any more than the tyrant could if they had succeeded.

If one wishes to decide this question by a dogmatic deduction of legal grounds, there can be much arguing pro and con; only the transcendental principle of the publicity of public law can free us of this prolixity. According to this principle, a people would ask itself before the establishment of the civil contract whether it dare to publish the maxim of its intention to revolt occasionally. It is clear that if, in the establishment of a constitution, the condition is made that the people may in certain cases employ force against its chief, the people would have to pretend to a legitimate power over him, and then he would not be the chief. Or if both are made the condition of the establishment of the state, no state would be possible, though to establish it was the purpose of the people. The illegitimacy of rebellion is thus clear from the fact that its maxim, if openly acknowledged, would make its own purpose impossible. Therefore, it would have to be kept secret.

This secrecy, however, is not incumbent upon the chief of the state. He can openly say that he will punish every rebellion with the death of the ring leaders, however much they may believe that he was the first to overstep the basic law; for when he knows he possesses irresistible power (which must be assumed to be the case in every civil constitution, because he who does not have enough power to protect the people against every other also does not have the right to command them), he need not fear vitiating his own purpose by publishing his maxims. If the revolt of the people succeeds, what has been said is still quite compatible with the fact that the chief, on retiring to the status of a subject, cannot begin a revolt for his restoration but need not fear being called to account for his earlier administration of the state.

2. We can speak of international law only under the presupposition of some law-governed condition (i.e., of the external condition under which right can really be awarded to man). For, being a public law, it contains in its very concept the public announcement of a general will which assigns to each his rights, and this *status iuridicus* must result from some compact which is not founded on laws of compulsion (as is the case of the compact from which a single state arises). Rather, it must be founded on a free and enduring association, like the previously mentioned federation of states. For without there being some juridical condition, which actively binds together the different physical or moral persons, there can be only private law; this is the situation met with in the state of nature. Now here there is a conflict of politics with morality (regarding the latter as a science of right), and the criterion of publicity again finds an easy application in resolving it, though only if the compact between the states has been made with the purpose of preserving peace between them and other states and not for conquest. The following cases of the antinomy between politics and morality occur (and they are stated with their solution).

a) "If one of these states has promised something to the other, such as aid, cession of some province, subsidies, and the like, and a case arises where the salvation of the state depends upon its being relieved of its promise, can it then consider itself in two roles: first as a sovereign (as it is responsible to no one in the state), and second as merely the highest official (who must give an account to the state)? From this dual capacity it would follow that in its latter role the state can relieve itself of what it has obliged itself to do in its former role." But if a state (or its chief) publicizes this maxim, others would natu- 384 rally avoid entering an alliance therewith or ally themselves with others so as to resist such pretensions. This proves that politics with all its cunning would defeat its purpose by sincerity; therefore, that maxim must be illegitimate.

b) "If a neighboring power becomes formidable by its acquisitions (*potentia tremenda*) and thus causes anxiety, can one assume because it *can* oppress that it *will*? And does this give the lesser power, in union with others, a right to attack it without having first been injured by it?" A state which made known that such was its maxim would produce the feared evil even more certainly and quickly, for the greater power would steal a march on the smaller. And the alliance of the smaller powers would be only a feeble reed against one who knew how to apply the maxim *divide et impera*. This maxim of political expediency, if made public, would necessarily defeat its own purpose, and hence it is illegitimate.

c) "If a smaller state is so situated as to break up the territory of a larger one, and continuous territory is necessary to the preservation of the larger, is the latter not justified in subjugating the smaller and in incorporating it?" We easily see that the greater power cannot afford to let this maxim become known; otherwise the smaller states would very early unite, or other powers would dispute the prey, and thus publicity would render this maxim impracticable. This is a sign that it is illegitimate. It may be unjust to a very high degree, for a small object of injustice does not prevent the injustice from being very great.

3. I say nothing about the law of world citizenship, for its analogy with international law makes its maxims a very simple matter to state and evaluate.

Thus in the principle of incompatibility between the maxims of international law and publicity we have a good distinguishing mark for recognizing the nonconformity of politics with morality (as a science of right). Now we 385 need to know the condition under which these maxims agree with the law of nations, for we cannot infer conversely that the maxims which bear publicity are therefore just, since no one who has decidedly superior power needs to conceal his plans. The condition of possibility of international law in general is this: a juridical condition must first exist. For without this there is no public law, since all law which one may think of outside of this, in the state of nature, is merely private law. We have seen that a federation of states which has for its sole purpose the maintenance of peace is the only juridical condition compatible with the freedom of the several states. Therefore the harmony of politics with morals is possible only in a federative alliance, and the latter is necessary and given a priori by the principles of right. Furthermore, all politics has for its juridical basis the establishment of this harmony to its greatest possible extent, and without this end all its sophisms are but folly and veiled injustice. This false politics outdoes the best Jesuit school in casuistry. It has *reservatio mentalis*, wording public compacts with such expressions as can on occasion be interpreted to one's own advantage (for example, it makes the distinction between *status quo de fait* and *de droit*). It has *probabilism*, attributing hostile intentions to others, or even making probabilities of their possible superior power into legal grounds for destroying other, peaceful, states. Finally, it has the *peccatum philosophicum* (*peccatillum, bagatelle*), holding it to be only a trifle when a small state is swallowed up in order that a much larger one may thereby approach more nearly an alleged greater good for the world as a whole.*

The duplicity of politics in respect to morality, in using one branch of it or the other for its purposes, furthers these sophistic maxims. These branches

---

*The precedents for such maxims may be seen in Counsellor Garve's treatise, *On the Union of Mortality with Politics* (1788). This worthy scholar admits in the beginning that he is not able to solve the problem completely. But to approve of this union while admitting that one cannot meet all objections which may be raised against it seems to show more tolerance than is advisable toward those who are inclined to abuse it.

are philanthropy and respect for the rights of men, and both are duty. The former is a conditional duty, while the latter is an unconditional and absolutely mandatory duty. One who wishes to give himself up to the sweet feeling of benevolence must make sure that he has not transgressed this absolute duty. Politics readily agrees with morality in its first branch (as ethics) in order to surrender the rights of men to their superiors. But with morality in the second branch (as a science of right), to which it must bend its knee, politics finds it advisable not to have any dealings, and rather denies it all reality, preferring to reduce all duties to mere benevolence. This artifice of a secretive politics would soon be unmasked by philosophy through publication of its maxims, if they only dared to allow the philosopher to publish his maxims.

In this regard I propose another affirmative and transcendental principle of public law, the formula of which is:

"All maxims which *stand in need* of publicity in order not to fail their end agree with politics and right combined."

For if they can attain their end only through publicity, they must accord with the public's universal end, happiness; and the proper task of politics is to promote this (i.e., to make the public satisfied with its condition). If, however, this end is attainable only by means of publicity (i.e., by removing all distrust in the maxims of politics), the latter must conform to the rights of the public, for only in this is the union of the goals of all possible.

The further development and discussion of this principle I must postpone to another occasion. But that it is a transcendental formula is to be seen from the exclusion of all empirical conditions (of the doctrine of happiness) as material of the law, and from the reference it makes to the form of universal lawfulness.

If it is a duty to actualize (even if only through gradual approach in endless progress) the state of public law, and if there is well-grounded hope that this can actually be done, then perpetual peace, as the condition that will follow what has erroneously been called treaties of peace (but which in reality are only armistices) is not an empty Idea. On the contrary, as ways and means are gradually found, we hope at an ever-increasing pace, perpetual peace is a task that grows ever nearer to achievement.

XI
What Is Enlightenment?

Editor's Introduction

This classic manifesto of the ideal of freedom of thought and press was published in the *Berlinische Monatsschrift*, a leading periodical of the German Enlightenment, one month before Kant's *Idea for a Universal History* appeared in the same journal, but it could have been composed at any time during Kant's career. Though written before Kant's troubles with the Berlin government over his freedom to lecture and write on religious subjects, it anticipates the stand which ten years later he was to make against the restrictions imposed upon him. It lays down the conditions on which the political progress foreseen in the *Idea for a Universal History* and *Perpetual Peace* can be effectuated.

The translation is by the Editor and was first published by the University of Chicago Press, 1949, and republished in 1963 in Kant on History (Bobbs Merrill).

What Is Enlightenment?

Enlightenment is man's release from his self-incurred tutelage. Tutelage is man's inability to make use of his understanding without direction from another. Self-incurred is this tutelage when its cause lies not in lack of reason but in lack of resolution and courage to use it without direction from another. *Sapere aude!*[1] "Have courage to use your own reason!" — that is the motto of enlightenment.

Laziness and cowardice are the reasons why so great a portion of mankind, after nature has long since discharged them from external direction (*naturaliter maiorennes*), nevertheless remains under lifelong tutelage, and why it is so easy for others to set themselves up as their guardians. It is so easy not to be of age. If I have a book which understands for me, a pastor who has a conscience for me, a physician who decides my diet, and so forth, I need not trouble myself. I need not think, if I can only pay — others will readily undertake the irksome work for me.

That the step to competence is held to be very dangerous by the far greater portion of mankind (and by the entire fair sex) — quite apart from its being arduous — is seen to by those guardians who have so kindly assumed superintendence over them. After the guardians have first made their domestic cattle dumb and have made sure that these placid creatures will not dare take a single step without the harness of the cart by which they are confined, the guardians then show them the danger which threatens if they try to go alone.
36 Actually, however, this danger is not so great, for by falling a few times they would finally learn to walk alone. But an example of this failure makes them timid and ordinarily frightens them away from all further trials.

For any single individual to work himself out of the life under tutelage which has become almost his nature is very difficult. He has come to be fond of this state, and he is for the present really incapable of making use of his reason, for no one has ever let him try it out. Statutes and formulas, those mechanical tools of the rational employment, or rather misemployment, of his natural gifts, are the fetters of an everlasting tutelage. Whoever throws them off makes only an uncertain leap over the narrowest ditch because he is not accustomed to that sort of free motion. Therefore there are only few who

[1] "Dare to be wise!" (Horace, *Ars poetica*).

have succeeded by their own exercise of mind both in freeing themselves from incompetence and in achieving a steady pace.

But that the public should enlighten itself is more possible; indeed, if only freedom is granted, enlightenment is almost sure to follow, for there will always be some independent thinkers, even among the established guardians of the great masses, who, after throwing off the yoke of tutelage from their own shoulders, will disseminate the spirit of the rational appreciation of both their own worth and every man's vocation of thinking for himself. But be it noted that the public, which has first been brought under this yoke by their guardians, forces the guardians themselves to remain bound when it is incited to do so by some of the guardians who are themselves incapable of any enlightenment — so harmful is it to implant prejudices, for they later take vengeance on their cultivators (or at least on those whose ancestors had cultivated them). Thus the public can only slowly attain enlightenment. Perhaps a fall of personal despotism or of avaricious or tyrannical oppression may be accomplished by revolution, but never a true reform in ways of thinking. Rather, new prejudices will serve as well as old ones to harness the great unthinking masses.

For this enlightenment, however, nothing is required but freedom, and indeed the most harmless among all the things to which that term can properly be applied. It is the freedom to make public use of one's reason at every point. But I hear on all sides, "Do not argue!" The officer says: "Do not 37 argue, but drill!" The tax-collector: "Do not argue, but pay!" The cleric: "Do not argue, but believe!" Only one prince in the world says: "Argue as much as you will and about what you will, but obey!"

Everywhere there is restriction on freedom. But what sort of restriction is an obstacle to enlightenment, and what sort is not an obstacle but a promoter of it? I answer: The public use of one's reason must always be free, and it alone can bring about enlightenment among men. The private use of reason, on the other hand, may often be very narrowly restricted without particularly hindering the progress of enlightenment. By the public use of one's reason I understand the use which a person makes of it as a scholar before the reading public. Private use I call that which one may make of it in a particular civil post or office which is intrusted to him. Many affairs which are conducted in the interest of the community require a certain mechanism through which some members of the community must passively conduct themselves with an artificial unanimity, so that the government may direct them to public ends, or at least prevent them from frustrating those ends. Here argument is certainly not allowed — one must obey. But so far as a part of the mechanism regards himself at the same time as a member of the whole community or of a society of world-citizens, and thus in the role of a scholar who addresses the public (in the proper sense of the word) through his writings, he certainly can argue without hurting the affairs for which he is in part responsible as a passive member. While it would be ruinous for an officer in service to quibble about the suitability or utility of a command given to him by his superior, he must obey; but the right to make remarks on errors in the military service and to lay them before the public for judgment cannot equitably be refused him as a scholar. The citizen cannot refuse to pay the taxes imposed to him; indeed, an impudent complaint at those levied on him can be punished as a scandal (as it could occasion general refractoriness). But the same person nevertheless does not act contrary to his duty as a citizen when, as a scholar,

38   he publicly expresses his thoughts on the inappropriateness or even the injustice of these levies. Similarly a clergyman is obligated to make his sermon to his pupils in catechism and his congregation conform to the symbol of the church which he serves, for he has been accepted on this condition. But as a scholar he has complete freedom, even the calling, to communicate to the public all his carefully tested and well-meaning thoughts on that which is erroneous in the symbol and to make suggestions for the better organization of the religious body and church. In doing this, there is nothing that could be laid as a burden on his conscience. For what he teaches as a consequence of his office as a representative of the church, this he considers something about which he has no freedom to teach according to his own lights; it is something which he is appointed to propound at the dictation of and in the name of another. He will say, "Our church teaches this or that; those are the proofs which it adduces." He thus extracts all practical uses for his congregation from statutes to which he himself would not subscribe with full conviction, but to the enunciation of which he can very well pledge himself because it is not impossible that truth lies hidden in them, and, in any case, there is at least nothing in them contradictory to inner religion. For if he believed he had found such in them, he could not conscientiously discharge the duties of his office; he would have to give it up. The use, therefore, which an appointed teacher makes of his reason before his congregation is merely private, because this congregation is only a domestic one (even if it be a large gathering); with respect to it, as a priest, he is not free, not can he be free, because he carries out the orders of another. But as a scholar, whose writings speak to his public, the world, the clergyman in the public use of his reason enjoys an unlimited freedom to use his own reason and to speak in his own person. That the guardians of the people (in spiritual things) should themselves be incompetent is an absurdity which amounts to the eternalization of absurdities.

But would not a society of clergymen, perhaps a church conference or a venerable classis (as they call themselves among the Dutch), be justified in obligating itself by oath to a certain unchangeable symbol in order to enjoy an

39   unceasing guardianship over each of its members and thereby over the people as a whole, and even to make it eternal? I answer that this is altogether impossible. Such a contract, made to shut off all further enlightenment from the human race, is absolutely null and void even if confirmed by the supreme power, by parliaments, and by the most ceremonious of peace treaties. An

age cannot bind itself and ordain to put the succeeding one into such a condition that it cannot extend its (at best very occasional) knowledge, purify itself of errors, and progress in general enlightenment. That would be a crime against human nature, the proper destination of which lies precisely in this progress; and the descendants would be fully justified in rejecting those decrees as having been made in an unwarranted and malevolent manner.

The touchstone of everything that can be concluded as a law for a people lies is the question whether the people could have imposed such a law on itself. Now such a religious compact might be possible for a short and definitely limited time, as it were, in expectation of a better. One might let every citizen, and especially the clergyman, in the role of scholar, make his comments freely and publicly (i.e., through writing) on the erroneous aspects of the present institution. The newly introduced order might last until insight into the nature of these things had become so general and widely approved that through uniting their voices (even if not unanimously) they could bring a proposal to the throne to take those congregations under protection which had united into a changed religious organization according to their better ideas, without, however, hindering others who wish to remain in the older. But to unite in a permanent religious institution which is not to be subject to doubt before the public even in the lifetime of one man, and thereby to make a period of time fruitless in the progress of mankind toward improvement, thus working to the disadvantage of posterity — that is absolutely forbidden. For himself (and only for a short time) a man can postpone enlightenment in what he ought to know, but to renounce it for himself and even more to renounce it for posterity is to injure and trample on the rights of mankind.

And what a people may not decree for itself can even less be decreed for ⁴⁰ them by a monarch, for his lawgiving authority rests on his uniting the general public will in his own. If he only sees to it that all true or alleged improvement stands together with civil order, he can leave it to his subjects to do what they find necessary for their spiritual welfare. This is not his concern, though it is incumbent on him to prevent, to the best of his ability, one of them from violently hindering another in determining and promoting this welfare. To meddle in these matters lowers his own majesty, since by the writings in which his subjects seek to present their views he may evaluate his own governance. He can do this when, with deepest understanding, he lays upon himself the reproach, *Caesar non est supra grammaticos*. Far more does he injure his own majesty when he degrades his supreme power by supporting the ecclesiastical despotism of some tyrants in his state over his other subjects.

If we are asked, "Do we now live in an *enlightened age?*" the answer is, "No," but we do live in an *age of enlightenment*. As things now stand, much is lacking which prevents men from being, or easily becoming, capable of using their own reason in religious matters correctly, with assurance and free from outside direction. But, on the other hand, we have clear indications that the field has now been opened wherein men may freely deal with these things and that the obstacles to general enlightenment or the release from self-imposed tutelage are gradually being reduced. In this respect, this is the age of enlightenment, or the century of Frederick.

A prince who does not find it unworthy of himself to say that he holds it to be his duty to prescribe nothing to men in religious matters but to give them complete freedom while renouncing the haughty name of *tolerance*, is himself enlightened and deserves to be esteemed by the grateful world and posterity as the first, at least from the side of government, who divested the human race of its tutelage and left each man free to make use of his reason in matters of conscience. Under him venerable ecclesiastics are allowed, in the role of scholars, and without infringing on their official duties, freely to submit for public testing their judgments and views which here and there diverge from the established symbol. And an even greater freedom is enjoyed by those who are restricted by no official duties. This spirit of freedom spreads beyond this land, even to those in which it must struggle with external obstacles erected by a government which misunderstands its own interest. For an example gives evidence to such a government that in freedom there is not the least cause for concern about public peace and the stability of the community. Men work themselves gradually out of barbarity if only intentional artifices are not made to hold them in it.

I have placed the main point of enlightenment—the escape of men from their self-incurred tutelage—chiefly in matters of religion because our rulers have no interest in playing the guardian with respect to the arts and sciences and also because religious incompetence is not only the most harmful but also the most degrading of all. But the manner of thinking of the head of a state who favors religious enlightenment goes farther, and he sees that there is no danger to his sovereignty in allowing his subjects to make public use of their reason and to publish their thoughts on a better formulation of his legislation and even their open-minded criticisms of the laws already made. Of this we have a shining example wherein no monarch is superior to him whom we honor.

But only one who is himself enlightened, is not afraid of shadows, and has a numerous and well-disciplined army to assure public peace can say: "Argue as much as you will, and about what you will, only obey!" A republic could not dare say such a thing. Here is shown a strange and unexpected trend in human affairs in which almost everything, looked at in the large, is paradoxical. A greater degree of civil freedom appears advantageous to the freedom of mind of the people, and yet it places inescapable limitations upon it; a lower degree of civil freedom, on the contrary, provides the mind with room for each man to extend himself to his full capacity. As nature has uncovered from under this hard shell the seed for which she most tenderly cares—the propensity and vocation to free thinking — this gradually works back upon the character of the people, who thereby gradually become capable of managing freedom; finally, it affects the principles of government, which finds it to its advantage to treat men, who are now more than machines, in accordance with their dignity.* 42

I. KANT

Königsberg, Prussia
September 30, 1784

*Today I read in the *Büschingsche Wöchentliche Nachrichten* for September 13 an announcement of the *Berlinische Monatsschrift* for this month, which cites the answer to the same question by Herr Mendelssohn. But this issue has not yet come to me; if it had, I would have held back the present essay, which is now put forth only in order to see how much agreement in thought can be brought about by chance.

Bibliographical Essay

The Introductions to the selections in this volume end with brief bibliographies which should be especially useful for beginning study. The following informal bibliography is a guide into more extensive and deeper study of Kant's philosophy, though it also includes titles of books which will be of help even when a reader is making his first acquaintance with Kant.

Over two thousand books and articles on Kant were published before his death in 1804. In our own times, an average of more than two hundred books and articles are added every year. A complete bibliography is impossible, but it would also be useless since there is so much that is repetitious, ephemeral, or misinformed. Even a bibliography of *good* books on which scholars might agree would be too long for practical purposes. This bibliography, designed for students and restricted (with four exceptions) to books in English, must be somewhat arbitrary and subjective in its selection and evaluations. I have tried (but failed) to limit the number of books cited (other than translations of Kant's works) to one hundred and have chosen mostly books published since the end of World War II, when there occurred a marked increase of interest in Kant's philosophy among American philosophers, and the study of Kant became a part of the standard curriculum in philosophy and the history of ideas.

I. TRANSLATIONS OF WORKS BY KANT

There is not yet a uniform complete edition of Kant's works in English, but one is planned for publication during the next decade. All the most important writings, however, have been repeatedly translated, and many of the books and papers of less importance exist in at least one English translation. Bibliographical information about the translations of the material included in this book is given at the end of the Editor's Introduction to each selection. Of Kant's writings not included in this volume we list the recommended translations. The order is approximately that of the publication of the original Kantian writings.

Universal Natural History and Theory of the Heavens (1755). The partial translation by William Hastie (1900) includes some other Kant writings on geology and astronomy. Also translated in full by Stanley L. Jaki (1981).

The Latin dissertations from 1755 to 1770 translated in *Kant's Latin Writings* (1987) by L. W. Beck and John A. Reuscher. (Two later unpublished Latin papers are included also in this volume.)

Proof of the False Subtlety of the Four Syllogistic Figures (1762), in T. K. Abbott, *Kant's Introduction to Logic* (1885).

The One Possible Basis for a Demonstration of the Existence of God (1762). Translated by Gordon Treash (1979) in the Abaris Janus series of bilingual editions of philosophical classics.

Observations on the Feeling of the Beautiful and Sublime (1764), translated by John T. Goldthwaite (1960).

Dreams of a Spirit-Seer (1766), translated by John Manolesco (New York, 1960) with a long introduction on Kant's interest in the occult.

On the First Ground of the Distinction of Directions in Space (1768). This important essay on incongruent counterparts, which determined the course of development of Kant's theory of space, is translated by John Handyside in his edition of *Kant's Inaugural Dissertation* (1929) and by D. E. Walford in *Selected Pre-Critical Writings* (1968).

Conjectural Beginning of Human History (1786), important both for Kant's philosophy of history and philosophy of religion, was translated by Emil Fackenheim and published in Beck's *Kant on History*[1] (1963).

What is Orientation in Thinking? (1786) in Beck's *Kant's Critique of Practical Reason and Other Writings on Moral Philosophy* (1949).

Metaphysical Foundations of Natural Science (1786), an important work transitional between the *Critique of Pure Reason* and the *Opus posthumum*, translated by James W. Ellington (1970).

First Introduction to the Critique of Judgment (1790) was discarded by Kant because of its length. It was published as a separate book by Kant's student J. S. Beck under the title *On Philosophy in General* and has been translated into English three times, most recently and skillfully by Werner Pluhar in his translation of the complete *Critique of Judgment* (1987).

On a Discovery According to Which Any New Critique of Pure Reason is Rendered Superfluous by an Earlier One (1790) was Kant's reply to J. A. Eberhard, a Wolffian philosopher, who asserted that Wolff had explained the possibility of synthetic a priori judgments. Translated by Henry E. Allison as appendix to his book *The Kant-Eberhard Controversy* (1973).

On the Failure of All Attempted Philosophical Theodicies (1791) is translated as an appendix to Michel Despland's *Kant on History and Religion* (1973).

Religion within the Limits of Reason Alone (1793), translated by H. H. Hudson and T. M. Greene (1935); the reprint in the Harper Torchbook series (1960) has an important introductory commentary by John R. Silber.

On the Old Saw: "That May be Right in Theory, but it Won't Hold in Practice," (1793) an interesting work in political theory, translated by E. B. Ashton (1974) and by H. B. Nisbet in *Kant's Political Writings*, edited by Hans Reiss (1970).

The End of All Things (1794), a strange and difficult essay in the philosophy of history, translated by Robert Anchor in Beck's *Kant on History* (1963).

Metaphysics of Morals (1797), consisting of two parts: I. *Metaphysical Elements of Justice*, translated by John Ladd (1965). Part II: *Theory of Virtue*, translated by Mary J. Gregor (1964).

On an Alleged Right to Lie out of Altruism (1797), in which Kant argued that it would be wrong to tell a lie even in order to save the life of an innocent person.[2] This little

---

[1] *Kant on History* includes also the translation by Robert Anchor of Kant's reviews of Herder's *Ideas for the Philosophy of the History of Mankind.*

[2] It is noteworthy that Kant does not deny this alleged right to lie because of any inconsistency with the categorical imperative; in fact his argument is very "un-Kantian," but a genuine Kantian argument can be given in support of this alleged right. H. B. Acton (*Kant's Moral Philosophy*, p. 65) says Kant's "supreme principle of morality does not entail that basic moral rules cannot have exceptions, but only that the permissible exceptions are universalisable maxims."

essay has done more than Kant's most vigorous critics to throw a bad light upon his ethical theory; much ink has been spilt in attempts to explain it away. It is translated by Beck in the 1949 edition of *Kant's Critique of Practical Reason*.

Anthropology from a Pragmatic Point of View (1798), based on Kant's lectures dealing with anthropology, psychology, and ethics as guides to the good life, translated by Mary J. Gregor (1974) and by Victor L. Dowdell and H. W. Rudnick (1978).

The Strife of the Faculties (1798), three independent essays on the relation of philosophy to theology, on the question of progress in history, and on the practical regimen of life. Translated in the Abaris Janus bilingual edition (1979) by Mary J. Gregor.

Logic (1800), based on Kant's lectures, translated by Robert S. Hartman and W. Schwartz (1974).

Lectures on Ethics. A composite of students' lecture notes over a period of years, translated by Louis Infield (1930 with many subsequent editions).

Lectures on Philosophical Theology, translated by Allen W. Wood and Gertrude M. Clark (1978).

Lectures on Pedagogy exists only in a poor edition by Annette Churton (University of Michigan Press, 1960) and in E. F. Buchner's *The Educational Theory of Imanuel Kant* (1904; reprint 1971). The German original, "arranged" by Kant's colleague Rink, is itself of doubtful authenticity.

What Real Progress Has Metaphysics Made in Germany Since the Time of Leibniz and Wolff? Kant prepared this paper about 1790 for submission to the Berlin Academy when the Academy offered a prize for the best answer to that question, but did not submit it. It was first published by Rink in 1804 and translated by Ted B. Humphrey (Abaris Janus Series, 1983).

Philosophical Correspondence 1755–1799, a useful and interesting collection of letters to and from Kant, translated by Arnulf Zweig (1967).

II. REFERENCE BOOKS ON KANT

There is no good reference work in English on Kant. Stockhammer's *Kant Dictionary* (1960) is useless. But with only a smattering of German, one can make good use of the following research tools which direct the inquirer to the desired texts: Rudolf Eisler, *Kant-Lexikon* (1930; later reprints) with article-length entries under the most important terms; Heinrich Ratke, *Systematisches Wörterbuch zu Kants Kritik der reinen Vernunft* (1929) which gives brief references to important passages in the *Critique* and *Prolegomena;* Gottfried Martin, *Sachindex zu Kants Kritik der reinen Vernunft* (1967), a computerized index to the most important technical terms in the *Critique;* and *Personenindex zu Kants gesammelten Schriften* (1969) by Katherina Holger *et al.,* which lists every reference Kant makes to a person.

Kant-Studien (published quarterly in Germany, with articles in French, German, and English) periodically publishes comprehensive bibliographies on Kant. The *Newsletter* of the North American Kant-Society publishes annual bibliographies, edited by Manfred Kuehn. A large pamphlet, *Selected Bibliography on Kant* by Ralph C. S. Walker, is helpful. It can be purchased from the Sub-Faculty of Philosophy, 10 Merton Street, Oxford.

III. BIOGRAPHIES OF KANT

The best biography in English is Ernst Cassirer's *Kant's Life and Thought* translated by James Haden (1981). This not only gives the essential facts about Kant's life and career but also serves as a highly instructive introduction to his philosophy. An older work, *The Life of Immanual Kant* by J. H. W. Stuckenberg (1882; reissued, 1987) is less philosophical and more anecdotal. Though we now know much about Kant that Stuckenberg could not have known, no fundamental feature of Kant's intellectual portrait as drawn by Stuckenberg has had to be changed as a result of later research.

IV. OVERALL SURVEYS OF KANT'S THOUGHT, SUITABLE FOR INTRODUCTORY STUDY

There are probably more overall surveys of Kant than of any other modern philosopher, and more are published almost every year. Any choice of the "best" is likely to be controversial. I have chosen eight, any one of which will give the reader a good orientation.

(a) Edward Caird. *The Critical Philosophy of Kant* (two volumes, 1889). This large, classical, work places Kant as a half-way house on the road to Hegel, and much criticism of Kant tacitly repeats Caird's criticisms. It is the most demanding of the books listed under this heading, and may be too demanding for the beginner.

(b) A. D. Lindsay. *Kant* (1934). Much briefer and easier to read than Caird, but gives very much the same kind of interpretation.

(c) I list two books which should be read together: Stephan Körner's *Kant* (Penguin, 1955; reprint 1982) and Richard Kroner, *Kant's Weltanschauung* (translated by John E. Smith, 1956). Körner's book is a lucid and sympathetic account of Kant written in full realization that contemporary analytic philosophy forces some fundamental revisions in Kantian philosophy, yet at the same time builds upon quasi-Kantian foundations. Kroner, on the other hand, sees Kant primarily as a moral philosopher rather than an epistemologist, and shows how Kant's theoretical philosophy may have grown out of his fundamental moral commitments. Kroner and Körner together show the very great variety of Kantianisms.

(g) Frederick Copleston. *A History of Philosophy,* vol. 6 Part i: *Kant* (1960; also available as paperback apart from the series). Copleston's well-known history of philosophy includes an entire volume on Kant, and covers the ground methodically and patiently, though somewhat tediously.

(h) John Kemp. *The Philosophy of Kant* (1968). A very clear textbook introduction to Kant's whole philosophy; the briefest and most elementary of the books listed here.

(i) H. J. De Vleeschauwer. *The Development of Kantian Thought* (translated by A. R. C. Duncan, 1962). A condensation of De Vleeschauwer's magisterial three volume French commentary on Kant's major works.

(j) Lewis White Beck. *Early German Philosophy: Kant and his Predecessors* (1969) Chapter xvii. Especially emphasizes Kant's relation to his German intellectual environment and traces major themes throughout his career.

V. KANT'S THEORY OF KNOWLEDGE

Kant's theory of knowledge can be dealt with in two ways: by expounding, interpreting, and evaluating the text of the *Critique of Pure Reason,* following more or less closely the sequence of topics in that book; or by dealing with one or more epistemological topics without focussing narrowly or exclusively upon the text of the *Critique.* Naturally the dividing line between them is not very sharp, but they can best be discussed by distinguishing commentaries from other studies.

A. Commentaries on the *Critique of Pure Reason*

Norman Kemp Smith's *Commentary on Kant's Critique of Pure Reason* (1918; many reprints) is the best known commentary. It is filled with historical explanations, detailed exegesis of single sentences, and sharp critical analyses. It is comprehensive and clear. It is marred, however, by a hobby horse Kemp Smith borrowed from some earlier German commentators, namely, the conviction that the *Critique* was hurriedly thrown together from bits and pieces of manuscript written over a twelve-year period, without much care whether they consistently fitted together or not. To support this, Kemp Smith ferreted out difficulties often overlooked by more sympathetic or less critical scholars, since each inconsistency he could find strengthened his case that the *Critique* was a "patchwork." Critics of this extraordinarily instructive and persuasive book, however, point out that many of the apparent inconsistencies it discovered are *only* apparent, and that the *Critique* has a unity and deeper consistency that Kemp Smith missed.

Kemp Smith's principal opponent was his fellow Scot, H. J. Paton, whose *Kant's Metaphysic of Experience* (two volumes, 1936) is a fine exposition of Kant's book, a defense of the integrity of the Kantian text, and an attack on many of Kemp Smith's putative discoveries of irreconcilable conceptions. Paton, however, dealt only with the Transcendental Analytic. Somewhat in Paton's spirit, W. H. Walsh's *Kant's Criticism of Metaphysics* 1975) continues the commentary through the Dialectic. Advice: read a chapter of the *Critique of Pure Reason,* and then compare Kemp Smith's, Paton's, and Walsh's interpretation of what you have just read.

A Short Commentary on Kant's Critique of Pure Reason by A. C. Ewing (1936) is a compromise between Kemp Smith's negative and Paton's positive evaluation of the *Critique.* It is probably the best *introductory* work on the *Critique.*

T. D. Weldon's *Kant's Critique of Pure Reason* (1945; second edition, 1957) is especially instructive in its first edition. Between the editions, Weldon became more interested in "linguistic philosophy" and this perhaps introduced some distortions (at least of emphasis) in the treatment in his second edition.

Jonathan Bennett's two volumes, *Kant's Analytic* (1966) and *Kant's Dialectic* (1974), are hard-hitting analytical investigations of Kant's arguments and conclusions. In spite of a certain prosecutorial style, Bennett is skillful and fair-minded, and Kant comes out of the inquisition looking pretty well.

C. D. Broad's *Kant, An Introduction* (1978) is based on his Cambridge lectures. Like everything Broad wrote, this is marked by a meticulous dissection of arguments and interesting experiments designed to make them work better. Unfortunately the book is harmed by one fundamental error on Broad's part, viz., he thinks Kant meant by "intuition" what Broad meant by "sense-datum", and this ruins many of his expositions. Where this error plays no part, Broad's assessment of Kant's arguments is sound and instructive.

Kuno Fischer was one of the leading Kant scholars in Germany a century ago. From his many-volumed *History of Philosophy* a part was translated under the title: *A Commentary on Kant's Critic of Pure Reason,* with a commentary on *it* by the translator, John Pentland Mahaffy (London, 1866; reprint, 1976). The book is historically important in its own right.

Other commentaries of more limited scope are: Karl Aschenbrenner, *A Companion to Kant's Critique of Pure Reason* (1983); H. W. Cassirer, *Kant's First Critique* (1954); Felix Grayeff, *Kant's Theoretical Philosophy. A Commentary on the Central Part of the Critique of Pure Reason* (1970); and T. E. Wilkerson, *Kant's Critique of Pure Reason. A Commentary for Students* (1976).

B. Studies of Kant's Theory of Knowledge

The most widely discussed and influential Kant book since the war is probably Sir Peter Strawson's *The Bounds of Sense* (1966). Its subtitle is "An Essay on Kant's *Critique of Pure Reason,*" but it perhaps could be called almost as well a "commentary"; its principal interest, however, is not the historical one in explaining and clarifying the text of the *Critique,* but in Strawson's use of the *Critique* as a part of his own "descriptive metaphysics." The parts in which Kant develops his psychology of the cognitive faculties and his transcendental idealism are severely criticized and rejected. On the other hand, one should read also R. P. Wolff's *Kant's Theory of Mental Activity* (1963) and Henry E. Allison's *Kant's Transcendental Idealism* (1983) which respectively emphasize these parts condemned by Strawson. Ralph C. S. Walker, *Kant* (1978) in the well-known series "The Argument of the Philosophers", likewise offers a defense of transcendental idealism.

Douglas P. Dryer, in his *Kant's Solution for Verification in Metaphysics* (1966), examines the methodology by which Kant hoped to establish metaphysics as a science with its own verification procedures; in so doing he referees many contemporary controversies over Kant and gives a good, but difficult and unnecessarily prolix, survey of much modern work on Kant.

H. A. Prichard's *Kant's Theory of Knowledge* (1909; reprint 1976) is a merciless attack on Kant from the point of view of English commonsense realism. Many of his arguments against Kant, some based upon patent misunderstandings, are repeated, often without acknowledgment, by later writers.

There is often only an artificial distinction between epistemology and philosophy of science, and the two fields notably overlap in Kant's works. Gordon G. Brittan *Kant's Theory of Science* (1978) deals with Kant's reconstruction of Newtonism. Arthur Melnick's *Kant's Analogies of Experience* (1973) is a brilliant interpretation of that chapter in the *Critique,* and deals with substance and causality also from the point of view of relativity physics. The Second Analogy of Experience is one of the most hotly debated parts of the *Critique,* and many articles have been published about it. I might mention my *Essays on Kant and Hume* (1978), which contains six pieces on it, and Harper's and Meerbote's *Kant on Causality, Freedom, and Objectivity* (mentioned below). Gerd Buchdahl, in his *Metaphysics and the Philosophy of Science* (1969) historically and conceptually analyzes the development of scientific constructions from Descartes to Kant and follows this with a deep analysis of Kant's conception of the law of nature. John McFarland (*Kant's Concept of Teleology,* 1970) and Clark Zumbach (*The Transcendent Science: Kant's Conception of Biological Methodology,* 1984) explain and evaluate the philosophy of science found in Part II of the *Critique of Judgment* and show its relation to the mechanistic conception of nature in the first *Critique.*

James Ward's *A Study of Kant* (1922; enlarged edition, 1976) is a brief exposition of most important themes in the *Critique,* but is noteworthy because of its extensive treatment of Kant's theory of self-knowledge. Carl Amerik's *Kant's Theory of Mind* (1982) deals with this problem through an analysis of the chapters on the Paralogisms of Reason, which it connects with Kant's practical philosophy; the book is unnecessarily difficult, and is not for beginners.

Gordon Nagel, *The Structure of Experience* (1983) deals with the Analytic of Principles. Robert B. Pippin, *Kant's Theory of Form* (1982) makes use of new ideas developed by Paton, Beck, Allison, and Prauss on the relation of objects of experience and things in themselves. A different standpoint on this problem is occupied by John N. Findlay in his *Kant and the Transcendental Object* (1981). Richard Aquila (*Representational Mind,* 1983) is almost unique in his emphasis upon "intentional analysis" in Kant's epistemology. One of the most fascinating books on Kant is Robert E. Butts's *Kant and the Double-Government Methodology* (1984). The title is a metaphor for Leibniz's distinction between the realm of nature and the realm of grace and Kant's between the sensible and the intelligible world. Butts holds that the conception of the latter involved also Kant's interest in Swedenborg, in his *Dreams of a Spirit-Seer.* The book is off the beaten track, and every reader will find something new and unexpected in it. Butts also edited a volume of papers by various authors, *Kant's Philosophy of Physical Science* (1987).

Some of the best articles on Kant's theory of knowledge have been repeatedly collected into anthologies (some of which include also papers on other important areas of Kantian thought). The best ones are, in alphabetical order: L. W. Beck, *Kant's Theory of Knowledge* (1974), containing a selection of papers from the *Proceedings of the Third International Kant Congress* (1972), and *Kant-Studies Today* (1969); Bernard den Ouden and Marcia Moan, *New Essays on Kant* (1987); William A. Harper and Ralf Meerbote, *Kant on Causality, Freedom, and Objectivity* (1984); J. N. Mohanty and R. W. Shahan, *Essays on Kant's Critique of Pure Reason* (1982); Terence Penelhum and J. MacIntosh, *The First Critique* (1969); Ralph C. S. Walker, *Kant on Pure Reason* (1982); W. H. Werkmeister, *Reflections on Kant's Philosophy* (1975); R. P. Wolff, *Kant* (1967); Allen W. Wood, *Self and Nature in Kant's Philosophy* (1984). One of the most interesting anthologies is Moltke Gram's *Kant: Disputed Questions* (1968; revised ed., 1984). Gram took three central problems (the patchwork theory, the metaphysical vs. the epistemological interpretation, and the analytic-synthetic distinction), selected opposing articles on these topics, and (to use Kant's words in another context) "set them quarreling." These confrontations are unusually instructive.

In referring to Gram's book I mentioned that there was a controversy between the epistemological and the metaphysical interpretations of Kant. While most Anglo-American responses to Kant have been strongly affected by modern logical, analytic, and linguistic concerns and have been favorable to Kant perhaps because of his reputed opposition to speculative metaphysics, a dominant movement in German philosophy interprets him as the *restorer* of metaphysics, not *der Alles-Zermalmende* (the one who destroys everything). Most works from this movement remain untranslated into English, but mention should be made of Karl Jaspers, *Kant* (English translation, 1962) and Gottfried Martin, *Kant's Metaphysics and Theory of Science* (English transl., 1962). In contrast to Martin's book, Heidegger begins his *Kant and the Problem of Metaphysics* (English translation 1962) with the bold statement *"The Critique of Pure Reason* has nothing to do with the 'theory of knowledge'" (p. 21). The book tells us far more about Heidegger than about Kant; a more instructive Kant book is Heidegger's *What is a Thing?* (1967). The influence of these Kant-interpretations has not been widely felt in America, but there have been three native books belonging in this tradition: John Sallis, *The Gathering of Reason* (1980), Charles Sherover, *Heidegger, Kant, and Time* (1971) and the anthology, *Kant and Phenomenology*, edited by Thomas M. Seebohm and Joseph J. Kockelmans (1984). It should not be thought that all the writers mentioned in this paragraph represent the same substantive point of view; they are affiliated only through their common opposition to the more widespread analytic epistemological currents of present-day Anglo-American philosophy.

VI. KANT'S MORAL PHILOSOPHY

A good brief survey of Kant's ethics, which has the merit of dealing lucidly with disputed points, is H. B. Acton's *Kant's Moral Philosophy* (1970).

The historical development of Kant's mature ethical theory has been traced by Paul A. Schilpp in his *Kant's Pre-Critical Ethics* (1938; second ed., 1960; reprint, 1976); Keith Ward in *The Development of Kant's View of Ethics* (1972); and L. W. Beck in the first chapter of his *Commentary on Kant's Critique of Practical Reason* (1960).

More commentaries have been written on the *Foundations of the Metaphysics of Morals* than any other modern ethical treatise. At the head stands H. J. Paton's *The Categorical Imperative* (1948), from which almost all recent study of Kant's ethics takes its start. A. R. C. Duncan's *Practical Reason and Morality. A Study of Kant's Foundations for the Metaphysics of Morals* (1957) and Sir David Ross's *Kant's Ethical Theory. A Commentary on the Grundlegung* (1954) differ sharply with Paton's interpretation. T. C. Williams (*The Concept of the Categorical Imperative*, 1968) makes a good effort at adjudicating the issue between Paton and Duncan. *Kant on the Foundation of Morality* by B. E. A. Liddell (1970) is part commentary and part translation, and can be highly instructive when one is first reading the *Foundations*. Robert Paul Wolff's *The Autonomy of Reason. A Commentary on Kant's Groundwork of the Metaphysics of Morals* (1973) is a controversial book largely on the concept of the self and freedom in the *Foundations*. Wolff has also edited a useful anthology of papers on the *Foundations*, which he has published in a single volume with Beck's translation (Bobbs-Merrill, 1969).

Beck's *Commentary on the Critique of Practical Reason* (1960) is the only full study of the second *Critique*, and has had the effect of broadening the base of discussion beyond the better known *Foundations*. Allen Wood, in *Kant's Moral Religion* (1970), differs from Beck's account of the *summum bonum*, and lines between their contrasting interpretations can be traced in much of the subsequent secondary literature. Robert J. Benton has extensively criticized Beck's account of the deduction of the moral law, in his *Kant's Second Critique and the Problem of Transcendental Arguments* (1977). These books should be read together.

Mary J. Gregor's *The Laws of Freedom* (1963) is the only exhaustive study of the *Metaphysics of Morals*, but Jeffrie G. Murphy (*Kant: The Philosophy of Right*, 1979) and Susan M. Shell (*The Rights of Reason*, 1980) have dealt with some of it.

An analytical, somewhat ahistorical, exposition and critique of Kant's ethics is found in Bruce Aune's *Kant's Theory of Morals* (1979), not a book for beginners.

One of the deepest and most perplexing problems of Kant's philosophy is that of freedom, and almost every book on Kant must deal with this question, as he himself did in book after book. Three books almost exclusively on it are: W. T. Jones, *Morality and Freedom in the Philosophy of Kant* (1948), singular in its emphasis upon the *Critique of Judgment;* Bernard Carnois, *The Coherence of Kant's Doctrine of Freedom* (1987); and Wolff's *The Autonomy of Reason* (cited above).

One of the principal objections to Kant's ethical theory is that he was an "empty formalist" who denied all values except those of punctilious obedience to the moral law. The *locus classicus* of this criticism is to be found in Hegel, and in the present century the chief exponent of this interpretation was Max Scheler in his *Formalism in Ethics and Non-Formal Ethics of Value* (English translation 1973). This misinterpretation is usual in oversimplified textbook accounts of Kant's ethics, because it makes it easy to set up neat antitheses between teleological and deontological ethical systems, as Sir David Ross did. In recent years there has been a reaction against this view and a new emphasis upon Kant's awareness of the legitimate purposiveness of moral action. Among many books which are revisionist in this way, including some which go perhaps too far in this direction, are: John E. Atwell, *Ends and Principles in Kant's Thought* (1986), Thomas Auxter, *Kant's Moral Teleology* (1982), J. Gray Cox, *The Will at the Crossroads* (1984), Hardy E. Jones, *Kant's Principle of Personality* (1971), P. C. Lo, *Treating Persons as Ends* (1987), and Rex P. Stevens, *Kant and Moral Practice* (1981). Onora Nell's *Acting on Principle: An Essay in Kantian Ethics* (1975) is a defense against the criticism that Kantian ethics is "empty", and in it she makes a strong case for regarding the categorical imperative as a decision-principle.

The intrinsic importance of Kant's ethics can best be appreciated by reading significant recent ethical treatises which are not professedly about Kant's ethical theory, but which show Kant to be a central source of many ideas in the forefront of contemporary debate in moral philosophy. The list of books which do this is long, but I will mention only four: Kurt Baier, *The Moral Point of View* (1958); Alan Donagan, *The Theory of Morality* (1977); John Rawls, *Theory of Justice* (1971), about which a great deal has been written concerning how "Kantian" or "anti-Kantian" Rawls is; and Marcus W. Singer, *Universalization in Ethics* (1961).

VII. THE THIRD *CRITIQUE*

H. W. Cassirer's *Commentary on Kant's Critique of Judgment* (1938; reprint 1970) is likely to be disappointing because of its gaps; Cassirer analyzes only about one-third of the sections in the *Critique* and omits some of the most interesting, difficult, and important. R. A. C. Macmillan's *The Crowning Phase of the Critical Philosophy* (1912; reprint 1976) studies the *Critique of Judgment* from the standpoint of its integrative role in the whole Kantian corpus, but its flowery style may put some off. Approaching the calibre of a commentary is Werner Pluhar's long and learned introduction to his translation of the *Critique* (1987). I have already referred to McFarland's and Zumbach's books on teleological judgment in section V, B.

The best general account of the first part is Donald Crawford's *Kant's Aesthetic Theory* (1974), where Kant's views are clearly and interestingly presented, with just the right amount of criticism and emendation. Much longer and more difficult, but repaying the effort to read it, is Paul Guyer's *Kant and the Claims of Taste* (1979). Guyer and Ted Cohen have produced an anthology of previously unpublished papers,

Essays on Kant's Aesthetics (1982). There is a collection of valuable papers by Eva Schaper, *Studies in Kant's Aesthetics* (1979). Israel Knox, *The Aesthetic Theories of Kant, Hegel, and Schopenhauer* (1958) relates Kant's theory to other great classics in the philosophy of art.

VIII. OTHER AREAS

Theology and Philosophy of Religion

C. C. J. Webb's *Kant's Philosophy of Religion* (1926; reprint 1970) is the standard, conventional work on this subject. On the metaphysical problem of theism, see F. E. England, *Kant's Conception of God* (1929) and, better, Allen W. Wood, *Kant's Rational Theology* (1978) and *Kant's Moral Religion* (1970).

Social and political philosophy

See Frederick P. Van de Pitte, *Kant as Philosophical Anthropologist* (1971). Patrick Riley's *Kant's Political Philosophy* (1983) is probably the most helpful book on this subject; it contains a useful chapter on recent criticisms of Kant's political writings. Carl Joachim Friedrich's *Inevitable Peace* (1948) is about *Perpetual Peace* and the history of the idea of a league of nations. Hannah Arendt's *Lectures on Kant's Political Philosophy* is an informal mixture of sketchiness, paradox, and profundity. Hans Saner's *Kant's Political Thought* (1973) has been extravagantly praised by Hannah Ahrendt and sharply condemned by Jeffrie Murphy as "dreadfully inane."

Philosophy of History

William A. Galston's *Kant and the Problem of History* (1975) is a competent but unexciting exposition. Yirmiahu Yovel, *Kant and the Philosophy of History* (1980) and W. J. Booth, *Interpreting the World* (1986) are books which give a complete rereading of Kant's historical thinking. Instead of dealing with his philosophy of history as an appendage to his writings on ethics, metaphysics, and epistemology, these authors read the rest of Kant's works in the light of his philosophy of history. Booth even speaks of "Kant's other Copernican Revolution," and Yovel sees the *summum bonum* as an historical goal.